Canadian Advertising in Action

Canadian Advertising in Action

Second Edition

Keith J. Tuckwell
St. Lawrence College
Adjunct Instructor, Queen's University

PRENTICE-HALL CANADA INC., SCARBOROUGH, ONTARIO

Canadian Cataloguing in Publication Data

Tuckwell, Keith J. (Keith John), 1950-
  Canadian advertising in action

ISBN 0-13-118829-1

1. Advertising. 2. Advertising - Canada. I. Title.

HF5823.T83 1992   659.1   C91-094320-6

©1988, 1992 Prentice-Hall Canada Inc., Scarborough, Ontario

Prentice-Hall Inc., Englewood Cliffs, New Jersey
Prentice-Hall International, Inc., London
Prentice-Hall of Australia, Pty., Ltd., Sydney
Prentice-Hall of India Pvt., Ltd., New Delhi
Prentice-Hall of Japan, Inc., Tokyo
Prentice-Hall of Southeast Asia (Pte.) Ltd., Singapore
Editora Prentice-Hall do Brasil Ltda., Rio de Janeiro
Prentice-Hall Hispanoamericana, S.A., Mexico

ISBN 0-13-118829-1

Acquisitions Editor: Jacqueline Wood
Developmental Editor: Linda Gorman
Copy Editor: Jamie Bush
Production Editor: Norman Bernard
Production Coordinator: Florence Rousseau
Cover Image supplied by Image Bank
Cover and Interior Design: Monica Kompter
Page Layout: Suzanne Boehler

1 2 3 4 5   AG   96 95 94 93 92

Printed and bound in the U.S.A. by Arcata Graphics

To Esther...and our children, Marnie, Graham and Gordie

Contents

Part Two Advertising Planning   79

Part Three Creating Advertisements And Commercials   161

Part Five Specialized Forms Of Advertising   431

Preface

The 2nd edition of Canadian Advertising in Action has been revised according to feedback from current adopters. Adopters expressed a desire for maintenance of practical applications and more extensive use of examples to demonstrate key concepts. The addition of a second colour was also recommended.

The original concept of the book has not changed. The book provides a careful balance between theory and practice, with a primary focus on advertising planning. Advertising-planning concepts are presented in the context of corporate planning and marketing planning. The relationships between the various plans are explored as students learn how advertising plans are developed from initial concept to finished creative and media plans. All advertising principles are presented from a Canadian perspective. The concepts developed herein are relevant to business students, marketing students, and advertising students, as well as to future managers who are embarking on a career in advertising.

New examples and advertising illustrations have been integrated into the text along with a series of "Advertising in Action" vignettes. The vignettes provide additional practical illustrations of key concepts in each chapter. In addition, part-ending "Illustrative Cases" have been added to highlight important concepts from various sections of the text.

Some organizational changes have been made to improve the flow of information. Issues related to strategic planning have been consolidated in chapter 5; thus, some information formerly included in chapter 4 has moved to chapter 5. The chapter on sales promotion has been repositioned and now appears as chapter 13. Statistical media data which formerly appeared in all media chapters has been consolidated in chapter 8: "Advertising Research."

"Advertising Planning—A Campaign Simulation" remains as a unique feature of the text. This integrated experiential-learning assignment immerses the student directly in the advertising-planning process and reinforces the procedures presented in the book. The experiential-learning component can be implemented as the students learn the appropriate theory. The book is organized into six distinct sections:

PART ONE - ADVERTISING TODAY

The initial section presents an overview of the advertising industry today and the organizations that compose the industry. The relationships between agencies and clients are explored along with some of the controversial issues facing the industry today.

PART TWO - ADVERTISING PLANNING

This section examines the relationships between marketing and advertising planning, illustrating how both types of plans contribute to achieving company objectives. Topics such as consumer behaviour, market segmentation, and target marketing are explored in detail. The organization and content of marketing plans and advertising plans are also presented.

PART THREE - CREATING ADVERTISEMENTS AND COMMERCIALS

A detailed discussion of creative planning is presented in this section. The initial chapter focuses on the development of creative objectives, strategies, and tactical considerations for producing effective print and broadcast advertising. The research techniques and information sources used in this advertising industry are also examined.

PART FOUR - MEDIA PLANNING

The initial chapter in this section is devoted to media planning and gives consideration to the development of media budgets, media objectives, strategies, and tactics. Subsequent chapters evaluate the use and effectiveness of the various media alternatives—specifically, print, broadcast, direct advertising, and out-of-home media.

PART FIVE - SPECIALIZED FORMS OF ADVERTISING

This section centres on specific-interest topics of advertising and promotion. The first chapter presents a variety of sales-promotion techniques that are often integrated with advertising strategies. This is followed by discussion of business-to-business advertising and retail advertising. The intent is to highlight the strategic-planning considerations that are unique to these forms of advertising.

PART SIX - EXPERIENTIAL LEARNING

"Advertising Planning—A Campaign Simulation" is an experiential-learning component designed to simulate planning procedure used in advertising today. The intent of this integrated exercise is to provide students with an opportunity to apply the theory they have learned and appreciate the interaction needed to develop an advertising campaign.

The format of the chapters is consistent throughout the book. Chapters start with a list of learning objectives directly related to key concepts presented in the chapter. Chapter summaries are located at the end of each chapter, along with review questions and discussion questions. The questions are designed to serve two purposes: to reinforce key concepts presented in each chapter, and to stimulate discussion on issues and problems confronting advertising practitioners today. An "Illustrative Case" appears at the end of each part of the text.

The Appendices contain a selection of laws and regulations that govern Canadian advertising, along with an advertising lexicon that defines key terms.

SUPPLEMENTS

A more comprehensive supplements package is available with the 2nd edition. The Instructor's Manual, the Test Item File, and the Transparency Masters have been published together as an Instructor's Resource Manual. The following materials therefore are now available for Canadian Advertising in Action.

INSTRUCTOR'S MANUAL

Prepared by the author, the manual includes learning objectives, chapter highlights, answers to review and discussion questions, a master list of overhead transparencies, and a summary of the planning simulation.

TEST ITEM FILE

An expanded list of multiple-choice and true and false questions appears in the manual.

COMPUTERIZED TEST ITEM FILE

The test item file is available in 3 1/2" and 5 1/4" format IBM-compatible disks.

TRANSPARENCY MASTERS

Culled from the textbook, or specifically designed to complement chapter content, these masters may be copied onto acetates for use in class.

VIDEO

A series of award-winning ABC videos helps illustrate important advertising concepts, shows how companies tackle real life problems, and contains dozens of features to enliven and enrich lectures. A videoguide, collating video clips relating to coverage in the text, is also available.

COLOURED ACETATES

A comprehensive set of full-colour overhead transparencies provides additional figures and illustrations to supplement the material found in the text. Numerous advertisements from a variety of sources are also included.

Acknowledgements

Many organizations and individuals have contributed to the development of the 2nd edition of this text. I would like to sincerely thank the following organizations for their special cooperation and contribution.

A.C. Nielsen Company of Canada Limited
Apple Canada Inc.
Atlantic Packaging Products Limited
Baker Lovick Advertising
Banff Centre for Conferences
BBM Bureau of Measurement
Beatrice Foods Inc.
BMW Canada Inc.
Calvin Klein
Campbell Soup Company Limited
Canada Life Assurance Company
Canadian Airlines
Canadian Advertising Foundation
Cap Communications Limited
Coca-Cola Canada Limited
Dofasco Inc.
Donner Schur Peppler Advertising
Eveready Canada Inc.
Federal Express Canada Limited
Ford Motor Company of Canada Limited
Honda Motor Company of Canada Limited
Jaguar Canada Inc.
Labatt Breweries of Canada Limited
Molson Breweries of Canada Limited
Murad Communications
Newspaper Marketing Bureau

Ontario Hydro
Power Broadcasting Inc.
Radio Bureau of Canada
Report on Business Magazine (The Globe and Mail)
S.C. Johnson & Son, Limited
St. Lawrence Broadcasting Limited
Telecom Canada
Tetra Pak
Toshiba of Canada Limited
Trans Ad, A Jim Pattison Company
TVB Television Bureau of Canada

From Prentice-Hall Canada Inc., I would like to thank the project editor, Ruth Bradley-St-Cyr, for her work on revising the text. Thanks also to editors Linda Gorman, Jamie Bush, and Norman Bernard for masterminding the production side of things. Also, a special thanks to Yolanda de Rooy for consultations along the way.

Finally, another big thank you to the Tuckwell family for their patience and understanding once again. To Esther, Marnie, Graham, and Gordie...thank you.

Advertising Today

The purpose of this book is to examine what is involved in the management and planning of advertising. Part One describes what advertising is all about, and identifies who is involved in the Canadian advertising industry.

Chapter 1 examines the role of advertising and its relationship to other marketing activity. You will be reading about various forms of advertising, about conditions necessary for advertising to be effective, and about the organizations that compose the industry today. The chapter ends with a discussion of the issues the industry is currently facing.

Chapters 2 and 3 focus on the activities of the two primary groups in the industry: the advertisers (referred to as the client), and the advertising agencies. The chapters describe their roles and responsibilities in the advertising process. Most importantly, you will be learning about working relationships that must exist between the client and the agency if effective advertising plans and activities are to be developed.

CHAPTER 1 Advertising Overview

In studying this chapter, you will learn

- The role of advertising and its relationship to marketing

- The distinctions between the various types of consumer and business-to-business advertising

- The conditions that are necessary for advertising to be effective

- The composition of the Canadian advertising industry

- The role that laws and regulations play in guiding Canadian advertising

- The basic social issues confronting advertising in Canada

THE IMPORTANCE OF ADVERTISING

Advertising is undoubtedly the most visible form of marketing today, and as we move further into the 1990s it will become an increasingly exciting and dynamic career field for students. Advertising is all around us, and we as consumers underestimate the influence it has on us. Have you ever really thought about the influence that advertising has on you? Consciously or subconsciously, advertising messages are in contact with us each day. Take a few moments to go through the following steps, and you will start to see the extent to which advertising influences you:

1. Consider the number of hours you spend watching television each day. Multiply by seven to arrive at your total weekly viewing hours, and then multiply by 12 the average number of commercials shown each hour. How many commercials were you exposed to?
2. Consider the number of hours you spend each day listening to a radio, even if you spend these hours doing something else as well. Duplicate the exercise above and arrive at the total number of radio advertisements you are exposed to each week.

Figure 1.1   Canada's Top 20 Advertisers

		Total (in thousands)
1.	The Thompson Group	$75 777.2
2.	General Motors of Canada	68 332.9
3.	Government of Canada	67 313.8
4.	Procter & Gamble	67 224.1
5.	Sears Canada	63 937.6
6.	Molson Breweries of Canada	52 664.5
7.	Paramount Communications	44 705.2
8.	Unilever	43 799.9
9.	Cineplex Odeon	42 865.2
10.	John Labatt Limited	40 849.5
11.	Kraft General Foods Group	39 011.6
12.	George Weston Limited	37 907.4
13.	Eaton's	37 575.2
14.	Ontario Government	35 877.7
15.	McDonald's Restaurants of Canada	32 479.6
16.	BCE Inc.	31 943.6
17.	Kellogg Canada	29 914.6
18.	Imasco	28 959.9
19.	Toyota Canada	28 215.7
20.	Ford Motor Company of Canada	28 215.7

Source: Adapted from "Canada's Top Advertisers," *Marketing,* April 8, 1991, p.47.

3. Take the newspaper you read regularly and do a physical count of the number of advertisements that appear in the paper on any given day. Multiply this by seven if it is a daily paper.
4. Now consider your excursions to and from school each day. How many messages do you see at bus shelters, subway stops, on transit cards inside buses and subway cars, and on outdoor posters along street sides?

In addition, you are exposed to ads in magazines, on shopping carts, even in movie theatres and restaurants. The list could go on and on, but by now you can readily see the potential influence of advertising. Advertising in Canada is big business! In fact, it is expected that, by 1991, the amount spent on advertising in this country will exceed $10 billion. Furthermore, the largest single advertiser in Canada is the Thompson Group, which spent $76 million on advertising in 1991. Other large advertisers include General Motors ($68.3 million), Procter&Gamble ($67.3 million), and Sears Canada ($63.9 million). It is important to note that the federal government is also a large advertiser. In 1990, the government was the third largest advertiser, with expenditures totalling $67.3 million. Refer to figure 1-1 for a list of Canada's top 20 advertisers, and the amount each spent on advertising.[1]

THE ROLE OF ADVERTISING

Advertising is best defined in terms of its purpose. It is a persuasive form of marketing communications designed to elicit a positive response (usually a purchase) from a defined target market. While advertising can accomplish specific tasks, such as increasing the public's awareness of a product or service or inducing trial purchase through a promotion incentive, its basic role is to influence the behaviour of a **target market** (or **target audience**) in such a way that members of the target market view the product, service, or idea favourably. Assuming that consumers develop a favourable attitude toward a specific service or brand of product, advertising attempts to motivate them to purchase that service or brand of product. Advertising can be both an informative and a persuasive form of communication.

Very often, the public measures the success of an advertising campaign strictly in terms of product sales. But there is *no direct relationship between advertising and sales*. A major problem with linking sales directly to advertising is that other variables, not just advertising, influence the consumer's decision-making process. Advertising does not operate in a vacuum; it is a subset of marketing and promotion activity. With respect to the planning and implementing of marketing activity, advertising is one component of the process, together with sales promotion, personal selling, public relations, and event marketing and sponsorship. Marketing decisions regarding such matters as product, price, and place all have an effect on sales. Hence it is the four "P" activities (product, price, promotion and place) that are directly related to sales. It is neither reasonable nor practical to isolate one variable, such as advertising, and hold it responsible when sales decline. All variables must be analyzed in relation to one another and to the specific goals each was planned to achieve. Figure 1.2 reviews the position of advertising in the marketing process.

Figure 1.2 Advertising: its position in the marketing process

ADVERTISING AND ITS RELATIONSHIP TO MARKETING

The marketing concept states that *all business planning revolves around the consumer.* All the resources of a firm should be directed at determining and satisfying consumers' needs in ways that will provide for long-term profitability. Many researchers and market planners now believe that contemporary marketing activity has gone well beyond the marketing concept. Kotler and McDougall state that the newest concept is the **societal marketing concept:**

> The societal marketing concept holds that the organization's task is to determine the needs, wants, and interests of target markets and deliver the desired satisfactions more effectively and efficiently than competitors in a way that preserves or enhances the consumer's and society's well-being.[2]

The *societal marketing concept* suggests that identifying and satisfying consumers remains the cornerstone of marketing, but that the element of competition has been added. It is competitive activity that influences most advertising and marketing strategy in today's marketplace. Many practitioners feel that satisfying customer needs better than the competition is the key to success. In certain product categories, wars have erupted, as one brand chases market share at the expense of another brand. For example, the comparative campaigns launched by Pepsi-Cola against arch-rival Coca Cola, initially via the "Pepsi Challenge Taste Test," and later by the "Taste Above All" campaign, created much controversy in the marketplace. Campaigns such as these, typical of the new style of marketing, place the competition front and centre in the marketing process.

It is important to note also that the societal marketing concept focuses on the well-being of consumers and of society generally. Today, consumer and environmental groups often attack companies and industries that market products of questionable quality or products that are harmful. Certainly we are living in an era of "green marketing" or an era of "environmental-friendly" marketing. Today, marketing organizations are very conscious of how the public perceives their activity. Being sensitive to the environment is a priority, and many companies take steps to inform the public of any actions they have taken to preserve the environment (see figure 1.3). In these situations, the effective use of advertising is a means to an end. It is nothing more than a marketing vehicle for reaching consumers with a positive message.

Figure 1.3 An advertisement that stresses environmental sensitivity

THIS IS A ^*Recycled* JUICE BOX.

So are some park benches we could show you. And road pylons. Pallets. Tree planters. And a whole list of other useful items, now made mostly from wood.

The fact is, juice boxes can now be recycled.

Through a proven new technical process, sponsored in part by Tetra Pak -- the leading manufacturer of juice boxes in Canada – empty juice boxes, along with their straws and wrap can now be combined with waste plastics and turned into a sturdy new

material called Superwood® lumber. And Superwood lumber can be used to make anything from picnic tables to picket fences.

The Town of Markham, Ontario has already taken the initiative, by adding juice boxes and all plastics to their Blue Box collection program. And Tetra Pak is working to get similar programs adopted in other municipalities right across Canada.

We all have to do our part to improve the environment. It's a commitment

we at Tetra Pak have made to ourselves and to Canada.

Juice boxes – because they use so little raw materials to begin with – have always produced less waste than other forms of packaging. Now that they can be recycled, they will produce even less waste. And help conserve our forest resources at the same time.

That means that juice boxes now make even better sense for your family and for your children.

And for your children's children, too.

TETRA PAK ®

Get all the facts about juice boxes and our environment. Write Tetra Pak Inc., 200 Vandorf Road, Aurora, Ontario L4G 3G8.

Courtesy: Tetra Pak Inc.

ADVERTISING — WHAT IT ISN'T

As indicated in figure 1.2, advertising is a subset of promotion within the framework of all the other variables involved in the marketing-planning process. At this point, it is necessary to distinguish between the various promotion variables often confused with advertising. These other variables often play an equal role with advertising in determining the success or failure of a product or service. To generate maximum impact on a target market, all promotion variables must work together.

Sales Promotion

Sales promotion includes activities that are designed to achieve immediate purchase-response on two fronts. First, there are promotion incentives offered to the *trade* (i.e., to wholesaling and retailing distributors). These are meant to cause greater volume of product to move through the channel. Incentives of this nature could include volume rebates, temporary price discounts, and cooperative advertising.

Second, there are promotions directed at consumers to help pull the product through the channel or create short-term volume increases. The incentives used to achieve these goals include coupons, cash refunds, free samples, and contests. Most of these promotion incentives rely on advertising to communicate the promotion. Again, all promotion-mix variables must work together to create impact in the marketplace.

Public Relations

Public relations refers to a firm's communications with its various publics. These publics include shareholders, employees, suppliers, the government, customers in the channel, and, finally, the consumer. So far as its role in the marketing process is concerned, public relations is distinguished from advertising in that it is more often viewed as a corporate function (i.e., it deals more with corporate image than with product image), and as such, its communications are often related to the firm as a whole.

Publicity is the communication of newsworthy information about a product, service, idea or company, such as the launching of a new product, the opening of a new location, or the achieving of a milestone. Such information is presented to the media through a press release. Unlike advertising, publicity communications are not paid for by the client (other than the preparation of the release), so the firm accepts whatever media coverage it receives.

Adverse reaction by consumers and governments to a product, because of poor product performance or product recalls, forces a manufacturer to respond via public-relations activity. The final outcome of a negative reaction to a product, service or business often depends on how effectively public relations is handled. Refer to the Advertising in Action vignette "Perrier Bounces Back" for an illustration of advertising and public relations working together.

Advertising in Action
Perrier Bounces Back

In January 1990, the world's trendiest mineral water was recalled around the world after traces of benzene, a poisonous chemical, were found in some bottles in the United States. A widespread poison scare is not on any company's list of planned activities. Clearly, Perrier had to act quickly, and the public had to be assured that the problem was being attended to.

In Canada alone, 20 million bottles were removed from the market. The parent company in France traced the problem to a dirty filter in one of its production facilities. The Canadian market was estimated to be worth $200 million in sales revenue at the time, and Perrier's market share in Canada fell into the 40% to 50% range. With so much at stake, how Perrier handled its comeback was crucial. It was a classic test of "crisis management", a test which companies do not plan for but must be prepared for on a moment's notice.

The product was off the market for three weeks, much to the delight of competitive brands. How the public would react to Perrier's return was unknown; consumers can be fickle. Upon Perrier's return, advertising and other forms of print communication simply stated that "the problem had been fixed," and reassured customers that Perrier water was "still as pure as it's been for thousands of years." The public was encouraged to contact the company directly through a toll-free 1-800 number if more information was required.

On the packaging side of things, the new bottles included a red and white label below the green Perrier label stating "new production." All of Perrier's actions reassured the public. Oh yes, the cost? The cost of the recall and reintroduction in Canada alone was $5 million. Imagine the financial impact worldwide!

Adapted from Martin Mehr, "Perrier is back," *Marketing*, March 12, 1990, pp.1,13.

Packaging

Packaging is a form of marketing communications, but it is not a form of advertising. It is very often the focal point of an advertising message, particularly in the introduction stage, when brand-name and package awareness are critical aspects of communications. However, packaging is an element of product strategy. As such, packaging is treated separately from advertising.

THE FORMS OF ADVERTISING

Advertising can be divided into two broad categories: *consumer advertising* and *business-to-business advertising*.

CONSUMER ADVERTISING

Consumer advertising refers to persuasive communications designed to elicit a purchase response from consumers. Advertising directed at consumers is subdivided into four types: national advertising, retail advertising, end-product advertising, and direct-response advertising.

National Advertising

National advertising is the advertising of a trademarked product or service wherever that product or service is available. In spite of its name, national advertising is non-geographic. National advertising messages communicate a brand name, the benefits offered, and the availability of the product or service. Advertising messages for products such as Molson Canadian, Tide detergent, Ford automobiles, Nabob coffee, and Apple Computers are all classified as national advertising (see figure 1.4).

Retail Advertising

As the name implies, **retail advertising** is the advertising that a retail store does in order to communicate store image, store sales, and the like. Usually, the retailer advertises the lines of merchandise it carries, which include generic brands, private-label brands, and national brands. The framework of retail advertising can thus be expanded to include the re-advertising of national brands.

Retail advertising includes advertising by large department stores such as The Bay, Eaton's or Zellers, and the advertising of weekly specials by stores like Safeway, Super Value, or IGA. The advertising done by specialty stores, such as Tip Top, Black's Cameras and Kettle Creek Canvas Company, also belongs to this category.

End-Product Advertising

End-product advertising is the advertising done by a firm that makes part of a finished product. Advertising of this nature encourages consumers to look for this particular component when buying a final product. For example, a consumer will take a roll of film to a camera shop to have the film processed into pictures, which is the finished product. Kodak spends a considerable amount of its advertising dollars convincing consumers to have their film processed on Kodak paper if quality prints are what they desire. More recently, the inclusion of "NutraSweet" in numerous food and beverage products has resulted in campaigns urging consumers to look for the NutraSweet designation on product labels.

Direct-Response Advertising

Direct-response advertising is advertising directly to consumers. The product is marketed directly: traditional channels of distribution are not utilized. Special tape and compact-disc offers are good examples of this type of advertising. Such offers are communicated to consumers through commercials on local television stations, national and regional magazines, and direct mail. Consumers traditionally purchase this type of product in music stores or department stores.

Figure 1.4 An advertisement from a national advertiser stressing the brand name and benefits offered

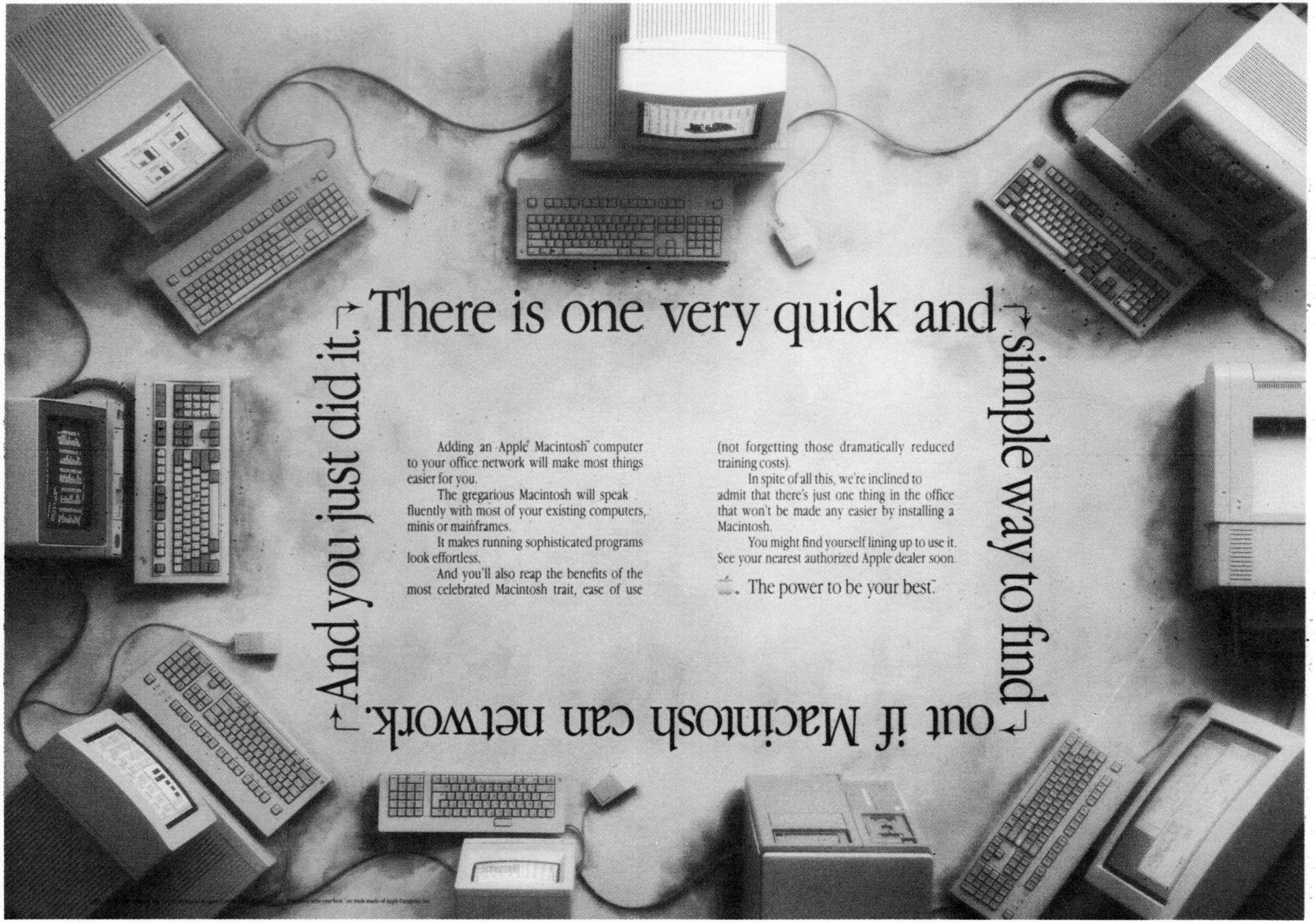
There is one very quick and simple way to find out if Macintosh can network. And you just did it.
Adding an Apple® Macintosh™ computer to your office network will make most things easier for you.
The gregarious Macintosh will speak fluently with most of your existing computers, minis or mainframes.
It makes running sophisticated programs look effortless.
And you'll also reap the benefits of the most celebrated Macintosh trait, ease of use (not forgetting those dramatically reduced training costs).
In spite of all this, we're inclined to admit that there's just one thing in the office that won't be made any easier by installing a Macintosh.
You might find yourself lining up to use it. See your nearest authorized Apple dealer soon.
The power to be your best.™

Courtesy: Apple Canada Inc.

Direct marketing is becoming an increasingly popular and dominant force in the Canadian advertising scene. Mail and telephone (telemarketing) are the media most closely associated with this type of activity. It is used frequently in business-to-business advertising also.

BUSINESS-TO-BUSINESS ADVERTISING

Business-to-business advertising refers to advertising directed by business and industry at business and industry. This type of advertising uses trade magazines as its primary vehicle. Advertising to professional groups (doctors, lawyers, accountants, etc.) is an example of this form of advertising. The major types of business-to-business advertising are trade advertising, industrial advertising, advertising to professionals, and corporate advertising.

Trade Advertising

Trade advertising is advertising done by manufacturers, and it is directed at channel members. The objective of trade advertising is to communicate a convincing message that will encourage middlemen to carry and resell the product. Messages usually stress that the product is a success (thereby suggesting that other middlemen have accepted the product), that the manufacturer will offer promotions to help resell the product, and that profit margins are based on average selling prices. This type of advertising is communicated to customers in such industry-related publications as *Canadian Grocer*, *Hardware Merchandising*, and *Foodservice & Hospitality*.

Industrial Advertising

The name says it all. **Industrial advertising** is advertising by industrial suppliers to industrial buyers. The decision whether to purchase capital equipment, accessory equipment, fabricated parts, and raw materials may be influenced most by personal selling. However, advertising in industrial publications or direct-response advertising can stimulate initial awareness of a product and develop sales leads. Maclean Hunter Business Publications provides numerous publications for industrial advertisers in a variety of specialized industries. Included are *Heavy Construction News*, *Canadian Packaging*, *Materials Management and Distribution*, and *Canadian Datasystems*.

Advertising to Professionals

As with industrial advertising, manufacturers can direct messages to professional groups to increase awareness of and knowledge about the product. Drug manufacturers, for example, can communicate with the medical profession through publications such as *The Medical Post*, *MD*, and *Diagnosis*. The legal profession can be reached through magazines such as *Canadian Lawyer* and the *Lawyer's Weekly*. Other professions have similar types of publications.

Corporate Advertising

Corporate advertising focuses on the broader services of a company or on the company as a whole. The nature and intent of corporate communications are varied. Corporate advertising may attempt to create or improve a firm's image in the mind of the public, or it may communicate a company's stance on a particular issue that affects it directly. The ad for Canada Life in figure 1.5 is an example of a corporate message. Very often, this type of advertising is the responsibility of the organization's public-relations department.

Figure 1.5   A corporate message that stresses image and the range of services offered

Courtesy: Canada Life Assurance Company

CONDITIONS NECESSARY FOR USING ADVERTISING EFFECTIVELY

Since advertising is the most visible form of marketing activity, people often view it as a quick fix for problem situations. The opposite is closer to reality. For advertising to be effective, certain conditions must be favourable. Those managers and planners responsible for the advertising function must analyze these factors and judge whether advertising will contribute to the achievement of marketing objectives. In effect, this form of appraisal is the initial step in the advertising-planning process. The steps in the appraisal process and their relationship to advertising planning are illustrated in figure 1.6.

Figure 1.6 Appraising the opportunity for advertising: factors to consider

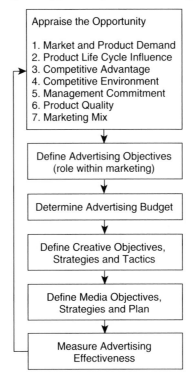

Appraise the Opportunity

1. Market and Product Demand
2. Product Life Cycle Influence
3. Competitive Advantage
4. Competitive Environment
5. Management Commitment
6. Product Quality
7. Marketing Mix

Define Advertising Objectives
(role within marketing)

Determine Advertising Budget

Define Creative Objectives,
Strategies and Tactics

Define Media Objectives,
Strategies and Plan

Measure Advertising
Effectiveness

Market and Product Demand

Assuming that customer needs have been properly identified, advertising's first task is to stimulate demand for the product or product category. The introduction of a new product concept is quite a challenge, since the marketing and advertising activity must first make customers recognize a need, then stimulate a purchase response based on that recognition.

If a market and product already exist, the advertiser will analyze the primary-demand trends and selective-demand trends. *Primary demand* refers to demand for the product category (product class). For example, the demand for camcorders must be positive if brands within this category are to be advertised successfully. Positive demand obviously provides the best economic environment to advertise in. The converse is also true. It can be very expensive to advertise in markets where primary demand is declining, since such a decline indicates that consumers are developing a preference for newer types of products.

Selective demand refers to demand for a specific product (brand) within a product category. When selective demand is positive, growing from year to year, the decision to advertise is relatively simple. However, the company must eventually decide at what point it will reduce or eliminate advertising support. Does a firm support brands with profit potential, or does it attempt to protect brands for which selective demand has declined? An examination of the influence of the product life cycle on advertising activity will help to resolve this question.

Product Life Cycle

Closely related to primary demand and selective demand, in terms of its influence on advertising decisions, is the **product life cycle**. The critical stages for advertising are the product's *introduction* and *growth* stages. The amount of money allocated to advertising and the advertising strategies implemented will change as a product moves through its life cycle. If its advertising strategies are based solely on life-cycle theory, a company spends heavily in the product's introduction stage to stimulate demand and create brand awareness. This short-term commitment results in long-term profitability, particularly if the commitment is made during stages where advertising plays a significant role. Commitment to advertising is critical at this early stage, enabling the brand to grow before new and competing innovations occur.

In the growth stage, competition is intense. A client company's commitment to advertising must continue as its product strives for growth or tries to defend its position in the marketplace. Here, the decision to advertise is a relatively easy one, since growth is usually rapid. Deciding how much to spend is more difficult. It is possible that competitors with less market share but with ambitious growth plans may force another company to spend more on advertising its product than it desires to spend.

When a product is in the mature stage, advertising is usually less important. Assuming that new strategies are not implemented to rejuvenate the product, funds formerly allocated to advertising the product may be shifted into other areas such as sales promotion and price discounting.

Competitive Advantage

Advertising contributes to the achievement of marketing objectives for a product when the advertising message can be based on the product's *competitive advantage*—that is, when the product offers something unique and desirable to a market segment. A product's having features that differentiate it from the competition is crucial for advertising, since a distinctive message must be planted in the minds of consumers. In deciding what to communicate, the advertiser has several options: demonstrating the product's superiority, capitalizing on product innovation, drawing upon the product's hidden qualities, or associating the product with a certain lifestyle.

Demonstrating Superiority   The most common way to demonstrate the superiority of a given product is to compare it to other products on the basis of their similar attributes. For example, Ruffles-brand potato chips used television to demonstrate that consumers who were asked to make a taste comparison preferred Ruffles to another leading brand. In the toothpaste market, Crest (Procter & Gamble) and Colgate (Colgate-Palmolive) both use their superior records of cavity prevention and their endorsement by the Canadian Dental Association to demonstrate their superiority over other brands.

Superiority over the competition can take many forms, such as superior economy, efficiency, dependability, and reliability. The claims for products such as the EveReady Energizer battery relate to how long the batteries last (which translates into savings for the consumer in the long run), while a budget hotel chain such as Journey's End touts the high quality and low price of its rooms.

Capitalizing on Product Innovation   In the coffee market, several product innovations, when introduced, became the focal point of advertising messages. For example, freeze-dried instant coffee was an innovation that led to claims of improved taste for a brand like Taster's Choice. Nabob's technological advances in packaging, specifically the vacuum-sealed package for its coffee, together with the advertising that stressed the coffee's freshness, distinguished this brand from all its competitors. Figure 1.7, the outdoor poster for Toshiba, uses the expression "Televisionary" as a means of promoting its technological innovation. Toshiba claims that it delivers tomorrow's technology today.

Figure 1.7   An advertising message that stresses technological innovation

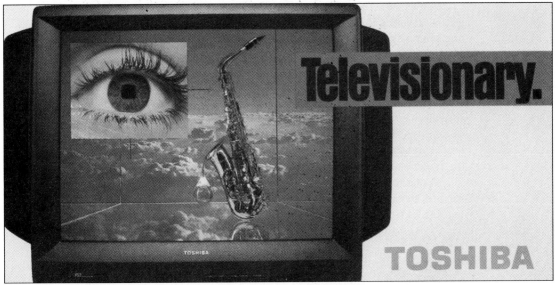

Courtesy: Toshiba of Canada Limited/Consumer Electronics Sector

Drawing Upon Hidden Qualities   Stressing hidden qualities is a popular means of differentiating one product from another. A hidden quality refers to some unique feature that is of benefit to consumers but that they cannot see, feel, or taste. Vitamin C is the benefit sought in numerous frozen and canned fruit juices. Retsyn is a special ingredient added to Certs that differentiates it from other brands of breath mints. The company that produces Tums experienced dramatic sales gains when it started to promote the calcium the product contained.

Lifestyle Associations   A more recent phenomenon in advertising is the progressive use of lifestyle associations to differentiate one product from another. The use of lifestyle-advertising appeals is popular in product categories where brand alternatives offer similar benefits to consumers. Perhaps the most frequent user of lifestyle advertising is the beer industry, where sports, leisure, recreation, and social settings are used to advertise specific brands. Such advertising often comes under attack from consumer groups, since the "implied good times" associated with the product only represent part of the story. Many point to the fact that the excessive use of a product such as alcohol is harmful. Some of these concerns are examined in greater detail later in this chapter.

Competitive Advertising Environment

The advertising for competitive products also influences what role advertising plays in a product's promotion. Assume that a product is not a major player in a market dominated by a few other brands that invest heavily in advertising. These leading brands would have a high-market-share/high-advertising-share relationship. **Advertising share** refers to the investment in a product's advertising expressed as a percentage of total market investment in advertising. Under such circumstances, the company selling the "minor league" product may look at alternative, less costly methods of attracting consumers, such as sales promotion or lower-pricing strategies.

Conversely, if a company does decide to pursue advertising, it must do so at competitive levels if it is going to penetrate through the clutter of messages issued by all brands in the marketplace. To proceed on this basis requires a long-term commitment to advertising.

Product Quality

Since most firms are operating within the framework of the marketing concept or the societal-marketing concept, it is often presumed that quality products are being manufactured and marketed. This situation cannot be taken for granted, however, since inferior products that do not meet consumers' expectations are being withdrawn from the marketplace all the time.

Most advertising communicates a brand name and a primary selling message, and attempts to create for the product a favourable image that consumers will respond to. In effect, advertising communicates a promise about a product to consumers (telling them what the product will do for them). Since advertising to stimulate trial purchase is implemented at very high cost, it is imperative that the product live up to consumer expectations so that repeat purchase occurs in the long term. Investment in advertising is wasteful if the product being marketed is of inconsistent quality.

Management Commitment

The perception that a client company's management has regarding the usefulness of advertising is also important. A management group that views advertising as a short-term expense will not be committed to a plan that requires a long-term investment. Budget cuts are likely to occur during the course of a year, and since advertising is highly visible on the profit-and-loss statement, advertising is one of the first items reviewed in a profit-squeeze situation if senior management is not committed to advertising. Such action greatly disrupts an advertising plan, since stated objectives have to be reassessed in the wake of reduced financial support for advertising. In the long term, cutbacks to the advertising budget have harmful effects on product development in the marketplace.

Conversely, senior management that views advertising as a long-term investment is usually more willing to commit funds to see a campaign through to the finish. Obviously, such an attitude provides a preferable operating environment for advertising.

The Marketing Mix

A company must consider the role of advertising within the marketing mix prior to deciding whether or not to advertise. For advertising to contribute effectively, it must be integrated in such a way that all marketing-mix variables work together. For example, the message content must be congruent with the quality of the product and the pricing structure. Do all the variables communicate the same message and meet the expectations of the intended target market? Will the product be available in locations where the target market normally shops? Since all of these variables must come together in an integrated marketing plan, the role of advertising must be carefully defined before any advertising activity is embarked upon.

Appraising the opportunity for advertising involves a careful review of the variables discussed in this section. If the results of such an analysis are favourable, then investment in advertising is warranted. If the results are unfavourable, the firm should perhaps investigate alternative means of encouraging product development.

COMPOSITION OF THE ADVERTISING INDUSTRY

The Canadian advertising industry comprises three primary groups: the advertisers, the advertising agencies, and the media. All advertising revenues generated in Canada are the result of advertisers' print ads and broadcast commercials being placed by advertising agencies in the media. The advertisers are the companies whose investment in advertising is largely responsible for keeping the other two component groups in business.[3] Other organizations that support these primary groups include advertising-production companies, audience-measurement and research companies, media-support services, and regulation and control agencies.

PRIMARY INDUSTRY GROUPS

Advertisers (The Client)

Canadian advertisers include manufacturers, retailers, service firms, governments, and non-profit organizations. Among the largest advertisers in Canada are Procter & Gamble, John Labatt Limited, General Motors, and Kraft General Foods. Advertisers such as these and others are represented by the Association of Canadian Advertisers. The ACA's mandate is "to exercise leadership in advancing the advertising interests and responsibilities of advertisers in Canada."[4] The objective of the ACA is to work for the creation of an environment that allows advertisers maximum opportunity to advertise responsibly and professionally. There are seven areas of action in which the ACA concentrates its work: government relations, membership education, organization effectiveness, public understanding, inter-association relations, advertising efficiency, and issue management.[5]

Advertising Agencies

Advertising agencies are service organizations responsible for creating, planning, producing, and placing advertising messages for clients. The largest advertising agency in Canada is Maclaren: Lintas Inc., which billed (placed) a total of $220 million in measured media in 1989.[6] There are different types of agencies. Some are classified as full-service agencies since they provide a complete range of services to their clients. Others are specialists that only offer limited services in areas of expertise.

The Institute of Canadian Advertising (ICA) is the national association representing full-service advertising agencies. The work of the ICA may be divided into two broad categories: external and internal. The external mission of the ICA is to act on behalf of the agency industry as spokesperson, negotiator, and defender of advertising. Its role is to discourage regulation, improve regulatory procedures, support self-regulation, and fight for the freedom to advertise. Its internal mission is to undertake tasks that promote the growth of all full-service agencies. In this role, the ICA promotes the general business of advertising and particular member services to potential advertisers, improves agency operations by offering educational programs, and provides leadership in the development of ethical practices.[7]

Media

The Canadian media are divided into three broad categories: broadcast, which includes radio and television; print, which includes newspapers and magazines; and out-of-home media, which is used for transit and outdoor advertising, and other unique forms of advertising such as elevator advertising and aerial advertising.

ADVERTISING SUPPORT GROUPS AND ASSOCIATIONS

Advertising Support Companies

This group is made up of research companies that measure and evaluate the effectiveness of advertising messages. Other support firms include photographers and illustrators (who convert agency ideas and concepts into finished advertisements), radio and television commercial production houses, print production specialists, music and sound production and editing companies, and media representatives who sell time and space for particular media. These support-service groups operate behind the scenes, and awareness of their existence, role, and function is low.

Media-Support Services

All major media in Canada have a support group whose primary mandate is to educate potential advertisers about the merits of their particular medium. Acting as a resource centre of information, each of these organizations attempts to increase its medium's share of advertising revenue in the marketplace. Where appropriate, these organizations also liaise with governments and the public on matters of interest. This group includes the Television Bureau of Canada (TVB), Radio Bureau of Canada (RBC), Newspaper Marketing Bureau, Magazines Canada, Canadian Business Press, and the Outdoor Advertising Association of Canada.

Research and Audience-Measurement Companies

Advertising planners working with limited budgets are constantly evaluating the various media alternatives in order to develop the most effective and efficient media mix. To make sound media decisions requires a factual and objective information base. Media research, therefore, is concerned with quantitative measures of media exposure. In Canada, there are numerous independent organizations that compile and publish reliable measurement data. What follows is a brief discussion of the role and nature of the major research and audience-measurement organizations.

BBM Bureau of Measurement   The BBM is a non-profit organization whose membership comprises advertisers, advertising agencies, and broadcasters. Its mandate is to compile reliable audience estimates by conducting surveys of network television and of market-by-market and station-by-station television. BBM also surveys radio and produces similar data for all member stations. While BBM is currently diary-based, it is in the process of converting to market-driven television audience meters (TAM).

A.C. Nielsen Company of Canada Limited   Subscribers to research information supplied by A.C. Nielsen include broadcasters, advertising agencies, and advertisers. Nielsen offers two basic services for television: the Nielsen Television Index (NTI) and the Nielsen Broadcast Index (NBI).

The NTI is a national service that estimates network audiences 52 weeks a year for the five commercial television networks: CBC, CTV, Global, Radio Canada and TVA. Since September of 1989, network television audiences have been measured by the Nielsen People Meter, an electronic measuring device. The NBI measures television station and program audiences in 42 local markets across Canada.

Audit Bureau of Circulations   The ABC is a non-profit organization composed of advertisers, advertising agencies, and publishers of newspapers and magazines. The objectives of the Audit Bureau are to issue standard statements of circulation—or other data—reported by members, to verify the figures shown in these statements, and, with complete objectivity, to disseminate the data that has been reported.[8]

Canadian Circulations Audit Board   The CCAB is a national non-profit organization, formed primarily to audit the circulation of members' publications and to issue standardized statements for the use of advertisers and their advertising agencies. The CCAB provides audited circulation data regarding trade and professional publications, farm papers, paid-circulation consumer magazines, community weekly newspapers, controlled-circulation magazines, and publications distributed in bulk.

*A*DVERTISING LAWS AND REGULATIONS

The advertising industry in Canada is a highly regulated industry. Regulation and control come from two primary sources: the Canadian Radio-television Telecommunications Commission (CRTC), which governs all broadcasting laws, including advertising; and the Canadian Advertising Foundation (CAF), which administers regulations based on codes of practice voluntarily established by the Advertising Standards Council (ASC).

The mandate of the CRTC is to enforce Parliament's intent that the national broadcasting system serve the national purpose. This regulatory body legislates

- Canadian ownership/control of broadcast outlets
- License applications and renewal of all broadcast outlets
- Commercial content and Canadian content
- Cable TV licenses (application, renewal and fee structures)

With regard to advertising, the CRTC approves all commercial scripts for foods, drugs, alcoholic beverages, and cosmetic products.

The Canadian Advertising Foundation is an umbrella organization that speaks on behalf of all advertisers, advertising agencies, and media. The organization coordinates the industry's response to vital issues that affect the entire advertising community. The role of the CAF is to improve the public's understanding of advertising and how it works and to help maintain industry standards and codes of ethics.[9]

With regard to maintaining industry standards, the Advertising Standards Council enforces codes of practice. It is responsible for vetting commercials which, whether through the orientation of their message or through their placement within childrens' programs, are directed at children of 12 and under. It also reviews and clears commercials for feminine sanitary-protection products and cosmetics.

Complete details on the various broadcasting codes administered by the Advertising Standards Council and information on government legislation administered by the CRTC can be found in Appendix I.

CRITICISMS OF CONTEMPORARY ADVERTISING

The voices that speak against advertising are many. They can be found in national and provincial legislatures. They can be found in consumer groups. They can be found in churches, universities and in magazine articles.[10]

Advertising is an industry that is often under attack. Some major issues faced by the advertising industry are discussed in this section.

SEX-ROLE STEREOTYPING AND THE USE OF SEX IN ADVERTISING

The advertising industry is constantly being attacked for its portrayal of women. Advertising for product categories such as alcohol, food, personal-care, and household-products often presents women in subservient roles. Such portrayals are strongly linked to the traditional roles of men and women in society and to outdated consumer patterns whereby the male head of the household was responsible for major purchasing decisions. (See the sections on demographics in chapter 4 for further discussion.) Equally controversial is the use of women and men in provocative poses to promote the sale of a product.

As early as 1979, the CRTC established a Public Sector Task Force to examine the portrayal of women in the broadcast media. This review indicated that many advertisements were insulting to women. Major concerns raised by the task force centred on the portrayal of the sexes: specifically, the predominance of male authority figures, the use of sexual innuendoes, and the exclusion of ethnic and older women. At the same time, the industry itself, through the Advertising Advisory Board (AAB), then known as the Canadian Advertising Advisory Board (CAAB), volunteered a list of nine proposals, presented in the form of action statements, aimed at encouraging a more realistic portrayal of women and men by advertisers in Canada. These guidelines recognized the changing roles of women and men and encouraged advertising to present a more realistic picture of the sexes: men and women would be shown as equally able; sexist language would be avoided; and a balance between the sexes in the decision-making process would be depicted.

The entire issue was re-examined again in 1986, and the findings of the CRTC were almost predictable. It reported that self-regulation had not succeeded in eliminating sex-role stereotyping, and that there was a need for regulation and legislation in order to eliminate the problem. It recommended penalties for advertisers who failed to comply with guidelines.[11] As a result of these and other investigations into this issue, many advertisers have changed their style of advertising and are presenting messages showing women in more progressive and contemporary roles and occupations. Others, however, have not changed.

Even though regulations have been tightened in the industry, the issue of sex in advertising (does advertising sell sex and does sex sell products?) remains controversial. It seems that sex is a staple ingredient of many things we enjoy—it is in the

Advertising in Action
Does Sex Really Sell?

Is sex in advertising really an issue? Does advertising sell sex, and if so, does sex sell the product? A few examples suggest that it does.

Let's first consider Beeman's gum. Its now classic commercial titled "Girl Watching" was a hit with males everywhere. If you are not familiar with the commercial, it showed nothing but beautiful, tightly-clad women strolling along the waterfront to the sound of "I'm a man, yes I am and I can't help but love you so."

Research conducted by Beeman's had led to the unsurprising conclusion that gum-chewing males have a passion for beautiful females, so the decision was made to give the target market what it wanted. The commercial made unabashed use of sex. And apparently it worked; Beeman's is now a top-selling brand. Prior to the use of this advertising theme, Beeman's gum didn't have any image to speak of.

Next, Molson's encountered much controversy for its Canadian ad "The Rare Long-Haired Fox." The controversy started when the Toronto Transit Commission decided to pull the ad from its vehicles, stating that it violated its guidelines regarding sexual exploitation. The copy of the ad read in part: "The fox is an attractive creature with sleek hair and lovely colouring. Her superior agility and intelligence enable her to outrun and outwit other animals, such as wolves." In the television commercial, the fox only wears a bikini, and the camera briefly pans over her body.

Finally, a bar poster for Carlsberg Light beer walks the fine line between sexy and sexist. In the poster, a bathing-suit-clad woman appears in an archway set against a striking blue sky. An anonymous arm props up a case of Carlsberg Light in another archway. LaRue

Shields, the creative director of the ad, stated that the target market "wants to see a woman," adding that women do wear bathing suits and that "there is nothing depicted in the ad that is out of the ordinary."

Glen Cavanaugh, the national-brand-development manager at Labatt Breweries of Canada, said that the poster "strives to be sexy, not sexist." He also reported that women who were shown the ad informally were not offended by the image; rather, they found it "interesting."

The Rare Long-Haired Fox.

Molson Canadian. What Beer's All About.

Adapted from Laura Medcalf, "Bathing beauty helps turn beer ad into art form," "*Marketing*, October 15, 1990, pp.1,3.

books we read, in the films we see, and in the music we listen to. Sex has been known to stimulate the sales of cosmetics and perfumes, blue jeans, motorcycles, beer, and even pantyhose. Advertising messages for Obsession, a Calvin Klein perfume, are quite provocative. Their use of unclad bodies in advertising messages is now commonplace, but still controversial.

If sex is readily assimilated into so many other areas of our lives, why is its role in advertising regarded with such suspicion? Part of the answer to this question revolves around the use of women as sex objects to sell products such as beer. Refer to the Advertising in Action feature "Does Sex Really Sell?" and the advertisement that accompanies this feature for help in formulating your own opinion.

COMPARATIVE AND MISLEADING ADVERTISING

In **comparative advertising**, two or more competing products are compared on the basis of a common attribute (taste, performance, etc.). The Canadian food-and-beverage industry is probably the largest user of comparative advertising. In recent years, the public has been exposed to the claims and counter-claims of Pepsi-Cola and Coca-Cola Classic, Diet Pepsi and Diet Coke, 7Up and Sprite, to name a few.

The *Manual of General Guidelines for Advertising* points out that "consumer information often becomes more meaningful through factual comparisons." However, the *Manual* goes on to say that "this form of advertising is susceptible to abuse and can lead to unfair representation or false disparagement of competition."[12] Several issues prevail in the area of comparative advertising. Many argue that comparisons which are false, unfair, or misleading can result in an unwise buying decision being made by consumers. Also, there is the risk that the data being used to compare the products may lack substantiation.

In Canada, one of the most celebrated comparative advertising campaigns was launched by Pepsi-Cola. Pepsi-Cola came under review by the advertising Standards Council for false and misleading advertising during the so-called "Cola Wars." In one commercial, a Pepsi truck was shown passing a Coca-Cola truck, an image which might have left consumers with the wrong impression. In actual fact, Coca-Cola was the leading brand at the time, so any message that implied otherwise was false and misleading. In a more recent case, Victor Kiam and his company, Remington Products, and their agency, Grey Advertising of Toronto, were charged with false and misleading advertising by the Marketing Practices Branch of the Department of Consumer and Corporate Affairs. Certain claims for the Micro Screen Ultimate shaver were disputed. The Crown disputed the advertised claims that the Micro Screen "shaves as close as a blade and closer than any other electric shaver", "gets whiskers others leave behind", and that "in independent tests, approximately 70% said it shaves closer than any other electric shaver." The Crown argued that such performance claims were not supported by proper and adequate tests.[13] Remington was found guilty in an Ontario Court and was fined $75 000.

There is no specific body that regulates comparative advertising in Canada. The Marketing Practices Branch of Consumer and Corporate Affairs monitors complaints and brings charges forward when necessary. The industry regulates itself through the

Advertising Standards Council of the Canadian Advertising Foundation. Clause 6 of the Canadian Code of Advertising Standards states that

> Advertisements must not discredit or attack unfairly other products, services, or advertisements, or exaggerate the nature or importance of competitive differences. When comparisons are made with competing products the advertiser must make substantiation available promptly upon the request from the Council.[14]

For more details on guidelines governing comparative advertising, the reader should refer to Appendix I.

ADVERTISING TO CHILDREN

Advertising messages directed at children often bypass parents. As a result, parents are concerned about the content of these messages, which could have a powerful influence on their child's behaviour.

Some of the criticism of advertising directed at children centres on conflicts between children and parents over purchases. The children start demanding higher-priced "in" goods when parents prefer to buy less expensive alternatives. Toys and clothing products are often the centre of this dispute. A criticism often directed at advertisements for toys is that they disappoint children by making exaggerated and unfulfillable claims for their products. A product that is made to look fascinating on television may lead to a complicated and frustrating experience for a young child when the toy is purchased. Finally, young children who cannot distinguish commercials from program content may become confused. For example, many of the popular children's programs today such as "Ghostbusters", "Teenage Mutant Ninja Turtles", and "Super Mario Brothers 3" are all closely tied into the marketing and merchandising activity of toy and game manufacturers.

The largest of the advertisers that direct messages to children are toy and food-product manufacturers. Products such as pre-sweetened cereals, candies and chocolate bars, cakes and cookies, and fast-food restaurants advertise heavily to children. Demonstrating the impact such messages have is the fact that, though it might be the parents that decide to eat out at a restaurant, more often than not it is young children who decide which restaurant.

Perhaps the real issue is whether advertising directed at children should be allowed. At what age do they understand that the purpose of the ad is to sell them a product? Children are vulnerable, and there is clearly a need for some form of protection. Since 1980, Quebec has banned altogether advertising to children under the age of 13. Advertisers such as toy and food manufacturers feared that other provinces would follow, but such has not been the case. Under the Quebec legislation, companies such as Toys 'R Us, Dare Foods and Kraft General Foods have all faced charges. The ban itself has created problems of another nature. The loss in advertising revenues has meant less funding for children's programming in the French language. Consequently, French Canadian children are watching more English-language programming, a situation which undermines the promotion of the French language. Quebec is now rethinking the ban on children's advertising.

For more information on broadcast codes governing advertising directed at children, refer to Appendix I.

ADVERTISING OF TOBACCO AND ALCOHOL

The advertising of products generally deemed to be harmful presents challenges for those companies which manufacture and market such products. Alcohol and tobacco manufacturers are criticized by consumer groups for the manner in which they advertise, even though they are promoting legally-sold products that generate significant tax dollars for governments.

One of the more common objections of consumer groups is that advertising promotes the sale and consumption of alcohol and tobacco, products that are potentially harmful to health. Consumers also affirm that the manner in which manufacturers appeal to target groups is objectionable (for example, the use of sex and sex-role stereotyping, youthful presenters, and lifestyle associations). According to the Non-smokers Rights Association, the distinctive lifestyle-oriented promotional campaign for the mint flavour of Cameo Special, a campaign which included outdoor posters and point-of-purchase displays, "was a blatant play for the youth market."[15] The critics charge that smoking does not enjoy the positive image it once had and that, as a result, the industry, in order to survive, is resorting to desperate measures such as appealing to youthful targets.

On the industry side of the issue, the products are legally marketed, yet manufacturers must deal with substantial government laws, both federal and provincial, restricting how and where their products are advertised. The latest controversy is the federal legislation (Bill C-51), which banned most forms of tobacco advertising effective January 1, 1989. Under the ban, outdoor advertising can continue until January 1991, and point-of-purchase material can remain until January 1993. Event marketing and sponsorship can continue at 1989 spending levels as long as the sponsor is identified by a corporate name, not a brand name. Rothman's president, Patrick Fennel, is vehement in his response to legislation banning the promotion of tobacco products. He states that such legislation "blocks the free flow of information about a legal product, and to ban commercial speech about a legal product is to distort the economic voting process that is central to our system of consumer sovereignty."[16]

Legislation governing the advertising of alcohol products varies from one segment to another (the segments being hard alcohol, beer and wine). Hard alcohol may not be advertised on television or radio, although the industry has appealed to the CRTC to allow television advertising. The hard-alcohol industry claims that current regulations are discriminatory. Advertising for beer and wine is allowed on television, but commercials must be approved by the CRTC in advance. To be approved, the ad must not promote general use, but promoting brand preference is acceptable. To the credit of the industry, it is the beer, wine and alcohol manufacturers, not the government, that allocate a considerable amount of money each year to promoting responsible consumption.

Summary

Advertising is defined as any paid form of nonpersonal presentation and promotion of goods, services, or ideas by an identified sponsor. The specific role of advertising is to influence favourably potential customers' responses to a product by communicating relevant information about the product, such as how the product will satisfy a need.

Advertising may be divided into two broad categories: consumer advertising and business-to-business advertising. Consumer advertising is used by companies that produce national brands and by retailers. It includes direct-response communications. Business-to-business advertising includes trade, industrial, professional and corporate advertising.

For advertising to be effective, certain conditions must be favourable: there must be market and product demand, the product must be at an appropriate stage in the product life cycle, the product should have a competitive advantage, the advertising environment must be correct, the product must be of adequate quality, and management must be committed to advertising the product.

The Canadian advertising industry comprises three primary groups and numerous support groups. The primary groups include the advertisers (client), the advertising agencies, and the media. Support groups include the Association of Canadian Advertisers, the Institute of Canadian Advertising, and numerous media associations. Regulation and control of the advertising industry comes under the jurisdiction of the federal government, through the Canadian Radio-television and Telecommunications Commission, and under voluntary regulations administered by the Canadian Advertising Foundation.

Some of the major issues confronting the industry include sex-role stereotyping and the use of sex in advertising to sell products, comparative advertising practices, advertising directed at children, and advertising of tobacco and alcohol products. In response to criticism from a variety of sources, the industry has established codes of practice to cover these issues.

Review Questions

1. What is the role of advertising? How does it relate to the marketing concept?
2. Explain the differences between advertising, sales promotion, and public relations.
3. Identify and explain the types of
   i) consumer advertising
   ii) business-to-business advertising
4. Advertising can be effective only under certain conditions. What are these conditions and why is each important?

5. What roles do the Canadian Radio-television and Telecommunications Commission (CRTC) and the Canadian Advertising Foundation play in the advertising industry?

Discussion Questions

1. "Advertising portrays women in subservient roles." Is this statement valid today? Explain why or why not.
2. Collect some print advertisements for a product that uses sex as its central means of appealing to its target market. Analyze the advertisements for applicability and potential impact. Do you agree or disagree with this type of advertising practice? Present viewpoints to substantiate your position.
3. "Is comparative advertising a wise investment or a waste of money?" Discuss this issue.
4. Should advertising bans apply to products sold legally in Canada? Discuss this issue.

CHAPTER 2

Advertising Management–The Client

In studying this chapter, you will learn

- The various organization systems for managing the advertising function
- The skills required to function effectively in the position of advertising manager
- The position, role and responsibility of the advertising manager
- The criteria and procedures a client follows when selecting an advertising agency

Discussion in this chapter focuses on the **advertising manager** and on his or her role and responsibility within the client organization. How do organizations vary in their management of the advertising function, and how do they go about selecting the advertising agency that will be responsible for handling their advertising needs? In this selection process, the advertising manager plays a key role. Depending on the size and nature of the organization, the title of the advertising manager may vary. Other similar titles might be director of advertising or manager of marketing services; or the advertising-management function could be included among the responsibilities of the marketing manager. While recognizing these title variations, this chapter will use the term advertising manager.

Chapter 2 is closely related to chapter 3, which deals with the advertising agency. In industry jargon, these two organizations—the client organization and the advertising agency—are the "client side" and the "agency side," respectively.

CLIENT-SIDE ADVERTISING MANAGEMENT

Management of the advertising function usually falls under the jurisdiction of the marketing department in an organization. Thus it is very common for numerous managers to be directly or indirectly involved with the task of advertising. The number of managers involved depends on the size and nature of the organization and on the relative importance advertising plays in the marketing of the products. For example, in a large organization that utilizes the brand-management system, numerous managers may be involved in advertising. Junior-level managers are active in the day-to-day affairs, while senior-level managers are active in the approval process. In some organizations, approvals may be required from a brand manager, from all members of the marketing-management ranks, and, finally, from the president of the company. Obviously, all managers are concerned about the quality and content of the messages communicated about the company and its products.

In other organizations, an advertising manager may have greater responsibility for advertising, and may not require approvals from others prior to implementation. In smaller advertising organizations (particularly those lacking marketing-resource depth), it is quite common for senior-level executives to be more actively involved in day-to-day advertising affairs. A discussion of the various advertising-management systems follows.

ORGANIZING THE ADVERTISING FUNCTION

There are several ways in which advertising can be organized and managed in the client organization. It can be organized by management system, usually a product-management or category-management system, which is popular among consumer-packaged-goods companies such as Coca-Cola, Pepsi-Cola, Kraft General Foods, and Procter & Gamble. Other alternatives include geographic-location, or regional, organization, a target-market organization, or organization by function (by type of activity).

Category- or Product-Management System

In the **product-management system**, all company brands are divided up so that certain individuals (brand managers) are responsible for the marketing activity of a brand or group of brands. A brand manager, or product manager, works with others in the organization and with external suppliers such as advertising agencies, promotion houses, research firms, and package suppliers. The brand manager/product manager is responsible for planning and managing a brand or a small group of brands. Depending on the size of the organization, the brand manager reports to a category manager (an individual responsible for a large group of similar products) or to a marketing manager. For multi-product companies, this system *ensures that all products receive equal attention in the planning area, even though certain products may have a higher marketing profile.*

Internally, this system encourages friendly competition, as managers compete for the resources of the firm (people, time, and money) to ensure that their product receives the attention it deserves. A diagram of the product-management system is presented in figure 2.1. In this illustration, it is assumed that the product managers are responsible for the planning of all four Ps, as well as advertising, and, as a consequence, would deal directly with the agency on creative and media assignments. Other firms may integrate an advertising manager into the product-management system, owing to the specialized nature of this marketing variable.

Figure 2.1   Product-management system

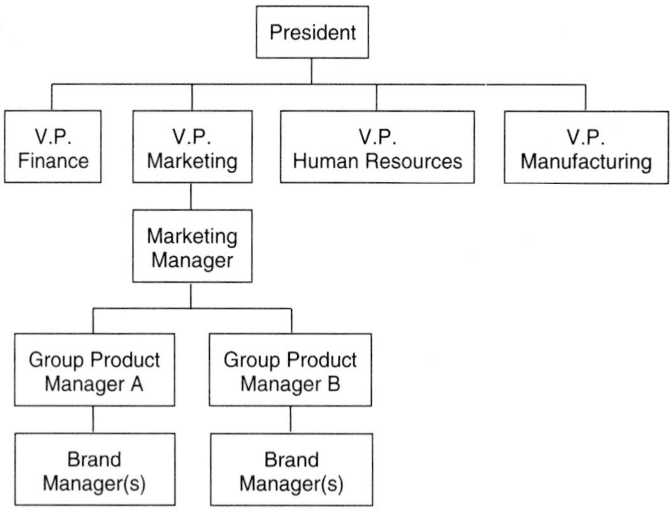

Advertising responsibility at group and brand level.

Geographic Management

In a **geographic-management system**, advertising is organized according to region, the assumption being that *advertising must be tailored to meet the varying needs of different regions.*

Figure 2.2   Geographic-management system

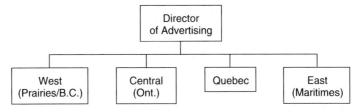

In Canada, the diversity of geographic locations, languages, and cultural backgrounds necessitates different advertising strategies. For example, an organization such as McDonald's will implement, in addition to national advertising strategies, regional campaigns that reflect local needs and shopping patterns. In addition, independent owner/operators of McDonald's outlets develop their own local-market advertising, geared directly to the target audience in the immediate area.

In the geographic-management system, advertising executives should be located in the areas where they are responsible for advertising. Labatts Breweries of Canada is a company with many national brands and regional brands. Consequently, it uses regional brand managers as well as national brand managers. These regional managers would report directly to a national advertising manager, who would be responsible for co-ordinating the advertising function. Refer to figure 2.2 for a diagram of a geographic advertising-management system.

Functional Management

In organizations that use a **functional-management system**, responsibility for advertising *is divided up on the basis of type of activity*. For example, extremely large companies may have separate departments responsible for various promotion and communications components. A public affairs department may be responsible for corporate advertising communications and public-relations activity, while other departments may be responsible for consumer-product advertising, trade advertising, or sales promotion. Another option is to divide responsibility by area of specialty, between a creative department and a media department. In this last situation, where a company is actually performing two functions—devising strategy and executing strategy—the organization is using what is referred to as an in-house agency which could be staffed by creative and media specialists. Refer to figure 2.3 for a diagram of a functional-management system.

Figure 2.3   Functional-management system

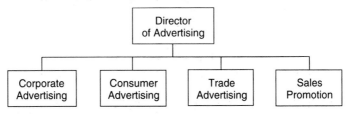

Target-Market Management

In a **target-market management** system, the organization recognizes that *different customer classes with different needs require different advertising strategies.* Such a system makes sense for multi-division companies dealing with diverse target markets. A company with both industrial and consumer customer bases would utilize different strategies when communicating with these targets. For example, a pharmaceutical manufacturer selling a product to the medical profession would require detailed, technical advertising to help convince doctors of the product's benefits. Communicating the benefits of the same product to the ultimate consumer would require a different advertising strategy. The same could be said of a business-equipment manufacturer (e.g., a micro-computer firm), which would direct different messages to industrial, institutional, and consumer user groups. In the case of different targets, communications may be more effective if the organization of the advertising function is based solely on the customer's needs. A diagram of the target-market management system is included in figure 2.4.

Figure 2.4   Target-market management system

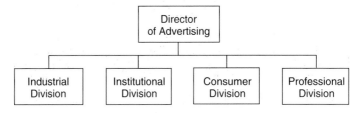

These traditional systems of advertising management are now being challenged by the changes occurring in the worldwide marketplace. The following section discusses some of these changes and their implications for the management of advertising.

Global Management of Advertising

Numerous changes in the marketplace are forcing companies to rethink how advertising is managed. Among these changes are the Canada-U.S. free trade agreement, the opening of Eastern European and USSR markets, and the elimination of trade barriers within the European Economic Community by 1992. Occurrences such as these will alter the patterns of global advertising.

In advertising, clients will increasingly look to agencies that have worldwide affiliations. Ideas that are developed in one country may be considered for another so that economies of scale are achieved. The often used expression, "Thinking globally and acting locally," is now a common salute among multinational advertisers. For example, an independent survey conducted by *Marketing News*, in the United States, showed that an overwhelming majority (84%) of marketing executives believe that regionally targeted advertising is the best approach for internationally marketed products. Moreover, 89% foresaw a future trend toward global advertising that is more visually uniform but has a culturally specific message.[1]

Similar thinking prevails in Canada, given the trends in the global marketplace. In a speech to the Advertising and Sales Club of Toronto, Peter Mills, the president of Baker Lovick Advertising, cited several trends that will cause change in Canada. Of significance were his comments about "the globalization or North Americanizing of marketing and communication strategies," and his suggestion that "English Canada is increasingly being seen as part of an English-speaking North American market in which there are more similarities than differences." [2] Contemporary marketing and advertising managers are redefining geographic targets in terms of north-south corridors as opposed to Canada's east-west divisions, with Canada being grouped with states like New York, Ohio, Minnesota, Michigan, and Washington.

The perceived similarity between Canadian and U.S. markets will influence the management of advertising. If U.S. head-office marketing departments and their advertising agencies can develop campaigns that work for the Canadian as well as for the U.S. market (e.g., common visuals, distinctive message), the cost savings will be significant. The marketing and advertising functions in Canada could be eliminated.

THE ADVERTISING MANAGER

Since responsibility for advertising management varies among advertising and marketing organizations, discussion here will centre on the general aspects of the advertising-management function. Regardless of position title, advertising management will be viewed in terms of the skills required, the role, and the responsibility.

THE NATURE OF THE BEAST

The advertising manager must possess the proper mix of management skills in order to function properly in the position and must, at the same time, produce the best quality of advertising for the company. What skills are required for such a task? Since the position revolves around the planning function, the basic skills required are a mixture of analytical/planning skills, leadership skills, and a combination of knowledge and experience. Let's briefly discuss each component.

Analytical and Planning Skills

The advertising manager must be able to define problems and, ultimately, recommend appropriate means of resolving them. The manager is responsible for collecting and analyzing research data which, once analyzed, provides advertising direction. With respect to planning, the manager prepares appropriate documentation to brief agency personnel on such necessary matters as establishing objectives and strategies.

Leadership Skills

The advertising manager acts, externally, as a liaison between the client and the agency, and, internally, works with other managers and staff people on an equal basis. The advertising manager must *solicit the co-operation of others if effective advertising is to result.* Internally, co-ordinating activities with sales managers, research managers, and product managers is mandatory; externally, the advertising manager must stimulate agency people to put maximum effort into creative and media recommendations.

Knowledge and Experience

Being an advertising manager does not require a background in art or media. Since much of the work is delegated to specialists, the manager primarily requires knowledge of procedures: such as how advertising is developed from start to finish, and what to ask for from the specialists at any given stage in the process. Also, the manager must *know what information and direction to provide external suppliers with in order to get maximum effort from them.* Obviously, the experienced manager can offer insight into all of these areas, and will possess the proper skills to co-ordinate the advertising activities of a company. By and large, however, the job demands a people-oriented individual, since the human element (i.e., people developing ideas) is the major resource in advertising. People who get along on both a personal and business level foster a better working environment.

POSITION, ROLE, AND RESPONSIBILITY

The position of advertising manager is usually a mid-management position in the client organization. Frequently, the advertising manager reports to a director of marketing or vice-president of marketing. Position titles that sometimes incorporate the advertising-management function are marketing-services manager, which implies a broad range of duties that include advertising; or director of advertising.

The advertising manager's position in the client organization is outlined in figure 2.5. Figure 2.5 also outlines the flow of communications between the advertising agency and the client at mid-management and senior-management levels. For the sake of convenience, the diagram assumes the use of the brand-management system of advertising planning, in which co-ordination of advertising activity for all company products falls under the jurisdiction of the marketing-services manager or advertising manager.

Figure 2.5   Position of advertising manager in consumer goods organization

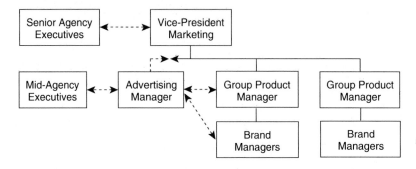

---▶ = Client-Agency Communications Flow

As well as developing overall marketing objectives and strategies, the advertising manager is supposed to develop and implement effective and efficient advertising plans (creative and media) that will contribute to the achievement of specifically stated marketing and advertising objectives. Given this general role, what does the advertising manager do? The following are the key areas of responsibility.

Advertising Planning and Budgeting

Working with other marketing managers, the advertising manager will contribute to the marketing plan. At this stage, advertising would be recognized as one element in the marketing mix; hence, the role it will play in the achievement of objectives will be clearly identified. When the marketing plan is developed, general budget guidelines will be established that will aid in the development of a more comprehensive advertising plan at a later point. *The expertise of the advertising manager will be called upon when budget requirements are being established in the marketing plan.*

Activity Co-ordination with Other Marketing Variables

The expression "a chain is only as strong as its weakest link" applies well to advertising and to its role in the marketing process. To be effective, advertising must work together with other marketing variables (product, price, place, and other promotion variables), and, when appropriate, call upon the resources available in other marketing areas, particularly marketing research, so that better advertising plans can be developed.

Other activities closely associated with advertising are sales promotion and marketing research. It is quite common for promotion activity to become part of the advertising communications process, as when, for example, coupons, refunds, contests, and premium offers are used at various stages of the product life cycle. Therefore, the advertising manager is responsible for *integrating promotion activities and plans with advertising activities and plans.*

Marketing and advertising research play an active role in the advertising-development process. Creative messages can be tested at various stages as a way of measuring their potential effect on the target market. Integration of research information is vital for developing effective communications. In these areas (promotion planning and research), the advertising manager works closely with external supply firms to devise and implement promotion activities and research programs. Once advertising and promotion plans have been finalized, the advertising manager is often responsible for distributing plan details to sales-management personnel. Communication of advertising details to the sales force is vital, since the information can be used to inform customers of programs that will help them resell company products.

Monitoring the Advertising Program

In this area, the advertising manager *ensures that advertising execution is in accordance with the actual plan.* For example, the manager may request a post-buy media analysis to ensure that desired reach levels were actually achieved. Also, the manager carefully reviews budgets and planned media expenditures throughout the year, making changes when necessary. To illustrate: competitive activity might dictate an increase in spending, so the manager must know what options are available on short notice. Or, a company may be facing a profit-squeeze situation, and spending on advertising might have to be reduced. In this case, the manager must know what flexibility there is for cancellation of media.

Evaluating the Advertising Program

The advertising manager is *accountable for the success or failure of company advertising programs*. Most advertising plans are based on quantifiable objectives, and whether these objectives are achieved can be determined through some form of advertising research. For example, a campaign may be designed to increase consumers' awareness of a product to a certain level, to generate sales leads, or to communicate a specific message. To measure the success of a commercial or print advertisement, the manager may conduct research at various stages (pre-test and post-test research). The evaluation process is critical, as the advertising manager must make recommendations for changes in advertising direction if research information so dictates. Also, research at carefully timed intervals, for any campaign, often helps in identifying potential trouble spots before they become problems. Advertising research is discussed in detail in chapter 9.

Liaison with Advertising Agency

Advertising managers are the direct link with the advertising agency, and hence they are in constant contact with agency personnel, checking the status of assignments and projects the agency may be working on.

As a liaison, one of the manager's key responsibilities is *providing the agency with appropriate information when new assignments occur*. For example, if a new advertisement or commercial is to be devised, the advertising manager will compile a creative briefing document outlining appropriate information regarding advertising background, and marketing and advertising objectives.

As the person in the middle, the advertising manager is often in the hot seat, because individuals and their egos must be satisfied at both ends of the advertising spectrum (client side and agency side). The manager is responsible for developing advertising that will be acceptable to all company personnel, who must approve the program (based on client input). Let's examine this situation more closely.

From the viewpoint of the agency, the advertising manager is the person it must satisfy first. If the manager does not like a particular creative or media recommendation, the chances of its being seen, let alone approved, by others on the client side are minimal. Being an experienced critic, and knowing client personnel and their expectations, the manager will provide the agency with input so that changes to the proposal can be made prior to the corporate-approval stage.

On the client side, once the creative or media assignment meets the specifications outlined in the marketing plan or briefing document, the advertising manager must carry the agency proposal through the corporate-approval network. At this stage, the idiosyncrasies of senior executives often come to the forefront. These executives offer opinions on how the advertisement or media proposal could be improved. The advertising manager must remain objective and use whatever selling skills are necessary to combat unnecessary changes to agency proposals. The ongoing requests for changes to the proposal that result from the corporate-approval system (and from attempting to satisfy each individual manager) often have a negative impact on client-agency relations.

Hiring and Firing of Advertising Agencies

Since the advertising manager is in constant contact with the advertising agency, he or she is in the best position to evaluate the agency's advertising needs (i.e., the work requirements and expectations of the agency). Also, the advertising manager is probably in the best position to evaluate the performance of the agency. While other marketing executives are involved in the selection and evaluation of an agency, the advertising manager has additional clout, owing to his or her close working relationship with the agency.

In this area of responsibility, the advertising manager must foster an atmosphere that will *stimulate the agency to produce creative and media recommendations that meet the needs of the client organization.* Many argue that this is the agency's responsibility, and that the agency needn't be motivated by the advertising manager, while others argue that it is a "people business," with success depending upon the existence of strong working relationships between the client and agency. Therefore, if agency performance is missing the mark, or if the working environment becomes strained due

Advertising in Action
Hired to Be Fired

Coaches of all professional sports teams know that the clock starts ticking as soon as they take over the reins. How many managers did George Steinbrenner go through in his tumultuous years as owner of the New York Yankees? How many coaches have the Toronto Maple Leafs had in the past 10 years? It's performance that counts, and in both New York and Toronto the coaches or managers weren't producing, so they were gone!

What does this have to do with advertising? Quite simply, the "what-have-you-done-for-me-lately" attitude is very prevalent in the advertising industry. Agencies are hired by clients to produce results—sales results! If the results aren't there—it's good-bye!

In the past few years, 1987 stands out as a banner year for saying good-bye. That year, a modern-day record was set. It was estimated that $281 million in billings (the value of media purchased on behalf of advertisers) moved from one agency to another. The previous year had also been record-breaking, but the amount that changed hands was a mere $213 million. There must have been a lot of unhappy clients. Among the winners and losers in 1987:

1. Ford Motor Company of Canada took its $25 million from Vickers and Benson Advertising and gave it to Young and Rubicam.
2. Toyota fired Ronalds-Reynolds, in favour of Saatchi and Saatchi. Twenty million dollars changed hands.
3. Nissan fired Ted Bates Advertising and Stratton Pearson Martin and Holman, and consolidated its account with Chiat/Day/Mojo. Eleven million dollars changed hands.

Other big moves included General Motors ($20 million), Ontario Lottery Corporation ($14 million), and Zellers ($14 million).

Adapted from "The Hammer was down," *Marketing*, January 4, 1988, pp.1,3.

to personality conflicts or other factors, the advertising manager may recommend to senior company executives a change of agencies. When changes are necessary, the advertising manager will be a key player in the search for and selection of a new agency. The firing of an agency and the hiring of another is a common circumstance in the industry. See the Advertising in Action vignette "Hired to be Fired" for more details.

SELECTING THE ADVERTISING AGENCY

Selecting a new advertising agency is a major decision for any company, since that decision can have a significant impact on the company's long-term sales and profit performance. In effect, the advertising agency is responsible for the care and maintenance of the client's most important asset—its reputation with the consumer.[3]

There is no ideal procedure for selecting an advertising agency; procedures used in the industry today vary from one advertiser to another. Regardless of the process, however, a major player is always the advertising manager. Since the advertising manager works directly with the advertising agency, it is critical that the right choice be made, since the payoff is a lasting working relationship that should ultimately boost company sales and profits. A company's association with an advertising agency should be viewed as a long-term partnership in which both parties can grow and mature while achieving mutual benefits. Because of this association, other key marketing executives should be actively involved in the selection process also.

The steps involved in selecting an advertising agency are briefly summarized in figure 2.6 and discussed in detail in the following section.

Figure 2.6 Six-step procedure for selecting an advertising agency

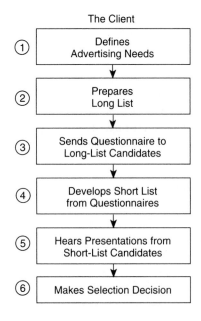

SIX-STEP PROCESS FOR SELECTING AN ADVERTISING AGENCY

1. Identify Advertising Needs

The first step is to assess the company's operations to determine advertising strengths and weaknesses. Essentially, this process will clarify what the *client requires* of an advertising agency. Much like a job description, a specific definition of needs enables advertisers to more easily sort through the variety of services offered by agencies.

Depending on the size and nature of the company, and on the importance of advertising to that company, the needs will vary. A written checklist of requirements, which takes into account both present and future needs, is essential in the selection process. This type of checklist allows the client to match its own needs against agency services in an objective manner. Once this objective evaluation is complete, the client can consider the "people-chemistry" aspect (i.e., would we enjoy working with these agency people?).

A typical list of needs might include some or all of the following elements.

Development Of:
 Marketing Plans
 Product Strategies
 New Product Planning
 Advertising Strategies
 Sales Promotion Concepts

Marketing Counsel On:
 Product Mix
 Pricing
 Target Marketing

Public Relations:
 Product Publicity

Creative Work On:
 Media Advertising
 Point-of-Purchase Material
 Sales Aids (brochures, etc.)
 Package Design

Marketing Research On:
 Creative and Media Evaluation

Media:
 Planning
 Buying

Prior to searching for a new agency, the client must be sure that change is what it really wants. Before dissolving the relationship, the client should candidly discuss matters with the current agency to see if the agency can be made to handle the account

Advertising in Action
It's Up for Grabs—$20 Million

In the world of advertising, it is the working relationship between a client and its agency that provides the impetus for progressive advertising campaigns. Much like a marriage, however, the client-agency relationship is not always without problems. Very often, the harsh realities of business dictate change, and change can happen suddenly and without warning. The reasons for change are many. Some of the ones most often cited are poor chemistry between client and agency personnel, philosophical differences in creative direction, agency mergers that create brand-assignment conflicts, and poor sales results.

The process of review is normal procedure in the industry, according to Ken Lambert, the director of marketing at Canadian Airlines International. Nineteen ninety was time for a review in his organization. There was no public criticism of the organization's current agency, McKim Advertising of Vancouver, and the fact that this was a client-agency relationship involving some $20 million and spanning some 40 years was inconsequential.

Canadian Airlines followed normal procedure. The first step was to clearly establish needs. Lambert stated, "We are simply looking for change. We'll be looking for a multinational agency that can handle us around the world, as opposed to just in Canada. And we are looking for a new agency in terms of creative bent—one we consider to be leading-edge. We want to enter the 1990s on a global basis, with a new look." In an open competition, McKim Vancouver was invited to submit a bid to retain the account, but they declined.

The next step was to formulate a long list of prospective agencies. This was accomplished by means of a credentials questionnaire. To be included on the long list, participating agencies had to demonstrate multinational capabilities, interesting and unique creative product, and strong account support. The goal was to find the best eight or nine agencies for the long list, and three or four for the short list.

Four agencies made the short list: Chiat/Day/Mojo, a relative newcomer to the Canadian scene, but with strong U.S. connections; Maclaren:Lintas Inc., Canada's largest advertising agency; Ogilvy & Mather, a worldwide agency; and BCP Strategy Creativity, a Montreal agency that already handled Canadian's English and French-language advertising in Quebec. As part of the competition, all four agencies had to prepare creative project presentations.

Following the presentations, Lambert announced that Chiat/Day/Mojo had won the account. Admitting that all four agencies had strong presentations, Lambert said that "it was the attitude of Chiat/Day/Mojo and their ability to get into the minds of the business traveller that influenced the decision." In a competitive situation, Chiat/Day/Mojo showed that it could quickly grasp what were Canadian's needs.

None of the finalists had any airline experience to draw upon, and, in summing up the process, Lambert felt that this was an advantage. His feelings were that Chiat/Day/Mojo could deliver a "fresh look." One of Lambert's aims was that the new agency not be shackled to or harnessed by creative ideas from the past.

Adapted from Randy Scotland, "Canadian Airlines up in the air," *Marketing*, July 2, 1990, p.1., and from "C/D/M nabs Canadian," *Marketing*, September 10, 1990, pp.1,3.

better. This is generally a last-ditch attempt, however, and perhaps a waste of time if the client has conducted proper evaluations on previous occasions.

The decision to seek another agency is a critical step, as the flow of normal business activity is disrupted while a new agency becomes acquainted with the new account. Nevertheless, account hiring and firing is a common phenomenon in the advertising industry. *Marketing* magazine and *Playback Strategy* both publish, on a regular basis, summaries of account switches. Refer to the Advertising in Action feature "It's Up for Grabs—$20 Million" for an illustration of the reasons and procedures for selecting a new advertising agency.

2. Develop a "Long List" of Agencies

At this stage, the client compiles a long list of 10 to 15 agencies whose services appear to match its advertising requirements. This matching process is based on information collected from several sources:

1. The Institute of Canadian Advertising can provide details regarding the size and type of its member agencies' (in this case, full-service agencies') operations.
2. *Canadian Advertising Rates and Data* (CARD) identifies personnel listings for Canadian advertising agencies.
3. *The National List of Advertisers* identifies advertisers, their present agencies, and the product lines assigned to agencies; this list enables advertisers to exclude from consideration agencies that have potential account conflicts (i.e., agencies that handle competitors' product lines).
4. Visits to Agencies. An informal visit to prospective advertising agencies will give the company a feel for the agencies' working environments and, perhaps, for the people employed there.

3. Submit Questionnaire to Long-List Candidates

Questionnaires are commonly used to assess potential agencies. The purpose of the questionnaire is to collect preliminary information about each agency so that company personnel can determine which agencies can best meet the company's advertising needs (from criteria established in step 1). A *briefing document* normally accompanies the questionnaire. The briefing document should describe the company and product lines, and give information regarding involvement with other agencies (multi-agency companies), and regarding the product and market in question. Confidential information need not be transmitted; however, product information should provide agencies with basic insight into the client's current advertising and marketing situation. This document is important to the agency, enabling its members to assess their capacity to meet the needs of the potential client. At this point, the agency can decide if the account is worth pursuing.

4. Develop a "Short List"

At this stage, all agency replies to the questionnaire will be evaluated in terms of how well they answer the needs established in step 1. Usually three to four agencies make the short list, and each is invited to make a credentials presentation. Agencies excluded from the long list should be informed and provided with reasons why they did not make the short list.

5. Credentials Presentation

In a credentials presentation, the contenders on the short list are given the opportunity to introduce their account-service, creative, and media people. Since the presentation is a key part of the decision-making process, it is important that all agencies base their presentations on specifications established by the client.

There are, normally, three types or levels of credentials presentations:

1. *Capabilities Presentations:* these are limited to the presentation of the agency's experience, service facilities, and people.
2. *Strategic Presentations:* these involve a presentation of the agency's ideas regarding the client's marketing situation and strategies.
3. *Creative-Project Presentations:* these call for a more thorough presentation, involving an actual marketing/advertising situation; the agency must develop and present creative, and possibly even media, recommendations based on client-supplied objectives.[4]

If a creative-project presentation is required, the client should be prepared to underwrite the costs involved. It should also be noted that many agencies are not in favour of speculative project presentations. These agencies believe that such presentations are of little value because they are based on the incomplete data normally supplied by the client. Also, the agency is giving up valuable resource time that could have been directed at handling the affairs of current clients. Clients who do not require speculative presentations will base their assessment of an agency's strategic thinking and creative ability on its performance with other clients. A list of satisfied clients suggests a lot about an agency's ability.

Regardless of the type of presentation, it should be made by those agency people who will be actually working on the account. This gives the client the opportunity to judge the agency's ability and its compatibility with the client's marketing personnel.

6. Make the Selection Decision

Based on the quality of the presentations and an objective assessment of the agency and the personnel who will be handling the account, a decision is made.

As stated earlier in the chapter, the client-agency relationship is really a business partnership; therefore, a formal agreement between both parties should be drawn up. To avoid any misunderstandings, both parties should, as they draw up the documents, consider the method of compensation to be used (for discussion of the fees versus commissions methods of compensation, see chapter 3), billing and payment details, itemized lists of the services required of the agency, and an understanding of the review and evaluation procedures for both parties.

For more detailed insight into the use of questionnaires in the agency-selection process, refer to the sample questionnaire model included in the Part One case "Working Together: The Client and the Agency."

Summary

Advertising management usually comes under the jurisdiction of the marketing department. The size and marketing sophistication of the organization often dictate how advertising is managed. In large organizations, the system used to manage the advertising function can be based on product, on geographical area, on function, or on target market. Large organizations often integrate the advertising responsibility with other marketing functions. Other organizations may utilize an advertising manager, responsible for advertising activity only.

The advertising manager's main role is to develop and implement effective advertising plans. The qualities required to perform effectively in the role of advertising manager include analytical and planning skills, leadership skills, advertising knowledge, and experience. Responsibilities include planning and budgeting, co-ordination of advertising with other marketing activity, liaising with the advertising agency, and securing executive approval to implement advertising plans. Once plans are implemented, the manager is responsible for evaluating advertising, for which he or she is held accountable.

Since advertising managers are constantly communicating with the advertising agency, they play a major role in the search for and selection of new agencies and, should the need arise, in the firing of current agencies.

Review Questions

1. What characteristics do the leading advertisers in Canada have in common?
2. What are the alternative management systems for managing the advertising function? Briefly describe each system.
3. What are the basic skills required to be an effective advertising manager?
4. Identify and explain the role and responsibilities of the advertising manager.
5. What is the six-step procedure for selecting an advertising agency?

Discussion Questions

1. Advertising is a specialized area and should be managed separately from other marketing activities in the client organization." Discuss this statement.
2. Speculative presentations are of little value," say many advertising agencies. Discuss this statement from (i) the agency viewpoint, (ii) the client viewpoint.
3. Review the advertising vignette " Hired to be Fired." What are your own viewpoints on the premise of this vignette?

Advertising Management– The Agency

CHAPTER 3

In studying this chapter, you will learn

- What are the largest advertising agencies in Canada
- The role and responsibilities of agencies in the advertising process
- The distinctions between the various types of advertising agencies
- How the organization and management of advertising agencies are distributed by functional area and position title
- The ways advertising agencies are compensated
- The relationships that exist between agencies and clients
- How agencies and clients evaluate each other's performances

Advertising agencies exist to help companies communicate with the public and to aid in the marketing of a company's product. The agency is a service company *that provides an essential link between the client (advertiser) and the public.* When the client company hires an advertising agency, it gains access to types of expertise it does not possess itself. Specifically, the client company gains access to creative and media specialists who will be responsible for planning and implementing vital components of the overall marketing plan.

ADVERTISING AGENCIES IN CANADA

The precise number of Canadian advertising agencies is unknown, but the October 1990 issue of *Canadian Advertising Rates and Data* (CARD) lists over 500. This list includes full-service agencies, creative and media specialists, and small-, medium-, and large-size agencies.

Figure 3.1   Canada's Top 10 Advertising Agencies

1989	*Rank by Billings* *($ million)*
1. Maclaren:Lintas Inc.	220.0
2. Cossette Communications-Marketing	215.4
3. FCB/Ronalds-Reynolds Limited	202.0
4. J. Walter Thompson Company Ltd.	195.0
5. Young & Rubicam Limited	193.8
6. McCann-Erickson Advertising Ltd.	190.9
7. McKim Advertising Limited	185.3
8. Ogilvy & Mather (Canada) Limited	183.0
9. Saffer Advertising Inc.	180.0
10. Vickers & Benson Advertising Ltd.	169.1

1990	*Rank by Revenue* *($ million)*
1. McKim Advertising Ltd.	33.4
2. MacLaren:Lintas Inc.	33.3
3. Cossette Communication-Marketing	32.8
4. Young & Rubicam	30.0
5. McCann-Erickson Advertising Ltd.	27.9
6. Baker Lovick Advertising	27.3
7. Ogilvy & Mather (Canada) Ltd.	25.4
8. J. Walter Thompson Company Ltd.	23.8
9. Grey Canada	21.7
10. Saffer Advertising Inc.	20.9

Source: Adapted from "Canada's Top Agencies," *Marketing*, December 10, 1990.

Canadian advertising agencies are ranked according to their annual media billings or their revenues. The term **media billings** is defined as the total dollar volume of advertising handled by an agency; that is, the amount of time and space handled by an agency in one year. Currently, the largest advertising agency in Canada with respect to media billings is Maclaren: Lintas Inc., which has annual billings of $220 million. There are only three agencies in Canada billing in excess of $200 million.[1] By revenues, the largest agency in Canada is McKim Advertising Limited. For a complete list of the 10 largest agencies in Canada by billings and revenues, refer to figure 3.1.

Some advertising agencies on these lists have their origins in Canada, including McLaren Advertising and Saffer Advertising Inc. However, a majority of the largest agencies are subsidiaries of major U.S. agencies, and are associated with related agencies around the world. Included in this category are agencies such as J. Walter Thompson, Ogilvy & Mather, Vickers & Benson, Leo Burnett, and McCann-Erickson.

THE ROLE OF THE ADVERTISING AGENCY

Advertising agencies perform various functions, tailoring their services to meet the specific needs of individual clients. The actual degree of the agency's involvement and responsibility may vary from one client to another, depending on such factors as the size and expertise of the client company. For example, large advertisers such as Procter and Gamble, Kraft General Foods, or Coca-Cola are normally equipped with marketing expertise in the form of a group of in-house executives whose function is marketing management. Under these circumstances, the agency's role will likely be confined to the communications area. The agency will develop and implement creative and media plans. For small advertisers, many of whom may lack marketing skills, agencies can provide marketing-planning assistance that will complement overall client operations, not just advertising.

In the marketing decision-making and planning processes, agencies can provide assistance to clients in the following areas:

- Clearly defining and understanding the nature of potential target markets
- Defining the unique selling points of a product and developing positioning statements regarding competitors
- Developing recommendations on how to effectively communicate with the target market (What media? How often? How long?).

Making good decisions in these areas may require marketing research. Information obtained through marketing research will provide the framework for developing a strategic marketing plan and advertising plan. Since the relationship between a client and agency is essentially a partnership, each will make contributions to the planning and decision-making process. In summary, the services that the advertising agency offers are experience and expertise in communications, planning assistance, and objectivity in the planning process.

Experience and Expertise in Communications

Clients normally develop a comprehensive marketing plan that embraces all elements of the four Ps (product, price, place, and promotion). The agency will develop, in more detail, elements from the promotion component of the plan. Specifically, the agency will utilize the guidelines and objectives established in the marketing plan to develop and execute an advertising plan that will contribute to the achievement of the client's objectives.

Planning Assistance

The agency, through its account group (account executives and account supervisors), provides assistance not only in advertising, but also in the other areas of marketing. Depending upon the internal structure of the client, the account group of an agency might be used as an external planning group. Such external planning may be used in the areas of marketing research, sales promotion, and public relations.

A Sense of Objectivity in the Planning Process

A tendency among many advertisers is to utilize advertising that suits the company's established style or image. Often, clients view change in direction as a risk. The use of familiar-looking campaigns is a safe strategy, but it is not necessarily the most effective means of communicating with a target market. The advertising agency is not directly associated with the internal environment, and hence can provide an objective viewpoint that might offer alternative directions and recommendations for communicating with target markets. This external position can result in the development of customer-oriented campaigns, rather than company-oriented campaigns.

*T*YPES OF ADVERTISING AGENCIES

We noted in chapter 2 that the client must use certain criteria to select a suitable agency. Generally, this review takes into consideration factors such as agency size, the service mix the agency is capable of providing, the compatibility of agency personnel, and other intangible factors. The choice of who you hire to plan, prepare, and deliver a message is difficult. Choosing the right help for your needs should mean cost-efficient, effective advertising which achieves desired results in a traditionally expensive area (advertising).[2]

Now let's examine the types of advertising agencies operating in Canada. Our classifications are based on the characteristics mentioned earlier.

THE NATURE OF SERVICES PROVIDED

In terms of the services they provide, agencies can be subdivided into three distinct groups: full-service agencies, creative boutiques, and media-buying services. Freelancers comprise a fourth group who provide certain services; however, they usually work independently for any of the three primary groups.

Full-Service Agencies

Full-service agencies appeal strongly to larger advertisers, which need the variety of services offered. Services most often provided by full-service agencies are *product and marketing research, creative planning, creative development and execution, media planning and placement, sales promotion,* and *public relations.* The latter is provided by a related or affiliated agency if it is not included in an agency's list of services.

Traditional full-service agencies such as Maclaren: Lintas, Young and Rubicam, and McCann-Erickson are normally divided into three functional areas: account management (sometimes referred to as account services or client services), creative, and media. The primary functional areas report to a central authority, often the agency president, and there is a central administrative body responsible for accounting functions within the agency. There are Canadian-owned agencies in which the top of the agency structure is the president and/or board of directors. There are also international agencies in which the structure culminates in international management that has varying degrees of involvement and authority.[3] Figure 3.2 illustrates the internal structure of a typical full-service advertising agency.

Each of the three primary functional areas of a full-service agency plays a vital role in the development of advertising for clients. The *account-management* group works with the client in developing the advertising approach and objectives, and oversees the whole process as it moves through the agency. The *creative* group develops words and artwork that are in keeping with the advertising objectives. The *media group* develops the placement plan determining where the advertising should be placed, for how long, in what media, and so forth. Some agencies may also have a research group that provides basic market information to assist in developing advertising objectives and strategies or in evaluating the effectiveness and efficiencies of various media buys and other forms of market research.[4]

Figure 3.2 Organization structure for a typical full-service advertising agency

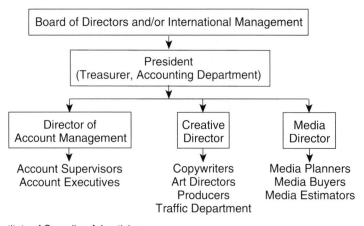

Source: Institute of Canadian Advertising

Creative Boutiques

Creative Boutiques are agencies specializing in the development of creative ideas and their execution for clients' advertising campaigns. In a world of specialization, it is now quite common for an advertiser to divide its advertising assignments between agency specialists, one of which is a creative boutique. Creative boutiques are usually formed and staffed by personnel previously employed by creative departments of full-service agencies; their key personnel, due to past performance, have excellent credentials within the industry.

According to Eric Miller, of Miller Myers Bruce Dalla Costa Inc., a successful Canadian boutique, these agencies "are an efficient way for companies to concentrate their advertising dollars into the creative product rather than in other areas of less value to advertisers."[5] Using advertising and marketing objectives as a guideline, a creative boutique concentrates on producing the single most important component of a campaign—the sales message. Creative boutiques are quite successful in attracting clients from full-service agencies. Very often, clients remain loyal to their creative talent as it moves from one type of agency to another.

Direct-Response and Retail Agencies

Many of the smaller advertising agencies can be classified according to the nature of the accounts (clients) they have. For example, an agency can develop a reputation for being a packaged-goods specialist, an industrial specialist, or a retail specialist. Among agencies that specialize, two distinct groups are worthy of mention: *direct-response agencies* and *retail agencies*. The advantage of using a specialized agency is clear. The personnel of such an agency know the business and marketing environment, and with their expertise they can provide more effective advertising plans for clients.

Direct-Response Agencies Examples of direct-response agencies include Wunderman Worldwide, an agency devoted solely to direct-response advertising; JWT Direct Response, and V&B Direct Marketing. The latter two are subsidiaries of full-service agencies, J. Walter Thompson and Vickers & Benson, respectively. These agencies and others recognized that there was a growing use of direct-response advertising, and that direct-response clients could be served more effectively by a separate agency, staffed by specialists. Additionally, direct-response clients (not to mention the subsidiary agencies) can benefit from the wealth of services provided by the parent agency whenever needed.

Retail Agencies Several agencies are recognized as retail specialists. The largest agency in this category is Saffer Advertising Inc., which billed $180 million in 1989, ranking ninth among all agencies in Canada in terms of size. Other retailing agencies include Palmer Jarvis Advertising (ranked 20th with $85 million in billings), and Kert Advertising (ranked 43rd, with $32.6 million in billings).[6]

Retail agencies came to the forefront in Canada in the early seventies. While full-service agencies during this period showed little interest in handling such accounts, other agencies and individuals, such as Morris Saffer, perceiving an opportunity,

Figure 3.3 The three largest retail advertising agencies

Agency	*Accounts (Selected List)*
Saffer Advertising Inc.	Simpsons, Home Hardware, Black's Photo, Fairweather, Domino's Pizza, GM Dealers of Ontario
Palmer Jarvis Advertising	Canada Safeway, Woodward Stores
Kert Advertising Ltd.	Shoppers Drug Mart, Pharmaprix, Hudson's Bay, Standard Optical

Source: Marketing, "Canada's Top 100," December 15, 1989, p.25.

pursued and created better advertising for retail operations. To counter the growth of retail agencies, some major full-service agencies eventually established retail groups on staff, or set up separate retail divisions to meet the different needs of this type of advertiser.

Retail agencies sell to retailers using concepts similar to those used by brand advertisers. Their task is to position the retailer within the competitive environment, and to attract potential customers by presenting a favourable image of the retailer. In the case of a national chain store, the advertising challenge is no different than that posed by a national brand.

Figure 3.3 identifies the three largest retail agencies in Canada and provides a selected list of some of the accounts they handle.

Media-Buying Service

A **media-buying service** is a media-specialist agency responsible for planning and purchasing the most cost-efficient media for a client—responsible, that is to say, for gaining maximum exposure to a target market at minimum cost. In addition, a media-buying service often obtains government and other clearances for advertisements, makes sure that each ad runs as scheduled, and generally takes care of administrative work associated with the media-buying transaction.

Since efficiency is important, the use of a media-buying service might generate cost savings that can be re-invested in the creative product. Indeed, the use of creative boutiques and media-buying services together could provide the best of both worlds for advertisers. However, full-service agencies argue that they can handle both services equally well for their clients, and under one roof, too.

Canada's oldest and largest media-buying service is based in Toronto, and is appropriately named Media Buying Services Ltd.

Freelance

Freelancers are self-employed, independent creative specialists who offer their services both to advertisers and to advertising agencies. A freelancer is usually an ex-agency employee skilled in a certain area such as graphic arts, copywriting, art direction, or audio-visual production. Such individuals are often used by agencies when heavy workloads prevail, or when new, fresh ideas are needed.

THE SIZE OF THE ADVERTISING AGENCY

Typically, agencies are classified as being large, medium, or small, depending on their annual media billings. Established benchmarks used to classify the size of an agency within the industry are as follows:

Annual Billings ($ million)	*Size Classification*
Under 20	Small
Under 50	Medium
Over 50	Large

In December of each year, *Marketing* publishes a list of the top 100 agencies in Canada. Based on the latest list (December 1989), there are 27 large agencies in Canada. The remainder are classified as small to medium-sized agencies. Consequently, it can be stated that a relatively small number of large agencies control or place the majority of media dollars in Canada.

Large Agencies

Size is a factor clients consider when selecting an advertising agency. Generally, there is a size correspondence between clients and agencies, although there are exceptions to this rule. It is quite common for large advertisers to migrate towards large agencies, since the needs of both parties are similar. This often results in a successful working relationship. Conversely, a small client with a limited budget could be lost in the shuffle at a large agency. Since a small client offers little financial incentive to the agency, whose compensation is based on commission, the agency's best resources may never come to bear on the needs of a small client. As a result, smaller clients may be better suited to smaller and medium-size agencies.

With few exceptions, agencies in the large classification are full-service shops. Also, recent trends indicate a movement towards super- or mega-agencies, the result of mergers between agencies already classified as large.

Medium and Small Agencies

Agencies with annual media billings of less than $30 million are faced with two basic options. They can remain on the small side and perhaps offer their clients better personal service, or they can graduate upwards into the large classification by hiring and developing creative talent that will attract larger clients. Regardless of the direction chosen, there are opportunities for small agencies in Canada. Small agencies can seek accounts not happy with the services provided by large agencies, or accounts not happy with conflicts arising from agency mergers or account switching. Small agencies also benefit clients by being cost-competitive. Since overhead costs are lower in a small agency than in a large one, hourly fee schedules charged a client can be comparatively low.

A traditional argument against the use of a small agency is that such an agency lacks creative and managerial depth. The quality of output in a smaller agency could be low in relation to that of larger agencies, for the latter have the resources to offer competitive salaries to top-quality talent. Also, if an agency must go outside its organization for the resources needed to satisfy the needs of a client, the client may be better suited to a larger agency.

RECENT TRENDS IN THE AGENCY BUSINESS

Mergers and Acquisitions in the 1980s

From the mid-1980s to 1989, the advertising industry went through a period referred to as "merger mania." The impact of mergers was felt directly in Canada, with top-line shops such as Maclaren, Ronalds-Reynolds, Doyle Dane Bernbach, F.H. Hayhurst and Foster Advertising disappearing. Some of them resurfaced under a new shingle and with new partners.

Much of the merger mania is attributed to Maurice and Charles Saatchi of London, England, whose ambition was to establish the world's largest advertising-agency conglomerate. Their idea was based on the conviction that what clients needed in the belt-tightening environment of the day was a global perspective that would eliminate costly duplications of effort in different countries. They claimed that economies of scale would bring huge benefits to multinational advertisers such as Procter & Gamble—and that Saatchi and Saatchi was the agency to handle such a business worldwide.[7]

The Saatchi brothers went on a buying spree that involved the acquisition of Hayhurst Advertising (to form Saatchi and Saatchi Compton Hayhurst), Baker and Spielvogel, and Ted Bates Advertising, all in 1985 and 1986.[8]

In 1987, Ronalds-Reynolds was bought by Foote Cone and Belding, which resulted in the formation of FCB/Ronalds-Reynolds. The following year, New York's Interpublic Group bought two premier agencies in Canada in back-to-back deals, forming Maclaren: Lintas Inc (now Canada's largest full-service agency), and Foster/McCann-Erickson (which now operates under the McCann-Erickson name).

The benefits of mergers and acquisitions are seen to be as follows:

1. A larger combined operation that can offer more services and international connections to existing clients.
2. The opportunity to pick up international assignments from the new parent agency. The marketplace is no longer Canada; it is the world.
3. Expanded opportunities to exploit the free trade agreement with the United States and the coming relaxation of trade barriers in Europe.[9]

Since globalization is an issue in marketing and advertising today, companies that develop marketing plans internationally will benefit from dealing with a mega-agency worldwide. If strategic directions are employed in many countries, it seems logical that an agency in one country can tap into the resources of another to develop local creative executions that complement the overall international approach.

Client Demands for Additional Services

In the latter half of the 1980s, clients altered their spending patterns by emphasizing direct marketing, event marketing, and sales promotion, and de-emphasizing media advertising.

For most agencies, which had been focusing on media spending, such a change by the client was dramatic and sobering. Agencies discovered that they could not meet all of the marketing needs of their clients. Competition from specialist agencies intensified, and many traditional full-service agencies responded by establishing in-house or satellite operations to satisfy other promotional needs. Clients, however, were not convinced that traditional agencies could provide such services as expertly as specialists could. The latest strategy devised to meet the expanded needs of clients is to form an association (alliance or joint venture) with a specialist. Saatchi and Saatchi was an agency that failed when it alone attempted to offer specialized services to its clients. In 1989, it formed an association with Taylor-Tarpay Direct Advertising, a leading specialist in the direct-response field.[10]

Centralized Media Buying

In a span of less than two weeks in 1990, two of Canada's leading advertisers— Labatt's Breweries of Canada and Hiram-Walker Allied Vintners—took more than $60 million in media billings away from existing brand-advertising agencies (full-service agencies with media departments) and consolidated the business under media-specialist companies.

Hiram-Walker moved $10 million in media buying to Media Buying Services Limited and Labatt's announced that it had bought Harrison Young Pesonen and Newell, one of Canada's largest independent media-specialist companies, through its jointly owned entertainment conglomerate, Supercorp. In the process, Labatt's moved $50 million worth of media planning and buying out of its brand agencies and into its new media subsidiary company.[11] For some insight into how the Labatt's move affected the advertising agency, refer to the Advertising in Action vignette "The Parting of the Ways."

The decisions to centralize media in both cases was not intended to reflect negatively on the performance of existing agencies. Dennis Stoakes, vice-president of Media at Hiram-Walker, said the decision to centralize was based on "the clear cut benefits of dealing with an independent third party for media planning and buying. We are looking to bring added value to our media investments."[12]

The trends toward specialization in marketing services is leading to a redefinition—or clarification—of the role of advertising agencies. According to Stoakes, "advertisers go to agencies for excellent creative and if more agencies relinquish media planning and buying to the specialist shops they can devote all of their energies to developing excellent creative."[13]

This trend is the reverse of what was occurring in the late 1980s. During the past decade, advertisers were looking to their agencies for more services. In response, agencies added services and staff to accommodate the retail, public-relations, direct-marketing and sales-promotion needs of clients. Such a turnabout will affect these agencies. First, full-service agencies could follow the lead of Maclaren: Lintas and set up a stand-alone media operation. Maclaren: Lintas established Media Initiative in 1990. Second, full-service agencies may have to accept the departure of the marketing-services functions recently added so that they can concentrate on their primary function—the creation of ads. It is also conceivable that medium-sized agencies, to

Advertising in Action
The Parting of the Ways

In a two-week period, advertising agency Scali McCabe Sloves (Canada) Limited lost two national accounts in Canada worth $17 million in billings. Labatt's Breweries of Canada dropped Scali from its agency roster by announcing that J. Walter Thompson would be taking over the Labatt's Blue assignment. Labatt's Blue is the company's flagship brand. The Labatt's decision was bad news, coming as it did shortly after Scali lost the business provided by Swedish automaker AB Volvo, an account worth about $2 million in billings.

The Volvo account was lost because of "false advertising" by Scali's parent company in New York. The parent company was forced to resign its $40 million North American Volvo account after admitting that a Volvo television commercial, which only ran in parts of the United States, was rigged to demonstrate the superiority of the Volvo automobile. The ad in question showed a row of cars being crushed by "Bear Foot," a giant pickup truck with huge tires. In the demonstration, all of the cars are crushed except the Volvo 240 station wagon, which remains intact. Volvo, which has a worldwide reputation for credibility and safety, acknowledged that the advertisement dramatizing the strength of its cars was phony. For the dramatization, the Volvo was reinforced while the other cars were weakened.

Volvo was forced to publicly admit its wrongdoing as part of a lawsuit settlement brought forward by the Attorney General of Texas. As part of the settlement, Volvo also had to place disclaimer advertisements in the markets where the original ad had run. The disclaimer was in the form of an open letter from Joseph L. Nicolato, president and CEO of Volvo Cars of North America. The letter stated that the commercial incorrectly depicted the car-crushing competition (it was not a real competition but the advertisement implied that it was) and that the ad's production team "apparently made modifications to two of the vehicles." Mr. Nicolato admitted that no Volvo could withstand being run over by a monster truck.

Volvo officials were unwilling to speculate at the time about how the problem might affect its relationship with Scali McCabe Sloves, but it was only a week later that Scali resigned the account. Not a surprising announcement, to say the least.

After Scali lost the Labatt's Blue business, an official at the agency's Toronto office attempted to soften the blow of the announcement by saying, "losing the Labatt's business will free the ad agency to bid for new accounts. The time and effort the agency spent on the Blue business prevented us from putting the attention we would have liked to put into new business." In sharp contradiction, an industry source stated that Scali's strength was understanding the beer drinker and coming up with concepts. The agency's weakness was that it couldn't take the idea and put it on film. This weakness ultimately resulted in the loss of the Labatt's account.

Adapted from Barry Meier, "Volvo pulls phony ads boosting strength of car," *The Whig-Standard*, November 6, 1990, p.28, and Marina Strauss, "This Blue's not for you," *The Globe and Mail*, November 15, 1990, p.B1.

keep pace with the trends, will merge, forming new companies that will specialize in independent services (e.g. creative and media services).

ROLES AND RESPONSIBILITIES OF AGENCY PERSONNEL

We know that advertising agencies are divided into three primary functional areas: account-management, creative, and media (refer to figure 3.2). Large agencies may include additional departments, embracing such functions as marketing research, sales promotion, and public relations. The following sections summarize the roles and responsibilities of these functional areas and of the key personnel working within these areas in typical large and medium-sized agencies.

Account Management

As the name implies, account-management staff are responsible for managing the affairs of the agency's clients. Account personnel perform a dual function: they are both *consultants* and *co-ordinators*. The task of account personnel is to understand totally the client's business so that they can

- Advise the client on a variety of marketing, strategic, and financial issues
- Identify and motivate the correct agency resources to build the client's business
- Co-ordinate overall agency involvement and projects between client and agency [14]

Account-management personnel must understand the major marketing issues facing the client and, using all available resources of the agency, recommend a course of action to the client. Thus, they are actively involved in the planning process and in presenting client work to the client for approval. They are expected to be experts on the ultimate consumer of a product or service, and to understand how the client's business relates to, and is perceived by, the consumer.

The account-management group includes an account executive, an account supervisor, and an account director.

Account Executive Often viewed as occupying an entry-level position, the **account executive** is responsible for *client contact, project planning, budget control, preparing annual advertising plans,* and *advising on strategic issues.* He or she is usually helped by an account supervisor. Basically, an account executive liaises between the client and agency, and communicates frequently with the personnel in the client organization who are responsible for the advertising function (advertising manager, product manager, etc.). An account executive is usually responsible for one or several clients, depending on the size and resources of the agency.

Account Supervisor As a middle manager, the **account supervisor** manages a group of account executives, and is therefore responsible for an expanded list of clients. Job functions include strategic planning, market analysis, competitive-activity analysis, and analyzing and capitalizing on business-building opportunities. In such a position, the supervisor must look beyond the scope of current projects and assignments, and assist in developing the future direction of a product or service.

Account Director The **account director** deals directly with senior members of the client organization, and is responsible for how the agency performs in handling client accounts. Specific responsibilities include long-term planning, deployment of agency personnel, and overall account profitability. Also, the account director is responsible for working with senior agency executives from other functional areas in seeking new business for the agency.

Creative Department

The Creative Department is responsible for the development of communication ideas and concepts. Once these are created, members of the Creative Department must sell them to the client; once the client approves them, the Creative Department must execute the creative. Heading up the Creative Department is the **creative director**, who oversees the development of all agency creative. The creative director is ultimately responsible for maintaining a high standard of creative quality on behalf of the agency. In such a position, the creative director must motivate the staff of copywriters and art directors who work directly on client assignments.

Copywriter The responsibility of the **copywriter** is to convert information provided by the client and account personnel (information concerning unique selling points, target-market profiles, purchase motivations, etc.) into an effective, persuasive sales message. The message must be presented in such a manner that it stands out and has relevance to potential customers. The copywriter develops the main idea of the advertisement presentation in conjunction with art directors, then creates its various verbal components: the headline, sub-headlines, and body copy or text.

Art Director Using the same information resources as the copywriter, the **art director** is responsible for developing a visual communication which, combined with the copy, elicits a favourable reaction from the target market. Art direction requires knowledge in specialized areas such as typography, graphic arts, and photography. An art director need not be an artist, but must understand the production process, and be capable of directing artists and technical-production specialists.

In summary, while the jobs of copywriters and art directors are separate, individuals in these positions usually work as a team on client assignments. Over a period of time, such a working relationship provides continuity and consistency in the creative product solicited by the client.

Print and Broadcast Production Manager **Production managers** are responsible for preparing print advertisements or broadcast commercials. Since production is an activity that involves execution, it requires co-ordination with numerous external suppliers. In print production, these external supplies may be typesetters and lithography shops; in broadcast, they may be actors, directors of film and music, and cameramen.

The production manager offers technical advice about such matters as production-cost estimates, and ensures that all activities are completed within scheduled timeframes—publishers' material deadlines or television air dates, for example. Often, a *traffic manager* is responsible for ensuring that the final product (print ad or broadcast commercial) reaches the media destination on time.

Media Department

The Media Department is responsible for the *planning and placement of advertising time and space*. The proliferation of media forms, the escalating cost of media, and the use of computers in the planning process have added to the complexity of the media responsibility. The functions of the Media Department are as follows:

1. *Media Planning* The plan that documents how the client's money will be spent to achieve advertising objectives is prepared and presented at this stage.
2. *Media Buying* Once approved, the elements necessary to execute the media plan are purchased. The objective when buying is obviously to achieve the most at the least expense—that is, to achieve maximum impact and reach at the lowest possible cost to the client. Each purchase must be checked to see that it ran correctly. Sometimes, media buys must be upgraded in mid-stream to compensate for audience loss (actual audience versus plan-estimated audience).
3. *Media Research* Larger agencies have a Media-Research Department that provides up-to-date information regarding audiences and circulation. Such data is used frequently when alternative media forms (television, magazine, newspaper, etc.) are being compared, or when the respective abilities of specific media to reach a certain target market are being compared. With advancing computer technology, many agencies have on-line access to computer data banks containing media-audience information. A number of independent research firms tap into these data banks in order to provide media analysis for agencies without on-line capabilities. More complete details on media research are included in chapter 9.

Position responsibilities in the Media Department are distributed among the media buyer, the media planner, the media supervisor, the group head (or associate media director), and the media director.

Media Buyer The responsibility of the **media buyer** is to develop an intimate knowledge of the media marketplace and be aware of all developments affecting media buying. Buyers must evaluate and make decisions on the competitive claims of the various media, in order to make the most efficient and effective buys for their clients.

Media Planner **Media planners** assess the strengths, weaknesses, cost efficiencies, and communications potentials of various media, in order to develop a media plan. The ability to communicate is vital for planners, since they must sell the plan twice— first within the agency, and then to the client. Since the client's money is on the line at this stage, planners must be ready to address all of the client's concerns. Media plans have been known to go through numerous revisions prior to client approval.

Media Supervisor The **media supervisor** is generally responsible for a team of media people, and for co-ordinating the efforts of buyers and planners during the development and execution of the media plan.

Media Group Head (Associate Media Director) As a senior manager, the **group head**, or **associate media director**, carries an administrative workload and is responsible for the management of the Media Department. The associate director provides counsel to media supervisors and is involved in major client presentations of media plans.

Media Director The responsibility of the **media director** depends on the size of the agency. In smaller agencies, the director is involved in planning and buying media. In a larger agency, the director is more of an administrator. As a senior manager, the director is ultimately responsible for the philosophy that governs the media-planning function in the agency and is accountable to the client for media planning and placement. Working with other senior executives, the media director usually plays an active role in business presentations to new clients.

≡ *M*ANAGING THE CLIENT'S BUSINESS

Several factors influence the professional relationship that exists between the client and the agency.

Agency Teams

The amount of time an agency spends with a client and the personnel it allocates to serve the needs of the client have impact on the client-agency relationship. Agency management will form teams, or account groups, that will work together on a client's business. The employees who make up an account group vary from one agency to another, depending on such factors as the size of the agency and the various levels of personnel resources available. Generally, an account group includes the following:

- Account executive
- Account supervisor
- Art director
- Copywriter
- Media buyer
- Media planner

Keeping an account group together over a number of assignments benefits both the client and the agency.

Familiarity with Business The client will keep the account group up-to-date on the changing business environment in which it operates. Ongoing knowledge of product, market, and competitive activity assists the account group in its own internal planning, and the group can draw upon its past experience with the client when considering new directions to pursue.

Consistency in Approach Since the basic function of the advertising business is to develop ideas that will assist in the selling of a product, a sense of consistency is important. The task of the account group is to develop a strategy that will work over a long period of time. Within the long-term strategy will be the flexibility to develop and execute new plans when needed. By contrast, if a client were to do business with an agency that experiences a rapid turnover in creative personnel, the client would likely be forced to accept different ideas and contrasting styles that would not enhance the long-term marketing-planning process.

The Team Concept—Agency and Client   The relationship between the agency and the client is a business partnership. The client should know exactly whom it is dealing with in the agency, should trust them and have confidence in them. In essence, the client team and agency team are separate in terms of formal organization, but must work together, harmoniously, to achieve success. Clients who are subjected to changing personnel within an account group may question the value that the agency places on their business. Conversely, the agency may, by keeping an account group together, imply that a client's business is important and that it is trying to serve the client more effectively.

Competing Accounts

Agencies are exposed to extremely confidential client information when developing advertising plans. As a consequence, agencies will not, as a rule, accept assignments from an advertiser who is in direct competition with a current client. Numerous conflicts develop as an agency seeks new business. When agencies merge to form larger agencies, competing accounts are often brought together. In such a case, one of the clients (usually the smaller, in terms of media dollars) will opt to take its business elsewhere, or the agency will resign the client's business.

Agency of Record

Many large advertisers (companies with numerous divisions or multi-product lines) distribute their advertising assignments among several advertising agencies. From the client's viewpoint, dividing the business among several agencies is advantageous in that the different products will receive more attention and service than would be possible if all assignments were given to one agency. Since the agencies are competing with each other for new business, all of them seeking further assignments from the client, their performance on the products they handle will be of a high quality. Dividing up the assignments, in other words, should positively affect the quality of the creative work.

On the media side, the client often appoints an **Agency of Record**(AOR). This is a central agency responsible for media negotiation and placement, and it is often used by multiple-product advertisers that use more than one advertising agency. An AOR facilitates efficiency in the media-buying process, often making greater discounts available to the client by purchasing all media on a corporate (large volume) basis. The AOR is responsible for corporate media contracts under which other agencies will issue their placement orders. Also, the AOR keeps a record of all advertising placed, and is responsible for final allotment of time and space in a media schedule.

AGENCY COMPENSATION

How an advertising agency is paid, and how much money it makes, is an issue frequently on the minds of both client marketing executives and agency managers. Marketing executives often argue that their agency is asking for too much money, or they feel they are paying for services not really required. Agency managers, on the other hand, feel that the profit margins on some of their accounts are too low in relation to the amount of resources allocated to the client.

There are two basic methods of compensating an advertising agency for the services it provides: the commission system or the fee system. Many variations of these two systems exist, since client and agency often blend the two systems.

The Commission System

The commission system has been used in one form or another for the past hundred years. At the turn of the century, the commission rate was 10%, and as time passed, the rate increased to 13%. As of 1918, the American Association of Advertising Agencies was successful in raising the commission to 15%, where it has remained for 70 years. In the latest reports published by the Institute of Canadian Advertising, approximately 84% of agency income under this system actually comes from commissions; the remainder comes from fees.[15]

Using the commission system, the agency receives a *15% rebate* from the media cost, with the exact amount of the rebate depending on the dollar volume purchased in a medium on behalf of the client. The media allows accredited advertising agencies to buy advertising time and space at a *15% discount off quoted rates*. This discount is granted to the agency for its work in selling the client the campaign, choosing the medium, creating and producing the advertising material, looking after copy and media research, doing all paperwork related to the transaction, and paying the media.[16]

The *15% commission is based on the purchase of time and space only.* To illustrate the commission principle, let's assume that a total media purchase amounted to $100 000. The commission calculation would be as follows:

Media Purchased (Total $)	$100 000
Commission Rate (15%)	× .15
Agency Commission	15 000
Balance due Media ($100 000 – 15 000)	85 000

Not all agency services are covered by the 15% commission. Production costs, which include the costs of producing print advertisements and broadcast commercials, are paid for by the client as an additional expense. The traditional rate for production services provided by the agency has been a mark-up of 17.65% on invoice costs to yield the agency a 15% commission for handling the transaction.

For example, the agency-commission principle for production services assumes that the cost of producing a single 30-second television commercial is $80 000. The commission calculation would therefore be as follows:

Commercial Production Cost	$ 80 000
Agency Commission (17.65%) ($80 000 × .1765)	+ <u>14 120</u>
Client Pays Agency	$ 94 120

In this example, the client pays the agency $94 120. The client is then responsible for paying the external suppliers who were employed to produce the commercial.

The Fee System

Several options are available if a fee system is used to compensate an advertising agency. Some of the more common options are minimum guarantees, hourly rates, and costs plus profits.

Minimum Guarantee The minimum-guarantee structure puts a floor under the agency's compensation. Client and agency establish a minimum income figure, including a profit, by making assumptions about the level of service required for a period of time, usually a year. Payments to the agency are made monthly. Commissions are credited against these payments, and the agency retains the excess of commission over the aggregate payment during the contract year.

Hourly Rates Using this system, the agency assigns an hourly rate to those employees who have direct contact with the client. The rate is designed to recover agency costs and includes a profit margin. There are two basic versions of the hourly-rate system:

- The agency credits all commissions against the accumulated hour charges.
- The agency retains any commission in excess of the accumulated hourly charges.

To illustrate the application of hourly rates, let's consider the following example:

Employee Costs:

Salary	$36 000
Benefits	<u>6 000</u>
Total Costs	$42 000
Agency Estimate of Time Spent on Account	1 200 hours
Direct Hourly Rate (42 000 / 1 200)	$35/hour

Costs Plus Profit With the costs-plus-profit system, the amount paid the agency covers the agency's direct costs, indirect costs (heat, light, and power), and profits. When overhead costs are factored into a fee system, the total costs of all people employed in the agency—including those who do not work directly on a client's business—are taken into account, along with other costs. In effect, indirect costs are added to direct costs, along with a provision for profit.[17]

To illustrate the application of the costs-plus-profit system, let's consider the following example:

Total Direct Client Payroll Costs	$550 000
Total Indirect Costs, Other Overhead Costs plus Profit	$1 512 000
Overhead Factor ($1 512 000/550 000)	2.75

This overhead factor of 2.75 can be applied against a particular account group working with a particular client to arrive at a monthly billing. The calculation would be as follows:

Total Salaries (Account Group)	$275 000
Overhead Factor	2.75
Total Fee Required ($275 000 × 2.75)	$756 250
Fee Per Month (756 250 / 12)	$763 000

WHICH SYSTEM OF COMPENSATION IS BEST?

Each of the two basic systems, commissions and fees, has advantages and disadvantages. Theoretically, the best system is the one that will produce the best quality of advertising for the client. A successful campaign brings success (profits) to both the client and the agency.

According to Keith McKerracher, president of the Institute of Canadian Advertising, in today's competitive, cost-conscious environment, "there is little question that the commission system alone is declining as the favoured compensation method, because 15% is no longer adequate compensation for the tasks agencies are required to perform. A figure set in 1918 cannot adequately cover all agency expenses and still provide a profit."[18]

A blended system, which combines elements of both commissions and fee systems, is gaining in popularity. This movement is based on the notion that agencies' profit levels have not been adequate, a principle to which clients agree. The increased use of fees suggests that supplemental income is vital if profits are to increase to reasonable levels. Dissenters contend that more extensive use of fees is a reaction by agencies that need to cover the lower profits that have resulted from lower media-spending by clients.

The Commission System—Advantages and Disadvantages

The advantages of the commission system are as follows:

1. The system is simple, and since both clients and agencies are familiar with the procedure, there is a motivation to create advertising that will run for extended periods of time. The result would be larger media budgets and greater commission for the agency. Also, commissions force the agency to manage time more efficiently, since costs, overheads, and profits all come out of the commission.

2. The client obtains all of the agency services without having to decide what it actually needs or is willing to pay for. As a consequence, there is little friction between the client and agency.

The disadvantages of the commission system are as follows:

1. Agencies make excess profit from accounts (brands) that bill large annual amounts, and lose on small-budget accounts (brands). This may not be reasonable, since workload is not constant from one client brand to another, or from

one account to another. For example, the agency is overcompensated when it places the same ad over and over again.

2. Commissions represent risks if the agency is handling new-product business. The high failure rate of new products means that the agency may not generate sufficient commissions to cover its resource investment in a new product.

3. Since agency income is directly linked to the client's media spending, it could conceivably influence an agency's recommendation on media selection.

4. When a client cuts the budget (a move called a profit squeeze), agency income is also affected, because the costs initially incurred by the agency were based on the prospect of higher commissions. Conversely, the agency may enjoy a windfall if the budget is suddenly increased.

The Fee System—Advantages and Disadvantages

The advantages of the fee system are as follows:

1. Since the fee system covers both costs and profits, the emphasis on money is removed from the relationship. Consequently, the agency can focus all of its attention on producing the best quality work for the client.

2. A more professional client-agency relationship develops. The client feels there is more objectivity to agency recommendations, since agency profit is not linked with the client's media budget. It also encourages the client and agency to make more efficient use of time.

3. The client's expectations of the agency are documented in a contract. Consequently, agency performance can be monitored and evaluated in relation to the fees paid during the life of the contract. In essence, the client can maintain control of spending by requesting only services it considers important.

4. Clients with large budgets can save money, particularly if the salary demands of the agency's creative department (traditionally a high-salary area) are low.

The disadvantages of the fee system are as follows:

1. Guaranteed incomes may stifle the agency's incentive to produce good creative or to look for media-cost efficiencies. In short, the system lacks incentive for productivity.

2. Fees admit clients into the agency's financial affairs, enabling them to consider variables such as the time spent on the account, and the salaries of the employees. These, having become known, are open to question. Also, there may be a conflict if the client hears the clock ticking each time it communicates with the agency.

3. The fee system generates paperwork for both client and agency; there are monthly transactions and a balancing at the year's end.

With regard to which system of compensation is best, it really depends on the expectations of both the client and the agency. Regardless of the system used, a contract should outline the expectations of both, consider the needs of the client, and calculate the resources the agency must allocate to satisfy those needs. The client will decide if it can afford the cost of the service. In developing the compensation system, client and agency should ensure that the system chosen does the following:

- Provides adequate professional service to the advertiser
- Fairly compensates the agency for its work
- Provides an incentive to both the advertising agency and client
- Is simple to operate
- Can be reviewed periodically (i.e., is flexible and capable of being changed as needs and conditions change)

Refer to the Advertising in Action vignette "New Incentive Plans on the Horizon" for more insight into new and creative ways of compensating advertising agencies.

≡ *C*LIENT-AGENCY RELATIONSHIPS

The professional and personal relationship that exists between a client and an agency has an influence on the quality of advertising produced. It has been said that when the agency-client relationship is a partnership, the relationship is long-term. If the relationship is a buyer-vendor one, the association is much more likely to be short-term.

The connection between client and agency is often very delicate, and it can be broken for a variety of reasons. Deteriorating relationships contribute significantly to the amount of account shifting that takes place in Canada each year. As explained in chapter 2, **account shifting** refers to the movement of an advertising account from one agency to another. In 1987 alone, a total of $281 million worth of media buying switched hands. The biggest account moves that year involved Ford Motor Company of Canada ($25 million) and Toyota ($20 million).[19]

There are a variety of reasons why so much advertising changes hands each year; most of these reasons have to do with the client-agency relationship, or lack of it. Following are some of the more common reasons for account shifting:

1. Clients are dissatisfied with the quality of the advertising or of any of the other services provided by the agency.
2. There are philosophical differences between client and agency in terms of management style and approach, only detected after the association has begun. For example, the two parties might not agree on the direction the advertising should take.
3. The absence of the team concept—the relationships between people do not develop, whether because of poor communications, differences in needs, or bad attitudes.
4. Clients decide to consolidate their business with fewer agencies (multi-product advertisers)—often, the re-organization of client-management structures leads to changes in advertising assignments.

Advertising in Action
New Incentive Plans on the Horizon

In the wake of many changes in the world of advertising—changes such as the move toward creative and media specialization and toward globalization—more and more advertisers are abandoning the 15% commission system once considered obligatory.

In the United States, DDB Needham Worldwide developed an incentive plan whereby it would be rewarded with up to 33% more than its normal compensation if sales increased by an agreed-upon amount. It also stood to lose 30% of its income on the assignment if the goals were not met. Agency employees who produced the results would get a two-thirds cut of the bonus. The offer was open to all DDB Needham's U.S. and Canadian accounts, which included McDonald's, Ralston-Purina, and Volkswagen.

According to Keith Reinhard, chairman and CEO of DDB Needham Worldwide, the plan was created in response to "expressed need on the part of clients for more agency accountability." As part of the deal, the client must agree to maintain the quality of its product, and the price and distribution of the product must be comparable with those of the competition; and the client must agree to sustain agreed-upon consumer support levels.

In another move in Canada, Kraft General Foods, one of the largest advertisers in the country, announced a new compensation plan that will pay a 16% commission to those agencies responsible for KGF brands that exceed expectations; a 14% commission to agencies meeting business expectations satisfactorily; and a 13% commission for an unsatisfactory performance.

Agencies involved in this new performance plan include many of Canada's largest—J. Walter Thompson, Leo Burnett, McKim Advertising, Young and Rubicam, Grey Advertising, and Ogilvy & Mather. To say the least, the agencies' reactions to the new plan were guarded. Andy Krupski, president of J.Walter Thompson, would only say that "It will reward good advertising." Mike Furber, director of business development at Young and Rubicam, was more direct in pointing out the drawbacks. His concern was the three-percentage-point difference in compensation. He said that the "spread could mean the difference between making a profit or none at all," and that agencies were running lean already.

Adapted from Cyndee Miller, "DDB Needham payment plan won't work," *Marketing News*, June 25, 1990, p.5., and "Silence greets agency plan," *Playback Strategy*, November 5, 1990, pp.1,2.

5. Conflict situations may arise owing to account re-alignments in the U.S. (shifts at the U.S. parent agency often create shifts in Canadian subsidiaries). Also, agency mergers, in Canada or internationally, can bring competing accounts under one roof, which creates a need for one account to switch to another agency.

AGENCY AND CLIENT EVALUATIONS

To encourage the best possible relationship between clients and agencies, and to clearly review the expectations of both, it is necessary for clients to conduct *agency evaluations* at planned intervals. Also, since the agency invests considerable resources into its client's business, it should have the opportunity to review the performance of the client. A good working relationship depends on honest, open communications at both ends.

It is usually the advertising agency that takes the fall when advertising does not meet the expectations of the client. Among the shortcomings that a client might ascribe to its agency are a high degree of personnel turnover, understaffing, and lack of interest. But the client's role in the advertising process must also be evaluated. The shortcomings of agency performance are well documented; the shortcomings of the client have received much less attention. Among the problems that agencies have with their clients are poor communication of objectives and strategies, lack of senior management involvement, and indecisiveness.

A document published by the Institute of Canadian Advertising (ICA) summarized the findings of an Advertising Age Survey of 50 corporate advertising managers

Figure 3.4 Agency-client relations

Bad Habits as Advertisers See Them
(all lists in descending order of importance)

Of Advertisers:	*Of Agencies:*
• Not providing enough information	• Personnel turnover
• Expecting too much	• Understaffing
• Too many approval levels	• Lack of interest in clients' business
• Lack of direction, objectives, strategy	• Blind defensiveness
• Not sharing total market approach	• Inexperienced account people
• Arbitrary changes in direction	• Late delivery and unresponsiveness
• Indecisiveness	• Too loose, unstructured
	• Tendency not to listen

Bad Habits as Agencies See Them

Of Advertisers:	*Of Agencies:*
• No strategy, no clear objectives	• Late delivery, poor follow-through
• No top management involvement	• Not cost conscious
• Failure to level with agency	• Personnel turnover
• Don't know/care about agency finances	• Don't share the facts
• Expect magic answers	• Take client for granted
• Inconsistency of advertising funds	• Interest in new business
	• Politics
	• Lack of written reports, estimates

Source: Institute of Canadian Advertising

and agency executives and consultants. The document outlined the most important shortcomings of both clients and agencies; these are summarized in figure 3.4. The purpose of reviews and evaluations is to flag potential problem areas, so that the appropriate corrective action can be taken to restore the relationship. Additional benefits of the evaluation process are that

- It will establish criteria for judging the quality of advertising.
- It will provide both client and agency with an opportunity to judge the competency of their respective staffs (i.e., their effectiveness, personal growth potential, etc.).
- Each evaluation will provide benchmarks for subsequent reviews.
- Each side will gain an appreciation of the problems the other party experiences—understanding alone can help improve the relationship.
- Wasteful activity and other cost inefficiencies can be identified and corrected.[20]

For more complete details on the client-agency evaluation process, refer to the Part One case, "Working Together: the Client and the Agency," which contains sample documents modelled after those used to quantify the performance of agencies and clients.

Summary

Advertising agencies provide a variety of services to their clients, but their primary role is to provide experience and expertise in the communications process. In this area, the agency provides planning assistance and contributes an objective viewpoint to that planning process.

Advertisers must evaluate the services provided by agencies, and decide whether to utilize a full-service agency or hire some type of specialist that may nor may not offer all of the services required by the client. The specialists available to the client include creative boutiques and media-buying services, retail agency specialists, and direct-response advertising specialists. The size of the advertising agency in relation to the size of the client is another factor a client considers when selecting an agency. In recent years, certain trends have forced traditional agencies to redefine their role. The major trends influencing the role and functions of contemporary agencies include merger and acquisition strategies among agencies, clients' demands for additional promotional services, and centralized media buying.

Traditional, full-service agencies are managed in specific functional areas: the Account-management area, the Creative Department, and the Media Department. Account-management personnel consults with clients and co-ordinates activity within the agency. The Creative Department develops communication concepts, and the Media Department plans and places advertising time and space. The services an agency provides to a client are usually handled by an account group or team, which includes an individual from each of the functional areas.

A major factor in client-agency relationships is the method by which the agency is paid. Two systems are used to compensate agencies: a commission system, according to which the agency receives a percentage of the value of media purchased by an agency for a client; or a fee system, which is based on the services requested by the client. Since the relationships between clients and agencies are often volatile, account shifting is a common occurrence in the industry. To overcome this and to foster better working relationships, both clients and agencies conduct ongoing performance reviews of each other.

Review Questions

1. What is the role of the advertising agency in the advertising process?
2. What are the differences between a full-service agency, a creative boutique, and a media-buying service?
3. What are the roles and responsibilities of the
   i) Account-management group?
   ii) Creative Department?
   iii) Media Department?
4. What is an Agency of Record?
5. Explain the concept of agency teams. Why is the team concept important to the client?
6. Identify and explain the two primary methods of compensating an advertising agency.
7. A client spends $1 750 000 on network-television advertising and another $150 000 on print advertising. The cost of producing two television commercials was $240 000, and the production charge for the print advertisements amounted to $15 000. How much commission does the client's advertising agency earn, given that the agency is compensated by commission?

Discussion Questions

1. "The commission system is an equitable system of compensating agencies today." Discuss this statement.
2. "The agency-client relationship is a partnership." Discuss the significance of this statement. What are the ingredients for success?
3. Review the Advertising in Action vignette "New Incentive Plans on the Horizon." What is your opinion of the new incentive plan put forth by Kraft General Foods?

Illustrative Case for Part One

Working Together: The Client and the Agency

In chapters 2 and 3, much of the discussion focused on the need for a good working relationship between a client and the advertising agency. In such a relationship there are bound to be times when problems will surface that will place a strain on the partnership.

For example, a client may not be satisfied with the quality of creative material the agency is developing. Perhaps the client has research evidence that justifies such dissatisfaction. Or perhaps there are some personality conflicts between people on both sides of the relationship. From the agency viewpoint, perhaps agency personnel feel uninformed regarding certain issues and, consequently, that their job is more difficult to perform than it should be. Or perhaps the agency feels that the demands of the client are unrealistic.

Regardless of what the situation is, it is of paramount importance that the chemistry between the two organizations be good. Both organizations will be working together very closely, so harmony is crucial to the relationship. A good working environment should result in prosperity for both organizations. To ensure that such a relationship exists, a client will spend considerable time selecting an advertising agency. Chapter 2 outlined the steps in the selection process. Also, it is important that the working relationship be evaluated periodically, so that potential problems are flagged before they fester into real problems. The review and evaluation process was discussed in chapter 3.

Included in this illustrative case are sample documents that the client uses in selecting an advertising agency (see exhibit 1). While referring to the document, note the nature of specific details sought in the questionnaire stage of the process. Included as well are some sample documents used by both organizations to evaluate the performance of the other on a quantitative basis (see exhibits 2 and 3). Certainly, areas of performance that, in the evaluation process, are perceived to be unacceptable or marginal, poor or fair will be the topic of discussion between the two organizations.

Exhibit 1   Agency selection questionnaire

Agency Selection Questionnaire

SECTION I—BASIC FACTS

1. AGENCY NAME

2. ADDRESSES

TOTAL NUMBER
OF EMPLOYEES

Head Office:

Branches:

3a. OWNERSHIP

☐ Public Company   ☐ Limited Partnership   ☐ Private Company   ☐ Chartered Federally   ☐ Provincially

3b. NAMES AND TITLES OF PRINCIPAL SHAREHOLDERS/PARTNERS

4a. PRINCIPAL CLIENT LIST	YEAR ACQUIRED	SENIOR CLIENT PERSON DEALT WITH	MAY WE CONTACT? YES NO
1.			☐ ☐
2.			☐ ☐
3.			☐ ☐
4.			☐ ☐
5.			☐ ☐
6.			☐ ☐
7.			☐ ☐
8.			☐ ☐
9.			☐ ☐
10.			☐ ☐

Exhibit 1   continued

4b. SPECIFIC NUMBER OF CLIENTS IN EACH SIZE CATEGORY

UNDER $100,000 _____ $100,000 to $500,000 _____ $500,000 to $1 Million _____

$1 Million to $3 Million _____   Over $3 Million _____

5a. LIST CLIENTS GAINED OVER PAST 24 MONTHS

_____

_____

_____

_____

_____

_____

5b. LIST CLIENTS LOST OVER PAST 24 MONTHS	YEAR ACCOUNT ACQUIRED	REASON FOR LOSS (Attach longer explanation if desired)
_____	_____	_____
_____	_____	_____
_____	_____	_____
_____	_____	_____

6a. APPROXIMATE AGENCY BILLINGS

This year (estimated) $_____   Last year $_____   Year before $_____

6b. WHAT PERCENTAGE OF YOUR BILLINGS ARE:

		6c. HOW DO YOUR BILLINGS BREAK DOWN BY THE VARIOUS MEDIA?	
Consumer packaged goods	_____ %	Newspapers	_____ %
Consumer durables	_____ %	Consumer Magazines	_____ %
Industrial products	_____ %	TV	_____ %
Office and commercial products	_____ %	Radio	_____ %
Retail advertising	_____ %	Outdoor	_____ %
Service organizations	_____ %	Business & Financial Press	_____ %
Agency of Record	_____ %	Sales promotion/Collateral Materials	_____ %
Other	_____ %	PR/Publicity	_____ %
		Other (specify)	_____ %

6d. WHAT PERCENTAGE OF YOUR BILLINGS ARE FOR:

English language advertising   _____ %

French language advertising   _____ %

continued

Exhibit 1   continued

SECTION II—FACILITIES, EXPERIENCE
AND OPERATING METHODS

7. NUMBER OF PEOPLE BY DEPARTMENT

	Head Office	Branch	Branch	Branch	Branch	Branch
Account Management						
Creative — Copy						
— Art						
Media — Planning						
— Buying						
Production						
Research and Planning						
Billing and Checking						

8a. WHICH TYPE OF COMPENSATION ARRANGEMENT DO YOU PREFER?

☐ Commission   ☐ Fee   ☐ Combination

8b. IF "COMBINATION", PLEASE COMMENT ON WHICH SERVICES YOU FEEL MERIT SPECIAL FEES:

_____

_____

_____

_____

_____

_____

_____

_____

_____

9a. DO YOU HAVE A FORMAL COST ACCOUNTING SYSTEM, WHEREBY YOU KNOW THE PROFIT PICTURE ON EACH ACCOUNT?

☐ Yes   ☐ No

9b. IF "YES", DO YOU REVIEW ACCOUNT PROFITABILITY WITH YOUR CLIENTS?

☐ Yes   ☐ No

Comment _____

_____

Exhibit 1   continued

10. PLEASE COMMENT ON THOSE ACCOUNTS ON WHICH YOU FEEL YOU HAVE MADE A SIGNIFICANT CONTRIBUTION TO THE CLIENT'S SUCCESS.

11. PLEASE COMMENT ON BOTH THE OPERATING AND THE CREATIVE PHILOSOPHY OF YOUR COMPANY.

12. COMMENT ON THE PROCEDURES THAT YOUR AGENCY FOLLOWS TO EVALUATE QUALITY OF WORK SPECIFICALLY WITH REGARD TO:

Development of Advertising Strategy:

Development of The Creative Product:

DATE THIS QUESTIONNAIRE COMPLETED:

BY: _____

Name   Title

continued

Exhibit 2   Sample agency review checklist

Sample Agency Review Checklist

Agency Review Checklist

Company review _____   Period under review from _____ to _____

Title _____   Division, department or

Agency representative _____   product, if applicable _____

Title _____   _____

	UNACCEPTABLE	MARGINAL	SATISFACTORY		EXCELLENT	
	1	2	3	4	5	6

Art
1. Overall quality of work.
2. Well thought out to meet the creative strategy.
3. More effective than competitive work.

Production
1. Faithful to creative concept and creative execution.
2. Prepared on time, within budget.
3. Control of outside services.

Media
1. Soundness of media research.
2. Effective and efficient media strategy and alternatives.
3. Achieve objectives within budget.
4. Negotiates and executes program smoothly.
5. Periodic review of plan and budget.

Account management
1. Motivates and involves all agency resources.
2. Continuity and professionalism.
3. Adequate meaningful contact.
4. Knowledge of account/ product-market.

Exhibit 2   continued

	UNACCEPTABLE	MARGINAL		SATISFACTORY		EXCELLENT
	1	2	3	4	5	6

Financial/Administrative

1. Competitive bids obtained and submitted.
2. Maintains adequate files/ submits detailed invoices.
3. Billing is timely/reflects smooth accounting.
4. Administratively and financially stable.

Research

1. Internal capabilities meet needs.
2. Control of outside services.
3. Utilizes existing research.
4. Adequate testing of creative product.

Performance

1. Continues to grow with company.
2. Keeps schedules.
3. Reacts well to criticism.
4. Takes initiative and speaks out.
5. Performs efficiently and effectively.

Staffing

1. Depth and professionalism throughout agency.
2. Depth and professionalism on the account.
3. Management spends time and effort on account.

General

1. Background knowledge of markets and products.
2. Understanding of advertising fundamentals.
3. Adherence to company policy.
4. Responsive to requests.

continued

Exhibit 2 continued

	UNACCEPTABLE	MARGINAL		SATISFACTORY		EXCELLENT
	1	**2**	**3**	**4**	**5**	**6**
Strategy						
1. Knowledge of company business.						
2. Knowledge of competition.						
3. Ability to define problems.						
Planning						
1. Assistance in establishing objectives.						
2. Contribution to marketing plans.						
3. Presentation of plans and programs.						
Creative						
1. Innovative and successful creative concepts.						
2. Accurate interpretation of problems/solutions in creative product.						
3. Ability to stay within established criteria.						
4. Cost consciousness.						
Copy						
1. Overall quality of work.						
2. Well thought out to meet the creative strategy.						
3. More effective than competitive work.						

Exhibit 3   Sample client review checklist

Client Review Checklist

Period under review from ⎯⎯⎯⎯⎯⎯⎯⎯⎯⎯⎯⎯⎯ to ⎯⎯⎯⎯⎯⎯⎯⎯⎯⎯

Prepared by ⎯⎯⎯⎯⎯⎯⎯⎯⎯⎯⎯⎯⎯⎯⎯⎯⎯ Title ⎯⎯⎯⎯⎯⎯⎯⎯

Agency ⎯⎯⎯⎯⎯⎯⎯⎯⎯⎯⎯⎯⎯⎯⎯⎯⎯⎯⎯⎯⎯⎯⎯⎯⎯⎯⎯

Discussed with client representative ⎯⎯⎯⎯⎯⎯⎯⎯⎯⎯⎯⎯⎯⎯⎯

	POOR	FAIR		GOOD		EXCELLENT
	1	2	3	4	5	6
Briefing						
1. Outline of corporate and marketing goals.						
2. Objectivity of market analysis.						
3. Depth of market analysis.						
4. Sharing confidential information.						
5. Allowing agency to dig for more information within company.						
Management involvement						
1. Appropriate amount.						
2. Timeliness of involvement.						
3. Clear direction.						
Expectations from Advertising						
1. Understanding of role in marketing mix.						
2. Clear positioning of product or service.						
3. Appropriateness of budget for task.						
Strategy setting						
1. Co-operates in strategy setting.						
2. Allows proposals to alter old strategies.						
3. Investment in research.						
4. Willingness to innovate.						

continued

Exhibit 3   continued

	POOR	FAIR		GOOD		EXCELLENT
	1	2	3	4	5	6
Creative						
1. Enthuses creative team.						
2. Allows creative latitude.						
3. Risks unknown.						
4. Gives time for new approaches to work.						
5. Provides good creative input.						
6. Criticism is constructive.						
Approvals						
1. Clear chain of approvals.						
2. Consistency of approval levels.						
3. Explaining rejection.						
4. Understanding of costs.						
5. Speed of approval.						
Deadlines						
1. Reasonable length.						
2. Accepts uncontrollable factors.						
Financial						
1. Understanding the financial arrangement.						
2. Prompt clearance of queries.						
3. Prompt payment.						
4. Timely budget information.						
The overall relationship						
1. Regularity of evaluation.						
2. Openness.						
3. Working to improve.						
4. Fairness of criticism.						
5. Good motivator.						

Advertising Planning

This section concentrates on the central theme of the text—the *planning* of the advertising effort.

Chapter 4 provides the foundation for advertising planning by establishing the relationships of plans at three different levels of an organization. The process is considered in the context of corporate planning, marketing planning, and advertising planning. The use of market-segmentation and consumer-behaviour concepts is presented in the context of advertising planning. The chapter ends with a discussion of the importance of *positioning* in advertising planning.

Chapter 5 describes the organization and content of typical marketing and advertising plans, in order to establish the relationships between the two plans and to provide the reader with an appreciation of the role and importance of planning in the development of advertising.

P A R T II

Relationship with Marketing– Understanding Customers

CHAPTER 4

In studying this chapter, you will learn

- The way in which advertising uses market-segmentation and consumer-behaviour concepts to advantage
- The distinctions between demographic, psychographic, and geographic segmentation variables
- The influence of consumer behaviour on purchase decisions
- The information needed to identify and select target markets
- The definition of positioning, and how it is used in marketing and advertising

This chapter is devoted to the principles of market segmentation, consumer-behaviour characteristics, and positioning concepts. In the context of marketing and advertising planning, it is imperative that organizations understand the customers that they intend to appeal to through advertising. In this regard, it is essential to analyze demographic, psychographic and geographic trends so that target markets can be identified and pursued.

MARKET SEGMENTATION AND CONSUMER BEHAVIOUR

As discussed in chapter 1, most organizations today have adopted the societal marketing concept; they exist to satisfy the needs of their customers. Furthermore, a company must satisfy needs better than does the competition in order to survive and grow in the marketplace. Market segmentation flows logically from the marketing concept. Current business thinking has it that it is unrealistic to presume that any product can satisfy the needs of a majority of people. Instead, marketing-oriented companies identify attractive market segments (target markets) to pursue.

Market segmentation refers to the process of dividing a large market into smaller homogeneous markets (segments) based on common needs and/or similar lifestyles. Market segmentation is one of the most important factors in marketing and advertising planning. In advertising, information about potential customers has three specific applications: in positioning the product, in selecting the correct media for advertising messages, and in creating the messages themselves.[1]

ADVERTISING APPLICATIONS OF MARKET SEGMENTATION

Positioning

Positioning refers to the place a brand occupies in the minds of consumers. Advertising plays a major role in securing for the brand a position in the consumer's mind, that is, in creating a favourable and lasting impression that will penetrate perceptual barriers. Think about fast-food restaurants. Why does McDonald's or Burger King come to mind first? Now imagine a soft drink. Either Coke or Pepsi immediately springs to mind, doesn't it? The reason is that advertising, in combination with other marketing variables, influences consumers' perceptions of any particular brand. Positioning will be discussed in more detail later in this chapter.

Media Strategy

Advertisers are concerned with effectively and efficiently reaching their target markets. Media groups are concerned with attracting potential advertisers to their medium. Consequently, much media research is conducted to gather information on

Figure 4.1   An advertisement that demonstrates lifestyle positioning, appealing to upscale bold achievers

Jaguar XJ12 Vanden Plas
With perfection, there is no compromise.

Jaguar Vanden Plas was created for those who cannot abide anything less than perfection. Its taut, yet fluid lines are sculptured evidence of the coachwork genius of Vanden Plas' master designers and builders. On the continent and, in fact, around the world their skills are legendary.

Lustrous, hand-rubbed burl walnut veneers crown the dashboard and door panels. Fine-grained, supple leathers are painstakingly cured, matched, and fitted to specially contoured seats. Passengers can relax in an environment cloistered from road, wind, and other distractions outside the world of Vanden Plas. Twin swivel reading lamps cast a gentle but effective light for those rear seat passengers who choose to read or engage in other cerebral pursuits.

An array of electrical amenities are at your complete disposal. A 4-speaker AM/FM stereophonic tuner and cas-

sette deck; automatic climate control; cruise control; power windows and sun roof; and central door locking are only a few of the standard features.

In power, performance, and dependability, Vanden Plas is unmistakably Jaguar. Beneath its graceful form, Vanden Plas is driven by the smooth, silently powerful 5.3 litre

V-12 May head engine. To assure the precise handling characteristics set for all Jaguars, Vanden Plas' 12-cylinder engine has been teamed with road and race proven handling systems. The outcome is an extraordinarily gifted automobile.

Extensive factory quality control programs and exhaustive North American testing have resulted in the most dependable line of Jaguars ever built. No idle claim, but a fact supported by a new warranty that is among the finest in the world. Please ask for details.

For more information on the XJ12 Vanden Plas or other fine Jaguar cars, contact your nearest Jaguar dealer, or send your business card to Jaguar Canada Inc., Indell Lane, Bramalea, Ontario L6T 4H3.

JAGUAR
A BLENDING OF ART AND MACHINE

Courtesy: Jaguar Canada Inc. Reprinted with permission.

the types of people who read, who listen to, and who watch the various media. With such data available, advertisers are better able to select the appropriate media vehicles with which to reach their target markets.

Creative Strategy

Information about market segments is important when creative strategies are being developed. Extensive demographic and psychographic knowledge results in more effective and convincing messages. What is it that triggers a response? Do consumers respond more positively to rational or to emotional appeals? Are they influenced by the use of celebrities to present a product? Having answers to these sorts of questions about consumers can help advertisers choose the tone, style, and mood of communications. For example, the lifestyle of the target market influences the decisions that are made regarding the surroundings and activities presented in a commercial. Will an advertiser show a business executive at work in the hustle and bustle of a large city, or in a more relaxed environment, participating in some recreation on the weekend? Such decisions are based on information obtained from market segmentation. Figure 4.1 shows an advertisement that focuses on the lifestyle of the target market.

CONSUMER BEHAVIOUR

Consumer behaviour can be defined as the acts individuals perform in obtaining and using goods and services, including the decision-making processes that precede and determine these acts.[2] A firm understanding of how behavioural tendencies apply to purchase decisions is of significant benefit to the marketing organization. Because of the dominant role that segmentation plays in the marketing of products and services, there has been considerable growth in primary research into consumer behaviour.

From a purely competitive viewpoint, marketers must have access to data concerning consumers' buying habits in order to develop more convincing communications programs that will stimulate response by the target market. Consequently, large sums of money are allocated to marketing research to find answers to the following major questions:

- Who makes the buying decision?
- How do they buy?
- Where do they buy?
- When do they buy?
- Why do they buy?

For any product, retail store, or company, answers to the above questions will provide valuable input into four-P activity. A discussion of the psychological and social factors influencing consumer behaviour is a useful preliminary to the study of segmentation techniques and their uses.

Psychological Factors

The primary psychological factors in consumers' behaviour and purchase decisions are needs, motives, perceptions, and attitudes. In any purchase-decision situation, the initial step for the seller is to make an individual recognize a need; the next step is to provide enough stimulation that the individual is motivated to take action to satisfy the need.

Needs and Motives *Needs* suggest a state of deprivation; the absence of something useful. *Motives* are the conditions that prompt the action that is taken to satisfy the need (the action elicited by marketing and advertising activity). The relationship between needs and motives is direct with respect to marketing and advertising activity. Such activity must sufficiently develop the target market's need—through an appealing presentation of appropriate benefits—that the target is motivated to respond by purchasing the product or service.

Maslow's *hierarchy of needs* and *theory of motivation* have had a significant impact on marketing and advertising strategies. The theory is based on the principle that needs can be classified from lower level to higher level, and it rests on two prevailing assumptions:[3]

1. When lower-level needs are satisfied, a person moves up to higher-level needs.
2. Satisfied needs do not motivate. Instead, behaviour will be influenced by needs yet to be satisfied.

Maslow states that individuals move through five levels (see figure 4.2):

1. *Physiological Needs*: hunger, thirst, sex, shelter
2. *Safety Needs*: security, protection, comfort
3. *Social Needs*: sense of belonging, love from family and friends
4. *Esteem Needs*: recognition, achievement, status, need to excel
5. *Self-Actualization Needs*: fulfillment, to realize potential (achieve what you believe you can achieve)

Numerous advertising examples can be cited to demonstrate advertising applications of Maslow's need theory. Pepsi-Cola appealed to physiological needs in a television commercial showing people sweltering at the beach on an extremely hot day.

Figure 4.2   Maslow's hierarchy of needs

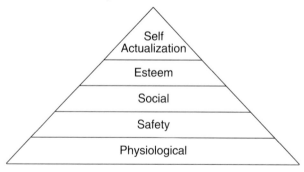

Source: "Hierarchy of Needs" from *Motivation and Personality, 2nd ed* by Abraham H. Maslow Copyright 1954 by Harper & Row, Publisher, Inc. ©1970 Abraham H. Maslow. Reprinted by permission of publishers.

Over a loud speaker came the sounds of swallowing (which was meant to impress consumers with the thirst-quenching power of the soft drink). The swallowing sound drew the throngs of people from the beach to a nearby Pepsi drink stand. Safety needs are used to motivate people to purchase automobile tires, life insurance, and retirement-savings plans. The desire to be accepted by peers (that is, the need for social satisfaction) is commonly appealed to in the advertising for products such as deodorants, toothpaste, and breath mints. Advertising for products in these markets tends to appeal to one's social consciousness. Esteem needs are addressed in commercials that portray people in successful business roles and occupations; the senior executive travelling first class on an airline is one example (see figure 4.3). Lotteries such as 6/49 appeal to consumers' self-actualization needs, to their desire for the easy life that can be obtained by winning big (a dream only possible if a ticket is purchased). Also, the armed forces' use of phrases such as "Choose a career, live the adventure" and "Be all that you can be" appeals to self-actualization needs.

Perceptions Perception refers to the manner in which individuals receive and interpret messages. From a marketing point of view, how individual consumers perceive the same product can vary considerably. Perceptual images are based on influences such as advertising, packaging, pricing, and so on. It should be noted that consumers are not aware of all that goes on around them; they are quite selective about messages they receive. Which messages they select to receive depends on their level of interest and need requirements. There are three levels of selectivity:

1. *Selective Exposure*: our eyes and minds only notice information that is of interest to us.
2. *Selective Perception*: we screen out messages and information that are in conflict with previously learned attitudes and beliefs.
3. *Selective Retention*: we remember only what we want to remember.

Theories of perception help explain why all people do not respond to all advertising and marketing activity. Quite simply, they do not notice it. However, if a consumer is contemplating a purchase—let's say the first purchase of an expensive audio component set—he or she will be interested in learning about the product. Thus the consumer will become receptive to advertising messages for audio components, while screening out other messages.

It is estimated that individuals are exposed to as many as a thousand messages a day, so it is virtually impossible for consumers to retain all of them. The challenge for advertisers is to communicate messages that will break through perceptual barriers. This is what creative strategy and execution are all about—designing advertisements that will command attention and compel the reader, listener, or viewer to take action.

Attitudes Attitudes are an individual's feelings, favourable or unfavourable, towards an idea or object (the advertised product). Virtually everyone has had a sour experience with a product. When people say, "I'll never buy that again," for whatever reason, they usually mean it. A bad experience creates an attitude that no amount of advertising will overcome.

Figure 4.3 An advertisement that appeals to the esteem needs of the business traveller

Our world revolves around you.

We know the feeling. Tight schedules. Back to back meetings in different cities. Being away from your city, away from your home. Because of the demands of travelling on business, we've gone to great lengths to make things easier and more comfortable for you when you travel with us. Our business is making yours fly.

Canadi⬛n

Our world revolves around you.

Canadian is a registered trademark of Canadian Airlines International Ltd.

Courtesy: Canadian Airlines

Marketers and advertisers have found that advertising designed to change attitudes is an expensive proposition. It is preferable to tailor the presentation of products to the widely held attitudes of the target market. Let's review two examples that illustrate the importance of attitudes. In the early eighties, a milk-based beverage with the brand name "Super 2" was launched in Ontario. Available in a variety of flavours, the product was positioned as a thirst-quenching alternative to soft drinks. The target market, composed mainly of teens, did not respond and the product failed. Teen attitudes were such that soft drinks were the preferred thirst quencher. Subsequent campaigns by the Ontario Milk Marketing Board successfully repositioned milk as a product that can be enjoyed at times of the day other than meal times. Had this attitude change preceded the launch of Super 2, the flavoured milk product might have been more successful.

Coca-Cola is currently trying to persuade the American public to consider Coke as a breakfast-drink alternative. In test-market situations, Coca-Cola is being advertised as a drink to enjoy early in the day, at times when other drinks, such as orange juice and apple juice, are popular. Despite the marketing expertise of Coca-Cola, and all of the resources it has to commit to this marketing effort, the prospects of success remain bleak, given the strongly held attitudes of consumers.

Social Factors

Social factors influencing the purchase-decision process stem from reference groups and from the role and status an individual has within a group.

A **reference group**, or **peer group**, is a group of people with a common interest that influences their attitudes and behaviour. Reference groups that people are commonly associated with include co-workers, sports teams, hobby clubs, fraternal organizations, and schoolmates. For a member of a group, there is considerable pressure to conform to the standards of the group, to "fit in." The consumer's desire to fit in definitely influences the types of products he or she purchases. For example, a young woman who has joined a downtown fitness studio may decide to purchase fashionable sportswear after her first fitness workout. During the first visit she may have found that she was inappropriately dressed. Fitting in becomes a priority to the extent that she is willing to purchase the "correct" workout gear. This type of behaviour is related to a "lifestyle-associations" factor, which has always been a strong influence on new members of any group.

DEMOGRAPHIC SEGMENTATION

With **demographic segmentation**, target markets are identified and pursued on the basis of variables such as age, gender, income, occupation, education, marital status, household formation, and cultural mix.

Age

Traditionally, the age group comprising people of 18 to 34 years of age has been given the most attention by marketers and advertisers, since this group spends the most on consumer goods and services. This strategy will begin changing in the present decade, as the Canadian population ages. Over the next decade (1986 to 1996), there will be a 7% decline in the number of Canadians under the age of 35.[4] Baby boomers will be entering middle age, and this group will become the major buying influence. It is estimated that, by 1996, there will be 1.6 million more people in the 35-to-49-year age group, an increase of 32.4% from 1986. In addition, the "grey revolution" will be increasingly apparent. By 1996, almost 7.6 million Canadians, representing 28% of the population, will be over the age of 50, compared to 22% in 1986.[5]

The impending over-50 age group is expected to be quite different from that of past generations. Current emphasis on health and physical well-being suggests that they will not be "old" either physically or in their outlook. They are also expected to retain the spending patterns of their younger days. It is anticipated that, increasingly, marketing and advertising plans will isolate and pursue these older groups (35 to 49, 50 to 64, and 65 plus). New products will be positioned to appeal to the needs of older age groups, and existing products will have to be repositioned in order to survive.

Gender

Gender has always been a primary means of distinguishing product categories—personal-care products, magazines, athletic equipment, and fashion are all categorized according to the gender of the buyer. More recently, the automobile market has recognized the benefits of gender segmentation, particularly since more and more women are buying cars. General Motors estimates that two-thirds of car purchasers are influenced by women in some way, and women purchase for themselves at least half of the popular sports cars (the Pontiac Fiero, for example, is popular with women).[6]

In the more expensive sports-car category, Mazda RX models and Toyota Celica have successfully positioned themselves to appeal to women with professional career aspirations. BMW traditionally targeted its advertising to the upscale male market, but recently it introduced to the Canadian market a model specifically for women, the 325i Cabriolet. The car was priced in the $40 000 range, and positioned as a less expensive alternative to the Mercedes Benz SL roadster; it is meant to appeal to upscale, career-minded women. Women are a growing segment for BMW, and in 1986 represented 20% of its total sales.[7] The Mazda Miata, a small sports car with a 1950s styling launched in 1989, has proven to be as attractive to female as to male buyers. The original thought was that the Miata would only appeal strongly to males.

The primary reason marketers focus on gender segmentation is the increasing economic power of women. Also, with more household responsibilities being shared, marketers and advertisers will be re-evaluating their positioning strategies for products and services that at one time were used by only one of the sexes.

Income, Occupation, and Education

Generally, these three variables have a close relationship with each other. Higher incomes are usually associated with certain occupations (the professions), which, in turn, are usually associated with a background of higher education. For example, it is a generally accepted fact that doctors, dentists, and lawyers are earning incomes above that of the average Canadian.

In Canada, there are some regional disparities in household incomes, with many regions suffering from higher-than-average rates of unemployment due to the depressed state of Canada's resource and manufacturing industries. However, wealthy Canadians now form a larger segment of the population than ever before, due mainly to the number of dual-income families. These households are defined as having an income in excess of $50 000 annually. The average income of Canadian households in 1990 was slightly over $57 000. This more affluent group represents a notable opportunity for advertisers, since the top 20% of affluent families account for 47% of education expenditures, 44% of savings and financial securities expenditures, 42% of recreation expenditures, and 42% of gifts and charitable donations.[8]

The occupations of individuals can be divided into three broad categories: white-collar, blue-collar, and professional. When trying to approach customers on the basis of occupation, marketers have two basic alternatives. They can identify occupation groups that have an interest in their product, or they can position their product so that it appeals to a certain group. While professional occupations are perceived to be the highest paying and so to offer the most spending potential, marketers do not ignore the spending potential of high-earning blue-collar workers. Highly skilled blue-collar workers can earn more than some professionals. The needs of the occupation groups may vary, but many have the income to buy.

Given the aging trends of the Canadian population, an increasing proportion of Canadians will be in these affluent income groups. What effect will this have on marketing strategy? With the emergence of a more mature, affluent target market, which already places an emphasis on fitness and on the home as an entertainment centre, marketers anticipate that demand will remain high for fitness and leisure products, for foods and beverages that match a healthier lifestyle, for home-entertainment units, high-quality fashion, and travel. Marketers will appeal to these targets on the basis of affluence, status, and achievement, using strategies that are in line with the target's income and occupation.

In response to the needs of an older but healthier consumer, Joseph E. Seagram launched V.O. Light in 1990, a new rye with 30% fewer calories and 30% less alcohol than the standard rye. According to John Bailey, vice-president of marketing, "Seagrams is aligning with better drinking behaviour, moderation and less calories."[9]

Marital Status and Household Formation

Marriage and divorce statistics for the period between 1980 and 1985 indicate a decline in the number of marriages each year, and a high but relatively stable divorce rate. These factors have created new household formations: greater numbers of bachelor households and greater numbers of single-parent-family households. Despite these trends, the absolute number of households is rising. Between 1986 and 1991, the number of households is expected to increase by 2.7% per year on average, which means an addition of 1.2 million households over five years.[10]

As of 1986, four out of five Canadian families were either the traditional family composed of husband, wife, and children, or the family composed of single parent and children. Growth in the number and size of traditional families has slowed due to delays in marriage, to the number of single-parent families, and to the aging population, now moving past the prime family-forming years. Another significant trend is the growth of the "singles" segment, due in part to the postponement of marriage and to a high divorce rate. Single-person households now account for 20% of all Canadian households.[11] The resulting household formations are illustrated in figure 4.4, which shows the family life cycle.

Knowing the stage a family has reached in the family life cycle offers insight into the family's purchase decisions. **Family-life-cycle** theory is based on the assumption that a family's needs change as it progresses through various stages. Needs change with variables such as age, income, marital status, and the presence of children. According to life-cycle theory, as individuals grow older and as their incomes rise, their overall financial burden eases. Consequently, different types of purchase decisions occur at each stage. To illustrate the application of this concept simply, the purchase priorities of a young family with children will be quite different from those of older married couples with no children living at home.

In other situations, a family must be considered as a purchasing unit. Consequently, the actual impact each person has on the purchase decision depends on the type of product or service under consideration. Traditionally, purchase decisions of a family were related to the role of each member in the family unit. In recent times, the roles of family members have changed dramatically, and the distinctions between the roles of the male and female heads of the household are vague. Among the factors contributing to these role changes are the increased presence of women in the workforce, the increasing number of single-parent families, and the increasing need for two incomes for families to survive (economic necessity).

From a marketing and advertising viewpoint, it is essential to determine who has the most influence. Is it the female head, the male head, or a combination of the two, and is the decision made with or without the influence of children? Once this is known, appropriate messages can be delivered by the most effective medium to the decision maker. Traditionally, purchase decisions have been classified as husband-dominant, wife-dominant, or shared equally. Despite role changes, product categories still perceived as being husband-dominant include life insurance, outdoor equipment, and garden supplies. Wife-dominant purchases include appliances, furniture, carpeting, and kitchenware. This is not sex-role stereotyping; it is simply indicative of traditional—and actual—purchase patterns. Obviously, both husband and wife may share in the decisions to buy and in the utilization of any of these items. Generally, the more expensive a product or service is, the greater the likelihood of a shared decision.

The presence and influence of children is another complicating factor for the marketer. For example, the parents may decide to dine out at a restaurant, but the children may select the actual restaurant, choosing one which is more in line with their tastes. To avoid potential conflict, parents will go along with such decisions; hence the frequency of visits to such restaurants as McDonald's, Burger King, Wendy's, and so forth.

Demographic shifts in Canada are changing the nature of the life-cycle concept, and these changes must be considered when contemporary marketing and advertising activity is being developed. What has changed is the time an individual spends at each

Figure 4.4 An overview of the traditional family life cycle and buying behaviour

Stage in family life cycle	Buying or behavioral pattern
1. Bachelor Stage: Young single people not living at home	Few financial burdens. Fashion opinion leaders. Recreation-oriented. Buy: basic kitchen equipment, basic furniture, cars, equipment for the mating game, vacations.
2. Newly Married Couples: Young, no children	Better off financially than they will be in near future. Highest purchase rate and highest average purchase of durables. Buy: cars, refrigerators, stoves, sensible and durable furniture, vacations.
3. Full Nest I: Youngest child under six	Home purchasing at peak. Liquid assets low. Dissatisfied with financial position and amount of money saved. Interested in new products. Like advertised products. Buy: washers, dryers, TV, baby food, cough medicines, vitamins, dolls, wagons, sleds, skates.
4. Full Nest II: Youngest child six or over	Financial position better. Some wives work. Less influenced by advertising. Buy larger-sized packages, multiple-unit deals. Buy: many foods, cleaning materials, bicycles, music lessons, pianos.
5. Full Nest III: Older married couples with dependent children	Financial position still better. More wives work. Some children get jobs. Hard to influence with advertising. High average purchase of durables. Buy: new, more tasteful furniture, auto travel, nonnecessary appliances, boats, dental services, magazines.
6. Empty Nest I: Older married couples, no children living with them, head in labour force	Home ownership at peak. Most satisfied with financial position and money saved. Interested in travel, recreation, self-education. Make gifts and contributions. Not interested in new products. Buy: vacations, luxuries, home improvements.
7. Empty Nest II: Older married couples, no children living at home, head retired	Drastic cut in income. Keep home. Buy: medical applicances, medical-care products that aid health, sleep, and digestion.
8. Solitary Survivor, in labour force	Income still good but likely to sell home.
9. Solitary Survivor, retired	Some medical and product needs as other retired group; drastic cut in income. Special need for attention, affection, and security.

Source: Phillip Kotler and Gordon H.G. McDougall, *Marketing Essentials* (Scarborough: Prentice-Hall Canada Inc., 1985) p.110. Reprinted with permission.

Advertising in Action
Demography Forces Change

Demography is the statistical study of human populations. Very simply, it is the analysis of numerical facts—how many teenagers there are, how many baby-boomers, how many senior citizens; how many people were born in a year and how many people died; and how many immigrants entered the country and how many people left. According to David Foot, an economist at University of Toronto and a noted demographer, we collectively—meaning governments, businesses, and economists—generally ignore what statistics are telling us. This may sound incredible, but Foot bases many of his own conclusions on one simple assumption: he maintains that "75% of just about everything, including the future, is explainable to demographics."

What's happening with demographics in Canada? The critical statistic is the bulge in the middle; no, not the waistline but the segment of the population, commonly referred to as baby-boomers, that represents one-third of the population, almost nine million people. Their presence is the result of the most prolific burst of fertility ever seen in any developed country in this century (proven statistically by analyzing demographic trends).

Baby-boomers are the core of Canada's population, and they will remain that way until about 2040, at which time most of them will be dead. If you are contemplating starting a new business, consider the funeral business. It can be projected that between 2020 and 2040 there will be the highest demand ever for this type of service. Pure and simple, as this segment of the population ages, it will have a profound effect on the future.

Demographic soothsayers believe that demographics alone will make Canada more productive. Their argument appears sound as they predict that the country will change from one of abundant labour and scarce capital to one of scarce labour and abundant capital. For that reason alone, output per person will increase, a trend that has already occurred in Europe and Japan.

Certainly, the aging population will have a direct impact on future marketing and advertising strategies. The eighties were the years of the light products—light beer, light soft drinks, light salad dressings, light desserts—all products that catered to the health-conscious attitudes of the aging population. This trend is expected to continue.

As regards the world of advertising, the baby-boomers in their younger years have been influenced by lifestyle appeals—"the bars, the beach, the parties," the fun-and-games youth-oriented approach. This cannot last. Our attitudes, our opinions, our lifestyles change as we grow older. We don't necessarily slow down, but we do things differently and we do develop new interests. Bearing this in mind, products will have to be repositioned in the aging consumer's mind if they are to survive. There will be a shift toward a more straightforward, factual, quality-driven style of advertising. Appeals will be made to the rational side of the consumer's mind rather than to the emotional side.

If you consider, as well, that baby-boomers will become wealthier as they grow older, the prospects brighten for sharp marketers and advertisers. As the kids leave the nest, the older adults will have more disposable income to play with—it will be time for them to really enjoy life, finally! We can look for more trips to far away and exotic destinations, more upscale kitchen appliances, and well-built, fully equipped smaller homes (assuming that the real-estate and home-building industries will survive the slide expected in the nineties). Everything electronic will continue to appeal to older age groups. Expect family rooms, within 10 years, to have entertainment centres covering entire walls, with components such as TVs integrated in "surround-sound" stereo, with high-definition flat and square TVs integrated with VCRs, audio equipment, digital audio tape recorders, and home computers. Before the end of the century, 3-D hologram movies could be part of the same system.

If this really is the future, consider that the big advertisers in the year 2000 and beyond will be the high-technology firms that produce and market these electronic gadgets. Move over Procter & Gamble and Coca-Cola, here come Sony, Panasonic, Hitachi and Toshiba!

Adapted from Daniel Stoffman, "Completely predictable people," *Report on Business Magazine*, November 1990, p.78, and information contained in Clarkson Gordon/Woods Gordon, *Tomorrow's Customers Today*, 1989.

stage. It is quite clear that the family of the nineties will be different from the families of previous decades. For more details on these trends and their implications for marketing and advertising activity, refer to the Advertising in Action vignette "Demography Forces Change."

Cultural Mix

Culture refers to the behaviour an individual learns while growing up, behaviour which feeds into a strongly held value system. Peoples' values can change. The hippies of the sixties gave way to the "me" generation of the seventies, which in turn evolved into the "yuppies" and parents of the eighties. As each decade passed, individuals' values changed (different needs, different attitudes, different responsibilities developed). We now live in a very materialistic society, and individuals constantly strive to possess more. Values are such that possession of a good-quality house or automobile is taken as an indication of success. In previous times, social values dictated saving rather than spending.

The Canadian birthrate is declining on an annual basis, and it is expected that, as a result, immigrants will account for most of whatever growth occurs in the 1990s. Canada's ethnic diversity represents new opportunities for Canadian advertisers. Existing within Canadian culture are many diverse subcultures—subgroups within a larger cultural context which have distinctive lifestyles based on religious, racial, and geographic differences, while retaining important features of the dominant Canadian culture. Canada's subcultures are evident in cities where parts of the urban and suburban neighbourhoods are occupied by large ethnic populations. Very often, these ethnic groups are served by their own media. Marketing organizations are now paying more attention to ethnic groups, and are developing specific marketing and advertising activities for them. Refer to figure 4.5, an advertisement of the Mercury Tracer aimed at the Chinese market.

With Canadian cities becoming more cosmopolitan as a result of immigration, companies are adjusting to the changing realities. Sun Life Assurance Company is

Figure 4.5 Chinese advertisement for Mercury Tracer

Courtesy: Ford Motor Company of Canada Ltd. and Vickers & Benson Advertising Ltd. Reprinted with permission.

one of those companies. Known as the Forever Bright Insurance Company in the Chinese community, it generates 10% of its insurance volume from ethnic marketing. The company makes extensive use of Chinese-language newspapers, Chinese TV, and Chinese agents.[12]

PSYCHOGRAPHIC SEGMENTATION

Demographics has been the traditional method of segmenting markets, but in today's competitive business environment, it is only one of the methods that must be used. Contemporary marketing organizations have added a more sophisticated variable, referred to as psychographics. The combination of demographic and psychographic information provides the marketing organization with a better understanding of its target market. Marketers not only know who buys, but why they buy.

Psychographics examines individual lifestyles in terms of activities, interests, and opinions. Information concerning lifestyle can explain why two people who are demographically identical behave in different ways—in particular, why they purchase totally different types of products and services. Therefore, when organizations target their products psychographically, advertising messages are in line with the lifestyle of the target market. Essentially, the personality of the product matches the personality of the target.

Psychographics and psychographic research are phenomena that have developed in response to the changing values of the baby-boom generation as it proceeds through life. The stages passed through by a single individual during his life are similar to the stages passed through by a whole generation. New needs emerge for the individual as attitudes, beliefs, and opinions change.

Psychographic research was pioneered by Stanford Research Institute in California (now SRI International), in 1976. At that time, SRI profiled nine American lifestyles: survivors, sustainers, belongers, achievers, emulators, I-am-Me's, experientials, the societally conscious, and integrateds.[13] In Canada, numerous psychographic research studies have been conducted, resulting in a variety of descriptive classifications. Goldfarb Consultants of Toronto has divided Canadians into six psychographic cells, in two broad segments: *traditionalists* and *non-traditionalists*.[14] A brief description of the psychographic cells, along with some marketing implications, follows in the next section.

CANADIAN PSYCHOGRAPHIC CLASSIFICATIONS

Traditionalists

Day-to-Day Watchers These people, who make up 25% of the population, represent the status quo who watch the world pass by. They dislike society's unremittingly fast pace. For them, family satisfaction takes priority over the satisfaction of the individual. They are motivated by security and loyalty factors, and familiar products appeal to them. In terms of marketing, they are influenced by the dominance of a brand name, by authority figures as presenters of products, and by quality. They respond to promotions (which encourage them to obtain what they cannot afford) and watch a great deal of television.

Old-Fashioned Puritans Representing 18% of the population, they are a group who prefer simpler times. The family is important to them, but their individual ethics dominate. They are firm believers in government, law, and social order. They shop for value at established stores. They are motivated by value, and by a combination of reasonable price and good quality. Therefore, they respond to messages stressing good value. They purchase large sizes (to save money), and they will respond to coupons if they perceive that value can be had from them.

Responsible Survivors These people, counting for 12% of the population, represent the frugal segment. They are somewhat insecure about spending, and shop for the lowest price. Income is not a factor; they have money, but do not enjoy spending it. This group is motivated by price, and likes generic products, low-end retailers, and so on. Marketing activity should emphasize price to attract responsible survivors, and since television is important in their lifestyle, it is an effective medium for advertising.

Non-Traditionalists

Joiner Activists Representing 16% of the population, joiner activists are idealistic dreamers looking for self-improvement. They reject the status quo, are liberal-minded, and make rational decisions. This group is motivated by information (they evaluate their options before making a purchase decision). Marketing and advertising activity should use techniques that appeal to rationality and should stress quality, service, and dependability. Because joiner activists are information-oriented, a variety of media can be used to reach them (television, radio, newspapers, magazines).

Bold Achievers People of this type (15% of the population) are aggressive, confident individuals who set high goals for themselves. They aspire to be at the top, to lead, to obtain power and responsibility. They are innovators and as such are willing to try new products. Achievers can be motivated on an emotional level by status-, prestige-, and success-based appeals. They will purchase products that reflect their success. They tend to respond to premium prices, expensive packaging, and exclusivity. They do not want products that others can have easily.

Self-Indulgents Making up 14% of the population, self-indulgents are a group resenting authority. They are "me-first" types, heavily into self-gratification. They have impulsive tendencies, even in major purchases, because they seek instant gratification. Products that differentiate them from their peers have strong appeal. Price is not a factor; gratification is very much a factor. Carefully planned advertising (short and to the point—they do not have much time) is effective, and it should highlight gratification.

Psychographic information shows how an individual's interest in a product depends on his or her lifestyle. Automakers produce and market a range of automobiles to satisfy the lifestyle requirements of the Canadian lifestyle groups. Trendy sports

Figure 4.6   Sample questions for collecting psychographic data

1. To collect information on likes, dislikes and attitudes of consumers (usually a scale of 1 to 5 is used with 1 being strongly agree and 5 strongly disagree)
   - I go out with friends a great deal of the time.
   - I generally achieve what I set out to do.
   - I like to think I'm a bit of a swinger.
   - An important part of my life is dressing smartly.

2 .i) To collect information on principles, values and aspirations of consumers (a scale is used to rank statements based on degree of importance)
   - Getting married, having a happy marriage
   - Respect for authority
   - Commitment to the work ethic
   - Promotion of conservation and the fight against waste in society
   - College education

   ii) To determine people's opinions (again, a scale is used to determine the strength of respondents' convictions)
   - Capital punishment should be reinstated
   - It is important that children receive religious training
   - A woman should not work outside the home unless her household needs the money.

3. To collect information on activities and participation (scales used to determine frequency of participation)

a) How often do you personally participate in these activities?
   - Jogging/Running
   - Golf
   - Downhill skiing
   - Fishing
   - Gardening
   - Dancing
   - Entertaining at home
     etc.

b) How often do you attend these events?
   - Movies
   - Live theatre
   - Ballet or Opera
   - Baseball, Hockey
     etc.

cars with European styling appeal to the bold achievers, while a family station wagon or a mini-van appeals to the old-fashioned puritans.

Other product categories for which psychographic segmentation has been used to advantage include soft-drink beverages, beer, alcohol and tobacco, sports-equipment and leisure-sportswear, and fashion retailing, to name a few. Where the purchase of clothing is concerned, stores such as Holt Renfrew and other upscale boutiques appeal to bold achievers and self-indulgents. The middle-of-the-road groups, such as old-fashioned puritans, are likely to shop for clothing in established department stores such as the Bay, Simpsons, and Eaton's, and in national chains such as Fairweather, Tip Top, and Susy Shier. In contrast, responsible survivors are likely to purchase clothing in discount department stores such as K-Mart, Zellers and Woolco, and in low-end retail chains.

The lifestyle approach to marketing and advertising is the result of greater use of psychographic research in Canada. Marketing organizations can classify those who buy their products in terms of demographic variables such as age, sex, and occupation. Nevertheless, two individuals who look the same and live side by side in any area of Canada can have entirely different lifestyles. It is their psychographic profile, obtained through research, which indicates the differences between people and the reasons why they buy certain products. Psychographic research is research that determines the activities, interests, and opinions of consumers (commonly referred to as AIO's). As to how psychographic information is collected, refer to figure 4.6 for some sample research questions.

Psychographics allows marketing organizations to position their products better in the marketplace. It allows advertising messages to associate a product with a particular lifestyle. The beer industry in Canada is a heavy user of psychographic-based advertising. Some brands are positioned to appeal to the blue-collar male worker (e.g., Budweiser), while others are positioned to appeal to socially active couples in their twenties who enjoy good times together (e.g., Molson Canadian). Potential users of a brand who identify with the particular lifestyle presented in an advertisement for the brand, may become more receptive through being exposed to the message.

THE BEHAVIOUR BEHIND PSYCHOGRAPHICS: PERSONALITY AND SELF-CONCEPT

Personality refers to a person's distinguishing psychological characteristics, those characteristics which lead that person to have relatively consistent and enduring responses to the environment in which he or she lives. Personality is influenced by self perceptions, with perceptions being influenced in turn by physiological and psychological needs, by family, culture, and reference groups.

The **self-concept**, or self-image, theory states that our actions, including our purchase decisions, are dependent upon our mental conception of self. Why do we pay a much higher price for a designer-label suit or dress when more economical alternatives are available? Our purchase of the designer label is based on the image we desire for ourselves. The self has four components: the real self, the self image, the looking-glass self, and the ideal self.[15]

1. *Real self* is an objective evaluation of the individual—you as you really are (reality is distorted by the other "selves").
2. *Self-image* is how you see yourself. You might, for example, see yourself as a swinger (which may not be reality).
3. *Looking-glass self* is the way you think others see you (one can project different images to different people).
4. *Ideal self* is how you would like to be (your aspirations).

Marketing organizations can use the self-concept theory to advantage. Marketers and advertisers know that, human nature being what it is, many important purchase decisions are based on the looking-glass self or the ideal self. Therefore, products and services that seem to bring closer this goal of the ideal self are appealing to the consumer. For example, a young business executive climbing the corporate ladder will have definite goals and aspirations, based on a positive self-image. Such an individual will purchase expensive business suits (of good quality, and conservative enough to project a certain image), join the appropriate clubs (fitness, golf, tennis, etc.), and probably drive a sporty car (perhaps a Japanese or European sports model). Purchase decisions like these are based not on where that person is but on where he or she is going—in their own mind, at least. Marketing organizations accentuate the image-making appeal of their products in order to woo purchasers who buy with the ideal self in mind.

As a concluding comment on the use of psychographic segmentation, a brief discussion of the advantages and disadvantages, as they apply to advertising, is warranted. On the positive side are the following advantages:

1. Lifestyle information—information concerning the activities, interests, and opinions of the target market—provides input that leads to more effective message development. The appeal techniques used (whether rational or emotional), the tone, the style, the mood, and the environmental surroundings used in an advertisement can all be based on the lifestyle of the target-market. If the message personality matches the target-market personality, the likelihood of the desired response occurring should increase.
2. The available data concerning the target market's media usage and consumption (what media they read, listen to, watch, and how much time they spend with it) provides input for better media strategy and execution.

On the negative side, advertisers should consider the following limitations:

1. It is unlikely that all people are the same in each lifestyle classification. In theory, all members would conform to some ideal representation, but realistically, of course, this is not the case. People are individuals, so it is to some extent inaccurate to perceive them in terms of groups that have the same tendencies.
2. The lifestyle approach may not be appropriate for certain product categories. Since a single product can appeal to several lifestyle groups, there is the problem of determining how to communicate with each group while making the product appealing to all.

Marketers and advertisers should use psychographic information with a certain degree of caution. Psychographic information can only enhance demographic knowledge; it is not a substitute for it.

GEOGRAPHIC SEGMENTATION

Geographic segmentation refers to the division of a geographically expansive market (Canada) into smaller geographic units (the Atlantic Provinces, Quebec, Ontario, the Prairies, and British Columbia). The availability of psychographic information about target markets has complemented the use of geographic segmentation. Knowing more about targets in the various regions—their behaviour, attitudes, and interests—helps marketers and advertisers to develop marketing and advertising plans. Gone are the days when a national brand could successfully apply an Ontario-based campaign to all parts of Canada.

The region with the most obvious difference is Quebec, whose language and cultural characteristics necessitate the use of different marketing and advertising strategies. For example, a prominent Quebec entertainer or sports personality who endorses a brand will have much more influence there than a nationally known celebrity. The same situation holds true in other regions. When all segmentation variables are combined (demographic, psychographic, and geographic), it is clear that the activities that will influence a Montreal-based, French-speaking business executive will be very different from those influencing a rural Prairie farmer. Consequently, marketing organizations must make assessments on a regional basis, and, when positioning their products, give consideration to regional differences and influences. For more details on regional differences and their influence on advertising, refer to the Advertising in Action vignette "Culture Important to Ultramar."

Geographic regions are further subdivided by geographic segmentation into urban (downtown), suburban, and rural households. It is estimated that approximately 75% of Canada's population lives in areas classified as urban. Not surprising, then, is the fact that successful marketing and advertising plans have an urban orientation. The type of family portrayed in an advertisement and the type of activity or situation they are shown to be engaged in tend to be "urban." In relation to other segmentation variables, the attitudes, opinions, and lifestyle of a downtown urban dweller may be quite different from those of the suburban dweller. For example, in many city neighbourhoods today, there is a higher incidence of younger, upscale households (refer to the different household formations discussed earlier). The inhabitants may be single, cohabiting instead of being married, and living in apartments, condominiums, or renovated housing.

In contrast, the suburban household may be more traditional in nature. Suburban dwellers are likely to be married, have children, own a large family automobile, live in new houses, commute downtown to work, and so on. Both of these groups may require the same products; however, the strategies used to reach these groups can be quite different. Similar comparisons can be made between the urban dweller and the rural dweller. The differences in need, attitude, and outlook on life create constant challenges for the marketing and advertising of products and services.

Advertising in Action
Culture Important to Ultramar

Ultramar is a major player in the retail gasoline business in Quebec and the Atlantic provinces. The company operates 1600 outlets and holds 20% of the market share. Generally speaking, the products that Ultramar sells are generic in nature; that is, it would be difficult for consumers to distinguish Ultramar's home-heating fuel, gasoline or industrial fuel from those of their competitors.

However, this fact did not dampen the marketing initiative of the company. In 1990, the company restructured itself internally so that marketing could play a more prominent role in company operations. According to Tony Di Gennaro, the company "saw an opportunity to concentrate on each of its products and position each with a personality." In positioning its Ultra Plus line, a new mid-priced gasoline, Ultramar's goal was to communicate that Ultra Plus provides the "best quality/price ratio for those people who plan to keep their cars longer."

A key decision that the company made involved the development of different advertising creative for the French Quebec and English Atlantic provinces. Citing several differences, Di Gennaro said "the English Quebecker is different from the English Maritimer, and there are differences in the Newfoundland market again."

In a pure marketing move, Ultramar launched Ultra Plus at the same price as the regular-grade Ultramar gasoline. The thinking was simple—once customers tried and were satisfied with the performance of Ultra Plus, they would stay with it when the price moved up to its normal level.

On the creative side of things, a general advertising concept was developed, but the nuances of the geographic markets were also considered with the help of information provided by consumer research. A humorous concept was tested in both French and English. The French commercial shows a man treating his car as if he were its "papa," tickling it and talking to it. The commercial went over well in French but the English market perceived the same message differently. They felt the man loved his car too much, even more than his family. Consequently, a new English concept had to be developed. The end result was total disparity in terms of look and feel between the English and French commercials. The French version did not include children and the car was given a name—"Cocette." In the English version there is much less affection shown toward the car, and a different kind of house is shown as the backdrop.

In this example, Ultramar recognized that there is a need to consider even subtle differences in language and culture when developing creative. It proves that a well-intended message can be misinterpreted by the target market. If such situations are not detected early, the results could be devastating. Advertisers would be making costly mistakes if they worked from the assumption that what works well in English-language markets will work just as well in French-language markets, and vice versa. At times there is a definite need to have alternative creative approaches.

Adapted from Gail Chiasson, "Cultural differences shown in creative," *Marketing,* November 19, 1990, p.15.

BEHAVIOUR-RESPONSE SEGMENTATION

Behaviour-response segmentation is used in conjunction with other segmentation variables, and divides buyers into groups according to the occasions they have for using a product (why they need it), to the benefits they desire from a product, to the frequency with which they use it, and to the degree of their brand loyalty.

Occasion for Use

This form of segmentation uses situations to optimize consumption of the product. For example, products such as milk and orange juice have been successfully repositioned in the market by advertisements showing the products being used at times other than traditional mealtimes. Other products are associated with special occasions. Flowers and chocolates, for example, are promoted heavily around Valentine's Day and Mother's Day.

Benefits Desired

In this case, marketers and advertisers are familiar with the buyer-behaviour influences discussed earlier in this chapter. If the target market is rational in nature, the benefits advertised will relate to quality, price, efficiency, dependability, and so on. If the target is influenced by emotion, different elements can be used in the advertising presentation (sex, fear, love, etc.). A product such as blue jeans provides a good illustration of these distinctions. An inexpensive, private-label brand purchased at a junior department store will perform the same function as the high-priced, designer-label brand purchased at a high-end fashion retailer. The reason why people buy one brand of jeans instead of another is based on a combination of demographic and psychographic variables.

Usage Rate

Frequency of use is an important segmentation variable. Marketers and advertisers conduct research to distinguish the characteristics of a heavy user from those of a medium or light user. Very often, the "80/20 rule" comes into play, that is, 80% of product volume comes from 20% of the users (heavy users). To attract more heavy users, marketers and advertisers use the heavy-user demographic and psychographic profile in presenting a product. The product will be positioned and the benefits communicated in a manner that will attract those potential users. A firm may also decide to pursue the light and medium user. Many more of these users would have to be attracted to the product in order to generate the sales volume generated by a heavy user. Also, trying to appeal to users with different backgrounds, attitudes, and lifestyles can complicate the development of marketing and advertising strategies and executions.

Loyalty Response

The degree of consumers' brand loyalty has an influence on segmentation strategy. As with usage-rate segmentation, the marketing firm should conduct research to determine the characteristics of brand-loyal users. Messages can then be developed, based on such knowledge, to attract users with similar profiles and behavioural tendencies.

From a marketing viewpoint, consideration must be given to users with varying degrees of loyalty. For example, marketers of a brand of detergent will develop promotional activities that are defensive in nature (e.g., coupons on the package for the next purchase, or a contest to generate multiple purchase) and direct them towards medium- and very loyal users, while using more aggressive tactics (e.g., trial coupons delivered by the media) to attract somewhat loyal users of competitive brands. Recognizing that brand switching does occur, marketers and advertisers must be concerned with customers at both ends of the loyalty spectrum.

IDENTIFYING AND SELECTING TARGET MARKETS

The market-segmentation and consumer-behaviour concepts discussed in the previous sections of this chapter provide the theoretical foundation of contemporary marketing strategies. The knowledge that a marketing organization has about its various target markets helps with advertising planning as well. Knowledge pertaining to who buys and why they buy is used to position products better, to develop more convincing messages, and to utilize media that will effectively reach the target. The target-marketing process involves three steps: identifying the market segments, selecting the market segments that offer the most potential, and positioning the product so that it appeals to the target market.

Identification of Market Segments

In defining market segments, marketing organizations profile potential user groups (segments) on the basis of their demographic, psychographic, and geographic characteristics. Essentially, the profile is a detailed description of the primary user. Secondary users' profiles may also be developed (which will involve different characteristics, habits, interests, etc.).

Selection of Opportune Target Markets

Of the segments identified as being potential users, which segment (target market) provides the greatest potential for the company? A multi-product firm competing in diverse markets will develop distinct marketing and advertising plans directed at target markets where the perceived profit potential is greatest.

Positioning of Product to Appeal to the Target Market

When positioning a product in the market, the marketing organization is concerned with designing and marketing a product that will meet the needs of the target. In this process, the organization will develop an image for the product and place it in the minds of the target, making the product appeal to members of the target market so that they will purchase it.

POSITIONING

Positioning can be defined as the selling concept that motivates purchase, or the image that marketers desire a brand or a company to have in the minds of consumers. The use of positioning strategies is much more frequent in today's marketing and advertising activity because of the increasing level of competition among products. Positioning is a strategy based on competition. It involves designing a product and marketing it to a target market in such a way that it will be distinguished from the competition. The manner in which a product is distinguished will have an effect on buyers' perceptions of the product and on the position the product occupies in the buyer's mind. Therefore, positioning is a means of segmenting a market in two different ways:

- Designing and marketing a product to meet the needs of a target market (marketing)
- Creating the appeals that will make the product stand out in the minds of the target market (advertising)

POSITIONING AND MARKETING

In the context of marketing, positioning is concerned with matching the right product with the needs of the target market. This matching process requires that marketers of a product assess competitive marketing activity to determine opportunities worth pursuing. In figure 4.7 a market is being analyzed on the basis of value—the relationships between price and quality. The assumption in this example is that price and quality are important purchase influencers, and that four competing brands exist on the market:

> Brand A—low price, low quality
> Brand B—high price for quality offered
> Brand C—medium price and quality
> Brand D—high price, high quality

A fifth competitor (E) is considering entrance into the market. Among the variety of alternatives available, Brand E could be located on the grid (market) so as to compete directly with an existing competitor, or it could be located so as to appeal to a different market segment. As shown in figure 4.7, Brand E was positioned to appeal to a segment demanding higher quality at a reasonable price. In this case, the firm will be sacrificing profit margin on each unit sold, since it will be more costly to manufacture and market a higher-quality product that stays within the price parameters of this market segment. However, if the marketing activity is effective in communicating the value offered, sufficient unit volume could be generated to compensate for lower profit margins. Such are the decisions of business.

Figure 4.7 Market positioning grid

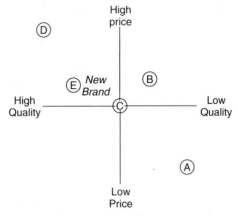

Based on the knowledge that price and quality are important factors to consumers, Brand E perceives an opportunity to market a high-quality product at a more reasonable price than its competitors.

POSITIONING AND ADVERTISING

Advertising will help position a product in the market, and influence what image of the product is retained in the mind of the consumer. Some of the more common advertising-positioning strategies are head-on comparisons, product differentiation, technical innovation, brand dominance, and lifestyle orientation.

Head-On Positioning (Comparative Positioning)

In head-on positioning, one brand is presented as equal to or better than another brand. This positioning is usually initiated by the number two brand in a market as a means of challenging the leader. The strategy is to show admitted users of a competitive brand showing preference for the advertised brand. The "Pepsi Challenge" is now a classic example of such head-on positioning. Its latest challenge occurred in the summer of 1990, when the Pepsi train caravan made stops all across Canada encouraging consumers to experience the taste of the Pepsi product. In the shampoo/conditioner market, two leading brands are going head-to-head for supremacy. Both Pert Plus and Pears Plus are claiming superiority over the rival brand, with each brand basing its claims on the preferred attributes of the product. Both products contain shampoo and conditioner properties in one package.

Head-on positioning requires financial commitment from the initiator, since the brand leader is likely to counter-attack with increased media spending. In so doing, however, the brand leader is not likely to make counter claims, preferring instead to let its number one position and product benefits work for it. In other words, it will use brand-dominance positioning.

Figure 4.8 An advertising message designed to communicate brand dominance

Courtesy: Coca-Cola Ltd.

Brand-Dominance Positioning

Brands that are established market leaders can utilize their market-share position to advantage when it comes to planting an image in the minds of their target market. Their advertising messages are designed to clearly state or imply that the product is successful, a market leader, highly acceptable to a majority of users, and so on. The Coca-Cola campaigns centring on the themes "Coke Is It", "It's the Real Thing", and "Can't Beat the Real Thing" exemplify campaigns designed to communicate brand dominance. Refer to figure 4.8 for an illustration.

Product Differentiation

Product differentation is a strategy that focuses on the unique attribute of a product—that feature which distinguishes it from all of the other products. The 7-Up "Un-Cola" campaign provides a classic illustration of product differentiation. In this campaign, 7-Up was presented as a crisp, clear, caffeine-free alternative to the more dominant cola brands. 7-Up was attacking a perceived weakness in the cola products—the presence of caffeine. A brand of toothpaste might be distinguished by its ability to prevent cavities, freshen breath, whiten teeth, or perhaps to perform all of these functions. A key selling point for a battery would be how long it lasts. In this market, Eveready claims that "Nothing lasts longer." Refer to figure 4.9 for an illustration.

Technical-Innovation Positioning

Technical innovation is more important for a company as a whole than for individual products. Companies seeking to establish for themselves an image of continual

Figure 4.9   A message that clearly stresses product differentiation

You've got to be good to finish last in this class.

Absolutely nothing lasts longer.

Courtesy: Eveready

Figure 4.10 An advertisement that demonstrates positioning by technical innovation

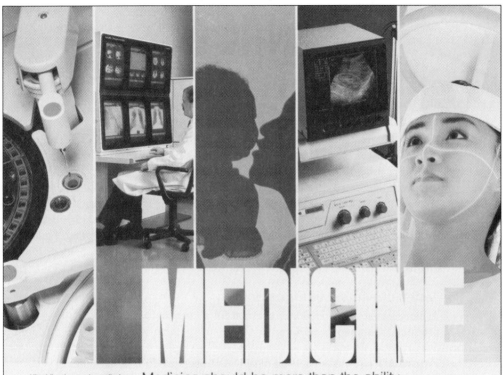

Hitachi's advances in medical electronics extend to automatic blood chemistry analysis, a Picture Archiving and Communications System, diagnostic ultrasonics and Magnetic Resonance Imaging.

Medicine should be more than the ability to treat or cure. The best care and treatment come from precise diagnosis.

Medical electronics have brought marvelous progress to diagnostic medicine in recent years. Great strides have been made in biochemical analysis, electron microscopes and medical information systems. Another shining example is the advent of imaging equipment which uses magnetic resonance to display even the most subtle changes in body chemistry.

Hitachi's scientists and engineers are now at work on an innovative system which will make it feasible to store, retrieve and use comprehensive diagnostic data from a wide array of imaging equipment — from the most sophisticated Magnetic Resonance Imaging units (MRI) to nuclear medicine, ultrasonic scanners and X-ray CT, to name just a few. This Picture Archiving and Communications System (PACS) should lead not only to more precise diagnosis but also to formation of research and-education information networks which use medical image data to the fullest.

Hitachi is also developing highly advanced electronic microscopes for exploring the world of micro-fine objects — indispensable in basic studies of medicine and biology. And we are creating medical equipment such as an automatic blood chemistry analyzer and an information processing system.

We link technology to human needs. We believe that Hitachi's advanced technologies will result in systems that serve peoples' needs more precisely and fully than ever before. Our goal in medicine — and communications, energy and transportation as well — is to create and put into practice innovations that will improve the quality of life the world around.

HITACHI

Hitachi, Ltd. Tokyo, Japan

Courtesy: Hitachi Ltd., Tokyo, Japan. Reprinted with permission.

technical leadership will use advertising to do so, positioning themselves on the leading edge of technology. Such a positioning, instilled in their customers' minds, will benefit such companies when they are introducing new products to the market. Hitachi Ltd. of Tokyo is such a company. One particular print advertisement (see figure 4.10) documented the company's contribution to the field of medical electronics. All of Hitachi's ads state its ambition as a company, which is to put into practice innovations that will improve the quality of life around the world. Hitachi Ltd. is active in medical electronics, communications, energy, and transportation around the world; through advertising its technical innovations, Hitachi makes certain that the world knows this.

Lifestyle Positioning

In crowded markets, where product attributes are perceived as being similar by the target market, firms must look for alternate ways of positioning their products. The use of psychographic information has allowed advertisers to develop campaigns that are based on the lifestyle of the target market. Essentially, the product is positioned to "fit in" or match the lifestyle of the user. As indicated earlier in this chapter, people are influenced by higher-level needs, by their looking-glass selves and ideal selves, and by their activities, interests, and opinions. These influences form the foundation of lifestyle advertising, and products that appeal to targets on the basis of these influences may have a greater chance of breaking through perceptual barriers.

Generally, lifestyle positioning through advertising uses emotional appeals such as love, fear, sex, humour, and so on, in order to elicit a response from the target. An example of such lifestyle positioning is the Chanel No. 5 perfume advertisement that shows a sunbathing female at one end of a swimming pool and, at the other end of the pool, an imaginary male who lunges into the pool and then approaches the female. Their slogan, "Share the Fantasy," piqued the imaginations of potential customers. In the beer market, the advertising for brands such as Canadian, Carlsberg, Blue, and Labatt's Dry uses lifestyle situations successfully. Typical advertisements show the target market enjoying activities such as volleyball at the beach, parties around the pool, and informal get-togethers in a pub. These are situations that the brand's target market would like to participate in. If potential users are seeking the type of lifestyle portrayed in the advertisement, they are apt to respond more favourably towards the ad, and this could lead to the purchase of the product.

REPOSITIONING

So far, we have discussed only the initial positioning of a product in the marketplace and in the minds of consumers. But the competitive market requires that positioning strategies be capable of being readily changed. It is unrealistic to assume that the position a brand adopts originally will remain the same throughout its life cycle. Products will be repositioned according to the prevailing environment in the market. Repositioning a product involves changing the place it occupies in the consumer's mind in relation to competitive products. The need to reposition a product occurs for two primary reasons. First, the marketing activity of a direct competitor can create the need to reposition a product; second, the changing preferences of the target market can make it necessary for a product to adapt.

Reacting to Competitive Activity and Positioning

This situation is best explained by example. In April 1985, Coca-Cola undertook a major repositioning of its flagship brand. Coca-Cola stunned the competing soft drink manufacturers, its own bottlers, and its consumer franchise by altering its formula. Coca-Cola was repositioned as a slightly sweeter, less filling soft drink. The company began the repositioning in the United States (Canada followed shortly thereafter) when it realized that its share of supermarket sales was slightly behind that of Pepsi-Cola. The new formula was extensively tested among consumers, who preferred it both to the original Coca-Cola and to Pepsi-Cola. However, by July of 1985, the company announced the return of the original product as Coca-Cola Classic. Coca-Cola's attempt at repositioning had failed. The company had underestimated consumers' emotional attachments to the original product—there was significant public outcry over the change, particularly among loyal users. Some believe that the brand loyalty for Coca-Cola had gone beyond *brand insistence* (that is, a consumer thinking that he or she must have a particular product and no other), to the point where it was a product that could not be changed.

Reacting to Changing Consumer Preferences

Analyzing consumer trends leads to repositioning strategies. The real demographic trends discussed earlier will force existing brands to reposition in order to survive in the marketplace.

A current example of repositioning may be seen in the fast-food restaurant industry. In the eighties, the trend towards eating more meals out of the home was a boon for restaurants such as McDonald's, Burger King, Wendy's and Harvey's. However, as consumers became bored with the hamburger, the same restaurants had to react or risk losing business to competitors offering other specialties, such as chicken and pizza. Consequently, menus were expanded to include broader-based entrée items, and hours of operation were extended to appeal to the early-morning and late-night customers.

In the beer market, Carlsberg dropped, in 1989, its strategy of focusing on its Danish heritage, in favour of a more contemporary style. The new strategy was to attract an older, more sophisticated beer drinker. According to Glen Cavanaugh, the national brand manager, "Research showed that the European link conjured up a traditional, old-fashioned and somewhat out of date image. Carlsberg drinkers aren't party animals but they enjoy drinking in small groups. It's a sociable beer, but in previous campaigns, there was no such component."[16] Changes in positioning, then, come out of demographic and psychographic shifts in the market, which companies must analyze continuously.

The demographic, psychographic, and geographic segmentation variables, as well as the positioning concepts discussed in this chapter, are discussed further in chapters 5, 6, and 10.

Summary

Market segmentation and knowledge of consumer behaviour are important factors in marketing and advertising planning. Both have a direct impact on product positioning, media strategy, and creative strategy.

Adequate knowledge of psychological, social, cultural and personal influences provides essential input into advertising strategy. In terms of segmentation, organizations must identify their target markets as precisely as they can. Good use of information provided by demographics (which provides information concerning the consumer's age, gender, income, occupation, education, marital status, household formation, and cultural mix), psychographics (which provides information concerning the consumer's activities, interests, and opinions), and geographics (which focuses on consumers' regional location or location within a region) enhances the quality of marketing and advertising plans.

Behaviour-response segmentation is integrated with other segmentation variables. In this type of segmentation, targets are analyzed with regard to the occasions they have for using a product, the benefits they desire from a product, the frequency with which they use a product, and the degree of their loyalty to a brand.

Positioning a product is an important part of pursuing target markets, and advertising plays a key role in positioning. Positioning involves designing a product or service to meet the needs of a target market, and then creating appropriate appeals to make the product stand out in the minds of the target-market members. Common positioning strategies include head-on comparisons, product differentiation, technical innovation, and brand-dominance and lifestyle techniques. As a product matures, factors such as competitive activity and changing consumer preferences will force a re-evaluation of positioning strategies.

Review Questions

1. Identify advertisements or advertising campaigns (brand and theme) that reflect the application of Maslow's hierarchy-of-needs theory. Provide examples for each level of needs.
2. What is the difference between demographic segmentation, psychographic segmentation, and geographic segmentation?
3. What impact does the family life cycle have on advertising activity?
4. What influence will the ethnic diversity of the Canadian population have on marketing and advertising strategies in the 1990s?
5. How do advertisers use the "self-concept" theory to their advantage? Provide two advertising examples to illustrate your explanation.

6. Briefly explain the four divisions of behaviour-response segmentation.
7 Explain the relevance of "positioning" and "repositioning" in advertising.
8. Briefly explain the differences between
   i) culture and subculture
   ii) needs and motives
   iii) ideal self and looking-glass self
   iv) selective exposure, selective perception, and selective retention

Discussion Questions

1. The economies of a national creative plan outweigh the need for numerous regional creative plans." Discuss this issue, using some products of your choice as examples.
2. The value of lifestyle advertising is very questionable, as little is actually said about the product." Evaluate the validity of this statement, using examples of your own choice.
3. To succeed in the future, products and services must be repositioned to appeal to older target markets." Comment on the implications of this statement.

Marketing Plan/ Advertising Plan

CHAPTER 5

In studying this chapter, you will learn

- The distinctions between and the relationships between the various types of business planning

- The influence of various stages of the product life cycle on advertising planning

- The organization and content of a marketing plan and of an advertising plan

- The relationships between a client marketing plan and an agency advertising plan

Business planning is an integrated process that involves planning at three distinct levels of an organization: corporate planning, marketing planning, and advertising planning. Students must understand the planning process and appreciate the interaction of plans at these different levels.

There are no design norms against which marketing plans and advertising plans are measured. The design and content of plans vary considerably from one organization to another. The design and structure of any plan are entirely dependent upon the needs and often on the marketing sophistication of the firm developing the plan. Lengthy, comprehensive plans are not necessarily good plans. A good plan provides direction for a product, service or company, outlines key activities to be implemented, and provides a means of measuring the success or failure of the plan. In this regard, there are no limitations placed on the design, organization, and content of a marketing plan or of an advertising plan.

This chapter illustrates the *typical content* of marketing and advertising plans, and it includes an alternative model to show how plans may vary.

BUSINESS-PLANNING PROCESS

A discussion of any form of strategic business planning should touch on three variables: objectives, strategies, and execution (tactics). Let's first define these planning variables:

1. **Objectives** are statements that outline what is to be accomplished in the corporate, marketing, or advertising plan.
2. **Strategies** are statements that outline how the objectives will be achieved. Strategies usually identify the resources necessary to achieve objectives (funds, time, people, type of activity, etc.).
3. **Execution (Tactics)** is defined as tactical-action plans that outline specific details of implementation, which, collectively, contribute to the achievement of objectives. Tactical plans usually outline the specific activity, the cost, timing, and who is responsible for implementation.

A diagrammatic presentation of the business-planning process as it applies to marketing and advertising is provided in figure 5.1. First let's establish and define some basic terminology:

1. **Planning** is the process of anticipating the future business environment, and determining the courses of action a firm will take in that environment. For example, a firm will look at trends in the areas of demography, the economy, changing technology, politics, and culture, and then develop a plan that will provide for growth in changing times.
2. **Strategic planning** is the process of determining objectives, and identifying strategies and tactics (activities, resources, and action plans) that will contribute to the achievement of objectives.

Figure 5.1 Business planning process — marketing and advertising orientation

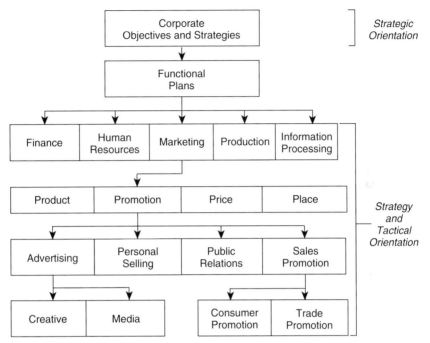

Each level of planning provides guidance for the next level. Advertising plans are integrated into marketing plans which are approved by senior executives of the organization.

Strategic planning is done at all levels of the organization, in all functional areas. Corporate planners, such as the chief executive officer, president and vice-presidents, will develop broadstroke corporate plans. The vice-president of marketing and marketing managers are guided in their individual-product planning by the objectives and strategies in the all-encompassing corporate plan. Finally, the advertising manager will consider the direction provided in the marketing plan (specifically, the marketing objectives and strategies) to develop the advertising plan.

In examining figure 5.1, we find that the business planning throughout the organization begins and ends at the corporate or senior-management level. The process starts with senior management formulating financial objectives for the organization (objectives regarding sales, profits, and return on investment). In the case of marketing and marketing plans, objectives, strategies, and tactics will be developed for each individual product, and their collective accomplishment will contribute to the financial well-being of the organization. Those who develop the individual-product plans will consider the marketing mix (product, promotion, price, and place), the characteristics of the target market, and positioning concepts when developing marketing objectives and strategies. Our primary concerns are advertising and promotion. The advertising manager will work closely with the advertising agency to develop the appropriate advertising objectives, strategies, and tactics. How well the advertising activities are carried out, how successfully the advertising objectives are achieved, will indirectly influence the achievement of marketing objectives. (Recognize that product, price, and place are influences also.)

The planning process discussed above shows the relationship between one plan and another. The saying "A chain is only as strong as its weakest link" applies to those relationships. Strategic planning attempts to co-ordinate all activity in such a manner that elements from various areas work harmoniously. In the case of marketing and advertising, all activity must present a consistent image of the company or of its product, in order to create a favourable impression in the minds of consumers. One weak link in the chain can create conflict or confuse the target market. For example, the selling price of a product may be too high in relation to the customer's perception of the product's quality. Inconsistent activity spread over numerous company products could seriously disrupt attempts to achieve marketing and corporate objectives.

*T*YPES OF BUSINESS PLANNING——*MARKETING APPLICATION*

Figure 5.1 divides business planning into three different categories: corporate planning, marketing planning, and advertising planning.

CORPORATE PLANNING

Corporate planning usually begins with the development of a **mission statement** for the organization. This is a statement of purpose for the organization, and reflects its operating philosophy. Such statements are based on the opportunities the company sees for itself in the marketplace. Mission statements are market-oriented; they will only work for the company if its products are designed and marketed according to the demands of the customers. Stemming from the marketing concept, mission statements not only recognize customers' needs, but also consider the competition, and, in this connection, the need to produce quality products for longer survival. The sample statement below could be a mission statement for a communications company:

> ABC Corporation is a company dedicated to producing quality
> products and services to meet the communication needs of business
> and industry.

Since corporate plans provide direction to all functional areas of the company, they tend to be long-term in nature (encompassing three to five years), broad in scope, and considerate of the overall well-being of the organization. Now let's examine the differences between corporate objectives and strategies.

Corporate Objectives The nature of **corporate objectives** varies considerably from one organization to another. Generally, however, corporate objectives focus on market share for a particular market, total company sales and profitability, return on investment, the corporation's aspirations regarding diversification and acquisition, and so forth. Some corporate objectives might be as follows:

> *Sales*: to increase total company sales from $250 million to $325
>   million in the next three year period.
> *Market Share*: to control 35% of the Canadian soft drink market
>   within three years, an increase of four share points.

Similar statements can be developed for other objectives. These objectives, decided upon by senior management, provide the framework for more detailed functional plans in the operating areas of the company such as marketing, finance, manufacturing, and human resources.

Corporate Strategies After the corporate objectives are confirmed, the organization must identify the **corporate strategies**, which outline how the objectives will be achieved. The factors that the organization considers in developing corporate strategies are marketing strength, the degree of competition that exists in markets the company operates in, financial resources (such as the availability of investment capital or the ability to borrow required funds), research and development capabilities, and management commitment (i.e., how much priority will be given to the goals the company sets for itself).

As in the case of objectives, corporate strategies can go in numerous directions. To illustrate the concept of strategy development, let's assume a company has established market growth as a primary objective. This company could develop a strategy for growth based on any one of the directions that follow, or any combination thereof:

1. *Penetrate Current Markets More Aggressively with Marketing Activity* Pepsi-Cola's use of the Pepsi Challenge (comparative taste tests) as a marketing platform is a good example of aggressive marketing activity. Aggressive activity by one firm can force other major competitors to compete as aggressively, with no real change occurring in the marketplace. However, constant pressure and share gains by Pepsi-Cola in the supermarket soft-drink business did result in a recipe change for Coca-Cola.

2. *Pursue Market Development by Entering New Markets with Current Products* McDonald's Restaurants began with suburban locations (where most of the people lived). Having established a base market, the company began to move into downtown locations (where the people work) and highway restaurants on major autoroutes.

3. *Develop New Products or Improved Products for Current Markets* This strategy is largely a response to consumers' changing attitudes towards and preferences for product categories. Breweries, for example, have all entered the market with a variety of light beers, using established brand names (Blue Light, Carlsberg Light, etc.). In the past few years, dry beers have become popular.

The light-beer and dry-beer market segments presented growth opportunities in a total market that was beginning to stagnate. The introduction of environmentally friendly products is another example of this strategy. These products are marketed in accordance with prevailing consumer attitudes.

4. *Acquire a Competitor to Secure a Stronger Market Position* Acquisition strategies have been more predominant over the past decade than at any time previously. The recent merger of Kraft Foods and General Foods, two very large food companies, to form the Kraft General Foods Group, and the merger of Pacific Western Airlines with Canadian Airlines to form Canadian Airlines International are examples of this strategy.

5. *Diversify Into New Markets* The decision to diversify into new markets often represents risk, as current management often lacks expertise in the market entered. Nonetheless, the pursuit of growth can involve diversification strategies.

Molson Breweries is a company that uses acquisition strategy and diversification strategy to advantage. Molson's entered into a strategic alliance with Elders IXL Limited of Australia. The alliance combines the brewing operations of Molson's Breweries of Canada with those of Elders' Carling O'Keefe Breweries of Canada Limited, resulting in an equally-controlled Canadian-based partnership known as Molson Breweries. As a diversified company Molson owns Diversey Corporation, a cleaning and sanitation supply firm; Beaver Lumber, B.B. Bargoon's, Lighting Unlimited and Aikenhead Hardware, all retail merchandising firms; and the Club de Hockey Canadien Inc., the Montreal Forum and Molstar Communications, all sports and entertainment businesses.

MARKETING PLANNING

Marketing planning is defined as planning activities that relate to the achievement of marketing objectives.[1] Marketing planning involves the development of marketing objectives, strategies, and executions for all products and services within a company. The integrated results of decisions on product, price, promotion, and place are outlined in marketing plans for each product. The sum of all the decisions made for all products will be, ideally, the achievement of all marketing objectives. In contrast to corporate plans, marketing plans are short-term (one year), specific in scope (since they deal with individual products and services), and subject to being changed on short notice because of economic concerns or concerns about competitive activity.

Marketing Objectives

Marketing objectives are statements identifying "what" a product will accomplish in the course of one year. Typically, marketing objectives concentrate on sales volume, market share, and profit (net profit or return on investment), all of which are quantitative in nature and hence measurable at the end of the planning cycle. Objectives that are qualitative in nature could include new-product introductions (line extensions such as new sizes or flavours), product improvements, and packaging innovations.

To illustrate the concept of marketing objectives, let's consider the following example statements:

> *Sales Volume*: to achieve a unit volume of 500 000 units by next year, an increase of 10% over last year.
> *Market Share*: to achieve a market share of 25% in 12 months, an increase of two share points.
> *Profit*: to generate a before tax profit of $750 000 in 12 months.
> *Product:* to introduce a new package size to the market in next year's third quarter.

Marketing Strategies

Marketing strategies are, essentially, the "master plans" for achieving marketing objectives. They can be defined as the process of identifying target markets and planning means of appealing to those targets with a combination of marketing-mix elements (the four Ps) within budget constraints. This definition identifies three important variables in the strategic marketing-planning process: the target market, the marketing mix, and the budget. Let's examine each variable in greater detail.

Target Market When developing a marketing plan, the manager will identify targets that represent the greatest opportunity and potential. Is there one primary user group, or are there several different user segments who can use the product or service to advantage? In answering these types of questions, the manager will define target markets in terms of demographic, psychographic, and geographic variables.

Marketing Mix At this stage of the planning process, the role and importance of each variable in the marketing mix, and the sub-variables of each, will be identified. The task is to develop a plan of attack that will enable all four-P variables to work together to achieve marketing objectives. The following questions might be asked: In terms of promotion, which is our major area of concern? What roles will advertising, consumer promotion, and trade promotion play in the overall mix of activity?

Budget The corporate plan has already identified a total marketing budget for the company, a budget that takes into account the overall profit concerns for the forthcoming year. That budget must be distributed among all company products and services, according to the needs of each. Managers responsible for product planning must develop and justify a budget that will allow the implementation of the strategies identified in their marketing plan, while obtaining financial objectives identified for the product (refer to the sample objectives presented earlier in this chapter). The final step in the budgeting process at this stage will be to allocate funds to the various activity areas (advertising, marketing research, consumer promotion, trade promotion, etc.).

Marketing Execution

Often referred to as **marketing tactics**, this type of planning focuses on specific program details that stem directly from the strategy section of the plan. In general terms, a tactical plan outlines what activity will be done, how much it will cost, what the timing of the activity will be, and who will be responsible for it. It should be noted that detailed advertising plans will be developed separately by the advertising agency. If advertising is a key element in overall marketing strategy, then advertising strategy and tactics will be integrated into the marketing plan in summary form.

ADVERTISING PLANNING

Similar to marketing planning, advertising planning involves the development of appropriate objectives, strategies, and tactics. Initially, the primary objective of the advertising must be stated. For example, is advertising intended to increase brand awareness, to create brand preference, or to change an attitude? Once this is established, strategies are devised and tactical decisions made in two areas: creative and media.

Advertising strategies are based on decisions made regarding eight different variables that we will refer to as the eight Ms. These variables are merchandise, markets, motives, message, media, money, measurement, and management. Figure 5.2 presents a summary of these advertising planning variables.

Merchandise

An important decision within a company involves determining which products will benefit from advertising support. Rarely are all products advertised, so a company must develop some criteria on which to base this decision. These criteria often include sales potential (future growth), profitability, stage in the product life cycle, and competitive activity. Judging from any combination of these factors, a company will decide on which products will be advertised, and to what extent they will be supported financially (the budget decision).

Figure 5.2   Decision variables affecting advertising planning: the eight Ms

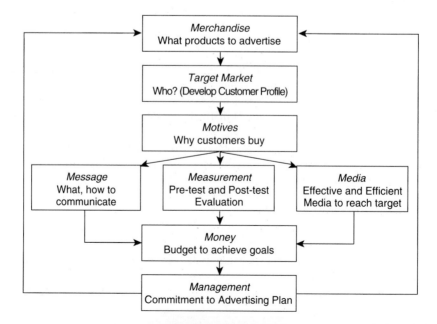

Markets (Target Markets)

The decision concerning markets involves identifying desirable target markets (i.e., identifying the customers with the greatest potential to use the product or service). The advertiser will identify a target market that is defined by some combination of demographic, psychographic, and geographic variables. The process of compiling this type of target-market information yields valuable clues as to how to communicate with the target (i.e., what type of message and media would be most effective).

Motives

It is not only necessary to know who buys, but, more important, to know why they buy. Research that generates **psychographic data** (data that concerns activities, interests, and opinions, commonly referred to as AIO's) provides added insight into how to market and advertise a product to a target market. Companies that understand the purchase-decision processes of their target markets (e.g., are they rational or emotional about a given genre of product?) have a distinct advantage when it comes to developing message and media strategy. This type of research is expensive, but well worth the investment if it contributes to the success of an advertising campaign.

Message

Assuming that the company has adequate insight into the target market and its motives for buying, the next decision concerns the presentation of the message. The advertiser and the advertising agency must decide on the content of the message (i.e., what to communicate), and the appeal techniques, tone, and style of the message (i.e., how to communicate). Proper consumer research should provide insight into what are effective means of influencing potential users. This area deals with the development of creative objectives and strategies that serve as blueprints for the development of everything from a single advertisement to a complete campaign.

Media

Choosing which media to use to reach the target market constitutes a major decision. Again, the collection of psychographic information provides insight into the most effective ways to reach a target market. Basically, an advertiser is concerned about two factors when developing a media plan, **effectiveness** and **efficiency**. The advertiser attempts to develop a media plan that will provide maximum impact (effectiveness) at minimum cost (efficiency). Key decision areas in a media plan are: what media to utilize, how often to deliver messages, for what length of time to run the campaign, and in what markets to provide advertising coverage.

Money

Establishing the budget that is to be available for advertising is a major decision area. Among the various methods that can be used to develop a budget, there are some that estimate sales first and then base the advertising budget on sales. Other methods develop the budget first; these methods essentially presuppose that advertising is an effective means of achieving sales objectives. Regardless of the method used, the advertising budget must be carefully calculated and rationalized by the manager responsible for it so that the advertising plan can be implemented as recommended.

Measurement

To evaluate the effectiveness of current advertising, and to provide input into the development of future campaigns, advertisers must allocate sufficient funds for research. The potential effectiveness of advertising strategies can be evaluated at various stages of the production process—prior to media placement (i.e., pre-test situations), during a campaign, or after a campaign has been implemented (i.e., in post-test situations). The decision whether to conduct research is critical, since considerable amounts of money can be wasted in commercial production and media placement if, because of inadequate research, the message does not perform as intended.

Management

The attitude toward advertising held by the senior management group in any company has a significant impact on the other variables discussed in this section. For advertising to be effective, there must be a long-term commitment from senior executives. That is, they must view advertising as an investment from which a pay-off is yielded at a later date. Unfortunately, many executives, posing as investment-minded advertisers, become short-term thinkers when faced with a profit-squeeze situation in any fiscal year. At such times, advertising budgets are axed! Such decisions are likely to be counterproductive over a longer period of time, for they prevent the advertising plan from being implemented as originally recommended. Such decisions are the realities of business, however, and all those responsible for advertising (both client managers and agencies) must work within this environment.

Refer to the Advertising in Action vignette "Honda Resolves an Image Problem." This vignette shows how marketing research information has an impact on advertising decisions. Specifically, it should clarify for the reader the relationships between the target market and their motives for buying, and the influence this information has on message and media strategy.

Advertising in Action
Honda Resolves an Image Problem

Based on an on-going consumer tracking study, it was apparent that the Honda Accord target consumer perceived the Accord as being relatively weak on the image dimensions relating to comfortable space for the family.

This perception was most likely the result of the residual image of the original Honda cars in Canada (i.e., people still associated a Honda automobile with a *small* economical car).

With the launch of a new, more spacious, fourth-generation 1990 Accord, the company had the opportunity to address and correct this perception, which was somewhat limiting sales growth potential. The details of the creative plan follow.

Creative Objectives

1. To position the Accord as the benchmark in family sedans.
2. Strategic focus was to be placed on the improved space (perceived weakness) as well as on the handling and roadholding characteristics (perceived and actual strength).

Creative Strategy

1. To capitalize on the launch of the new 1990 Accord by focusing on the issues most important to the Accord target consumer.
2. To present this information using the established Honda tone of voice which is preemptive, provocative, relevant and human.

Target Market

Males and females, 25-49 years of age, with a household income of $35 000 and over who have a practical need (contemporary lifestyle) for a four-door sedan but who are unwilling to be satisfied with space and utility alone. Status and drivability are as important as the functional values.

Creative and Media Execution

1. A two-tiered campaign of television supported by magazine was developed.
2. There were three separate double-page spreads that ran consecutively to form a synergistic execution designed to position the Accord as the benchmark in family sedans. Refer to the Honda print illustra-

tions (see pages 124, 125, and 126) to see the relationships between target market needs and message strategy and execution.
3. Specifically, each spread focuses on different strategic issues, namely, styling, roominess/space, and roadholding.

> **Styling:**
> "Presenting the 1990 Accord. The Sedan that Rewards all Your Senses"
> **Roominess / Space:**
> "A Cure for Cabin Fever."
> **Roadholding / Technological Advancement:**
> "Handling Inspired by the Curvature of the Earth."

In spread B (page 125), the headline "A Cure for Cabin Fever" is used. An inviting line that suggests there is spacious room that will help cure that ancient illness of being locked up in a small place. "Cabin Fever."

The body copy explains Accord's increase in headroom, legroom, footroom, seating capacity, and cargo space. The copy also describes features that make driving a whole lot more pleasurable, like increased visibility, new heating and cooling systems, Unibody construction, and one-piece dash to remove squeaks and noise.

All these improvements are summed up by a line that all consumers, adults, or adolescents, can relate to: "A place where you may never hear 'How much farther to go Dad?' again."

These magazine executions, coupled with the television campaign focusing on the improved space issue and the drivability of the Accord, have been very successful in achieving the desired positioning of the Accord.

Information courtesy of Honda Canada Inc. and their advertising agency, Doner Schur Peppler Advertising.

Presenting The 1990 Accord.
The Sedan That Rewards All Your Senses.

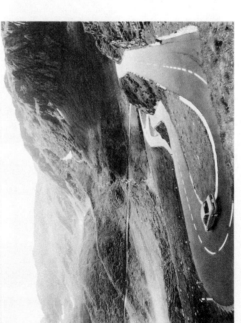

A Cure For Cabin Fever.

Enter now into the most spacious Accord ever. A place where you may never tear. "How much farther to go Dad?" again.

The lengthened cabin and significantly larger glass area create a bright, airy relaxed environment of total comfort with almost 300° of unrestricted view.

Accord's new ventilation system is quieter and more efficient while providing up to 500 cubic metres per hour of air flow in a much improved cooling and heating system.

Headroom has comfortably increased by 35 mm. Front seats are now 35 mm longer with 30 mm more underseat footroom for rear passengers.

The rear seat is contoured for better comfort and support with 40 mm additional legroom. A seamless, soft-touch motif is carried throughout.

The Accord's instrument panel is a quarter industry-leading one piece design. The analogue instruments and controls are in clear sight and easy reach.

1990 Accord

Remember your next Honda. It's a simple fact of life.

Passive restraint seat belt system not available in Canada.

≡ *A*DVERTISING PLANNING AND THE PRODUCT LIFE CYCLE

The product life cycle has significant influence on marketing and advertising planning. A **product life cycle** is defined as the movement of a product through a series of four stages, from its introduction to its eventual withdrawal from the market. Figure 5.3 illustrates the product life cycle. Life-cycle theory posits that a product starts out slowly in the introduction stage; experiences rapid sales increases in the growth stage; experiences marginal growth or decline each year as it matures; then enters the decline stage, where sales drop off at a much faster rate each year. The life-cycle concept is popular from a strategic-planning viewpoint. Presupposing that the characteristics of each stage are quite different, the life-cycle theory suggests that different strategies be utilized in each stage.

This section of the chapter examines the four stages of the product life cycle, and discusses some of the advertising implications of each stage.

Introduction Stage

The introduction stage is a period of slow sales growth; a new product idea is being introduced to the market. Losses are frequently incurred due to the high initial investment required to launch a product. High investment in advertising at this stage is a sign that a company is committed to building a viable market position.

Figure 5.3   Product life cycle and advertising stages

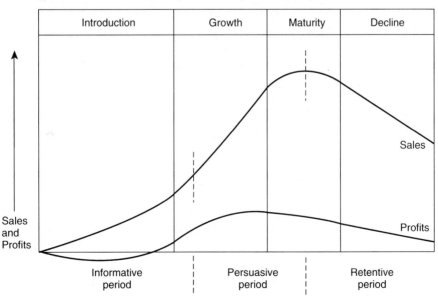

Advertising objectives focus on the creation of primary demand. The critical first step toward gaining consumers' acceptance of a new product is to make them recognize in themselves a need for the product or product category. Advertising endeavours to have the brand name and package register in the consumer's mind. Also, a new product launch is very likely to involve promotion incentives to stimulate trial purchase.

Advertising strategists believe that if these objectives are to be accomplished, the product must enter the market with a sizeable budget behind it so that high reach and frequency can be obtained. **Reach** refers to the number of people (households) exposed to a particular message, while **frequency** refers to the average number of times a household is exposed to a message. Since this is the period in which first purchases are made, marketers are concerned with reducing the consumer's risk in making such a purchase (i.e., the risk inherent in paying for an unknown). Consequently, advertising messages often include incentives, such as coupons or other special offers, in order to give the consumer the sense of not being able to lose with this purchase.

Viewed from a tactical viewpoint, introductory advertising often adopts an *informative* tone and style while stressing the brand name and package. Frequently, advertisers will *not* include members of their perceived target market in introductory ads. Although initial research may have identified a potential target market, many marketers prefer to let the marketplace determine who purchases the product. Therefore, media vehicles offering mass appeal to generally defined audiences are quite appropriate for satisfying reach objectives in the introductory stage. A more precisely defined target market, based on research into actual purchasing experience, can be used to advantage in developing strategies in later stages of the product life cycle.

Growth Stage

As indicated by the sales curve in figure 5.3, the product's growth stage is the period of rapid consumer acceptance. It is also a period in which profits rise significantly. Several competitive brands will enter the market to get a piece of the action, which means that the original product must continue to invest aggressively in advertising to build market share.

At this stage, advertising objectives perform a dual role. There is ample opportunity yet to attract new users, so creating awareness remains a priority. Since competitors have entered the market, advertising objectives must focus on **brand preference** (i.e., selective demand for a particular brand) also. Consequently, trial-purchase incentives and repeat-purchase incentives are incorporated into advertising messages.

Depending on the degree of competition, the advertiser will either maintain spending levels established in the introduction stage or increase them. Aggressive competitors seeking market share can force advertisers of the original brand to spend more than they desire to spend. Competition forces advertising messages to focus on product differentiation so that customers have a sound reason to buy the product. Target markets are more *precisely* defined at this stage, so advertisers can manipulate the reach and frequency variables in order to attract more users of a particular demographic or psychographic target market, and to get maximum efficiency out of scarce media dollars.

Creative executions become more *persuasive* in tone and style in the growth stage, and utilize **appeals** such as sex, love, fear, humour, and facts in order to stimulate both rational and emotional buying motives. A greater variety of promotion incentives are utilized, since trial and repeat purchase are both important in the growth stage. Added to the use of coupons, quite commonly, are such promotions as refunds and contests, which generate multiple purchase by interested consumers. Media execution is much more precise in the growth stage. Wherever possible, media vehicles are selected that have an audience composition closely matching the target-market profile.

Mature Stage

The mature stage is characterized by a slowdown in sales growth (*marginal growth* and *marginal decline*); the product has been accepted by a majority of its potential buyers. Profits stabilize and begin to decline because of the expenses incurred in defending the brand's market-share position. This happens when low sales growth among competitors intensifies competition (and thus increases marketing and advertising spending) at a time when management should be more concerned with controlling product costs. Consequently, many fringe brands unable to cope with such costs drop out at this stage, leaving the market to a core group of competitors.

Marketing and advertising objectives can be quite *defensive* in nature in the mature stage. The focus will be on maintaining market-share position. Implementing activity that will rejuvenate the product (delay the inevitability of decline) is a more offensive strategy.

Should a defensive strategy be adopted, advertising budgets will be established at a level that will maintain the brand's market-share position. The tone and style of messages will be *retentive*, that is, they will reinforce past messages and emphasize the brand name. Since maintenance of current customers is a priority, there is often greater spending on promotion activity than on media advertising. Promotions that encourage brand loyalty are even more popular at this stage than at the growth stage. These promotions include product-delivered coupons (in-pack, on-pack, etc.), refunds, contests, and premium offers, all of which are designed to achieve multiple purchase.

Advertisers that opt to *rejuvenate* a product adopt a more aggressive attitude. Strategies will be implemented to extend the product life cycle. Strategic options available include modifying or improving the product, presenting new uses for the product (and thereby increasing frequency of use), or attracting new user segments to the product. Regardless of the strategic option selected, advertising will play a key role in communicating the new direction. Since a new initiative is being undertaken, advertising budgets may increase in the short term. Over the longer term, less expensive promotion alternatives, which protect profit margins, may prevail. Over the life of a product, numerous life-cycle extensions may be pursued.

Decline

The decline stage is the period when sales begin to decline rapidly and profits erode. Products become obsolete as many consumers shift to more innovative products entering the market. Price cuts are a common marketing strategy at this stage, as competing brands attempt to protect their share in a declining market.

Product objectives in the decline stage centre on planning and implementing withdrawal from the market, because the costs of maintaining a product in decline are quite high. There is little sense in supporting such a product with advertising. Investment in advertising is cut so that profit is maximized and funds are generated that can be invested in new products with greater profit potential. Since companies do not have the resources to support all products equally, it is wise to have products at various stages of the product life cycle, so that marketing and advertising activities and spending requirements can be effectively managed within financial constraints.

We have mentioned three different advertising stages in the product life cycle: *informative*, *persuasive*, and *retentive* stages. These refer to the tone and style of the advertising communications used at the various stages of the product life cycle. With reference to figure 5.3, informative communications occur in the introduction and early growth stages. When competitors enter the market with their own advertising messages, all products must be more persuasive in tone. Persuasive communications occur in the growth and early mature stages of the life cycle. Retentive or reminder messages are used in the late mature stage, when competitive advertising is less intense.

LIMITATIONS OF PLANNING BASED ON PRODUCT-LIFE-CYCLE THEORY

Although the product life cycle is commonly used to develop marketing and advertising strategies, there are certain limitations associated with it. As William Band states, "If you assume a business will inevitably mature, and then decline, rest assured that's exactly what will happen."[2] Band's statement could be a reflection of a company's attitude: those companies which stay too close to life-cycle planning will encourage a defeatist attitude among managers. Instead of assuming that maturity and decline are inevitable, managers should strive for innovation—and generally play an aggressive role in striving for future success (acting in the market, as opposed to reacting to the market).

The mature stage is the critical stage. Does management take action to rejuvenate the product? Is there adequate management commitment to rejuvenation plans under consideration? One of the better examples of taking action occurred in the grocery-retailing business in Ontario. In the mid-seventies, Loblaws was a large grocery distributor floundering in a sea of red ink, lagging well behind Dominion, the established leader. The Loblaws image was dated, and their store interiors reflected a bygone era. Loblaws went on the offense and invested heavily in store-design changes, introduced a complete line of generic "no-name" products, and presented a more contemporary image to grocery shoppers. Loblaws is now a highly profitable retailing operation. Coincidentally, Dominion began to flounder in the wake of this competitive activity and subsequently did little to correct the situation. As a result of its inertia, Dominion is on the verge of disappearing from the market entirely. The Atlantic and Pacific Tea Company (A&P) purchased control of Dominion in the mid-eighties, and has been converting the more profitable locations to A&P stores. Loblaws has boldly moved into newer, attractive areas such as "President's Choice" products and "green" products as a means of staying current.

ORGANIZATION AND CONTENT OF A MARKETING PLAN

A **marketing plan** is a planning document prepared on an annual basis for a product, service, or company. While the format and content of marketing plans can vary, the plan usually contains the same basic information:

- A review of market, product, and competitive activity
- Identification of problems and opportunities
- A positioning statement
- Specific marketing objectives, strategies, and tactics
- Appropriate budget and financial information

This section of the chapter presents a detailed review of the contents of the marketing plan, based on the planning model included in figure 5.4. This planning model suggests that a marketing plan can be divided into two major sections: background analysis and the actual marketing plan, which is based, in turn, on the background analysis and direction provided by corporate-planning activities.

BACKGROUND ANALYSIS

The basic purpose of the background analysis section is to

- Identify problems and opportunities for a product, service, or company by analyzing market, product, and competitor performance within a specific market
- Provide input for the development of marketing objectives, strategies, and tactical plans, based on conditions that exist in the marketplace
- Provide senior-level planners with adequate information so that they will understand what contributions marketing (and advertising) will make in achieving corporate objectives

Market Analysis
In this section of the plan, various subjects are analyzed and presented.

Market Size and Growth For planning purposes, it is imperative to include a perspective on recent growth trends in the market. It is quite common to include a five-year historical perspective, an estimate for the current year, and a projection for the year in which the plan will be implemented (a plan for 1992 would probably be prepared very early in 1991).

Regional Market Importance In this section, key regions will be identified (e.g., problem regions where brand development has been slow, or regions where promising

Figure 5.4 Sample marketing plan model

A. Background	B. Marketing Plan
1. Market Analysis a) Market Size and Growth b) Regional Market Importance c) Market Segment Analysis d) Seasonal Analysis e) Consumer Data f) Category and Brand Loyalty g) Pack-Size Trends h) Media Expenditures	**1. Positioning Statement** **2. Marketing Objectives** a) Volume b) Market Share c) Profit d) Other Product-Related Objectives
2. Product Analysis a) Shipments b) Market Share c) Distribution d) New Product Activity e) Profit Improvements f) Creative g) Media h) Sales Promotion i) Marketing Research	**3. Marketing Strategies** a) Target Market Identification b) Marketing Strategies • Product • Price • Promotion • Distribution • Research c) Budget
3. Competitive Analysis a) Market Share b) Segmentation Trends c) Regional Share Trends d) Assessment of Marketing Activity e) Competitive Innovations	**4. Marketing Tactics** a) Detailed Plans for: • Product • Price • Promotion: Creative, Media, Sales Promotion • Distribution • Profit Improvement **5. Financial Summary**
4. Problems and Opportunities a) Problems b) Opportunities	**6. Marketing Budget** **7. Promotional Calendar**

opportunities are presented). A common practice is to devise development indexes showing what are the regions of strength and weakness for a product category within a market, or for a brand within a product category. For example, the penetration of a brand in a specific region could be compared to population or household patterns, or brand penetration could be compared to category penetration within a region. The sample advertising plan for the Mercury Tracer, which appears at the end of Part Two, utilizes development indexes in the planning process. Regional analysis is also intended to point out urban-versus-rural trends, such as the importance of a city (Vancouver) within a region (British Columbia) in terms of market-volume importance.

Market Segment Analysis In this section, the various segments of a total market will be analyzed in terms of their *volume importance* and *growth rates*. Marketing planners will determine areas of priority, basing their judgements on which segments are growing or declining. Segmentation trends for the coffee, dog-food and soft-drink markets might be considered thus:

> *Coffee:*
> • Instant *versus* Ground Coffee
> • Regular *versus* Decaffeinated *versus* Flavoured Coffee
>
> *Dog Food:*
> • Canned *versus* Soft-Moist *versus* Dry Dog Food
>
> *Soft Drinks:*
> • Regular *versus* Diet Soft Drinks
> • Colas *versus* Other Flavours.

A firm must also decide whether to gain access to basic market information. Although such information is costly, it is readily available through research organizations such as the A.C. Nielsen Company of Canada Ltd. The Nielsen Retail Index, which collects data from the grocery and drug trades in Canada, provides an assortment of information to interested clients. The information available includes volume and market-share trends, distribution and inventory information at the retail level, as well as advertising and pricing information for all major brands in a variety of product categories.

Seasonal Analysis This section of the plan will indicate the significance of any seasonal or cyclical fluctuations that occur during the course of a planning year. For example, soft-drink sales will escalate in the hot summer season and the Christmas season, while other products and companies may have a variety of seasons. A sporting-goods manufacturer marketing golf, tennis, hockey, football, and basketball equipment will be involved in a variety of seasons. Observing seasonal shifts in sales volume is an important part of market analysis; such shifts have a direct impact on marketing and advertising planning, for they show planners what is the best time to promote a product.

Consumer Data The intent of this section is to profile the current users of the product. In addition to current targets, new targets worthy of pursuit may also be identified. A target market profile based on any combination of the following factors will be included:

> • **Demographics**: age, income, sex, occupation, education, etc.
> • **Psychographics**: attitudes, interests, and opinions (the lifestyle of the target)
> • **Geographics**: location of the target, either by region or by urban-versus-suburban-versus-rural considerations

Category and Brand Loyalty Marketers can utilize loyalty information to their advantage in the planning process. Research information, available from a variety of sources, will provide insight into the degree of loyalty customers have towards a product category or a particular brand within a category. Are current customers very loyal, somewhat loyal, or subject to a high degree of brand switching? Marketers who can develop profiles of loyal users will develop plans to attract more people of the same type. If users of competitive brands are disposed to brand switching, or if current brand users like to try competitive brands, appropriate action can be built right into the marketing plan. The more precise the target information base, the more effective and efficient the marketing plans will be.

Pack-Size Trends In many product categories, particularly packaged-goods categories, volume trends and growth rates are analyzed in connection with pack size. Which sizes are most popular, and which are least popular with the target market? Will future growth occur in regular size, single-serving size, family size, or economy size?

Depending on the market, other considerations may be important. For example, volume trends may be analyzed on the basis of flavour, scent, or product format, as in the following examples:

Soup: analyzed on the basis of flavour variety

Deodorant: analyzed on the basis of product format: aerosol, pump-spray, roll-on, or stick. The scent of the deodorant may also be important.

Regardless of the nature of the analysis, the market planner wants to discover the areas of growth and decline. Where should the planning emphasis be in the short term and the long term?

Media Expenditures Advertising media expenditures are the most visible form of marketing support for a product. Information regarding trends in product-category and individual-brand media expenditures is available through marketing-research sources. Marketers frequently analyze media expenditure in connection with share performance to determine the impact of their plans and activities. The intent of this section of the plan is to establish such relationships between media expenditure and share performance and to highlight the relative importance of advertising expenditures.

Product Analysis

The part of background analysis that is concerned with product analysis highlights the actual performance of the product in the marketplace. Typical information concerns shipments, market share, distribution, new-product activity, profit improvement, creative analysis, media, sales promotion, and marketing research.

Shipments (Volume) With respect to volume trends in the market, how has the product performed? This subsection usually includes a historical volume summary, a revised estimate for the current year, and a projected volume figure for the year being planned, based on historical trend and planned activities. Such information is usually presented in terms of *absolute volume* each year, with the corresponding growth rates shown.

Market Share It is important to assess the past share performance of a brand in terms of national and regional performance. Market-share information is the clearest indicator of how well a brand is performing. Regional breakdowns are crucial, because regions analyzed in the plan must be identified as problem or opportunity markets. A brand that is strong nationally may not be strong in every region. Also, a weak national brand may have some regional areas of strength. Such information definitely affects the direction of a marketing plan.

Distribution Very similar to market share, this subsection summarizes brand performance in terms of distribution. What is the current level of distribution nationally or regionally? Is distribution strong in cities or in rural areas, in chain stores or in smaller independents? The answers to these types of questions influence the marketing plan, particularly the trade-promotion section of the plan. It should be noted that plans to improve the level of product distribution have a significant impact on volume in the planning year.

New-Product Activity This subsection briefly reviews the success or failure of any new products introduced in the past few years. New products, in this case, are defined as new pack sizes, flavours, product formats, and so forth, all sold under the same brand name. The market planner identifies what effect the new product volume has had on sales volume since the introduction.

Profit Improvement Senior management is always interested in knowing which activities implemented in the past year had a positive effect on the profitability of the product. In this subsection of the plan, a brief review of price increases and cost-savings programs is included. Cost-savings programs might include reducing the cost of the product formula (e.g., using less expensive ingredients or packaging).

Creative Analysis of creative direction is extremely important to marketing and advertising planners. This subsection reviews the creative strategies utilized in the past year or recent years. Product analysis should include a recommendation, based on other background factors and on any consumer research that may have been conducted in advertising, as to whether current creative is worthy of maintenance or if new directions should be explored.

Media As with creative analysis, the current media situation should be reviewed to determine whether new directions should be explored. A factor that is typically considered in this area of a marketing plan is **advertising share**, which refers to one product's media spending expressed as a percentage of the total product category's media spending. Other factors studied are media-usage patterns (the amount invested in television, radio, magazines, etc.), and certain spending allocations, such as spending by season or by market.

Sales Promotion This subsection briefly outlines the various consumer-promotion and trade-promotion activities implemented in the past year. **Consumer promotions**

involve activities intended to generate trial purchase and repeat purchase; these are duly detailed here. A review of **trade promotions**—and the amount spent on deal allowances, performance allowances, and co-operative advertising—is important.

Marketing Research If research has not been discussed in any other subsection of the plan, this subsection reviews the research activities initiated in the past year—product-comparison tests, new-product evaluations, and creative testing are examples of such activities.

Competitive Analysis

In this section of the plan, the major competitors will be identified and their performances analyzed. The purpose of analyzing competitors is to flag recent occurrences that have had an impact on the market. The combination of market analysis, product analysis, and competitive analysis provides direction to those developing a new marketing plan, and gives to senior managers—who may be unfamiliar with the intricacies of each market the company is involved in—a better perspective on what is happening.

The information about the major competitors that is usually included in the plan concerns market share, segmentation trends, regional share trends, competitive marketing activity, and competitive innovations.

Market Share A review of share performance in the past year or recent years is important, for it enables planners to identify which competitors are "trending" upwards or downwards. In the case of those competitors that are showing market-share improvement, a close examination of their marketing activity should be included so that relationships between activity and performance can be established.

Segmentation Trends As with market share, it is important to identify which competitors are strong or weak in the various product segments of the market. The competitive forces may be different in the various segments of the market. For instance, the dog-food market in Canada is dominated by a few large companies. Ralston-Purina is the market leader, even though it does not compete in all segments. Its strength in dry dog food compensates for its absence from the canned segment of the market. From this example, it can be seen that a segmentation-trends analysis of the competition is important to the marketing plan.

Regional Share Trends All major competitors must be analyzed regionally to determine their market-share strengths and weaknesses in the various geographic areas of Canada. Very often, national brands have varying levels of market-share strength across the country. Also, there can be regional brands that are dominant in only one region. Kokanee, for example, is the leading brand of beer in British Columbia, the only region it is sold in. Analyzing different competitors in different regions can influence the marketing activities planned by an organization.

Assessment of Competitive Marketing Activity The activities that have played a role in influencing the volume and market-share performances of competitors should be presented in this section of the plan. Any of the various marketing-mix-activity areas (i.e., product, price, promotion, and distribution) could be deemed important.

The knowledge and experience of the market planner will determine what competitive activity is included for assessment in the marketing plan.

Competitive Innovations In addition to its regular product activity, did the competition introduce any new product or packaging innnovations to the market in the past year or recent years? What effect did these innovations have on the market (in terms of share performance) or on the consumer (in terms of purchase influence)? Any major shifts in marketing strategy by the competition must also be identified. For example, did any competitors shift funds into more trade spending and away from consumer spending? Did any competitors place less emphasis on advertising and more emphasis on other activity, such as pricing? Were any new advertising strategies implemented, in terms of new creative or new media utilization?

Problems and Opportunities

Based on a thorough analysis of the market, and of product and competitive activity, this section of the marketing plan identifies the problems and opportunities facing a product in the next planning year. Problems and opportunities are usually presented in a list format, and are precise in their wording. The purpose of these lists is to provide the planner with direction when developing marketing objectives, strategies, and tactics in the new marketing plan.

The nature and content of the problem-and-opportunity section depends entirely on the analysis of any given market, product, and competitive situation. The examples cited below are simply intended to illustrate some typical problems and opportunities which result from a background analysis. Bearing in mind that the list provides *direction* to the new marketing plan, some areas of consideration may include

- *New markets to pursue*—the demographic, psychographic, and geographic areas that require special attention
- *Potential product activities*—product improvements, new product concepts, line extensions, and new packaging
- *Pricing alternatives*—the flexibility or risks associated with price increases implemented to improve profit margins
- *Channels of distribution*—options for expanding distribution in current channels, or developing new channels
- *Budget allocations*—new directions for allocating marketing funds (trade spending versus consumer spending)
- *Promotion activities*—potential changes in direction for creative strategy and media strategy
- *Marketing research*—identification of the role research will play in future programs

MARKETING PLAN

The section of the marketing plan that is actually a *plan* usually includes a positioning statement, a complete list of marketing objectives, and a presentation of the marketing strategies and tactics needed to achieve those objectives. In addition, a budget allocation and financial summary are included, along with a promotional calendar outlining key details of plans to be implemented.

Positioning Statement

Positioning, as discussed earlier, refers to the selling concept that motivates purchase of a product or, in other words, to the desirable image of a product that a company would like to place in the minds of customers. The positioning statement outlines the product concept. Effective positioning statements are realistic, specific, and uncomplicated. They are working statements from which relevant substrategies (relating to product, price, promotion, creative, and media) can be developed. To illustrate the concept of a positioning statement, let's consider the following hypothetical examples:

> Tooruff dog food [a brand of dry dog food] will be positioned as the only dry dog food which combines four flavours in every package and offers complete and balanced nutrition.
>
> Hal and Edna's Gift Shop [a retail giftware shop] will be positioned as a specialty boutique which satisfies all the giftware needs of area consumers through a mix of quality products and personalized services.

Marketing Objectives

Marketing objectives are statements identifying "what" a product will accomplish in the forthcoming year. Objective statements should be specific, and expressed in *quantifiable* terms wherever appropriate, to permit accountability (i.e., to make objectives the means of determining success or failure).

Objective statements consider problems and opportunities identified in the first section of the marketing plan, and are in line with the corporate objectives established by senior management. Some examples follow.

> *Sales Volume*: to achieve a volume of 100 000 units in 1990, and an increase of 15% over 1989.
>
> *Market Share*: to increase market share to 20% in 1990, an increase of two share points over 1989.
>
> *Distribution*: to improve current levels of distribution in Quebec by increasing distribution from 50% to 65% in the forthcoming year.
>
> *Product*: to test a new product formulation in the British Columbia market in the third quarter of 1990.

Marketing Strategies

Marketing-strategy statements are essentially the "master plans" for achieving marketing objectives. In a planning document, the marketing strategies usually consider three basic variables: the target market, marketing strategies, or marketing-mix variables (the four Ps), and the budget required to implement recommended activities.

Target Market Based on the consumer data presented in the background section of the plan, a profile of the target market is developed. Primary targets and secondary targets may be identified according to the objectives that are established for the product. The following example demonstrates the precise nature of target market profiles:

> *Age*: 25 to 49 years
> *Sex*: male and female
> *Income*: $40 000 plus annually
> *Occupation*: business or professional
> *Education*: college or university
> *Location*: cities of 100 000 plus population
> *Lifestyle*: progressive thinkers and risk takers who like to experiment with new products; interested in the arts, entertainment, and vacation travel.

Strategy statements indicate "how" objectives will be achieved. In effect, they outline the relative importance of the four Ps and how they will be utilized to accomplish marketing objectives. As well, strategies will provide the framework for specific action plans (tactics) for each of the four Ps.

In general terms, some considerations for marketing strategy could be as follows:

1. *Product Strategy* With respect to marketing objectives and strategies, product-related strategies focus on a variety of concerns. For example, are product improvements required? Should cost-savings programs be investigated with a view to improving the product's profit margins? Does consumer research show that the current product should be revised to meet new or changing consumer needs? And finally, are any new products required to meet new consumer needs and expectations in the marketplace? Answers to product-related questions such as these often provide direction to marketing-strategy statements.

2. *Pricing Strategy* Pricing strategy is usually based on three primary factors. First, pricing strategists will consider the product's innovativeness and uniqueness, often choosing higher price options for product offerings that will seem unique to the customer's mind. Second, pricing strategists will consider the nature and degree of the competition. If products in the market are similar ("me-too products"), prices will be comparable. Third, pricing strategists will consider profits (i.e., profit objectives). The marketer needs to establish a pricing structure that covers all costs and provides an adequate rate of return to the organization.

3. *Distribution Strategy* Products can be sold through direct channels (i.e., from manufacturer to industrial user or consumer) or indirect channels (i.e., from manufacturer to a variety of distributors to industrial user or consumer). Channel choice depends on factors such as the perishability and complexity of the product. In these cases, the channels used are generally direct, while more standardized products use indirect channels.

Considering that a certain level of distribution already exists, the marketing strategy must indicate how to improve (expand) the current level of distribution (assuming that distribution is a marketing objective).

4. *Promotion Strategy* In terms of promotion strategy, the role and importance of each of the various substrategies should be identified. For example, what role will creative, media advertising, sales promotion, and personal selling play in the efforts to achieve marketing objectives? These components must work together towards a common goal.

Budget The marketing plan includes a budget request that is in line with corporate objectives and specific marketing objectives for the product. Very often, the budget will have been approved before the marketing plan is submitted. Budgets are frequently struck as part of an organization's long-range financial-plan forecasting. The budget, along with supporting rationale to justify the expenditure, is included in the strategy section of the marketing plan.

In order to illustrate application of these marketing-strategy concepts, let's consider the strategy statements that follow—those of a hypothetical hamburger chain starting up in Calgary, Alberta. This new hamburger chain, called Benny's Hamburger Emporium, would like to accomplish the following marketing objectives:

1. To achieve a 10% share of market in the first full year of operation, based on the opening of five new outlets
2. To appeal to the young adult segment of the population, 18 to 34 years of age, single or married

The corresponding marketing strategies for Benny's Hamburger Emporium are as follows (note that product strategy is included with promotion strategy):

1. ***Promotion Strategy***
   a) To position Benny's as a unique eating experience, based on their quality and variety of internationally flavoured recipes, served in an upscale art-deco environment, with friendly, efficient service
   b) To extend media advertising throughout the year, using a combination of local radio and print media
   c) To utilize promotion-oriented advertising during a two week period in each quarter of the year to build volume—encouraging store traffic and trial purchase
2. ***Pricing Strategy***
   a) To establish a premium price menu, based on the quality of ingredients (100% Grade "A" beef), slightly larger portions than the competition, and the availability of fresh condiments
3. ***Distribution Strategy***
   a) To locate each outlet in high traffic areas, close to transit systems, shopping malls, and major traffic thoroughfares
   b) To decorate each outlet in art-deco furniture, modern artwork, and hanging potted plants to reflect a contemporary image

4. ***Research Strategy***
   a) To conduct consumer research during the media campaign to measure the impact and awareness of Benny's advertising

Marketing Tactics (Activity Plans)

The marketing-tactics section of the marketing plan communicates details of the specific activities that will be implemented in the forthcoming year. In essence, tactics are an extension of the strategies, and outline the timing, costs, and often the personnel responsible for implementing the activity.

Product-activity plans typically include details regarding product testing, research-and-development programs, the financial impact of pending product changes, and the timing and costs of any new activities.

Details regarding *price* increases are also included. For example, the timing of the increase, the amount of the increase, the effect on retail price, the financial impact, and any potential risks associated with the increase are all considered essential items of information.

A *promotion* summary is incorporated into the plan, and is often derived from the advertising plan developed by the advertising agency. For each of the three main areas, creative, media, and sales promotion, a summary of objectives, strategies, and tactics is commonly included. Key details are communicated to senior management in the marketing plan.

Tactics used to accomplish distribution objectives are usually closely related to trade-promotion plans. Consequently, relevant details regarding deal allowances and co-operative advertising programs are included in the tactical section of the plan.

Tactical considerations for profit improvement in the forthcoming year and subsequent years should also be included in this section of the plan. Therefore, any details concerning cost-savings programs—such as the savings activity, the amount to be saved, and the timing of such activity—are noted.

Financial Summary

As a summary of the entire marketing plan, a statistical presentation of key product-performance indicators is commonly included. Variables such as sales volume, market share, gross profit, marketing budget, and net profit before tax are presented in the financial summary. Senior executives who approve marketing plans are interested in trends, so a predetermined number of years' actual performance is presented, along with the latest financial estimates for the current year, and, of course, the projected figures for the forthcoming year.

Marketing Budget

Similar to the financial plan, a detailed budget is included that indicates all activity areas in which funds will be spent. Major expenditure areas such as media, consumer promotion, trade promotion, and marketing research are often subdivided into more specific areas. For example, a media budget allocates funds for all specific media to be utilized in the planning year. The consumer-promotion budget might be divided into areas such as coupons, samples, refund offers, and so on.

Promotional Calendar

The purpose of the promotion calendar is to illustrate, in chart form (usually a one- or two-page format), the activities that are planned for the planning year. Promotion calendars typically include and summarize all media, consumer, and trade-promotion activities, and indicate the markets the activities are scheduled for and the timing of the activities.

ORGANIZATION AND CONTENT OF AN ADVERTISING PLAN

Prior to discussing the various components of an advertising plan, let's briefly review the objectives of advertising. Advertising should take consumers through a series of stages so that their reaction to the product is favourable. Each advertising objective is examined briefly below.

Awareness

An awareness campaign is designed to create initial awareness or to increase awareness for a specific product that has a predetermined target market.

Acceptance

When *gaining acceptance* is the objective, advertising positions the product in the customer's mind so that it is viewed as an attractive purchase alternative. The consumer realizes that the product will satisfy a need. For example, the Canadian government spends a considerable amount on advertising Canada as a vacation destination in the northern and central United States. The goal is to get Canada into American consumers' frame of reference when they are considering vacation travel.

Preference

When the objective is *preference*-related, advertising's goal is to have consumers prefer and purchase one brand instead of another, given a choice. The objective is that the brand in question secure a special status in the customer's mind. A brand for which there is preference may be the brand which, owing to advertising, has the highest "top of mind" awareness or the brand which has proven, through usage, to be satisfactory. For example, the Nike campaign, "Just Do It," featuring celebrities such as Michael Jordan and Bo Jackson, serves to distinguish Nike from Reebok and other competitors.

Buying Intentions

Advertising intended to stimulate *buying intentions* is advertising that will "prep" people to buy a specific brand. Any advertisement that offers some form of promotional incentive will get people ready to buy. To illustrate, let's assume that Speedy Muffler and Midas Muffler are both running television campaigns to generate awareness, acceptance, and preference. Let's assume further that both are perceived as equals by customers in a local market. Therefore, if one muffler shop runs a special on brakes or a new muffler system, it may be just enough to motivate action (i.e., potential purchase) by the target market.

Purchase Response

A multitude of factors influence the actual purchase, so it is difficult, if not impossible, to link advertising directly to *purchase response*. Among the various forms of advertising, only direct-response advertising can be linked to actual response, since it is designed to encourage immediate action.

ADVERTISING PLAN

An **advertising plan** is a planning document, usually prepared by an advertising agency for its client. For any product, service, or company, the plan includes a sum-

Figure 5.5   Sample advertising plan model*

1. Advertising Objectives
2. Advertising Strategies
3. Creative Plan
   a) Creative Objectives
      • What to communicate
   b) Creative Strategy
      • How to communicate
   c) Creative Execution
      • Specific communication tactics
4. Media Plan
   a) Media Objectives
      • Who
      • What
      • When
      • Where
      • How
   b) Media Strategies
      • Criteria for Researching Target Market
      • Rationale for Media Selection
   c) Media Execution
      • Media Cost Summaries (Budget Appropriation)
      • Media Schedules
5. Sales Promotion Plan
      • Activities
      • Budget

*Assumes adequate input from background section of the marketing plan.

mary of advertising objectives and strategies, and is subdivided into creative and media sections. Figure 5.5 includes a sample advertising plan model.

Certain information must be available to the agency responsible for developing an advertising plan. This information is the same as that which appears in the background section of a marketing plan. The client and agency will discuss this information via a creative-briefing document. Given the availability of adequate background information, the first task is to establish a list of advertising objectives.

Advertising Objectives

Advertising objectives define the role advertising will play in selling the client's product or service, and in achieving a stated marketing objective. A good statement of objectives will make it possible to quantify the success or failure of advertising by establishing the minimum levels of awareness and purchase motivation that advertising must achieve. It should also provide a description of the target market to be reached by advertising.

To illustrate the advertising-objective concept, we shall refer back to Benny's Hamburger Emporium, the hypothetical restaurant opening up in Calgary. Benny's advertising objectives will be to generate awareness and purchase interest among consumers, and to remind and motivate them to dine at any of Benny's conveniently located outlets. Specifically worded advertising objectives are as follows:

1. To achieve a minimum awareness level of 70% amongst men and women 18 to 34 years of age in Calgary
2. To motivate at least 25% of the defined target market to try one of Benny's hamburgers, on the basis of trial incentives to be included in print advertising.

Advertising Strategies

Advertising strategy provides a broad outline of how elements of advertising will be deployed to achieve objectives. It often contains a positioning statement (discussed under "Marketing Plan" earlier in this chapter) for the product or service to be presented to the consumer, a comment on the allocation of funds, any special advertising features (e.g., promotion incentives) to be used, and a statement concerning the role that research will play. In conjunction with the overall planning sequence, both advertising objectives and strategies provide direction for the creative and media plans that follow.

Creative Plan

The creative plan, which documents specific creative objectives, strategies, and tactics, outlines the means of accomplishing stated advertising objectives.

Creative Objectives Included in this component of the creative plan are statements that indicate "what" information is to be communicated to the target audience. Objective statements usually outline the key benefit of a product and any product-support claims (i.e., reasons why people should buy the product).

Creative Strategy Creative strategies are statements that indicate "how" a message is to be communicated to the target audience. Strategy deals with the image that should be conveyed in the communication, along with factors such as tone, style, and appeal techniques.

Creative Execution Included in this section of the creative plan is a brief description of the tactical considerations concerning how to generate impact on the target audience. Considerations might include what candidates might act as presenters in commercials, which vehicles are most appropriate to communicate benefits and create the desired image, the size of print ads, and the use of colour, to name only a few.

Media Plan

The media plan documents specific media objectives, strategies, and tactics for accomplishing stated advertising objectives.

Media Objectives This section of the media plan details specific objectives, based on the following variables:

- Which target market is to be reached?
- What is the message to be communicated?
- When is the best time to advertise to reach the target?
- Where are the priority markets to advertise in?
- How (with what reach, frequency, and continuity) will advertising be implemented?

Media Strategy The media-strategy section gives more specific details on the variables identified in the objective section. The intention is to rationalize the recommendation of certain media activities and directions—the use of specific media vehicles, the amount spent on each medium, the timing of media, and the weight levels to be purchased in various markets.

Media Execution In terms of the advertising plan, media execution refers to the visual presentation of media strategies. Information on media spending, media timing, market coverage, media usage, and so on is presented in chart form so that the client organization can quickly grasp how its funds will be spent.

Sales-Promotion Plan

If promotion incentives are to be integrated with the advertising activities, a sales-promotion section should be included in the advertising plan. Objectives of the promotions (e.g., to secure trial purchase, repeat purchase, or multiple purchase) should be documented. A summary calendar outlining the activities and the costs associated with the promotion must be included where applicable. As per the marketing plan discussed earlier in this chapter, sales-promotion budgets will very likely be separate from the advertising-media budget.

ALTERNATE PLANNING FORMATS

The marketing-plan and advertising-plan formats presented in this chapter are comprehensive in nature. As indicated at the start of the chapter, there are no design and

Figure 5.6   Alternate planning model, Marketing Plan/Advertising Plan

A. *Recommendations*
1. Budget summary review which includes:
- Marketing Objectives
- Marketing Strategies
- Key Objectives and Projects for planning year
- Sales, Budget, Profit
(Last Year Actuals vs Current Year Estimates vs Plan Year Projections)

B. *Business Review*
1. Market Review
- Volume and Growth Trends
- Segmentation Trends
- Seasonal Influences
2. Product Performance Review
- Shipments
- Market Share
- Activity Review (product, price, promotion, distribution)
3. Competitor Review
- Market Shares
- Key Marketing Activities

C. *Industry/Category Outlook*
1. Industry and Market Segment Forecast
2. Problems and Opportunities

D. *Advertising Plan*

1. Communications Plan
- Objectives
- Strategies
- Execution
2. Media Plan
- Objectives
- Strategies
- Execution

3. Sales Promotion
- Objectives
- Strategies
- Execution
4. Advertising Research
- Plan

format norms, and the length and detail of plans vary considerably from one organization to another. To illustrate how plans can vary, refer to figure 5.6—an alternate planning format. The model is a streamlined version of a combination marketing plan/advertising plan. It combines certain components of the two plans and attempts to convey important data and information in more summary form. For example, advertising objectives are integrated with creative objectives in a section entitled "Communications Plan"; background information is more consolidated; in terms of sequence, the recommendations precede the market and product-analysis sections.

Summary

The quality of marketing and advertising planning in an organization is influenced by the business-planning process itself. In terms of advertising, three different but related plans are important: the corporate plan, the marketing plan, and the advertising plan. Each plan involves the development of appropriate objectives, strategies, and tactics, and when one plan is complete, it provides direction to the next plan. The marketing plan, for example, directs the advertising plan.

When an advertising plan is being developed, strategic decisions are based on eight different variables: merchandise, markets, motives, messages, media, money, measurement and management. Advertising planning is also influenced by the product life cycle. Throughout the product life cycle, strategies will change in accordance with new consumer preferences and competitive activity.

A marketing plan usually includes detailed information about the following areas: the market, the product and the competition; problems and opportunities; marketing objectives, strategies, and tactics; and a budget and other related financial information.

The advertising plan identifies the advertising objectives to be accomplished and delineates strategy in two key areas: creative and media. The creative plan includes creative objectives (i.e., what to communicate), creative strategies (i.e., how to communicate) and tactical considerations regarding the presentation of the message. The media plan states the media objectives by answering who, what, when, where and how. The media strategies rationalize the use of media alternatives, and treat in more detail considerations of timing, market coverage, and scheduling of messages.

Finally, a sales-promotion plan may be included. This plan outlines the complementary activities designed to encourage trial purchase, repeat purchase, or trade support, and the costs associated with each activity.

Review Questions

1. What is the relationship between a corporate plan, a marketing plan, and an advertising plan?
2. In this chapter, marketing strategies are described as the "master plans" for achieving marketing objectives. In the context of planning, what does this mean?
3. What are the "eight Ms " of advertising planning?
4. Compare and contrast the role and nature of advertising as it is used in the introduction and growth stages of the product life cycle?

5. Distinguish between
   i) Advertising objectives and strategies
   ii) Creative objectives, strategies, and tactics
   iii) Media objectives, strategies, and tactics
6. What influence will a precise target-market profile have on the development of creative strategies and media strategies?

Discussion Questions

1. "Good strategy, poor execution" versus "poor strategy, good execution." Which scenario will produce the best results? Support your position with an appropriate rationale.
2. Analyze the Mercury Tracer advertising plan and campaign included at the end of Part Two. If you were to assume the roles of creative director and media director in an advertising agency, what changes would you recommend to this plan? Present an appropriate rationale to support your changes.

Illustrative Case for Part Two

Advertising plan example — Mercury Tracer

The purpose of including the Mercury Tracer Advertising Plan is to demonstrate a practical application of the various elements of an advertising plan. While the Tracer plan does not include every element of an advertising plan, it definitely illustrates the relationships between the various sections of the plan. It also verifies that the plan formats used in industry vary from one organization to another, depending on their own specific needs.

Readers should note the use of lists and statistical charts in the Tracer advertising plan. This type of presentation format clearly highlights the planned activities and the supporting rationale for the recommendations put forth in the plan. For the reader's benefit, selected creative execution illustrations are also included. You may wish to review the creative objectives and strategies, and draw your own conclusions as to how effective the execution is in achieving stated objectives and strategies.

Exhibit 1   Print advertisement for Mercury Tracer

Courtesy: Ford Motor Company of Canada Limited

Mercury Tracer
Advertising Plan

Ford Motor Company of Canada Limited

I. **MERCURY TRACER**
 COMMUNICATIONS OBJECTIVES
 AND STRATEGIES

MERCURY—TRACER

Sales Objective
 The Model Year 1987 sales forecast is 12 000 units.

1987 M.Y. Communications Objectives and Strategies

Objective 1
 Establish awareness of the all new Mercury Tracer.

Strategy
 Position Tracer as a stepup subcompact offering best in class quality, spirited performance and a high level of standard features.

Objective II
 Establish Tracer as a subcompact that is fun to own.

Strategy
 Use highly emotive messages and create a personality for Tracer.

Positioning*
 Mercury Tracer is a quality-built subcompact to meet the demands of today's young stylish car buyer who wants more than just transportation.

Tone
 Emotional
 Exciting

Target Group
 Sex: 60% Male
 Age: 24-45
 Education: Slightly above average
 Household Income: $25 000 +

*Positioning to be tested.

FORD MOTOR COMPANY OF CANADA, LIMITED MODEL YEAR 1987 MEDIA PLAN TRACER

Prepared by: Vickers & Benson Advertising Ltd.

Date: May 28, 1986

MEDIA OBJECTIVES

1. TARGET GROUP
   —Adults 24-45, 60% Male/40% Female
   —$25 M+ household income
   —Post-secondary + education

2. TIMING — SEASONALITY
   —Support must recognize launch date (October 2/86) and periods immediately prior to sales peaks: October—November and April—June. (See chart—Mercury Franchise)

EMPHASIS	PERIOD
PRIMARY	October–December 1986 (Launch)
SECONDARY	April–June 1987 (Key Sales Period)

   RATIONALE
   —While the October launch is critical, some support in 2nd Quarter 1987 is judged necessary as:
   a) Greater unit volume will be available in Spring
   b) Need to provide presence during key sales period

3. REACH/FREQUENCY
   —Launch: Maximize both <u>reach and frequency</u>
   —Follow-Up: <u>Reach</u> emphasis
   —Planning Guideline will be:

	% REACH 3 + TIME/4 WEEKS	
MEDIA EMPHASIS	LAUNCH	FOLLOW-UP
HIGH	75%	60%
MEDIUM	70%	55%
LOW	60%	50%

4. REGIONALITY/MARKET COVERAGE
   —National English and French.
   —Emphasis on Quebec, B.C. and Toronto.

RATIONALE

—Some degree of national support is required for the Launch.

—However, the alignment of advertising weight must recognize sales potential for Tracer (i.e. exploit regions/markets with high Basic Small category penetration): B.C. and Quebec—Primary; major markets in Ontario—Secondary (Volume).

REGION	% POP	% INDUSTRY SALES	% CATEGORY SALES	C.D.I.*	MEDIA IMPORTANCE
B.C.	11.7	8	11.2	140	High
Prairies	17.2	15	11.4	76	Low
Ontario	36.1	42	33.6	80	Medium
Quebec	26.3	27	34.6	128	High
Atlantic	8.8	8	8.3	104	Low

(Source: POLK 1985, Basic Small)

*Category Development Index

The Top 10 Markets within these regions which will be emphasized due to volume potential are indicated in the following chart.

MARKET	% POP	% INDUSTRY SALES	% CATEGORY SALES	C.D.I.*
Toronto	13.0	17.4	14.1	81
Montreal	11.8	11.3	11.9	105
Vancouver	5.6	4.5	6.0	133
Ottawa	3.1	3.3	2.9	88
Calgary	2.5	3.1	2.5	81
Winnipeg	2.5	2.1	2.0	95
Quebec City	2.4	2.3	3.0	130
Edmonton	2.7	2.8	2.4	86
Halifax	1.2	1.6	1.8	113
Hamilton	2.2	1.4	1.4	100
Total 10 Markets	47.0	49.8	48.0	

*Category Development Index

—In addition to the above Top 10 Small Car markets, Tracer support should also recognize Markets 11-20 (Small Car)

MARKETS 11-20	(Total Small Car)
Kitchener	Oshawa
London	St. Jerome
Windsor	Trois Rivières
Victoria	Regina
Sherbrooke	Moncton

PLAN SUMMARY

PERIOD	MEDIUM	WEEKLY REACH/FREQ		FLIGHT REACH/FREQ	
		R/F	GRPS	R/F	GRPS
Intro Qtr	TV (Tracer)	60/2.0	120 (Avg)	85/7.1	600
(Oct-Dec)	TV (All-Line)	52/1.8	95 (Avg)	87/7.6	665
	Total TV			92/13.7	1 265
	Outdoor	40/1.9	75	76/11.8	900
	Total Media	70/2.4	166 (Avg)	95/22.8	2 165
Ist Qtr	TV (All-Line)	60/1.8	110	83/6.6	550
2nd Qtr	TV (Tracer)	55/1.8	100	83/6.0	500
	TV (All-Line)	45/1.6	75	70/3.2	225
	Total TV			87/8.3	725
	Radio	50/4.0	200	65/12.3	800
	Total Media	65/1.8	117	92/16.6	1 525

NOTE: Planned Sable paid media launch reach/frequency was 95/29.9
SOURCE: TV—CMDC R/F Guides
Outdoor—Mediacom/Harris Adults 25-49
Radio—Harris
Intermedia—Harris. Assumes equivalent message delivery by medium.

PLAN SUMMARY—REGIONAL ALIGNMENT

REGION	IMPORTANCE	% IMPRESSIONS	INDEX VS POP	% $	% CATEGORY SALES
Atlantic	Low	4.3	49	3.7	8.3
Quebec	High	31.4	121	30.9	34.6
Ontario	Medium	38.2	105	36.4	33.6
Prairies	Low	12.3	72	15.1	11.4
B.C.	High	13.5	115	13.8	11.2

PLAN RATIONALE
1. MEDIA SELECTION
   —A media mix will be used to launch and support Tracer in M.Y. 1987.
   TELEVISION: Recommended as the primary medium as:
   a) Provides efficient reach of the national target group. In line with the media strategy, television is the most cost efficient medium to reach amass, national target. The medium has a potential daily reach of 84% of all Adults, a level which comes to 98% over a week (Spring '85 BBM).
   b) Provides efficient, national coverage of both urban and non-urban markets, while permitting tailoring of weight to market potential.

c) Delivers <u>high, continuous frequency</u>. This supports the objective of maximizing both reach and frequency. Due to television's high reach potential and the amount of time spent with the medium (an average of 26.6 hours weekly per capita), it is the most cost-efficient medium in which to build the rquired effective frequency levels.

d) <u>Creatively</u> television is the most intrusive medium available, capable of forcefully communicating the new Tracer.

OUTDOOR

—Outdoor backlights will be used during the initial launch period.

a) Outdoor is an effective medium in which to develop <u>high message frequency</u> in line with the strategic objective.

b) <u>Demographically appropriate</u> against the car owner/driver consumer.

c) <u>Visual medium</u>, capable of communicating the Tracer design.

—Backlights have been recommended over posters due to their greater impact, durability and visibility during late Fall.

—<u>At this time, inventory is available</u>. Should there not be sufficient inventory at time of approval, alternate media will be investigated.

—The use of more than one medium to launch a new nameplate is considered necessary as it:

—Extends reach

—Equalizes message frequency against light users of primary medium.

RADIO: Recommended as a support medium during the late Spring as:

— Ability to provide <u>high reach and frequency</u> against the executional target (Adults 25-49) and efficient <u>message concentration</u>.

— Concentrates messages against <u>key volume markets</u>.

— Environmentally appropriate (drive time periods).

— Provides message continuity and frequency immediately prior to peak June sales at a time when television viewing begins to decline.

— Image transfer with primary medium (television): audio.

2. DEVELOPMENT OF SUPPORT MEDIA MARKET LIST

—OUTDOOR has been planned in the top 20 small car markets where it is available. These markets represent 66% of total small car unit sales.

—RADIO has been recommended in:

a) B.C. and Quebec: top 20 markets which fall in these regions.

b) Ontario: only the 2 major volume markets (Toronto and Ottawa).

3. DEVELOPMENT OF TELEVISION WEIGHT LEVELS

— As required, media weight has been aligned with identified regional opportunities.

REGION	RANK	LAUNCH OBJECTIVE		BASE OBJECTIVE	
			GRP	R/F	GRP
R/F					
Atlantic	Low	110	60/1.8	75	50/1.5
Quebec	High	180	74/2.4	110	60/1.8
Ontario	Medium	150	68/2.2	100	55/1.8
Prairies	Low	110	60/1.8	80	50/1.6
BC	High	180	77/2.4	110	60/1.8

Note: Due to lesser fragmentation, a lower weight level is required in Atlantic to deliver 50% reach level (CMDC Guides).

— During the initial launch flight (October), a flat schedule at the recommended launch weight levels has not been planned for executional reasons. During the weeks of October 13 & 20, Ford will be up against World Series (General Motors).

— Total weekly television does not increase during periods of special events; rather, available viewing is concentrated against the special property.

— Consequently, high weight levels have not been recommended during these 2 weeks. Television execution will avoid purchase of programs running head-to-head with World Series games where possible.

— During preceding weeks, Baseball Playoffs (open to Ford) will be investigated.

4. TELEVISION EXECUTION
   — Program purchase will focus on those program types with high target group reach and composition.

PROGRAMS	ENGLISH CANADA			FRENCH CANADA		
	% TARGET	INDEX	RANK	% TARGET	INDEX	RANK
Sports	30	106	4	31	109	4
Comedy	26	87	6	22	81	6
Suspense/Drama	28	96	5	28	98	5
News/Documentaries	42	100	2	56	114	2
Movies	51	104	1	60	117	1
Variety	13	79	7	21	77	7
Mini-Series	32	105	3	38	101	3

Source: PMB 85: Base = Adults 18+, Target = Sub-Compact Owners, Programs = Watch Very Often.

5. ALTERNATE MEDIA

NEWSPAPER, while appropriate for a new car announcement, has not been recommended due to high absolute cost. (One newspaper insertion is approximately equivalent to 12 weeks of outdoor.)

SMALL CAR MARKETS	COST/INSERTION PAGE B&LC
	$ (000)
1-10	142.0
11-20	31.5
21-30	20.9
Mandatory Markets	<u>10.8</u>
TOTAL	<u>205.2</u>

<u>MAGAZINES</u>, while visually appropriate, have not been recommended for 4th Quarter launch activity as the budget cannot support a tertiary medium in 4th Quarter without decreasing the required 2nd half support. Further, corporately Ford will have a strong magazine presence for other car lines in 4th Quarter and the addition of another nameplate to magazine would necessitate several multiple insertions per issue which is counter to the Ford Corporate philosophy.

6. <u>ALIGNMENT OF MEDIA WEIGHT BY MONTH</u>

—The recommended scheduling of media weight satisfactorily addresses seasonality <u>and</u> anticipated volume availability.

<u>MONTH</u>	<u>MEDIA</u>	<u>GRP'S</u>	<u>% WEIGHT</u>
Oct.	TV & Outdoor	685)	
Nov.	TV (All-Line) & Outdoor	850)	51
Dec.	TV (All-Line) & Outdoor	630)	
Jan.	–	–	
Feb.	TV (All-Line)	110)	13
March	TV (All-Line)	440)	
April	–	–	
May	TV & Radio	1 125)	
June	Radio	400)	36
July	–	–	
Aug	–	–	
Sept	–	<u>–</u>	<u></u>
TOTAL YEAR		4 240	100

(Note: Above assumes equivalent message impact by medium)

II. MERCURY TRACER
RADIO SCRIPTS
T.V. SCRIPTS

copy   Vickers & Benson Advertising Ltd.   Toronto/Montreal

Client:	FORD MOTOR COMPANY OF CANADA LIMITED	Job No.
Product:	Mercury Tracer	Date Jan. 20, 1987
Medium:	Radio :30 "Extraordinary" National	Version No. DWM/cs/5

MUSIC UP   <u>AS RECORDED</u>

ANNCR: The extraordinary Tracer. So complete, all it needs is you.

SINGERS: HEY TRACER...

ANNCR: Mercury Tracer "LS" with a tough 1.6L overhead cam engine, front wheel drive and four wheel power disc brakes.

A classy little car that's sporty outside and loaded on the inside.

SINGERS: SO COMPLETE,
...ALL IT NEEDS IS YOU.

ANNCR: With a great fuel economy, four wheel independent suspension, and AM/FM electronic cassette radio.

SINGERS: HEY TRACER.

ANNCR: Mercury Tracer. The complete car, at your Mercury dealers.

V&B

copy

Vickers & Benson Advertising Ltd. Toronto/Montreal

Client:	FORD MOTOR COMPANY OF CANADA LIMITED	Job No.
Product:	Mercury Tracer	Date Jan. 20, 1987
Medium:	Radio :30 "Fun-To-Drive" National	Version No. DWM/cs/6

MUSIC UP   <u>AS RECORDED</u>

ANNCR: If you've been looking for a fun-to-drive sporty little car...

SINGERS: HEY TRACER

ANNCR: Look no further. Mercury Tracer is here. So complete, all it needs
            is you.

            Tracer comes with a long list of standard features that leaves
            virtually nothing to be desired.

SINGERS: SO COMPLETE,
            ...ALL IT NEEDS IS YOU

ANNCR: Experience a great looking state-of-the-art car today and bring the
            fun back to driving.

SINGERS: HEY TRACER

ANNCR: The import Ford built.
            Now at your Mercury dealers.

V&B

copy

Vickers & Benson Advertising Ltd. Toronto/Montreal

Client	FORD MOTOR COMPANY OF CANADA LIMITED	Job No.	T-10486
Product:	Mercury Tracer	Date	Jan. 20, 1987
Medium:	TV:30 "Hey Tracer"	Version No.	DWM/LE/cs/10

AS RECORDED

VIDEO	AUDIO	
OPEN ON A YOUNG GIRL DRIVING HER TRACER ALONG STREET. PEOPLE ARE SITTING TALKING AT OUTDOOR CAFE. THEY LOOK IN UNISON AT TRACER AND THEN PULL OUT OLYMPIC JUDGING CARDS. THEY ALL SHOW "10". THEY ALL SMILE. SUPER MERCURY TRACER.	ANNCR:	Mercury Tracer. We put more in, so you get more out of life.
	SINGERS:	Hey Tracer...
CUT TO AN EMPTY ROAD SHOT. THERE IS A BIG HILL. OVER THE TOP OF THE HILL WE SEE A CANOE AND THEN WE SEE A MERCURY TRACER CARRYING IT.	ANNCR:	With a tough 1.6L overhead cam engine and front wheel drive for lots of power and traction.
SUPER: MERCURY TRACER		
WE SEE A LITTLE GIRL AND HER FATHER WALKING TOWARDS THEIR TRACER.		
CUT TO FATHER SMILING OVER HIS SHOULDER INTO BACK SEAT. CUT TO BACK SEAT: HIS LITTLE GIRL IS SITTING THERE ALL DRESSED UP IN "MOMMY'S" CLOTHES, COMPLETE WITH PEARLS AND HUGE PICTURE HAT.	ANNCR:	A classy little car that's sporty outside and loaded on the inside.
SUPER: MERCURY TRACER.	SINGERS:	So Complete, so fine.. ..all it needs is you.
CUT TO CLOSE-UP OF YOUNG GIRL IN TRACER LOOKING AT SIGNS THAT SAY "LAST PHONE AND GAS FOR 500km". SHE GRINS AND SHRUGS LOOKS AT BOYFRIEND AND TAKES OFF UP THE MOUNTAIN ROAD IN TRACER.	ANNCR:	With great fuel economy, power brakes and four wheel independent suspension.
	SINGERS:	Hey Tracer.

V&B

Creating Advertisements and Commercials

In Part Two of the text, the relationships between marketing and advertising were established, and a detailed review of the marketing- and advertising-planning processes was presented. Clearly, the content of a marketing plan or advertising plan affects the direction taken in creative planning.

The purpose of this section is to describe the creative-planning process in detail, to distinguish between creative objectives, strategies, and execution considerations, and to describe the responsibilities of the client and the agency in the creative process. This is accomplished in chapter 6.

Chapter 7 presents the production considerations for both print and broadcast media. Chapter 8 examines the role that research plays in advertising. The chapter presents the techniques for measuring and evaluating the effectiveness of creative, and describes in detail the types and nature of media-research information available to advertisers, agencies, and the media.

PART III

CHAPTER 6 Creative Planning

In studying this chapter, you will learn

- About the stages in the creative-development process
- To distinguish between client responsibility and agency responsibility in the creative process
- The factors that influence the development of creative objectives and strategies
- The role and purpose of objective statements and strategy statements in advertising
- The various appeal techniques used in advertising today
- The various considerations for presenting advertising messages

Developing the actual message to be advertised is the next step in the advertising-planning process. The creative plan is a logical extension of the marketing plan and advertising plan discussed in the previous chapter. Essentially, the marketing plan provides valuable input to the creative team (i.e., art director and copywriter) at the advertising agency.

Students must appreciate that the actual advertisements that they see, read, and listen to are simply the outcome of the planning process. It is in the planning stages for both creative and media that client-agency interaction is at its peak, and any discussion that takes place results in clear direction for the development of advertising messages.

This chapter focuses on the creative-planning process and the relationships between the client and the agency in that process. The concepts of creative objectives, creative strategies and creative execution are examined in detail, and numerous advertisements and campaigns are included to illustrate these concepts.

CREATIVE - DEVELOPMENT PROCESS

To provide direction for creative development, there is a significant amount of discussion between the client and advertising agency, so that both parties can agree on a plan of action. The creative-development process can be subdivided into five distinct stages (see figure 6.1).

Figure 6.1   Creative-development process

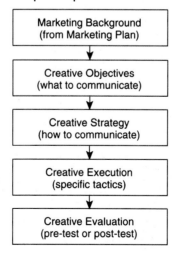

Communication of Marketing Background

From the marketing plan, the client compiles a document containing information that will be relevant to the agency creative team (i.e., creative directors, art directors, and copywriters). This document is often referred to as a *creative brief*. The purpose of the brief is to provide a framework for discussion between the client and the advertising agency. The creative brief includes some or all of the following components: a market profile, a product profile, a competitor profile, a target-market profile, additional marketing information, and a proposed budget.

Market Profile This is usually a quantitative and qualitative review of market trends and competitive activity in the context of variables such as

- Market size (in terms of dollars, units, etc.)
- Market growth rates
- Competitor-product profile (i.e., the unique selling points of competitive products)
- Advertising history (an evaluation of competitors' creative and media strategies)
- Media usage and expenditure trends

A sound knowledge of these variables provides the creative group with a reasonable perspective on the overall market situation, provides insight into the relative strengths and weaknesses of competitive products, and indicates the importance of advertising for each competitor.

Product Profile This section of the creative brief communicates the important aspects of the product or service to be advertised. Included is the product positioning statement, the product description (i.e, a description of its physical characteristics), a discussion and ranking of the unique selling points and their corresponding consumer benefits, and an evaluation of current and past creative direction.

Competitor Profile To provide the creative team with a more complete perspective on what is happening in the marketplace, a discussion of competitive advertising activity is essential. A qualitative assessment of the creative direction of competitors, in terms of what and how they communicate, would be part of the creative-briefing process.

Target-Market Profile A thorough understanding of the customer is vital for the creation of an effective and convincing advertising message. The client must provide a complete profile of the target market that includes all relevant demographic, psychographic, and geographic information, along with any other information obtained from research (e.g., information concerning buying motives) which might influence the development of the advertising message.

Additional Marketing Information The relationship of advertising with other elements of the marketing mix should be clarified. While the product-positioning statement will provide basic direction, often more specific strategy information regarding product, price, place, and promotion is necessary. With respect to product strategy, for example, is the product perceived to be of high, medium, or low quality by current customers? Is the price level low or high, and what is the perceived value of the product in the minds of current customers? For devising promotion strategy, the creative team must know if any sales-promotion incentives, such as coupons, refunds, and contests, are to be included as part of the creative-development process, or if they will be handled separately.

Proposed Budget To put the creative plan into perspective, the client should provide a budget guideline. How much money is available will determine whether the use of certain media is restricted or eliminated, and this, in turn, will affect creative strategy and execution.

Creative Objectives

Creative objectives are the marketing objectives and strategies extended into the creative area. Much of the marketing background discussed earlier (e.g., product positioning, unique selling points, consumer benefits) is really the basis of creative messages.

Positioning Positioning, as mentioned earlier, refers to the selling concept or message that motivates consumers to purchase a particular product or service. In terms of advertising, positioning refers to the message or image of the product to be instilled in the customer's mind by advertising. Thus a positioning statement has an influence on the content of creative-objective statements.

Creative Objectives These are statements that clearly indicate what information is to be communicated to a target audience. Although the formats may vary, objective statements usually contain the following basic elements:

1. *Key-Benefit Statement* This is a statement of the basic selling idea, service, or benefit that the advertiser is promising the consumer. This benefit or key fact is the primary reason the consumer has for buying the product instead of any competitive product. Additional supplementary benefits may be described in another objective statement.
2. *Support-Claims Statement* This statement describes the principal characteristics of the product or service, the characteristics that substantiate the promise (i.e., the promise made in the key-benefits statement), usually offering a reason why the customer should buy the product. For example, support claims could be based on technical-performance data or consumer-preference data generated from marketing research.

The objective behind these statements is to provide the customer with both a promise and a proof of promise; to assure buyers, in other words, of the quality of what they are purchasing.

For example, a tire manufacturer may stress "safety" in its advertising, referring to advanced technology in tread design and scientific testing of the product. A deodorant manufacturer may stress "effective protection against wetness and odour," basing this promise on a new formula containing an active ingredient that acts as both an anti-perspirant and a deodorant.

Creative Strategy

With the content of the message confirmed, the next stage is to develop the creative strategy. In contrast to the first two stages, the agency's creative team plays a dominant role here, in the creative-development process. In essence, the client is paying the agency primarily for the strategy (i.e., the ideas and concepts used in presenting the message). Sound strategies, in accordance with creative objectives, are the foundation of successful advertising campaigns.

The creative strategy is a statement of *how* the message is to be communicated to the target audience. It is a statement of the character, personality, and image that the agency will strive to develop for the client's product or service. Strategy is reflected in the mood, tone, or style of the advertising. A product may appeal to a potential buyer on the basis of emotion, humour, or product comparison. The tone may be informative, persuasive, entertaining, or warm in nature. From an endless list of strategic alternatives, a strategic plan of action is developed.

Creative Execution

The execution stage of the creative-development process is concerned with two main areas: *tactical considerations* regarding how to present the message (and to generate impact on the audience), and *production considerations* regarding the media to be used.

Tactical Considerations At this stage, the agency's creative team evaluates specific ideas about how to present the client's product or service. These ideas, often referred to as "tactics," are simply more precisely defined strategies. Tactics undertake to answer such questions as the following:

- What is the best or most convincing way to present a product so that the consumer will be motivated to take the desired action of purchasing the product?
- Does the advertisement use a demonstration, a product (brand) comparison, a testimonial, or a celebrity spokesperson?

Production Considerations As indicated earlier, the media budget has probably already restricted the use of certain media. Budget considerations may also affect the production of advertising messages. Considering the media which is to be used, the client must communicate to the agency any production restrictions.

For example, if television is being used, what is the commercial length (15 or 30 seconds)? For what tactical purpose is television being used? How many commercials will be needed (one commercial, or a pool of commercials on the same theme)? If print is being used, what are the size specifications (one page or less)? Are there any restrictions on the use of colour (black and white, spot colour, or four-colour process)?

Once any production considerations have been noted, the agency creative team can start developing the creative in the form of radio scripts, television storyboards, and rough layouts for the various forms of print advertising.

To demonstrate the application of creative objectives, strategies and execution, and the relationships between each, refer to figure 6.2. This figure contains the

Figure 6.2   Telemarketing customer service creative workplan and customer service storyboard (creative execution)

TELECOM CANADA
"Customer Service"
30 sec. TV

TELEMARKETER: (UNDER)
Well in your city Sir...
BOSS: My competitive edge.
Customer Service...
Nationwide... through
Telemarketing.
LUMLEY: Glad to be of help.

BOSS: It's that simple.
LUMLEY: Here Chief.

BOSS: Customer Service...

uh, your filbert flange won't
mesh with your grappel
grommet.

BOSS: No problem! Lumley!

BOSS: See, a satisfied
customer is a repeat
customer.

LUMLEY: You're welcome.
BOSS: We make grappel
grommets?

LUMLEY: 23,000 a day.
BOSS: Awesome!

ANNCR V.O.: Telemarketing.
Today's way to operate.

continued

Figure 6.2 continued

TELEMARKETING - CREATIVE WORKPLAN

AWARENESS TV SPOT

KEY FACT

Business enterprises are constantly searching for new accessible alternatives in order to improve profitability. This market is now ready for a system/program that integrates Telecommunications, direct marketing and MIS to satisfy this need. Although T/M is not new in its essence and, indeed, it is just another application of BLD, a T/M system proposes a fresh approach to conducting traditional marketing operations.

PROBLEM THAT THE ADVERTISING MUST SOLVE

The advertising must avoid any responses from the target group that may suggest that there is nothing new about T/M.

ADVERTISING OBJECTIVE

To generate awareness and interest for T/M.

TARGET GROUP

Primary   :   CEO's and Senior Marketing Management
Secondary :   Marketing and Sales Management

CREATIVE STRATEGY

A. Promise

    A T/M program will improve your "profitability."

B. Reason Why

    Because a T/M program will make your marketing operations more "cost-effective."

C. Tone

    • look of efficiency
    • contemporary
    • entertaining
    • warm

D. Creative Guidelines

    • Consistent with existing BLD campaign (i.e. use of Larry Mann).
    • Positive reinforcement (rather than reprimand).
    • Telecom Canada animation logo.
    • Creative can consider having the setting within a T/M centre.

Courtesy: Telecom Canada and Publicité McKim Ltée. Reprinted with permission.

creative workplan and actual storyboard execution for the very successful "Telemarketing" campaign by Telecom Canada. The creative workplan is divided into the following areas: "Key Fact" (i.e. major benefit), "Problem That Advertising Must Solve," "Advertising (Creative) Objective," "Target Group and Creative Strategy (Promise, Reason why, Tone, and Creative Guidelines)."

Figure 6.2 is an awareness advertisement designed to show how customers can improve profitability through telemarketing, a program which integrates telecommunications, direct marketing, and management-information systems. This advertisement was part of an umbrella strategy used by Telecom Canada to promote "business long distance." The campaign, which features Larry Mann in "The Boss" role, first aired in 1981. Various executions were developed, all within the same creative strategy, since the campaign was very successful. It wasn't until 1990 that Telecom Canada decided to move away from this strategy and on to something new. An illustration of the new strategy appears later in this chapter.

Creative Evaluation

Once the ideas and concepts have been developed by the agency, they are presented to the client for approval. The creative team and the account executive are usually involved in this process. Knowing that the client must make a critical decision (i.e., whether to proceed with production), the agency must sell its concepts to the client. Even if the client approves the concept, it is entirely possible that the concept will be tested with consumers before the client commits to the production process.

Depending on how much money the client is willing to invest in research, advertising can be tested at numerous stages of the development process. To prepare for evaluation by the client, which is the first critical test, the agency should know in advance the client's procedure for evaluating creative. Since the agency provides the advertising expertise, and the client is paying for this service, the evaluation of creative is done by means of a "managerial approach." In this regard, members of the client organization must restrict their impulse to assess the creativity on personal, subjective bases; they must keep in mind that the client delegated the creative task to the agency. However, if a "to-proceed-or-not-to-proceed" decision must be made, the client reserves the right to conduct consumer research prior to making the decision.

Clients using the "managerial approach" for evaluating creative may apply some or all of the following criteria:

1. *In terms of content, does the advertisement communicate the creative objectives?* The client reviews the creative for the primary message and support claims outlined in the creative brief.

2. *In terms of how the ad is presented (strategy and execution), does it mislead or misrepresent the intent of the message?* The client must be concerned about the actual message and any implied message contained in the creative. Once the creative is approved, the client is responsible for the truthfulness of the message content. In today's advertising environment, legal counsel often decides on the content of advertisements.

3. *Is the advertisement presented in good taste?* The client must also be concerned about the danger of alienating potential users of the product or service owing to the manner in which the message is presented. As well, the client may review the style of the advertisement in light of corporate image.

4. *Should the advertisement be researched?* When it comes to assessing the impact and effectiveness of the advertisement, subjective judgements by the client have the disadvantage of not being quantifiable. Prior to spending money on production, the client may decide to conduct consumer research to seek quantifiable data that will aid the decision-making process.

5. *Does the advertisement represent the quality expected of the creative team?* The client must be convinced that the members of the creative team gave the assignment their best effort. If the client has any suspicions in this regard, the underlying cause of the suspicion must be investigated. If the creative team's performance does not meet expectations, the following questions should be asked: Was there enough time? Were they adequately briefed? Were they familiar with the evaluation process?

The evaluation process can take place at virtually any stage of the creative-execution process. A television commercial, for example, could be evaluated by the client and the consumer at the storyboard, rough-cut, or finished-commercial stage. While it is not practical to test commercials at all stages, if the quality or effectiveness of the commercial should ever come into question, then the client should conduct research to avoid costly and embarrassing errors in judgement. Refer to figure 6.3 for a summary overview of the content of a typical creative workplan.

The Advertising in Action vignette "Breaking New Ground—The Black Label Story" draws the relationships between marketing background, creative objectives and strategies, creative execution and creative evaluation.

Figure 6.3   Content of a typical creative workplan

Creative Objectives:
Statements of *what* is to be communicated
  1. Key Consumer Benefit (Key Fact)
  2. Support Claims

Creative Strategy:
Statements about *how* message is to be communicated
  1. Reason for buying (motivation)
  2. Appeal Techniques
  3. Tone and Style
  4. Theme Considerations

Creative Execution:
Specific details for presenting message
  1. Tactical Considerations
  2. Production Considerations

Advertising in Action
Breaking New Ground—The Black Label Story

Marketing and advertising beer in Canada is big business. Canadians quaff about 460 million gallons of suds annually, worth about $2.5 billion, and the big two companies, Labatt's and Molson's (Molson's and Carling O'Keefe merged in 1989), control 95% of all beer sales, with a combined output of 75 different brands of beers. Together, these two giants will spend about $100 million annually advertising and promoting their beer. Only the auto industry spends more.

Carling faced a big problem in 1988. The market was stagnating and the company was floundering. For any brand, growth was hard to achieve, and what growth did occur had to be taken out of the hide of another brand, hopefully a rival brand. What, then, did Carling have in mind when it decided to revive Black Label?

Here was a brand that was popular in the fifties and sixties with the blue-collar crowd—it was all but dead in the eighties, with a market share of 0.5% and an advertising budget of only $150 000 (peanuts in relation to typical advertising budgets in the industry). What the company executives did know was that it was much cheaper to revive an old brand than to launch a new brand. So, despite the years of neglect suffered by Black Label, Carling discovered that there were still people around who could remember the old slogan, "Hey Mabel, Black Label!"

Two veterans of the beer industry collaborated on the relaunch of Black Label. David Barbour was the executive vice-president of marketing who had recently come to the company from Molson's. He was the individual who would ultimately approve a rather daring campaign. Robin Milward was the vice-president of advertising, and a former executive with MacLaren Advertising who had gained "beer experience" on the Molson Canadian brand. Both were new to the company and both were faced with the challenge of doing something exciting in the beer market. Against incredible odds, the pair decided to relaunch Black Label. Their first step in determining how best to do it was to appoint an advertising agency with absolutely no experience in beer advertising. They viewed this as a plus. The agency appointed was Palmer Bonner BCP, a medium-sized Toronto agency.

Both the client and the agency realized that research was the next step. Knowledge of consumer attitudes and preferences is essential to the development of any campaign. Through research, the agency inadvertently discovered that Black Label was extremely popular in downtown bars in Toronto and Montreal, among a certain type of crowd. "It was the brew of choice of new-wave trendies who like to dress head to toe in funeral black. They were nonconformists who worshipped black—and Black Label was their beer." Such knowledge set the stage for creative development, but, before the agency proceeded, it was decided to conduct some research into focus groups to collect more psychographic information—to probe the attitudes of this new-wave beer drinker.

Research revealed that Black Label drinkers were "ardent individualists that preferred jazz, classical music, and underground bands—not rock. They preferred to drink in small groups—not crowds. They were educated, artistic, and musical." More importantly,

continued

this group despised mainstream beer-advertising and clearly indicated that they would reject Black Label out of principle if such an advertising direction was pursued.

Now the agency had some ammunition. The next step was to clarify the positioning of Black Label. The agency decided that "they would pitch Black Label not to the converted, but to the slightly disaffected mainstream beer-drinker who was ready for a change, who secretly admired the trendies and wanted to share their on-the-fringe lifestyle." The associate creative director at Palmer Bonner, Paul Hains, was given the challenge of developing the ads that would make it happen. His challenge was unique—to create advertising for people who hated advertising. He knew he would be heading in a new direction.

It was in June 1988 that the first wave of Black Label commercials hit the airwaves. Both the agency and Carling were nervous about them, but they eagerly awaited the consumer's reaction. The ads were different: black and white had replaced the usual colour; cool sex replaced hot sex; and loud music was not so loud. There were no parties; there wasn't a beach in sight; and there was no bottle or pouring of beer. There was lots of reverse imagery, a red label, and the now famous theme line—"The Legend is Black."

Yes, the campaign was successful. It was applauded by the industry as breaking new ground, and it did win the big advertising awards that year. In terms of sales, the campaign did a whole lot more than expected. David Barbour said it best: "I have never worked on a campaign that resulted in such a quick jump in sales." But hold on. What lies ahead? Certainly not complacency. Black Label has been successfully repositioned as the brand for the avant-garde—but the challenge now is to protect that position. Here comes Carlsberg!

Adapted from "What? No bimbos?" *Report on Business Magazine*, December 1988, pp.68-75.

RESPONSIBILITIES FOR CREATIVE DEVELOPMENT

With the creative-development process covered, let's briefly review the procedure, considering the primary areas of responsibility for both the client and advertising agency. Figure 6.4 illustrates in diagram form the respective responsibilities of clients and agencies.

Client Responsibility

The client's initial task is to provide enough marketing and product background, based on the creative-development procedure outlined earlier, so that the agency understands the situation it is dealing with. The client also plays a dominant role in developing a list of creative objectives. Considering the client's knowledge of the target market, it must be accountable for the content of the message.

Through consultation with the agency's creative team, the client will have some (limited) input into the development of creative-strategy statements. The agency might gain broadstroke direction by noting the client's preference for emotional appeals or humorous appeals, but strategy is largely the domain of the agency.

Figure 6.4 Client-Agency responsibility in the creative-development process

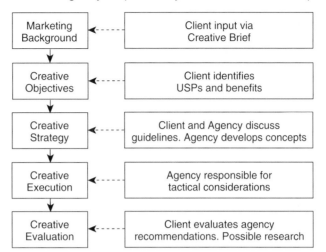

The last area of client responsibility is the creative-evaluation process. Since it is the client's money that is on the line, the client has every right to make qualitative- and quantitative-research assessments at any stage of creative execution.

Agency Responsibility

The agency's first task is to familiarize itself, through consultation with the client, with the intricacies of the marketplace. Once the creative objectives have been agreed to, the agency must develop a more precise creative strategy. The creative team works on numerous ideas and concepts, and develops a shortlist of possibilities that look promising. Creative-execution details are considered, so that the product may be presented in a convincing and believable manner. When the creative team has completed the creative assignment, in the form of rough layouts for print, storyboards and scripts for television, and so on, the ideas are submitted to the client for approval.

Depending on the outcome of the evaluation process, the agency either proceeds with creative execution, or goes back to the drawing board to make modifications or to develop new ideas.

*P*ROVIDING CREATIVE DIRECTION

So far, this chapter has dealt with the stages of the creative-development process. To understand how client and agency come to agree on an advertising direction, it is important to understand the process of analysis that determines what and how messages will be communicated. Since the content and style of an advertisement or advertising campaign are another means of distinguishing one product from another, client and agency must try to gain an advantage over competitors by making the right choices about how to present and what to present in a message. The next section examines the various factors that influence the development of creative objectives and strategies.

FACTORS INFLUENCING THE DEVELOPMENT OF CREATIVE OBJECTIVES AND STRATEGIES

Product Characteristics

It is important to clearly identify the basic performance characteristics and advantages that the product or service has to offer. This is often referred to as the *unique selling proposition* (USP). The USP, expressed as a consumer benefit, might be economy, safety, variety, durability, efficiency, or what have you. Once the USP has been identified, it should become the focal point of the advertising message. In the Westin Hotel advertisement (see figure 6.5) the unique selling point is the service provided by the hotel.

Product-Related Features

To distinguish between comparable brands (i.e., products that have the same characteristics), additional features may be considered as possible influences on the purchase decision. That is to say, if all major brands are relatively equal in terms of quality, performance, and price, a related feature may differentiate one brand from another. Proper communication of that related feature could influence the purchase decision. An example of a product-related feature might be a guarantee, a warranty, or a promise of quick delivery.

Target Market

The better the knowledge of the target market, the easier the task of developing advertising messages. If adequate resources are committed to collecting research information—to identifying and understanding the motivations behind consumers' purchases—such information can be used to develop convincing messages. The ability to associate product benefits with buying motives or to present a product in a manner that appeals to a certain lifestyle is part of developing creative-objective and creative-strategy statements.

With respect to demographics and psychographics, the Canadian advertiser faces the dilemma of how to best approach the French-language market. Advertisers recognize that French Canadian consumers are distinguished by language, culture and social traditions (all arguments in favour of original French creative). However, by adapting English-language campaigns to the French-language market, economies of scale are achieved in production costs.

Price

Price, particularly a price that is high in relation to prices of competing products, is often viewed as a disadvantage, and is thus often rejected as an element to advertise. However, advertising can develop a strong, positive image for a product over a period

Figure 6.5 An advertisement that presents service as the unique selling point

Advertisement courtesy of Westin Hotels & Resorts

of time, and if the price-quality relationship is handled properly, a higher price need not be a disadvantage.

For example, if product offerings are comparable in terms of quality, an advertiser may decide to develop a message that focuses specifically on quality. The perceptual image of quality would help justify the price of the product to consumers. Very often, advertisers will use the "you-deserve-better" approach, or the "aren't-you-worth-it?" appeal technique. Conversely, a product that advertises on the basis of lower price to distinguish itself will often attempt to show product equality at a better price. Appealing to rational buying motives in a convincing and believable manner can influence consumers to purchase a product.

Product Reputation

Although creative objectives and strategies change over time, and advertising campaigns come and go, quite often there is some element from previous campaigns that is retained in new creative execution. An investment in advertising over an extended period of time will help create a distinctive brand image or develop a reputation, and there is always a risk of damaging an established image when an advertiser decides to change something that is working.

For example, a good slogan may outlast numerous advertising campaigns because the slogan is closely associated with the brand name and has high recall with consumers. Consider the following examples:

- *Coca-Cola*: "Can't Beat the Real Thing."
- *Maxwell House Coffee*: "Good to the last drop."
- *Ford Automobiles*: "Quality is Job One."
- *Pepsi-Cola*: "The choice of a new generation."

Also, a character or spokesperson may be closely associated with a product. The following are some examples:

- *Kellogg's Frosted Flakes*: Tony the Tiger
- *Green Giant*: the Jolly Green Giant and Sprout.
- *Pillsbury*: the Pillsbury Doughboy.
- *Breton Crackers and Dare Cookies*: the Dare Bears.
- *Post Raisin Bran*: the California Raisins

Elements such as these have had longevity, and therefore must be considered when new creative directions are being developed.

The Competitive Situation

The nature of other brands in the marketplace and what they are promising should be considered when creative objectives and strategies are being developed. In looking at the competition, the advertiser should analyze its strengths and weaknesses, and use the analysis as a guideline for creative direction. The direction an advertiser takes may be similar to or totally different from that of the competition.

Figure 6.6   Factors influencing the development of creative objectives and strategies

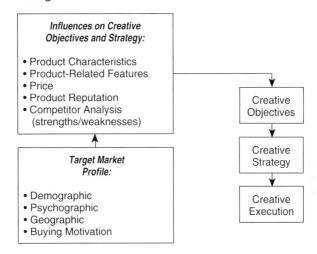

For example, 7-Up utilized the "Un-Cola" theme to advantage in the past, and, more recently, used the "clear, clean, and no caffeine" theme in advertising messages. The development of this message was based on a perception that cola-based products have a weakness—they contain caffeine. 7-Up used this strategy to appeal to a segment of the soft-drink market that was concerned about the ingredients in cola products.

Competitive analysis may also have an impact on the tone, style, and appeal techniques used in advertising. Generally, if one product uses a particular style of advertising (e.g., humorous or emotional) effectively, it may not be in the best interests of a competing product to use the same style, since the products would not be clearly differentiated.

The direction finally taken by a product may be similar to that of the competition. For example, in a highly advertised product category, where all brands are comparable in terms of quality and price, advertisers may resort to lifestyle advertising. In the Canadian beer market and the cola segment of the soft-drink market, various brands compete for and advertise to a socially active target market through lifestyle advertising. Refer to figure 6.6 for a summary of the various factors influencing the development of creative objectives and strategies.

THE PURPOSE OF OBJECTIVE AND STRATEGY STATEMENTS

A significant amount of time, effort, and thought goes into the creative-planning process. For the benefit of the advertiser and the advertising agency, it is important to develop clearly defined creative-objective and creative-strategy statements for the following reasons:

1. *To Provide Continuity in Advertising* Over a period of time, the advertised product will stand for something specific in the mind of the consumer. Relative to the positioning statement discussed earlier in this chapter, carefully worded objective and strategy statements will lead to advertising execution that will achieve distinctiveness in a competitive market.
2. *To Provide Guidance for Agency Creative Team* In effect, a carefully articulated creative strategy sets the limits within which an agency will exercise its creative imagination. In this regard, the statements should be specific, yet allow enough latitude for the presentation of new ideas and concepts.
3. *To Provide a Framework for Evaluation* Creative-objective and creative-strategy statements provide a common denominator to which both the client and agency can refer when evaluating the merits of a creative submission.

Figure 6.7 summarizes the factors to consider in creative planning and indicates the relationship between creative objectives, creative strategy, and creative execution.

CREATIVE OBJECTIVES OF ADVERTISING

The basic task of advertising is to influence consumers to feel positively toward an idea, product, or service. More specifically, advertising will inform, persuade, and remind customers about the benefits of using a particular brand. Advertising objectives usually centre on increasing the level of consumers' awareness of a particular product or service (brand name), or on establishing preference for the product or service in the mind of the consumer. Also, advertising objectives can focus on securing trial purchase by consumers, particularly if sales-promotion incentives are part of the advertising message.

Once the advertising objectives are established, the creative objectives can outline the content of the intended message, for which there is an endless list of possibilities for any given product or service. The stage the product has reached in its life cycle and the competitive environment in the marketplace often influence the content and nature of the advertising message. For example, in the introduction and growth stages of the product's life cycle, the message content deals with the unique selling points and benefits available to the consumer. Advertisers attempt to differentiate their product or service from competitive alternatives. In the mature stage, the message content shifts in order to increase frequency of use by consumers, to expand the variety of uses current customers have for the product, or to attract new users to the existing product.

The list of creative objectives below is intended as a useful generalization about typical aims and orientations of message content.

To Communicate Unique Attributes and Benefits

In this case, the advertising makes a promise and backs it with some form of proof. For example, a creative objective might read as follows:

Figure 6.7 Detailed checklist: creative strategy and plan

Factors to Consider:
1. Brand Name and Perceived Image
2. Primary Consumer Benefit (unique selling points)
3. Product Performance versus Competition
4. Product Characteristics (taste, colour, texture, scent)
5. Product Form (solid vs liquid, cream vs gel, etc.)
6. Product Formula (active ingredients and applicable benefits)
7. Packaging (glass, plastic plus applicable benefits)
8. Sizes Available (small, large, family size)
9. Pricing (high vs low plus value relationships of price and quality)

Each section of the Creative Strategy and Plan should consider:

Creative Objective
1. Who is the Target Market?
   —demographic, psychographic, geographic profile
2. What is the Primary Product Benefit?
   —when ranked, which benefit is most important to target market?
3. How does the product compare to competitive brands?
   —comparable, superior (research data to verify)

Promise and Benefit
1. What does the product deliver?
   —state the basic promise in a way that allows the question
   "why should the consumer buy this product?" to be answered simply.

Support
1. What is in the product which supports the benefit statement?
   —usually based on product form, formula or characteristics

Creative Execution
Decide on
1. The specific advertising media
2. Length of broadcast copy (15/30/60 seconds)
3. Colour and size of print ads.
Remember
1. Cost considerations and restrictions
2. Mandatories which must be included.

Objective 1 To demonstrate the superior taste of the product, in relation to competitor offerings.

Proof Use comparative taste tests and research survey data to verify preference claims.

Objective 2 To communicate a price savings for consumers, while providing a product of equal quality (performance) to other leading brands.

Proof Show typical consumer using the lower-priced and high-priced product. If there is not a noticeable difference, the message will appeal to the rational buying motives of the consumer. ABC laundry detergent and its "can you tell the difference, no I can't tell the difference" campaign uses the price savings approach successfully, implying that the consumer gets good quality at a better price.

The Ontario Foodland advertisement contained in figure 6.8 is a good example of an ad that simply concentrates on the product's unique attributes (in this case, the superior taste of fresh-grown fruits and vegetables). The intent of the campaign was to promote the great taste of Ontario fruits and vegetables, with the essence of the campaign being captured in the slogan "There's no taste like home." This particular campaign was designed to build on the success of the "Good-things-grow-in-Ontario" slogan, which created high awareness levels of the quality and diversity of Ontario foods.

The creative objectives and strategies for the Ontario Foodland campaign are as follows:[1]

Creative Objectives:
1. To convince consumers to purchase Ontario-grown food products
2. To increase consumer understanding (and hence the value) of the Ontario Foodland symbol

Creative Strategies:
1. To make the strongest, most relevant product claims
2. To increase symbol understanding and value by tying it to product claims
3. Support individual products within an overall campaign framework (similar format and style)

Target:
The primary food shopper, with emphasis on mothers, aged 25 to 49

To Increase Frequency of Use

When a product is firmly established in the market (i.e., when it has reached the mature stage in its life cycle), the marketing objectives for it usually centre on converting light or casual users into heavy users. Advertising can play a role in this campaign to increase frequency of use by showing alternative uses for the product.

Campaigns by marketing boards such as the beef-marketing board or Canada Pork, the pork-marketing agency, are designed to encourage consumers to use beef and pork more frequently. In 1990, Canada Pork launched a print campaign that used the line, "If you think pork's fat, you're living in the past." One way of increasing consumption is to dispel a misconception—in this case, that pork is a fatty product. The ads explained that pork is 23% leaner than it was five years ago, due to better breeding and feeding.[2]

Figure 6.8 An advertisement concentrating on unique attributes alone —taste

Courtesy: Ontario Ministry of Agriculture and Food. Reprinted with permission.

In another campaign, the orange-juice industry encourages consumers to think of orange juice as a thirst quencher for "any time of the day," not just for breakfast time.

To Communicate Variety of Use

Another option for an established product is to encourage current users to use the product more heavily. Since the benefits of the product are known by users, the costs associated with increasing usage are much less than those required to attract new users.

A classic example is Cow Brand Baking Soda, which experienced significant sales growth when communications illustrated its versatility as a rug and refrigerator deodorizer and as a water softener for the bath. More recently it has been positioned as a natural "green" product useful as a tub and tile cleanser and for other household cleaning functions. Not only did current users purchase more of the product, but new users were attracted also.

In the running-shoe market, many leading brands such as Nike and Reebok promote the merits of their cross-training shoes. The versatility of these shoes—their suitability for many sports—provides added value to consumers.

To Attract New Targets

Advertising can play a key role in "repositioning" a product in the marketplace. In the case of mature products that are experiencing marginal sales growth or decline, making the product appeal to different user segments represents an opportunity for advertisers.

One of the classic examples of this is the advertising of Johnson & Johnson shampoo. Originally positioned as a product only for babies and young children, the brand experienced success when advertising repositioned the brand to appeal to parents. Since the brand appeals to all family members, the additional benefit for consumers is purchase economy, since only one brand need be purchased.

More recently, Tums (a brand of stomach antacid) experienced significant market-share increase when communications focused on its calcium content. The calcium message in the advertising for Tums appealed to a segment of the market concerned about their daily calcium intake. In another instance, some existing cereals experienced success when advertising for them appealed to the health-conscious attitudes of Canadian consumers. Post Grape Nuts is one such example. Once the fibre component of the cereal was publicized, the product became attractive to this health-conscious target market. Kellogg's Frosted Flakes is now advertising to adults, using phrases such as "you enjoyed it as a child, so why not buy it now?"

To Communicate Product Improvements

In the late-growth and early-mature stages of the product's life cycle, marketing strategies often deal with product changes and improvements, in order to keep the product competitive. This strategy is very popular in the food industry (where advertisements often focus on a product's new and improved taste) and the household-products industry (where messages focus on improved product performance).

In this situation, advertising messages must make the consumer aware of the improvement. This strategy is often used as a defensive measure to entice current users to stay with their current brand rather than switch to a newer brand that may be offering trial-purchase incentives.

To Introduce Line Extensions

Similar to the above situation, the late-growth and early-mature stages of the product's life cycle represent opportunities to introduce new lines (i.e., new sizes, new flavours, new forms of the existing product, etc.). While the existing product will still be advertised, the thrust of the advertising will shift to the "new" variations on the product.

A brand of toothpaste might introduce a new "gel" formula with a promise and benefit centred on fresher breath. Both Crest and Colgate introduced flavours suitable for kids (sweeter) in an attempt to make brushing teeth a more pleasant experience for kids. Advertising for the new line benefits the existing product also, since both are marketed under the same brand name. In this case, advertising helps in the introduction of a new line and presents it in such a way that it appeals to a different segment of users, basing this appeal on the new segment's primary reason for buying toothpaste. Overall, advertising will contribute to the expanded presence of the product line in the marketplace.

To Communicate Promotion Incentives

Very often, sales-promotion incentives are incorporated into advertising campaigns. For example, if one of the marketing objectives and advertising objectives is to "stimulate trial purchase," it is very likely that the print advertisements will include coupon incentives.

In other situations, advertising may temporarily depart from normal creative objectives and strategies. It may ignore unique selling points and benefits, and focus only on the brand name and promotion. For example, the automobile industry promotes rebates, low financing, and special-option packages (sometimes free) as a means of stimulating sales.

To Communicate a Favourable Corporate Image

In addition to product-oriented advertising, a company can implement advertising campaigns that benefit the company as a whole. Multi-product firms may run a corporate-advertising campaign as part of their "corporate-responsibility" positioning. Alcan returned to the advertising scene in 1990 with a $1.2-million print campaign aimed at building awareness of the company's involvement in the business and daily life of other countries around the world. It was also intended to boost the pride of the company's own employees.[3] Although the success of corporate campaigns is difficult to measure, these efforts may have indirect impact on a company's individual company products.

CREATIVE STRATEGY

Creative strategy deals with how an advertised product will appeal to its target market. The use of appeal techniques and the tone and style of an advertisement are the elements that stimulate interest in and desire for a product. The following section elaborates on some of the more common appeal techniques used in advertising today.

APPEAL TECHNIQUES

Positive Appeals

When positive appeals are used in advertising, the product promise and benefits (i.e., the primary reason for buying the product) are associated with the positive, enjoyable experience the product will bring to the consumer. The mood, tone, and style of the advertising are upbeat, and are intended to leave a favourable impression with the consumer.

Following are some examples of positive appeals:

1. *Canadian Egg Marketing Agency:*
   The "Get Crackin" campaign presented in rapid succession a delicious-looking selection of egg dishes.
2. *McDonald's Restaurants:*
   A young girl making her first purchase, independent of adults, is presented as having a positive experience. More recently, McDonald's has moved to a faster paced style of advertising that uses lots of music and the slogan "Food, folks and fun."
3. *London Life Insurance:*
   The "Freedom 55" campaign stressed the benefits of life insurance for the living, a unique approach in an industry that is strongly associated with the negative. The campaign illustrated living patterns that everyone, not just high-income earners, can enjoy through careful retirement planning.[4]

Negative Appeals

For negative appeals, the product promise and benefits are based on an experience the potential buyer can avoid by purchasing the advertised product or service. Very often, the use of "fear" is associated with negative appeals.

Following are examples of negative appeals:

1. *American Express Traveller's Cheques:*
   A variety of typical travel situations are presented in which the travellers lose their traveller's cheques. Their fear and anxiety are minimized when they find out how easily the cheques are replaced.

2. *Royal Trust:*
A commercial shows a distraught woman (recently widowed) pondering her personal financial situation now that her husband is gone. It is a strong message for the need to plan ahead financially.

Factual Appeals

In this appeal technique, the promise and benefits are presented in a straightforward, no-nonsense manner. The benefits are stated in a factual way. Proprietary medicines—such as cough and cold remedies, nasal sprays, and liniments that relieve the tension of aching muscles—are product categories for which a factual advertising approach is frequently used. Their appeal is to the rational buying motives of consumers, and they employ a no-nonsense, here's-what-the-product-does approach.

Telecom Canada's new campaign does just that. Using the theme "Long distance business sense," problem situations faced in business are presented and then resolved when the merits of long-distance telephone services are considered. Refer to figure 6.9 for an illustration.

Comparative Appeals

When comparative appeals are used, the benefits of the advertised product are presented through comparison of those attributes that the product shares with competitive brands—attributes which are important to the target market, usually the primary reason for consumers' buying the product. Comparative appeals can be indirect, in the form of a comparison with other unidentified leading brands, or direct, with the other brand mentioned by name.

In recent years, the use of comparative appeals has come to the foreground owing to campaigns dubbed as the "Cola Wars." The ongoing battles for softdrink supremacy have resulted in extended use of comparative-advertising appeals. In the "Un-cola wars," 7Up and Sprite did battle. In another arena, Nike uses the slogan "Just Do It," while Reebok, the arch rival, says, "Don't just do it.Do it right."

The decision to use a comparative campaign involves an element of risk. For the initiator, usually the number two brand in a market, comparative campaigns can be very expensive. To participate in a potential battle with a competitor requires long-term financial commitment from the initiator, since there is always the danger of retaliation by the market leader. For example, there is an on-going battle between Eveready and Duracell in the battery market, with both brands claiming they last longer than their rival.

This commitment factor demands that advertisers of a product analyze the competitive situation carefully prior to making the decision to proceed with a comparative campaign. Such campaigns, if used carefully, are effective in the following situations:

1. A new or unknown product needs public awareness; the comparison of the unknown product with the market leader has the effect of giving importance to the unknown product.

Figure 6.9 An advertisement that uses a factual approach while appealing to rational buying motives

CLIENT: NEWFOUNDLAND TELEPHONE
PRODUCT: Business Long Distance
TITLE: "Winning Team"
LENGTH: :30 sec. TV

LAURA: Michael, the
Martinson account is driving
me crazy...

MICHAEL: We were just
talking about that.

LAURA: They say they don't
see me enough. But I can't
make that trip every week.

REP: Have you thought
about team selling?

MICHAEL: Laura, this is
Sandy from Newfoundland
Telephone.

REP: What if you had a
partner here, a telephone
specialist we could help
train.

They phone your clients
once a week. You work as
a team.

LAURA: Makes sense.

ANNCR. VO: Long distance
business sense.

Getting close to your
customers can give you
the edge.

NEWFOUNDLAND TELEPHONE.

Courtesy: Telecom Canada

2. The goal is to plant doubts about a rival product. If the ad is convincing, loyal users of the competing product are likely to try the challenger at least once (trial purchase).

Avoid comparative ads when

1. The product benefit being compared is one of marginal interest.
2. The product's only advantage is price; rivals can neutralize the ad campaign simply by lowering their price.[5]

Humorous Appeals

When an advertiser uses humorous appeals, the promise and benefits of the product are presented in a light-hearted manner. The use of humorous appeals is often questioned by advertisers, since the campaign could suffer from premature wearout after few exposures: when the humour is familiar, it is no longer funny. Also, the use of humour allows for a great deal of creative latitude, and some advertisers argue that the humour gets more attention than the product. If the brand-name recall is low after research testing, the problem is often attributed to the excessive use of humour in the advertising for the brand.

Although there are disadvantages in using humorous appeals, many products have been successful with them. These successes would indicate that humorous appeals can be persuasive in getting customers to take the desired action. Very often, campaigns using humour require that the strategy be used in a pool of commercials.

Following are some examples of ad campaigns that use humour:

1. ***Fibreglass Pink Insulation (Fibreglass Canada Inc.):***
   Fibreglass Pink uses Don Cherry (of Hockey Night in Canada and Grapevine fame) and his dog, Blue, in its latest television and radio spots. In typical Don Cherry style, the vocal portions of the ads are humorous, if not outrageous.
2. ***Anacin***:
   Same family, different presenter. In a more subtle form of humour, Anacin uses Rose Cherry (wife of Don) to pitch the merits of fast pain relief. She indicates that, for her, headaches are frequent (the perils of living with Don and Blue), saying, "I know headaches, and having someone talk your ear off for 35 years doesn't make it any easier."

Emotional Appeals

Advertisers who use emotional appeals successfully are doing so by arousing the feelings of the audience, or by showing the psychological satisfaction that can be gained by using the product.

Following are some examples of advertisements that use emotional appeals:

1. **Michelin Tires**:
   The ad shows a small baby in diapers, rotating in a Michelin radial tire. A male and female voiceover (the voices of the parents) discuss the safety aspects of Michelin tires, arriving at

the inevitable conclusion that they should purchase Michelin tires.

2. ***Diamonds are Forever***:
   Televison commercials promoting the purchase of diamonds for those very special occasions appeal directly to the consumer's heart by showing the loving relationships between happily married couples.

Sexual Appeals

The use of sexual appeals in certain product categories has become increasingly popular in recent years. For product categories such as cosmetics, colognes, perfumes, and lingerie, sex is used as an effective motivator.

Calvin Klein has been accused of aggressively using sex to sell its products, particularly its line of designer blue jeans. More recently, the company has been criticized for its "Obsession" campaign (male and female colognes). See figure 6.10 for an illustration. Rightly or wrongly, the company continues to use sex because the products are selling well.

Courtney and Whipple, in their research findings, report that

> An attractive, sexy, or nude female can increase the attention getting power of an ad, especially among male audiences. Under some complex conditions, that model may increase favourable evaluations of the brand and intentions to buy it.[6]

The research goes on to state that the attractiveness of the model and her appropriateness to the advertised product is what commands attention. Clearly, however, explicit sexuality increases the risks for the advertiser, since it may alienate some consumers. Labatt's Dry beer used sexual appeals in its "La Goddess" series of commercials. In one commercial, a man enters the bar, quickly scans the room, and zeroes in on "La Goddess," who is seated at the bar smiling, and striking a rather provocative pose.

Lifestyle Appeals

Advertisers who use lifestyle-appeal techniques are attempting to associate their brand with the lifestyle of a certain target audience. This type of appeal is part of Pepsi-Cola's claim and slogan "The choice of a new generation." Refer to figure 6.11, a magazine advertisement for Pepsi-Cola. Background information on that campaign is as follows:

1. ***Advertising Direction***:
   Music and entertainment celebrity endorsements
2. ***Creative Objectives***:
   To build Pepsi's contemporary brand image
3. ***Creative Strategy***:
   a) To use growing consumer interest in contemporary music and entertainment, and capitalize on the emerging trend of rock videos

Figure 6.10 An advertisement that uses a sexual-appeal technique

Courtesy: Calvin Klein Ltd.

Figure 6.11   An advertisement that demonstrates a contemporary image through life-style associations (target market 18-34 years, male emphasis)

PEPSI. THE CHOICE OF A NEW GENERATION.

Courtesy: Pepsi-Cola Canada Ltd. and J. Walter Thompson Canada Ltd. Reprinted with permission.

        b) To build strong association between Pepsi and contemporary music/entertainment in advertising, promotion, tour sponsorships, and point-of-sale material

    4. *Target Market*:

        Eighteen to 34 years of age, with emphasis on teen males.[7]

The Pepsi-Cola campaign uses celebrities such as Michael Jackson, Lionel Ritchie, Glen Frey, and Don Johnson in television commercials.

The key to the success of this type of campaign is in the association. If an individual feels him- or herself to be part of the advertised trend, in this case a more youthful generation, then he or she is likely to purchase the product, even if only on a trial basis.

Lifestyle appeals are becoming increasingly popular, owing to the greater availability of psychographic information about Canadian consumers. However, lifestyle advertising is problematic in that it involves little attempt to differentiate one brand from another. Usually, the advertisements focus on the lifestyles of the target market, instead of on the product benefits. For products such as beer and soft drinks, where competing brands are comparable in quality, the overuse of lifestyle advertising by many brands creates a situation in which any one brand can only benefit marginally from its use.

CREATIVE EXECUTION

Once the strategy has been developed, the creative team must decide how to best present the product so that the message will have maximum impact on the target market. Creative execution deals more specifically with tactical considerations and is the stage where ideas are converted into reality. Some of the more commonly used presentation tactics are testimonials, endorsements, product-as-hero tactics, product demonstrations, torture tests, and product comparisons.

Testimonials

In a **testimonial ad**, a typical user of the product presents the message. Since real people are used, as opposed to professional models and celebrities, the message is usually perceived as believable, even though the presenter works from a carefully prepared script. Procter and Gamble Canada Ltd. has used testimonials effectively for Tide in the company's "Could-you-write-a-commercial-for-Tide?" campaign. Numerous creative executions were developed for this strategy. The use of third-party endorsements enhances the credibility of the advertising claims. Refer to figure 6.12, an advertisement for Ontario Hydro, for an example of a testimonial ad.

Endorsements

An **endorsement** essentially amounts to a celebrity testimonial, whereby the advertiser is attempting to capitalize on the popularity of a "star." Television and movie personalities, along with music and sports stars, form the basis of celebrity endorsements. Some of the more prominent celebrities endorsing products today are Bo Jackson for Nike and Pepsi-Cola, Michael Jordan for Nike and Coca-Cola, and Joe Montana for L.A. Gear products.

In this age of more sophisticated consumers, the advertiser must be very careful if it selects this method of presenting its product. It must be careful about who it selects to present the product. According to research conducted by the Creative Research Group in Toronto,

Figure 6.12   An advertisement that uses the testimonial approach

"The heat pump's meant a lot to our store in terms of both air flow and cash flow."

John Prinzen, Owner/Manager, Stamford Pro Hardware, Niagara Falls

"We've had the dual-fuel heat pump system almost four years now, since we opened our new store here. It's been great. Heating, cooling and saving us money.

"We have a similar system at home and it works so well that we wanted one for the store too.

"The system costs less to heat and cool than other systems because it makes more efficient use of energy, switching between gas and electricity.

"It's easy to service and maintain so that cuts operating costs and down-time. It's also flexible. You can relocate it if your store changes or gets bigger.

"We didn't think of it at first, but there are no roof openings so no one can get into the store through the roof.

"Sum it up? I'd have to say we're very comfortable with it. And it keeps our customers very comfortable too."

For more information on how a dual-fuel heat pump can benefit your business, contact: Ontario Hydro, Commercial Marketing Department, 700 University Avenue.

1-800-263-9000

Ontario Hydro

Courtesy: Ontario Hydro

Advertising in Action
Corporate Pitch Men

"Shaves close as a blade, or your money back." Who said that famous line? If you said Victor Kiam, you are right! Victor Kiam is one of the best known of the corporate executives now doing television commercials for their own products. His are the Remington products. The other well-known executive is David Nichol of Loblaw's fame.

Back to Victor. He is best known as the bathrobe-clad huckster who liked the Remington shaver so much he bought the company. He is also known as the gizmo and gadget man of personal-care products, having added a string of new products to the Remington line-up. The new products included Fuzz Away, a device for removing pills and fuzz from sweaters and other garments; the Smooth 'n Silky women's shaver; the Right Angle beard and mustache trimmer, and even a machine-washable neck tie.

Kiam leapt from salesperson (of Pepsodent and Playtex bras) to corporate bailout artist in 1979 when he used $750 000 of his own money to launch a $25 million leveraged buyout of Remington. Only 10 years later Remington is the world's second largest producer of electric shavers. Along the way, Kiam's advertising efforts have given him celebrity status—he is seen in scores of commercials around the world, peddling his wares in at least 15 different languages.

Kiam is a very successful man, and advertising helped launch that success. His most successful enterprise is probably himself, an enterprise built on his own persona. He is an author of the best-selling book *Go For It! How to Succeed as an Entrepreneur*, and on the banquet circuit he commands and gets a $25 000 public speaking fee.

Among the concerns that come with using an executive as a spokesperson is whether the executive is believable and can deliver a unique message. This is hardly a concern of Kiam's. He candidly states, "If a commercial is going to be successful, the individual has to say something no one else can say." And what does the advertising industry think of the Kiam style of advertising? Apparently, everyone is not a fan. The Canadian trade publication *AdWeek* gave Kiam its "badvertising award" in 1985.

Loblaw Companies Limited started using David Nichol for entirely different reasons back in the early 1970s. David Nichol is a recognizable figure in Canadian households due solely to his on-camera appearances to promote the merits of shopping at Loblaws. Why did he get into the advertising game? Loblaws had been using actor William Shatner (of Captain Kirk and "Star Trek" fame) as its primary spokesperson, but needed a way to counter the perceptions of Loblaws that were left by a vicious price war with its rivals—A&P, Dominion and Steinbergs. Loblaws had come out of the price war with a high-price image. Nichol figured that the most convincing way to tell people that Loblaw's prices were right would be to have the guy whose job was on the line do it. Turns out, he was right!

His first script was quite to the point: "If you were the president of Loblaws, would you go on TV and say you had the lowest prices if it weren't true?" So successful were the commercials, Loblaws stopped using its advertising agency and developed its own commercials in-house. A studio was built next to Nichol's office This move produced significant cost savings.

continued

Nichol wrote all the scripts and filmed them a dozen or so at a time at a cost of about $1500 apiece—a neat and tidy operation, to say the least! His commercials have covered everything from corporate image and President's Choice products to no-name products and "green" products.

And what about fame and success? Well, the company promoted Nichol in 1985, and he stopped doing the commercials for a while, but by then, he says, "We had gone from having the worst price image, to the best." More recently he has been the chief presenter in the print medium for Loblaw's *Insider's Report*, a publication extolling the merits of product lines that Loblaws imports from around the world—products that offer good value to their shoppers—and he is back on television extolling the virtues of Loblaw's environmentally-friendly products.

Adapted from Mark Evans, "Star CEOs get in the picture," *Financial Post*, August 11, 1990, pp.1,4, and from Gerry Blackwell, "The Italian ladies point and stare," *Canadian Business*, November 1988, pp.88, 100, and from Bertrand Marotte, "Victor Kiam and the American Way," *Financial Times*, October 30, 1989, p.3.

heroes put before an informed public will lose some credibility because the consumer is more inclined to recognize that the spokesperson is being well paid to endorse the product.[8]

Another problem associated with using celebrity endorsements is overexposure for the celebrity. A celebrity who represents numerous products may not be readily identified with any one product.

In a related form of testimonial and endorsement advertising, chief executive officers of big corporations are becoming celebrities in their own right. For more details read the Advertising in Action feature "Corporate Pitch Men."

Product as Hero

In the case of **product-as-hero** presentation tactics, the advertiser presents a problem situation (i.e., using negative appeal strategy) which is quickly resolved when the product comes to the rescue. The advertisers of Glad Garbage Bags have used this technique effectively for many years. In many commercials, other brands of garbage bags are shown ripping open, leaving a mess. The obvious message is that the use of Glad Bags prevents such situations from happening. In this example, the execution effectively dramatizes the durability of the Glad product.

Product Demonstrations

The use of **demonstrations** is quite common in advertising centred on the performance of the product. Several execution options are available to the advertiser. For example, a "before-and-after" scenario is a strategy commonly used for diet-related products, where the message implies usage by the presenter. Such a technique is suitable for both print and television media, although with television the technique is much more effective. A second strategy is to simply demonstrate the product at work—a technique commonly used for advertising household products such as oven cleaners, tub and tile cleaners, and floor wax. Typically, such advertisements show how easy the product is to use.

Torture Tests

In a **torture test**, the product is exposed to exaggerated punishment or abuse in order to substantiate a product claim that is known to be of interest to consumers. The Timex watch campaign showing that the product "Takes a licking and keeps on ticking" is perhaps the classic case of creative execution that uses torture testing. In a demonstration of strength, Krazy Glue shows a workman hanging upside down from a steel girder. The only thing holding up the man is the glue. Torture tests tend to be exaggerated, but they do leave a lasting impression.

Product Comparisons

Although already dealt with in more detail in the creative-strategy section of this chapter, a few execution considerations regarding product comparisons should be considered here. To be used successfully, the attribute singled out for comparison must be of value or highly interesting to the target market. So as not to mislead the consumer in the message, the competitor must be identified fairly and properly, and the advertiser must be able to substantiate its claims with independent, objective research. Legal and ethical considerations aside, comparative advertising, if used properly, can present a convincing argument to consumers.

CREATIVE EXECUTION—PRE-PRODUCTION

With creative strategy and tactical details confirmed, attention shifts to the production requirements of the campaign. Production requirements are determined by media usage. For example, storyboards must be prepared for television, scripts for both radio and television, and rough layouts and designs for print advertisements.

Very often, the content of the ad, if not the budget, restricts or makes necessary the use of certain media. For example, demonstrations are effective on television, while factual details are best left to magazines and newspapers. If sales-promotion activity is to be part of the creative execution, a media mix may be required, with broadcast media being used for building awareness and print media being used to communicate details.

In addition, the pre-production stage should review any mandatory items that must appear in an advertisement or commercial. These might be the use of product or company logos in a certain place, suggestions for scenes and settings for a commercial, or directions as to whether the execution is to be consistent or different from creative used in the past.

Summary

The creative-planning process involves five distinct stages: detailing relevant marketing and product background; identifying creative objectives, strategies, and execution details; and, finally, evaluating creative recommendations.

Compiling background on the market and the product is the responsibility of the client and a necessary step that enables the agency to proceed with creative development. In determining creative objectives (i.e., what to communicate) and creative strategies (i.e., how to communicate), advertisers must evaluate various factors. These factors include product characteristics and related benefits such as price and reputation; the target market and why it buys; and competitive activity.

Creative objectives are closely linked to the product objectives and positioning statement included in the marketing plan/advertising plan. Creative strategy is the responsibility of the agency, and is concerned with tone, style, and appeal techniques. Some common appeal techniques are positive and negative approaches, the use of factual information, competitor comparisons, humour, emotion, sex, and lifestyle appeals.

In terms of creative execution, the primary concern is to make an impact on the target market. Considerations in this area include whether to use testimonials, endorsements, product-as-hero tactics, demonstrations, or characters. The final stage, creative evaluation, involves client-management's appraising and approving (or disapproving) of the agency's creative recommendations. It may also involve conducting consumer research to evaluate the potential impact the advertisement or campaign will have on the target market.

Review Questions

1. What are the five stages in the creative-planning process?
2. Identify and briefly describe the components of creative-objective statements.
3. What is the basic difference between creative strategy and creative execution?
4. What is meant by the "managerial approach" to evaluating creative output?
5. Identify and briefly explain the factors that influence the development of creative objectives and strategies.
6. What purpose do creative-objective and creative-strategy statements serve?
7. Briefly describe the appeal techniques commonly used in advertising.
8. Explain the difference between the following creative tactics:
   i) testimonials and endorsements
   ii) product demonstrations and product-as-hero tactics

Discussion Questions

1. Review the vignette "Corporate Pitch Men." What is your opinion of business executives being used as spokespersons for their products. Is it an effective strategy or not? Refer to examples other than those cited in the text to substantiate your opinion.

2. The "managerial approach" to evaluating creative was discussed in the chapter. Do you think this activity by the client impedes the creative process in the advertising agency? Discuss.

3. "Humorous advertising campaigns are effective in the short term, but do little to achieve long-term objectives for a product or service." Agree or disagree. Cite some specific examples to substantiate your position.

Creating Print and Broadcast Advertising

CHAPTER 7

In studying this chapter, you will learn

- The role of the creative team in developing the creative concept
- The roles and responsibilities of the copywriter and art director
- The design principles and creative considerations for developing print and broadcast advertising
- The various types of print layout options
- The functions of the various sections of a television commercial
- The production stages of television and radio commercials

This chapter examines in greater detail the execution stage of the creative-development process. Focusing on the differences between print and broadcast media, it examines the roles of the copywriter and art director, and how they interact with each other. Finally, some of the techniques they use to develop ads for the various media are presented.

A significant amount of a client's advertising budget can be tied up in production expenses. The combination of production expenses and the high cost of media time and space places pressure on the agency to produce creative that sells the client's product or service. Theoretically, the various elements of an advertisement or commercial must work together effectively to present a convincing message. In essence, the message must create a favourable impression in the mind of a consumer, as quickly as possible. For those who earn a living developing advertising and commercial concepts for written media, the challenge is to stop readers at a certain page, to make them *read* the headline and then *progress* through the advertisement. With television, the task is to keep viewers in the room and mentally alert during commercial breaks. To understand how these challenges are met, one must first understand the communications process itself.

THE COMMUNICATIONS PROCESS

An overview of the communications process is presented diagrammatically in figure 7.1. The process begins with a *sender* (in this case the advertiser) who develops a message to be transmitted by the *media* (television, radio, magazine, newspaper) to a *receiver* (the consumer or business user).

It must be recognized that competitive products may also be sending similar messages to the same target market. This is referred to as **noise**. If the message can break through the noise of competitive messages, and if it is relevant to the receiver (i.e., if its benefits satisfy a need), then the product may become a preferred alternative. In this case, *positive feedback* comes in the form of a purchase of the product. However, if the message cannot break through the noise (if it is dull, uses the wrong appeal techniques, or is misunderstood by the target), there is little chance that the product it

Figure 7.1 The communications process

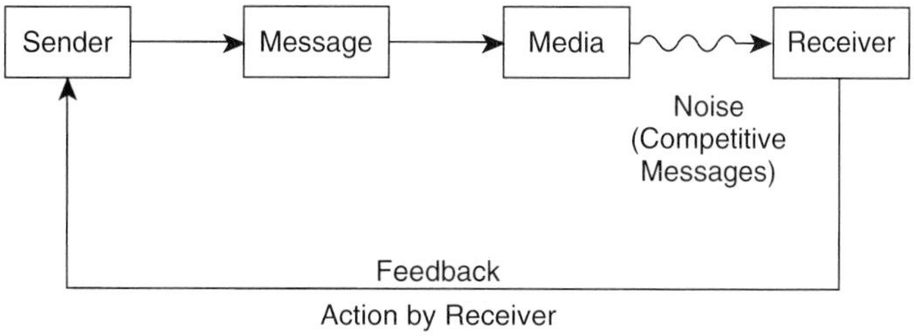

advertises will be bought. This is a form of negative feedback, and it indicates that creative strategy needs to be re-evaluated.

Studies have been conducted into how advertising messages influence consumer behaviour. Such studies determine advertising's effect on the various behavioural stages an individual passes through before making a purchase decision. The theories so developed are referred to as **hierarchy-of-effects models**, and are very similar to the AIDA formula that is strongly associated with personal selling. (AIDA refers to Attention, Interest, Desire, and Action.)

DAGMAR is a theoretical model that helps advertisers examine the effect advertising has on the decision-making process of consumers. DAGMAR is an acronym for Designing Advertising Goals, Measuring Advertising Results. It was a research study originally sponsored by the Association of National Advertisers (a U.S. association) and written by Russell H. Calley. According to Calley, it is difficult to directly link advertising to sales; what can be measured is how well the message communicates. That is to say, the effectiveness of the message in getting attention, gaining awareness, and stimulating consumers' interest in and preference for a particular product—this can be measured and evaluated. The evaluation is important not only as a measure of the performance of an individual ad, but also as a measure of its performance in relation to competing ads. An advertisement that succeeds in all of these respects increases the likelihood that consumers will purchase the product advertised. As a consequence, clients and advertising agencies conduct extensive consumer research to evaluate advertising. The results of research do offer suggestions on how to improve the quality of the message.

Calley states that individuals pass through four behavioural stages: *awareness*, *comprehension*, *conviction*, and *action*.

Awareness   In the awareness stage, the customer learns of something for the first time. Obviously this learning can only occur if one is exposed to a new advertisement.

Comprehension   By the comprehension stage, interest has been created. The message is perceived as relevant, and the product, judged from the information presented, is considered useful. The product becomes part of the customer's frame of reference.

Conviction   The customer's evaluation of the product's benefits (as presented in the advertising) leads to a decision. The product is viewed as satisfactory, and has gained preference in the customer's mind. The customer may be sufficiently motivated to buy the product.

Action   In this stage, the desired active response occurs. For example, a car advertisement may motivate a customer to visit a dealer's showroom; a coupon may motivate a reader to clip it out for more information or for use in an initial purchase.

Role of the Creative Team

A common practice among advertising agencies is to have a copywriter and art director work together under the supervision of a creative director as a "creative team." This team is responsible for developing the advertising concepts for a group of clients and their products. One benefit of the team approach is that the team becomes familiar with clients' products and needs and comes to understand the idiosyncracies and expectations of the client executives who must approve the team's creative recommendations. Perhaps the greatest benefit of the team concept, though, is that it provides consistency to campaigns that stretch over an extended period of time. The creative team includes a copywriter, an art director, and a creative director.

Copywriter The **copywriter** is responsible for developing the headline, the body copy, and the signature (i.e., the combination of logo and slogan) in a print ad, and the script in a broadcast advertisement.

Art Director The **art director** is responsible for developing the layout (the overall "look" of the ad) through the use of photographic and line-drawn illustrations in print, and storyboards in television. (A **storyboard** is a series of sequential frames that indicates the development of a television commercial.)

Creative Director The **creative director** is the administrative head of the creative department, responsible for motivating copywriters and art directors and maintaining the quality standards of the agency's creative recommendations. (The creative director may also perform copywriting and art-direction functions.)

The teamwork approach is important here for two reasons. First, a half-hearted effort will destroy the "total ad." Second, the team members are judged solely on the quality of their work, so rising within the organization—acquiring higher status, bigger accounts, and recognition by one's peers—is directly linked to effort. In summary, the copywriter and art director must complement each other, appreciate each other's talents, and enjoy working together as a professional team.

For some practical insight into the challenges and successes of a creative director, refer to the Advertising in Action feature "A Creative Master."

The creative team develops the creative concept or central theme/idea (as it is often referred to in the marketing plan, the advertising plan, or both). The **creative concept** is the basic selling message an ad attempts to communicate to a consumer. In the case of Telecom Canada, the central theme was that "long distance telephone makes good business sense." From this central theme, the copywriter and art director developed a series of commercials and print advertisements (e.g., different problems and situations would have been presented, but the solution remained the same—long distance).

It is the creative execution, in both print and broadcast, that brings these themes to life. When the concept or theme is established, the creative team develops the appropriate combination of copy and illustration, trying to devise an effective means of conveying the concept or theme. Refer to the Telecom Canada advertisement in figure 7.2 ."(p. 204)"

Purpose of Creative Concept (Central Theme)

The creative concept serves four basic purposes. It provides clues as to how to attract attention, it can clarify the product's key benefit, establish its uniqueness, and help position the product in the customer's mind.

Advertising in Action
A Creative Master

In Canadian advertising circles, Brian Harrod stands out as the master of art direction. So successful has he been that he is the undisputed role model for all young creative types. A tribute to his success is that he is one of the very few people to have risen from the ranks of art direction to lead an entire advertising agency. Brian Harrod is the Harrod of Harrod and Mirlin, a medium-sized advertising agency based in Toronto.

Within the industry he is admired by colleagues—described as remarkable, amazing and incredible by fellow art directors, copywriters, photographers, and film directors. How did he reach such lofty status? His success stems from an overwhelming desire to achieve, and from attributes such as dedication, discipline, and natural inclination. What follows is a brief look at a man who has done more than just survive in the jungle of advertising.

Harrod and Mirlin is a highly respected agency admired for its creative flare. Accounts are blue chip and include Christie Brown and Company, Nabob, Levi Strauss, Nabisco, and Moosehead Breweries. Some of these accounts have been with Brian since his very early days in advertising with McCann-Erickson. The agency was started with the financial assistance of one of the largest conglomerates in the advertising world—the Interpublic Group (New York), which also owns Brian's former agency, McCann-Erickson.

It was Brian's entrepreneurial instincts and desire for freedom to be honest that prompted him to form his own agency. Both he and his copywriting partner, Ian Mirlin, did not want to be subject to the whims of accountants and other business-oriented executives who weren't as committed to the profession of advertising as they were. His first attempt at breaking away from the big agencies was in 1985 when he left McCann to join Miller Myers Bruce DallaCosta as a partner. The addition of a Harrod and a Mirlin made this the longest agency name in the country, and it caused problems internally. After a frustrating few years as low man on the totem pole, the offer came in from Interpublic to form a new agency—an offer that couldn't be refused.

Harrod and Mirlin started small. Beginning as a staff of four, the team is now composed of 50 hard-working individuals. The owners—or at any rate, those to whom the names on the letterhead belong—are in a unique position with Interpublic. They do not really own the company but have the power to make all decisions—not just the creative decisions. They are responsible for their own destiny. Harrod views this situation as a big plus. "What tends to happen if you finance it yourself is that all you worry about is money. Instead of what you do best."

Despite much success and countless awards for creativity, Brian is his own biggest critic. About his own agency he candidly states, "I believe that right now our agency is not doing as good work as it should." Now that's being honest! On the subject of Canadian advertising, he is equally candid: "Canadian creative has never been as bad as it is now." For proof, he points to the industry's lack of representation among winners of North American and International advertising awards. Again on the subject of his own agency, he says, "I think we're doing good work by Canadian standards, but that was never our intention. I always envisioned this agency doing some of the most outstanding advertising in North America." To clients already satisfied, this should come as good news—the best is yet to come!

What has made Brian successful? His colleagues have offered some insight.

Brian Kay, the agency's director of account services, has been associated with Brian since the mid-70s when they both worked at McCann-Erickson. Kay states that "Brian was a better account guy than I was." He understood the client and got right into every aspect of their business and their problems.

Ian Mirlin, his long-time partner in creative collaboration, admires Brian's energy (he is a fitness fanatic who walks 12 flights of stairs to reach the office every day). He is always doing ads—on napkins in restaurants, on slips of paper in airports—the mind is always grinding away. Mirlin adds that Brian is a driven man, obsessed with the need to over-achieve, perceiving that failure is just below the surface.

Dennis Huggett, vice president of business development at Christie, likes the way Brian immerses himself in the client's business. At Christie, "he got right into the long term planning, and over the years has been involved in the conception of several new products. Trust builds with this kind of relationship."

In a business of inflated egos, modesty is another characteristic Brian possesses. He keeps a low profile, shuns the local watering holes popular with others in advertising, and stays away from the awards galas. With clients, he maintains his composure and rarely gets angry (at least not on the surface) when the client pecks away at his creative ingenuity. He admits there are times when he should be tougher with a client, but gentle persuasion and open negotiation are more to his liking.

What about advertising bothers Brian Harrod? As art director extraordinaire, he is driven crazy by "ads that use visuals to repeat what the headline says." Last-minute focus groups initiated by the client when creative is finally ready for approval are another real sore spot. At a time when highly paid client executives should be earning their keep, they bail out, letting a focus group make the big decision. Regarding research, Brian agrees with its use as completely as possible prior to starting the creative. "If you do any research at all it should be just as a disaster check."

Yes, Brian has survived in the ad game and he will undoubtedly prosper for many years to come. Of his various accomplishments, he is particularly proud of his tutoring of up and coming young art directors. He is even more proud of the impact he has had on Christie advertising. Consumers trust Christie, and that trust is largely due to the style and voice of Christie advertising over the years— advertising that originated in the creative mind of Brian Harrod.

Adapted from Pat Annesley, "The life of Brian," *Marketing*, October 29, 1990, pp.24,28.

Attracting Attention The finished advertisement or commercial must grab the customer's attention quickly, while communicating the key benefit. The advertising illustration in figure 7.3 communicates the most important feature of the Toshiba Turbo copier—it operates at two speeds. It is the action-oriented visual that grabs your attention first. The visual works well with the headline, so the reader can grasp the message quickly.

Figure 7.2 An advertisement that shows how the telephone can be used to resolve business problems

CLIENT: BELL CANADA
PRODUCT: Business Long Distance
TITLE: "Point Of No Returns"
LENGTH: :30 sec. TV

JEFF: This is the eighth
return in three days, Paul!

PAUL: Look, I bust my butt
trying to sell this stuff...
JEFF: Yeah, and as soon as you
sell them they get returned.
PAUL: It's gotta be the
instructions.

SECRETARY: Excuse me,
the Bell rep's here.

REP: Hi.
JEFF: Look, I don't really
think talking to Bell can
help me right now.

PAUL: Wouldn't mind talking
to the people who keep
returning this new product
of ours.

REP: Why don't you have
them call you? Put an 800
number on everything.
Packaging, instructions...
it's easier for them to call
and find out how the thing
works, than it is to return it.

PAUL: Makes sense.
ANNCR. VO: Long distance
business sense.

Call us.

Courtesy: Telecom Canada

Figure 7.3   A visually effective advertising message

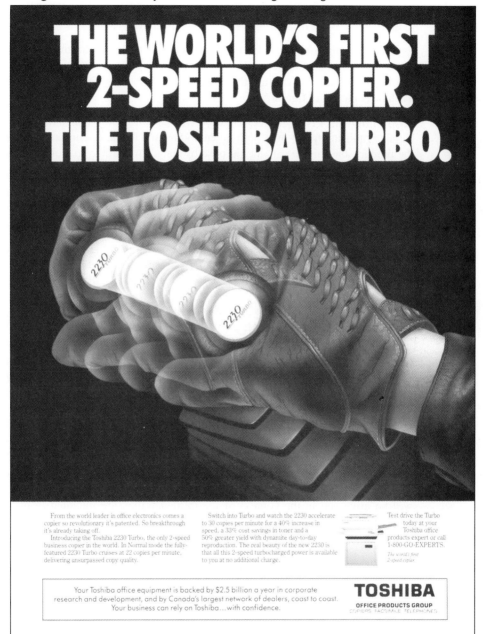

Courtesy: Toshiba of Canada Limited, Office Products Group

Clarifying the Key Benefit Where necessary, the key benefit can be elaborated on by substantiating any promises or claims made in the advertisement. This task is generally accomplished by the illustration and body copy.

Establishing Uniqueness Ads must be unique and work only for the advertised product. Every effort should be made to avoid similarity between competitive messages, for such similarity may confuse the consumer. Note the way details are clarified in the Toshiba copier ad in figure 7.3.

Positioning the Product To make an impression on the consumer, the product should dominate the ad. It is not uncommon for the theme or concept to overshadow the product, but this defeats the purpose of the ad. According to Robert Levenson, a former creative director with Doyle Dane Bernbach (New York),

> If you fall in love with the brilliance of a commercial, take the product out. If it's still brilliant, it's no good. The commercial should crumple when its reason for existence is taken away.[1]

In the maze of competitive advertising, the central theme of an advertisment serves as the means of presenting a product's benefits more persuasively.

PRINT ADVERTISING

In print advertising, the central idea is primarily conveyed through the headline and visual illustration. Both elements work together to produce a single message. As a unit, the headline and illustration must attract attention and create sufficient interest so that the reader moves on to the body copy, which, in turn, must sufficiently amplify on the promise made in the headline or illustration.

The Copywriting Function

The major areas of concern for the copywriter are the headline and subheadlines, the body copy, and the signature elements of an advertisement. Each of these elements will be discussed in the context of the influence they are intended to have on the reader.

Headlines The primary purpose of the headline is to command the attention of the reader. According to David Ogilvy (Ogilvy & Mather Advertising, New York), "Headlines get five times the readership of the body copy. If your headline doesn't sell, you have wasted your money."[2] There is no magic formula for distinguishing a good headline from a bad headline, but some research indicates that short headlines are more effective than long. These conclusions are somewhat consistent with the readership patterns of average consumers, who tend to scan ads and only stop if something grabs their attention—the headline!

To attract the attention of readers, various types of headlines are commonly used. They are as follows:

1. *Promise* This type of headline (obviously) makes a promise to the reader. Other copy, or illustrations, substantiate the promise.

   Four Seasons Hotel: "A Good Hotel Reacts to Your Requests, a Grand Hotel Anticipates Them"
   Toshiba Office Products: "Reliability runs in the Toshiba family"

2. *Curiosity* This type of headline tries to make the reader inquisitive enough to seek more information (to look for an explanation).

   Blue Nun Wine: "The Nun Who Came to an Intimate Evening"

   Beatrice Light Yoghurt: "Once You've Tasted Less, You'll Want More"

3. *How To* This type of headline is similar to a promise but is presented in a different way. The headline subtly suggests that the ad copy will provide the consumer with a way to save, or a way to improve, or a way to be generally better off.

   Kraft Barbecue Sauces: "How to Teach an Old Dog New Tricks"

4. *News* A news headline expresses urgency or a situation of importance to the reader. Words commonly used in news headlines are "Introducing!," "Here Now!," "Finally!"

   Digital Equipment of Canada Ltd.: "Digital Has It Now"
   Canadian Imperial Bank of Commerce: "Introducing the Commerce Self-Directed RRSP"

5. *Command* A command headline politely makes a request of the reader.

   Head & Shoulders Conditioning Shampoo: "Try New Head & Shoulders Conditioning Shampoo"
   Libby's Baked Beans: "Taste What's New from Libby's Beans"

Subheadlines A subheadline (subhead) is a smaller headline that amplifies the main point of a headline. It makes it possible to keep the headline short, and acts as a breaker between the headline and the body copy. It is more common, however, to take the reader directly from the headline to the body copy and/or illustration. The Toshiba facsimile advertisement in figure 7.4 exemplifies the use of a subheadline and all of the other elements of an advertisement. Note how the subheadlines in this advertisement help maintain interest and move readers into the more detailed body copy.

Body Copy The **body copy** is the informative or persuasive prose that elaborates on the central theme of the advertisement. The body copy helps create preference by providing information the consumer needs as a basis for making a purchase decision. Body copy is the substantiation—the proof of promise or product claims. It is a device that integrates headline with illustration. In the Toshiba advertisement in figure 7.4, the body copy explains the three benefits presented in the subheadline.

Figure 7.4 An advertisement demonstrating the transition from headline to subheadline to body copy

Courtesy: Toshiba of Canada Limited, Office Products Group

Carefully worded body copy also promotes action on the part of the consumer. In the Toshiba advertisement (figure 7.4), the reference to the 1-800 telephone number is an attempt to promote immediate action.

There are three different types of body copy commonly used in print advertising:

1. **"Reason-Why" Copy** This is straightforward copy relating the product's benefits to customers' needs. Typically, a reason-why headline resolves a problem the reader may encounter.

2. **Dialogue Copy** In the case of dialogue copy, the message is delivered from a spokesperson's point of view (i.e., in the form of a testimonial or endorsement).

Figure 7.5 A copy-oriented message

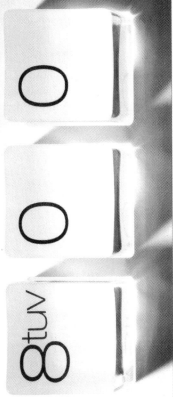

These three numbers can help you win the battle for business.

In the 90's, business will be won or lost on an increasingly important aspect of your business: customer service.

Those who ensure customer satisfaction will create loyal, repeat business, which in turn, translates into higher volume, market share and profit.

NBTel 800 Service is a powerful advantage that keeps the lines of communication open from sale to delivery to product support.

A SATISFIED CUSTOMER IS A REPEAT CUSTOMER

Research shows that frustrated customers are more likely to switch to the competition than complain. However, these same customers say they'd likely to give repeat business to any operation that resolves their problems quickly. With a toll-free 800 number, your customers have easy and direct access, helping them to solve their small problems before they become big enough to drive their business away.

IMPROVE YOUR CUSTOMER SERVICE BEFORE AND AFTER THE SALE

When you promote an 800 number on your packaging and advertising, you give your customers the opportunity to phone you directly. You'll be able to quickly answer questions about price, selection and delivery.

After the sale, you'll be able to answer questions about assembly, operation, repairs and warranty—all in a friendly, efficient manner.

At the same time, you can take advantage of this direct customer contact by encouraging and taking new orders.

TOLL-FREE FAX MEANS BETTER CUSTOMER SERVICE

In addition, with 800 Service, you have the option of offering your customers toll-free facsimile service.

Your customers in Canada, the US and Overseas will be able to contact you instantly, however they choose.

As global competition becomes more intense, this advantage will give you the edge you need to succeed.

WINNING THE BATTLE FOR BUSINESS

In the coming decade, the battle for business will be redefined. And those who understand the importance of customer service will be the victors.

To find out more about 800 Service and how it can give you every advantage on the new global playing field, call 1-800-567-7000 ext. 22. And discover how 800 Service makes good business sense.

1-800-567-7000
Ext. 22

Long Distance Business Sense.

NBTel

Nationwide Communications through Telecom Canada

Dialogue copy can stand alone, but it is commonly integrated with other types of copy.

3. **Narrative Copy** With narrative copy, the message is presented in the third person. Using this type of copy can be problematic; it must be very good to hold the reader's attention.

How long should body copy be? Advertising practitioners have varying opinions on this subject. Generally, people read more of the copy if they are interested in the product or the idea communicated in the advertisement. People accept and read advertising messages more readily when trying to decide on a major purchase. The body copy provides the information that helps the consumer decide. Refer to the Telecom Canada advertisement in figure 7.5 for an illustration of this principle.

Three general rules have been established regarding the length of body copy, but it should be kept in mind that the creative team does not have to follow rules to develop persuasive advertising.

1. Short copy is most appropriate for image advertising. The illustration plays a key role in portraying a certain image, and lengthy copy would detract from it.
2. Purchase value has a bearing on copy length. The higher the cost of the product or service, the more likely that the consumer will use advertising as a source of information, and thus more copy is necessary.
3. Copy for new products may be longer than copy for established products. More copy is needed in the informative stage of advertising than in the retentive stage, where short messages are used to remind consumers of product benefits.

Signature The final copy element in a print advertisement is the signature. Often referred to as a **tagline**, the signature can include a company or product logo and a product or company slogan. A logo or logotype refers to the distinctive copy style that identifies the company or product. Logos are used in advertising to provide a common corporate identity to all products of a multi-product firm (e.g., a corporate logo appears in all ads for individual products). The purpose of the signature is to achieve the following:

1. To summarize the concept or central theme of the advertisement. For example, the logo and slogan can reinforce a key benefit or reinforce a company position that applies to several products.
2. To position the product in the customer's mind. For example, the logo and slogan will appear in all forms of advertising and be a selling message in itself. Recognizing that readers may pass over body copy entirely, the signature must leave an impression with the consumer. In addition, the signature provides continuity from one advertisement to another.

The purpose of slogans is illustrated in the examples below and in figures 7.2 through 7.5 (where their relationship to the other elements of the advertisements can also be seen).

- "Your business can rely on Toshiba...with confidence."
- "Bell...Answering your call."

- "Jaguar...The Blending of Art and Machine."
- "The ultimate driving experience...BMW."
- "Apple...The power to be your best."

The Art-Direction Function

The primary responsibility of the art director is to design the layout of the advertisement. **Layout** refers to the design and orderly formation of the various elements of an advertisement within specified dimensions (size specifications). The layout combines the illustration with the copy and offers an overall impression of what the final advertisement will look like.

In designing a layout, the art director will progress through three design stages: the thumbnail sketch, the rough art, and the comprehensive.

Thumbnail Sketch **Thumbnail sketches** are a series of small, experimental drawings of various ideas and design concepts. Their purpose is to identify a few options for more extensive design development.

Rough Art **Rough art** refers to the drawing of an ad that is done in actual size (derived from the best of the thumbnail sketches), with the various elements of the ad included so that their size and position are shown—the location of headline, body copy, and illustration.

The rough art work and copy sheet (where precise copy is composed) are usually presented by the agency to the client for approval. Again, several options may be presented, with the preferred option progressing to the next stage of design.

Comprehensive (Mechanical Art) In a **comprehensive**, or comp, the copy and illustration are in final form and are pasted into place. The comprehensive indicates what the actual ad will look like when it appears in print. It is often referred to as camera-ready art, because the artwork is photographed to obtain negatives for printing.

Computers now make a significant contribution to almost every step of the creative process, playing a role in determining how well, how fast, and at what cost print ads are developed. In the age of the computer, copywriters and art directors can conduct quickly many "what-if" experiments with their raw ideas. Also, the near typeset quality of layouts is more effective in selling ideas to clients, and revisions wanted by clients can be completed in hours instead of days. Once a layout is approved, the mechanical artwork only takes one extra day.

Design Principles Affecting Layouts

The client and agency strive for distinctiveness in their ads in order to break through the clutter of competition. To achieve that distinctiveness, the art director considers such factors as balance, unity and flow, the use of colour, size alternatives, the use of white space, and the use of artwork and photography.

Balance **Balance** refers to the relationship between the left side and right side of an advertising layout. Formal balance occurs when both sides are equal in weight. If different weights are assigned the various elements of an ad, there is informal balance.

Figure 7.6 An advertisement that effectively blends the headline, illustration, and body copy

FAR FROM
THE MADDING
CROWD.

The BMW 5-Series automobiles have a singular presence that sets them apart. These elegant sports sedans have the effect of creating their own environment, one which leaves their occupants untouched by the turmoil of city streets.

The new M5 shown above has an even further distinction. This stems in part from the fact that it has been hand crafted by our BMW Motorsport Division who design and build our racing cars.

Starting with the beautiful BMW 5-Series, they incorporated in the new M5 a powerful 24-valve, 310 hp engine, making the M5 the fastest production sedan in the world.

This latter side of its nature is revealed in the twisting turns of M5 country where it also proves itself to be one of the safest sedans in the world. A meticulously fine-tuned suspension system has given the M5 road-holding ability that one automotive writer has called magnetic. It's forgiving nature makes the M5 simply exhilarating to drive.

With its Motorsport heritage, it is fair to say of this automobile that it takes the BMW 5-Series to a further stage of its evolution.

THE ULTIMATE DRIVING EXPERIENCE.

FOR MORE INFORMATION ON BMW, PLEASE SEND YOUR BUSINESS CARD TO A. OSBORNE AT BMW CANADA INC., P.O. BOX 5324, VILLE SAINT-LAURENT, QUEBEC, H4L 4Z9

Courtesy: BMW Canada Inc.

Figure 7.7 Reader's eye movement

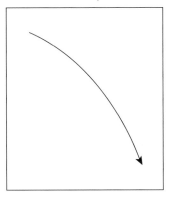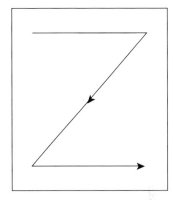

Flow of reader's eye from left to right and top to bottom

Unity **Unity** refers to the blending of all elements of an ad to create a complete impression. The headline, visual and body copy must work together to create an impression. Refer to the BMW advertisement in figure 7.6 for an example of an ad in which these elements work together effectively.

Flow **Flow** refers to the movement of the reader's eye—from left to right and top to bottom—when he or she is exposed to a print advertisement (see figure 7.7). When some people scan an advertisement, their eyes may move diagonally, from upper left to lower right. Others may follow a "Z" pattern, with eyes moving left to right across the top, then diagonally, from upper right to lower left, and then across the lower portion of the page to the right corner. Such reading patterns suggest the ideal locations for various elements of a print ad. For example, most headlines appear at the top to attract attention and state the key point of the ad. The illustration is used as background to the entire page, or in the middle section of the page, with body copy. The signature (summary message) usually appears in the lower right-hand corner of the page, along with any purchase incentives to encourage action. Signatures are strategically located to make an impression on those who skip the body copy.

Colour and Contrast Colour, or contrast in colour and style, can be an effective attention-grabber. In a black and white medium, reverse printing (white letters on black background), or spot colour may attract more attention. In a colour medium, where photography prevails, black and white photos, line drawings, or spot colour can distinguish one ad from another.

Size The decision to use a full page, double-page spread, or fractional page (1/2 page, 1/4 page, etc.) has an impact on how effectively an advertisement draws readers. Sometimes, small ads can achieve the same result as larger ones (which is a boon to the client paying the bill), but generally speaking the full-page ad gets higher readership than a smaller ad.

Bleed Pages In the case of a magazine, a **bleed page** is an advertisement in which the dark or coloured background extends to the edge of the page (often explained as an arrangement where the colour appears to run off the page). The BMW advertisement in figure 7.6 is an example of an ad that bleeds on three sides of the page. Most magazines offer bleed flexibility; some charge a premium for its use. A bleed page attracts more attention (21% more) and preference (22% more) than a non-bleed page.[3]

Artwork Versus Photography The two basic illustrating devices are photography and drawn (or painted) illustrations. In the case of a four-colour medium such as magazines, logic suggests that colour photography be used, but the end product will, of course, be similar to numerous other ads in the same publications. An artist's drawing, even a black and white drawing, may command a higher level of attention through contrast. The opposite is true of newspapers.

Generally, a good photograph will be most effective in conveying realism, emotion, or urgency. But there are benefits to using drawings. Drawings free artists to create the desired impression in their own style. The end product can exaggerate or accentuate in ways a photograph cannot often match.

White Space **White space** is the part of an advertisement that is not occupied by other elements. Margins, for example, are considered white space. The careful use of white space can be an effective means of providing contrast and of focusing attention on an isolated element. White space is also the means of achieving an uncluttered appearance.

Clarity and Simplicity Any elements that do not serve a specific function should be eliminated. Too much variety in type style, too many reverses or illustrations, and unnecessary copy should be excised. To achieve the desired impact, the ad should be pleasant to the eye and easy to read. The Labatt's Dry advertisement in figure 7.8 demonstrates the principles of white space, clarity, and simplicity at work in a poster format.

For more details on design principles and the effect they have on readers, refer to the Advertising in Action feature "What Research Says About Design."

Types of Layouts

The creative team considers the factors discussed in the preceding section when positioning the various elements in an ad for layout. With its decisions depending on the importance of an illustration and the need for explanatory copy, the creative team must blend all elements together to create an overall "look" for an advertisement. Some of the more common layout options used in advertising today are posters, vertical and horizontal splits, multiple illustrations, long copy, and insert layouts.

Poster The **poster** layout relies almost entirely on visual impression. The advertisement is picture dominant, with a minimum of copy. The BMW advertisement in figure 7.6 and the Labatt's Dry advertisement in figure 7.8 are examples of a poster layout.

Vertical Split In a **vertical-split** layout, the copy dominates one side of the ad, the picture dominates the other side (left side versus right side). Vertical splits are popular when a double-page spread (two pages) is used. Single-page ads can be divided by an imaginary line down the middle of the page.

Figure 7.8 A poster advertisement that uses to advantage the design principles of balance, unity, flow, white space, and clarity

Courtesy: Labatt Breweries of Canada

Advertising in Action
What Research Says About Design

Hidden camera tests have revealed that when readers leaf through pages of magazines, the average ad has less than half a second to grab their attention. This doesn't leave much time for reading headlines and body copy, but a catchy illustration may get a reader to stop for a longer length of time.

The results of many research studies conducted by the Starch and Gallup organizations have to be considered when copywriters and art directors design advertisements. Some key findings of the research indicate that

1. Colour significantly outscores black and white in readership.
2. A picture should take up at least half the page.
3. A photograph works better than a drawing.
4. Single pictures covering the entire width of the page are more visible than other picture combinations.
5. If people are used in the illustration, eye-to-eye contact with the reader is an attention-getter.
6. Interest scores for full page ads are greater than for fractional pages.

Robert Cohen, president of the Cohen Group, Toronto, runs seminars called "Winning the Ad Game." He has some other ideas on how to design the perfect print ad.

Headline: Only 30% of the readers read the headline, so it must be placed close to the illustration if it's going to grab the reader's attention. Headlines should be simple and less than 12 words. The type should be black print on a white background—white on black looks good but it is harder to read.

Illustrations: Seventy percent of readers notice an illustration. To get attention, it should occupy 60% of the space. Colour has impact (cost will increase by 25%, readership by 100%). Photographs grab attention better than drawings do because people identify with them more easily. Men identify more readily with photos of men and women more readily with women.

Body Copy: Only 5% of people seeing an ad will read all of the body copy. A column format for body copy is more pleasing to the eye than any other format is. The copy should be clear, fresh, memorable and believable. The message and images should be relevant to the target reader and should communicate a clear benefit to him or her.

Sub Headlines: Sub headlines are noted by 15% of readers. Since they draw the reader into the body copy, they should be bolder and done in a larger typeface than that used for the body copy.

Signature: Signatures are read by 10% of those looking at the page. They should include the company logo and an address and telephone number.

According to Cohen, advertisements created under these guidelines may not win any awards, but they will get the message across safely and simply. And that is the job of any ad—to sell the product.

Adapted from Jo Marney, "Gotcha!" *Marketing*, February 22, 1988, p.14, and from "General rules for the perfect print ad," *Marketing*, June 26, 1989, P.B14.

Figure 7.9   An advertisement using a horizontal split layout

The chefs of the Four Seasons Hotel Philadelphia.

A Good Hotel Reacts To Your Requests.
A Grand Hotel Anticipates Them.

A grand hotel should be judged not simply by how quickly it responds to your requests, but by how few requests you find it necessary to make in the first place.

Thus, at Four Seasons, we devote an enormous amount of time to anticipating precisely what the changing needs and desires of our guests are likely to be.

Our exclusive Alternative Cuisine menu selections, for example, were developed in anticipation of the growing number of people who've become careful about calories —yet no less discriminating about taste.

We also recognize that while business travellers

© 1986 Four Seasons Hotels, Ltd.

generally want to eat in a city's best restaurants, they don't necessarily want to leave the hotel to do so. Which is why you'll find 4-star restaurants in all our hotels.

And we realize that the rigors of business travel often dictate irregular hours. So we offer 24-hour room service —with food prepared by our highly acclaimed chefs.

But the Four Seasons philosophy of anticipating needs rather than reacting to them extends considerably beyond the kitchen.

We've anticipated, for instance, that many people don't want travel to disrupt their daily routines—which is why we provide jogging

maps and workout gear in all our hotels, and health clubs in many of them.

And since many of our guests prefer to travel with only carry-on luggage, we offer overnight pressing and shoe shining, so whatever you bring will look fresh in the morning. And we furnish our rooms with bathrobes, hair dryers and other essentials that might not fit into a single overnight bag.

We've anticipated all this and more because at Four Seasons we staunchly believe that a grand hotel should adapt to its guests. Not the other way around.

UNITED STATES
Austin (1987)
Boston
Chicago:
 The Ritz-Carlton
Dallas/Las Colinas:
 The Mandalay
 Las Colinas Inn and
 Conference Center;
 Four Seasons Fitness
 Resort and Spa.
Houston:
 Four Seasons,
 Inn on the Park
Los Angeles (1987)
New York:
 The Pierre
Newport Beach
Philadelphia
San Antonio
San Francisco:
 The Clift
Seattle:
 The Olympic
Washington, D.C.
CANADA
Edmonton
Montreal
Ottawa
Toronto:
 Yorkville,
 Inn on the Park
Vancouver
UNITED KINGDOM
London:
 Inn on the Park
Call (800) 268-6282
or your travel agent.

Four Seasons Hotels

Courtesy: Four Seasons Hotels. Reprinted with permission.

Figure 7.10 An advertisement demonstrating the use of multiple illustrations, reason-why body copy, and formal balance of top and bottom, and left side and right side

Courtesy: Canon Canada Inc. Reprinted with permission.

Horizontal Split The **horizontal split** divides the page across the middle. A common format is to have picture-domination at the top and copy-domination at the bottom. The Four Seasons Hotel ad in figure 7.9 is an example of a horizontal split.

Multiple Illustration In the **multiple-illustration layout**, a series of illustrations are presented, either in sequence, or showing a variety of related features and benefits. The Canon copier advertisement in figure 7.10 illustrates this concept.

Long Copy The **long-copy** advertisement is copy-dominated, with limited or no use for illustrations. The Telecom Canada ad in figure 7.5 is an example of a long-copy ad.

Insert Layout In the **insert layout**, a secondary visual illustration appears as an "insert" on the page. Inserts are commonly used to emphasize the product or package.

*C*REATIVE CONSIDERATIONS FOR OTHER PRINT MEDIA

Typically, the layout and design considerations for both newspaper and magazine media are quite similar. But other print media possess different characteristics, and present different problems and opportunities for the creative team to explore.

Outdoor Advertising

A research study conducted by Perception Research Services (U.S.) indicated that 75% of all individuals who see an outdoor board are likely to be drawn to the name of the product advertised, so bold identification of the name is important. In addition, factors such as size and the use of cut-out extensions affect the attention-getting ability of the board. *Cut-out extensions* are outdoor designs that go beyond the perimeters of the standard space. Cut-outs lead to higher levels of readership and more repeat examination by readers.[4]

Other design factors important for outdoor advertising include the simplicity of the design and the use of colour. Since outdoor is often used as a complementary medium (in conjunction with a primary medium such as television), the outdoor message should contain creative concepts from the other media. This is referred to as the *integrative concept* of creative design.

Here are some basic rules of thumb for outdoor layout and design:

- Use bold colour and high contrast
- Use typefaces that are simple, clear, and easy to read
- Size the copy and place it appropriately in relation to the product[5]

Transit Advertising

Owing to the fact that the transit rider is sometimes moving and sometimes standing still, certain design considerations are particularly relevant to both interior and exterior transit advertising.

Figure 7.11   A brief message that grabs the consumer's attention

Courtesy: Trans Ad, A Jim Pattison Company

Interior Transit   With interior transit, the advertiser can use time to advantage. The average length of a ride is 28 minutes, so copy and illustrations can be detailed. Alternatively, short and quick messages tend to be read and re-read by idle passengers. The Scrabble ad in figure 7.11 is an example of an ad that grabs attention quickly and will be read frequently by passengers.

Exterior Transit   Exterior transit advertising reaches pedestrians and travellers in other vehicles. Since travelling displays on buses are often viewed from an angle and a distance, bold type, punchy copy lines, and absolute simplicity are preferable.

Point-of-Purchase Advertising

Point-of-purchase is another form of "reminder" advertising that uses the design concepts of another medium, that is, it may be similar in appearance to ads designed for newspapers or magazines. Point-of-purchase advertising encourages impulse buying and influences last-minute choices between comparable brands. When it comes to retail-display materials, which include **display shippers** (merchandise packaged for stores that have display materials), posters, shelf-talkers (small posters at shelf locations), and ad pads, the design must provide what the point-of-purchase industry refers to as the four I's: impact, identification, information, and imagery.

Impact   The display must generate immediate impact. It must say "Here I Am, Buy Me."

Identification   The brand or business name must be boldly displayed. Identification must link the message to the source.

Information   In brief format (i.e., in the copy and the illustration), the display must provide the consumer with a reason to buy.

Imagery   The overall impression must be relevant to the customer. As in a print ad, the various elements of a display must blend together to make a complete message.

Direct Mail

In sharp contrast to other forms of print advertising, successful direct-mail campaigns are governed by a different set of copy, layout, and design rules. Direct mail, particularly direct mail sent to business customers, is generally rather dry and copy-oriented. However, considering the audience (i.e., business customers with rational buying motives), the use of hard facts in the communications process is appropriate. In support of long copy, David Ogilvy states: "Long copy sells more than short copy, particularly when you are asking the reader to spend a lot of money."[6] Design factors considered important in the business-to-business direct mail marketplace are as follows:

1. White space is not important; every line should be used to communicate details.
2. A coupon or reply card is considered mandatory; such items make it possible to track returns and to measure conversion to actual orders.
3. Copy tone should be upbeat (positive) at all times, and illustrations should only be included when they serve a useful purpose; otherwise, stay with copy domination.
4. The copy should be closing continuously (i.e., it should be continually asking for the order). As with any ad, the reader's interest will steadily fade, so, like an effective salesperson, the copy must "close" early and often.

TELEVISION ADVERTISING

The nature and content of a television commercial derive from the same base of information as print advertising, but there are obvious differences. Print advertising uses space, whereas television advertising is concerned with the use of time, and since the message is delivered within a period of time, the creative team is concerned with the "flow" of the commercial from beginning to end.

The Sections of a Television Commercial

A television commercial is typically divided into three distinct sections: an opening, a middle, and a closing.

Opening   The purpose of the opening section is to grab the viewer's attention and introduce the key benefit before the audience "disappears" physically or mentally. A common means of attracting attention is to present a problem situation that must subsequently be resolved.

Middle The purpose here is to communicate the bulk of the message. This section must hold the viewer's interest by elaborating on the single most important benefit of the product or service in an interesting manner, clearly identifying the name of the product or service.

Closing The closing section of a commercial, which is usually the final few seconds, will definitely focus on the product's name and package, if applicable. It may repeat a promise and should suggest some course of action to the viewer (e.g., "call or write for information," or "visit your dealer for a test drive").

Let us examine the case of the Bell Canada commercial that was displayed in figure 7.2. In the opening section, the problem of returned merchandise is presented. This introduction is accomplished in the first three frames.

In the middle section, the commercial shows that the problem can be resolved if the customer considers using Bell's 1-800 telephone service—which allows quick communications between a buyer and a seller. Interest in the service is created in frames four through seven.

In the closing section, a summary is attempted in phrases such as "makes sense," and "Long distance business sense," phrases which express the theme of this advertisement and others like it in the campaign. There is also a call for action in the inclusion of Bell's 1-800 number on the screen in the second to last frame. The close is accomplished in the final three frames.

Designing Television Commercials

In designing a television commercial, the creative team first develops the central concept or theme, and then creates a story around it. In the development stage, the creative team is concerned with the sequence of events in the ad, and the team creates a storyboard for this purpose. A **storyboard** is a set of graphic renderings (an artist's rough version of a finished commercial) in a television-frame format, with appropriate copy showing what the commercial will look like. An alternative to the storyboard is a complete script, which details in words the audio and visual elements of the commercial. Common practice is to have the description of the visual on one side, and the audio on the other. Refer to the Apple television script in figure 7.12. It is on the basis of these scripts that clients approve advertising campaigns, so scripts must plant a good visual impression in their minds. Once approved, these scripts are used as the guideline for producing the commercial.

Creative Considerations for Television

The creative team must consider several factors when trying to design a television commercial that will stand out from the clutter of competing commercials. Considering the context in which commercials appear (six in a cluster during a station break), the need for a commercial to break through a viewer's perceptual barriers is paramount.

Unity Viewers do not distinguish the opening, middle, and closing sections of an advertisement as they watch. Instead, they perceive the ad as a continuum of action focussed on a central idea. The commercial, therefore, must flow logically: present the problem, provide an explanation and solution, and then suggest action.

Figure 7.12 An example of a script used in producing a television commercial

```
┌─────────┐
│ BAKER   │   TELEVISION
│ LOVICK  │
└─────────┘
```

CLIENT	APPLE CANADA	DATE THIS DRAFT	JULY 4/90
PRODUCT	MACINTOSH (Split :60)	DATE DNHW & C.R.T.C.	
COMMERCIAL NO.	AMN 0076	DATE CLIENT APPROVAL	
TITLE	Testing/Yesterday	DATE FINAL AS RECORDED	

VISUAL	AUDIO
JOHN, BOSS OF A BIG INSURANCE COMPANY IS STARING OUT OF HIS OFFICE FROM BEHIND THE GLASS, OBSERVING HIS PEOPLE WORKING. HIS ASSISTANT ED ENTERS.	ED: You've been staring out there all day. What are you doing?
CUT TO EMPLOYEE WHO IS WORKING ON THE MAC. NEXT TO HIM IS A VACANT DESK WITH AN UNUSED IBM COMPUTER.	JOHN: Trying to figure out which computer is the most powerful.
CUT BACK TO JOHN AND ED. JOHN CONTINUES STARING INTENTLY OUT OF HIS OFFICE.	ED: Well that's easy. The one with the most memory... megahertz...MIPS...you know.
CUT TO JOHN'S POV. ANOTHER WORKER COMES UP TO MAC DESK.	JOHN: No, I don't think so...
WORKER STANDS AND WAITS TO USE THE MAC.	...I think the most powerful computer is the one that people actually use.
CUT TO JOHN'S POV. KEN LEAVES THE MAC. MICHELLE SITS DOWN AND STARTS USING IT.	(MUSIC). V.O.: Macintosh has the power to change the way you look at computers.
SUPER: (LOGO) THE POWER TO BE YOUR BEST.	
JOHN LOOKS AT ED AS IF TO SAY "WAKE UP".	(CUT MUSIC) ED: That's not really a fair comparison. People like using the Mac.

continued

Figure 7.12 continued

BAKER LOVICK | TELEVISION

CLIENT	**APPLE CANADA INC.**	DATE THIS DRAFT **SEPT. 25/90 R1**
PRODUCT	**MACINTOSH**	DATE DNHW & C.R.T.C.
COMMERCIAL NO.	AMN 0076	DATE CLIENT APPROVAL
TITLE	Testing/Yesterday	DATE FINAL AS RECORDED

VISUAL		AUDIO
OPEN ON NONDESCRIPT PC COVERED IN COBWEBS.	MUSIC:	DRAMATIC TO MATCH PICTURE.
CUT TO MAC CLASSIC AS KEYBOARD AND MOUSE ARE PLACED IN FRONT OF IT.	ANNCR.:	At Apple, we believe the most powerful computer in the world is one that people actually use.
CUT BACK TO PC DECAYING.	SFX:	(DECAY SOUND).
CUT TO PLUG GOING INTO BACK OF MAC CLASSIC AND HAND TOUCHING MOUSE TO TURN COMPUTER ON.		One that comes complete and ready to run in minutes, not hours.
CUT TO REALLY DECAYED P.C.	SFX:	(DECAY SOUND).
CUT TO MAC CLASSIC SCREEN AS MULTIPLE PROGRAMS FLASH ON IT.		One that runs thousands of programs and has built-in networking.
CUT TO PC ALMOST TOTALLY DECAYED.	SFX:	(DECAY SOUND).
CUT TO CLASSIC SCREEN AS $1,349 APPEARS ON IT.		And one...that everyone can afford.
PULL BACK TO SHOW WHOLE MAC CLASSIC.		Introducing the Macintosh Classic...
PULL BACK TO SHOW REMAINS OF PC BESIDE IT AS PC DUST BLOWS AWAY.		At $1,349 it makes everything else look like yesterday's news.
SUPER: APPLE LOGO. THE POWER TO BE YOUR BEST.		MUSIC: STING.

Courtesy: Apple Canada Inc.

If a commercial is understood to be a 15-, 30-, or 60-second film, this flow strategy makes sense. In the case of the Bell Canada commercial discussed earlier, the central idea is the plotline—the dramatization of the business problem that the Bell 1-800 service can resolve. The interaction between the characters in the commercial is designed to maintain the viewer's attention.

Integration of Audio and Video In a commercial, the voice and action should be in unison: if a benefit is shown, it should be discussed at the same time. The product should be the main element of the commercial; the creative team will consider using sound effects and music, where appropriate, but in so doing they must recognize that their purpose is to enhance the product message, not to overwhelm it.

Special Effects Special effects are such devices or techniques as animation, trick photography, or supers. A **super** is copy superimposed onto a picture in a television commercial, as is done with the phone number and corporate name and logo in the Telemarketing commercial. As with sound effects and music, special effects are meant only to enhance the commercial message.

Pace The content of a television commercial is designed to fit a time limit of either 15 seconds, 30 seconds, or 60 seconds. Using the time limit as a guideline, the creative team must come up with a message that will communicate itself at a suitable pace. In recent years, the 15-second commercial has become popular with advertisers, as it saves money in media time. However, scaled-down versions of 30-second commercials do not have the same impact. It is preferable to use the time constraint as a guideline from the beginning and develop an original commercial designed to suit the 15-second period.

The product and product image have an effect on the pace of a commercial. For example, a commercial for a perfume product may suggest romance and use emotional situations in the communications process. In this situation, the pace is likely to be slow. In contrast, a commercial for a soft drink aimed at a youthful target market may use fast-paced rock music to create the appropriate image for the product.

Live Action Versus Animation Live action involves using real-life situations and real people in a commercial. The real people may be the average person, or an actor or actress. Animation is a technique whereby hand-drawn cartoons or stylized figures and settings are given movement and visual dimension. Some commercials combine live action and animation. (Remember the commercials for Kellogg's Frosted Flakes that showed Tony the Tiger sitting at a table with real people and "communicating" with them?) The Pillsbury Doughboy live-action commercials employ another animation technique.

There are advantages to both live-action and animated ads. A live-action commercial can generate a sense of realism and immediacy. As well, personalities can be used as persuasive presenters, and effective locations can be selected in which to shoot the commercial. The animated commercial is potentially entertaining; the advertiser can use a fantasy situation to advantage, and the commercial will no doubt be unique in its animation techniques. Animation is becoming more innovative as technology advances. New computer-assisted television cameras that control camera movement, complex effects from multiple exposures of the same frame, and computer-generated graphics have added to the quality of animated commercials.

Television Production Stages

The creative team and the account executive are responsible for presenting the storyboard and script to the client for approval. Several alternatives may be presented, and the client will certainly offer some feedback (positive and negative) as it reacts to the ideas and concepts being recommended. With a significant amount of money on the line at this stage (i.e., actual production costs plus the cost of media time), both the agency and client want the message to be right.

Once the concept, storyboard, and script have been approved by the client, the commercial goes into production. The production process involves four separate stages: *securing cost quotations, preproduction, production,* and *postproduction.*

Cost Quotations   The task of producing the commercial is the responsibility of a production house (i.e., a specialist in commercial production). Evaluating production-cost estimates from various production houses is a critical assignment, as the costs of producing a 30-second, live-action commercial—without celebrity talent—can easily exceed $100 000.

The normal procedure is for the agency to solicit estimates from two or three suppliers, who bid competitively on the job. Presuming that all are capable suppliers (i.e., that they have good track records, good crews, etc.), the lowest bid will be accepted. To estimate costs, the production house will use the storyboard and script as a guideline, and add in other costs normally associated with commercial production. Some of the factors that can cause commercial-production costs to be high are as follows:

- Travel to distant locations
- Use of celebrity talent (although such talent may be paid for by the client through a separate contract)
- Complexity (which calls for a large crew and many cameras)
- Special effects
- Studio rental charges
- Use of animals
- Costs of the director (good ones can be expensive)
- Additional days for production (time is money, after all)

Production is a one-time cost, except for the talent used in the commercial. Talent can include actors, models, musicians, and so on. Talent is paid union-scale for an appearance in a commercial, and an additional payment, known as a **residual**, is made to the talent each time the commercial is broadcast. Therefore, the costs of the talent increase with the frequency and coverage of the media buy.

Preproduction   At this stage, a meeting is held with representatives of the production house, the agency (i.e., the creative team), and the client. The purpose of the meeting is to plan production. The storyboard and script are reviewed, and final decisions and arrangements are made. Prominent areas of discussion are casting, the use of secondary suppliers (e.g., music specialists, editors, and mixers), and finding appropriate props, costumes, and film locations. Agreement by all parties on all details is essential.

If an announcer is required for the commercial, the decision on who the announcer is going to be will be determined in the preproduction meeting. Announcers in a commercial do not appear on screen, but are heard as a **voice-over** that communicates a key point. Refer back to figure 7.2, the Telecom Canada ad, or to figure 7.12, the Bell Canada ad, for examples.

If music is to be part of the commercial, the advertiser has several options, depending on the price it is willing to pay. For the highest cost, specific music can be requested (usually such music is under copyright by the original musician or producer). An advertiser using a current rock tune would fall into this category. As an alternative, original music scores can be prepared by music writers and arrangers. Less costly alternatives include the use of pre-recorded music, prepared and distributed by recording studios, and the use of public-domain music, which is music whose copyright has expired.

Production The actual shooting (production) of the commercial can be very long and tedious, but since time is money, every effort is made to complete the task as quickly as possible. However, quality is also paramount. So when scenes are shot, it is common to try several takes to get them right. The director may adjust the lighting, for example, a process that often requires two or three good takes of each scene.

Scenes do not have to be shot in sequence. For example, scenes without sound, which do not require a full crew, can be done last. Finally, considerable time is lost between scenes as cameras are moved, actors briefed, lights reset, and so on. It is important that there is continuity from scene to scene; otherwise, the finished commercial will appear disjointed. As discussed earlier, the concepts of "time" and "flow" are critical to the success of the message.

Postproduction The postproduction stage involves putting the commercial together, and requires a co-ordinated effort between the director, film editor, and sound mixer. The normal procedure is to assemble the visuals and the sound separately, without extra effects such as dissolves, titles, or supers.

Postproduction activity can be described in a series of steps, which are as follows:

1. *Rough Cut* A *copy* of the original film, referred to as a *work print*, is used in editing as a way of preventing damage to the original. The film editor reviews all footage and splices together the best takes to form a **rough cut**.
2. *Interlock* The **interlock** is the *synchronization* of sound and picture by means of a special editor's projector. The synchronized film and sound are projected onto a large screen to provide a feeling of what the finished commercial will be like. At this stage, scenes can be substituted and music added or deleted at the discretion of the creative team or client.
3. *Addition of Optical Effects* The movement from one scene to another in the rough cut and interlock is usually "abrupt." Optical effects, such as dissolves,

are added to make the transitions from scene to scene appear smooth. These dissolve effects involve **fades**, whereby one scene fades away and another gradually appears, and **wipes**, whereby one scene pushes the other away. Other options include the use of split-screen techniques, or the addition of **supers** to the film.

4. *Mixed Interlock* With the sound track and film edited, additional audio elements can be added in a mixing section. Sound effects dubbed in to other elements are referred to as a **mixed interlock**.

5. *Answerprints* The final postproduction step results in the **answerprint**. This is where film, sound, special effects, and opticals are combined and printed. The answerprint is presented to the client for approval, and duplicates are made for distribution to television stations.

*R*ADIO *ADVERTISING*

Like television execution, radio execution focusses on the effective use of time and on making the commercial flow from beginning to end. The creative team develops the concept or central theme in script form, which indicates the words to be spoken and provides direction regarding the use of sound effects and music.

Creative Considerations for Radio Commercials

Radio commercials must grab the listener's attention immediately and hold it until the end. This is a challenging task; there is a tendency for listeners to "tune out" quickly if they are not interested.

Radio is used by listeners who are generally doing something else as well (e.g., reading, driving, sun bathing). To command attention, therefore, the ad must be catchy and memorable. Some rules of thumb to follow in the creation of radio advertising include the following:

1. Mention the advertiser's name often. Many practitioners suggest that the brand or company be mentioned three times during a 30-second commercial.
2. Be conversational, but use short words and sentences.
3. Centre the message on one significant idea. Variations of the key message should be made repeatedly.
4. Use sound effects to create a *visual* image. Radio advertising, to be effective, must activate the listeners' imaginations.
5. Make the tone of the radio commercial positive, cheerful, upbeat.

An example of a radio script is included in figure 7.13

Types of Radio Commercials

Generally, radio commercials can be divided into four categories: *musical commercials, slice-of-life commercials, straight announcements,* and *personality announcements.*

Figure 7.13 Radio script for a "slice of life" commercial. Script includes audio for character presenters, audio for announcer and special effects.

DMB&B

D'Arcy Masius Benton & Bowles Canada Inc.
2 Bloor Street West, Toronto, Ontario M4W 3R3
(416) 922-2211

AS RECORDED AT
AIRWAVES AUDIO

Print/Radio

XX

		Date:	February 6, 1987
Client:	Pitney Bowes	Revision:	3
Product Division:	Mailing Systems	Ad/Commercial No.:	
	(WEIGHING MACHINES)	Docket No.:	
		Title/Length:	"RETURN TO SENDER" (MOM)
		Publication/Ad Size:	:30 RADIO SPOT

SFX:	(MAN HUMMING, INTERRUPTED BY PHONE BUZZING)
MAN:	Yes?
SEC'Y:	Your mother the weightlifter called, sir.
MAN:	Oh yes, it was her birthday yesterday.
SEC'Y:	Oh yes, that reminds me. Her present was returned, marked "INSUFFICIENT POSTAGE".
MAN:	(GASP)
SEC'Y:	Do you want me to send it out again in today's mail, dear?
MAN:	(TO SELF) She's comin' after me.
SEC'Y:	Sir?
ANNCR:	TRAGEDIES LIKE THESE CAN BE AVERTED WITH A PITNEY BOWES ELECTRONIC MAILING SCALE. THAT WAY, YOU ALWAYS PAY CORRECT POSTAGE, EVERY SINGLE TIME. PITNEY BOWES. SYSTEMS AND SERVICE THAT JUST WON'T QUIT. CALL US. WE'RE IN THE WHITE PAGES.
SFX:	(PHONE BUZZ)
SEC'Y:	Your mummy's here, sir.
MAN:	(SCREAM)

Courtesy: Pitney Bowes Canada Ltd. and DMB&B D'Arcy Masius Benton & Bowles Canada Inc. Reprinted with permission.

Musical Commercials For commercials where music is to play a major role, there are several alternative ways of "deploying" music: a commercial may be all music, as in the case of many softdrink ads; music jingles may be interspersed with spoken words; or orchestral arrangements can be used.

Slice-of-Life Commercials Much like a television commercial, a "slice-of-life" situation involves the presentation of a problem and then of product benefits that will resolve the problem. Effective use of listeners' imaginations enhances slice-of-life commercials.

Straight Announcements With these commercials, the message simply states the facts. The message is relatively easy to prepare and easy to deliver. Music may be used in the background.

Personality Announcements This alternative differs from the first three alternatives in that the advertiser gives up the control of commercial delivery. In a personality announcement, the disc jockey presents the message in his or her own style. The radio station is provided with a feature sheet that outlines the key benefits and the product slogan. The DJ develops the specific wording for the message.

Radio Advertising—the Production Process

In the case of a radio commercial, the finished product is a mixed tape that contains all of the spoken words, music, and special effects. For radio-commercial production that involves a production house, the basic steps in the process are as follows:

1. Once the script and the production costs have been approved by the client, the commercial producer selects the studio and the casting director.
2. The casting director finds appropriate actors for slice-of-life commercials and the right voices for announcement-type commercials.
3. If music is required, the decision whether to hire a composer or use stock music is made. Decisions regarding the use of special effects are also finalized.
4. The director supervises rehearsals, and several commercial readings are made so that the agency and client have a selection to choose from.
5. Music and sound are recorded separately and mixed to form a master tape. The tape is duplicated for distribution to radio stations.

Summary

For both print and broadcast media, creative execution is the responsibility of the copywriter and art director under the supervision of the creative director. They work together as a creative team, and their primary role is to develop the creative concept or central theme that will differentiate the advertised product from competitive offerings.

The creative concept serves four basic functions. It should attract attention, clarify the key benefit, establish product uniqueness, and assist in positioning the product in the customer's mind.

In developing print and broadcast messages, the creative team considers the behavioural stages an individual passes through prior to making a purchase decision. These stages are awareness, comprehension, conviction, and action. The tools employed to penetrate the customer's perceptual barriers are numerous. For example, the copywriter is responsible for the headline, the body copy, and the signature, and the art director is responsible for the illustration; the two join forces to create a complete message—an impression on the customer. In print advertising, the impression is affected by variables such as balance, unity, flow, the use of colour and size, white space, and the use of artwork or photography in illustrations.

Other print media have unique creative considerations. Outdoor messages must be simple in design and use bold colours; point-of-purchase advertising must likewise be brief, but also convincing to promote impulse purchasing. Transit ads have a more captive audience (often idle), and therefore their messages can be more detailed. In the case of direct mail, particularly business direct mail, long copy is the standard rule of thumb.

For television commercials, the element of flow is the critical creative consideration. Variables such as integration of audio and video, the use of music and special effects, and the pace of the commercial are also significant in that they, too, have an impact on the viewer. In commercial production there are four stages: obtaining cost estimates, preproduction, production, and post-production.

Radio commercials are also concerned with flow. Effective commercials tend to be positive and upbeat in tone, conversational in nature, and focused on one central idea. Radio ads that involve the listener's imagination have proven to be successful. The production process is very similar to that of television.

Review Questions

1. Distinguish between the roles and responsibilities of the copywriter and the art director in the creative process.
2. What does the term "creative concept" refer to? What is its purpose?
3. Identify the basic elements of a typical print advertisement and describe the primary purpose of each.
4. What are the stages in the design of a print layout?
5. What are the factors affecting the design and layout of print advertising? Briefly discuss the influence of each.
6. Distinguish between the following:
   i) balance versus unity (print advertising)
   ii) vertical split versus horizontal split

iii) poster versus long copy
iv) unity versus pace (television advertising)
v) live action versus animation (television)
vi) rough cut versus interlock versus answerprint

7. What are the various sections of a television commercial? Explain the role of each section.
8. Identify and briefly explain each stage in the television-production process.
9. What are the different categories of radio advertising?

Discussion Questions

1. Read the Advertising in Action vignette "What Research Says About Design," contained in this chapter. Select a few of the advertisements included in the chapter and assess their potential effectiveness in light of the rules of thumb presented in the vignette.
2. "Given the nature of the job, the creative team should not be assigned to any one client (product) for too long." Discuss this statement from the viewpoint of the client and the agency.
3. "Tell more, sell more." Discuss this statement in the context of print advertising.

CHAPTER 8 Advertising Research

In studying this chapter, you will learn

- About the various organizations involved in advertising research
- The various types of research utilized in the advertising industry
- The basic stages in the advertising-research process
- The measurement techniques for evaluating creative effectiveness
- About organizations involved in the media-research process
- The way in which the media uses research data

≡ Advertising and the Research Process

As advertising is a component of the marketing process, so advertising research is a component of marketing research. Marketing research refers to the systematic gathering, recording, and analyzing of data to resolve a marketing problem. Marketing research serves two primary functions:

1. *To develop new knowledge*—for example, to develop an understanding of the markets a firm is considering entering, to develop demographic and psychographic profiles of potential users.
2. *To provide information to assist in the decision-making process*—that is, to reduce the risks associated with a certain decision. If, for example, a choice between two comparable options had to be made, research would provide information regarding which option would have the most influence on the target market.

The role and importance of marketing research is illustrated in figure 8.1. Within the organization structure, marketing research is viewed as a service function that undertakes investigations and activities that benefit the planning and management of the four Ps (product, price, place, and promotion). Research also serves to identify the potential target markets to which a company will appeal.

Advertising research provides information useful in the preparation or evaluation of an advertisement, commercial, or other elements of a complete campaign, including media alternatives and usage. In general terms, advertising research investigates variables such as what message to send, how to send it, how effective the message is, and what media is best to reach the target market.

ORGANIZATIONS INVOLVED IN ADVERTISING RESEARCH

Organizations that play an active role in the advertising-research process include advertisers, agencies, marketing-research firms and consultants, and media and media

Figure 8.1   Position of marketing research in the marketing environment

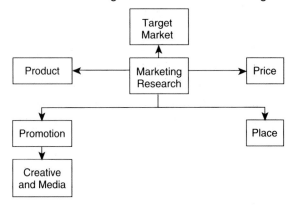

associations. The research done by media and media associations is chiefly intended to convince advertisers to use a particular medium. This type of research determines the size of audience an advertiser can potentially reach by a particular medium as well as the basic demographic profile of that audience. The main thrust of research done by advertisers and marketing-research companies is towards obtaining information about the effectiveness of a message directed at a target audience.

Advertisers

The largest advertisers in Canada, excluding the governments, are consumer-goods or packaged-goods companies such as Procter & Gamble, Unilever, and Kraft General Foods. Generally, it is large packaged-goods companies that spend the most on advertising research. Smaller firms are active in research, of course, but larger multi-product firms with significant advertising budgets place more emphasis on research.

Very often, the kind and quantity of research conducted by a company is determined by the management philosophy respecting the usefulness of research data and information. Some companies do not spend much on research since they would rather allocate the funds to advertising or to some other form of marketing activity. Since research is a highly specialized field, the assignments are usually contracted out to independent researchers. Specialists not directly linked to the sponsoring company provide objectivity in the analysis and interpretation of data.

Advertising Agencies

A few of the larger agencies in Canada have their own marketing-research or advertising-research departments. Research in an agency is centred on two main areas: creative and media. In the creative area, agencies will be involved in pre-testing and post-testing of advertisements and commercials. The pre-testing of ideas, concepts, and partially finished advertisements and commercials is essential to determining whether the strategies and executions being developed are going to have a positive influence on the target market. Post-testing is done to evaluate the effectiveness of the entire campaign. Research results provide input for future change.

In the media area, agencies must be well informed of media developments (audience reach, rates, etc.), and therefore they tap into on-line media-data banks. Computerized media information and analysis assist the media-planning function.

Marketing-Research Firms

Marketing-research firms are the specialists who conduct research for both advertisers and agencies. Using the problems and objectives provided by the client, the research firm develops a proposal that details the procedure for collecting information, the vehicles to be used in gathering it (e.g., questionnaires and experiments), and the costs associated with the research. Projects undertaken by research specialists typically cover areas such as consumers' message-recall and recognition, purchase motivation, and evaluations of creative alternatives for effectiveness.

Media and Media Associations

The various media rely on research information to demonstrate their ability to meet the needs of advertisers (their ability to effectively and efficiently reach certain target groups, their degree of local market coverage, and so on). Associations involved in media research include the Television Bureau, the Print Measurement Bureau (PMB Data Bank), the Newspaper Marketing Bureau (NADbank), and the Canadian Outdoor Measurement Bureau. Research data from these organizations is presented later in this chapter.

Specific media vehicles (e.g., magazines, newspapers, radio stations) conduct research among their current audiences in an attempt to improve the quality of their product. By meeting the expectations of current audiences, they demonstate the potential to attract a larger audience and to gain a larger market share.

OVERVIEW OF THE RESEARCH PROCESS

Research studies can be classified according to the source of the information, to the research design, and to the nature of the information sought.

Research by Source of Information

Research data can be obtained through primary or secondary research sources.

Primary Research **Primary research** refers to data observed, recorded, and collected specifically with a view to resolving an identified problem, and it is usually available at high cost to the sponsor. In advertising, creative research relies mainly on primary data to show whether creative approaches are acceptable.

Primary research involves three different methodologies: *surveys*, which involve the use of questionnaires via telephone, mail, or personal interview; *observation techniques*, either personal or electronic; and *experimental procedures* involving controlled environments and changing stimuli. All of these methodologies can be adapted to suit any angle of advertising research.

Secondary Research **Secondary research** refers to data compiled and published by others for purposes other than resolving a specific problem; it is usually available at a reasonable cost.

In advertising, secondary sources are frequently used to gain access to media information that benefits media analysis and planning. Such information is available through the media, media associations, governments, and trade and business publications.

Research by Design

Design classifications refer to how the research procedure is organized and implemented to accomplish a stated task. Research is either custom-designed for a specific sponsor, or it is designed in such a manner that numerous sponsors can participate.

Custom-Designed Research This is a form of primary research whose objective is to resolve a specific problem or to obtain specific information. A procedure will be developed and a research instrument designed to perform a specific task only. Creative research into recognition and recall of message content uses custom-designed studies.

Omnibus Studies These are often referred to as "syndicated services," operating as they do on the principle of collaboration. So that costs of research are kept at a reasonable level, numerous clients participate in a study, or numerous subscribers share the costs of accessing specific types of research data. The services of A.C. Nielsen (television ratings), the Print Measurement Bureau (data on magazines), and NADbank (data for newspapers) are syndicated services offered to all subscribing members.

Research by Nature of Information Sought

With respect to the nature of information sought, research can be classified as qualitative or quantitative.

Qualitative **Qualitative research** involves collecting data from small sample sizes. A *focus group* is a small (eight to 10 people) representation of a large target, brought together to discuss advertising ideas, concepts, and executions from a non-professional perspective.

Typically, qualitative research is implemented in the early stages of the creative-production process (concept testing, for example, is done via rough ads and storyboards) to determine if the directions under consideration will have a positive influence on target-market responses.

Quantitative **Quantitative research** attempts to quantify feelings, attitudes, and opinions. A quantitative study relies upon a structured procedure (e.g., a questionnaire) and a larger, representative sample size (100 to 200 respondents is a common sample size for creative research, while media research uses much larger samples).

Quantitative research is often done prior to final commercial production to confirm that the creative approach is in line with client and target-market expectations. The decision to proceed with expensive production is easier if supported by reliable research data. This type of research is also common in post-campaign evaluations of communications effectiveness.

STEPS IN THE ADVERTISING-RESEARCH PROCESS

Before conducting a research study, the client and the agency generally start with a situation analysis. The purpose of a situation analysis is to review all background information, consult with experts in the field of concern, and obtain information from appropriate secondary sources. The situation analysis should provide the information needed to define the project direction for research. The project direction states the problem to be resolved or the basic purpose of the research.

At this stage, a specialist-research firm usually becomes involved. The researcher outlines the procedure for and costs of obtaining information and data. The steps in the process are outlined in figure 8.2 and below.

Figure 8.2 Advertising-research process

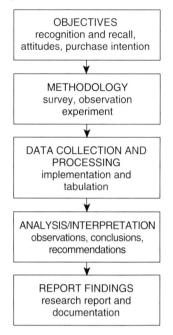

1. State Research Objectives

Objective statements outline what the research is intended to accomplish. For example, common advertising-research objective statements refer to consumers' recognition and recall of the product's name and primary selling message; attitudinal measures such as believability, acceptability, and ease of understanding; and the degree of purchase intent resulting from message exposure.

2. Establish Methodology

This stage considers the means by which the data will be collected. Other areas considered are the sample design (i.e., who the respondents are, how they will be recruited, and how many are required), and in what location the research will be conducted (in-home, shopping malls, etc.).

3. Collect and Process Data

In this stage, trained interviewers conduct the research according to instructions they have received regarding methodology. Once completed, the data is entered into a computer, and tabulations and cross-tabulations of raw data are printed out. Cross-tabulations refer to data about subgroups, usually tabulated according to demographic variables (i.e., analysis of responses by age group, by income, by education, etc.).

4. Analyze and Interpret Data

The research firm interprets the raw data during the next stage. Each question is analyzed, and observations are noted. All data are interpreted in light of the problem under review or the objectives of the research study.

5. Present Findings

In the final stage, the research firm develops a research report that summarizes the findings of the research and states recommendations based on those findings.

CREATIVE RESEARCH

Creative research is the process of evaluating and measuring the effect of an advertising message on a target market. At this stage, the particular medium for delivering the message has been determined, and the creative concept developed to a rough or final stage.

Pre-testing

Pretesting is the process by which an advertisement, commercial, or campaign is evaluated before final production or media placement, so that the strengths and weaknesses of a strategy and execution may be determined.

Post-testing

Post-testing is the process of evaluating and measuring the effectiveness of an advertisement, commercial, or campaign during or after it has run.

The basic purpose of pre-testing is to gauge initial reaction and make changes where necessary, while post-testing provides information that can be used in future advertising planning.

The pre-testing and post-testing of creative is typically concerned with target markets, motives, and messages.

Target Markets Advertisers test creative on their target market to gauge the market's initial response to it. Information thus obtained indicates where changes to the creative might be appropriate, and helps the advertiser decide whether to scrap or continue in a certain creative direction.

Motives Using information about consumer motivation (obtained from marketing research), the advertiser can test messages in light of consumers' purchase motivations. The advertiser can measure the audience response to the appeal techniques used.

Messages Pre-testing and post-testing can determine if the message is getting through to its intended audience. Several aspects of the message can be evaluated. Often gathered, for example, are data regarding the audience's recognition and recall of the brand name, the primary selling message, and slogans. Also obtained are measures related to attitude—in particular, to such variables as believability, clarity, meaningfulness to the target market, and overall impact. Response to specific components of an advertisement such as headline, illustrations, and body copy can be measured as well.

MEASUREMENT TECHNIQUES FOR CREATIVE RESEARCH

The advertiser can obtain the benefits of pre-testing and post-testing if both are integrated into the creative-development process. The measurement techniques used for pre-test and post-test research, with few exceptions, are the same. In other words, a certain technique can be modified to accommodate the needs of a pre-test or post-test situation. Among the more common techniques used to measure the effectiveness of creative are recognition (awareness) testing, recall (comprehension) testing, and opinion-measure testing.

Recognition (Awareness) Testing

In **recognition tests**, respondents are asked if they can recall an advertisement for a specific product or any of the points made in the advertisement. For example, consumers who have read a publication where an ad has appeared are asked if they remember the editorial content of an advertisement, or the advertisement itself. A test of this nature can also measure the cumulative effect of a campaign in terms of the audience-awareness level for the advertised product (brand name).

Recall (Comprehension) Testing

Testing for **recall** is a method of measuring advertising impact. In either an aided or an unaided recall-testing procedure, respondents are asked to recall specific elements of an advertisement or commercial, such as its primary selling points, the characters used in it as presenters, and its slogans. In the case of an aided-recall test, the interviewer mentions a product class to determine whether the respondent can remember an ad for a specific brand in that product class. Depending on the nature of the research, additional details could be provided to stimulate recall. Numerous research firms offer services that employ the unaided-recall procedure. In this test procedure, respondents are asked questions about an ad without the benefit of having the ad in front of them. In some cases, the brand name is provided, and respondents are asked to recall and describe advertisements they remember for the product. Typically, such research obtains information on how the ad appeared to the reader, what readers perceive it to have said about the product (its selling message), consumers' interest in the product, and their purchase motivation. Although test scores are usually lower, many argue that these tests are more realistic, since no information is provided to respondents. The impact of the ad alone is tested.

Two of the more common methods for collecting recognition and recall information are Starch readership tests and day-after-recall tests.

Starch Readership Test A **Starch readership test** is a post-test recognition procedure applied to both newspaper and magazine advertisements. The main supplier in Canada is Daniel Starch (Canada) Ltd., an organization which offers the research as a syndicated service (i.e., many clients share in the costs of collecting the information and in the findings of the research). The objectives of a Starch readership test are to measure how many readers have seen the ad, and what percentage of those who saw it read it.

In terms of procedure, a consumer is shown a magazine, and once it has been determined that he or she has read it, an interviewer goes through the magazine ad by ad with the respondent. For each advertisement in the magazine (the entire magazine is "starched"), respondents are divided into three categories:

1. *Noted*—the percentage of readers who remember seeing the ad in this issue.
2. *Associated*—the percentage of readers who saw any part of the ad that clearly indicated the brand or advertiser.
3. *Read Most*—the percentage of readers who read half or more of the written material.

The client receives the issue of the tested magazine, with all readership scores for all advertisements shown. The benefits derived from this form of testing are as follows:

- The client can measure the extent to which an advertisement is seen and read.
- By reviewing the results for other ads that were tested, the client can determine how effectively its advertisement broke through the clutter.
- Viewed in the context of previous testing, the scores may indicate an increase or decrease in readership, and this information could provide some insight into what creative approaches to use in the future.
- Different ads can be tested over time so that the effectiveness of various layout and design options can be determined.

In addition to the standard service, clients can request that special or additional questions be asked for a particular ad, at additional cost. The purpose of these questions is to measure how attitude dimensions such as believability, acceptability, and purchase intention are affected by exposure to the message.

Day-After-Recall (DAR) In the broadcast media, particularly television, the use of **day-after-recall testing (DAR)** and various forms of opinion-measure testing is quite common. As the name implies, day-after-recall research is conducted the day after an audience has been exposed to a television-commercial message for the first time. By means of a telephone-survey technique, a sampling of the client's target market is recruited and asked a series of questions so that their exposure to, and recall of, particular commercials may be determined. Depending on the client's needs, day-after-recall testing can accommodate aided-recall or unaided-recall formats. The objectives of the test are to measure the extent of the respondents' brand-name recognition and their recall of the primary selling message.

The procedure for day-after-recall testing is as follows:

1. Establish if the respondent watched a particular program.
2. Establish if the respondent recalls a commercial for a product category, a brand name, or a commercial for the brand being tested.
3. To gauge the achievement of communications objectives, ask for details on what the respondent remembers and what ideas the ad actually communicated (in either aided or unaided format).
4. Ask for specific information about what the respondent likes and dislikes in commercials, about areas of disbelief or confusion, about purchase motivation, and so on.
5. Collect basic socio-economic data for the purpose of analyzing research information.

The actual quantified measures obtained in a DAR test are described as total-related-recall levels. Total related recall measures two dimensions of the test commercial: intrusiveness and impact. Related recall refers to the percentage of the test-commercial audience who claim to remember the test execution, and who are also able to substantiate their claim by providing some description of the commercial.[1] The higher the percentage, the more intrusive the message with respect to the audience. For measuring the impact a commercial has made on an audience, the total-related-recall score is broken down into categories: unaided (by brand name mention) versus aided; specific versus non-specific; communication-objective or selling-message playback; and central-situation playback.

The primary strength of the day-after-recall test is that the advertisement is evaluated in a natural setting (in the respondents' home, with the respondents unaware that they might be part of a test group). Assuming that a viewer's recall should be highest the day after he or she is exposed to a commercial (given that the test is never performed on the same day as viewing), the response of the target market will reflect the commercial's ability to break through the clutter. However, many argue that placing a commercial within a popular program distorts data and may inflate recall scores, while the noise of competitive commercials may have a negative impact on recall scores.

Opinion-Measure Testing

Opinion-measure testing exposes an audience to test-commercial messages in the context of special television programs. In terms of procedure, a group of people are seated around television monitors to view the program and commercials. For consistency, all instructions and questions are presented over the monitors via prerecorded videotapes. Respondents record answers by circling responses on a questionnaire.

The test commercial is usually presented twice during the program, in cluster situations. Position within the cluster changes with each showing. The commercial sequences contain a series of test commercials (several client sponsors share the costs of test procedures) separated by three unchanging control commercials. The objectives of this form of testing are three-fold:

1. It measures the extent of the audience's awareness of a commercial—that is, the extent to which the commercial breaks through the clutter. In an unaided format, respondents are asked to recall the brand name and product type correctly after being exposed to the commercial.

2. It measures the extent to which the main idea in the commercial has been communicated to the audience. Questions are tailored to accommodate specific client needs. Typically, communication evaluations examine the audience's response regarding
   • What was actually communicated
   • The likes and dislikes of the audience regarding the commercial generally, or characters specifically
   • Their attitudes regarding the ad's believability, acceptability, comprehensibility, information content, persuasiveness, and so on.

3. It measures the effect of the commercial on purchase motivation; the measurement is based on a comparison of pre-exposure brand-purchase data and post-exposure brand-preference information. The purchase-motivation score is derived from measuring that percentage of competitive-brand users (as determined by a pre-usage question) who chose the test brand after being exposed to the commercial (that is, they chose the test brand for inclusion in a market [prize] basket, an incentive for participating in the test).

This procedure is often referred to as a forced-exposure test, a name which suggests the potential weakness of the test: the artificial environment in which it occurs. The question is, can such an environment yield good results? On the positive side, the results for commercials are compared to results from previous tests, and since the procedure remains constant, the data should provide reasonable direction to advertisers.

TESTING FOR INVOLUNTARY RESPONSES

Advertisers also have access to a variety of physiological-testing methods that measure involuntary responses to a specific element of an advertisement. The physiological-testing procedures include eye-camera tests, telcommeter tests, pupillometer tests, and tachistoscope tests.

Eye-Camera Test

In an **eye-camera test**, consumers read an advertisement while a hidden camera tracks their eye movement. Such a test gauges the point of immediate contact, how a reader scans the various components of an ad, and the amount of time spent reading it.

Telcommeter Test

A relatively new testing procedure in Canada is the **telcommeter** (Telcom Evaluation Techniques, a subsidiary of Cogem Inc.), which has testing applications for print and television. The telcommeter is a device that pinpoints a person's focus of attention. The device determines which elements of a print ad are noted, in what order, and which ones are re-examined. It can also determine how long a person spends looking at or reading each element, as well as how completely each piece of copy is read.[2]

The telcommeter can test outdoor advertising, a medium largely ignored in communications testing. Respondents go on a simulated drive, facing a video screen on which a series of slides dissolve automatically from one to the next. Billboards and transit-shelter ads appear on screen, move closer, and pass by. The telcommeter measures which ads attract attention the quickest, how long the ads are viewed for, and what is read on each.

Pupillometer Test

A **pupillometer test** measures pupil dilation (enlargement) while a person is reading. Based on the psychological principle that people's pupils respond to appealing stimuli by dilating, such a test can determine whether people respond in a positive manner or a negative manner to the ad.

Tachistoscope Test

A **tachistoscope test** measures respondents' perceptions of different elements of an advertisement. In the test, an ad is flashed onto a screen for a fraction of a second and subjects are asked what they saw. In such a test, the stimuli can be altered—different elements of the ads are rearranged so that the effectiveness of each can be measured.

Testing procedures and the need for them are controversial issues in the industry, particularly among advertising agencies, whose work is being tested. Many creative directors argue that too much testing defeats the creative process (it stifles creativity) and that what people say in research and do in the real world can be completely different. For all this criticism of pretesting procedures, however, clients like to know how customers will react to their messages, preferably before they spend money on them. For some additional insight into a relatively new form of creative testing, read the Advertising in Action vignette "Pre-Testing: Is Any Test Valid?"

OTHER FORMS OF RESEARCH

Perhaps the most meaningful tests are those which measure an ad's actual influence on a target audience: did the target actually purchase the product or take advantage of a special offer because of the ad? Alternately, an advertiser may attempt to measure the influence of advertising in terms of product movement in the channel of distribution. Examples of tests of this type are inquiry tests (split-run tests), sales measurements, and controlled experiments.

Inquiry Tests (Split-Run Tests)

Using this test, an advertiser can measure the effectiveness of two or more advertisements at once. For example, an advertiser could run two different ads with the same coupon offer (the coupon being pre-coded differently for each of the two ads). The number of coupons redeemed for each ad may be indicative of the relative strength of the overall ad. Small-scale tests of this nature are excellent for determining which advertisement should be more widely distributed. This procedure can be adapted for use by direct-response advertisers who use return coupons of a "send-for-more-information" nature.

Advertising in Action
Pre-Testing: Is Any Test Valid?

Will a middle-aged man linger over an automobile ad featuring a leggy female model? Will a female spend more time perusing a cologne ad featuring a sparsely-clad male model in a romantic setting? These are the types of questions that advertisers like to have answered prior to spending a fortune on magazine space. In the past, advertisers have had to rely on the accuracy of a test subject's memory, and the usefulness of those results was debated. Now they can secure some additional insight into reader's reactions by using the "people reader," an invention of research expert Lee Weinblatt. Lee is a former advertising-research executive with the Interpublic Group of advertising agencies based in New York City. He formed his own company, Pretesting Co., in 1985 and has enjoyed success with the people reader and a few other advertising-research procedures.

How does the people reader work? It is a device that surreptitiously monitors the way people react to a magazine advertisement. It looks like a desk lamp with a chunky smoked-glass body. Behind the glass are two tiny remote-controlled video cameras, one that tracks eye movements and another that monitors which page is being perused. In effect, it records how a reader progresses through a magazine. Where does the reader stop, and for how long? This type of information is interesting to an advertiser and a publisher of a magazine.

Does the people reader work? Naturally, such a device has its critics, many of them advertising executives who have been stung by the results of such a test. Remember, it is the advertising agencies that come under attack,

since it is their messages that are tested by the procedure. According to a New York city advertising executive, "You can measure the body's response, but you can't make a leap to what is going on in a person's mind." It is virtually impossible, in other words, to link the physiological response to the psychological response. Nonetheless, an ad that stops a reader for a few seconds longer, or an ad that draws a smile from the reader, is probably going to be the ad that an advertiser will run with.

Weinblatt acknowledges that very few advertising agencies have said that what he does makes sense. But he also states that traditional forms of pretesting are too overt—their results are relatively meaningless since the respondent knows a lot about why he or she is being tested. For example, in the case of a television-commercial test, a client arranges to have an advertisement aired to test subjects during normal programming, and then interviews them the next day about their ability to remember the ad and their reactions to it (i.e., using day-after-recall procedure). Weinblatt argues that this procedure "provides at best a murky picture, often failing to measure the impact of subliminal messages." The strength of the people reader is its ability to detect responses consumers may not be aware of—now that's real!

Despite the criticism from many advertising agencies, clients and publishers find the results of the people-reader test interesting. Among Weinblatt's clients are many large advertisers, including Ralston-Purina, RJR Nabisco, and S.C. Johnson, and prominent publishers such as *Sports Illustrated* and *The New Yorker*.

Adapted from Edmund Andrews, "People Reader designed to monitor how people react to advertising," *Whig-Standard*, August 2, 1990, p.26.

Sales Measurements

Although it is difficult to link advertising directly to sales, many firms that purchase sales and inventory data from A.C. Nielsen Company of Canada Ltd. via the company's Retail Index do perceive relationships between the two. These relationships do not measure the effectiveness of the message, but consider the overall impact of advertising (message, media, amount of expenditure, and timing) on sales.

Briefly, a company such as A.C. Nielsen monitors the movement of merchandise at the retail level. Advertisers who purchase the Nielsen data regularly (it is issued bi-monthly) are made aware of their pre-campaign and post-campaign inventories at retail. During the campaign, A.C. Nielsen makes periodic inventory checks to monitor cumulative product sales and the trend of the sales. Once the campaign is over, post-campaign inventories can be monitored so that the extent of the advertising impact can be measured. A.C. Nielsen data regarding advertising expenditures (amount and timing) is available on a bi-monthly and rolling 12-month basis so that trends can be evaluated in comparison with those of a year before or with those from the latest 12-month period.

Controlled Experiments

To measure the potential impact of advertising activity on sales, an advertiser could set up a comparative situation in which the advertising activity used in the test market is different than that used in a a control market. To implement this type of test, the advertiser would select two markets that were closely matched in terms of demographics, shopping habits, and media-consumption habits. In the control market, a given set of planned marketing activities would prevail. In the test market, the advertising variable would be altered: different media might be used, or the expenditure level or the weight of advertising might vary. Sales would be monitored closely in both markets so that test results would be obtained and conclusions with regard to advertising effectiveness would be reached.

MEDIA RESEARCH

The primary objective of a media plan is to reach as many people as possible within a defined target market (a target whose identity is based on demographics, psychographics, and geographics) in a cost-efficient manner. In other words, the advertiser strives for maximum impact at minimum cost. Achieving this objective requires that both qualitative and quantitative analysis of the media alternatives be performed so as to determine which medium or which combination of media is best suited for the campaign. The analysis considers the class of media (e.g., television, radio, magazine, newspaper), the subclass of media, the specific media vehicles, and the scheduling of media time and space in a media buy.

Media information in Canada is available through a variety of sources. For media planners, there is available an abundance of quantitative data, based on demographic variables, that shows each medium's ability to reach target markets. The media environment in Canada is quite competitive, as each one is constantly striving for an additional share of the market. A medium seeking to increase its market share does well to provide media planners with the most reliable, objective information possible; only this way will a given medium be considered for use in an advertiser's media mix.

The various groups involved with media research in Canada include independent-research companies, media associations and bureaus, and individual media. Independent organizations that provide a significant amount of data include the A.C. Nielsen Company of Canada Ltd., the Bureau of Measurement (BBM), the Audit Bureau of Circulations (ABC), and the Canadian Circulations Audit Board (CCAB). Among the media groups, data is provided by the Television Bureau (TVB), the Radio Bureau of Canada (RBC), the Print Measurement Bureau (PMB), the Newspaper Marketing Bureau through their NADbank studies, and the Canadian Outdoor Measurement Bureau (COMB). In addition, individual media (specific newspapers or magazines) also conduct research, or use data compiled by media associations or independent-research organizations, to show the effectiveness and efficiencies of their medium. For example, local daily newspapers use NADbank data, and magazines use data from Print Measurement Bureau studies.

MEDIA RESEARCH—BROADCAST MEDIA

The organizations that compile broadcast-media data on a continuous (year to year) basis include A.C. Nielsen, the Bureau of Measurement, the Television Bureau of Canada, and the Radio Bureau of Canada.

BBM Bureau of Measurement

The BBM collects audience data through mailed surveys. Participants are asked to fill in a seven-day diary, recording all television viewing for all TV sets in the household, for each quarter hour of the day from 6:00 A.M. to 2:00 A.M. Information from returned diaries is keyed into computers for processing and verification.

As of March 1991, the BBM and A.C. Nielsen have agreed to jointly produce audience ratings. The agreement divides responsibilities between two equal partners. The BBM will continue using the diary system it now employs to measure market ratings, but will cease measuring networks by diaries. The BBM focus will be on collecting data concerning local markets, while A.C. Nielsen will electronically collect data for the network programs.

The BBM also conducts a "sweep" survey in the fall and spring covering 65 000 people (two years of age and older) in 46 television markets across Canada. The data collected during the ratings period is used to estimate the audiences of programs on individual stations. Ratings are audience estimates expressed as a percentage of a population in a defined geographic area.[3]

The television-market reports cover 46 Canadian markets—major markets such as Toronto, Montreal, and Vancouver are reported seven times a year. The key data reported is a measure of the size of the audience in relation to the time of day.

The BBM conducts surveys on radio markets also. Up to four times a year, and depending on the size and competitive nature of the market, BBM selects a random sample of telephone listings from over 400 sampling cells across Canada. Households are initially contacted by telephone. Once the names, ages, and sex of all household members are known, researchers design and select a sample that matches the Canadian population by size and location by demographic group. Diaries are then mailed to households for completion. The data collected generates information on average quarter-hour listening trends and cumulative audience estimates.

A.C. Nielsen Company of Canada

The data available through Nielsen concern channels tuned and audience composition. The Nielsen Television Index (NTI) Network Reports cover audiences for all programs, 52 weeks a year for national and regional networks. Network reports provide audience-viewing information 24 hours a day for the entire year. Data is organized on the bases of the age, education, income, and occupation of audience members. Nielsen has a sample panel of 1500 households collect data by an electronic-metering device known as the "people meter." Respondents indicate their viewing responses through the use of a remote-control device. Among the data recorded are program rankings and audience composition. Samples of the type of information compiled by A.C. Nielsen are included in figures 8.3 and 8.4.

For additional information on the Nielsen people meter, refer to the Advertising in Action feature "People Meter Sparks Controversy."

Television Bureau of Canada (TVB)

The TVB is a sales and marketing resource centre for the commercial television industry in Canada. Its mandate is to promote television as an effective advertising medium. Each year, this organization publishes a booklet, *TV Basics*, which contains the latest data on television trends. Information contained in this publication includes viewing trends by demographic and geographic variables, programming preferences by demographic variables, television-station circulation by sex and age for all station markets, and penetration statistics for Cable TV, Pay TV, and VCR households.

In addition, the TVB frequently conducts primary research, using independent research firms to gather information on the influence of television and television advertising in relation to the influence of media alternatives. In accordance with their mandate, and given the competitive nature of the media, television networks and individual stations can use such data, if it is favourable, to better position television as an advertising medium.

TELEVISION-VIEWING TRENDS

Have you ever thought about the amount of time you spend in front of a television? In Canada, 99% of the population aged two years of age and up live in households equipped with television sets. In fact, 56% have two or more sets in the household. On an average day, 78% of Canadians view television at least once. During prime time (7:00 to 11:00 P.M.) an average of 37.1% of adults will tune to the medium in any given quarter hour period.[4] Viewing patterns vary by week, day, by time of day, and by season.

Figure 8.3 Typical data compiled by A.C. Nielsen—CTV program rankings, by audience size

29

CTV

NIELSEN WEEK/SEMAINE
SEPT 18 SEPT, 1989

PROGRAM RANKINGS

CLASSEMENTS DES EMISSIONS

RANK RANG	PROGRAM/EMISSION	# STNS	DAY JOUR	AVG MINUTE (000) MOY PAR MIN	RANKING CLASSEMENTS			
					PUBLIC PRIMAIRE	HIGH SCHOOL SECONDAIRE	COLLEGE CEGEP	UNIVERSITY UNIVERSITE
	ADULTS 18+/ADULTES 18+							
1	COSBY	16	THU	1742	10	1	2	5
2	SISTER KATE	16	THU	1698	10	2	1	2
3	MURPHY BROWN	16	MON	1655	4	4	3	1
4	MATLOCK	15	TUE	1654	1	3	8	4
5	CTV SUNDAY MOVIE	16	SUN	1490	2	5	4	8
6	ROSEANNE	16	MON	1251	8	6	16	12
7	YOUNG RIDERS	14	THU	1222	6	8	18	11
8	DOOGIE HOWSER M.D.	13	MON	1187	3	18	5	12
9	HARDBALL	15	FRI	1111	19	7	9	16
10	W-5	22	SUN	1103	12	11	7	16
11	BLUE JAYS PRIME 2	20	WED	1102	14	10	17	3
12	DOOGIE HOWSER M.D.	14	MON	1076	4	19	14	10
13	ANYTHING BUT LOVE	16	MON	1075	7	12	20	23
14	MIDNIGHT CALLER	16	TUE	1034	9	17	14	26
15	B HOPE SALUTE-L.BALL	14	SAT	1006	13	13	23	14
16	MY TWO DADS	11	SUN	929	15	21	6	18
17	CTV NATIONAL NEWS	22	A-7	928	28	9	10	7
18	BLUE JAYS PRIME 1	19	WED	916	22	15	19	8
19	BLUE JAYS OFF PRIME	20	SUN	867	20	20	12	19
20	CHICKEN SOUP	16	MON	804	30	14	12	23
21	LIVE IT UP	22	MON	798	16	26	22	22
22	SISTER KATE	13	SUN	753	21	31	21	6
22	KATTS & DOG	16	SAT	753	18	28	11	32
24	MY SECRET IDENTITY	16	THU	736	30	16	27	15
25	BORDERTOWN	16	TUE	709	17	27	32	21
26	BLUE JAYS PRIME	18	WED	692	26	22	24	20
27	NIGHT HEAT	16	THU	671	24	25	24	25
28	ANOTHER WORLD	16	A-5	648	23	24	30	29
29	FREE SPIRIT	11	SAT	578	27	29	26	27
30	NICK & HILARY	12	FRI	577	25	30	27	31
31	LAST FRONTIER	16	FRI	508	35	23	29	27
32	SNOOPS	7	FRI	309	34	32	35	39
32	CAMPBELLS	16	SAT	309	32	33	40	35
34	HAVE FAITH	10	SAT	295	29	43	32	46
35	LITTLEST HOBO	15	SUN	283	33	37	34	42
36	CANADA AM	22	A-5	254	36	36	31	30
37	QUESTION PERIOD	22	SUN	197	40	34	44	35
38	SHIRLEY	16	A-5	174	37	38	38	35
39	ROMPER ROOM	13	THU	140	48	35	39	
40	WIDE WORLD OF SPORTS	21	SAT	129	44	40	40	41
41	5,4,3,2 - RUN	16	SAT	128	41	39	45	
42	CANADA AM INTRO	22	A-5	123	43	43	40	34
43	SECRET LIVES	8	THU	110	37	43		
44	PUTTNAM'S PRAIRIE	16	SAT	105	39	46		
45	ROMPER ROOM	14	WED	99	50	42	35	35
46	ROCKETS	16	SAT	95	42	48	46	33
47	SECRET LIVES	10	A-2	77	47	41	46	43
48	ROMPER ROOM	15	A-2	66	46	49	40	40
49	EXTRA EXTRA	16	SAT	46	45	51		44
50	SECRET LIVES	9	TUE	39	48	47		
51	ROMPER ROOM	13	FRI	37	51	50	37	44
	SECRET LIVES	7	FRI	IFR				

Courtesy: A.C. Nielsen Company of Canada Limited

Figure 8.4 Example of data compiled by A.C. Nielsen—Overnight ratings for January 28, 1990

A.C.NIELSEN METER OVERNIGHTS
NTI DIRECT
Preliminary Projections (1000)

DATA FOR 01/28/90

NTI DIRECT: TOTAL PROGRAM
DAYPART: PRIME DATE: 01/29/90

NETWORK # STNS	TIME	DUR MINS	(MTWRFSS) PROGRAM NAME EPISODE TITLE	Khlds. Total	Persons 2+	Adults 18-34	Females 18+	Females 18-49	Females 25-54	Males 18+	Males 18-49	Males 25-54	Teens 12-17	Children 2-11
CBC 35	6:00p	60	(S) MAGICAL WORLD DISNEY	943	1510	377	527	335	309	452	292	267	108	423
CBC 37	7:00p	60	(S) ROAD TO AVONLEA	1205	1883	302	926	453	430	574	216	225	97	286
CBC 37	8:00p	120	(S) RYL VARIETY PERFORM. (S)	1007	1627	281	827	338	335	604	281	279	53	143
CBC 37	10:00p	25	(S) CBC NEWS:SUN REPORT	832	1297	137	570	245	235	652	281	317	11	64
CBC 37	10:25p	26	(S) VENTURE	669	944	118	379	190	190	501	218	233	13	51
CBC 16	10:53p	5	(S) NATIONS BUSINESS	364	458	78	223	118	114	235	127	135	<<	<<
CBC 16	11:00p	30	(S) CBC LOCAL NEWS	245	324	50	139	88	81	177	122	140	<<	<<
CTV 9	7:00p	30	(S) MY TWO DADS 7212	135	219	42	77	29	19	123	74	82	<<	16
CTV 21	8:00p	60	(S) W-5 89-13	561	897	179	426	225	247	428	187	207	16	26
CTV 16	9:00p	120	(S) CTV SUNDAY MOVIE PLOT-HITLE	689	1222	419	526	333	343	597	362	331	28	70
CTV 22	11:00p	30	(S) CTV NATIONAL NEWS SUNDAY	736	1210	291	616	320	301	588	248	262	<<	<<

Courtesy: A.C. Nielsen Company of Canada Limited

Advertising in Action

People Meter Sparks Controversy

To an advertiser, how many people a message reaches and at what cost are crucial issues. How much a network or station actually charges for a 30-second commercial is an issue for the broadcasting industry. In bygone days, the data used to determine advertising rates was obtained from diaries. People were carefully recruited to record in a diary their household's viewing patterns over a one-week period. Information was collected at quarter-hour intervals, between 6:00 A.M. and 2:00 A.M. each day of the week. The diary was the norm for the industry, and its sponsors—the broadcasters, advertising agencies, and advertisers—were comfortable with the results it was producing. At least, they were comfortable until the people meter came along.

The advances of technology have added some fuel to the audience-information fire. Since 1988, A.C. Nielsen has been experimenting with and fine tuning the procedures needed for the electronic information-retrieval system it calls the "People Meter." Ultimately, the people meter will replace the diary. Nielsen claims that the people meter is much more accurate than the diary and that the sponsors will have much better information to do their media planning with. The immediate problem, however, and one that all sponsors are wrestling with, is the discrepancies between diary-generated data and people-meter-generated data. Data collected by diaries and data collected electronically over the same period produced different results. The electronic data indicated that:

1. Daytime viewing is higher then diary-based data would suggest.
2. Late-night television attracts greater numbers of night owls.

3. Children spend a greater number of hours watching television each week.
4. Viewing by males is relatively constant; viewing by females is down slightly.
5. Viewership of sitcoms in prime time is generally lower, as are documentaries and news.
6. Hockey audiences are down significantly.

Such information has sent the industry spinning, as rate structures for advertising are so closely pegged to audiences. Nielsen defiantly stands behind the accuracy of the people meter. Its role is not to produce data that the industry would like to see, but accurate information for all concerned parties to use.

To get a feel for the sophistication of the people meter, let's quickly examine how it works. The meter itself is about the size of a videocassette tape and is linked to the television like any other gadget—a VCR or a converter box, for example. It records who is watching (each member of a household is given a number that must be keyed in before viewing commences—reserve numbers are available for guests); the show and the station being watched (up to 200 stations can be recorded); whether the VCR is on (yes, the system distinguishes between a playback and a simultaneous recording); and it can tell if the television is being used as a video-game monitor.

For TV executives, this more accurate viewing system is a double-edged blessing. On one hand it is possible to measure which ad in a cluster of commercials gets the highest number of viewers (it should be noted that Nielsen currently only collects data concerning audi-

continued

ences of programs, but the technology is there to do commercials). If the first ad gets a higher number of viewers than the third, the network can charge a premium for the lead position. On the other hand, the broadcaster faces the dilemma of advertisers refusing to pay high rates for evening viewing hours (referred to as prime time) if there are fewer people watching than has been assumed.

Peter Sisam, a vice-president at CTV, acknowledges that only an electronic measuring device can keep up with what viewers watch. People have so much choice today because of the penetration of cable television and satellite dishes. VCRs, too, have altered viewing habits, allowing for "time shifting" (record now and play later), while remote con-

trols encourage "zapping" (switching channels at commercial breaks). It is Nielsen that keeps track of all of these viewing patterns—and it does it every three seconds the television is in use.

Nielsen sees the new system as a real planning tool for advertisers. They know that advertisers are anxious to obtain more accurate information about a medium they pay so heavily for. Since demographic information about the viewing audience is also compiled (enabling advertisers to know who is watching), advertisers will be able to target their television advertising dollars more wisely. Traditionally, television was a mass medium, but the era of television specialization may be just around the corner.

Adapted from Jamie Hubbard, "Television tunes in on fickle viewers," *Financial Post*, April 27, 1987, p.7.

Figure 8.5   Average per capita hours of viewing by age breaks, Canada

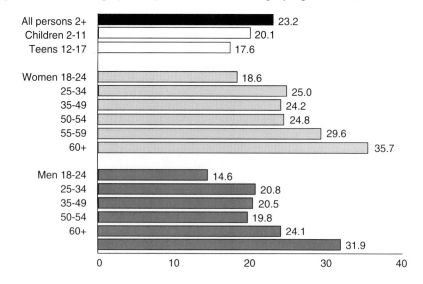

Source: BBM Bureau of Measurement (1989 Fall BBM Sweep Survey)

Average Weekly Hours Tuned

Among adults, the number of average weekly per-capita hours of TV viewing tends to increase with the age of the viewer. The least viewing is done by men aged 18–24. Per capita tuning levels in teens are lower than those of both children and adults. Men tend to view television less than women do. Refer to figure 8.5 for a summary of this tuning data.

Viewing by Day of Week

Among all people aged two years and older, viewing is lowest on Wednesday, Friday, and Saturday. Viewing peaks on Sundays. Among women aged 18 years and older, viewing tends to be higher during the week and lower on the weekend. Among men aged 18 and up, the opposite is true. Sample charts illustrating viewing trends by day of the week are included in figure 8.6.

Viewing by Time of Day

Most television watching (except that of children) is done during prime time: Monday to Sunday, 7:00 P.M. to 11:00 P.M. Monday to Friday, 6:00 A.M. to 4:30 P.M., represents the most popular viewing time for children. Daytime TV hours for children and women are almost twice as high as those for men. All demographic groups have relatively similar patterns for the Monday to Friday 4:30 to 7:30 P.M. daypart. A **daypart** is a block of time in a station's or network's daily programming schedule (e.g., a half-hour or one-hour period). A summary of this data appears in figure 8.7.

Viewing by Season

When television viewing is analyzed on a month-by-month or seasonal basis, the number of hours spent watching television is relatively constant across all age categories. Television viewing begins to soften in May, and definitely tapers off in June and July. Such factors as weather, outdoor activities, and people spending more time away from home account for the drop off in viewing during the summer. TV viewing is strongest in the months of November and February. Sample data regarding television viewing by season is included in figure 8.8.

VCR VIEWING PATTERNS, PAY-TV AND SPECIALTY SERVICE VIEWING

An average of four hours each week is spent on VCR usage. Relative to all TV viewing, VCR usage is higher in the evenings (Monday to Sunday) and on the weekends (6:00 A.M. to 7:00 P.M.). VCR reach is now in the 20% range, and its share of the total hours spent viewing television is 3.3%. VCR weekly reach has slackened in pace but continues to grow, while the share of total hours spent viewing television has levelled off.

Figure 8.6   Viewing trends by day of week

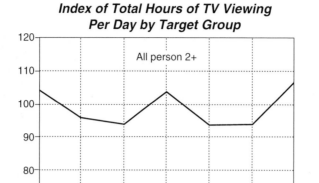

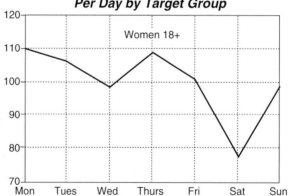

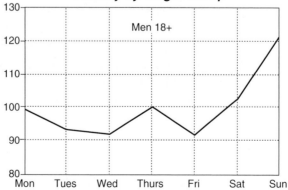

Source: BBM Bureau of Measurement (1989 Fall BBM Sweep Survey)

Figure 8.7   Viewing trends by time of day

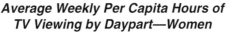

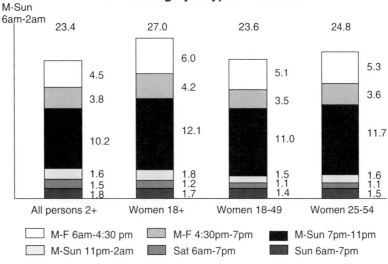

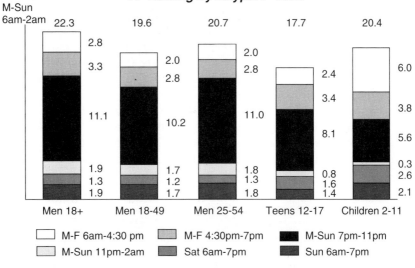

Source: BBM Bureau of Measurement (1989 Fall BBM Sweep Survey)

Figure 8.8 Weekly television-viewing trends by month of year for all persons two years of age and older

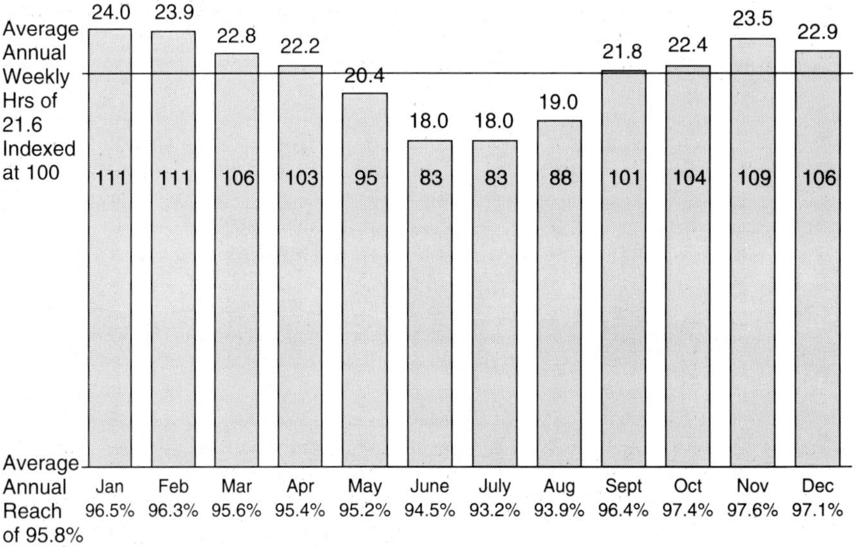

	24.0	23.9	22.8	22.2	20.4	18.0	18.0	19.0	21.8	22.4	23.5	22.9
Average Annual Weekly Hrs of 21.6 Indexed at 100	111	111	106	103	95	83	83	88	101	104	109	106
	Jan	Feb	Mar	Apr	May	June	July	Aug	Sept	Oct	Nov	Dec
Average Annual Reach of 95.8%	96.5%	96.3%	95.6%	95.4%	95.2%	94.5%	93.2%	93.9%	96.4%	97.4%	97.6%	97.1%

Source: BBM Bureau of Measurement (1989 BBM Network Reports)

Since the addition of some Pay-TV and Specialty Services to the basic cable-converter service in 1988, weekly reach continues to gain strength in these areas. Similarly, the weekly share of hours tuned continues to increase. For more details on VCR and Pay-TV viewing patterns, refer to figure 8.9.

RADIO BUREAU OF CANADA (RBC)

The Radio Bureau of Canada is a sales and marketing resource centre serving the commercial radio broadcasting industry. The Bureau provides statistical data to advertisers and agencies that allows them to make objective assessments regarding how to best use radio as an advertising medium.

In conjunction with the BBM, the Bureau conducts a Radio Product Measurement Study (RPM) in selected major markets. The RPM study is designed to generate information about retail and national-product categories, and other media-usage data. RPM provides advertisers and agencies with radio-station and daypart-audience composition for specific product-user groups.[5]

RADIO LISTENING TRENDS

The radio listenership is divided between AM and FM stations. Generally, AM stations reach more of the Canadian population than do FM stations. Among all people aged seven and older, AM stations have a 53% share of total hours tuned compared to a 47% share for FM. In this section we present some basic information about radio-listenership patterns.

Figure 8.9 Trends in VCR and pay-TV usage

1. VCR's Weekly Reach and Share of Hours, All Persons 2+

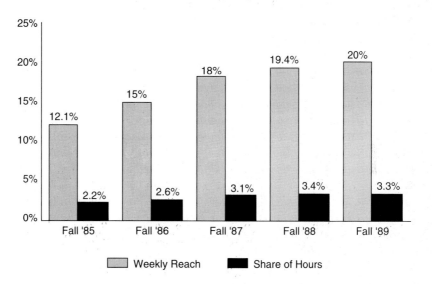

2. Pay-TV/Specialty Services' Weekly Reach and Share of Hours, All Persons 2+

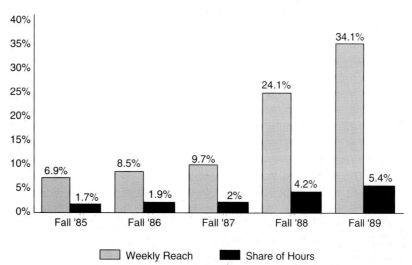

Source: BBM Bureau of Measurement (1989 Fall BBM Sweep Survey)

Figure 8.10 The importance of breakfast-time reach in radio

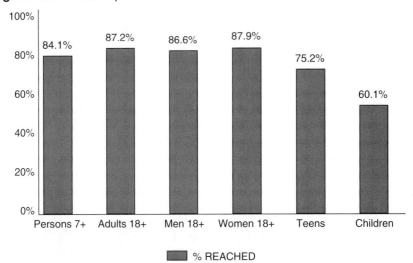

Source: Radio Bureau of Canada. The graph is based on material collected by BBM Bureau of Measurement (Fall 1989).

Listenership by Daypart

Radio listenership by daypart is almost the inverse of television. Generally, radio is very popular in the morning but listenership tapers off as the day progresses. Among all Canadians aged seven years and older, the breakfast-time period involves listening by up to 84% of the population. Figure 8.10 presents additional details on the breakfast-time reach of radio.

In terms of audience composition by daypart, the morning and mid-morning time blocks are popular with men and women 18 years of age and older. The late afternoon and evening are more popular with teens.

Listenership by Day of the Week

The weekday reach of radio is high. Among adults 18 years of age and older the average reach is 95%. On weekdays, adults spend an average of 3.7 hours listening to the radio. Teens and children spend fewer hours listening to radio. Radio's reach is extremely consistent during weekdays, but it does drop off on the weekends. More information on day-of-the-week listening patterns is included in figure 8.11.

Listenership by Season

Radio reaches adults consistently throughout each season. Year round, adults spend more than 20 hours per week listening to radio. Figure 8.12 presents more information on seasonal listening patterns for radio.

Figure 8.11 Day-of-the-week listenership patterns by age and by day of the week

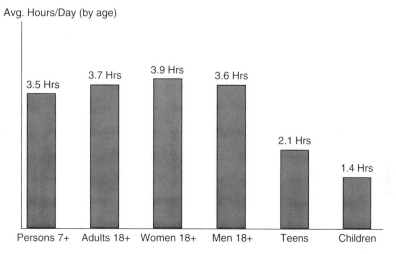

Avg. Hours/Day (by age)

3.5 Hrs	3.7 Hrs	3.9 Hrs	3.6 Hrs	2.1 Hrs	1.4 Hrs
Persons 7+	Adults 18+	Women 18+	Men 18+	Teens	Children

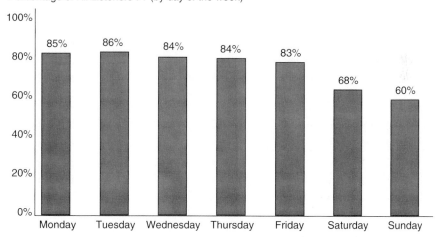

Percentage of All Listeners 7+ (by day of the week)

85%	86%	84%	84%	83%	68%	60%
Monday	Tuesday	Wednesday	Thursday	Friday	Saturday	Sunday

Source: Radio Bureau of Canada. This graph is based on material collected by BBM Bureau of Measurement (Fall 1989).

MEDIA RESEARCH—PRINT MEDIA

The companies and organizations involved in print-media research include the Audit Bureau of Circulations, Canadian Circulations Audit Board, Print Measurement Bureau, Newspaper Market Bureau, and Canadian Outdoor Measurement Bureau.

Figure 8.12   Radio listenership by season (adults 18 years of age and older)

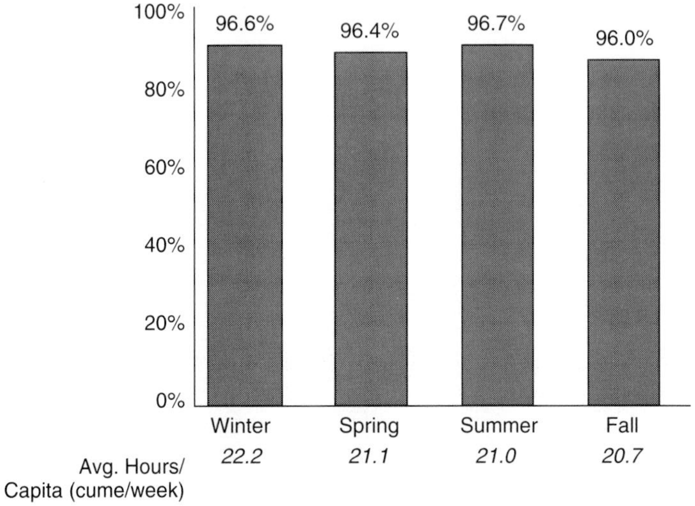

Season	Winter	Spring	Summer	Fall
Listenership	96.6%	96.4%	96.7%	96.0%
Avg. Hours/Capita (cume/week)	22.2	21.1	21.0	20.7

Source: Radio Bureau of Canada. This graph is based on material collected by BBM Bureau of Measurement (1989).

Audit Bureau of Circulations (ABC)

The ABC is responsible for issuing standardized statements verifying circulation statistics for paid-circulation magazines (consumer and business publications) and a majority of daily newspapers in Canada. All publications that are members of ABC receive an audited **publisher's statement**. This statement is the authority on which advertising rates are based (verified circulation is used to establish the advertising rate base as shown in the publication's rate card). Refer to figure 8.13, a sample publisher's statement for *Equinox* magazine. A publisher's statement includes the following information:

1. *Average Paid Circulation for the Latest Six Months* In addition to the six-month trend, average circulation is shown for regional and metropolitan editions.
2. *Paid Circulation for Each Issue in Last Six Months* This circulation figure includes single copy sales and subscription sales, the combination of which gives the total paid circulation.
3. *Analysis of Total New and Renewal Subscriptions* This analysis gives information concerning prices, terms, sales sources, and the use of premiums in subscription selling.
4. *Additional Circulation Information* This takes into consideration
   • Magazines issued to subscribers after subscription has elapsed (a three-month grace period is allowed for auditing)
   • The use of incentives (such as lengthier subscriptions for the same price) to encourage prompt payment
   • How the magazine is sold at retail (is it returnable or non-returnable?)

EQUINOX - THE MAGAZINE OF CANADIAN DISCOVERY

CLASS, INDUSTRY
OR FIELD SERVED: Magazine of Canadian Discovery

[1] AVERAGE PAID CIRCULATION FOR 6 MONTHS ENDED JUNE 30, 1986

Subscriptions:	154,308
Single Copy Sales:	12,281
AVERAGE TOTAL PAID CIRCULATION	166,589
Advertising Rate Base	160,000
Average Total Non-Paid Distribution 4,012	

[1a] AVERAGE PAID CIRCULATION of Regional, Metro and Demographic Editions

None

[2] PAID CIRCULATION by Issues

Issue	Subscriptions	Single Copy Sales	Total Paid
Jan. Feb.	158,974	11,547	170,521
Mar./Apr.	153,550	12,326	165,876
May/June	150,399	12,970	163,369

ANALYSIS OF TOTAL NEW AND RENEWAL SUBSCRIPTIONS

Sold during 6 Month Period Ended June 30, 1986

[3] AUTHORIZED PRICES:
(a) Basic Prices: Single Copy $3.50 22,160
(b) Higher than basic prices: Foreign, 1 yr. $40.00 air mail 18,394
(c) Lower than basic prices: 1 yr. (6 issues) $21.00; 2 yrs. $42.00; Foreign, 1 yr. $25.00 surface mail ... None
     Subscriptions: 1 yr. (6 issues) $15.97, $17.00, 7 issues $17.00, 5 yrs. (30 issues) $64.70 ... None
(d) Association subscription prices 278
     Total Subscriptions Sold in Period 40,554

[4] DURATION OF SUBSCRIPTIONS SOLD
(a) One to six months (1 to 3 issues) .... None
(b) Seven to twelve months (4 to 6 issues) 32,624
(c) Thirteen to twenty-four months 7,652
(d) Twenty-five to thirty-six months .... None
(e) Thirty-seven to forty-eight months .... None
(f) Forty-nine months and more 278
     Total Subscriptions Sold in Period 40,554

[5] CHANNELS OF SUBSCRIPTION SALES
(a) Ordered by mail and/or direct request
(b) Ordered through salespeople
     1. Catalog agencies and individual agents 28,493
     2. Publisher's own and other publishers' salespeople 12,061
     3. Independent agencies' salespeople .... None
     4. Newspaper agencies .... None
     5. Members of schools, churches, fraternal and similar organizations .... None
(c) Association memberships .... None
(d) All other channels .... None
     Total Subscriptions Sold in Period 40,554

continued

EQUINOX - THE MAGAZINE OF CANADIAN DISCOVERY	Publisher's Statement	For 6 Months Ended June 30, 1986

MAGAZINE PUBLISHER'S STATEMENT

EQUINOX - THE MAGAZINE OF CANADIAN DISCOVERY

CAMDEN EAST, ONTARIO K0K 1J0

AVERAGE PAID CIRCULATION
For Six Months Ended
June 30, 1986

166,589

Publisher's Compilation - Subject to Audit

Audit Bureau of Circulations
900 N. Meacham Road, Schaumburg, IL 60173-4968

Figure 8.13 continued

6. USE OF PREMIUMS:
(a) Ordered without premium.
(b) Ordered with material reprinted from this publication
(c) Ordered with other premiums. See Par. 11(a)
Total Subscriptions Sold in Period:

23,960
None
16,594
40,554

ADDITIONAL CIRCULATION INFORMATION

7. POST EXPIRATION COPIES INCLUDED IN PAID CIRCULATION (PAR. 1):
(a) Average number of copies served on subscriptions not more than three months after expiration 10,277

8. COLLECTION STIMULANTS: .... None

9. BASIS ON WHICH COPIES WERE SOLD TO RETAIL OUTLETS:
Fully returnable 100.00%

10. CANADIAN PAID CIRCULATION BY ABCD COUNTY SIZE based on May/June, 1986 Issue

November/December, 1983 issue used in establishing percentages.
Total paid circulation of this issue was 1.93% less than average total paid circulation for period.

County Size	No. of Counties	% of Canadian Population	Subscription Circulation Copies	% Total	Single Copy Circulation Copies	% Total	Total Circulation Copies	% Total
A	56	62%	89,135	62.00	7,782	60.00	96,917	61.84
B	57	18%	23,002	16.00	5,188	40.00	28,190	17.99
C	46	9%	17,252	12.00			17,252	11.00
D	106	11%	14,377	10.00			14,377	9.17
TOTAL CANADA	265	100%	143,766	100.00	12,970	100.00	156,736	100.00

EXPLANATION OF ABCD COUNTY SIZE

A—All counties which are, in whole or in part, within the boundaries of Census Metropolitan Areas.
B—All remaining counties which are, in whole or in part, within the boundaries of Census Agglomerations of 25,000 population or over and other counties containing a place of 25,000 or more population not officially designated as Census Agglomerations.
C—All remaining counties which are, in whole or in part, within the boundaries of Census Agglomerations of less than 25,000 population and other counties containing a place of 10,000 or more population.
D—All remaining counties.

11. EXPLANATORY:
Latest Released Audit Report Issued for 12 months ended June 30, 1985.
Variation from Publisher's Statements

Audit Period Ended	Rate Base	Audit Report	Publisher's Statements	Difference	Percentage of Difference
6-30-85	(a)	156,233	156,111	+122	+0.08
6-30-84	(b)	136,557	137,233	−676	−0.50
6-30-82	(c) 75,000	122,926	121,845 *	+1,081	+0.89

*Initial Audit for 6 months ended June 30, 1982 - Publisher's Statement not required for this period.

(a) Effective 1/1/85 changed from 145,000 to 160,000.
(b) Effective 1/1/84 changed from 125,000 to 145,000.
(c) Effective 1/1/83 changed from 75,000 to 125,000.

(a) Par 6(c): A paperback book. The Whales of Canada, with no advertised value was offered with subscriptions at prices shown in Par 3.

12. GEOGRAPHIC ANALYSIS OF TOTAL PAID CIRCULATION for the May/June, 1986 Issue

Total paid circulation of this issue was 1.93% less than average total paid circulation for period.

PROVINCE	Subs.	Single Copy Sales	TOTAL	%
Newfoundland	871	60	931	0.57
Nova Scotia	4,360	376	4,736	2.90
Prince Edward Island	467		467	0.29
New Brunswick	2,496	242	2,738	1.68
Quebec	7,906	602	8,508	5.21
Ontario	65,969	7,227	73,196	44.81
Manitoba	6,463	298	6,761	4.14
Saskatchewan	7,154	332	7,486	4.58
Alberta	19,582	1,645	21,227	12.99
British Columbia	26,976	2,188	29,164	17.85
Northwest Territories	888		888	0.54
Yukon Territory	543		543	0.33
Miscellaneous				
Unclassified	91		91	0.05
TOTAL CANADA	143,766	12,970	156,736	95.94
British Commonwealth	866		866	0.53
United States	4,297		4,297	2.63
Foreign	1,470		1,470	0.90
Unclassified				
Military or Civilian Personnel Overseas				
GRAND TOTAL	150,399	12,970	163,369	100.00

We certify that all data set forth in this Publisher's Statement are true and report circulation in accordance with Audit Bureau of Circulations' Bylaws and Rules.

EQUINOX - THE MAGAZINE OF CANADIAN DISCOVERY, published by Equinox Publishing, 7 Queen Victoria Road, Camden East, Ontario, Canada K0K 1J0.

MARGARET HEWITT
Circulation Manager

DANNY R. BEDFORD
Controller

Date Signed, July 31, 1986.

Printed in U.S.A.

Courtesy: Equinox Publishing. Reprinted with permission.

5. *Paid Circulation by County Size* This involves a review of circulation by size of market (four different county sizes are included, based on population density).
6. *Geographic Analysis of Total Paid Circulation* This is a study categorizing circulation by province, territory, and foreign subscriptions.

Canadian Circulations Audit Board (CCAB)

The CCAB is responsible for auditing the circulation data of member publications, and issuing standardized statements for use by advertisers and advertising agencies. Members who subscribe to auditing by the CCAB include business and industry publications, consumer magazines, community newspapers, and controlled-circulation (i.e., free-distribution) magazines. In the case of a controlled-circulation publication, audited statements from the CCAB contain the following information:

1. *Type of Circulation* This includes both the method of distribution and the areas of distribution.
2. *Field Served and Recipient Qualification* Distribution to a pre-determined target, based on demographic data.
3. *Circulation by Issues* This gives circulation data for the last six months.
4. *Average Paid Circulation per Issue* This is the average paid circulation against which advertising rates are applied.
5. *Average Audited Circulation at the End of Previous Audit Periods* Circulation for the last four audit periods (two years) reveals circulation-growth trends.
6. *Analysis of Geographical Distribution of Circulation* This examines circulation by each province and territory, and all of Canada together.
7. *Analysis of Circulation by Type of Recipient* This gives the location of selected homes or other locations (e.g., hotels) where the magazine is distributed.

The Use of Audited Circulation Data Audited circulation data provided by the ABC or CCAB provides several benefits to the advertiser and the advertising agency.

1. Circulation figures, current versus past, can be analyzed with a view to determining whether the publication is growing or declining in popularity.
2. The circulation audience of the publication can be compared with the target market of the advertiser.
3. Efficiency comparisons (i.e., comparisons of the amounts being spent on reaching the target audience) can be made with competing publications reaching similar target audiences to determine which publications are the most cost-effective.

Print Measurement Bureau (PMB)

The PMB provides standardized readership information for members, which include advertisers, agencies, publishers, and associate members. More recent studies (from 1983 on) have been expanded to include data concerning people's exposure to other media, their lifestyles, and their product usage.

A *Product Profile Study* is published annually by the PMB. Each year, PMB obtains over 13 500 completed questionnaires; what is published is based on the latest two years of data. PMB data consists of the following: readership data, inter-media exposure information, product-usage data, and brand data.[6]

Readership Data Data concerning total and primary readers is available for individual publications. This information provides assistance in determining the most efficient publication mix for diverse advertising campaigns. Readership data is also broken down as follows: total Canada, English and French Canada, and key markets (i.e., Toronto, Montreal, and Vancouver); it is also broken down according to demographic variables (i.e., age, sex, income, head of household, principal shopper, occupation, household size and composition).

Inter-Media Exposure Information Data concerning people's exposure to other media, including television, radio, newspaper, outdoor, and transit, is collected in each research study. Knowing what media an advertiser's target market is exposed to can assist the advertiser in developing a more efficient media mix to reach that target.

Product-Usage Data Data is compiled for over 800 products in a variety of product categories, including food, personal-care products, beverages, leisure activities, financial services, tobacco, alcohol, and many more. The information permits extensive cross-tabulations with media habits, demographics, and lifestyle data. Analysis of product-usage data can answer such questions as "Do users of my product read magazines more than they watch television?" or "What are the demographics of heavy users of my product?"

Brand Data Usage data concerning specific brands is recorded. Sponsors may include questions about specific brands, but at additional cost. This opportunity allows advertisers and agencies to determine the demographic and media-exposure profiles of users of specific brands within a product category.

An example of product-usage data is found in figure 8.14. Here, product-usage information is correlated with the magazines that product users read. The chart shows which magazines are more popular with product-category users (i.e., magazine readers) generally, and heavy, medium, and light users specifically.

Data provided by the PMB's product-profile studies are beneficial to advertisers and agencies in the media-planning process. Based on cross-tabulations of data concerning media, product, brand, and lifestyle, the information can be used to identify target markets more precisely, to assist in budget allocation, and to inform decisions regarding media selection and placement.

Newspaper Marketing Bureau

The Newspaper Marketing Bureau acts as a marketing arm for the daily-newspaper industry in Canada. Through NADbank, a newspaper-audience data bank, data concerning local-market newspaper coverage is provided so that individual daily newspapers can present themselves as viable advertising alternatives.

The NADbank readership data is updated annually and compiles information concerning 53 dailies in 32 markets across Canada. For readers 18 years of age and

Figure 8.14 Print Measurement Bureau—Example of product-usage data by magazine readers

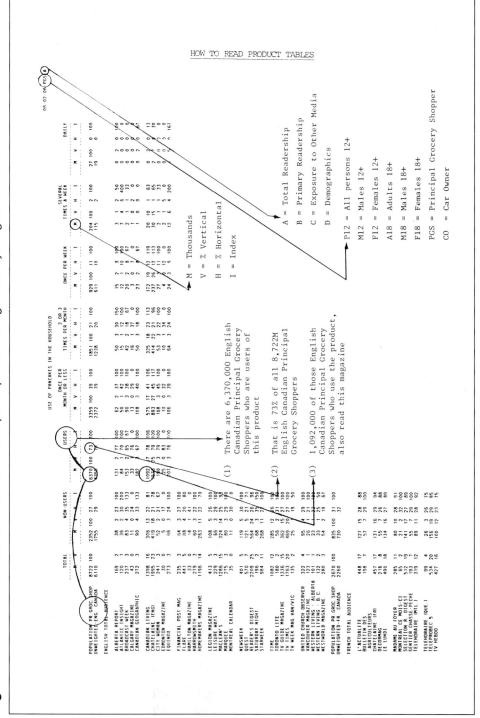

Courtesy: Print Measurement Bureau. Reprinted with permission.

Figure 8.15 A summary of newspaper reach among adults — NAD bank' 90 Readership Results

National—31 Markets

	Read Yesterday Mon-Fri(%)	Read Mon-Fri Cume(%)	Read Last Weekend(%)
Adults 18+.....	68	83	75
Men 18+.....	74	87	77
Women 18+.....	62	79	73

By Community Size (Adults 18+)

Adults 18+	Read Yesterday Mon-Fri(%)	Read Mon-Fri Cume(%)	Read Last Weekend(%)
1 Million +......	64	81	74
100 000-1 Million.....	71	85	76
Under 100,000.....	76	88	73

By Region (Adults 18+)

Adults 18+	Read Yesterday Mon-Fri(%)	Read Mon-Fri Cume(%)	Read Last Weekend(%)
Maritimes.....	75	91	74
Quebec.....	63	78	72
Ontario.....	69	84	78
Prairies.....	73	87	77
British Columbia.....	67	85	66

Source: Newspaper Marketing Bureau

over, NADbank provides readership data for a variety of demographic variables. For example, in a seven-day cycle, newspapers reach 88% of the portion of the population that is over the age of 18. In cities whose population exceeds one million, the reach is 87% of the adult population. For more information concerning the reach of newspapers, refer to figure 8.15.

Similar to the PMB with its product profile studies, NADbank also includes measures of product usage, lifestyle, and the leisure activities of the readers reached by newspapers. Other categories of interest to advertisers relate to what merchandise the consumer plans to buy in the next 12 months, and what stores are shopped at most frequently by category. A sample of NADbank data for the *Vancouver Sun* is illustrated in figure 8.16.

Figure 8.16   Nadbank data concerning the *Vancouver Sun*

	TOTAL ADULTS 18+	% OF MARKET	% READ THE VANCOUVER SUN MONDAY-FRIDAY CUME	SATURDAY
TOTAL MARKET	1 045 000	100%	60	49
General Characteristics				
SEX				
Male	505 800	48	61	53
Female	539 200	52	59	45
AGE				
18–24	177 400	17	63	37
25–34	251 100	24	62	49
35–49	252 200	24	62	54
50+	364 300	35	56	51
HOUSEHOLD INCOME				
Less than $25 000	357 800	34	55	40
$25 000–$34 999	234 200	22	60	48
$35 000–$49 999	193 600	19	62	51
$50 000+	259 400	25	66	59
OCCUPATION				
White-collar worker	457 400	44	65	54
Blue-collar worker	222 700	21	61	46
Manager/Owner/ Professional/Executive	172 800	17	68	59
EDUCATION				
Some high school or less	196 100	19	45	27
High school graduate	321 700	31	58	50
Some post secondary	306 300	29	63	48
University graduate+	201 600	19	74	66
MARITAL STATUS				
Single/Widowed/Divorced/ Separated	418 300	40	53	39
Married/Living together	619 300	59	65	55
TENURE				
Own	631 000	60	63	55
Rent	401 200	38	55	39

Data illustrates readership analysis for selected demographic and other variables
Courtesy: Pacific Press Ltd. Reprinted with permission

Figure 8.17 Outdoor advertising circulation—superboards and bulletins

SECTION V – SUPERBOARDS & BULLETINS

General Information:
Superboards are large display units at select, high circulation locations. Hand-painted or printed designs are rotated to different locations in each market every 60 days to provide market coverage at the required Gross Rating Point level over the contract term. Series 10 Superboards are 10'6" x 46'9" (3.2 x 14.3 m) and Series 14 Superboards are 14' x 48' (4.3 x 14.6 m).

SUPERBOARDS

		ESTIMATED 1985 POPULATION	No WHEN AUDITED	SUPERBOARDS '14 AVG DAILY CIRC. GROSS	IN-MARKET AVG DAILY CIRC.	No WHEN AUDITED	SUPERBOARDS '10 AVG DAILY CIRC. GROSS	IN-MARKET AVG DAILY CIRC.	AUDIT DATE COMB IMPROVED AUDIT	VERIFIED INTERIM AUDIT
Maritimes	Halifax (CMA)	285,700	5	16,700	14,980	–	–	–	June/84	–
	St. John's, Nfld.	163,000	–	–	–	1	23,380	18,704	–	June/83
Quebec	Quebec City (CMA)	606,600	–	–	–	19	17,800	15,967	–	July/84
	Trois-Rivieres & Dist.	122,500	–	–	–	3	18,300	16,415	July/84	–
	Sherbrooke (CA)	123,100	–	–	–	3	14,000	12,558	Sept/84	–
	Montreal (CMA)	2,851,000	39	48,400	43,899	35	29,300	26,575	May/84	–
Ontario	Ottawa (CMA)	738,900	–	–	–	20	16,300	14,784	June/84	–
	Toronto (CMA)	3,170,400	53	37,100	34,447	43	26,100	24,234	July/84	–
	Hamilton (CMA)	552,600	3	45,400	41,087	23	23,400	21,177	July/84	–
	Kitchener (CMA)	301,400	–	–	–	5	14,940	12,086	–	June/84
	London (CMA)	295,000	–	–	–	60	17,600	14,238	July/84	–
	St. Catharines & Dist.	355,600	–	–	–	17	13,400	12,060	June/84	–
	Windsor (CMA)	244,900	–	–	–	32	16,400	14,711	–	Feb/84
	Thunder Bay (CMA)	123,100	–	–	–	13	10,600	9,010	–	June/84
	Brantford & Dist.	98,300	–	–	–	3	15,500	12,540	June/83	–
Manitoba	Winnipeg (CMA)	590,500	14	34,300	30,767	46	30,300	27,179	–	June/84
Saskatchewan	Regina (CMA)	175,800	–	–	–	17	19,700	15,760	–	June/84
	Saskatoon (CMA)	174,000	–	–	–	15	15,800	11,850	–	June/84
Alberta	Calgary (CMA)	688,900	34	30,461	27,324	6	11,650	10,450	–	June/84
	Edmonton (CMA)	746,700	26	30,000	26,910	22	21,700	19,465	–	June/84
British Columbia	Vancouver (CMA)	1,356,600	–	–	–	19	23,390	21,987	–	June/84

BULLETINS

Painted units size 16' × 40'.

		EST. 1985 POPULATION	No. WHEN AUDITED	GROSS AVG. DAILY CIRC.	IN-MARKET AVG. DAILY CIRC.	AUDIT DATE COMB IMPROVED AUDIT	VERIFIED INTERIM AUDIT
Alberta	Edmonton — Street Art Communications	746,700	10	31,800	28,525	March/84	–

Courtesy: Canadian Outdoor Measurement Bureau. Reprinted with permission.

Figure 8.18   *Report on Business Magazine*'s profile of its readers

THE SURVEY
OF MANAGERS
AND PROFESSIONALS

HIGHLIGHTS OF REPORT ON BUSINESS MAGAZINE

Report on Business Magazine consistently delivers an upscale audience to the advertiser.

- 85% of readers are between 25 - 54 years of **Age.**

- 90% of readers earn **Personal Income** in excess of $30,000.

- Over 70% of readers have a **Household Income** in excess of $50,000.

- Over 66% of readers are at least **University Graduates.**

- 64.6% of readers are **Senior Managers.**

- Our readers take over one million **Business Trips** a year.

- 1 in 3 of our readers carries an **Investment Portfolio** in excess of $50,000.

Courtesy: *Report on Business Magazine*

Canadian Outdoor Measurement Bureau (COMB)

COMB is responsible for auditing the circulations of outdoor posters, superboards, mall posters, backlit posters, and street-level advertising (e.g., transit-shelter ads, pillar ads). Circulation data concerning all outdoor media except mall posters is based on municipal and provincial traffic counts, and converted to circulations according to an established traffic-variation factor. COMB currently uses an *average occupancy factor* of 1.75, which represents the average number of people in an automobile.[7] Mall counts are based on observation (head counts) in each location by an independent research firm.

Some outdoor boards contain a number of messages rather than a single message. These boards, referred to as *trios* or *post-turns*, carry three messages posted on triangular louvres, with each message rotated sequentially. Circulation figures for trios are calculated at 60% of the traffic count for the location.[8] A sample of quantitative-circulation data for outdoor poster advertising is included in figure 8.17.

THE USE OF RESEARCH DATA BY INDIVIDUAL MEDIA

The specific media vehicles often conduct their own marketing research, or utilize research data provided by independent sources such as those described above. The purpose of this data is to provide advertisers and agencies with objective, reliable information showing the relative strengths of the given medium as an advertising vehicle.

Individual media such as newspapers and radio also provide advertisers and agencies with data to assist them in the decision-making process. The information contained in figure 8.18 illustrates how the *Globe and Mail's Report on Business Magazine* uses research data to convince advertisers that it is a worthy advertising medium. The statistical data shows the extent of the executive-level readership of the *Report on Business Magazine*.

Summary

Owing to the large amount of money at stake in an advertising campaign, advertisers attempt to protect their investment by conducting various forms of research. Advertising research provides advertisers with information that is useful in the preparation and evaluation of the communication and in decisions regarding the use of media alternatives.

Advertising research is classified by source of information (primary or secondary), by the design of the research (custom-designed or omnibus studies), and by the nature of the information sought (qualitative or quantitative).

Creative research is concerned with gathering information useful in the preparation or evaluation of the message. Pre-testing procedures can be implemented to measure the potential effectiveness of a message that is in the development stages. Post-testing procedures can be implemented during or after the campaign to test for variables such as the audience's message awareness, message comprehension, and opinion measures. A variety of recognition- and recall-testing procedures are available for such tests.

The objective of a media plan is to achieve maximum impact on the audience at minimum cost. Media research plays a key role in achieving this objective by identifying the most cost-effective alternatives for reaching a target audience. Most information is available through a variety of sources, including research companies such as A.C. Nielsen, and various associations and bureaus such as BBM Bureau of Measurement, Television Bureau (TVB), and the Print Measurement Bureau (PMB). These media sources provide information about readership, listenership, and viewership patterns, to assist the advertiser in the media-selection process.

Review Questions

1. What are the steps in the advertising-research process? Briefly describe each step.
2. What is the difference between pre-testing and post-testing?
3. What is the difference between recognition testing and recall testing in creative research?
4. What are the readership dimensions measured in a Starch recognition-test procedure? Briefly describe each dimension.
5. What is the nature and content of a publisher's statement as verified by the Audit Bureau of Circulations?
6. What type of data is provided to advertisers by the Print Measurement Bureau?
7. Briefly explain the following terms as they relate to marketing or advertising research:
   a) primary research versus secondary research
   b) custom-designed research versus omnibus studies
   c) aided recall versus unaided recall
   d) opinion-measure testing
   e) quantitative research versus qualitative research

Discussion Questions

1. "Too much research hinders the creative-development process." Discuss this statement from the viewpoint of an agency's creative director and a client's advertising manager.

2. "How people say they will react and how they actually react can be entirely different." Discuss this statement in the context of how creative-research data should be interpreted.
3. "The increasing penetration of VCRs and Pay-TV services will dramatically influence the nature of commercial broadcasting." Identify and discuss some of the implications of these innovations for commercial broadcasters.

Illustrative Case for Part Three

Advertising Research: Ontario Hydro's 1-800 Campaign

For many years, Ontario Hydro has been a significant advertiser. In this time, Hydro has experimented with many different advertising strategies and themes. Recently it settled on a preservation and conservation theme. Ontario Hydro is very concerned that the advertising it implements be effective. The goal of its advertising is to plant a message in the minds of its various target markets, a message that will result in more efficient use of a valuable resource. To this end, Ontario Hydro conducts extensive research during its advertising campaigns. In effect, Ontario Hydro listens to its customers and constantly looks for ways to improve its advertising. This case will show the reader how research is integrated into the advertising-planning process, particularly creative planning. Highlights of research studies are included so that the reader can see why Ontario Hydro implements the type of advertising it does. The case discusses the advertising of Ontario Hydro in 1989 and 1990. Discussion starts with a review of market research from the 1988 campaign. As you will see, the results of the research had a direct impact on the advertising developed for 1989-90.

BACKGROUND INFORMATION

A key aspect of the 1988 Ontario Hydro advertising was the implementation of a 1-800 service. The campaign was a multi-media campaign that used print, radio, television, and direct mail. Its purpose was to keep people informed about topics of interest to them, namely conservation, the environment, and safety. The 1-800 number allowed consumers to call Ontario Hydro to express opinions and obtain a wide variety of information. The ads set out to show real people, in real situations, talking about real issues. The campaign was a success. As of the end of 1990, over 300 000 calls were received. Hydro claims that their 1-800 Centre is the most sophisticated and up-to-date anywhere in Canada.

Ontario Hydro decided to continue with the conservation theme, basing its decision on marketing research. In 1988, Goldfarb Consultants conducted a research study to evaluate public reaction to the 1-800 Toll Free Service and to a refrigerator-thermometer campaign. The study was conducted in four cities.

Results were overwhelmingly positive in favour of both the concept of a dialogue toll-free number and the idea of using a thermometer to save energy. Exhibit 1 is a review of key research findings.

Exhibit 1   A review of key research findings—Ontario Hydro

SOME HIGHLIGHTS FROM THE RESEARCH
Attitudes Toward And Experience With The 1-800 Service

☐   Consumer experience in using the 1-800 number service in responding to the free thermometer offer has been overwhelmingly favourable. The vast majority experienced no trouble getting through to an operator (85%), were "very satisfied" with the way the Hydro operator handled their call (92%), and found the operators to be polite (98%), friendly (95%), efficient (96%) and helpful (93%).

☐   Overall consumer reaction to the idea of Ontario Hydro offering a 1-800 service is also very positive. Overwhelmingly, consumers feel it makes Ontario Hydro easier to deal with (90%) and more accessible (80%). In addition, two in three (67%) say they are likely to contact Hydro more often with a 1-800 service being available.

Reaction To The Thermometer Offer

☐   Overall consumer reaction to the thermometer offer is very positive. As many as six in ten (63%) considers this promotional offer an "excellent" idea and most everyone else (32%) considers it a "good" idea.

☐   The data also indicates that the free thermometer offer has reflected very favourably on Ontario Hydro's image among those consumers who participated in the program. As many as four in ten (43%) say their opinion of Ontario Hydro was favourably influenced, or changed for the better, as a result of this offer.

☐   A number of positive image messages about Ontario Hydro have also been conveyed to consumers by the thermometer offer. The message comes through very clearly that Ontario Hydro is interested in encouraging consumers to conserve or save energy or electricity (58%). In addition, the thermometer offer suggests to consumers that Hydro is concerned about and responsive to the consumer (30%), is interested in good public relations (23%) and better customer service (13%), and is generally a good company (21%).

Use Of The Thermometer

☐   The usage data collected in the survey indicates that:

• those who responded to the offer received their thermometer in an average of 2.9 weeks

• the vast majority (90%) of those who have received their thermometer are using it

• eight in ten (80%) believe it has helped them save energy

• half (46%) say they did have to adjust the temperature of their fridge, with most of these people setting it to a warmer (68%) rather than a colder (28%) temperature

• the average number of degrees of adjustment is 3.3 degrees Celsius or 5.3 degrees Fahrenheit.

Exhibit 1   continued

Advertising Recall

☐   The thermometer promotion ad appears to have worked very well in generating readership and conveying the intended message as indicated by the following data:

- eight in ten (82%) of those interviewed say they read the entire ad

- a high proportion of respondents play back that the main message of the ad was to promote tips on energy saving or efficiency (43%) or to promote interest in energy saving or conservation in general (13%).

☐   That is, a strong energy conservation or energy saving message comes through to consumers from the ad.

Interest In Other Similar Offers

☐   Interest is very high (95%) in seeing Ontario Hydro offer consumers other energy saving devices for the home in similar promotions of this type.

Interest In Using The 1-800 Number For Other Reasons

☐   Interest is also very high (90%) in making other kinds of information available to the public about Ontario Hydro's service, operations, and energy saving tips, through the 1-800 service.

☐   Interest is especially high in having the following available via the 1-800 service:

- information about ways to save energy and electricity
- information about ways to save on your electricity bill
- information about safety with regard to electricity.

CONCLUSIONS

☐   Overall consumer reaction to both the 1- 800 service and thermometer promotional offer has been very favourable. More such programs should be considered, incorporating and extending the use of the 1-800 service.

☐   This particular promotion has functioned successfully for Ontario Hydro on three levels:

1) It has provided a meaningful consumer benefit to Hydro's customers.

2) It has motivated consumers to take direct action to more carefully monitor and control their electricity consumption.

3) It has impacted favourably on Hydro's corporate image. In particular, it has helped convey and reinforce the perception that Ontario Hydro is accessible to the consumer, concerned about and responsive to the consumer, and interested in promoting and encouraging the wise, efficient use of energy.

☐   In addition, the study clearly suggests that having a 1-800 service available is a positive public and customer relations service for Ontario Hydro. It reflects favourably on Ontario Hydro's corporate image by making the corporation appear to be more accessible to the consumer, by making it easier for the consumer to deal with Hydro, by promoting direct interactive communication between the consumer and Hydro, and by making Hydro appear to be more personal and responsive to the consumer.

Courtesy: Ontario Hydro

1989 ADVERTISING CAMPAIGN — ONTARIO HYDRO

Note that the conclusions of the marketing research revealed a very positive response to the 1-800 service. In addition, Ontario Hydro benefitted in different ways: corporate image improved, as Ontario Hydro was perceived to be an approachable company that was more personal and responsive to the consumer. As a result of this information Ontario Hydro developed new television commercials and print executions for 1989. Refer to exhibits 2 and 3, two television commercials that focus on the "conservation" theme, and to exhibits 4 and 5, which focus on the "Hydro-is-listening" theme. Note the use of real people discussing real issues in each of the illustrations.

1990 ADVERTISING CAMPAIGN — ONTARIO HYDRO

For 1990, Ontario Hydro developed a new set of commercials for its energy-management advertising campaign. The commercials were designed with two clear goals in mind:

1. To encourage the people of Ontario to use electricity wisely, both at home and at work
2. To instill a positive attitude toward electricity conservation with a series of practical "How-to's"

To accomplish these goals a new theme was developed. The theme is expressed in two lines which work in concert.

"Be a power saver."
"Let's give tomorrow a hand."

The first line, "Be a power saver," is a positive call to action, encouraging people to get involved and jump on the growing energy-saving bandwagon. The second, "Let's give tomorrow a hand," provides the motivation—by using electricity more wisely today, we are investing in our future and that of our children.

Research has shown that people like the theme. They respond positively and they accept the challenge both of being a Power Saver and of giving tomorrow a hand.

"Lets give tomorrow a hand" asks people to co-operate by offering them a rationale for that co-operation; while "Be a power saver" tells people how they can co-operate and what they actually can do. Refer to exhibits 6 and 7 for examples of the creative executions in storyboard format. In exhibit 6, called "Grandfather," a man is depicted in the midst of an on-going series of wise-use activities; he is joined and helped by a visiting grandchild. In exhibit 7, called "Hands," the hands of several different people of all ages and from all walks of life are doing the things that make them Power Savers. The activities represented are typical of both residential and commercial situations.

Exhibit 2 An Ontario Hydro commercial that focuses on the conservation theme

Courtesy: Ontario Hydro

Exhibit 3   Another commercial focusing on conservation

 ontario hydro

CLIENT: ONTARIO HYDRO
PRODUCT: Demand Management
TITLE: "Laundry"
LENGTH: 30 seconds

HER: Here's your change.

HIM: Thanks, now I gotta wash 'em.

HER: They're pre-shrunk. Cash? Charge?

HIM: Yeah, but it helps to soften 'em up. I'm just gonna throw 'em in my folk's washer.

HER: Just by themselves?
HIM: Yeah.

HER: Do you know how much hot water that wastes?
HIM: Well yeah, but...

HER: If the washer isn't full, it's gonna cost you. Hot water. Electricity. Sign Here please.

HIM: But I gotta wear 'em tonight.

HER: Wear 'em the way they are. They look good on you.

HIM: Yeah?

HER: Yeah.

SFX: PHONE DIALS AND RINGS
OPERATOR: Ontario Hydro.

Courtesy: Ontario Hydro

Exhibit 4   One of the "Hydro is listening " commercials

Courtesy: Ontario Hydro

Exhibit 5 Another of the "Hydro is listening" commercials

People are talking.

"So has anybody got any bright ideas on how to bring down energy costs?"

"What exactly are they doing about acid rain?"

"They wouldn't put that on there if it didn't do anything."

Hydro is listening.

If you'd like to know more about how to save energy, or be safe with it, or about its effect on the environment, our lines are open. Call us weekdays between 8am and 6pm and ask for your free booklets.

1-800-263-9000
Ontario Hydro

Courtesy: Ontario Hydro

Exhibit 6   Creative execution in storyboard format—"Grandfather"

Ontario Hydro
Demand Management TV
-"Grandfather"

GRANDMA: Oh, he's off somewhere doing something. I saw him with his stepladder

and another box from the store. It's been like that for days. He's changing

lightbulbs all over the place to ones that use less electricity.

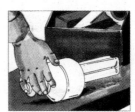

Good place to start saving money, he says.

Says all his friends are putting in

timers and dimmers and who knows what else. Said to me the other day, "See Betty,...

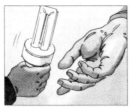

Be a Power Saver

you can teach an old dog new tricks."

Then he said for his next trick he was going to (fade out)

Ontario Hydro
Let's give tomorrow a hand.

Courtesy: Ontario Hydro

Exhibit 7 Another creative execution in storyboard format—"Hands"

Ontario Hydro
Demand Management TV
–"Hands"

ANNOUNCER: There are hundreds of simple ways

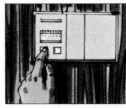

you can become a Power Saver.

Right at your fingertips.

Saving electricity.

Saving money.

For Today.

And Tomorrow.

Be a Power Saver

Ontario Hydro
Let's give tomorrow a hand.

Courtesy: Ontario Hydro

Media Planning

In Part Two of the text, the relationships between advertising and marketing planning were established, and a detailed review of the marketing- and advertising-planning processes was presented.

In Part Three, the creative-planning process was described in detail, and the relationships between creative objectives, strategies, and execution were established. The role of research in creative and media planning was also described.

The aim of this section of the text is to describe the media-planning process in detail: to consider budget limitations and to distinguish between media objectives, strategies, and execution. The responsibility of the client and agency in the media-planning process is also discussed. This is accomplished in chapter 9.

Chapter 10 reviews the print media, and chapter 11 the broadcast media. In both chapters, the pros and cons of the various media are presented, along with media-buying considerations and examples. Chapter 12 is devoted to direct-response advertising and out-of-home media, and the special considerations for media planning in these areas.

Budgeting and the Media Plan

In studying this chapter, you will learn

- The factors affecting the size of an advertising budget
- The methods of determining the size of an advertising budget
- The role and responsibility of the advertising manager in the budgeting process
- The impact that the four Ps have on media planning
- The distinction between media objectives and media strategies
- The factors that influence the development of media objectives and strategies
- The terminology used in media planning
- The steps involved in the media-selection process
- The role and responsibility of both client and agency in media planning

The process of developing a media plan is very complex. The task of an agency's media planners is to reach the desired target market efficiently. Although this objective may appear to be rather simple, the assignment is complicated by variables such as market information, media-reach information, consumers' media habits, and so on. Efficiency in media planning can be loosely defined as "gaining maximum impact or exposure at minimum cost to the client." The agency must develop and execute a plan that meets stated expectations within certain financial parameters.

Essentially, input from the client to the agency becomes the foundation of the media plan. The direction a media plan takes is largely based on the guidelines provided by the client's marketing plan and the advertising plan which client and agency agree to. It is important to realize that the media plan is a subset of a larger strategic plan, on a level with other planning variables such as promotion, pricing, creative planning, and product development. Since all variables stem from the overriding marketing strategy, they must work in unison to accomplish desired goals.

A budget is normally developed to establish the financial parameters for the media plan. The method used to devise the budget is the choice of the client.

With the budget defined, the advertising objectives are translated into media objectives and strategies. The purpose of this process is to identify which media are best suited to reach the target audience. Once the media vehicles are identified, a media schedule is developed which outlines the specific details of the plan (when, where, and for how long the messages will run). The process of developing media objectives, strategies, and tactics results in a comprehensive media plan that is presented to the client for discussion and approval.

THE ADVERTISING BUDGET

Determining just how much money to spend on advertising, for any period of time, is a problematic process the advertising manager must face each year. In striking a budget, the manager is concerned with two decision areas. First, how much will be spent in total? Second, how should the budget be allocated—by medium, geographic area, or time of year?

The investment paybacks from some expenditures can be calculated relatively precisely, but the payback from advertising remains rather vague. The advertiser must clearly understand the purpose of advertising and the value derived from advertising expenditures, since success requires a financial commitment over the longer term. To expect a fast return via higher sales in the short term is often unrealistic. All advertising executives must wrestle with this short-term versus long-term predicament. Quite often, budgets are slashed midway through a campaign to protect short-term profit margins, even though such a strategy may be in conflict with the advertiser's long-term expectations for the product: specifically, the expectations that its market-share position improve or that the level of consumers' awareness of the product rise.

The same principle applies to small businesses, particularly independent retailers, who tend to cut promotion expenditures when they find themselves in tight financial situations. Frequently, such cuts to the advertising budget only serve to accentuate the rough financial situation by reducing revenues further.

Advertising budgets are often the first items affected if short-term strategies prevail. Within a company, the money allocated to advertising could be one of the largest expenditures of the year. Thus, if short-term profit motives take over, money for advertising that is not yet spent during the year is subject to cancellation. It is because of this situation that budgets must be carefully developed and rationalized for approval by senior executives. The preservation of a sound market-share position, in the longer term, will largely depend upon a company's ability to maintain a reasonable advertising budget.

FACTORS AFFECTING BUDGET SIZE

In order to develop an advertising budget, the manager responsible for the budgeting function should analyze the several factors that will have an impact on the size of the advertising budget. Among such factors are the size of the customer base, the degrees of competition and demand, the stage the product has reached in its life cycle, the characteristics of the product, and the size of the company and its financial position. The importance of these variables may vary from one product to another, but, analyzed collectively, they provide insight into the amount of money required for advertising.

Size of Customer Base

As regards the size of the customer base, a clear distinction can be made between consumer markets and industrial markets. Organizations directing consumer products at mass target markets have a tendency to rely more heavily on advertising, while organizations directing products at industrial markets, which represent a more selective and geographically-centred audience, rely more on personal selling. Viewed from a budgeting perspective, the consequences are obvious. A competitive advertising budget is essential for the long-term success of any product in a consumer-oriented market. For industrial products, the money available for promotion will be wisely spent if less is allocated to advertising than to personal selling and sales-promotion budgets. The relative importance of advertising in the consumer-goods and industrial-goods markets is outlined in figure 9.1.

Degree of Competition

The amount of money spent on advertising by competitors may be the single most important influence on the size of a product's advertising budget. If nothing else, it is a useful indicator of how much money the company will have to spend to remain competitive.

Information on competitors' advertising spending is available to consumer-goods advertisers through marketing-research firms such as A.C. Nielsen. While past expenditure is well known, the advertising manager must also predict with reasonable accuracy what the main competitors will spend next year, for these projected expenditures can help him or her develop and justify a budget.

Figure 9.1 Relative importance of promotional tools in consumer-goods and industrial-goods markets

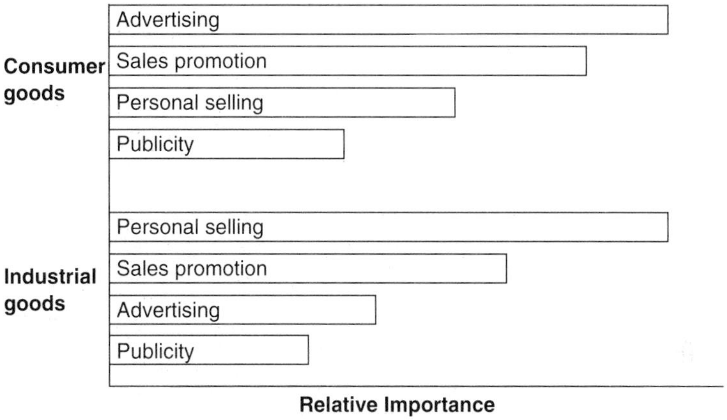

Consumer goods

| Advertising |
| Sales promotion |
| Personal selling |
| Publicity |

Industrial goods

| Personal selling |
| Sales promotion |
| Advertising |
| Publicity |

Relative Importance

Courtesy: Kotler and McDougall, *Marketing Essentials* (Scarborough: Prentice-Hall Canada, Inc., 1985), p. 311. Reprinted with permission.

For any brand, a decision must be made regarding how competitive the brand will be with respect to advertising expenditures. Although other factors or advertising objectives, such as the objective of increasing awareness levels, will influence this decision, the advertising manager must decide how his or her budget will compare to that of the competition.

In many markets, the competition is so intense that competitors force other advertisers to spend more than they would like to spend. Advertisers in such a position realize that not keeping pace with competitors would have a negative long-term impact on brand performance. For example, the recent dramatic increase in Pepsi-Cola's spending in Canada, on promotion of the Pepsi Challenge, forced Coca-Cola to respond with increased spending. While such retaliatory spending is not desirable from a profit viewpoint, it was essential in this case if Coca-Cola were to protect its number-one market-share position. Similar advertising battles rage on in other markets such as the headache-remedies market, where brands such as Advil, Nuprin, Tylenol, and Anacin protect share through constant investment in advertising.

Stage in the Product Life Cycle

The relative importance of advertising, and the budget required for advertising, varies from one stage in the product life cycle to another. Advertising is more important in the introductory and growth stages of the product life cycle than it is in the mature and decline stages.

Introduction Stage In the introductory stage, the advertiser is mainly concerned with creating a high level of awareness for the new product. Specifically, the advertiser will spend heavily to create awareness for the brand name and package. In relation to sales returns, the investment in advertising will be extremely high. Since the objective is brand development, it is quite common to have an advertising expenditure that exceeds the projected return in sales. Initial losses on a brand are tolerated, as long as the brand is expected to provide adequate profit levels in the long-term. The heavy expenditure on advertising in the introduction stage is a significant contributing factor in short-term losses.

Growth Stage When advertising managers are confronted with information about the advertising expenditures of the competition, their objectives change: instead of trying to create awareness of the brand, they seek to create preference for it. Securing growth and improving market share for a brand necessitate a budget that will attract users of competitive brands. Considering the overall objective of creating brand preference, a brand's advertising share is likely to exceed market share at this stage of the product life cycle. The advertising share is a measure of how much is invested in the advertising of one brand compared to the total industry advertising. For example,

	Investment in Advertising ($)	Advertising Share (%)
Brand A	250 000	41.7
Brand B	150 000	25.0
Brand C	200 000	33.3
Total Industry	600 000	100.0

Assuming that Brand A is the market leader and that advertising is an influencing factor in purchase, Brands B and C would have to increase their advertising expenditures significantly to overtake Brand A in the marketplace.

Mature Stage When the brand enters the mature stage, most advertisers shift the strategic focus from brand development to profit maximization. Rather than spending money on advertising, a company makes a conscious effort to preserve money wherever possible, thereby improving the profit margin for the product. A brand at this stage is in a maintenance position, and the advertising strategies are designed to prolong the mature phase as long as possible. The advertising budget is developed accordingly. For a brand to remain competitive at this stage, a budget that equates advertising share with market share is appropriate. The main concern is to spend just enough to sustain share position while increasing bottom-line profitability.

The mature stage is a time for life-cycle-extension strategies such as product modifications, new packaging, new varieties, and so on. If such strategies are implemented, the awareness-of-change advertising programs, which are needed to boost sales, will result in increased advertising expenditures. Unlike spending in other earlier stages, the spending on product changes is more short-term in nature.

Decline Stage As newer products take over the market and established products enter the decline stage, profit motives take priority. Advertising budgets are generally cut significantly or withdrawn entirely. The advertiser redirects whatever profits are generated by products in decline to other products in the development stages.

Product Characteristics

The nature of the product (the degree of its uniqueness) and its perceived value to potential customers can have an influence on the amount of money that is spent on advertising the product.

High-Interest Unique Selling Point   Clearly establishing in consumers' minds the perceived value of the unique selling point initially requires a large budget. For example, when Nabob Coffee introduced the vacuum-sealed package format as a new way of preserving its product's freshness, the company increased its advertising budget significantly to communicate its product advantage. The combination of the new package (offering better, fresher product) and the advertising effort made Nabob a legitimate contender in the coffee market. Once the brand is established, or when adequate levels of brand loyalty have been achieved, the investment in advertising can be reduced significantly.

Marginal Unique Selling Points   For product categories in which brands are similar (i.e., in which unique selling points can be easily duplicated), the amount spent on advertising is determined by the overall objectives for the brand. For example, if Brand A wants to remain competitive with Brands B and C, and these brands are spending more on advertising, then Brand A will be forced to spend heavily on advertising also. Conversely, Brand A may channel money into other marketing variables, remaining competitive by reducing investment in advertising. (Consider all of the brands that are available in the laundry-detergent market; only a minority of the popular brands spend heavily on advertising.)

Image and Lifestyle   Differentiating a brand on the basis of perceived image or lifestyle takes time, and, as a result, requires a significant budget on an ongoing basis. If similar brands adopt the lifestyle strategy in appealing to a similar target market, the increase in the advertising budgets may be out of all proportion to the potential return on sales. Certain segments of the brewing industry are in such a situation (e.g., Labatt's Blue, Carlsberg, Old Vienna, Canadian). All brands spend heavily in broadcast and print media to attract essentially the same target market.

The Nature of Management and the Organization

The size of a company and its financial position have an influence on the amount of money allocated to advertising. Smaller firms, with limited financial strength, will not have the budgets necessary to compete with larger firms. Also affecting the budget's size is senior management's perception of the value of advertising. As indicated earlier, expense-oriented managers who think only of the short term may be reluctant to spend scarce dollars on advertising; investment-minded managers, on the other hand, are more willing to take budget risks to encourage long-term brand development.

BUDGETING METHODS

Annual sales and profit projections are normally established at the corporate level of an organization. These projections often become guidelines for developing potential advertising budgets. An advertising budget can be developed in a variety of ways, each with its own pros and cons. Since no one method is ideal for all situations, it may be wise to compare a variety of methods so that the budget arrived at is realistic, given the competitive situation in the marketplace. Budgeting methods that predominate include: *percentage-of-sales, fixed-sum-per-unit-sold, industry-averages, advertising-share/marketing-share,* and the *objective*, or *task, method.*

Percentage of Sales

If a company uses the **percentage-of-sales** method, it usually forecasts sales-dollar volume for the forthcoming year and allocates a predetermined percentage amount of those sales to advertising. Management determines the percentage to be used. Percentages often used are past industry averages or simply the percentage the company has used in the past. The percentage-of-sales method of developing a budget has an obvious shortcoming. The philosophy underlying the method is that advertising results from sales, whereas the wiser manager prefers to believe that advertising results in sales.

The reason for the popularity of this method is not clear. Management may use it for its simplicity, and because it relates advertising expenditures directly to sales. The method tends to ignore the *interaction* between advertising and sales. If used, the budget implications are very predictable. If sales decrease, so does the budget, and vice versa.

The percentage-of-sales method may be appropriate for companies and products that face very similar market conditions year after year. However, if conditions are volatile, the advertising expenditure should change with the market. This may necessitate a change (increase or decrease) in the predetermined percentage allocated to advertising, or a comparison between the percentage-of-sales budget figure and a budget figure derived by another method.

Note: Depending on the competitive situation, on the stage the product has reached in the life cycle, and on other factors, the actual percentage allocated to advertising may vary as time passes. For example, a company may allocate to a new brand a very high percentage of the sales, say 200% (two dollars in advertising for one dollar in sales), in order to establish the brand's position (thus sacrificing short-term profit). Conversely, a mature brand may be allocated a reduced percentage so that profit margins may be improved.

Fixed Sum Per Unit Sold

The **fixed-sum-per-unit-sold** method of budgeting is very similar to percentage-of-sales in that the volume of product sold has a direct influence on the size of the brand's advertising budget. According to this method, the company allocates a predetermined amount to advertising for each unit sold. For example, if an appliance manufacturer estimates unit sales to be 120 000 in any given year, and they traditionally allocate $10 to advertising for each unit sold, the budget would be $1 200 000.

This method is suitable for products with a high unit price (appliances, automobiles). Similar to the percentage-of-sales method, the major weakness in using this method is that the budget fluctuates with changes in sales volume.

Industry Average (Competitor Spending)

Advertisers that use the **industry-average** approach base their advertising budgets on what competitors are spending. Depending on the performance objectives established for a product, the advertiser may choose to lag behind, be equal to, or exceed the spending of the competition. Using competitors' past expenditures as a starting point, advertisers attempt to forecast competitive advertising expenditures for the next year, and then they position their own budgets accordingly.

An advertiser may use historical industry averages as a starting point. For example, if a cosmetics company knows that the cosmetic industry historically spends 20–30% of revenues on advertising, then this range would provide a "safe" starting-point figure for a particular brand's budget.

Industry averages provide a good preliminary guideline. However, the influence of other variables may force the advertiser to modify this "starting point budget."

An alternative approach is to simply look at the average spending patterns of your closest competitors. For Example:

Brand A	400 000
Brand B	200 000
Brand C	300 000
Industry Average	*300 000*

Using this method, we see that Brand B is lagging behind its competitors. Assuming advertising is of equal importance to all brands, the company that produces Brand B would not anticipate much in the way of improved brand performance in the following year. As indicated, a weakness of this method is the assumption that advertising is of equal importance to all brands. On the positive side, it does provide a reasonable starting point (figure) in the budget development process.

Task (Objective) Method

The budgeting methods discussed so far fail to acknowledge that advertising is a potential means of achieving marketing objectives. Which comes first, the chicken or the egg? In contrast to other methods, the task or objective method shows how advertising can have an impact on sales. The **task method** involves a few basic steps: defining the task, determining the type and quantity of advertising needed, and determining the cost of the advertising recommendation.

Defining the Task   The task of advertising is often expressed in communications terms; usually, it is described as the task of achieving a specified level of brand awareness (e.g., "to increase brand awareness for Product X from 60% to 75% in the next year").

Determining the Type and Quantity of Advertising   The difficult part of the task method is determining the most efficient and effective ways of achieving the desired objectives. The myriad media options available suggest that knowledge and experience in media planning are essential for arriving at reasonable and reliable budget estimates.

The primary task of the media planner is to calculate the number of **impressions** required to reach the awareness objective. The term *impressions* refers to the total of all audiences delivered by a media plan. Also referred to as *total exposures*, it is calculated by multiplying the number of people who receive a message by the number of times they receive it. In this regard, the client is at the mercy of agency expertise. However, the client can subjectively analyze proposed budgets by referring to past spending trends for any particular product. Questions such as how much, how often, and how long to advertise are addressed at this stage of the task process.

Since many variables are considered in the task method, it is often viewed as the most scientific of the various methods. It is also argued that, if the input variables (media-planning variables such as reach, frequency, and continuity) are incorrect, it will lead to serious miscalculations for a budget.

Determining the Cost of the Advertising Recommendation This last step in the process is more mechanical in nature. Presuming there is agreement as to objectives and to the type and quantity of advertising required (i.e., the first two stages), the costs are calculated arithmetically according to media. Production costs are estimated, and the sum of all media and production variables becomes the advertising budget.

Because of its more precise methodology and because of the fact that it takes into account several variables, the task (objective) method is held in high regard in the industry today. However, there are some drawbacks:

1. It does not consider the profit objective for the product or company. Therefore, once a figure is reached, the company must decide if the investment is affordable. It may decide to re-evaluate its communications objectives in order to reduce spending and preserve desired profitability. The goal is to match reasonable budgets with reasonable objectives.
2. Facts and media knowledge are needed to complete the steps of the method. Thus budget responsibility shifts from the client to the agency—the client is relying heavily on a supplier to determine the budget. Such an arrangement can only work if there is a relationship of trust and confidence between the parties.

Share of Advertising/Share of Market

This budgeting method is based on the premise that "share of advertising will equal share of market." If advertising is, for all brands competing in the market, an important factor in the consumers' decision to purchase, such a premise has some merit.

If that premise is acceptable, it is clear that if the product's advertising budget is maintained at a competitive level, the product itself will remain competitive with the rest of the field. The best way to increase market share is to ensure that advertising share (share of industry spending) stays ahead of market share.

Consider the consequences for each brand as outlined in the following table:

Brand	Market Shares (%)	Projected Advertising Budget ($)	Advertising Share (%)	Consequences
A	40	5 000 000	50	share increase
B	30	2 500 000	25	decrease
C	20	1 500 000	15	decrease
D	10	1 000 000	10	maintenance
	100	10 000 000	100	

If the projected budgets came close to equalling actual spending in that year, advertising expenditures for Brand A would have been at a level greater than Brand A's market share, while those for Brands B and C would have been below market share. As a consequence, we would expect Brand A to achieve share increases while B and C suffer market-share declines.

The advantages of this method are as follows:

1. It forces a company to be aware of and to review competitors' spending.
2. It provides a reasonable starting point (guideline) for developing a budget.

The disadvantages are as follows:

1. Advertising is totally separated from consideration of other marketing variables.
2. It does not consider the profit motivation of the firm. Preoccupation with competitors' spending and with share objectives may actually force a firm to spend more on advertising than it can afford to spend.

Clearly, certain variables must be analyzed prior to the establishing of a working budget. Also, there are several budgeting methods to choose from, and this may result in a variety of budget figures. Since no one method is totally accurate, it is recommended that a company use several methods and compare the results of each prior to committing to a final advertising budget.

BUDGET ACCOUNTABILITY

The manager responsible for the development of an advertising budget oversees four areas: budget preparation, budget presentation, budget execution, and budget control.

Budget Preparation The manager's initial responsibility is the preparation of the budget. To accomplish this task, he or she analyzes the factors affecting the budget size and develops a budget based on the methods of choice.

Budget Presentation The next stage is to present the budget to senior executives for approval. Such a step is necessary, owing to the significant amount likely to be required and, consequently, to the visibility of an advertising budget within an organization. The presentation carefully rationalizes the budget required.

Budget Execution   Once senior management has approved the budget, the next step is implementation. Under the direction of the advertising manager, the agency is instructed to purchase the media (time and space), and to proceed with production.

Budget Control   The visible nature of advertising expenditures makes controls essential. The manager must keep track of expenditures in preparation for quarterly financial reviews. For example, the manager should know the spending patterns by media, region, time of year, or whatever. A comparison of actual spending versus planned spending is necessary should budget cuts be contemplated by senior management of the firm. Knowledge of what can be cancelled on short notice is the responsibility of the advertising manager.

*T*HE CANADIAN MEDIA

Net advertising revenues in Canada are estimated to have been approximately $8.46 billion in 1989. Figure 9.2 summarizes media revenue trends for the past three years. An analysis of these trends provides for some interesting observations. Of interest to students should be the fact that the most visible medium, television, is not the largest in terms of revenue. Television revenues rank third behind daily newspapers and direct-mail advertising.

The newspapers' lead in media revenues is largely owing to the amount of advertising dollars generated in local markets. Collectively, local advertisers, which comprise retailers and service companies, generate 71% of newspaper advertising revenues. In contrast, almost the exact opposite is true for television, as 75% of all

Figure 9.2   Canadian net advertising revenue, by medium ($ million)

	1987	*1988*	*1989*
Radio	648	706	748
Television	1177	1339	1416
Daily Newspaper	1278	1375	1443
Weekly Newspaper	514	576	628
Magazines, General	235	273	283
Business Papers	170	177	184
Other Print (incl. Direct Mail)	1700	1828	1979
Outdoor	610	659	718
Directories, Phone	700	834	931
Other Media	137	125	130
Total	7169	7892	8460

Source: Adapted from *Canadian Media Directors' Council Media Digest*, 1990-91, p.10.

Figure 9.3 Sources of revenues—1989, television vs newspaper

	National Revenue	Local Revenue	Total Revenue
Television($ million)	1062	353	1415
(%)	75	25	100
Newspaper($ million)	424	1019	1443
(%)	29	71	100

Source: Adapted from *Canadian Media Directors' Council Media Digest*, 1990-91, p. 11.

revenues are generated by national advertisers. Refer to figure 9.3 for national versus local advertising revenue ratios.

MEDIA CLASSIFICATIONS

The Canadian media can be classified by type of media, by audience reached, and by specific vehicle.

Classification by Type of Media

Media are differentiated by type, and divided into five categories: *broadcast media, print media, out-of-home media, direct mail*, and *specialized media*.

Broadcast Media The national English-language networks include CBC and CTV. Radio-Canada is the CBC French-language network. Regional English-language networks include ATV (Atlantic region CTV affiliates) and the Global Television Network. Regional French-language networks include Quatre Saisons and TVA, both based in Quebec. Specialty networks also offer commercial time and include MuchMusic, The Sports Network (TSN), Youth Channel, Vision TV, and CBC Newsworld. Specialty French-language networks include Musique Plus and Les Reseau des sports (RDS).

The Canadian radio media comprises 687 stations (385 AM and 302 FM). There is only one national network (CBC). Syndicated packages of news and event programming are offered to independent stations on a regional and national basis.

Print Media Daily and community newspapers (weeklies), along with magazines, comprise the print media. Currently there are 110 daily newspapers, 1056 community newspapers, and 534 consumer magazines listed in *Canadian Advertising Rates and Data*. These publications are controlled by relatively few organizations, among them Maclean Hunter, Southam Publishing, Thompson Publishing, and Metroland Publishing.

Out-Of-Home Media This is outdoor advertising, and includes posters and billboards, mall posters, pillar ads, transit-shelter advertising, and interior- and exterior-transit advertising.

Direct Mail Direct-response advertising is a medium based on communications mailed between sellers and buyers. Using lists, businesses communicate directly with predetermined buyers. Direct communications from businesses to buyers are usually kits or packages containing a sales letter, pamphlet or brochure, a purchase incentive (optional), and a reply card.

Specialized Media Included in this category are a variety of media: aerial advertising, airport displays, bench advertising, grocery-cart advertising, in-store advertising, theatre screens, and many more.

Classification by Audience

Effective and efficient media planning relies on the media planner's ability to match the product message with the right media in accordance with the consumer profiles of people who read, listen, and watch a particular type of media.

In Canada, *Canadian Advertising Rates and Data (CARD)* is a major source of information about audience characteristics. Media in *CARD* are divided into the following audiences:

- Daily newspapers
- Community newspapers
- Consumer magazines: this classification includes numerous subdivisions, such as business, women's, city, general-interest, sports-and-recreation, and many more
- University and school publications
- Farm publications
- Business publications: this classification also comprehends numerous subdivisions, including a variety of specialized-industry magazines, government publications, and general-interest magazines
- Radio stations and networks
- Television stations and setworks
- Other advertising: included here are outdoor, transit, and a variety of specialized media

Classification by Vehicle

Classification by vehicle refers to the specific medium within a type of medium. For example, to reach Toronto effectively via television, the following stations are available: CBLT (CBC), CFTO (CTV), Global, and City-TV (independent). Also, CHCH, a Hamilton-based station, has high reach in the Toronto market. Similar lists could be developed for specific radio stations covering a particular geographic area.

On the print side, consumer magazines are the type of media, while publications such as *Chatelaine, Reader's Digest*, and *Canadian Living* represent the vehicle classification. For daily newspapers, the specific vehicles are dailies such as the *Vancouver Sun*, the *Globe and Mail*, and the *London Free Press*.

DEVELOPING THE MEDIA PLAN

In chapter 5, discussion centred on the marketing-planning and advertising-planning processes. The guidelines resulting from these processes—the planning documents, particularly the advertising objectives and strategies—have a direct influence on the media plan and the planning process. The advertising objectives define the role advertising will play in marketing a product, service, or retail establishment. These objectives also provide a goal against which the actual results of advertising can be measured. Advertising strategy provides an outline of how the elements of advertising will be utilized to achieve the objectives. For example, advertising strategy (marketing strategy) usually includes a positioning statement, a comment on the allocation of funds by media, and information regarding the role of special advertising features such as coupons or contest-type promotions.

The **media plan** is a document that recommends how the client's advertising funds can best be spent to achieve their advertising objectives. The media plan includes a precise definition of the media objective, supporting strategic rationale, and (tactical) details concerning the execution of the plan. Since a significant amount of the client's money is usually at stake in any advertising campaign, the media planners' strategic arguments and tactical details are of high interest to the client. In this regard, the media plan provides a rationale for media selection and rejection, reach and frequency positions, for the duration of the plan, and so on. Communications between agency and client peak when media plans are presented. Media planners must present and defend their recommendations, and be prepared to consider client input. Clients do not question the expertise of the media planner, but media plans have been known to go through numerous revisions prior to client approval.

Let's examine the relationships between the marketing mix and the media plan. As indicated in chapter 4, the four Ps (product, price, promotion, and place) must work in unison to make a strong impact on the marketplace and on the consumers.

Impact of the Four Ps on Media Planning

Product Strategy   The best way to show the impact of product strategy on media selection and usage is by example. If a product requires demonstration, television is the best possible medium for showing the product in action. If the product is at a very early stage in the product life cycle, with a loosely defined target market, the company's objective for the product would probably be reach-related; under these circumstances television, which offers high reach within a short period of time, would, again, be the most effective medium. Later in the life cycle, when target markets, being based on actual purchase experience, are more precisely defined, more selective and precisely defined media can be used.

As well, advertisements for certain products are prohibited from appearing in some media. Tobacco and alcohol are not allowed to be advertised on television in Canada, and certain specific media have banned the advertising of specific "hazardous" products. Canada's oldest daily newspaper, the *Kingston Whig-Standard*, banned tobacco ads in early 1985, the first newspaper to do so.

Pricing Strategy   The price of the product, as well as the perceived image of the product that results from that price, also has an impact on the media-selection process. For example, an automobile such as Mercedes-Benz would probably choose to advertise in upscale business magazines whose readership is made up of people with higher financial status. *Financial Post Magazine* and *Successful Executive* may be appropriate matches for Mercedes Benz, while general-interest publications, such as *Reader's Digest* and *Maclean's*, may reach some of the company's target market, but not enough to warrant being selected.

Advertisers of products that are positioned in lower- to mid-price ranges and appeal to a broader range of consumer segments have more flexibility when it comes to choosing among the media options available. However, the scarcity of dollar resources demands that, within this flexible position, such companies be very selective about the media they choose.

Promotion Strategy At an earlier stage of the planning process (marketing planning), the budget is divided between advertising, consumer promotions, and trade promotions. Often, the integration of consumer-promotion activity into advertising dictates that certain media be used. For example, coupon campaigns utilize consumer magazines and newspapers. Promotions, such as contests and sweepstakes, may require a media mix of, say, broadcast media (for awareness) and print media (for communicating promotion details).

Place (Distribution) Strategy The relative importance of regional markets and urban markets has a direct impact on the amount of media time and space bought in any one area.

All things being equal, a product that enjoys a high level of national distribution may have its media budget divided proportionately, based on sales and volume, between the five geographic regions of Canada (the Maritimes, Quebec, Ontario, the Prairies, and British Columbia).

Others might argue that because of disproportionate advertising support in the past, sales are not proportionate to population patterns. Media considerations aside, this debate sparks considerable argument between marketing managers and regional sales managers on the client side. Sales managers can influence the number of media dollars allocated to their region, if they present a convincing argument that is based on marketing priorities.

In a very different way, poor distribution in a certain city or region can create an opportunity to increase media spending. For example, a company may allocate to a product that is performing poorly a disproportionately large amount of media support, at least temporarily, in hopes of correcting the problem. The increase in media spending can help "pull" the product through the channel. Given that there is a total budget ceiling, a disproportionate increase in spending in one region could result in less spending elsewhere, a potential problem in the making.

Creative Strategy or Media Strategy—Which Comes First?

Both creative strategy and media strategy are closely linked to the overall marketing plan. But which should come first? In some cases, it may be the media plan, since the media budget could restrict the use of certain media (e.g., television, if funds are limited), dictate the length of the message (15, 30, or 60 seconds) or the size of the message (full page or less). In other cases, the creative plan may influence the media plan. For example, creative planners may recommend the use of short commercial messages (15 seconds does the job), thus saving the client valuable media dollars.

Many practitioners suggest that creative strategy and media strategy should be developed together. Since both are based on the same core product and the same market information, the suggestion sounds reasonable. However, given the independent nature of the two agency departments (creative and media), combining the two activities is problematic. Also, with the recent growth of agency specialists, including creative boutiques and media-buying services, the two plans are often prepared quite separately. An advertiser, working with specialists, will probably develop the creative strategy first. Regardless of which comes first, it is imperative that the plans be compatible if they are to perform effectively with the other elements of the promotion mix and marketing mix.

Media Planning Media is the vehicle that carries a product's selling message to a predetermined target market. The selling success of any advertising campaign is, therefore, dependent upon the effectiveness of the media plan.

Media planning can be defined as the process of developing a plan of action for communicating messages to the right people (target market), at the right time, and as often and efficiently as possible. A media plan will utilize a single medium or a **media mix** (a combination of broadcast, print, and other media) to fulfill overall advertising objectives.

Media planning should flow logically from overall marketing and advertising strategy to meet the objectives specified in the marketing plan/advertising plan (chapter 5). Figure 9.4 illustrates a schematic diagram of the media-planning process.

Figure 9.4   Media-planning process

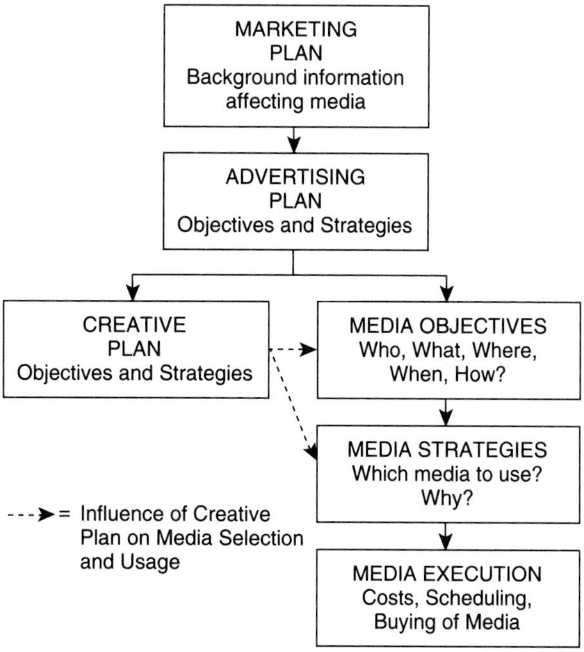

Advertising in Action
Super Bowl—Wise Investment or Waste of Money?

To advertise on the Super-Bowl broadcast is costly. With so much money at stake an advertiser has to be confident that the investment will produce the desired results—sales! The 25th version of what is now the single most watched sporting event in the world year after year was the most expensive one to date for advertisers.

For Super Bowl XXV, the cost of one 30-second commercial was pegged at $800 000. Ten years ago the cost was a mere $275 000. For ABC, the network airing the game, it will be their biggest payday ever. With 56 30-second spots sold out, revenues for the day will be in the $45 million range. Whether ABC will make a profit on the game is not clear, however, when the high cost of broadcast rights and production are considered.

What is the allure of the Super Bowl? In terms of events, it seems that this game is the *big event*. According to Jack Keiver, executive vice president of sales at ABC, "the game sells out every year and the game offers something special for advertisers who want to stand out."

Many advertisers, however, have begun taking a more critical look at the Super Bowl and are questioning the wisdom of paying such a high price for advertising over such a short period. If the game's a yawner, as was the 1990 version—a 55-10 drubbing of Denver by San Francisco—the audience sits back and pays less attention, especially to the advertisements. Toyota has been associated with the game for many years but opted out in 1991. They concluded that such an expense could not be justified.

Other companies use the game as a springboard for new ventures. People still talk about the Apple Macintosh commercial that ran during the 1984 game—a commercial that officially launched the Apple Macintosh. This year L.A. Gear will launch its Catapult line of shoes and Nike its Air 180s during the Super-Bowl broadcast.

For those who decide to advertise on the game and for those who don't—what will they get or what will they miss out on? Research conducted by Nielsen Media Research, and independent research by Cramer-Krasselt, a U.S. advertising agency, point out numerous benefits. These are:

1. The Super bowl will be the most watched show of the year. It will reach at least 100 million households, not to mention the countless televisions in bars and taverns across North America. On a list of the top 10 shows of all time, the Super Bowl holds five of those positions.

2. The audience is actually larger than that stated by Nielsen because of the viewing outside the home. The Super Bowl is a social event during which throngs of people huddle around a single television to watch the game in all kinds of locations.

3. Viewers tend to pay more attention to what's on the screen, even the advertising, than they do when watching other television programs.

4. The average prime-time commercial is remembered by 23% of the viewers the following day. Super Bowl commercials are remembered by 52% of the viewers.

5. The advertising during the game is perceived to be more interesting. No doubt firms like Apple, Nike and L.A. Gear produce commercials especially for the game. Sixty-two percent of viewers think the game commercials are more interesting than commercials in general.

Cramer-Krasselt, the agency who conducted research on the Super Bowl, did so for a good reason. For years they had been recommending the Super Bowl to Master Lock; one of its big clients. In fact, one commercial on the Super Bowl used up one-third of Master Lock's entire media budget for the year. Now that's significant.

Based on the data presented in this vignette, is such a decision vindicated? Would you invest this kind of money at one time?

Adapted from, Michael Lev, "Super bucks," *The Whig-Standard*, January 12, 1991, p.13.

The Advertising in Action vignette "Super Bowl—Wise Investment or Waste of Money?" discusses an interesting case in media planning. The glamour of the event itself has always been an attraction to many advertisers, but now many of these same advertisers are starting to question the wisdom of the investment. Examine some of the information in the vignette and form a position of your own. Would the Super Bowl be part of your media buy?

MEDIA OBJECTIVES

Media objectives are clearly worded statements that outline "what" the media plan is intended to accomplish. Within this framework, media objectives can be subdivided, and more precisely defined statements can be developed in response to the questions concerning who, what, where, when, and how.

Although answers to some of the above questions are often judged to be strategic elements of the media plan, they are intended to provide broad guidelines for more detailed strategic considerations (refer to figure 9.5).

Components of Media-Objective Statements

Who?   Who is the target market? A precise definition of the target market, derived from the marketing plan/advertising plan, provides the foundation for the media plan. A target-market profile defined in terms of demographics, psychographics, and geo-

Figure 9.5   Questions from which media objectives are derived

WHO	is the target market?
	—demographic, psychographic and geographic profile
WHAT	is the creative selling message?
	—brief description of key sales points
WHERE	are the priority markets?
	—regions and cities based on budget limitations
WHEN	is the best time to reach the target market?
	—season, time of day, day of week
HOW	many, how often, how long?
	—reach, frequency, continuity

graphics is input, and media planners use it to match the target with a compatible media profile (those who read, listen to, or watch a certain media).

What? What is the message to be communicated? A brief summary of the selling message should be included in the objectives statement. Note that the creative strategy may already be complete. As discussed earlier in this chapter, the message, and the manner in which it is presented, can have an influence on media selection.

Where? Where are the market priorities? This is a critical question, as most advertising campaigns are restricted by the size of the advertising budget. Based on directives from the client regarding which regions or cities have priority, and the media planner's ability to work efficiently with little money, decisions must be made as to whether to reach few markets more frequently or to go for more markets less frequently.

When? When is the best time to reach the target market? Certain product and target-market characteristics have bearing on this question. For example, the fact that a product is sold on a seasonal basis will directly influence media timing. A heavier media schedule in the pre-usage season may be recommended as a way of building awareness prior to the purchase period of the seasonal product.

Knowledge of the customer can also influence the timing of advertising messages. For example, is there a best time of the day, or better days of the week to reach the target?

How? How many? How often? How long? Several questions must be answered here. These questions are strategic considerations regarding reach, frequency, and continuity. Objective statements on these issues stem from more detailed media strategies. Strategy considerations will be discussed separately in this chapter.

MEDIA STRATEGY

Similar to other types of planning, media planning deals with the "how" problem: how best to advertise the product or service within the budget guidelines provided. The result of strategic media planning is a recommendation as to what media to use, along with supporting rationale detailing why certain media were selected and others rejected. In conjunction with media objectives, consideration is given to a host of factors that influence the choice of which media to use, how often to advertise, for what length of time to advertise, in what markets, and so on.

Numerous factors are considered when media objectives and strategies are being developed. A discussion of some of the more important factors follows.

Target Market

A well-defined customer profile must be provided to media planners. The more precise the target market definition is, the greater the likelihood of the planners' making a more effective and efficient media recommendation. For products and services whose target markets are more loosely defined (markets that include both sexes, a wider age range, no specific income requirements), the task of selecting the most effective and efficient media is less challenging.

Essentially, the task of the media planner is to match the advertised product's target-market profile with a compatible media profile such as the readership profile of a magazine or newspaper, or the listenership profile of a radio station. Theoretically, the more compatible the match, the more efficient the media buy. Depending on the media planner's knowledge about the target market (its characteristics, attitudes, interests, location, and so on), certain matching strategies can be considered.

Profile-Matching Strategy   In the case of a **profile-matching strategy**, the customer target market is carefully defined by demographic, psychographic, and geographic variables. If a profile-matching strategy is used, the advertising message is placed in media whose readers, listeners, or viewers have a profile that is reasonably close to the profile of the product's target market. All media do not offer complete compatibility. Certain media types are characterized as being general-interest, while others are seen as special-interest. For example, magazines such as *Financial Post, Canadian Business* and *Report on Business Magazine* appeal to a more selective target market, and may be suitable for a profile-matching strategy. The same could be said of television programs that appeal specifically to children, or sports programs that appeal to a predominantly male audience. Some of the benefits of sports advertising are presented in the Advertising in Action vignette "Sports Break through the Clutter."

Examine the profile presented in figure 9.6. *Your Money* (published by CB Media Ltd., Toronto) is positioned as "Canada's personal finance and lifestyle" magazine that offers advice about money and lifestyle features for successful Canadians. The readership profile presented in figure 9.6 suggests that advertisers who are appealing to an affluent, upscale market should consider *Your Money* as an appropriate advertising medium.

Shotgun Strategy   The nature of the word "shotgun" suggests that the target market for which the **shotgun strategy** is best suited is more general than other target markets and therefore that this strategy is more suitable for a product or service with widespread appeal. For target markets that are more loosely defined, particularly in terms of demographics, the media selected to advertise the product can be more general in nature.

Members of the audience watching a popular situation comedy during prime time (8:00 P.M. to 9:00 P.M.) will range in age from child to senior citizen, encompass both sexes equally, will cover the entire range of income groups, and will lead all kinds of lifestyles. For advertisers with sizeable media budgets, television is an effective means of reaching a broad target market. For advertisers with more limited media budgets, newspaper, transit media, and outdoor media can provide good reach at a lower cost.

Very often, advertisers implement a shotgun strategy for new products, going for high reach and frequency in order to create awareness. Although costly in terms of the amount spent on media, the strategy is sound, since it does not alienate potential consumers by being too selective. Certain segments of the market (opportunities) could be missed if more specialized media were used. Once the product is established in the market, and purchase experience and consumer research have led to the identification of buyers, then advertisers may be able to switch to a profile-matching strategy, utilizing more efficient media.

Advertising in Action
Sports Break through the Clutter

Finding the right medium to reach a target market is always the first challenge for the best of media planners. Once the right medium has been found, the challenge is to find a way of breaking through the clutter of advertising directed at the same target.

In today's cluttered media environment, sports advertising offers some solution to this problem. Essentially, sports advertising offers an advertiser four key benefits:

1. Generally, the sports advertising environment is less cluttered. In regular television programming, ads are placed in clusters (six to eight commercials back-to-back). In sports such as hockey, basketball, and football, commercials can only appear during breaks in the action. In effect, the ads run in isolation or in shorter clusters; thus, the potential effectiveness of the ad increases.

2. Sports advertising reaches a viewer who watches relatively little television, but that viewer tends to be upscale. Sports does attract a different audience than conventional programming—predominantly male, and upscale in terms of education, occupation, and income. Specifically, sports pro-

grams are effective at reaching the hard-to-reach business audience.

3. Sports reaches a large audience. Audience data confirms that sports programs are popular. In fact, five of the 10 most watched shows in Canada in 1990 were sports programs: Grey Cup (fourth), Blue Jays versus Athletics (fifth and tenth), "Hockey Night in Canada" playoffs (eighth and ninth).

4. The persona of the sport enhances the image of the advertiser. Sports programs tend to generate loyal audiences and advertisers can take advantage of loyalties by concentrating on one sport and thus appearing to be a larger advertiser than they really are. Molson's, for example, is a long time sponsor of "Hockey Night in Canada" and Labatt's has a strong association with Blue Jays baseball. Package buys such as the Olympic games offer national appeal; hence, many large companies such as Petro-Canada, Coca-Cola, and the Royal Bank of Canada use the games for broad awareness and image campaigns.

Adapted from Ann Boden, "A sporting chance to break through the clutter," *Marketing*, September 10, 1990, p.11.

Rifle Strategy   A **rifle strategy** is a matching strategy used in situations where the target market can be precisely defined by some common characteristic. The common characteristic could be employment in a certain industry, having a certain occupation, or having a particular leisure-time interest or hobby. In many situations, there is a specific medium that can reach this target market.

An interest in recreational downhill skiing, for example, could be the common characteristic of a group. The demographic profile of such a group could be diverse, but the fact that all members of the group ski is important to equipment manufacturers.

Figure 9.6   Readership profile—*Your Money* magazine

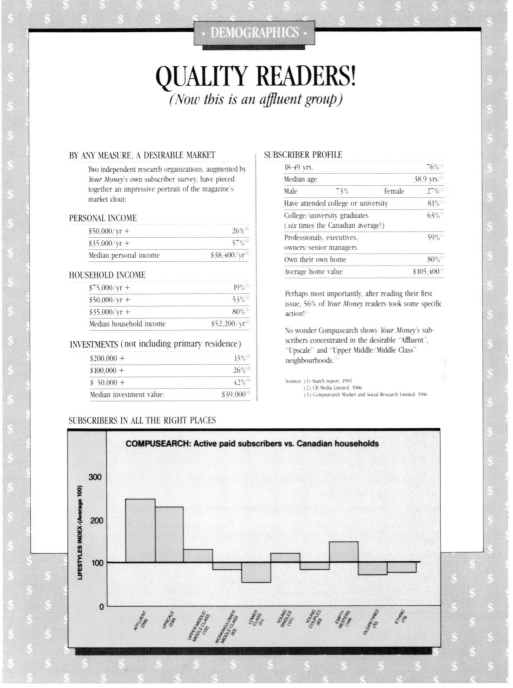

Courtesy: Your Money, CB Media Ltd. Reprinted with permission.

A specific medium can be used to reach the target group. *Ski Canada* (Maclean Hunter Ltd.) would be an appropriate match for the advertiser. For reaching the Canadian snowmobiler, either *Snowmobile* (SGF Publishing Inc.) or *Snowmobile Canada* (CRV Publishing Company Ltd.) would be an appropriate medium to select for a rifle strategy.

The rifle strategy is effective for advertising to the current users of a product or service. To reach potential users, media that appeal to a more general target audience would have to be integrated into the media plan.

Business publications, subdivided according to the nature of the target market, provide business and industrial advertisers with the means of reaching potential buyers directly and efficiently. For example, advertisers interested in reaching the hotel and restaurant trade could advertise in *Hotel & Restaurant* (Maclean Hunter Ltd.) or *Foodservice & Hospitality* (Kostuch Communications). Advertisers interested in reaching purchasing agents might consider *Purchasing* (Maclean Hunter Ltd.) or *Purchasing Management* (Clifford Elliot & Associates Ltd.). Business-to-business publications will be discussed in more detail in chapter 14.

Nature of Advertising Message

As discussed earlier, creative strategy and media strategy should be developed simultaneously for a coordinated effect in the marketplace. However, the nature of the message, determined by the advertiser's needs, often influences the media-selection process. If factual details such as technical data and performance ratings must be communicated, print media is the only practical option. If a promotion, such as a contest, is part of the advertising campaign, a combination of media could be recommended as the means of achieving a variety of objectives.

Reach/Frequency/Continuity/Flexibility

These strategic factors are grouped together because of their interaction in the media-planning process.

Reach **Reach** is the total, unduplicated audience potentially exposed, one or more times, to an advertiser's schedule of messages in a given period of time (say, a week). It is expressed as a percentage of the target population in a geographically defined area (e.g., a television station might reach 30% of a metropolitan market).

Reach is a term commonly used in broadcast media. To explain the principle of reach, assume a message on a particular station was seen by 20 000 households, in a geographic area of 100 000 households. Reach is calculated by the formula

$$\text{Reach} = \frac{\text{Number of households tuned in}}{\text{Number of households in area}}$$

To complete the example,

$$\text{Reach} = \frac{20\ 000\ (\text{tuned in})}{100\ 000\ (\text{in area})}$$

$$= 20\%$$

Frequency **Frequency** is the average number of times an audience is exposed to an advertising message over a period of time, usually a week.

Both reach and frequency variables are considered together in media planning. The media planner must delicately balance reach and frequency objectives within budget guidelines. A common dilemma faced by the media planner is whether to recommend more reach at the expense of frequency, or more frequency with less overall reach.

Impressions **Impressions** refers to the total audience delivered by a media plan, often referred to as "total exposures." You calculate it by multiplying the number of people who receive a message (reach) by the number of times they receive it (frequency).

To illustrate the concept of impressions, let's assume that a message on a television station reached 100 000 people, and that the message was broadcast three times a week for eight weeks. The calculation for the number of impressions would be

$$
\begin{aligned}
\text{Impressions} \quad &= \quad \text{Reach x Frequency} \\
&= \quad 100\ 000 \times (3 \text{ per week} \times 8 \text{ weeks}) \\
&= \quad 2\ 400\ 000
\end{aligned}
$$

The weight (amount of) advertising in a market is determined by a rating system. Media weight is expressed in terms of gross rating points (GRPs).

Gross Rating Points **Gross rating points** are an aggregate of total ratings in a schedule, usually in a weekly period, against a predetermined target audience. Reach multiplied by frequency equals GRPs.

To explain the principle of GRPs, let us assume that an advertiser will buy media time in both Toronto and Halifax. Since the markets differ in size, the potential reach is different in each case. Therefore, the absolute cost of advertising in Toronto would be greater than in Halifax. Considering this information, an advertiser could request equal GRP levels for each market by manipulating reach and frequency. The *costs* would be different, but the *weight* would be the same in each market.

To illustrate this concept (GRP's = Reach $\times$ Frequency), let us assume that a message reaches 15% of the target households three times in one week. The GRP level would be 45 (45 GRPs).

Average Frequency In any given market, each household does not receive the same number of exposures, due to the different viewing habits of the households. As a result, media planners think of frequency in terms of *average* frequency, based on the formula

$$
\text{Average Frequency} \quad = \quad \frac{\text{Total exposures of all households}}{\text{Reach (households)}}
$$

To illustrate this formula, let us assume that the total exposure of all households is 52 500, and the total number of households reached in one week is 15 000. The average frequency is as follows:

$$\frac{52\ 500}{15\ 000} = 3.5$$

To calculate the GRP level for the market, assume that the objective of the campaign is to reach 70% of the households. The GRP level would be:

$$
\begin{aligned}
\text{GRP} &= \text{Reach} \times \text{Frequency} \\
&= 70 \times 3.5 \\
&= 245
\end{aligned}
$$

In this example, enough spots would be purchased to add up to 245 GRPs.

Continuity **Continuity** is the length of time required to ensure that impact is made on a target market through a particular medium. It refers to the duration of the campaign. Media planners must juggle the reach, frequency, and continuity factors to obtain maximum benefit for the dollars invested in media. Quite often the continuity is the first of these variables to "give way" before budget restrictions.

Only the exceptional advertiser would purchase media time on an annual basis (52-week schedule). More moderate advertisers tend to stretch dollars over a one-year period by purchasing media time in "flights." Flighting is the purchase of media time and space in planned intervals, or **flights**. The term *hiatus* is used to describe the inactive period between flights. To understand the application of continuity and flighting, refer to figure 9.7. Flighting is a tactic used to stretch media dollars over an extended period of time, usually a one-year planning cycle.

Flexibility **Flexibility** is the ability to modify media-spending plans throughout the media-spending period. Flexibility is not a variable that influences the media-selection process. It is, however, important from the client's viewpoint, since rapidly changing conditions in the marketplace or within the company may require that media tactics be changed on short notice.

The flexibility of the chosen media—that is, whether the media will allow cancellation by a client who is in a profit-squeeze situation—must be known prior to media purchase. The various media stipulate lead times required for notification of cancellation. A media plan is, after all, exactly that, a "plan." During the year, "reality" sets in; that is, profit objectives of a short-term nature begin to look better than advertising objectives of a long-term nature.

Conversely, an advertiser may decide to purchase additional media. Competitive activity might dictate heavier-than-planned spending in a certain market. Often, media time is sold well in advance of air-date/publication-date, but the advertiser should be aware of the options that are available on short notice. Assuming that the creative material is readily available, newspapers and radio offer short-notice purchase flexibility.

Market Coverage

Market coverage refers to the identity and the number of markets in which advertising occurs over the course of the media plan's execution. Several coverage options are available to the advertiser. Market selection is often based on such factors as the level

Figure 9.7   Continuous advertising versus flighting

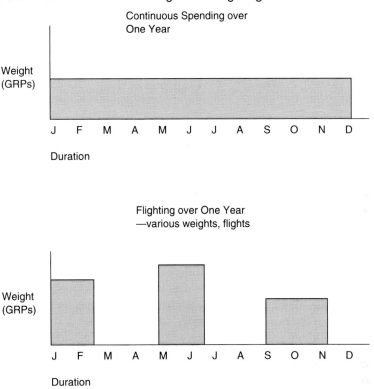

of distribution in a market (i.e., the availability of the product or service) and the importance of an area in terms of the sales volume generated there. An additional factor affecting market choice comes into play when an advertiser decides either to correct a problem or to pursue an opportunity through advertising. In either situation, the result is a disproportionate increase in media spending in the area of concern. Assuming there is an overall ceiling on spending, such a move involves a decrease of advertising in another region.

There are several market-coverage plans available to an advertiser.

National Coverage   National coverage involves having media coverage wherever the product is available. Assuming that a product is widely distributed, the advertiser can select media that have national scope. Network television and national editions of magazines are obvious choices. If urgency is a criteria in the decision-making process (as it usually is when a new product is being launched or a competitive activity is being reacted to), then newspapers in major metropolitan areas, which provide national coverage, are excellent vehicles to use.

Regional Coverage   If an advertiser chooses to advertise regionally, and to allocate media dollars accordingly, some equitable system of allocation must be devised so that all regions benefit from advertising. All regions do not require the same level of advertising weight; competitive-advertising and promotion factors vary from region to region, and this affects regional allocations and causes either upward or downward adjustments.

Assuming that Canada is divided geographically into five regions and that the regional volume importance (contribution to total volume) as shown below is accurate, then an advertiser would allocate $1 million in media dollars according to the following chart:

Geographic Regions	Regional Volume Importance (%)	Media Budget ($)
Maritimes	8	40 000
Quebec	28	140 000
Ontario	40	200 000
Prairies	12	60 000
British Columbia	12	60 000
Canada	100	500 000

This example only considers the level of brand development in each region. Additional considerations could be factored into the regional equations so that a more accurate allocation could be calculated. For example, one could compare the total volume of the market in each region to regional brand development in order to identify areas where potential increases and decreases in spending could be productive. When funds are being allocated and media are being purchased on a regional basis, such media as selective-spot television, radio, regional editions of magazines, and newspapers are attractive alternatives.

Key Market Plan A key market plan is a media plan according to which time and space are purchased in urban markets that have been identified as priorities. Providing coverage only in key markets is often considered as an option when budget constraints do not allow for much flexibility. In this situation, the advertiser uses a predetermined system to prioritize markets. Key markets could be identified nationally or regionally—according to population, for example.

To illustrate, let us assume that a product had reasonably good national distribution, but only enough funds to advertise in a selective list of markets. The media objective would therefore be to achieve adequate levels of reach and frequency in all cities of over 500 000 inhabitants. The media planner would consider the reach, frequency, and continuity factors for each market, and allocate the budget equitably to the cities in question. What cities would this plan cover? The illustration below indicates that media spending would be distributed among nine cities, which compose 46.4% of the Canadian population.

Total Market Area	Population (in thousands)	Canadian Total (%)
Toronto	3 649	13.8
Montreal	2 955	11.1
Vancouver	1 471	5.6

Ottawa-Hull	867	3.3
Edmonton	783	3.0
Calgary	683	2.6
Winnipeg	638	2.4
Quebec	635	2.4
Hamilton	571	2.2
	12 252	46.4

Source: Canadian Media Directors' Council Media Digest, 1990-91, p. 8.

While this system appears equitable, at least in the example, some cities and areas may never receive advertising support. Such decisions often create conflict between marketing/advertising managers and sales managers, who argue that they are short-changed in the media allocation process. The illustration, for example, does not include any city in the Maritimes. The advertiser would have to drop the population requirement down to the 300 000 range to accommodate Halifax. Even then, the markets of St. Catharines-Niagara, Kitchener, and London are ahead of Halifax.

Key market-coverage plans can accommodate media that have a more urban orientation or are more local in nature. Potential media alternatives include spot television, radio, daily and community newspapers, city magazines, outdoor media, and transit media.

Selective Plan In contrast to other market-coverage plans, a selective plan does not consider level of distribution, population by area, geographic product development, and the like. Instead, it attempts to reach a desired target market regardless of geographic location.

A selective-coverage plan is used in conjunction with a rifle strategy when a target market can be narrowly defined by a common characteristic. In this situation, a selective-coverage plan works because of the nature of the advertised product, the common characteristic of the target market, and the availability of a specialized medium. For example, *Photo Life* magazine would be an advertising vehicle appropriate for reaching a photography enthusiast. Direct mail offers the industrial or business advertiser a good opportunity to approach prospects on a selective basis. The use of specialized mailing lists can effectively match sellers with buyers, regardless of their geographic location.

Best Time to Reach Target Market

Media strategy must consider the "best-time" factor (i.e., what is the best time to reach the intended target market?). The best time could refer to the best time of year, the best season, the best time of day, or the best day of the week. If a new product is to be launched onto the market, should the advertiser intensify reach and frequency initially, or gradually build intensity over a longer period of time? These questions are addressed when decisions as to how to schedule media are being made. In most cases, the advertiser is working within a budget restriction, so the money available must be stretched over the entire media-planning period. Several scheduling options are available to the advertiser. Refer to figure 9.8 for a diagrammatic representation of each.

Even Schedule According to the **even schedule**, media time and space are purchased in a uniform manner, over a designated period of time. Such a schedule is usually a practical option for the largest of advertisers, who find it necessary to advertise on a steady basis, perhaps due to competitive factors.

Skip Schedule With a **skip schedule**, media time and space are purchased on an "alternate" basis—every other week or month. In terms of media usage, skip can refer to alternating media—magazines one month, television another month. A skip schedule is one method of stretching media dollars over an extended period of time, while maintaining the effect of advertising in the marketplace.

Figure 9.8   Media scheduling options

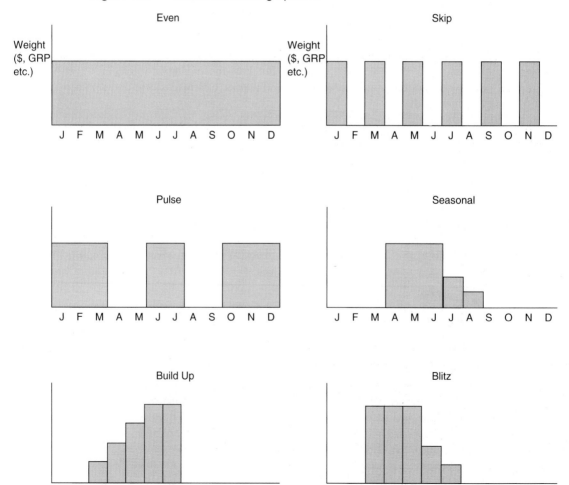

Pulse Schedule **Pulsing** refers to the grouping of advertisements (spending of media dollars) in *flights* over a predetermined length of time. **Flights**, as mentioned earlier, are the periods of time in which the product or service is advertised. In this case, a flight would be followed by a hiatus, followed by a flight, and so on throughout the year. The grouping of advertisements in flights contributes to the synergistic effect desired. In any particular flight, the weight of the advertising can be different.

Seasonal Schedule A seasonal schedule is used for products that are sold and purchased at traditional times of the year. Usually media advertising is heavy in the preseason, and then tapers off in the purchase season. Products may advertise lightly at other times of the year, but will increase weight considerably in the pre-selling season.

Build-Up Schedule A **build-up schedule** is characterized by low media weight initially, often due to selective use of media, gradually building to an intensive campaign in subsequent time periods, with an increase in media weight and the use of additional media.

Blitz Schedule The **blitz schedule** is often associated with the introduction of a new product, an event for which multi-media campaigns are implemented. To create high levels of awareness during the introductory period, advertising saturates the market, and then gradually tapers off. Another feature of this schedule is that certain media will be used less frequently as time goes on, or eliminated over the longer period of time.

Competitive Factors

Prior to committing to a plan, media planners should analyze the competitors' media-usage and expenditure patterns. What the competition is doing can help planners recommend a media direction for their own product.

Assume that a product has a large media budget and dominates other products because it is extensively advertised on television. Does a competitor attempt to compete at the same level in television (assuming adequate funds are available) or should its media planners choose for it another medium and media combination so that, by dominating the different media, the product can reach a similar target market? If funds are not adequate to allow direct competition, then a different media strategy must be considered. In this situation, the use of more selective media, which reach a defined target market, may be the most efficient and competitive approach to media planning.

Budget

All other media strategy considerations are affected by the budget, in one way or another. For example, a small budget can restrict the use of media, the extent of coverage, and the reach and frequency levels; a sizable budget can provide considerable flexibility with respect to the same factors. A large budget allows flexibility in the media-selection process, since a multi-media campaign can be considered. Media planners who face restrictions or smaller media budgets must be more selective in the evaluation process.

To maximize the potential of scarce media dollars, media planners often recommend a primary medium that provides an effective and efficient means of reaching a target market. Such a plan is referred to as a *concentrated media strategy*, since a majority of media dollars are allocated to a primary medium. The advantage of a concentration strategy is potential media-cost savings, since the purchase of one medium in larger quantities creates higher discounts. Then, after considering additional factors such as reach, frequency, market coverage, and the like, media planners will recommend secondary media. Secondary media are often used selectively, and serve to complement the primary medium. The result is a media mix that maximizes the use of scarce media dollars.

Alternately, a media planner could recommend that media dollars be distributed more equitably among several media types. Such a strategy allows the advertiser to reach the same target market in different environments—if members of the target market are not watching television in their leisure time, they may be reading. The strategy of distributing media dollars more equitably across several media is often referred to as an *assortment strategy*. Figure 9.9 summarizes the effect of budget size on media strategy.

Figure 9.10 provides a summary outline of all factors affecting the development of media objectives, strategies, and planning.

MEDIA EXECUTION

The final stage in the media-planning process is media execution. Media strategy determines the general type of media to use, and the reasons for using certain media instead of others. Media execution is basically the process of fine tuning strategy and translating it into specific action plans. These action plans, or tactics, can be divided into the following areas: evaluating cost comparisons so that a particular medium may be chosen over another; scheduling specific media in a planning format (calendar or blocking chart); developing budget summaries that outline media-spending details; and buying the media time when the plan is approved by the client.

The first major tactical decision involves choosing the particular medium (or media) that will best accomplish the media objectives and best allow the media strategies to be executed. This choice is based on a three-stage decision system, referred to as the media-selection process. This process involves

- Selecting the general type of media to use (media strategy)
- Selecting the class of media within the type
- Selecting the particular medium

This can be viewed as a "funnelling" process, since the focus of the media-selection process is moving from the general types of media to the specific medium. See figure 9.11.

Figure 9.9 Influence of budget size on media strategy

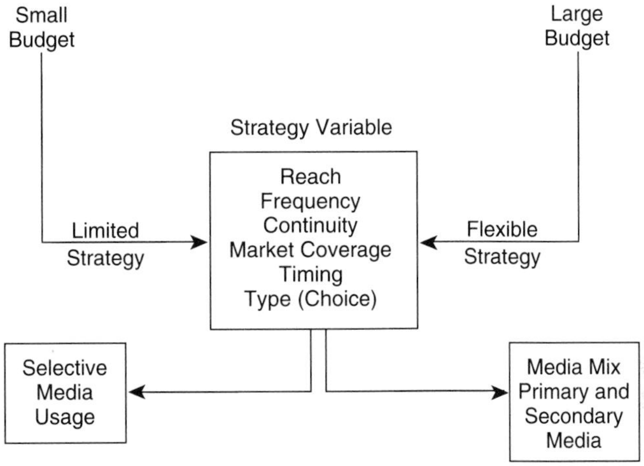

Figure 9.10 Media plan checklist

1. Target Market	— demographic, psychographic and geographic profiles
2. Reach, Frequency, Continuity	— how many, how often, how long?
3. Campaign Duration	— start and finish dates for planning period
4. Market Coverage	— national and regional considerations and priority of urban markets
5. Allocation of Funds	— based on brand development or category development (indexes often used)
6. Network versus Spot Considerations	— national, regional, and local market priorities
7. Buying Strategy	— prime time vs. fringe time vs. day time; seasonal influences
8. Media Selection	— which media and why?
9. Alternative Media	— considerations of and reasons for rejection
10. Cost Efficiency	— cost comparisons of specific media (cpm); effectiveness vs. efficiency

Figure 9.11   Media-selection process—magazine example

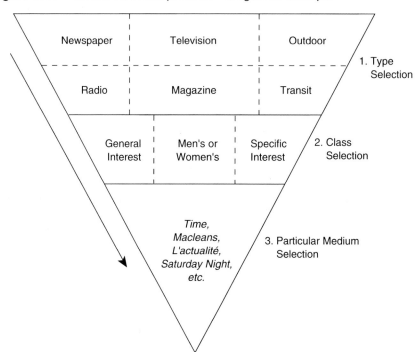

Media-Selection Process

Select General Type of Media   The first decision is one of selecting the type of media that will best allow the advertisers to meet the objectives for the product and to execute the advertising strategies that have been devised for the product. In the selection process, the various media types are evaluated and compared on the basis of how effectively and efficiently they reach the target market.

Select the Class of Media within Type   The second decision involves comparing the class options within the type of media recommended. For example, if magazines are recommended, what class of magazine should be used? Will it be general-interest, specific-interest, or a magazine tailored to the needs of men or women? If television was recommended, will it be network, selective-spot, or a predetermined major-market package?

Select the Particular Medium   The third decision of the media planner is one of recommending which particular medium within a class provides the most cost-efficient means of delivering the advertiser's message. For example, given that the male or female head of household is the intended target market, and magazines have been recommended, which publications are most cost-efficient? The recommendation may consider publications such as *Time*, *Maclean's*, *L'actualité*, *Reader's Digest*, and

Saturday Night. Depending on funds available, one publication or several might be recommended. If television were recommended, which network, or which station (to be purchased locally) ought to be part of a key market plan?

Tactical Considerations for Using a Particular Medium

The media planners must make recommendations concerning which particular medium within a class of media is the most cost-efficient means of reaching the intended target market. Factors affecting media objectives and strategy discussed earlier in the chapter influence this recommendation in general terms, but it is actual cost comparisons of particular media that have the most influence.

The evaluation of media alternatives based on cost comparisons is examined in more detail later, but, to briefly examine the process, let us consider the following magazine-related decision. All publications in the example are classified as women's consumer magazines. There are modest demographic differences between the readerships of the magazines, but the magazines are similar enough to be considered comparable alternatives for reaching Canadian women.

Specific magazines are compared on the basis of CPM (cost per thousand). **CPM** is defined as the cost incurred in delivering a message to 1000 individuals. The data required for the calculation is the cost of a comparable advertisement in each publication, and the circulation figures. The CPM calculation allows for easy comparison of magazines that have different rate structures and circulations. The formula for calculating CPM is as follows:

$$\text{CPM} = \frac{\text{Unit Cost of Message}}{\text{Circulation (000)}}$$

The CPM comparison of the three magazines is as follows:

Magazine National Edition English	Cost ($) (1 Page, 4 Colour)	Circulation (in thousands)	CPM
Chatelaine	29 200	1010.1	28.91
Canadian Living	18 055	558.5	32.33
Homemaker's	20 800	1600.0	12.99

This illustration reveals that *Homemaker's* reaches its audience at a lower cost per thousand than do the other two magazines. If the media planner were recommending a frequency strategy, *Homemaker's* might be recommended as the best alternative for reaching the same prospects many times. Conversely, if a reach strategy were recommended, all three magazines might be approved for use, but probably at various weight levels, due to the different CPM figures for each magazine.

The sample decisions outlined above are based solely on cost efficiency. Other, more qualitative factors are often considered in the decision-making process. Factors such as editorial content, quality of reproduction, and demographic selectivity can lead the media planner to prefer one magazine over another, even if the preferred magazine's CPM is greater than the other magazine's.

To broaden the perspective on tactical considerations, let us review some of the decisions that will affect what other media forms are chosen for use. Refer to figure 9.10; certain factors play a key role in the cost calculations for specific media usage. The following is a brief outline of some critical factors involved in evaluating broadcast, print, or other media.

Some tactical considerations for broadcast media are:

1. What levels of reach and frequency are required? Which is more important, reach or frequency?
2. In which days or months will commercials appear? (Seasonality often affects costs.)
3. Will commercials be placed in prime time or fringe time, or combinations of both?

Some tactical considerations for print media are:

1. How many advertisements will appear, and on which day (newspapers) or which weeks or months (magazines)?
2. Will preferred positions, such as covers in a magazine or specific pages in a newspaper, be purchased?
3. Are there special creative options to be considered, such as gatelegs (multiple-page foldouts) or use of spot or full colour?
4. What are the reach and frequency objectives?

Some tactical considerations for other media are as follows:

1. For outdoor advertising, what markets will be purchased, and what locations are preferred within a market?
2. For outdoor advertising, what kind of billboard will be used (poster or spectacular)? There are considerable cost variations.
3. For transit advertising, what markets will be purchased? Will interior or exterior transit be purchased, or a combination?

Media Scheduling and Budgeting

With the media-selection process complete, planners proceed to the final stage in developing the media plan: formulating a media schedule and related budget summaries. This portion of the planning document outlines for the advertisers how, where, and when the media expenditures are to occur.

The media schedule is normally presented in a calendar format (a blocking chart), and communicates specific details, such as market coverage, media usage, weight levels (GRPs, reach, frequency), and the timing of the campaign. Accompanying the schedule are budget-allocation documents. Typically, the media budget classifies spending allocations according to product (for multi-product advertisers), medium, region, and time of year (months, quarters, etc.).

Detailed expenditure plans are important to the client for budget-control purposes. As indicated in the strategy section of this chapter, flexibility in media planning is important, due to the possibility of rapidly changing conditions throughout a planning cycle. Budget-control documents are referred to often, particularly when cancellations are being considered.

Media Buying The task of the media buyer is to purchase the time and space according to the media plan. This requires the buyer to interpret the work of the media planners and to make decisions regarding actual buys. Buyers are also charged with the responsibility of making replacement buys if the original choice is unavailable.

Time is often a critical factor in the buying process. For example, in broadcast television, the CBC and CTV networks are booked in June to cover a 52-week period, starting in September, with bookings being non-cancellable. Spot television can be purchased any time during the year, assuming local-market availability. There is cancellation flexibility with selective-spot buying.

The role of the media buyer is to act as a "negotiator" with media representatives. His or her assignment is to maximize the efficiency of the media budget by seeking favourable positions and negotiating the best rates possible in light of the guidelines in the media plan. In essence, the buyer fulfills the schedule by putting the plan into action.

The Role of Computers in Media Planning

The process of media planning and buying has always been a complicated task. In recent years, the use of computers has proven to be of significant benefit. Owing to the myriad calculations that are involved in a media plan, it is not surprising that computers are playing a more dominant role. They have helped both small and large advertisers and advertising agencies. Sophisticated independent media services are now offering computer-assisted planning at costs attractive to smaller advertisers.

Harris Media Systems of Toronto provides advertisers and agencies with a host of computer media-planning and analysis services for most major media. The systems are offered in microcomputer mode, interactive mode, or through Harris Media's client service. For television planning, some of Harris' services include GRP per week by market, one-week reach and average frequency, multi-week reach, and multi-week reach and average frequency. Similar planning packages are available for other media.

Other companies that specialize in computerized services to assist in the media-planning process are Telmar Communications of Canada Limited and IMS (Interactive Market Systems Inc.)—both of Toronto. All of these firms are based in Toronto.

MEDIA PLANNING—ROLES AND RESPONSIBILITIES

Both the client and the advertising agency have roles to play in the media-planning process. The client provides the agency's media personnel with background information about marketing and advertising, along with broadstroke direction for developing the media plan. Similar to the creative plan, the media plan must flow from the marketing plan and advertising plan discussed in chapter 5.

Role of the Client (Advertiser)

Information typically provided to the agency by the client may include some or all of the following: a marketing profile, a product media profile, a competitor media profile, a target-market profile, media objectives, and a media budget.

Marketing Profile The marketing profile reviews the market size and growth trends. It also includes current and historical market-share trends, which give the media planner a perspective on what is happening in the market and the level of competition therein.

Product Media Profile Using the product media profile to review historical media usage and spending trends is often wise, prior to embarking on a new plan. A qualitative and quantitative evaluation of the strengths and weaknesses of past media plans provides input for new plans. If little else, such a review should induce strong feelings about what worked and what did not.

Competitors' Media Usage A summary analysis of competitors' media-usage and spending trends influences the strategic media direction chosen for the product. For example, what media do the competitors dominate? How much do they spend? Where do they spend it?

Target-Market Profile The marketing plan provides the media planner with a precise definition of the target market. All relevant demographic, psychographic, and geographic information available influences media strategy and execution. For example, what media strategy is chosen—whether profile matching, shotgun, or rifle— often depends upon the degree of target-market knowledge available. Knowing the activities and interests of the target market can enable media planners to choose the best times and places in which to advertise.

Media Objectives Broadstroke definition of what the media plan will accomplish is the responsibility of the client. Information regarding who, what, when, where, and how should be provided to the agency. The intent is not to restrict the agency in its thinking; on the contrary, the *detailed* consideration of these elements will be the responsibility of the agency media planners.

Media Budget Unless the task method of budgeting is to be employed, the media budget has already been allocated in the marketing plan. The relative importance of media, in comparison to other promotion plans, should be communicated to the agency media planners. The budget provides the framework within which the planners must develop strategies and achieve stated goals.

Role of the Advertising Agency

In an advertising agency, the **media director** is responsible for developing the overall media plan, and oversees the selecting, scheduling, and buying of time and space.

Reporting to the media director is a staff of media planners, buyers, and estimators. Media planners are specialists who put together the detailed media strategies and tactics. Their task is to consider the factors affecting the development of media objectives and strategies, which involves evaluating the client input, and to produce a plan of action that will meet the stated objectives. All details are presented to the client for approval in the form of a media plan.

Once the media plan has been approved, the time and space is purchased by the media buyers. Their mandate is to interpret the media plan, and purchase the best deals available through the various media representatives for the different media vehicles. As indicated earlier, computer sophistication has enhanced the ability of media planners and buyers. This being the case, a buyer's task is to deliver the maximum amount of impact (against a target audience) at a minimum of cost (client's budget).

Summary

A media plan is a document that outlines proposed means of gaining maximum impact or exposure for a product or service at minimum cost to the client. The initial step in developing a media plan is to establish a budget that sets the financial parameters for the planning process. With the budget defined, advertising objectives are translated into media objectives, strategies, and tactics.

Whether the budget devised is appropriate for a media plan depends largely upon the marketing sophistication of the organization. A variety of factors influence the potential size of an advertising budget, including the size of the customer base, the degree of competition the product will face, the stage the product has reached in the product life cycle, the product's characteristics, and management's commitment to advertising.

The media plan flows logically from the overall marketing strategy and advertising strategy so that the objectives specified in the marketing plan/advertising plan will be met. The media plan is divided into three basic sections: media objectives, media strategies, and media execution. Media objectives are statements that outline who (i.e., what the target market is), what (i.e., what the selling message is), where (i.e., where the markets to advertise in are located), when (i.e., when is the best time is to reach the target market), and how (i.e., how often and how long are needed to reach the target market). These objectives act as the framework for more detailed strategies and tactics.

Media strategy deals with the selection of appropriate media to accomplish media objectives. Strategies are affected by variables such as the characteristics of the target market, the nature of the message, reach and frequency objectives, the degree of coverage desired, competitive influences, and the budget.

Media execution is the section of the media plan that outlines the specific tactics for achieving the media objectives. In these detailed action plans are the specific media-usage recommendations, and summaries of how media funds will be allocated.

In the media-planning process, the client is responsible for providing the agency with adequate background information, information which is usually contained in the marketing plan. Using this information, the agency develops a detailed media plan and assumes responsibility for selecting, scheduling, and buying media time and space.

Review Questions

1. Identify and briefly describe the factors that influence the size of an advertising budget.
2. Contrast the strengths and weaknesses of the percentage-of-sales budgeting method with those of the task (objective) budgeting method.
3. What are the advertising manager's functional areas of responsibility in the budgeting process?
4. What are the basic differences between media objectives, strategies, and tactics?
5. Identify and briefly describe the components of media-objective statements.
6. Describe the differences between
   i) Profile-matching strategy
   ii) Shotgun strategy
   iii) Rifle strategy.
7. Briefly explain the impact that reach, frequency, and continuity have on strategic media planning.
8. What is the difference between a "key-market" media plan and a "selective" market plan?
9. What are the stages in the media-selection process?

Discussion Questions

1. "Media planning is an activity that should be in the hands of specialists." Discuss, in the context of clients doing their own media planning, the use of a full-service agency and a media-buying service (a specialist).
2. "The client is at the mercy of the agency's media recommendations." Is this a problem or not? Discuss.
3. "The budget should be based on the media plan, not the media plan based on the budget." Discuss from the perspectives of both the client and the agency.

Print Media— Newspaper and Magazine

CHAPTER 10

In studying this chapter, you will learn

- The classifications of newspapers and magazines available to the Canadian advertiser
- The advantages and disadvantages of newspapers and magazines as advertising media
- The considerations and procedures involved in buying newspaper and magazine space
- The basic terminology used in newspaper and magazine advertising

Newspapers in Canada

Newspaper publishing has changed dramatically in recent years. In the past decade alone, a new era of newspaper publishing has begun. Words and phrases such as *telecommunications, satellite transmission, laser beams, video-display terminals, electronic journalism, on-line systems, videotex,* and *data bases* have become buzzwords in the industry.[1] Typewriters have been replaced by video-display terminals, linotype machines by computers, and heavy plates for rotary presses by wafer-thin plates that are engraved photographically. Perhaps the most dramatic innovation has been the advent of national newspapers, which can be assembled and printed in a number of cities at the same time. The Toronto-based *Globe and Mail* is the Canadian innovator in this area, publishing at once in Toronto, Moncton, Montreal, Calgary, and Vancouver.

CANADIAN DAILY NEWSPAPERS

In Canada, there are currently 110 daily newspapers, with the largest in circulation being the *Toronto Star.* Average Monday-to-Friday circulation for the *Toronto Star* is 523 400, with Saturday circulation increasing to an average of 786 300. As of 1990, the total circulation of all Canadian daily newspapers was 5 387 300.[2]

The term **circulation** in print media refers to the number of issues sold. Circulation is defined as the average number of copies per issue of a publication that are sold by subscription, distributed free to predetermined recipients, carried within other publications, or made available through retail distributors.

It is estimated that daily newspapers reach one of every four Canadians on a daily basis. On a regional basis, Ontario has the largest number of daily newspapers, with 43, followed by British Columbia with 17, and Quebec with 11. Nine of the Quebec newspapers are French-language publications.

As indicated in chapter 9, newspapers are one of the largest generators of advertising revenues in Canada. The latest statistics show newspaper net revenues to be $1.5 billion annually, for an average share of advertising revenue of 17%. Newspaper revenues are generated from three advertising sources: retail advertising produces 54% of revenue, classified advertising 26%, and general (national advertising) 20%. Additional advertising revenue is generated through the distribution of preprinted inserts carried in newspapers.

Control and ownership of Canadian daily newspapers rests with three large firms. Torstar controls the *Toronto Star.* Southam Publishing also dominates the Canadian newspaper scene, with 14 dailies strung across the country. Their combined circulation of 1.5 million represents about 20% of all papers sold in Canada.[3] Southam has four entries in the list of Canada's top 10 dailies: *Vancouver Sun, Montreal Gazette, Ottawa Citizen,* and *Vancouver Province.* Thompson Newspapers is the other major

Figure 10.1   Canada's Top 10 Daily Newspapers

Market	Newspaper	Circulation (in thousands)
Toronto	*The Toronto Star*	523.4
Toronto	*The Globe and Mail*	330.0
Montreal	*Le Journal de Montréal (Tab.)*	321.6
Toronto	*The Toronto Sun*	282.3
Vancouver	*The Vancouver Sun*	207.1
Montreal	*La Presse*	205.3
Ottawa	*The Citizen*	184.5
Vancouver	*Vancouver Province (Tab.)*	182.3
Montreal	*The Gazette*	178.4
Winnipeg	*Free Press*	172.2

company in the business. Their largest newspapers are the *Globe and Mail* and *Winnipeg Free Press*. Refer to figure 10.1 for the list of Canada's top 10 daily newspapers and their circulations.

WEEKLY NEWSPAPERS

Weekly (or community) newspapers are generally smaller-circulation newspapers published once a week (sometimes more in larger markets), and directed at a local-area target audience. In comparison to dailies, the weekly newspaper is truly an advertising medium for the local market, appealing more to local, independent advertisers than to chain-store advertisers. One advantage weekly newspapers provide is that the paper actually stays in the home for a relatively long time, owing to its weekly distribution cycle.

Recently, weekly newspapers have started to become attractive vehicles for national advertisers. The circulation of these newspapers has increased due to the promotion of newspaper groups and networks, and they now reach the areas where most people live (in suburban areas around major urban centres). There are some 1056 community newspapers in Canada with an average weekly circulation of 11.7 million copies. In Canada, 63.2% of the population received and read a community newspaper in the past seven days.[4] In the Toronto area, for example, Metroland Publishing has a network of newspapers that reach a high percentage of the suburban population. Metroland's newspapers include the *Etobicoke Advertiser/Guardian*, *Mississauga News*, *Oshawa/Whitby This Week*, and the *Brampton Guardian*. In British Columbia, the *Now/Times Newspapers* reach over a quarter of a million people with community papers in Burnaby, New Westminster, Surrey/North Delta, and Port Coquitlam.

Despite these impressive figures, the 1990s are shaping up to be tougher times for newspapers. After almost a decade of revenue growth, the late 1980s were not kind to the industry. It was a period when advertising linage declined. This situation is forcing the industry to consider new strategies for marketing the medium in the nineties. For more insight into the situation, see the Advertising in Action vignette "New Strategies for Tougher Times."

SPECIALIZED NEWSPAPERS

In addition to dailies and weeklies, there are specialized newspapers published in Canada. These tend to concentrate on a particular area of interest. The typical specialized newspaper in Canada focusses on business and financial target markets. Included in this category are *Report on Business* (distributed via the *Globe and Mail*), *The Financial Post*, *Financial Times of Canada*, and *Les Affaires*.

NEWSPAPER FORMATS

Canadian newspapers are published in two formats: *tabloids* and *broadsheets*. Some terminology must be defined before a discussion of these will make sense. With regard to newspaper page configurations, and how advertising space is sold, the following are important terms: Canadian Newspaper Unit (CNU), Modular Agate Line (MAL), and gutter.

Canadian Newspaper Unit (CNU) **CNUs** make up standardized newspaper formats. A 13" wide broadsheet is divided into six columns, and a 10 1/4" tabloid into five columns; each unit is measured one column wide by 30 modular agate lines deep (2 1/8"). A full-page broadsheet contains 60 CNUs, a tabloid 30 CNUs.

Modular Agate Line (MAL) The **modular agate line** is a standardized unit of space equal to one column wide and 1/14" deep. Standard column widths are 2 1/16" in broadsheets, 1 15/16" in tabloids.

Gutter The **gutter** is the blank space in the inside-page margins, or the space between columns across the page.

Tabloids

Tabloids are flat, with only a vertical centrefold, and resemble an unbound magazine. In terms of size, the tabloid averages 10 1/4" (260 mm) wide and 13" (330 mm) deep. A tabloid page is divided into 30 equal modular units (five column units wide by six units deep). Each column measures 1 15/16" in width, and is separated by gutters. The depth of each unit is 30 modular agate lines. For advertising purposes, standardized ad sizes can be ordered in 25 combinations of these units, or ordered by modular agate lines and columns. The largest circulation tabloids in Canada are *Le Journal de Montréal* (321 500), the *Toronto Sun* (282 300), and the *Vancouver Province* (182 300). In total, there are 16 tabloids published in Canada, 11 of which are English-language and five French-language.

Advertising in Action
New Strategies for Tougher Times

To speak of tough times for newspapers is not to say that newspapers have lost their appeal with the Canadian public. In fact, the Newspaper Marketing Bureau reports that more than 66% of adult Canadians still read a daily newspaper regularly. Newspapers are an important source of information to people, be it global, national, business, sports, or entertainment information. To their advantage, newspapers are a medium that is referred to at the consumers' convenience—at home, on public transit, or at work.

Despite all that newspapers have to offer an advertiser, it is predicted that tough times lie ahead for them, and that new marketing strategies will be necessary if newspapers are to maintain a leadership position as an advertising medium. To illustrate what has been happening, newspapers controlled 27% of all advertising revenue in Canada 10 years ago. The most recent figure (1989) is down to 24%. Over the past decade, newspapers have lost revenue to other media.

Today's newspapers are slimmer than in the past, and the size of a newspaper is usually a direct reflection of advertising linage. Newspapers generate close to 75% of their revenues from retail advertising. In this day and age, the retailing sector is very weak—retailers are hurting and advertising budgets have been cut back. Also, the real-estate market is taking a beating and the automobile industry is slumping. These are two other large advertisers that have cut back on advertising, and newspapers have been affected by it. New forms of competition are also hurting newspapers. Direct marketing, free or specialized periodicals, and directories and catalogues are taking revenues from daily newspapers.

The challenge for dailies in the 1990s is to adopt a stronger marketing orientation to compensate for lack of growth in the economy and to react to moves being made by other media. To do this, the industry must pro-actively promote its two important strengths: high coverage of a local or regional market, and immediacy. Newspaper advertising has been traditionally sold on a "reach" or "coverage" basis. Now, newspapers must discover the strength of "frequency" and introduce a rate structure that encourages more insertions by advertisers. Further, satisfying readers will be of paramount importance. There is little doubt that newspapers will become smaller, but at the same time they should become more interesting.

What, then, can we expect of newspapers in the 1990s? Here's a list of possibilities:

1. Newspapers will broaden their appeal by sectionalizing, capturing reader's attention with departments on topics as diversified as health, leisure, and technology.

2. Colour, virtually unheard of 10 years ago, will be used extensively to appeal to a generation raised on video.

3. Newspapers will have a more contemporary look. Perhaps they will have a flashier look much like the look *USA Today* has now. Certainly, they will have to appeal to two different readers at the same time—one who wants in-depth stories and another who likes to flip through a paper casually.

4. Newspapers will be smaller in size, communicating through better editing and graphics rather than through sheer volume of words. Newspaper publishers will come to realize that a smaller, more interesting paper will be the recipe for success in the 1990s.

Adapted from Leonard Kubas, "Newspapers need new marketing strategies," *Marketing,* September 17, 1990, p.44.

Broadsheets

Broadsheets are much larger newspapers, with an approximate size of 13" (330 mm) wide by 22"(559 mm) deep. For broadsheets, a page is divided into 60 modular units (six columns wide by 10 units deep). Each column measures 2 1/16" in width, and is separated by gutters. The depth of each unit is the same as the tabloid, 30 modular agate lines. For advertising, there are 53 different combinations of sizes to choose from; ads can also be ordered by modular agate lines and columns.

The majority (94) of Canadian daily newspapers are published in broadsheet format, the largest being the *Toronto Star*, with an average daily circulation of 523 400, the *Globe and Mail* (330 000), and the *Vancouver Sun* (207 000).

For more information about advertising size combinations in newspapers, refer to figure 10.2.

Figure 10.2   Page configuration—broadsheets and tabloids, Canadian newspaper unit formats

Broadsheet

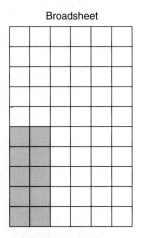

Tabloid

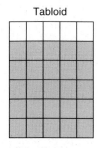

CNU format	CNU format
6-column broadsheet	5-column tabloid
page equivalent	page equivalent
(1 unit = 30 MAL in depth)	(1 unit = 30 MAL in depth)
5 units deep × 2 units wide	5 units deep × 5 units wide
OR	OR
150 MAL (modular agate lines)	150 MAL (modular agate lines)
× 2 columns	× 5 columns
(Total linage 5×2×30 = 300 MAL)	(Total linage 5×5×30 = 750 MAL)

*T*YPES OF NEWSPAPER ADVERTISING

The revenues generated by advertising significantly offset the production and overhead costs of publishing a newspaper. A common rule of thumb in newspapers is that advertising, on average, accounts for 60% of the space. The advertising layouts are put into position first, then the editorial content is arranged around the advertising. On days when the newspaper is larger, it is because of an increase in advertising revenues. For example, the Wednesday edition of many daily newspapers is often much thicker than the other days' editions, in part because of the addition of pre-printed inserts by supermarket chains.

There are two broad forms of advertising: *display* and *classified*. **Display advertising** is defined as any advertisement appearing in any part of the publication, excluding the classified section. Display advertising can be subdivided into two types: *general*, or *national, advertising*; and *retail advertising*. Preprinted inserts are another form of advertising that produces revenues for a newspaper. Let's now examine the various types of advertising in greater detail.

General Advertising (National Advertising)

General advertising, or **national advertising**, is sold to advertisers and advertising agencies by a national sales department or a media-representative firm. Advertisements of this kind normally feature products or services marketed on a national or regional basis, through a network of local retailers. Included in this category are advertisements for such products and services as brand-name food and beverages, automobiles, airlines, and banks and other financial institutions. Very often, ads placed by national advertisers include **hookers** (tags) identifying local retailers where the product can be purchased; a hooker is usually placed at the bottom of the advertisement. General advertising is usually placed by advertising agencies on behalf of the advertiser (client).

Retail Advertising

As the name suggests, **retail advertising** is used by such businesses as department stores, supermarkets, drug stores, restaurants, and shopping malls. Retail ads usually stress sale items and specials, or they re-advertise national brands that are carried by the retailer at special prices. Another important function of retail ads is the communication of store location and hours of operation. This type of ad is sold by a local newspaper's sales staff. As indicated earlier, retail advertising generates the majority of the newspaper's revenues. Also of note is the fact that retail advertisers pay as much as 50% less for advertising space than do national advertisers. The higher rates charged to national advertisers is a controversial issue in the advertising and newspaper industry.

Classified Advertising

Classified advertising appears in a much-read section of the newspaper, and in many of the larger dailies it has a full section to itself. It produces a considerable amount of revenue for a newspaper. Classified ads provide readers with opportunities to buy, sell, lease, or rent a variety of products and services such as jobs, houses, apartments, cars, recreational vehicles, furniture, and so on.

Preprinted Inserts

Daily newspapers and weekly newspapers receive additional revenues from the distribution of preprinted inserts. These inserts, often referred to as *supplements* or *free-standing inserts*, are inserted into the fold of the newspaper and look like a separate, smaller section. On any given day, it is not uncommon for a newspaper to include several different inserts. Large users of inserts include supermarkets, department-store chains, and automotive and hardware chains.

NEWSPAPERS AS AN ADVERTISING MEDIUM

ADVANTAGES OF NEWSPAPERS

Geographic Selectivity

Newspapers serve a well-defined geographic area (town, city, trading zone, etc.), so they are attractive to local merchants. For the national advertiser, newspapers offer placement on a market-by-market basis. The advertiser can select specific newspaper markets, or all the markets in a region. This makes spending economy available to the national advertiser.

Although predominantly local in nature, Canada's two largest dailies illustrate how newspapers can expand coverage into regional markets. The *Toronto Star* has excellent penetration in trading zones surrounding Metropolitan Toronto, and the *Globe and Mail* publishes an Ontario edition and National edition. Approximately 40% of the *Globe and Mail's* circulation is outside of Toronto.[5]

Coverage

In local markets, newspapers effectively reach a broad cross-section of the adult population. Current readership statistics show that newspapers effectively reach adults 18 years of age and over. The medium also offers high reach among all household-income, occupation, and education groups. For all of these demographic variables, readership increases proportionately to income, education, and occupation.

Flexibility

Newspapers provide several forms of flexibility. In terms of creative execution, the Canadian-Newspaper-Unit (CNU) system offers advertisers a multitude of size options. (Refer to figure 10.2.) In terms of placement, newspapers allow advertising to be placed with short lead times, as little as two or three days in most cases. By using newspapers, therefore, advertisers can react to competitive situations quickly.

Reader Involvement

Since subscribers pay for the newspaper, and since the content is news and current information, newspapers are a closely-read medium. Although readership patterns (how a newspaper is read) vary among individuals, 77% of all readers go through a newspaper reading whatever is interesting,[6] and 68% look at newspaper ads, whether interested in buying or not.[7] Such reading tendencies suggest a high possibility of exposure for products and services advertised in newspapers.

Creative and Merchandising Considerations

Since newspapers are a closely-read medium, and since ad-size options are many, advertisers are able to present messages that include long copy or factual information (as is not the case with broadcast media). Also, newspapers offer merchandise tie-in opportunities, such as co-operative advertising with local distributors, or ads containing coupons or other promotional incentives geared towards trial purchase.

Editorial Support

Newspaper content can offer positive benefits to advertisers. For example, a clothing-store ad that is placed in the fashion section of a newspaper will be seen by readers interested in fashion. Similarly, advertisements for sports-and-recreation products could appear to advantage in the sports section. It should be noted, however, that requests for specific positions in the newspaper add to the costs of advertising (i.e., a premium price is charged).

Suitability for Small Advertisers

To retail advertisers, particularly local-market independents, newspapers offer high reach and flexibility at relatively low cost compared to other media. Also, retailers lacking in advertising expertise can draw upon the creative services of the newspaper, usually at no extra cost.

DISADVANTAGES OF NEWSPAPERS

Short Life-Span

"There is nothing as stale as yesterday's news." This phrase sums up any newspaper's biggest drawback—a short life. Since a daily newspaper is only around for one day or less, the likelihood of an advertisement's receiving exposure is drastically reduced if the newspaper is not read on the day of distribution.

Lack of Target-Market Orientation

Excluding specialized newspapers, which have a more selective target-market reach (a reach determined by demographics), newspapers in general reach a very broad cross-section of the population. For advertisers using a shotgun strategy (mass reach), newspapers serve a purpose. But advertisers wishing to reach a target market that is upscale in terms of income, occupation, or education must recognize that newspaper advertising will reach many who are not in the target market, resulting in wasteful circulation. Therefore, advertisers with well-defined targets may find other media more appropriate.

Clutter

As a rule of thumb, 60% of a newspaper's space is devoted to advertising. Therefore, making an ad stand out and make an impression on the reader is a challenging creative task. The inclusion of advertising inserts on certain days compounds the clutter problem, as does the hasty manner in which people read newspapers.

Poor Reproduction Quality

Advertisers may compare newspapers to magazines on any number of bases. With respect to quality of print reproduction, newspapers compare very poorly. Detracting from the quality of the print production in newspapers are the quality and speed of the printing presses and the poor quality of newsprint used. However, newspapers have been putting offset presses (magazine presses) to greater use in recent years, and the quality of reproduction has improved, particularly in the areas of spot-colour and four-colour advertising.

High Cost

The high costs of newspaper advertising are a problem faced by national advertisers. National advertisers pay a line rate much higher than that paid by retail advertisers. Another cost-related problem for national advertisers is that continally adding markets to increase regional or national coverage adds considerably to the costs of newspaper advertising. An advertiser who chooses to advertise in 91 markets via 110 daily newspapers, with a 667 modular agate line ad in black and white, incurs a cost of $134 757. The addition of colour (4-colour process) increases the cost to $229 712. Although it is unlikely that any advertiser would adopt such a strategy or make such an expenditure, this example demonstrates that advertisers must consider alternative media if they desire to increase regional or national coverage for a product, or if the product's target market is precisely defined.

BUYING NEWSPAPER SPACE

The basic procedure for buying newspaper space is to determine the size of the ad to be run, either in Canadian Newspaper Units (CNUs) or modular agate lines. You determine the cost of the advertisement by multiplying the line rate by the number of modular agate lines purchased. Other factors that influence costs include the number of insertions, creative considerations such as the use of colour, and position charges, if applicable.

Determine Space Size

Newspaper space is sold on the basis of modular units (CNUs), whereby an advertiser requests an ad that is so many units wide by so many units deep. Alternatively, space can be sold on the basis of modular agate lines (MAL) times the number of columns required.

To illustrate the procedure for buying advertising space, let us assume that an advertiser is buying the shaded area of the broadsheet illustration in figure 10.2. The size requested in the insertion order would be

2 units wide by 5 units deep.

However, since each unit of depth contains 30 agate lines, the alternate order, in modular agate lines, would be based on the following formula:

Number columns wide × units deep × 30 = Modular Agate Lines

2 × 5 × 30 = 300 MAL

If an advertiser purchased the shaded area of the tabloid in figure 10.2, a total of 750 modular agate lines would be purchased, in accordance with the following formula:

Number columns wide × units deep × 30 = Modular Agate Lines
5 × 5 × 30 = 750 MAL

Rate Schedules

With regard to rate schedules, several factors must be noted. First, rates charged by line go down as the volume of the linage increases over a specified period of time. Second, costs for the addition of colour or preferred positions are quoted separately. Third, the line rates may vary from one section of the paper to another. For example, the transient rate for advertisers in the *Globe and Mail's* "Report on Business" section is higher than in the fashion, sports, or travel sections.

Line rate is defined as the advertising rate charged by newspapers for one modular agate line. See figure 10.3, the *Globe and Mail* rate card, for more details about line rates.

In this chart, the rates quoted start with a transient rate. Transient rates are defined as one-time rates, or base rates, that apply to casual advertisers. Discounts are offered to advertisers purchasing volume linage over a more extended period of time, usually one year.

To illustrate how costs are calculated in newspapers, let's develop a hypothetical plan based on the following information:

Newspaper:	The Globe and Mail—National Edition
Size of Ad:	4 units wide × 5 units deep
Rate:	Transient Rate—General Advertising
Frequency:	Once

The first calculation would be to determine as follows the total number of modular agate lines:

4 units wide × 5 units deep × 30 = 600 MAL

The next step would be to multiply the number of modular agate lines by the line rate by the frequency to determine the cost of the insertion. In this case, the 400 MAL rate would apply.

MAL × Line Rate × Frequency = Total Cost
600 × $19.48 × 1 = $11 688

Rates Based on Volume Purchased As indicated in the rate schedule in figure 10.3, the cost of each advertisement will be less if the volume of lines purchased meets or exceeds the line requirements on the volume scales. To illustrate the effect of such a situation on costs, let's assume the same information as in the preceding example, with one change. This time, the ad will run 10 times. In this example, the total lines purchased would be as follows:

4 units wide × 5 units deep × 30 × 10 insertions = 6000 MAL

Figure 10.3 The *Globe and Mail* rate card

THE GLOBE AND MAIL

1991 GENERAL ADVERTISING RATE SCHEDULE

News

Modular Agate Lines	National Edition and Report on Business	Ontario Buy	Metro Edition	Tombstones	Eastern Edition	Western Edition
Transient	$19.77	$17.66	$16.27	$24.71	$4.80	$5.04
400	19.48	17.40	16.02	24.35	4.64	4.89
950	18.90	16.87	15.54	23.63	4.46	4.70
1,700	18.37	15.94	14.68	22.96	4.28	4.51
3,500	17.24	14.82	13.61	21.55	4.02	4.23
7,000	16.47	14.32	13.17	20.59	3.84	4.04
10,000	16.12	14.08	12.93	20.15	3.72	3.91
17,000	15.77	13.83	12.70	19.71	3.66	3.86
25,000	15.51	13.60	12.52	19.39	3.59	3.79
33,500	15.27	13.36	12.33	19.09	3.57	3.72
50,000	14.81	12.90	11.89	18.51	3.50	3.65
70,000	14.32	12.43	11.42	17.90	3.35	3.50
100,000	13.84	11.98	11.03	17.30	3.21	3.37
135,000	13.35	11.54	10.64	16.69	3.12	3.28
175,000	12.84	11.10	10.23	16.05		

Multiple pages in same issue - *in lieu of volume discounts.*

	National Edition and Report on Business	Ontario Buy	Metro Edition
3 pages	$15.81	$14.12	$13.00
4 pages	14.82	13.25	12.17
5 pages	12.86	11.46	10.56
6+ pages	11.88	10.58	9.72

National Edition: Distributed across Canada - 330,000.
Ontario Buy: Ontario circulation including Ottawa - 229,000.
Metro Edition: Distributed throughout Ontario - except Ottawa - 211,000.
Estimated average daily circulation as of Oct. 1/90.

* Effective October 1, 1990
Balance effective January 1, 1991

Arts, Fashion, Sport, Travel*

	National Edition	Ontario Buy	Metro Edition
Transient	$13.25	$12.20	$11.07
400	12.35	11.32	10.18
950	11.55	10.53	9.38
1,700	10.91	9.87	8.74
3,500	10.18	9.14	8.01
7,000	9.94	8.89	7.76
10,000	9.88	8.85	7.71
17,000	9.82	8.80	7.65
25,000	9.77	8.73	7.59
33,500	9.69	8.65	7.52
50,000	9.65	8.60	7.46
70,000	9.58	8.55	7.40
100,000	9.54	8.51	7.36
135,000	9.51	8.47	7.32
175,000	9.48	8.44	7.29

Multiple pages in same issue*
- in lieu of volume discounts.

	National Edition	Ontario Buy	Metro Edition
3 pages	10.60	9.76	8.86
4 pages	9.94	9.15	8.30
5 pages	8.61	7.93	7.20
6+ pages	7.95	7.32	6.64

Earlugs

	Report on Business	Money & Markets	National & Int'l Reports	Facts & Arguments	Metro Edition Other features†	National features†
Transient/ per insertion	$718	$574	$610	$610	$368	$502
104-155 insertions	515	412	438	438	285	360
156-311	496	397	422	422	274	347
312 +	478	383	407	407	262	335

Report on Business (per MAL)

Appointment Notices	$36.44
Financial Notices	24.51
Bank Statements	7.00

Colour charges

	National Edition and Report on Business	Ontario Buy	Metro Edition
Black & 1	$2,867	$2,608	$2,400
Black & 2	4,178	3,801	3,495
Black & 3	5,689	5,174	4,760

Additional Information

- There is a $50 production charge for ads under 50 MAL that are not camera-ready.
- Minimum display space in News, Fashion and Report on Business is 30 MAL; unless specified, it is 15 MAL in other sections.
- Regional copy changes: $250 per plant
- Position charge: 25 per cent.
- Charge for Globe and Mail box number: $40.
- Cancellation charge: 25 per cent for ads cancelled after deadline. No cancellations accepted the day prior to publication.

Direct Response Advertising Insert Features

- Free information services for readers.
- Exceptional opportunities for effective, targeted marketing — giving a direct return on your advertising investment.
- Each perforated reply card on the insert has advertiser's message on one side; return address and postal licence number are on other side.
- Trim size of each card: 5½" x 3½".
- Camera-ready art or film negatives required.
- Process colour separations, if required, are at extra cost.
- Advertiser to provide Business Reply Card postal licence number with artwork for reply card.
- National distribution.
- CLOSING DATE: 28 days prior to publication.

Report on Business Action Response Cards

1991 Insertion Dates: 3rd Friday of January through May and July through November plus June 14 and December 13.

1991 Advertising Rates — Per Response Card:

1 x	$6,450
4 x	6,130
8 x	5,805
12 x	5,480

Travel & Tourism Direct Response in The Saturday Travel Section

1991 Insertion Dates: 3rd Saturday of each month.

1991 Advertising Rates — per response card:

1 x	$4,350
4 x	4,132
8 x	3,925
12 x	3,728

† Features: Arts, Fashion, Sport, travel.

Courtesy: *The Globe and Mail*

Based on the rate schedule (figure 10.3), the rate per line in the national edition would be $16.12. Therefore, the total costs of the campaign would be calculated as follows:

Total Lines Purchased × Line Rate   =   Total Cost
6 000   × $16.12   = $96 720

Where the cost of the advertisement in the original example was $11 688, the cost of each advertisement in this campaign would be $9672 ($96 720 divided by 10 insertions).

Space Contracts and the Short Rate

To facilitate the use of the volume-discount scale, large advertisers usually enter into a space contract with newspapers. This *space contract* is an agreement based on the following conditions:

- The advertiser *estimates* the amount of linage required for one year, but does not guarantee the purchase.
- The advertiser is billed during the year by the newspaper at the *estimated* rate.
- The advertiser agrees to a rate adjustment at the end of the year (positive or negative), based on the *actual* lines purchased.

To illustrate the use of a space contract, let's assume the estimated linage for the national edition of the *Globe and Mail* (figure 10.3) was 10 000 modular agate lines for a one-year period. The corresponding line rate would be $16.12. At the end of the year, the actual MAL purchase totalled 9000. What is the effect on costs for the advertiser?

Since the advertiser estimated that 10 000 modular agate lines would be purchased, the rate billed by the newspaper was $16.12 per line. However, since the advertiser only purchased 9000 lines, which was less than estimated, the line rate actually charged at the end of the year would be based on the $16.47 line rate. The difference between the two line rates is referred to as the **short rate**. In this example, the calculation would be as follows:

Costs Based on Estimated Line Rate
   10 000 lines × $16.12   = $161 200
Costs Based on Actual Line Rate
   10 000 lines × $16.47   = $164 700
Balance Due Newspaper   = $3 500

The advertiser would therefore *owe* the newspaper $3500, according to the terms of the space contract. Conversely, if the advertiser purchased more than the estimated number of lines, and graduated upward to the next level on the volume scale, the newspaper would *rebate* the advertiser the difference! For the benefit of advertisers contemplating more extensive use of newspaper advertising, space contracts can be back-dated so that previous advertising volume can be grouped together to earn volume rates. Transient rates apply to unsigned space contracts, and back-dating policies vary from one newspaper to another, but a 90-day period is quite common.

Position Charges

Since a disadvantage of newspaper advertising is clutter, advertisers and agencies normally request positions in the newspaper that are deemed to be favourable. The request may be for a particular section, or it could be for the first few pages of the newspaper. In the case of a broadcast, for example, advertisers commonly request a position above the fold. To keep advertisers satisfied, a newspaper will do its best to accommodate requests, but there are no guarantees that requests will be honoured.

For the privilege of having a preferred position in a newspaper, the advertiser must pay an additional charge, referred to as a position charge. The position charge is normally quoted as a percentage increase over the insertion cost. Referring to the *Globe and Mail's* rate card (figure 10.3), we see that a specific position request adds 25% to the cost of the insertion. The advertiser usually justifies the additional expense of a position request by referring to the improved recognition and recall that will result from the better position.

Newspaper publishers reserve the right to place advertisements at their discretion, unless a preferred position charge is paid. The placing of advertisements anywhere within the regular printed pages of a newspaper is referred to as **ROP (Run of Press, Run of Paper)**.

Colour Charges

Although newspapers are often referred to as the black and white medium, colour is available to advertisers provided they are willing to pay for it. Additional costs are incurred as the number of colours increases. Colour charges are normally quoted on the basis of black and one colour, two colours, or three colours.

With reference to the *Globe and Mail's* rate schedule (figure 10.3), the addition of one colour adds $2867 to each advertisement. The use of black and three colours adds $5689 to the cost of each advertisement.

Does the use of colour justify the additional expense? In making this decision, the advertiser must weigh the potential impact of colour on the reader against the cost of colour. In two separate research tests, the following was observed:

1. Southam Inc. evaluated a 1500 line (1250 MAL) black and white ad against a one-colour ad and a four-colour ad of the same size. Among readers who noted the ads, the scores were as follows.[8]

Advertisement Size	*Average Noting Score (%)*
1500 (1250 MAL) Black and White	25
1500 Black and One Colour	41
1500 Full Colour	54

2. In a *Toronto Star* split-run test, which compared a black and white ad with a black and one-colour ad, the following scores were achieved:[9]

   —Among men 18+, noting increased by 51%
   —Among men 18–29 years, noting increased by 50%
   —Among men 30–49 years, noting increased by 42%

Colour options available to advertisers include ROP colour, Hi-Fi colour, and spectacolour.

ROP Colour For **ROP colour**, often referred to as *spot colour*, the colour is printed by newspaper presses as part of a regular press run. The purpose of spot colour is to draw readers' attention to the ad (it often involves a coloured border or a coloured headline). ROP colour is available in most Canadian daily newspapers. Also, there is a minimum size-requirement for ads to which colour is going to be added.

Hi-Fi Colour Doing ads in *Hi-Fi colour* involves pre-printing rolls of high-quality colour advertisements so that these advertisements appear in a continuous wallpaper pattern, bleeding off the top and bottom of the page. **Bleeding** is the practice of printing to the very edge of the page, so that there is no margin.

Spectacolour An advertisement done in *Spectacolour* is a pre-printed advertisement in roll form, with a fixed width and depth dimension. The pre-printed advertisement is inset so that the pre-printed page is in register with other pages. Currently, there are only seven dailies in Canada which can handle spectacolour.[10]

Multiple-Page Charges

Multiple-page charges apply to advertisers who use multiple pages in a single issue of a newspaper. For example, supermarkets, department stores, and shopping malls often use double-page spreads or more pages to advertise weekly specials. In this situation, reduced line rates apply based on the number of pages purchased. Multiple-page rates are quoted in the *Globe and Mail's* Rate Schedule (figure 10.3).

Pre-Printed Inserts

Pre-printed inserts, such as advertising supplements for supermarkets and department stores, are inserted in and distributed by most newspapers. Costs are usually quoted on a cost-per-thousand basis, with rates increasing with the size of the insert. For example, a 24-page catalogue insert would cost more than a four-page folded insert.

Split Runs

A split run occurs when an advertiser uses the full circulation of the newspaper to run two different ads. During the press run, one ad is substituted for the other, so that half of the readers are exposed to one ad, the other half to the other ad. The availability of split runs allows an advertiser to test various layout and design concepts for effectiveness. For example, a variety of coupons could be included with a variety of ads; a comparative measure of the numbers of coupons redeemed for each ad would reveal which ad-coupon combination was most effective.

For newspapers such as the *Globe and Mail*, which are published by satellite in different regions, advertisers can alter advertising content from one region to another. The costs of the split-run service is nominal, while the benefits to the advertiser can be significant.

Insertion Orders

Details of a newspaper ad are communicated via an insertion order. The insertion order specifies pertinent details, including the size of the ad, the dates of its insertion, the use of colour, position requests, and the line rate to be charged. Closing dates and cancellation dates may also be included.

To verify that an advertisement actually ran, the agency or the advertiser receives a *tear sheet* from the newspaper. As the name implies, a **tear sheet** is an ad that the newspaper personnel extracts from the newspaper to illustrate to the advertiser how it actually appeared. Should there be any problems with the ad, such as poor production quality, the advertiser or agency might request a **make good**, a rerun of an ad at the publisher's expense.

Comparing Newspapers for Efficiency

In larger metropolitan markets, where several newspapers compete for advertising revenue, advertisers must make decisions regarding which papers to place advertising with. If using a shotgun strategy, the advertiser may use all newspapers. Conversely, if budgets are limited and target markets are more precisely defined, the advertiser may be more selective in the decision-making process.

Since the circulations and the costs of advertising (line rates) vary from one newspaper to another, the advertiser must have a way of comparing the alternatives. To make this comparison, the advertiser may use a standard figure called the CPM. **CPM** is the actual cost of reaching 1000 readers in a market. The formula for calculating CPM is as follows:

$$\frac{\text{Cost}}{\text{Circulation (000)}} = \text{CPM}$$

For an illustration of CPM for newspapers in the Toronto market, refer to figure 10.4.

As is shown by the data in figure 10.4, the CPMs of the newspapers vary considerably. It is strictly a quantitative measurement, and if the advertiser's decision regarding what newspaper to use were based solely on this principle, the decision

Figure 10.4 Comparison of newspapers based on the cost of reaching a thousand people

	Toronto Star	*Globe and Mail*	*Toronto Sun*
Rate per MAL	$14.71	$14.64	$5.00
Ad size	900 MAL	900 MAL	900 MAL
Ad Cost			
(Rate x size)	$13 239	$14 076	$4 500
Circulation	523 400	330 000	282 300
CPM	$25.29	$42.65	$15.94

Source: Adapted from data in *Canadian Advertising Rates and Data*, October 1990.

would be an easy one. The editorial content may be a factor, and in this case the content of the *Toronto Sun*, a tabloid, is quite different from that of the *Toronto Star* and that of the *Globe and Mail*. Also, the demographic profile of the readers can be a determining factor. The *Toronto Star* offers mass appeal to a broad cross-section of the Toronto population at costs that are very reasonable in comparison to those of the *Globe and Mail*. However, if the target market is more upscale in terms of income, occupation, and educational background, the *Globe and Mail* might be selected, despite the higher CPM. In summary, CPM is a quantitative figure that fluctuates with changes in the line rate or circulation: the higher the circulation, the lower the CPM. Advertisers can use it as a base guideline for comparing the varying cost efficiencies of specific newspapers that reach a mass target market.

MAGAZINES IN CANADA

There are currently 545 magazines published and distributed in Canada. Canadian magazines are divided into three broad categories: consumer magazines, whose publishers use demographics to target specific audiences; business magazines; and other magazines, which include religious and farm publications. Magazines are classified in many ways: by content and audience reached, by circulation, by frequency of publication, and by size and format.

CONTENT AND AUDIENCE REACHED

In terms of content and audience reached, publications fall into two major categories: consumer magazines and business magazines. Both categories include general-interest and special-interest publications. In both consumer and business magazines, the content is such that it has high interest among a precisely defined target market. A third classification, "other" magazines include farm, religious, and student-oriented publications.

Consumer Magazines

Canadian Advertising Rates and Data indexes 50 sub-classifications of consumer magazines, with the classification based on the publication's content and audience. There is a strong base of general-interest magazines, as well as a host of specialized categories such as art and antiques, children, entertainment, hobbies, sports and recreation, and women's. Figure 10.5 illustrates the concept of general-interest magazines and special-interest magazines.

Business Magazines

Business magazines can be broadly subdivided into subject areas such as trade, industry, professional, and institutional. Sub-classifications of these general areas would include broadcasting, data processing, engineering construction, food and food

Figure 10.5 General-interest and special-interest magazines

Category	Circulation
General-Interest	
Reader's Digest	1 323 348
Equinox	168 162
Harrowsmith	155 207
Leisureways/Westworld	1 376 198
Saturday Night	110 899
Special-Interest — Women's Classification	
ENGLISH:	
Recipes Only	1 289 000
Canadian Living	565 116
Flare	206 351
Chatelaine	955 609
FRENCH:	
Madame au Foyer	311 000
Chatelaine	242 796
Coupe de Pouce	144 359
Femme Plus	80 276

Source: Adapted from information in *Canadian Advertising Rates and Data*, October 1990.

processing, hardware trade, hotels and restaurants, photography, telecommunications, and many more.

Business publications tend to be very specialized, their content appealing to a particular industry, trade, or professional group. Being specialized, with a very well-defined target audience, such publications allow an efficient use of media dollars by advertisers.

Horizontal and Vertical Business magazines can also be classified as *horizontal* or *vertical*. A **horizontal publication** is one that appeals to people who occupy the same level of responsibility in a business—the senior-management level, for example. Horizontal publications tend to be more general in content, dealing with subjects such as business issues and trends, management-information systems, effective business-management principles, and so on. Examples of horizontal business publications are *Canadian Business, Financial Post Magazine, Report on Business Magazine*, and *Successful Executive*. Also classifed as horizontal are those publications aimed at people who have functions in their companies similar to those discussed in the magazine. A magazine such as *Modern Purchasing* would be directed at the purchasing managers and agents, in any number of different industries.

Vertical publications are magazines that appeal to all levels of people in the same industry. All specialized classifications and corresponding magazines fall into this category. *Canadian Grocer*, for example, appeals to those employed in the food-processing and food-distribution business in Canada, while *Food Service and Hospitality* magazine appeals to those employed in the restaurant, hotel, or food-service industry.

Additional details on business publications are included in chapter 14.

Other Magazines

Farm Publications Farm publications originated as general publications serving the farming community, but, like consumer and business magazines, have become a more specialized medium. Serving a variety of farm operations (dairy, cattle, fruit, etc.), magazine content deals mainly with issues concerning, and means of improving, farm operations and farm management. In 1989, farm publications accounted for $22 million in net advertising revenues.[11] Examples of magazines in this category are *Cattlemen, Canadian Fruit Grower, Country Guide,* and *Alberta Farmagazine.*

Religious Publications *Canadian Advertising Rates and Data* lists 20 publications in this category. Included are magazines such as *United Church Observer, Canadian Churchman,* and *Presbyterian Record.*

CIRCULATION BASE (DISTRIBUTION)

Canadian magazines are distributed on the basis of paid circulation (subscriptions and newsstand sales), or by free distribution to a predetermined target market. Magazines such as *Maclean's, Time, Chatelaine, Flare,* and *Canadian Business* rely on subscriptions, newsstand sales, and advertising space to generate revenues. Conversely, *controlled-circulation* magazines generate revenue from advertising space only. A controlled-circulation magazine is mailed free to a select group of individuals or to households that the publisher feels are in a unique position to influence sales. The individuals or households receiving the controlled-circulation magazine will have in common demographic cells that are attractive to potential advertisers.

Homemaker's/Madame au Foyer is an example of a widely distributed controlled-circulation magazine. Distribution is implemented by Canada Post. Other magazines, many of which have a city-lifestyle orientation, are examples of controlled-circulation magazines. Included in this group are publications such as *Toronto, Vancouver,* and *Ottawa* magazines. These are distributed to selected households, apartments, condominiums, and hotels in a defined geographic area.

FREQUENCY OF PUBLICATION

The frequency of publication varies considerably from one magazine to another. The more common frequencies are monthly and weekly; more limited frequencies are bi-weekly or quarterly. Some magazines publish 10 times per year (certain months combined) instead of monthly. The following is a sampling of magazines and their respective publication frequencies:

Magazine	*Frequency of Publication*
Canadian Business	12 Monthly
Reader's Digest	12 Monthly
Maclean's	52 Weekly
Time	52 Weekly
Harrowsmith	6 Bi-monthly
Equinox	6 Bi-monthly

SIZE AND FORMAT

Canadian magazines are published in three distinct sizes: digest, standard, and larger size. Owing to the rising costs of production, mailing, and distribution, there is currently a trend toward smaller-size publications.

Digest Size

The approximate dimensions are 5 1/2" × 7 1/4" (140 cm × 184 cm), with a two-column printing format. Popular magazines that come in this size and format include *Reader's Digest, Homemaker's, Recipes Only,* and *New Mother* (*Selection du Reader's Digest, Madame au Foyer, Bien Manger,* and *Mère Nouvelle*).

Standard Size

Dimensions of the standard size are 8" × 11" (203 cm × 279 cm), with a three-column printing format. Among the popular magazines that appear in this size and format are *Maclean's, Time, Canadian Business,* and *Equinox.*

Larger Size

The dimensions of larger magazines vary from one publication to another. *Marketing* is a larger-size business publication, with dimensions of 11 1/4" × 16 1/4" (286 cm × 413 cm). Being a larger size, *Marketing* is published in a five-column printing format.

MAGAZINES AS AN ADVERTISING MEDIUM

ADVANTAGES OF MAGAZINES

Demographic Selectivity

Magazines are often referred to as being a "class" medium rather than a "mass" medium. Both consumer magazines and business magazines have target audiences that are well defined by some combination of demographic variables. Therefore, advertisers with well-defined target markets can select specific magazines by using a profile-matching strategy (i.e., by selecting magazines whose audience closely matches the product's target market). The profile-matching strategy becomes a little more complicated when a group of comparable magazines compete for the same target audience. Nevertheless, demographic selectivity is the primary advantage of magazines.

For more insight into the demographic selectivity of magazines, refer to the Advertising in Action vignette "The Niche Medium."

Geographic Flexibility

Numerous high-circulation consumer magazines offer regional editions. An advertiser only wishing to advertise in a certain area, such as the Prairies or the Maritimes, may make use of the flexibility offered by regional editions, provided, of course, that the

Advertising in Action
The Niche Medium

Magazines only account for about 13% of Canadian advertising revenues, and yet they have the ability to give advertisers what they want most—direct reach to a precisely defined target. With such a powerful advantage, one would think that advertisers would be flocking to magazines, but such is not the case. The share of the Canadian advertising pie held by magazines over the past five years has remained relatively constant. But all of this might change in the future. State-of-the-art printing presses are churning out 1 600 000 four-colour pages an hour for consumption by eager readers across the nation.

There is a good reason for this speed. Quite simply, people are reading more. According to *Magazines Canada*, readers are looking for a focus, a perspective, and more importantly, analysis. Further, people are reading because of the information explosion that is all around us. The author of *Megatrends*, John Naisbett, puts it well: "We are drowning in information but starved for knowledge." Consequently, people are turning to magazines to make information make sense.

Television, radio, and newspapers all play an important role in advertising. Magazines, however, can convey detailed information for discriminating buyers who want the full story on a company's goods and services.

Among the various strengths of magazines, the strongest selling point is that it is a "precision marketing medium." Magazines offer selectivity, which allows advertisers to pinpoint people demographically, psychographically and geographically. They are read by quality, "volunteer" audiences, people with superb socio-economic characteristics, and magazines reach them when they are most receptive to ideas and information. It is the reader that controls when and where a publication is read.

In addition, for advertisers looking for reproduction quality, magazines are second to none. Powerful ads in a rich, quality colour are dependably reproduced and surrounded by editorial content the reader is interested in.

Advantages such as these augur well for the future of magazines. The age of instant communications has unleashed a deluge of data, and the very volume of information makes understanding it difficult. People will increasingly turn to magazines because of the medium's reflective, analytical nature.

Adapted from "Consumer magazines, the most versatile and cost-efficient medium," *Sales & Marketing Management in Canada,* March-April, 1988, pp.10-11.

regional readership is similar to the advertiser's target market. Regional editions also provide advertisers with the opportunity to increase spending on an "as-needed" basis geographically, while holding the line on spending in other areas of the country.

Currently, there are 26 publications offering some form of geographic flexibility. The largest publication doing so is *Chatelaine* (English and French). *Chatelaine's* regional editions include: Quebec English, Ontario English, Eastern English, Prairies English, and British Columbia. *Chatelaine* also prints a five-city edition that covers the key markets in Toronto, Montreal, Vancouver, Edmonton, and Calgary and that totals one-quarter of the national circulation.

The growth of city magazines, such as *En Ville Montreal, Toronto Life*, and *Vancouver*, gives advertisers both demographic selectivity and geographic flexibility. Although, owing to their regionality, city magazines are most suited to local advertisers, they also appeal to national advertisers because of their demographic selectivity.

Life Span

Because of the relative infrequency (in comparison to newspapers) with which magazines are published (weekly, bi-weekly, monthly), they offer the advertiser the benefit of permanency. Magazines remain in the home and are read intermittently over a period of time; hence, readers may be exposed to an advertisement several times during the life-span of the magazine (which means that the product gets repeat exposure at no extra cost). Some magazines, such as *Canadian Geographic*, may be retained in the home permanently as part of a collection.

Environment

Magazines are purchased and read because the editorial content is of specific interest to the reader; therefore, advertisers' messages may benefit in terms of prestige and believability from being associated with the magazine and the quality it represents. The receptiveness of the audience may also result in the magazine's being read at a more leisurely pace; this creates the potential for more detailed communications in advertising.

Quality of Reproduction

Magazines are printed on high-quality paper, by means of a four-colour process that creates a high-quality and attractive presentation of both editorial and advertising content. Recent innovations, such as bright metallic inks that create a striking visual effect, have added to the quality of reproduction.

Creative Considerations

As regards creative strategy and execution, magazines offer certain flexibility. For example, most magazines offer gatefolds (multiple-page foldouts), double-page spreads, bleeds, and can accommodate inserts and pop-up coupons (coupons with a perforated edge appearing on top of an advertisement for a product). Although the use of such options may increase the cost of advertising, the resulting distinction and potential impact on the reader may justify the additional expense.

Passalong Readership

Magazine space is sold to advertisers at costs that are based on the magazine's circulation and on the costs the magazine itself incurs in reaching that circulation. As well as being exposed to its primary readers, a magazine may be exposed to other readers. The actual readership of the magazine will be much greater than the circulation. A **primary reader** is a person who qualifies as a reader because he or she lives (works) in the household (office) where the publication is initially received. The **passalong**

readership is the average number of people who read a single copy of a publication. Therefore, the number of primary readers times the average number of readers per copy equals total readership. For the advertiser, the potential reach is greater, but all passalong readers may not be in the same target audience as the primary reader. Nonetheless, passalong readership represents bonus circulation at no additional cost.

DISADVANTAGES OF MAGAZINES

Lead Time

The use of magazines requires of the advertiser careful production planning that must begin well in advance of issue date. Since the layout and design of the magazine are finalized at an early point (in comparison to newspapers), advertisers must deliver finished production materials to the publisher well in advance of publishing date. Lead times may vary from one publication to another, but for a monthly magazine, eight weeks is the average lead time required for materials. For a weekly magazine, an average of four weeks is required. Long lead times do not allow advertisers the flexibility of changing advertising content should market conditions so warrant, nor can they increase advertising weight on short notice.

Clutter

Clutter in magazine advertising refers to the clustering of ads near the front and back of the magazine. Advertisers can partially overcome the problem by ordering preferred positions (covers), assuming such positions are available. Although covers are only available at higher cost, the resulting impact may justify the additional expense. Other position requests, such as being on the right side (as opposed to the left side), are available at no additional cost, but the publisher will not guarantee the position.

Cost

Magazine production costs, particularly for four-colour advertisements, are significantly higher than newspaper production costs. Because of these high production costs and because of the cost of space, magazines may not be an efficient buy for the local or regional advertiser, particularly if the regional target is small. Although many magazines offer regional editions, the absolute cost of advertising does not decline proportionately with the decline in circulation. In fact, the cost of reaching the regional reader is actually higher. National advertisers, with their larger budgets, can consider regional editions and the higher costs associated with them when market conditions warrant such activity.

Frequency

Although large mass-circulation magazines offer high reach to the advertiser, and specialized magazines offer selective reach, magazines do not offer the advertiser much opportunity to *frequently* reach the audience, because the distribution frequency of magazines is low. Building frequency in one publication is extremely difficult for advertisers. They can overcome this problem by adding magazines that reach similar target markets. But such a solution is expensive.

Figure 10.6 *Report on Business Magazine* rate card

1991 Advertising REPORT ON BUSINESS Rate Schedule

THE GLOBE AND MAIL — MAGAZINE

EFFECTIVE JANUARY ISSUE, 1991

4 COLOUR PROCESS	**1X**	**3X**	**6X**	**12X**	**24X**
PAGE	15,835	15,355	14,880	14,250	12,665
2/3 PAGE	12,345	11,975	11,605	11,110	9,875
DBLE 3/4 OR 1/2 HOR	10,605	10,290	9,970	9,550	8,485
1/3 PAGE	7,125	6,915	6,695	6,415	5,705
DBLE PAGE SPD	28,485	27,630	26,775	25,640	22,795
DBLE 1/2 SPD	19,085	18,510	17,945	17,175	15,265
IFC/IBC*	18,210	17,655	17,110	16,385	14,565
OBC*	18,990	18,425	17,855	17,090	15,190

B&1 COLOUR	**1X**	**3X**	**6X**	**12X**	**24X**
PAGE	13,955	13,540	13,125	12,570	11,170
2/3 PAGE	10,885	10,560	10,235	9,795	8,715
DBLE 3/4 OR 1/2 HOR	9,360	9,080	8,790	8,425	7,480
1/3 PAGE	6,280	6,100	5,905	5,650	5,025
DBLE PAGE SPD	25,135	24,385	23,625	22,620	20,105
DBLE 1/2 SPD	16,840	16,335	15,835	15,155	13,475

B & W	**1X**	**3X**	**6X**	**12X**	**24X**
PAGE	11,645	11,290	10,940	10,475	9,310
2/3 PAGE	8,845	8,580	8,315	7,960	7,075
DBLE 3/4 OR 1/2 HOR	7,560	7,345	7,115	6,810	6,055
1/3 PAGE	5,010	4,855	4,705	4,510	4,005
1/6 PAGE	2,560	2,485	2,410	2,310	2,055
DBLE PAGE SPD	20,945	20,315	19,690	18,850	16,760
DBLE 1/2 SPD	13,615	13,205	12,800	12,255	10,890
REPLY CARD (supplied) (must accompany full page)	7,560	7,335	7,110	6,805	6,055

****Covers are non-cancellable. Must be booked 30 days prior to display space closing***

- Combination Discount: All advertising in Report on Business Magazine, Domino and Destinations magazines may be combined for frequency discounts.
- Material close is 7 days following space close.
- Consecutive page discount available.
- Guaranteed position premium - 15% on earned space rates.
- Insert rates supplied on request.
- 3 Issue incentive : Space purchased in January, February and July issues will earn a 50% credit towards an August insertion.
- Appointment Notices - 10% discount on display rates.
- Annual Reports - available in the July issue -ROB 1000

Mechanical Specifications

Printing Method: Web Offset
Binding: Saddle stitched
Screen 133-120 lines final negative.

Colour specification for all color advertising

Supply 1 set of screened film negatives, 1 piece per colour, in exact registration, right reading, emulsion side down.

One set of proofs either Fuji Colour Art proofed using magenta #3 in the sequence black, cyan, yellow, magenta, or progressive proofs. Acromatic/GCR 80%, total film density 260%. (Please note colour key is not an acceptable colour proof).

Register marks should be centred on 4 outside edges of each film for all four colours. Only hard dot film is acceptable. All film must be dimensionally stable of identical gauge (.004") thickness with colours identified.

NOTE: All reverse type must be spread or released. All other mechanical specifications must meet MAC standards. Double page spreads require two sets of film or 1/4" overlap on each page if supplied on single pages.

Special Colour

A premium of $2,750 is required on PMS, ADPRO, Metallic or other special inks.

Page Sizes	Width			Depth	
Trim Size	206mm	(8 1/8")	x	273mm	(10 3/4")
Type Page	184mm	(7 1/4")	x	254mm	(10")
Bleed Page	215mm	(8 1/2")	x	283mm	(11 1/8")
D.P.S. Type Page	393mm	(15 1/2")	x	254mm	(10")
D.P.S. Bleed	421mm	(16 5/8")	x	283mm	(11 1/8")

Unit Sizes					
Page	184mm	(7 1/4")	x	254mm	(10")
Double Page Spread	393mm	(15 1/2")	x	254mm	(10")
Double 1/2 Spread	393mm	(15 1/2")	x	125mm	(4 15/16")
2/3 Page	118mm	(4 5/8")	x	254mm	(10")
1/2 Page Horiz.	187mm	(7 1/4")	x	125mm	(4 15/16")
Double 3/4 Column	117mm	(4 5/8")	x	187mm	(7 3/8")
1/3 Page Vertical	57mm	(2 1/4")	x	254mm	(10")
1/3 Page Square	117mm	(4 5/8")	x	125mm	(4 15/16")
1/6 Page Vertical	57mm	(2 1/4")	x	125mm	(4 15/16")

An additional 1/4" should be allowed for all bleed ads.

Keep all critical or illustrative material minimum 1/4" from final trim 8 1/8" x 10 3/4" including spread. Publisher reserves right to crop 3/16" from either side of all bleed ads to compensate for left or right hand page.

Issue and Closing Dates

Issue	**Space Closing**	**Distribution**
January 1991*	Oct. 29, 1990	Dec. 14, 1990
February**	December 3	Jan. 18, 1991
March	January 3, 1991	February 15
April	January 28	March 15
May	March 4	April 19
June	April 2	May 17
July***	April 29	June 14
August †	June 3	July 19
September	July 2	August 16
October ††	August 6	September 20
November	September 3	October 18
December	September 30	November 15
January 1992	October 28	December 13

* *Special Report - The World in 1991*
** *Special Report - Personal Finance*
*** *Report on Business 1000*
† *Special Report - Small Business*
†† *Special Report - Taiwan*

Reader Reply Service is included in all special issues at no charge.

Courtesy: *The Globe and Mail*

ADVERTISING FEATURES OFFERED BY MAGAZINES

Magazines have some special features that make the medium attractive to potential advertisers. The use of these features adds to the cost of advertising, however, so advertisers must carefully weigh the additional cost of these features against the potential impact their use will have on readers. These features include bleeds, gatefolds, preferred positions, inserts and reply cards, and split-run availability.

Bleeds

The term **bleed** refers to a situation where the coloured background of an ad extends to the edge of the page. An ad can bleed on some or all sides of the page, depending on creative strategy and execution. Magazines either build bleed charges into published four-colour rates, or quote the additional costs separately.

Gatefolds

A **gatefold** is an advertisement that folds out of a magazine (it could span two, three, or four pages). Gatefolds are usually used on special occasions. For example, a car maker may use gatefolds when launching a new line.

Gatefolds are normally located at the front cover, or near the front of the magazine. Since they are not used very frequently, and require significant lead time, most magazine rate cards state that rates are available on request.

Preferred Positions

Obtaining a preferred position in a magazine involves requesting a specific position within the magazine. Since the potential for an advertisement to be seen is very great if it is positioned on the inside-front or inside-back covers, such positions command a higher price than other positions. Cover prices for *Report on Business Magazine* are quoted in the rate card in figure 10.6. Note that the back cover costs $18 990, while the standard page rate is $15 835.

Inserts and Reply Cards

Practically any size of business-reply card or small multiple-page insert or booklet can be bound into a magazine. Business-reply cards are common in business publications, as are pop-up coupons and small recipe booklets in consumer publications. Note that in *Report on Business Magazine* (figure 10.6), a reply card must be accompanied by a full page of advertising. Other publications may have different policies.

Split-Run Availability

Similar to newspapers, a selected group of consumer magazines offer split-run availability. Assuming that all conditions are constant and that each of the two ads contains a coupon, the split-run availability can help advertisers determine which ad is more effective; they can compare actual customer responses to the coupon.

BUYING MAGAZINE SPACE

The procedure for buying magazine space is, first, to decide on the size of the ad, which involves choosing from among the variety of page options sold by the magazines under consideration. The rates quoted are based on the size of page requested. Other factors that could influence the cost of advertising in magazines include the frequency of insertions and appropriate discounts, the use of colour, and guaranteed-position charges.

Determining the Size of Advertisement

Magazines have a variety of page options or page combinations to select from. For example, *Report on Business Magazine* sells space in the following formats: 1 page, 2/3 page, double 3/4 column, 1/2 page horizontal, 1/3 page, double-page spread, and horizontal 1/2 page spread. Refer to figure 10.6 for a visual illustration of these formats.

Rate Schedules

The size selected for the advertisement determines the rate to be charged. In figure 10.6, rates are quoted for all page combinations sold on the basis of: (1) black and white, (2) black and one colour, and (3) four colour.

To illustrate how costs are calculated, let's consider a simple example. Assume an advertiser would like to purchase a one-page, four-colour ad in *Report on Business Magazine* during the months of January and February. Since the frequency of the advertising does not reach the first discount level (three insertions), the advertiser would pay the one-time rate. The cost calculation would be as follows:

One Page Rate × Number of Insertions = Total Cost

$15 835 × 2 = $31 670

Discounts

Advertisers who purchase space in specific magazines with greater frequency will qualify for a variety of discounts. The nature of these discounts may vary from one publication to another. Some of the more common discounts offered by magazines include *frequency* discounts, *continuity* discounts, and *corporate* discounts.

Frequency Discounts In magazines, a **frequency discount** refers to a discounted page rate, with the discount based on the number of times an advertisement is run. The more often the ad is run, the lower the unit cost for each ad. In the *Report on Business* rate card, the unit rate is reduced when the ad is run 3 times, 6 times, 12 times, and 24 times.

Continuity Discounts A **continuity discount** is an additional discount offered to advertisers who agree to purchase space in consecutive issues of a magazine (buying space in 12 issues of a monthly magazine, for example). When continuity discounts are combined with frequency discounts, lower unit costs per page of advertising result.

Corporate Discounts Large advertisers who use the same magazine to advertise a variety of products (note that such an advertiser would have to be a multi-product firm whose products have similar target markets) may qualify for **corporate discounts**. A corporate discount involves consideration of the total number of pages purchased by the company (all product lines combined), and a lower page rate for each product. Therefore, products that do not advertise frequently in a particular magazine may obtain a very favourable page rate if other company product lines advertise frequently in that magazine. As an alternative to using pages as the means of calculating volume discounts, magazines may use dollar-volume purchased as the guideline, and offer a percentage discount on total advertising dollar volume.

Other Discounts To see an example of other types of discounts, note that in the *Report on Business Magazine* rate card (figure 10.6), advertisers can combine pages from other *Globe and Mail* publications (*Domino* and *Destinations*) to earn a lower page rate.

Colour and Position Changes

Additional costs for the inclusion of colour, or for a guaranteed position, are quoted separately on the rate card. For a guaranteed position, such as the back cover or the inside-front and inside-back covers, the additional costs are usually in the +20% range. Rates for guaranteed positions are usually quoted as a percentage or a dollar-amount increase over the normal four-colour page rate. As for any regular page, the unit rate for a cover decreases as the frequency increases.

Buying Magazine Space—Sample Calculations

To illustrate the cost calculations of buying magazine space, let's develop an example based on the *Report on Business Magazine* rate card (figure 10.6) and on the following information:

> *Size of Ad:* one page, 4 colour; one double-page spread,
> 4 colour
> *Number of Insertions:* one page ad to run in 8 issues; double-page
> spread to run in 4 issues

The calculation for this buying plan will be as follows:

1. Costs for one page, 4 colour:
   Base Rate = the 6 times rate
   $14 880 × 8 = $119 040

2. Costs for double-page spread, 4 colour:
   Base Rate = the 3 times rate
   $27 630 × 4 = $110 520

3. Total Costs = $119 040 + $110 520
   = $229 560

Space Contracts and the Magazine Short Rate

To facilitate the use of discount scales offered by magazines, larger advertisers usually enter into a space contract with magazines they use frequently. The space contract provides an estimate of the advertising space required for a one-year period. At the end of the year, adjustments are made, positive or negative, when actual usage of space is known. Should advertisers not meet their estimates, a short rate would be due the publisher. To illustrate, let's assume the advertiser estimated that 12 four-colour pages would be purchased in *Report on Business Magazine*, but only eight pages were purchased by the end of the contract. The advertiser would be billed as follows:

Ran eight times but paid the twelve times rate
$8 \times \$14\ 250 = \$114\ 000$
Earned only the six times rate of $14 880
$8 \times \$14\ 880 = \$119\ 040$
Short Rate Due Publisher = $5040

In this example, the advertiser would owe the magazine $5040, according to the terms of the space contract. Conversely, if the advertiser purchased more than the estimated amount, to the point where another frequency discount plateau was reached, the magazine would rebate the difference to the advertiser.

Magazine Insertion Orders

Depending on the extent of an advertising campaign with any particular magazine, the advertiser may decide to enter into a space contract with the magazine, or place an insertion order on an "as needed" basis. To obtain the best possible rate, large advertisers will opt for the space contract. The space contract is not an order for a specific amount of space; rather, it protects the advertiser's right to buy space at a certain rate. Publishers retain the right to announce increases in rates at predetermined levels.

When the advertiser is ready to run an ad, an insertion order is sent to the magazine. The **insertion order** specifies the date of issue, the size of the ad, any applicable position requests, and the contracted rate. As indicated by the *Canadian Business* rate card, there are several important dates the advertiser should be familiar with: the issue date, the insertion-order date, and the material date.

Issue Date The issue date is the monthly date of issue (normally seven to 10 days prior to the actual month of issue).

Insertion-Order Date The insertion-order date is the closing date for ordering space (normally nine weeks prior to issue date for a monthly magazine).

Material Date The material date is the closing date for submitting production materials to the publisher (normally eight weeks prior to issue date for a monthly magazine).

These key dates vary according to the publishing frequency of the magazine.

COMPARING MAGAZINES FOR EFFICIENCY

Assuming that a decision has been made to utilize magazines with the understanding that magazines usually have a well-defined target audience based on demographic variables, advertisers must choose particular magazines to advertise in. Since costs and circulation figures vary, the advertiser must have a way of comparing alternatives. As with newspapers, CPM is an effective quantitative means of comparing competing magazines. In the case of magazines, the formula for determining the CPM is

$$\frac{\text{Cost per Page}}{\text{Circulation (000)}}$$

In most magazine classifications, there is usually a group of publications competing for the same market. For example, *Chatelaine*, *Homemaker's*, and *Canadian Living* compete against each other in the women's classification. Although the editorial content varies from one magazine to another, they do reach a similar target, so advertisers must look at the efficiencies of each.

Figure 10.7 contains the comparative calculations for three of the magazines in the women's classification. In terms of a purely quantitative measure, *Homemaker's* offers the best efficiency in reaching the target market. The CPM of *Homemaker's* is considerably lower than that of *Canadian Living*. It is the CPM, along with other factors, that is evaluated in the magazine-selection process. For large advertisers, selection is easier, because they can use combinations of magazines. For them, the question to be considered is how much advertising weight should be allocated to each competing magazine.

For additional information on how advertisers evaluate magazines refer back to chapter 8, "Advertising Research".

Figure 10.7   Comparative statistics used in making magazine advertising buying decisions

	Comparative Costs and CPMs		
	Homemaker's (English)	*Chatelaine* (English)	*Canadian Living*
One-time, 4-colour page rate	$20 800	$29 200	$18 055
Circulation	1 600 054	1 010 152	558 531
CPM	$12.99	$28.91	$32.33

Source: Adapted from information in *Canadian Advertising Rates and Data*, October 1990.

Summary

With respect to print media, the primary alternatives for an advertiser are newspapers and magazines.

Newspaper advertising is divided between daily and weekly publications. Dailies and weeklies attract both national and local advertisers, but most of their revenues are generated by local advertisers. A newspaper is published in one of two formats: the broadsheet, which is the larger, folded newspaper; and the tabloid, which is the smaller, flat newspaper. All newspapers receive revenues from four different types of advertising: national or general advertising, retail advertising, classified advertising, and preprinted inserts (flyers distributed via a newspaper).

As an advertising medium, newspapers offer the advertiser geographic selectivity, local-market coverage, and flexibility. Major disadvantages include the short life span, the lack of target-market orientation (demographic distinctions), and clutter. The rates charged an advertiser decrease as the volume of lines purchased increases, and are increased by position requests and requests for the use of colour.

Magazines are classified according to factors such as size and format, frequency of publication, circulation base, content, and audience reached. As an advertising medium, magazines offer target-market selectivity, quality in reproduction and editorial environment, and a life span that is longer than those of other media. On the negative side, significant lead time is required for materials; the use of colour raises costs; and clutter remains a problem.

Additional features of magazines which make them an attractive advertising medium include the use of bleeds and gatefolds. Magazine advertising rates depend on the size of the ad, the frequency of insertion, and the use of colour. A variety of discounts are available to advertisers who opt for magazine advertising.

Review Questions

1. What are the differences between general advertising, retail advertising, and classified advertising?
2. What are the advantages and disadvantages of using newspapers as an advertising medium?
3. In a city where more than one daily newspaper dominates the market, how would you determine which newspaper to advertise in, assuming you could only select one? What factors would enter into your decision?
4. Provide an explanation for the following newspaper terms:

a) hooker	f) ROP colour
b) MAL	g) spectacolour
c) transient rate	h) tear sheet

d) short rate
e) split run

i) make good
j) milline rate

5. Identify and briefly describe the various discounts frequently offered by magazines.
6. What are the advantages and disadvantages of using magazines as an advertising medium?
7. Explain the CPM concept, as it applies to the purchase of advertising space in magazines.
8. How does the magazine "short rate" work?
9. What is the difference between the following magazine terms:
   a) Paid-circulation magazine versus controlled-circulation magazine
   b) Vertical publication versus horizontal publication
   c) Primary reader versus passalong reader.
10. Provide a brief explanation of the following magazine terms:
    a) digest ad
    b) bleed ad
    c) gatefold
    d) reply cards
    e) insertion order date
    f) material date
    g) space contract
    h) split run
    i) preferred position

Discussion Questions

1. "Advertisers will receive greater value from advertising in a paid-circulation magazine than from advertising in a comparable controlled-circulation magazine." Discuss this statement, playing the role of publisher for each type of magazine.
2. "Paying a premium price for a cover position in a magazine is always a wise investment." Discuss this statement.
3. "The location of an advertisement in a newspaper is the key factor determining the success of the ad." Discuss this statement in the context of other variables you may judge to be important.

CHAPTER 11 Broadcast Media

In studying this chapter, you will learn about

- The organizations involved in the Canadian broadcasting industry
- The advantages and disadvantages of television and radio as advertising media
- The factors considered in, and procedures used for, buying television and radio time
- The recent technologies affecting commercial television in Canada

The latest statistics available reveal that 99% of Canadian households are reached by both television and radio. Such spectacular reach suggests that the potential impact of broadcast media on their audience is enormous. From an advertising point of view, the placement of messages in broadcast media offers the same high-reach/high-impact potential.

The broadcast media have other features which make them attractive to advertisers. First, both television and radio only require passive audience involvement: either medium can be there as background while a person is doing something else, yet the message can penetrate. Such cannot be said about print, which requires a more active (reading) involvement. Second, television and radio offer a sense of immediacy. The public regards the broadcast media as the most up-to-date source of news information, and refers to it first for late-breaking news stories.

In contrast to the print media, broadcast media is highly regulated through the Canadian Radio-television and Telecommunications Commission (CRTC). All broadcasters must apply and re-apply for station licenses, and they must abide by the broadcasting and advertising regulations established by the CRTC and other regulating bodies, including the Canadian Association of Broadcasters (CAB) and the Canadian Advertising Foundation (CAF). Some of the legal and regulating information that most affects broadcast advertising is outlined in Appendix 1.

New technologies in the broadcast industry have had an effect on conventional commercial broadcasters. The use of converters in television households, the growth of cable television, the introduction of pay television, which provides movie and specialty stations, and the use of satellite dishes—these are some of the new technologies that have had an impact on the public's television-viewing habits. A television market that was already fragmented is now fragmented even more due to the advent of these new technologies.

This chapter examines the use of television and radio as advertising media, and the advantages and disadvantages of each; it reviews the variety of rates and discount structures available to advertisers; and finally, it examines these new technologies, which are affecting the traditional broadcasting industry.

*T*ELEVISION

THE NETWORKS

In Canada, there are three different types of networks: national, regional, and specialty.

National Networks

There are three national networks. The Canadian Broadcasting Corporation (CBC) is a Crown corporation consisting of 10 English-owned-and-operated stations and 26 private affiliates. An affiliate is defined as an independent station carrying network programs. The full English network reaches 98% of English-language homes in Canada.

The CTV Network is a private English network of 16 member stations covering 97% of English-language homes. All stations have access to major markets across Canada.

Radio-Canada is the full CBC French network consisting of 20 stations. In terms of advertising, the network provides over 99% coverage of Francophones in Quebec.

Regional Networks

There are eight networks operating on a regional basis in Canada. English-language networks include the Atlantic Satellite Network, ATV, Maritime Independent Television, Global Television, and Saskatchewan Television. French-language networks are Quatre Saisons, Radio Quebec, and TVA/The Network Plan.

Specialty Networks

Ten specialty networks offer commercial time on a national basis. The English-language specialty networks include MuchMusic, The Sports Network (TSN), Vision TV, Weathernow, Youth Channel (YTV), and CBC Newsworld. French-language specialty networks include Musique Plus, Le Reseau des Sports (RDS), Metromedia, TV5, Chinavision (a Chinese-language station) and Teletino (an Italian- and Spanish-language station).

PAY TELEVISION

In Canada, Pay-TV is distributed to households via cable, although it can be received direct if a household owns a satellite dish. Pay-TV reaches 73% of Canadian households, and current licenses are held by the Family Channel, First Choice/Superchannel, Super Ecran, Cathay International, Teletino, Chinavision, TV5 Quebec, and Canal Famille.

A pay-per-view service is now being test marketed in three markets in Saskatchewan. The objective of the test is to determine if the need for such a service exists in Canada. Superchannel is the channel being tested. The goal of pay-per-view is to attract viewers who are presently renting movies from video stores.

VIDEOTEX

Using television as the medium of communications, interactive videotex provides two-way communication to the home. Among the participants in this form of communication are Bell "ALEX" and Videotron "Videoway."

ALEX is a mass-market consumer-information-and-transaction service offering details regarding a variety of goods and services such as travel, stock quotations, personal finance, and restaurant menus.

Videoway is currently a one-way system; however, it does offer viewers two-way interactive options so that they can select the news items they desire to see and the camera angles they would like to have as they watch hockey games broadcast from the Montreal Forum. The difference between Videoway and ALEX is that Videoway is a cable system, with the household TV acting as the terminal. It has the potential to offer services on a pay-per-view basis.

TYPES OF CONVENTIONAL TELEVISION STATIONS IN CANADA

Canadian television stations are available in two basic formats or frequencies: VHF and UHF. The broadcasting regulating body in Canada, the CRTC, assigns special frequencies to television stations:

VHF VHF refers to a very high frequency range for broadcasting, and runs from channels two through 13 on the television dial.

UHF UHF refers to an ultra high frequency range, and runs from channels 14 through 83 on the television dial.

In today's market, all new television sets are equipped with both VHF and UHF capabilities.

ADVANTAGES OF TELEVISION

Impact and Effectiveness of Message

Compared to all other media, television stands out as a multi-sense medium. Advertisers can use the combination of sight, sound, and motion television offers to create maximum impact on the viewing audience. Television viewing only requires passive involvement; viewers can be doing something else as they receive messages from the television. A third point related to impact and effectiveness is that, in a television buy, advertisers purchase commercial time for specific programs, and so may select programs that are compatible with their products.

High Reach

Television's reach, as has been mentioned, is astounding. Fully 99% of Canadians aged two years and over can be reached via television. In prime time, during the hours between 7:00 P.M. and 11:00 P.M., an average of 43% of Canadian adults tune into television in a given quarter-hour period. Reach statistics such as these make television extremely attractive to advertisers, particularly those who are targeting fairly general age categories. Consumer packaged-goods advertisers, the Canadian government, and producers of high-priced consumer durables all value the high reach available from television. Advertisers who purchase commercial time on top-rated shows such as "Cheers", "Roseanne", "Murphy Brown", and "60 Minutes" achieve high reach almost instantaneously.

Frequency Potential

Television is an expensive medium in absolute dollar terms, but advertisers who have large budgets at their disposal can use television effectively to build frequency. For example, an advertiser may purchase more than one spot within a certain program or during a certain daypart. Alternatively, an advertiser could build frequency by purchasing the same time slot in a program over a continuous period of time, for 13, or 26, or 52 weeks, say. In either case, owing to viewers' loyalty to a certain program or to the appeal a certain time period has for a particular target market, the target audience will be exposed to the same commercial message over an extended period of time. Since the repetition of messages is often the key to creating top-of-mind brand awareness among consumers, messages can be rotated vertically through the day, or horizontally during the week, to build frequency against a target audience.

Some Demographic Selectivity

Television is primarily a mass-reach medium, but has some potential for demographic selectivity. Because of the various age and sex classifications that television reaches, television advertising can reach certain demographic groups effectively at certain times. Further, certain types of programs may attract upscale, white-collar professional groups, while other programs may attract a predominantly blue-collar crowd. Programs such as "Hockey Night in Canada" and Blue Jays baseball are sold to advertisers on the strength of their potential to reach males of all ages.

Coverage Flexibility

Network advertisers receive good national coverage on both of the national networks (CBC and CTV). However, advertisers who, despite smaller budgets, still want to use television can purchase commercial air time from individual stations. Thus advertisers can be selective with regard to markets they advertise in. Consideration of variables such as competition and opportunity markets helps advertisers determine which markets to purchase. For network advertisers, additional advertising on selected stations can be used to increase the weight of advertising in a particular market when needed, say, to counter competitive spending. Figure 11.1 illustrates the coverage capability of CKCO-TV in the Kitchener-London area.

Demonstration Capability

Television offers creative flexibility. It is the appropriate medium for verifying a product's claims, because it can show the product being used, which provides proof. Convincing demonstrations provide potential customers with a reason to buy the product. In addition, television is an effective medium for building consumers' awareness of and ability to identify the packages of products, particularly the packages of new products.

DISADVANTAGES OF TELEVISION

High Cost

Television does offer high reach potential and relatively low CPMs, but in real spending terms, television is very expensive. The cost of a 30-second commercial on the CBC full network varies between a low of $3500 and a high of $25 500. On the CTV Network, the range is $8000 to $25 000.[1] Both networks negotiate rates on the basis of supply and demand.

Figure 11.1   Sample coverage map of a local television station

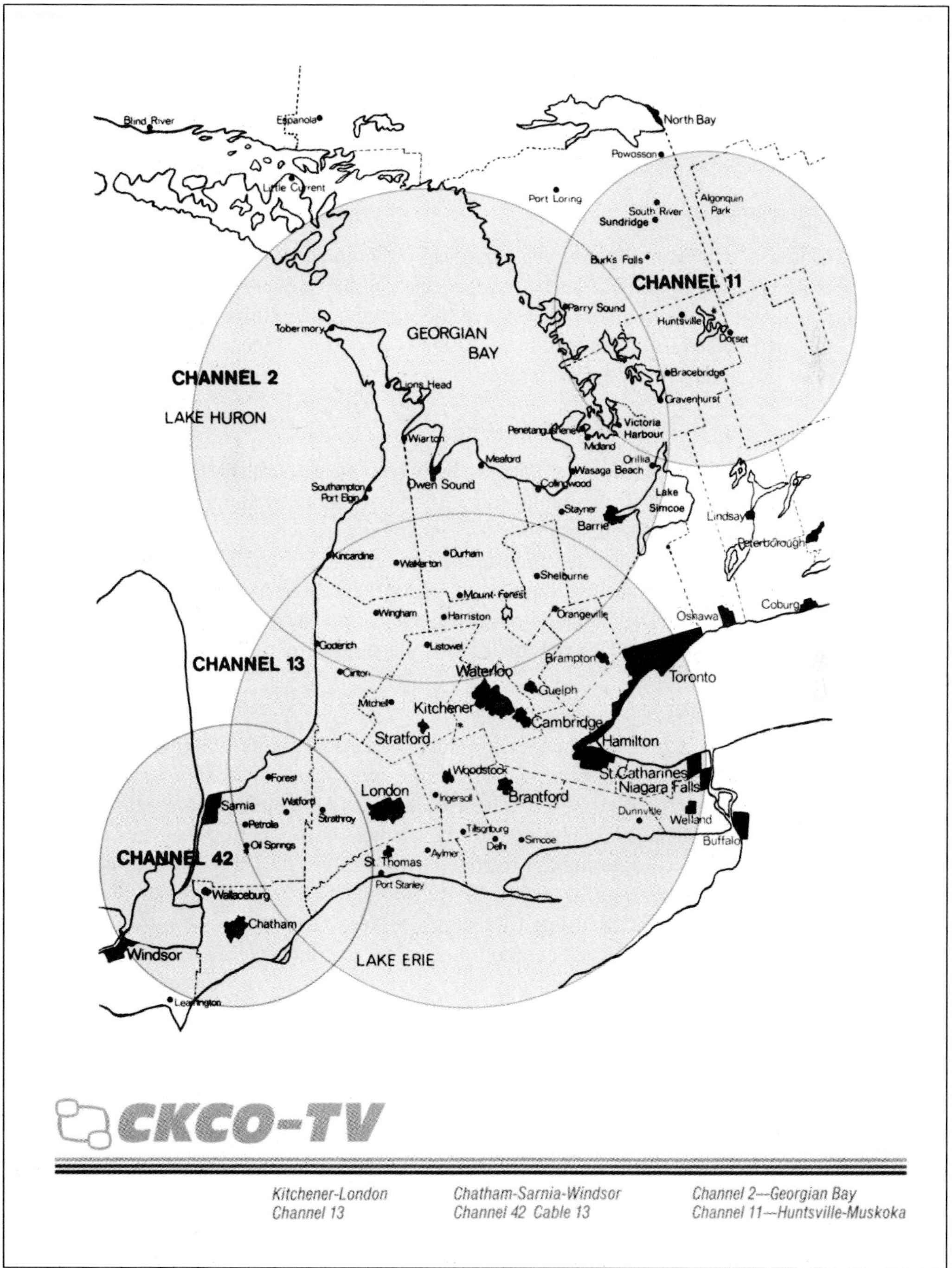

Kitchener-London
Channel 13

Chatham-Sarnia-Windsor
Channel 42 Cable 13

Channel 2—Georgian Bay
Channel 11—Huntsville-Muskoka

Courtesy: Cap Communications Limited

In addition to the cost of media time, television advertising involves high production costs; these costs for a finished commercial fall within a range of $80 000 to $150 000. To counter the high costs of television advertising, many advertisers are opting for 15-second commercials. However, 15s are sold at a premium rate of 65% to 75% of the cost of a 30-second commercial. In addition, the use of 15-second commercials adds to the clutter problem. For more information on the use of 15-second commercials, refer to the Advertising in Action vignette "Shorter is Better."

Clutter

Clutter in television refers to the clustering of commercials together during a program break. Since clustering of commercials occurs at planned intervals, and since a certain percentage of the audience may leave the viewing area during the break, many feel that particular placement within a cluster is important. Generally, the first and last positions in the cluster are preferable.

Lack of Target-Market Selectivity

As indicated by the list of advantages, television offers high reach to mass audiences, with some potential for reaching target markets that are defined in terms of age and sex. However, for advertisers with target markets precisely defined in terms of a combination of demographic, psychographic, and geographic variables, the use of television advertising is wasteful, since the message is received by many people outside the target definition. This reduces cost efficiencies considerably, so advertisers should consider other media that reach their target markets more efficiently.

Audience Fragmentation

The number of television channels available in a given market fragments the potential audience, thus reducing potential reach and increasing the costs of reaching those whom the message does reach. The problem of fragmentation is magnified by the intrusion of U.S. border stations into the picture. For example, the viewing options available in the Toronto market include CBLT (CBC), CFTO (CTV), Global, CITY-TV, CHCH-TV of Hamilton, CKVR Barrie, and CKCO-TV Kitchener, as well as three U.S. stations broadcasting from Buffalo, New York.

A less significant fragmentation problem is that the time a viewer spends with a satellite dish, a VCR, or with pay television reduces the amount of time he or she spends watching conventional television. Also of concern to advertisers are the recent phenomena of "zipping" and "zapping", both of which affect the viewer's potential to see an advertising message. **Zipping** refers to a method of reducing commercial viewing by using the fast-forward control on a VCR while watching a prerecorded television program. **Zapping** refers to the practice of switching channels by means of a remote-control device to avoid commercial messages.

Lack of Planning Flexibility

Television requires significant lead time from advertisers. For example, network buys are negotiated in the spring for a complete broadcasting year that commences with the new fall program schedule in mid-September. Network contracts are usually

Advertising in Action

Shorter is Better

In a time of rapidly rising television media costs, advertisers and their agencies are constantly looking for ways to spend money more effectively and efficiently. One option getting a lot of consideration is the 15-second spot (instead of the 30-second spot that has traditionally been the workhorse of the industry). All things being equal, if the creative aspect of a 15 is as effective as a 30, that is, if the message gets through with the same impact, then the advertiser will save money, since the actual rate paid for a 15 is usually 65% to 70% of a 30. The big issue, however, is whether a 15 can be as effective as a 30 in delivering the message.

The challenge for a media planner is to balance reach and frequency in the media equation so that the client's advertising objectives are achieved. In a campaign of straight 30-second commercials, the challenge is difficult. Now, the media planner has also to consider the element of commercial length.

In Canada, the 15-second commercial is still in its infancy. Trends in other countries do suggest that 15s will play a more dominant role in the television mix in the future. In some countries the 15-second commercial is now the norm, as is indicated by the following statistics:

Percentage of commercials in 15-second format

France	71
Japan	79
Spain	80
West Germany	50
Canada and U.S.	15

Media experts in Canada and the United States predict that, by 1995, the corresponding figure for 15s will be in the area of 60%.

Let's examine briefly a few known facts about 15-second commercials to determine if they are as effective as 30s:

1. In a recall and persuasion study conducted by Advertising Research Systems, Inc., 54% of respondents indicated comparable recall of 15s and 30s. There was little difference between the two formats in terms of persuasiveness.

2. A study by J. Walter Thompson (1987) reported that, with respect to recall scores, 15s had 65–70% of the effectiveness of 30s, with the average 15 scoring 16% as compared to the 23% scored by 30s. Subsequent studies by other organizations have confirmed these results.

3. A major concern about 15s, expressed often since their inception, is that they increase clutter and hence reduce the effectiveness of the television medium. Another J. Walter Thompson study indicated that viewers react negatively to the clutter of 15-second commercials. Viewers perceive that they are seeing more commercials and react negatively to this perception.

4. A large number of viewers do not associate shorter messages with the right advertiser. Research shows that the rate for misidentification rises proportionately as commercial length decreases. A McCollum/Speilman study shows 15s to be far less effective among adults over the age of 35 years.

What impact does this information have on the television media planner? Judging from this and other information, planners conservatively estimate that a campaign of nothing but 15-second commercials would have to increase in frequency by 30% during a four-week flight. This

continued

being the case, advertisers may wind up spending more on advertising. Remember that the price of a 15 is 65–70% of that of a 30. Given the frequency boost required to ensure the 15s achieve the desired intrusiveness levels, advertisers could spend more to achieve the same results previously generated by a pure 30-second campaign.

Now, if you were a media planner, would you recommend a 15-second campaign to one of your clients?

Adapted from Jo Marney, "Advertising quality is key in TV," *Marketing*, October 29, 1990, p.51., and Anne Parkes, "15s: They're short but are they sweet?" *Marketing*, February 1, 1988, pp.23-24.

non-cancellable, and spot advertising can only be cancelled on the basis of a minimum run and a specified notice period (e.g., advertising must run four weeks, and four weeks notice must be given prior to cancellation). Facing this, advertisers must be prepared to make an investment commitment to television advertising.

Creative Limitations

Television is a multi-sense medium offering significant impact capabilities, but a television commercial is very short (the normal length is 30 seconds; this is the length of 80–85% of all commercials sold).[2] As discussed earlier, there is also a movement towards 15-second commercials. It is questionable whether a 15-second commercial can achieve the same communications results as a 30-second spot. In both cases, time is essential, and as a result, only simple messages can be effectively communicated on television. Products and services whose selling points need to be communicated via long copy are better suited to print media. Television advertisements must focus on one major benefit of a product if communications are to be effective.

TYPES OF ADVERTISING TIME

When buying television time, the advertiser has three options: **network advertising** (either national or regional), **selective-spot advertising**, and **local-spot advertising**.

Network Advertising

Network advertising is suitable for advertisers whose products and services are widely distributed and who have relatively large media budgets. All stations composing the network (the CBC, for example, has 36 stations in its national network) carry a set of programs at a certain time—usually prime time, with some daytime. All commercial time is sold by the network. The advertiser must supply one commercial to a central source, and the message is fed across the entire network all at once.

The *advantages* of network advertising are as follows:

1. The advertiser can purchase many markets at a cost much lower than would result from using many individual stations. Therefore, under certain circumstances, network advertising can be cost-efficient.
2. Since network programs tend to be popular, advertisers reach a large national audience at a relatively low cost (CPM).

3. As regards production and traffic requirements, only a single film or tape need be in distribution, rather than numerous tapes for individual stations.

National-Spot or Selective-Spot Advertising

At a regional level or local-station level, stations fill in the balance of programming time with non-network programs, and sell commercial time directly to clients wanting to advertise in that market. Alternatively, the local station that carries network programs may have the opportunity to sell some advertising time directly to advertisers. For example, in network shows such as "Street Legal", "Dallas", or "Hockey Night in Canada", a certain portion of the commercial time available is allocated to local stations for selective-spot sales. In either case, advertisers would purchase time from the individual station, be it CBLT Toronto, CBOT Ottawa, or CBUT Vancouver. Each station from which time is purchased would require a copy of the commercial.

The *advantages* of selective-spot advertising are as follows:

1. It provides the network advertiser with the opportunity for incremental coverage; that is, advertisers wanting more frequency in certain markets would purchase more time from the key markets' local stations.
2. The selective-spot system allows advertisers with smaller budgets to pick and choose markets in which to advertise. They need select only those markets where their product has good distribution.
3. It provides some flexibility in the media-planning process. For example, advertisers can adjust their local-market advertising weight accordingly as local or regional market-share conditions change, as new opportunities are identified, or as competitors' media spending changes. Such variables must be considered in the planning stages, since the availability of good television time on short notice is virtually non-existent.

Both network-advertising and selective-spot sales are commissionable at the rate of 15% to recognized advertising agencies.

Local Advertising

Local advertising is basically the same as selective-spot sales, but the time is purchased by advertisers in local markets (retailers, restaurants, entertainment facilities, etc.). In contrast to network and selective-spot advertising, local advertising is non-commissionable. Since local-market advertisers do not usually work with an advertising agency, the individual television stations provide assistance in the development and production of commercials for local clients.

*T*ELEVISION ADVERTISING RATE STRUCTURES

In today's television market, the value of commercial time is largely dependent upon the laws of supply and demand. Generally speaking, the more popular the show, the larger the potential audience; hence, advertisers negotiate for time on popular shows, and since they are competing with other advertisers for a scarce resource (time available in any show), they force the price of the advertising spot up.

Demand pricing was an innovation introduced by the CBC Network in 1985. Today, both the CBC and the CTV Networks base advertising rates on the supply available and the demand in the marketplace. Traditionally, the advertising rates established for all shows were based on projected audience size. In essence, each show or time slot (AA, A, B, etc.) had a specific rate which was charged the advertiser, less any discounts offered by the network or station. On individual stations, rates are established on a grid schedule that bases the value of the ad spot on the popularity of the program and the size of its audience.

What factors affect the advertising rates charged or demanded by networks and stations? In general terms, factors such as the nature of the advertising purchase, the type of program, the time of day, the time of year, and the availability of discounts all influence rate structures.

FACTORS AFFECTING TELEVISION ADVERTISING RATES

Supply and Demand

For the CBC and CTV networks and for their member stations, it is market activity that establishes the price of an advertising spot. Advertising costs are based on basic economic principles, mainly the availability of supply and the demand exerted on that supply by competing advertisers. Under such conditions, prospective advertisers outline their advertising needs in terms of desired reach levels, frequencies, and so forth, and indicate how much budget is available, the ratio of prime time to fringe time required, and any seasonal implications. Working with the media, the network assembles a package; then, the price of the advertising is negotiated between the agency's media buyer and the network or spot-sales representative. Given the competitive nature of the market, this system places added pressure on media buyers, since the rates their clients pay for television advertising are dependent upon their ability to negotiate a deal.

Nature of the Advertising Purchase

Whether it is network advertising or selective-spot advertising being purchased is also a factor in television advertising rates. In the case of network advertising, placement is made on the basis of negotiation between the agency's media buyers and the media. The time is booked well in advance, usually in late spring for the following broadcast year, and heavier advertisers with program incumbencies obtain the more desirable programs. The CBC network explains the situation as follows:

> Each spring, upon announcement of its fall schedule, the network establishes a declaration date (referred to as D-Day) by which time most advertisers place their orders for the coming broadcast year.
>
> Every effort is made to accommodate each order as placed. If overbooking should occur as a result of the volume of orders, preference is allocated according to the following priorities:
>
> 1) Incumbency position   3) Volume of Contract
> 2) Length of contract   4) Start Date.[3]

The CTV network is booked in mid to late June to cover a 52-week period starting in September. At the time, advertisers may negotiate a particular rate for a certain package, but they may end up not obtaining the actual time they negotiated for on the basis of any of the four factors just listed. It is estimated that approximately 70% of available commercial time on the networks is sold by the declaration day.

Types of Programs

The nature of the program has a bearing on who watches, and on the size of the potential audience. Network and selective-spot advertising is sold on the basis of a regular program schedule that is established for the entire broadcast year. However, certain programs within a schedule may be designated as special buys, and are sold separately to potential advertisers. Examples of such programs include drama specials, miniseries, and sports programs such as "Hockey Night in Canada," "Expos Baseball," and the "World Figure Skating Championships."

In the case of sports programs, the hockey and baseball broadcasts appeal largely to a particular viewing audience (i.e., males of 18 to 49 years of age), and as a result are attractive to a particular type of advertiser. Since the network is seeking sponsors willing to make a long-term commitment over the entire season, separate rates and discount schedules apply to those who make such a commitment.

Dayparts (Time of Day)

Television can be divided into three broad time categories: prime time, fringe time, and daytime. Some stations make further subdivisions; they distinguish between early morning, mid-morning, and afternoon, all of which are in the daytime category. Since the type of audience and the size of audience varies according to daypart, so then must the rates for commercials within the dayparts.

Prime Time   Prime time is usually designated as the viewing hours between 7:00 P.M. and 11:00 P.M. (sometimes 6:00 P.M. to 11:00 P.M.). It is during prime time that most network shows are scheduled, and audience rates also peak during prime time. Rates for advertisers, though high during prime time, do vary from one show to another, depending on the program's popularity and reach potential. The types of programs available in prime time are those that appeal to a family audience (early evening) and those that appeal to an adult audience (later evening).

Fringe Time   Fringe time is usually defined as the time preceding or following prime time. For example, *early fringe* would be 4:00 P.M. to 6:00 P.M., and *late fringe* 11:00 P.M. to 1:00 A.M. In early fringe time, viewership is somewhat lower among the adult population, but high among kids returning home from school. As a result, early-fringe-time rates are lower than prime-time rates. Program content in this time period usually comprises comedy reruns, music videos, talk shows, and local programming. In late fringe time, viewership drops off significantly (after the national news hour) and advertising rates are adjusted accordingly.

Daytime   Daytime television runs from early morning (sign-on) to 4:00 P.M. The reach potential of television is relatively low in the morning, except the potential to reach young children. Television rates are lowest during the day. However, audiences increase during the day, and the rates are increased accordingly. The types of programs scheduled during the daytime range from news and information in the early morning, to kids' shows in the morning (non-commercial), to soap operas and quiz shows in the afternoon.

For a complete illustration of a weekly program schedule by daypart, refer to figure 11.2.

DISCOUNTS OFFERED BY TELEVISION

A variety of discounts are available to television advertisers, depending on the extent of their advertising commitment. Although the names and terms of the discounts vary from one network to another, or among individual stations, they do share common elements. In general terms, discounts are based on the amount of advertising time purchased, on seasonal factors, and on other factors important to the network or station.

Discounts Based on Amount of Time Purchased

Frequency Discount A **frequency discount** is usually earned through the purchase of a minimum number of spots over a specified period of time. Offered on a percentage basis, the discount increases with the number of spots purchase in the stated period of time. For example, the purchase of five to 10 spots per week may earn a 5% discount, 11 to 15 spots per week a 10% discount, and so on.

Volume Discount A **volume discount** is linked to the dollar volume purchased by the advertiser over a 52-week period. The greater the volume purchased, the greater the discount. The CBC offers a 2% discount to advertisers purchasing a minimum of $200 000, graduating up to 10% for a purchase of $1 600 000 per year.[4]

Continuity Discount **Continuity discounts** are earned when advertisers purchase a minimum number of designated spots over an extended period of time (usually 52 weeks, but the period may be shorter). The value of the continuity discount may increase with the number of spots purchased. For example, purchasing a minimum number of prime-time spots, say two per week over 52 weeks, may earn the advertiser a 4% discount. If the number increases to three spots, the discount may move to 6%, and so on.

Seasonal Discounts

The time of year has an effect on potential reach and the size of the television-viewing audience. As indicated in chapter 9, television viewing drops off in the summer season. Consequently, discounts are available to advertisers wishing to purchase commercial air time in non-peak seasons. The television seasons are as follows:

- *Fall*—mid-September through mid-December
- *Winter*—mid-December through mid-February
- *Spring*—mid-February through mid-June
- *Summer*—mid-June through mid-September

Figure 11.2 Sample program schedule

CKCO-TV

FALL 1990

TIME	MONDAY	TUESDAY	WEDNESDAY	THURSDAY	FRIDAY	SATURDAY	SUNDAY
5:45	The Ontario Report					**(6 a.m.)** George The Dog	**(6 a.m.)** McGowan's World
6:30	Canada A.M.					Paul Hann and Friends	Open Roads
7:00						The Rockets	People's Church
7:30						Wonder Why	
8:00						Winnie The Pooh	Sunday A.M.
8:30						Magic Circus	
9:00	Romper Room and Friends					OWL TV	
9:30	Witness To Survival	Secret Lives	Canada: In View	Secret Lives	In Shape For Life	The Campbells	
10:00	The Dini Petty Show					Time Exposures	Sunday Edition
10:30						Big Top Talent	
11:00	Morning Magazine					Brownstone Kids	Church Service
11:30	The Judge					Teen Video	
12:00	The Noon Report					Bowling For Dollars	Question Period
12:30	The Best of the Beverly Hillbillies					The Country Life	Littlest Hobo
1:00	Shirley					Saturday Afternoon Movie	Sunday Afternoon Movie I
1:30							
2:00	Another World						
2:30							
3:00	The Joan Rivers Show					Stars of Hockey	Sunday Afternoon Movie II
3:30							
4:00	Bewitched					Wide World Of Sports	
4:30	Head of the Class						
5:00	Cheers						Class Of Beverly Hills
5:30	Night Court						
6:00	The Scan Newshour					Scan Weekend	
6:30						Inside Entertainment	Provincewide
7:00	The Cosby Show					On Stage	
7:30	Murphy Brown	Cheers	Doogie Howser M.D.	Perfect Strangers	Parenthood	My Secret Identity	W5
8:00	Rescue 911	Matlock	Unsolved Mysteries	The Cosby Show	Full House	Katts and Dog	Am. Funniest Home Videos
8:30				Different World	Family Matters	Hogan Family	Am. Funniest Part 2
9:00	CTV Monday Night Movie	Roseanne	Jake And The Fatman	E.N.G.	Night Court	China Beach	CTV Sunday Night Movie
9:30		Bordertown			Babes		
10:00		Law And Order	Hunter	Knots Landing	Midnight Caller	Neon Rider	
10:30							
11:00	CTV National News						
11:30	The Ontario Report						
12:15	Sledgehammer						
12:45	Simon And Simon					Late Date Double Feature	Late Date Movie
1:15							
1:45	Magnum P.I.						

CTV
Tuned in to You

NETWORK

LOCAL

Courtesy: Cap Communications Limited

Summer Discounts The summer television season usually falls between the first week of July and early mid-September. Networks and stations usually offer discounts in the 20%–25% range during this period because of the decline in television viewing.

Summer Dividends As an alternative to lowering actual rates or offering a discount, some networks and stations offer *dividend announcements* based on the number of spots purchased. The dividend usually amounts to 20–25% of the total expenditure during the summer season.

A summary of the various discounts offered by the CBC is included in figure 11.3.

Other Discounts

Package Plans Networks and stations offer **package plans** in order to sell off fringe or daytime spots at a discount, sometimes in combination with the purchase of prime time. The nature of such plans varies considerably. An advertiser who purchases two prime-time spots per week in a popular American series may be required to purchase equivalent time in a prime-time Canadian series and/or equivalent time in daytime

Figure 11.3 Advertising discounts available in television

1986/87 NETWORK AND METRONET DISCOUNTS

52 Week Continuity Discount—10%
A 10% discount applies to purchases that contain a minimum of two designated prime units per week for 52 consecutive weeks.

26 Week Continuity Discount—5%
A 5% discount applies to purchases that contain a minimum of two designated prime units per week for a minimum of 26 weeks to a maximum of 51 weeks. A minimum of 13 weeks must run in the Winter or Summer periods or a combination thereof. Winter period: December 15, 1986 to February 22, 1987. Summer period: June 29, 1987 to September 13, 1987.

Notes: Continuity discounts (52 or 26 week) earned on either the Network or MetroNet are applicable to all other Network and/or MetroNet purchases during the contracted period.

For sales purchases, prime-time is defined as 6:00 p.m. to 11:00 p.m. Monday to Sunday. C.F.L., Hockey and Baseball can be used to establish continuity even though continuity discounts do not apply to these specific properties.

Winter Package Discount—10%
During the period December 15, 1986 to February 22, 1987 advertisers may qualify for a 10% discount, in addition to their earned discounts, on all programming (excluding specified sports packages), subject to package negotiations.

Summer Discount—20%
All units (excluding specified sports packages) aired during the period June 29, 1987 to September 13, 1987 will qualify for a 20% discount.

Summer Dividend Plan
Announcements aired in specified programs during the summer period will earn 20% of their value in dividend announcements.

Specials Package
Advertisers committing a minimum $100,000 budget upfront for special programming, prior to the end of June, qualify for an additional saving. Information on this special plan is available on request from your CBC sales rep.

Discount Averaging
Advertisers must calculate cumulative weekly discounts earned over the duration of the flight: divide by the total number of weeks and receive an average weekly discount that will be based on this prorated number.

 **CBC Television Sales** ON DEMAND!

Courtesy: Canadian Broadcasting Corporation. Reprinted with permission.

periods. Essentially, advertisers who demand the premium time spots must be ready to make sacrifices through the purchase of less desirable time also.

ROS (Run of Schedule) **Run of schedule** refers to a discount offered by a station to an advertiser who allows the station to schedule a commercial at its discretion, for any time in the programming day.

Pre-Emption Rates **Pre-emption** is a situation in which a special program, such as a mini-series, an entertainment special, or a hockey play-off, replaces a regularly scheduled program. For such programs, advertisers are usually determined well in advance, and they pay premium prices for the right to sponsor such shows. Advertisers of the originally scheduled show would be credited with equivalent air time at a later date.

ADVERTISING RATES BASED ON LENGTH OF COMMERCIAL

Most advertising-rate schedules supplied by the networks and stations, and the rates published in *Canadian Advertising Rates and Data*, are based on the purchase of 30-second units. Commercials that are longer in length—at 60, 90, and 120 seconds—are usually sold at two, three, and four times the 30-second rate.

More recently, 15-second commercials have become popular, as have "split 30s" (two 15-second commercials for the same product, one appearing at the start and one at the end of a commercial cluster). The trend toward 15-second commercials has posed scheduling problems for networks and stations, and their policies for acceptance vary. On average, the rates for 15-second commercials, as quoted in CARD, range from 65% to 70% of the 30-second rate. Split 30s are 130% of the 30-second rate.

*B*UYING TELEVISION TIME

In recent years, dramatic changes have occurred in television advertising. Factors such as audience fragmentation, the introduction of "people meters" (electronic devices attached to televisions to measure individuals' viewing patterns), 52-week audience measurements, and demographic and lifestyle influences have created a need for new approaches to buying and selling television time.

Media buying in television is a very complicated process that requires a high level of expertise on both sides of the negotiating table: that is, among the media buyers who represent their clients, and among sales representatives who represent the networks and individual stations. In a textbook of this nature, it is not possible to illustrate the negotiation process, as there is so much variation between the networks and stations with regard to rates and discounts. Instead, a brief overview of some of the key points for the major networks is presented below in the context of theory discussed earlier in this chapter. Also, a few illustrations of specific media buys are included in this section.

NATIONAL NETWORK RATES

Both the CBC and CTV networks negotiate commercial air time with advertising agencies on the basis of supply and demand. Such a system is predicated on the fact that television time is a commodity, and like all commodities, its price is affected by pressures and shifts in the marketplace.

The demand system is based on a standard grid card with varying price levels. The highest level on the CBC and CTV grids is in the $25 000 range for a high-demand 30-second spot in prime time. In this type of system, rates are adjusted periodically, and are affected by factors such as inventory of time available, projected audiences, continuity, and seasonality. When the agency and the network (or spot-sales representative) are negotiating the rates, other factors influence the price levels, including market competition, budget available, the ratio of prime to fringe time required, and program mix.

The CBC offers advertisers four different alternatives: full network, regional networks, MetroNet, and selective spot.

CBC Full Network The CBC's full network includes 36 stations from coast to coast. Advertisers supply one commercial to a central source for broadcast across the network. Ten stations are owned by the network, and 26 are affiliates.

CBC Regional Networks The CBC's regional networks include groupings of stations in geographic regions. There are four regions: Pacific (British Columbia), Western (Manitoba, Saskatchewan, and Alberta), Central (Ontario and Quebec English), and Atlantic (the Maritimes and Newfoundland).

MetroNet MetroNet is a group of 10 major market stations across Canada. Advertisers supply one commercial to a central source for broadcast across MetroNet.

Spot Sales In the case of spot sales, time is purchased by advertisers from any of the 10 CBC-owned stations that compose the CBC network. Commercial material must be supplied to each station purchased.

The CTV network negotiates commercial rates for 16 member stations in a network buy; otherwise, agencies can negotiate rates with member stations individually. CFTO-TV Toronto is the flagship station of the CTV Network.

LOCAL-MARKET TELEVISION RATES

In contrast to network rates, published rates for local-market television stations vary considerably. Nonetheless, the spot-announcement rates established by local stations also depend on the time classification (daypart) in which the commercial is scheduled to appear. As is shown by figure 11.4, the highest rates (AA) are charged for advertising between the hours of 6:00 P.M. and 11:00 P.M., Monday through Sunday. Reduced rates are offered in fringe and daytime periods.

Similar to the networks, the local-market station offers a continuity discount to advertisers booking a 52-week contract. In addition, CKCO-TV offers discounted rates for a specified seven-day reach plan. Reach plans running 52 weeks also earn the

Figure 11.4 CKCO-TV rate card

RATE CARD No. 47
EFFECTIVE: February 5, 1990
CKCO-TV
864 King Street West, Kitchener, Ont. N2G 4E9
SALES REPRESENTATIVES
Canada—Paul Mulvihill Limited:

Toronto   (416) 962-0080
Montreal   (514) 393-4101
Vancouver   (604) 684-6277

U.S.A.—Young Canadian Ltd.
New York head office   (212) 688-5100

Network Affiliation: CTV.
Rating Services: Nielsen, BBM.
Associations: CAB, CCBA, TvB Canada.

KITCHENER/LONDON
Channel 13

WINDSOR/SARNIA/CHATHAM
Channel 42

OWEN SOUND/GEORGIAN BAY
Channel 2

MUSKOKA
Channel 11

TIME CLASSIFICATIONS (Announcements placed in the minute adjacent to a higher time classification take the higher rate.)		30-SECOND ANNOUNCEMENT RATES
6:00 p.m. to 11:00 p.m. Monday through Sunday	AA	$1,265
4:00 p.m. to 6:00 p.m. Monday through Friday 12:00 noon to 6:00 p.m. Sunday 11:30 p.m. to end of Late News Package daily	A	$610
6:30 a.m. to 9:00 a.m. Monday through Friday 12:00 noon to 4:00 p.m. Monday through Friday 10:30 a.m. to 6:00 p.m. Saturday	B	$370
6:30 a.m. to 10:30 a.m. Saturday 6:30 a.m. to 12:00 noon Sunday 9:00 a.m. to 12:00 noon Monday through Friday End of Late News Package to 6:30 a.m. daily	C	$95

SEVEN-DAY REACH PLANS		
PLAN No. 1 — $4,130	**PLAN No. 2 — $5,140**	**PLAN No. 3 — $7,300**
2 Class AA 2 Class A 2 Class B 4 Class C	3 Class AA 2 Class A 2 Class B 4 Class C	4 Class AA 3 Class A 5 Class B 6 Class C

CONTINUITY DISCOUNTS:
A 52-week contract, booked in advance, is eligible for a 10% continuity discount on any individual announcement or Seven-Day Reach Plan which runs for the full 52-week period without hiatus.

TARGET GROUP PLANS:
3TR (10%) and 6TR (20%) discounts available on off-prime. (NOTE: Target Group Plans are not eligible for continuity discounts.)

SCAN NEWS PACKAGE:
A $100 premium to the AA rate is applicable to participants in Monday through Saturday 6:00 p.m. to 7:00 p.m.

FRIDAY & SATURDAY LATE DATE and SUNDAY AM:
A $50.00 premium to the C rate is applicable to participants wishing to isolate in these programs.

Courtesy: Cap Communications Limited

continuity discount. The **reach plan** is an interesting concept for television (it is more commonly used in radio as a way of selling off non-peak time). In the CKCO-TV reach plans, commercials are rotated vertically throughout the day, and horizontally during the week. Since the demographics of the audience change throughout the day, the number of people reached in a particular target group will vary with the schedule. However, with respect to the entire viewing audience, reach will be maximized, and the plan is purchased at a discounted rate. The advertiser saves about 15% in absolute dollars, a trade-off that must be considered against daypart scheduling.

TELEVISION BUYING—ILLUSTRATIONS

The concept of gross rating points (GRPs) was discussed in chapter 9—"Media Planning." When purchasing commercial air time in specific television markets, media buyers request a certain level of GRPs, basing their request on the reach and frequency objectives of the advertiser. The GRP concept offers a way of measuring the advertising weight levels in a market in terms of reach and frequency variables; it is based on the formula

GRPs = Reach × Frequency

Assume, for example, that a commercial message reaches 20% of target households in a market, and the commercial is scheduled five times in a week. The GRPs (weight) would be 100 (Reach 20 × Frequency 5 = 100). In another week, the reach may be 25% and the frequency four; in that case, the GRP level would remain at 100. Consequently, from week to week in a television advertising flight, the actual number of commercials varies depending on the estimated reach of the programs the ads appear on.

Since reach figures are discussed in the media negotiation process, it is impossible to illustrate in a sample buying plan the use of the GRP concept. However, to illustrate the basic use of a television rate card, and to illustrate the fact that rates fluctuate according to daypart (daypart rates are indicative of reach potential), a few examples will be developed.

If we use the CKCO-TV Kitchener-London Rate Card (figure 11.4) in conjunction with the buying-plan examples below, we come up with the following media-cost calculations:

Buying Plan One

> *Information* – 5AA spots per week
> – 3B spots per week
> – 52-week schedule
> – 30-second announcements

Cost Calculations On the basis of the above information, the advertiser qualifies for a continuity discount, which will be considered in the following cost calculations (the costs are taken from figure 11.4).

AA spots—5 spots per week × $1 265 × 52 weeks = $214 500
B spots—3 spots per week × $370 × 52 weeks   = 57 720
Gross cost   = 386 620
Continuity Discount × 10%   = 38 662
Net Cost   = 347 958

Assuming an advertising agency purchased the advertising time for the advertiser, a further calculation would be

Client is billed by agency	$347 958
Agency retains 15% commission	52 194
Media CKCO-TV receives	295 764

Buying Plan Two

The rates in this example are also based on the CKCO-TV rate card (figure 11.4).

Information – 7-day reach plan
– Plan 3
– 52-week schedule
– 30-second announcements

Cost Calculations In this example, the advertiser would buy time based on the discounted-reach-plan rate and also qualify for a continuity discount. The calculations would be as follows:

Reach Plan 3—$7 300 × 52 weeks   = $379 600
Continuity Discount × 10%   =   37 960
Net Cost   =   341 640

Assuming the time was purchased by an advertising agency, a further calculation would be as follows:

Client is billed by agency	= $341 640
Agency retains 15% commission	51 246
Media CKCO-TV receives	290 394

TECHNOLOGIES AFFECTING COMMERCIAL TELEVISION

Advertising revenues are the primary resource sustaining commercial-television broadcasting. Because of this, the television media, that is, the *conventional* television media, is concerned about the time potential viewers spend with pay-TV and videocassette recorders. Increased penetration by these technologies will reduce the amount of time viewers spend watching commercial television; hence, revenues from advertising may be reduced in the long term.

Advertisers are also concerned about the number of viewers watching commercial television, because rates are closely pegged to the number of people watching a particular program. Reduced audiences in the years ahead, combined with media rates that will gradually increase, will make television a less efficient advertising medium.

At present, in spite of inroads being made by these broadcasting competitors, the conventional commercial-broadcasting operations account for approximately 92% of television viewing in Canada. This figure represents the average weekly share of hours spent watching television by all persons two years of age and over in Canada. Conventional commercial broadcasting has been adversely affected by Pay-TV and VCR usage.

PAY-TV AND SPECIALTY SERVICES

In Canada, cable television has a penetration rate of 73%.[5] The growth of cable television affects advertisers in two ways. First, there is greater audience fragmentation, since more channels are available to the public. This lowers the reach potential of advertising messages. Second, the phenomenon of zapping comes into play. To eliminate commercial messages, viewers switch to other channels, via the remote control, during commercial breaks. Both of these developments will be drawbacks to television advertising in the future.

The advent of Pay-TV and specialty channels has led to a trend towards **narrowcasting**, which is specialized programming to attract or appeal to a narrowly defined target market (e.g., children or young adolescents). For the advertiser, narrowcasting, unlike convential television, offers potential target selectivity. As of fall 1989, Pay-TV reached 34% of all people two years of age and over, and accounted for 5.4% of viewing time on a weekly basis.[6]

VCR'S

With the movement towards home entertainment, VCRs have become a popular alternative to conventional commercial television in Canada. Almost two-thirds of households are equipped with videocassette recorders. As of 1989, the average weekly audience share was 3.3% among viewers two years of age and over, and average weekly reach was 20%. The threat of zipping (fast forwarding pre-recorded programs to avoid commercials) exists with the use of VCRs.

In summary, the growth of Pay-TV and VCRs will have a negative effect on conventional television in terms of its audience size and reach potential. Such trends will force advertisers to re-evaluate their media-spending patterns, particularly with regard to television.

RADIO

As of 1990, there were 385 AM and 302 FM radio stations operating in Canada. Collectively, these stations reach 94% of all persons seven years of age and over. FM reaches 63% of the same group of people.

Radio broadcasting in Canada is divided between the Canadian Broadcasting Corporation, which is funded by the government (or more precisely, by the taxpayers of Canada), and independently owned and operated stations that survive on advertising revenues. All AM stations are self-regulating, with no restrictions on the number of commercial minutes or on the placement of these minutes. FM stations are allowed 150 commercial minutes per day, with no restrictions on the number per hour or the number of commercial breaks.

AM VERSUS FM

Radio signals are transmitted by electromagnetic waves in two different ways: **AM (Amplitude Modulation)** and **FM (Frequency Modulation)**.

AM (Amplitude Modulation)

Amplitude refers to the height at which radio waves are transmitted. AM stations transmit waves by varying amplitude (amplitude modulation). AM waves initially travel close to the ground, and at night they are reflected back from the sky by a layer of electrical particles high above the earth. For this reason, it is quite common to pick up radio signals from distant U.S. stations at night, something that does not happen during the daytime. The very nature of AM radio provides stations with greater reach outside the station's area and makes it a suitable medium for car radios.

FM (Frequency Modulation)

Frequency refers to how fast waves travel in thousands of cycles per second (kilohertz). FM stations transmit waves by varying frequency (frequency modulation). FM waves travel in straight lines over shorter distances, but at frequencies above the static and noise level of AM. This results in clearer reception and better sound on FM stations.

In terms of reach, AM radio is more effective than FM, but both represent viable advertising alternatives for reaching local target markets. Refer to figure 11.5 for an illustration of reach effectiveness by demographic variables.

Figure 11.5   AM and FM radio—weekly reach and share of total hours tuned by demographics

CANADA	AM	FM	AM	FM
	Reach		Share	
	(%)	(%)	(%)	(%)
7+	71	63	53	47
Women 18+	74	64	55	45
Men 18+	72	66	51	49
Teens 12-17	65	62	49	51
Children 7-11	58	44	60	40

Source: BBM Bureau of Measurement (Fall 1989)

RADIO-STATION FORMATS

One of the major advantages of radio is its ability to reach selective target audiences. What audience is reached depends on the format of the station. **Format** refers to the type and nature of the programming offered by an individual station. Basically, the content is designed to appeal to a particular target group, usually defined by age. The content may be changed during the day to reflect **audience flow** (the process whereby audience demographics change according to daypart). For example, while adults listen to the radio frequently in the early morning, more female adults listen in the daytime, and more teens at night. In terms of station format, the style of music may change according to the needs of the different listeners during the day.

The most common radio-station formats in Canada are adult-contemporary, top-40, album-oriented-rock, gold, country, and classical.

Adult-Contemporary This type of station plays popular and easy-listening music, current and past, and generally appeals to an audience in the 25- to 49-year age range.

Top-40 This type of station plays the latest hits, mainly rock, and appeals to youthful targets, usually under 25 years of age. Top-40 stations are popular in urban AM-radio markets.

Album-Oriented-Rock This type of station plays a continuous collection of rock albums, and is quite popular with teens and adults. Basically, they are an alternative to the top-40 stations, and appear more frequently on FM than on AM.

Gold All adult-contemporary and top-40 stations usually incorporate some solid-gold hits into their program line-up. In recent years, gold has emerged as a format itself, largely based on the extreme competition in urban markets between top-40 stations. In Toronto, CHUM-AM, once the number one top-40 station, switched to a solid-gold format in 1985. Since that time, many other stations in urban markets have done likewise. The gold format appeals to a large demographic group (baby boomers) who prefer music from the sixties and seventies.

Country These stations play a variety of country music ranging from gold hits to current chart-toppers. The music played is in the contemporary or traditional Nashville, or Blue Grass, genre. Audiences tend to be blue-collar in nature, and cover a much wider cross-section of age ranges.

Classical Classical music is usually integrated into a station's program schedule to reflect audience flow, or as a programming alternative in markets served by only one radio station. CBC radio includes a significant classical-music component. Classical music generally appeals to more mature age groups with more extensive educational backgrounds and with occupations that require a more extensive education.

Other formats include ethnic/multicultural, jazz, middle-of-the-road, and urban-contemporary.

DETERMINING THE STATION FORMAT

When a radio station is determining its music-program format, be it specialization or music mix, local-market factors are considered. The main considerations are the age demographics of the local market and the number of competitive stations appealing to similar target audiences. Some generalizations can be made regarding this issue if we compare urban markets and small centre markets.

Urban Markets

In markets such as Toronto, Montreal, Vancouver, and Edmonton, radio stations with the same formats enter into a competitive situation, all trying to appeal to similar target markets (there are numerous top-40 stations in any one market). These stations rely on published reach levels to attract advertisers to their station.

Small Centres

In markets where only one or two stations serve the area, there is a tendency to adopt a more general musical format to meet the varying needs of a wider cross-section of age groups. Consequently, the music schedule varies with the audience flow during the day.

In summary, stations have two basic format strategies. First, the station can identify a specific target audience and design a musical format, such as top-40 or country, to appeal to them. Second, the station can appeal to a broad cross-section of the local market with a mix of music that varies according to daypart.

ADVANTAGES OF RADIO

Target-Market Selectivity

Because they tend to adopt a specific music format (rock, country, gold, etc.), radio stations appeal to more precisely defined demographic groups than do television stations. Consequently, advertisers can use a profile-matching strategy and select stations with audience profiles that closely match their target market. Even in smaller markets, where music formats change on a station and the audience flow varies by daypart, the advertiser can schedule radio commercials at the appropriate time of day so that dollars will not be wasted reaching people outside the target. For example, advertisers for soft drinks, snack foods, and fashion aimed at a youthful target would concentrate their advertisements in the evening time block, when the youthful target market is most likely to be listening.

Reach Potential

Since radios are almost everywhere—with multiple receivers in the home, carried around by teens with ghetto blasters, in the car, and at the beach—radio has the potential to reach large audiences, particularly if advertisers purchase from several stations in an urban market. In order to attract local advertisers, which provide the bulk of radio-station revenues, stations rely on reach figures to sell their medium. The application of reach statistics is illustrated in figure 11.6.

Figure 11.6 Tapscan rank report: weekly cume Kingston (central area)

Adults 18 — 49 — All Week

Station	Weekly Cume Estimates
1 CKLCLY	40 000
2 CFFXMK	25 300
3 CKLC	24 900
4 CFLY-FM	21 700
5 WCIZ-FM	17 500
6 CFFX	17 000
7 CFMK-FM	12 000

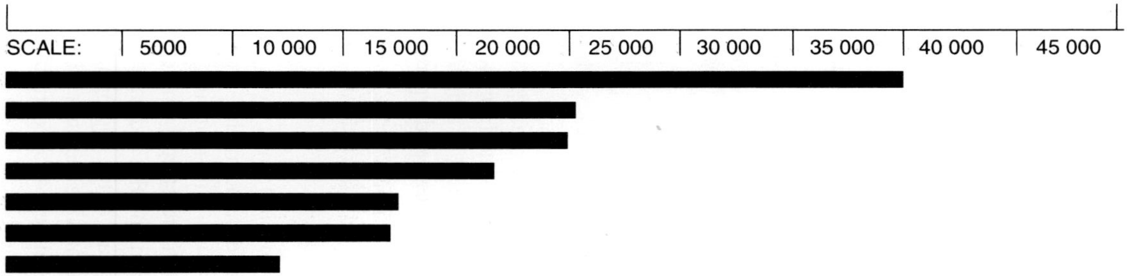

SCALE: 5000 | 10 000 | 15 000 | 20 000 | 25 000 | 30 000 | 35 000 | 40 000 | 45 000

Adults 25 — 54 — All Week

Station	Weekly Cume Estimates
1 CKLCLY	34 600
2 CFFXMK	23 800
3 CFLY-FM	22 200
4 CKLC	19 000
5 CFFX	15 400
6 WCIZ-FM	12 200
7 CFMK-FM	12 200

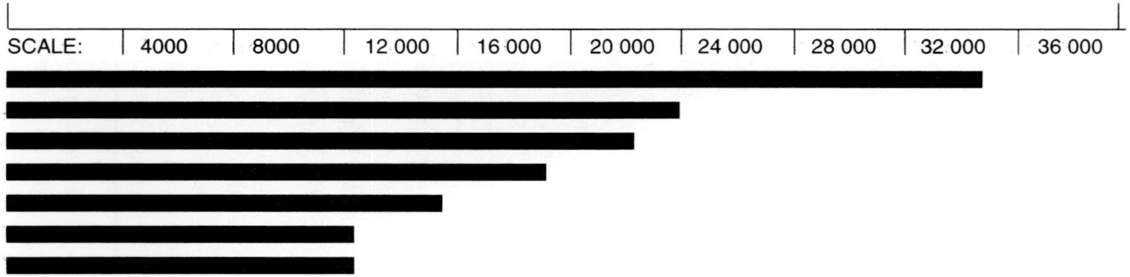

SCALE: 4000 | 8000 | 12 000 | 16 000 | 20 000 | 24 000 | 28 000 | 32 000 | 36 000

Source: St. Lawrence Broadcasting Company Limited. These graphs are based on data collected by BBM Bureau of Measurement (Fall 1990).

As discussed earlier in this chapter, the morning and evening drive times are popular tuning-in periods. Because they offer advertisers higher reach, these are the most expensive time periods for advertising. The *mobility* of radio has a positive influence on reach potential. Some research studies have shown that more time is spent with radios in drive time than is spent reading daily newspapers. Another factor affecting reach potential is *portability*. Radio is a popular medium out of doors in the summer, when people are away from competitive media. Many stations charge higher rates in the summer because of this higher reach potential.

Frequency

Radio is usually referred to as a *frequency medium*, a name which suggests what is probably radio's foremost advantage. If target market selectivity is used, an audience can be reached on several occasions throughout the day or week (vertical and horizontal rotation plans) at relatively low cost. For local advertisers wanting to advertise sales, radio is a preferable medium; numerous announcements can be scheduled for before and during the sale to stimulate immediate response from consumers. For national advertisers, the radio can boost frequency in key markets as needed. Because radio offers frequency at reasonable cost, advertisers can use it to supplement the reach of other media in a campaign.

Cost

The low cost of radio advertising attracts local clients to whom advertising otherwise would not be affordable. Radio advertising is cost-favourable in two areas. Production costs, first of all, are much less than they are for television, and changes to copy can be made on short notice. Second, in terms of time, the basic cost for each spot is relatively low (which makes radio an efficient means of reaching selective audiences), and numerous discounts are available for larger-volume advertisers. The combination of reasonable cost and frequency potential makes radio a good medium to supplement other media in a total campaign.

Flexibility

Radio offers flexibility in three areas: creative, time scheduling, and market scheduling. In terms of creative, copy changes can be made on short notice to meet the needs of changing competitive situations, and to meet the needs of local markets. According to Barry Agnew, director of marketing for The Bay, radio is now more important in his company's media mix. There is, he says, among advertisers,

> a major shift to radio to take advantage of its flexibility and lower front-end cost. With TV you had to buy 52 weeks, but radio allows The Bay to customize its creative for different marketplaces and it's ideal backup to newspapers.[7]

Other large retailers have also shifted more funds into radio. Woolco, for example, shifted its advertising spots for "$1.44 days" from television to radio. According to Brian Duckworth, director of advertising at Woolco,

Television production and time costs were certainly a factor, but so was the flexibility radio gave this one day event.[8]

With respect to scheduling, the lead time required is short (two weeks, or less in some cases); however, demand for popular stations in urban markets is quite high. Nonetheless, schedules can be "heavied up" (i.e., advertising can be increased) on short notice if the competitive situation so dictates.

Finally, media buying for radio is done on a market-by-market basis. Consequently, advertisers purchase only the markets they wish to advertise in. Because it offers selectivity with respect to the age and geographic location of the audience, radio can be an efficient media buy.

DISADVANTAGES OF RADIO

Audience Fragmentation

While reach potential is high, the audience is fragmented due to station format and to the demographic groups that competing stations appeal to. An advertiser wishing to reach the teen market in urban centres may have to purchase several stations in order to achieve adequate reach levels. Listener loyalty to a certain station contributes to the fragmentation problem. The net effect of fragmentation is that radio is recognized as a *low-reach/high-frequency* medium.

Message Retention

Several factors restrict the ability of radio messages to be retained. First, radio messages are short; there is limited opportunity for the communication of details in 30 seconds. Sixty-second commercials offer more creative flexibility, but they are less popular because of costs. Second, radio is a background medium often listened to while people are doing other things; therefore, attention levels of listeners are potentially lower. Third, clutter is a problem, particularly on AM stations. Finally, radio is a sound medium only, and as a result, there is no chance for the customer's mind to register the way a package looks (an important consideration for a new product), and there can be no product demonstration.

Media-Planning Considerations

For local-market advertisers, the advantages of radio outweigh the disadvantages. For national advertisers purchasing a large number of radio markets, other media factors must be considered. Generally speaking, radio time is in high demand, particularly among leading stations in urban markets. This makes it difficult for media buyers to purchase the specific times desired by their clients. Also, since there are more than 500 commercial stations from coast to coast, it is a difficult medium to co-ordinate in a media buy.

In assessing the merits and drawbacks of radio advertising, one would think it would be an attractive medium for national advertisers. This is not the case, however. For more details on this issue, refer to the Advertising in Action vignette "Radio: A Medium Taken for Granted."

Advertising in Action
Radio: A Medium Taken for Granted

Radio is an all-pervasive medium—it is with you at home, at work, and on the road. BBM Bureau of Measurement data show that radio reaches 94% of all people over the age of seven, that the average adult female listens to the radio for 22.4 hours a week, and that adult males tune in for 20.6 hours a week. Radio has also discovered the fine art of segmentation—appealing to different audiences through the use of specialized radio formats, a benefit that should be of high interest to advertisers.

When cost is built into the media equation, radio is even more attractive to advertisers. Research conducted by the CBS television network in the United States showed that radio commercials are between 77% and 83% as effective as television commercials in generating brand recall—at a small fraction of the time and production costs. A television commercial can cost about $150 000 to produce; the equivalent in radio would be about $15 000. So why is radio given short shrift by advertisers? It seems that, among national advertisers, radio-media recommendations are routinely dismissed, even when the disadvantages of advertising on television—the clutter problem, competition from VCRs, and couch potatoes zapping from station to station—are well known.

The reasons for national advertisers' disinclination to use radio are many. Some of the positions held by advertisers and their agencies about radio are as follows:

1. The medium is an afterthought or an adjunct to another campaign. In other words, only a small portion of a budget will be allocated to radio.
2. Radio ads are executed with little imagination. For example, most ads are radio versions of a television commercial, adapted somewhat to the different medium.
3. Agencies don't make as much money on radio; hence, they are reluctant to put their good people on radio assignments. Television is more glamorous than radio due to the elements of sight, sound, motion, colour, and the impact of surrounding programs.
4. Print offers visual power, and the prestige of the carrier helps the image of the advertiser. For example, an advertiser in *Financial Post Magazine* or *Maclean's* benefits from the association with the publication. Such potential for positive association does not exist in radio.

What, then, lies ahead for radio? Certainly, it will be tough to attract national advertisers. Some of them, however, already see the merits of radio and are doing something about it. In 1990, Procter & Gamble increased its radio budget by 25%. Automakers are turning to radio more frequently, and beer companies are finding radio effective in reaching younger targets at an age (19–25 years) when brand loyalties start to form.

It seems that there is a misconception about what radio can do for an advertiser, and its role in the media mix is misunderstood. Nobody would suggest that a national advertiser adopt radio as its primary medium, but it is clear that, if used properly, radio can complement a campaign. The industry will have to promote more effectively the key advantages of radio in the 1990s. These advantages—flexibility, targetability, intrusiveness, and cost-efficiency—should position radio well to meet the challenges of advertisers in the 1990s.

Adapted from Marina Strauss, "Advertisers neglect potential of radio," *Globe and Mail*, January 3, 1990, and Jo Marney, "Who's listening? Radio reaches everyone," *Marketing*, March 21, 1988, pp.13,15.

RADIO ADVERTISING RATES

The actual rates paid by radio advertisers are affected by several factors: the season or time of year where commercials are placed; the daypart or time of day for which the commercials are scheduled; the utilization of reach plans; the availability of discounts offered by individual stations. The type of advertiser (national or local) also has an impact on the basic rate charged to advertisers.

FACTORS AFFECTING THE COSTS OF RADIO ADVERTISING

Seasonal Rate Structures

Radio stations have moved toward grid-rate schedules that reflect seasonal fluctuations in listenership and reach potential. Refer to figure 11.7 for an illustration of specific grid-level rates. Generally, radio rates fluctuate with the seasons, as follows:

Time Period	*Rate*
May-August (summer) and December	Higher
September-October March-April	Mid-range
January-February	Lower

Dayparts

Since the size and nature of the audience vary according to the daypart, different rates are charged for each. Generally, the dayparts are classified as follows:

Classification	*Time*
Breakfast	6:00 A.M. to 10:00 A.M.
Midday	10:00 A.M. to 4:00 P.M.
Drive	4:00 P.M. to 7:00 P.M.
Evening	7:00 P.M. to Midnight
Night Time	Midnight to 6:00 A.M.

Dayparts vary from one station to another, some stations having more or fewer classifications than those listed above. In addition, weekend classifications are often different from weekday, as the listening patterns of the audience change on weekends.

Reach Plans

Radio advertisers can either purchase specific time slots and schedule a particular **rotation plan** during the length of the media buy, or they can purchase a **reach plan**. For the first option, a rotation plan, the advertiser specifies the time slots and pays the corresponding rate associated with it. There are two types of rotation plans available:

- *Vertical Rotation:* the placement of commercials based on the time of day (within various dayparts)

Figure 11.7 CKLC /CFLY rate card

RADIO KINGSTON
CKLC/CFLY
RATE CARD

A
Sound
Advertising
Combination

98·3 FLY·FM

EFFECTIVE October 1, 1990.

		7	6	5	4	3	2	1
Reach Plan CKLC - 20% Breakfast 30% Day, 20% Drive 30% Evening/Sunday	60 sec.	44.00	49.00	54.00	62.00	71.00	79.00	88.00
CFLY - 6:00 a.m. - 12 midnight	30 sec.	34.00	38.00	43.00	47.00	54.00	61.00	68.00
Breakfast CKLC - 6:00 -10:00 a.m. Monday-Saturday	60 sec.	60.00	65.00	72.00	79.00	88.00	98.00	109.00
CFLY - 6:00 - 12:00 midnight	30 sec.	45.00	49.00	55.00	60.00	67.00	74.00	82.00
Daytime CKLC - 10:00 a.m. - 3:00 p.m. Monday-Friday	60 sec.	45.00	50.00	58.00	64.00	73.00	82.00	92.00
10:00 a.m. - 7:00 p.m. Saturday CFLY - 6:00 a.m. - 12 midnight	30 sec.	34.00	39.00	44.00	49.00	55.00	62.00	70.00
Drive CKLC - 3:00 - 7:00 p.m. Monday-Friday	60 sec.	51.00	57.00	63.00	70.00	79.00	88.00	98.00
CFLY - 6:00 a.m. - 12 midnight	30 sec.	39.00	43.00	48.00	53.00	60.00	66.00	74.00
Evening/Sunday CKLC - 7:00 p.m. - 1:00 a.m. Monday-Sunday	60 sec.	40.00	44.00	49.00	57.00	65.00	68.00	76.00
6:00 a.m. - 7:00 p.m. Sunday CFLY - 6.00 a.m.- 12 midnight	30 sec.	31.00	34.00	37.00	43.00	49.00	53.00	58.00
Night Time CKLC - 1:00 a.m. - 5:00 a.m.	60 sec.	8.00	8.50	9.00	9.50	10.00	11.00	13.00
CFLY - midnight - 6:00 a.m.	30 sec.	6.00	7.00	7.50	8.00	8.50	9.00	11.00

Contract Buys

14 - 26 WEEKS	Grid 5
27 - 39 WEEKS	Grid 6
40 - 52 WEEKS	Grid 7

FEATURES: 52 WEEKS 6 per week GRID 6 plus 10%
3 per week GRID 5 plus 10%

Volume Discounts

300 Time	Grid 5
500 Time	Grid 6
1000 Time	Grid 7 -

99 Brock Street, P.O. Box 1380, Kingston, Ontario K7L 4Y5 (613) 544-1380

continued

Figure 11.7 continued

1990
Media Month

	M T W T F S S
SEPT. '90 Starts Aug. 27	
OCT. '90 Starts Oct. 1	
NOV. '90 Starts Oct. 29	
DEC. '90 Starts Nov. 26	
JAN. '91 Starts Dec. 31	
FEB. '91 Starts Jan. 28	
MAR. '91 Starts Feb. 25	
APR. '91 Starts Apr. 1	
MAY '91 Starts Apr. 29	
JUNE '91 Starts May 27	
JULY '91 Starts July 1	
AUG. '91 Starts July 29	

1991
Media Month

SEPT. '91 Starts Aug. 26	
OCT. '91 Starts Sept. 30	
NOV. '91 Starts Oct. 28	
DEC. '91 Starts Nov. 25	
JAN. '92 Starts Dec. 30	
FEB. '92 Starts Jan. 27	
MAR. '92 Starts Feb. 24	
APR. '92 Starts Mar. 30	
MAY '92 Starts Apr. 27	
JUNE '92 Starts June 1	
JULY '92 Starts June 29	
AUG. '92 Starts July 27	

CREDIT POLICY
1. Credit will be issued subject to a credit investigation.
2. Invoices due net 30 days, 2% discount if paid by 10th day of month following.
3. Invoices will be issued at the end of each month reflecting that month's advertising.
4. Overdue accounts will be charged interest at 2% monthly.
5. Accounts over 90 days will go to collection upon review.
6. Cash in advance is required for all concerts and accounts without credit history.

SHORT TERM GRID LEVELS
The Grids are set in advance and are estimated to be one Grid below their anticipated level. Changes in the Grids, if any, will take place Thursdays at 8:30 a.m. All Contracts booked must be at the current effective Grid for the air dates.

GRID LEVEL
December 31 - April 28	Grid - 4
April 29 - September 29	Grid - 3
September 30 - October 27	Grid - 4
October 28 - December 29	Grid - 3

STATION POLICIES
1. Reach Plan requires a minimum of 16 + AM/FM announcements.
2. Single Station Rates available upon request.
3. Features 52 weeks, short rate to appropriate seasonal Grid +10%.
4. R.O.S. Schedule and prices available only when Station on Grid 1.
5. Short rate to apply to all CONTRACT and VOLUME BUYS not fulfilled.
6. Contract rates net to CKLC/FLY-FM.

COMMERCIAL ACCEPTANCE
In order to maintain our high standards of Radio Broadcasting, all commercials must be approved by CKLC/CFLY Programming Departments before being aired. These departments may reject any scripts or produced commercials that, in their judgement do not meet the standards required for the environment in which they will be broadcast.

EVEN SCHEDULING
An equal distribution of commercials on one of the following combinations.

Monday - Friday	Tuesday, Thursday, Saturday
Monday - Saturday	Tuesday, Thursday
Monday - Sunday	Saturday, Sunday
Monday, Wednesday, Friday	

 99 Brock Street, P.O. Box 1380, Kingston, Ontario K7L 4Y5 (613) 544-1380

Courtesy: St. Lawrence Broadcasting Company Limited

• *Horizontal Rotation:* the placement of commercials based on the day of the week (same daypart on different days)

Earlier in the chapter, potential reach was identified as an advantage of radio. However, since listenership levels and the type of audience vary with the daypart, radio stations have developed reach plans as means of maximizing reach. In a reach plan, or *total audience plan* as it is often called, commercials are rotated through the various dayparts in accordance with a predetermined frequency, in order to reach different people with the same message. Reach plans vary from station to station. In many cases, the reach plan covers the entire week, while in other cases a separate reach plan is implemented on weekends.

The Radio Kingston CKLC/CFLY rate card shown in figure 11.7 divides the reach-plan spots equally between breakfast, daytime, drive time, and evening/Sunday dayparts. For the advertiser, the benefit of the reach plan is twofold. First, the reach potential is extended, and second, the rates charged for the reach plan collectively are lower (because of the discounts) than those that would result from the individual purchase of similar time slots. Reach plans do require a minimum spot purchase on a weekly basis.

Type of Advertiser

Radio advertising rates vary with the nature of the advertiser. National advertisers are charged the general (national) rate as published in *Canadian Advertising Rates and Data* (CARD). These rates are generally higher than rates charged to local advertisers (retail establishments, restaurants, etc.). Rates for national advertisers are commissionable to recognized advertising agencies at the rate of 15%. Retail rates, being lower, are non-commissionable, but owing to their importance in the local radio station's revenue mix, stations offer production assistance either at no cost or at reasonable cost to encourage retailers to advertise.

*B*UYING RADIO TIME

Radio stations' rate schedules usually quote a general advertising rate that is based on a seasonal grid schedule. For advertisers purchasing in large volume, certain discounts are available. This section discusses the variety of discounts usually offered by radio stations, examines some strategic decisions advertisers make when purchasing radio media, and then offers some examples to illustrate radio buying.

DISCOUNTS

Advertisers that purchase frequently from specific stations qualify for a variety of discounts. While the criteria for earning discounts vary from station to station, the discounts are similar in nature. Some of the more common discounts offered by radio are **frequency discounts**, **continuity discounts**, **weekly reach plans**, and **combination rates**.

Frequency Discounts A frequency discount is a discounted rate earned through the purchase of a minimum number of spots over a specified period of time, usually a week. Having earned such a discount, advertisers are referred to a lower-rate grid schedule, or they could be quoted a percentage discount, such as 5% for 15 to 20 spots per week, 8% for 21 to 30 per week, 10% for 31 plus spots, and so forth.

Volume Discounts With a volume discount, the advertiser is charged a lower rate for buying a large number of spots: the discount might be 5% for 260 spots, for example, or 10% for 520 spots.

Continuity Discounts With a continuity discount, the advertiser is charged a lower rate for making a contract buy that covers a specified period of time. At intervals of 26, 39, and 52 weeks, advertisers are charged according to a discounted grid schedule, or the percentage discount offered increases with the length of the contract.

Package Plans As discussed earlier in the chapter, radio can increase advertising reach—can gain access to a different audience—by rotating commercials through the various dayparts. To increase reach, stations offer reach plans or total audience plans that require advertisers to purchase a minimum weekly number of spots in return for a packaged discount rate, such as 12 spots per week divided equally between four dayparts.

Combination Rates It is quite common for independent radio stations to be controlled by one owner (e.g., two AM stations in different markets, or an AM/FM combination in the same market). To sell advertising time on both stations, or in both markets, to advertisers, the radio stations would quote discounted rates for the combination purchase.

ROS (Run of Schedule) A station may offer additional discounts to advertisers if allowed to vertically and horizontally rotate commercials through a schedule at its own discretion.

Premium Rates In contrast to discounts, premium-priced spots are also available to advertisers. For example, advertisers wishing to sponsor news, sports, or daily features and commentaries by radio personalities may do so if they are willing to pay a higher rate. The rate is justified by the loyal following of the audience that comes with such spots and is usually quoted as a percentage increase above a specified grid schedule.

STRATEGIC DECISIONS TO MAKE WHEN BUYING RADIO TIME

A basic procedure to use when considering the purchase of radio time is to make some strategic decisions regarding the following questions:

- How many commercials will be scheduled each week? (and how frequently will each be aired?)
- For what time of day and days of the week will the commercial be scheduled?

- Will the ads be scheduled to run through different seasons?
- What will the length of the campaign be in terms of weeks?
- If reach is a major factor, how many and what stations will be purchased in a market?

For the purposes of developing some radio-buying examples, continued references will be made to figure 11.7—the Radio Kingston CKLC/CFLY rate card. Let's try making some of these strategic decisions on the basis of the CKLC/CFLY rate card and the discount information discussed earlier in the chapter.

How Many Commercials Will Be Scheduled?

The CKLC/CFLY rate card quotes rates for both 30-second and 60-second commercials. Discounts offered are based on the volume of spots purchased over the length of the schedule, so consideration would be given to multiplying frequency each week times the number of weeks, to arrive at a total volume of spots. Discounts are offered when volume reaches 300, 500, and 1000 spots.

For What Time of Day (Day of the Week) Will Ads Be Scheduled?

At all grid levels, the rates for CKLC/CFLY vary according to daypart. Rates are highest in the breakfast time block, when the most people are listening, and decrease for other time blocks when audience numbers are reduced. Some rate distinctions are made by the day of the week. All day Saturday, for example, from 10:00 A.M. to 7:00 P.M., is considered the equivalent of 10:00 A.M. to 3:00 P.M., Monday to Friday. Since breakfast rates are the highest, all other time blocks are discounted.

The rate schedule illustrated in figure 11.7 quotes rates by daypart over a 7-level grid. The rates vary at each level of the grid. Grid levels 3 and 4 quote rates by season and grid levels 5, 6, and 7 quote rates by volume discounts and contract buys. Refer to figure 11.7 for detailed explanations.

For What Time of Year Will the Ads Be Scheduled?

Rate fluctuations are based on the seasonal shifts in radio's importance and effectiveness. In the CKLC/CFLY rate card, rates are highest from the end of April to the end of September and during the months of November and December. Rates in other times of the year are lower.

How Long Will the Campaign Be?

Continuity discounts, based on the length of the schedule, are also available. In the case of CKLC/CFLY, a discount is offered for contract buys, with rates discounted at intervals of 26, 39, and 52 weeks.

BUYING RADIO TIME—SAMPLE CALCULATIONS

To illustrate some basic cost calculations used in buying radio time, let's develop some examples based on the CKLC/CFLY rate card.

Example One

Buying Information	– 30-second spots
	– 10 breakfast spots per week
	– 15 drive spots per week
	– 12-week schedule

Based on the length of the schedule (12 weeks), the advertiser does not qualify for a continuity discount. Therefore, the first calculation is to determine the total number of spots in the buy, to see if the advertiser qualifies for a volume discount.

Total number of spots	=	spots per week × number of weeks
Breakfast	=	10 per week × 12 weeks = 120
Drive	=	15 per week × 12 weeks = 180
Total Spots		= 300

Based on the total number of spots (300), the rate charged will be from grid 5. In this case, the 30-second rate is $55 for breakfast, and $48 for drive time. The cost calculations are as follows:

Total Costs	=	number of spots × earned rate
Breakfast	=	120 spots × $55	= 6 600
Drive	=	180 spots × $48	= 8 640
Total Cost			= 15 240

Example Two

The advertiser would like to evaluate a reach plan (involving 16 commercials per week) against a specific buying plan. Details of each plan are as follows:

Plan A—Reach Plan (30-second spots)

Information	– involves 16 spots per week
	– rotated between breakfast, drive, day, and evening/Sunday
	– runs for 16 weeks, June through September.

Plan B—Specific Plan (30-second spots)

Information	– 8 breakfast spots per week
	– 8 drive spots per week
	– 16-week schedule

Cost Calculations for Plan A In this case, the advertiser qualifies for a continuity discount because of the 16-week schedule. Based on the rate card, the earned rate would be reach plan grid 4. The earned rate is $43 per spot. Therefore, the cost of the reach plan is

Total Cost	= total number of spots	× earned rate
	= 16 spots per week	× ($43 × 16 weeks)
	= $11 008	

Cost Calculations for Plan B The total number of spots in the buy are

Breakfast = 8 spots per week × 16 weeks = 128 spots
Drive   .= 8 spots per week × 16 weeks = 128 spots
Total Spots   = 256

Based on this calculation, the advertiser does not qualify for a volume discount, but, since the length of the contract is 16 weeks, a continuity discount does apply. The advertiser is charged the rate from grid 4. Therefore, the total costs for Plan B are as follows:

Breakfast = 128 spots × $55 = $ 7 040
Drive   = 128 spots × $48 = 6 144
Total Cost   = 13 184

In conducting a comparative evaluation of Plan A and Plan B, the advertiser must weigh the more selective reach potential of Plan B against the savings of Plan A. Perhaps the advertiser wants to reach business commuters in drive time to and from work. With Plan A the advertiser can reach a somewhat different audience by means of a daypart rotation of spots. The net result is a cost difference of $2176 in favour of Plan A. Should the advertiser decide, then, to go with the cost savings of Plan A, or with the more selective reach of Plan B at greater cost? Would you like to make the decision?

Summary

The Canadian television market comprises public networks, private networks, cable television, and pay-television networks. How people view television varies according to the time of day and the season. Television viewing tends to be lower in the morning, somewhat higher in the afternoon, and highest in the evening. As regards seasonal changes, viewership is much lower in the summer.

As an advertising medium, television's primary advantages include high reach, message impact and effectiveness, frequency (for large advertisers), and coverage flexibility. Disadvantages include high cost, audience fragmentation, and clutter.

Advertisers can purchase television time from the national networks, national or selective spots, or from local stations, depending on the degree of coverage they desire. The rates an advertiser pays are affected by supply and demand (CBC Network stations), the type of program purchased, and the daypart. Discounts are generally offered on the basis of frequency, volume, continuity, and season.

In contrast to television viewship trends, radio listenership peaks in the morning (6:00 A.M. to 10:00 A.M.), and tapers off as the day progresses. As an advertising medium, radio offers target-market selectivity, frequency potential (based on its relatively low cost), and coverage flexibility. Disadvantages include audience fragmentation, problems associated with message retention, and clutter.

Radio rate structures are affected by season (i.e., rates are higher in the summer), daypart, the use of reach plans, and the type of advertiser (local advertisers pay lower rates). Advertisers are offered discounts based on frequency, volume, continuity, and the use of package plans (reach plans).

Review Questions

1. Why do television and radio stations have different time classifications?
2. What are the primary advantages and disadvantages of television advertising for the national advertiser? For the local advertiser?
3. Explain the difference between network advertising and national, or selective-spot, advertising.
4. Identify and briefly explain the television discounts that are based on the amount of time purchased by advertisers.
5. Explain the following television terms:
   a) affiliates
   b) fragmentation
   c) simulcasting
   d) daypart
   e) zipping
   f) zapping
   g) clutter
   h) package plans
   i) ROS
   j) pre-emption rates
   k) GRPs
6. What does "station format" refer to in radio broadcasting?
7. What are the major advantages and disadvantages of radio advertising for the national advertiser? For the local advertiser?
8. What is a reach plan, and what benefits does it provide the advertiser?
9. If you made the decision to use radio in a city such as Vancouver, on what basis would you select specific stations? Discuss your reasons.
10. Briefly explain the following radio terms:
    a) audience flow
    b) combination rate
    c) vertical rotation
    d) horizontal rotation
    e) premium rate
    f) frequency discount
    g) volume discount
    h) continuity discount

Discussion Questions

1. What would be the potential effects on television rate structures if all rates established were based on supply and demand? Discuss.

2. "Expanded penetration of Pay-TV and VCRs will have an impact on traditional television viewing patterns." Discuss from the viewpoint of the advertiser.

3. Target-market selectivity is the key benefit of radio advertising. On what basis can the radio industry exploit this advantage in the 1990s? Discuss appropriate strategies the industry might use to attract advertisers.

Direct Advertising and Out–of–Home Media

CHAPTER 12

In studying this chapter, you will learn about

- The various types of direct advertising and out-of-home media advertising
- The advantages and disadvantages of direct advertising and out-of-home media
- The factors considered in and procedures used for buying direct mail and various forms of out-of-home media

The remaining two primary categories of media are discussed in this chapter. **Direct advertising** is a form of media advertising that communicates messages directly to marketing prospects. **Direct mail** is the most common means of delivering these messages, but other mass media may be used as well. Out-of-home media include outdoor advertising, transit advertising, and point-of-purchase display and advertising materials. This chapter presents the basic advertising alternatives, the advantages and disadvantages of each, and the procedures for buying media space for each alternative.

DIRECT ADVERTISING

Direct advertising is one segment of the direct-marketing industry in Canada, and it plays a major role in influencing consumer purchase patterns. A recent study (see figure 12.1) showed that direct sales to Canadian households, through a variety of communication and distribution channels, amounted to $2.4 billion. Personal selling contributed the most in terms of sales, followed closely by direct mail—one form of direct advertising.

Some distinctions should be made between the following marketing terms, which are often confused with each other:

1. **Direct marketing** is a marketing system, fully controlled by the marketer, that develops products, promotes them directly to the final consumer through a variety of media options, accepts direct orders from consumers, and distributes products directly to the consumer.
2. **Direct-response advertising** is advertising that prompts immediate action (e.g., a newspaper ad with a clipout coupon that can be sent in for more information about a retirement savings plan). Direct-response advertising is commonly communicated via direct mail or via any of the mass media.
3. **Direct advertising** is the process of advertising directly to prospects via mail, sales people, and dealers (e.g., direct mail, door-to-door flyers, telephone solicitation). Direct advertising does not use the traditional mass media.

Figure 12.1 Direct sales to Canadian households

Communication/ Distribution Channel	Value ($ Millions)	Share (%)
Personal Selling (e.g., house parties)	808.5	33.2
Mail	567.5	23.3
Door-to-Door	531.4	21.8
Manufacturer Shipped	378.9	15.5
Other	113.7	6.2
TOTAL	2 437.7	100.0

Source: Canadian Media Director's Council Media Digest, 1986/87 (Toronto: Maclean Hunter Ltd.), p.19.

4. **Direct mail** is a form of direct advertising communicated to prospects via the postal service.

Since direct mail is the primary medium for delivering direct-advertising messages, this chapter focuses mainly on various aspects of direct mail.

TYPES OF DIRECT MAIL

Sales Letters

The most common form of direct mail, the letter, is typeset and printed, and delivered to household occupants or to specific individuals at personal or business addresses. Letters are usually the primary communication in a mailing package, which typically includes a brochure, a reply card, and a postage-paid return envelope.

Leaflets and Flyers

Leaflets and flyers are usually standard letter-sized pages (8 1/2" × 11") that offer relevant information and are accompanied by a letter. The purpose of a leaflet is to expand on the information contained in the letter and to generate a response (i.e., to get the recipient to take action).

Folders

Folders are sales messages printed on heavier paper, and they often include photographs or illustrations. They are usually folded, and are frequently designed in such a way that they can be mailed without envelopes. Postage-paid reply cards are an important component of a folder.

Statement Stuffers

Statement stuffers are advertisements distributed via monthly charge-account statements (such as those one gets from Sears, Simpsons or The Bay). Capitalizing on the ease of purchasing by credit, such mailings make it very convenient to take action. Usually, the credit-card number is the only information the seller requires.

Catalogues

Catalogues are reference publications, usually annual, distributed by large retail chains and other direct-marketing organizations. Examples are the *Sears Catalogue* and *Regal Gifts*.

SOLO DIRECT MAIL VERSUS CO-OPERATIVE DIRECT MAIL

Direct-mail campaigns can be delivered to target markets, either by **solo direct mail** or by co-operative direct mail. Solo direct mail is specialized or individually prepared; direct-mail offers are sent directly to prospects via the mail. Solo-direct-mail pieces are commonly employed in business-to-business communications, supplementing the messages frequently communicated via traditional business publications. Refer to figure 12.2 for an illustration of a solo-direct-mail piece.

Figure 12.2   Sample content of a solo direct mailing (business-to-business advertising)

Courtesy: Pitney Bowes Canada Ltd. Reprinted with permission.

Co-operative direct mail is a mailing that contains special offers from non-competing products. They are quite commonly employed by consumer-goods marketers. A typical mailing would contain coupons for a variety of grocery, drug, and related products, magazine-subscription offers, preprinted envelopes offering discounted rates for film processing, and so on. Co-operative direct mailing has proven to be one of the most effective forms of print media for generating trial purchase. The median response rate for all products delivering coupons via co-operative direct mail is 9.8%.[1]

DIRECT MAIL AS AN ADVERTISING MEDIUM

In the words of Leslie Wunderman, the chairman of Young & Rubicam's Direct Marketing Group,

General advertising invites everyone to the party. It's kind of a mass blind date... We in direct marketing use a dating bureau called a database, which matches producers and consumers to each other one to one, demographically, psychographically.[2]

Wunderman's Statement indicates the primary advantages of direct-mail advertising: it has the ability to reach the right people (e.g., decision makers and influencers)—that is, it enables advertisers to be selective.

ADVANTAGES OF DIRECT MAIL

Audience Selectivity

Using direct mail, advertisers can reach targets that are precisely defined in terms of demographics—assuming that the organization acquires lists that identify its primary prospects. A good list results in minimal circulation waste. Additional discussion of lists appears later in this chapter.

High Reach

Solo direct mailings reach everyone the advertiser would like to reach, unlike other media, which only reach some portion of the target. For example, a life-insurance or credit-card organization wanting to reach all college graduates may be able to obtain access to such a list of students. For co-operative direct mailings (i.e., mass distribution to selected Canadian households), the national reach potential is very high. In this case, there is much circulation waste, but the response rates are usually adequate to cover the costs of mass mailings.

Geographic Flexibility

A proper mailing list offers an advertiser not only demographic selectivity but also the opportunity to deliver direct-mail messages *wherever* desired. This advantage is appealing to retailers and other local businesses that want to confine mailings to certain areas.

Creative Flexibility

Like advertising in business publications, direct mail offers the flexibility to include long copy (the longer the better, according to some practitioners) in advertisements. Since various pieces are often included in a single mailing, there is also flexibility in terms of style, length, and format. Generally speaking, a combination of formats in a single medium is effective. In this area, the advertiser is only limited by imagination, budget, and applicable post office regulations. Finally, because it provides the opportunity to include items (free sample packets) that will reach desired targets, direct mail is a good medium for distributing coupons, free samples, and trial offers.

Advertiser Control

For solo-delivered direct mail, the advertiser retains control over such variables as the circulation and the quality of the message. The message is printed by one source, which results in consistent quality of reproduction. This is in contrast to the situation advertisers find when running an advertisement in a variety of different newspapers, when the quality of reproduction varies from one newspaper to another.

Exclusivity

Another advantage of direct mail is that mailings delivered to the household do not compete with other media at the time they are received, though they do compete for attention with other mail. This is in contrast to the circumstances of ads in newspapers and magazines, which compete with other ads and with editorial content.

Response Rates

The success of a direct-mail campaign is measured in one way only—the sales generated by the mailing. As a rule of thumb, business-oriented direct mail receives 15% of the responses within the first week of the mailing. Early responses, used in conjunction with historical conversion patterns, can be used to project sales for a longer period of time. In this regard, the success of a direct-mail campaign can be determined in a short space of time. For co-operative direct mailings, coupon-redemption rates are higher than for other print-media alternatives, and redemptions peak in the third month of a typical direct-mail offer, at 12.6% of total redemption.[3]

DISADVANTAGES OF DIRECT MAIL

High Cost per Exposure

When the absolute costs of production, of renting or purchasing lists, of fulfillment (i.e., of stuffing and sealing envelopes), and of mailing are tallied, the total can be higher than it is for other print alternatives. Remember, though, that the selectivity of the medium reduces waste circulation.

Absence of Editorial Support

In comparison to magazines, which have the support of editorial content (which provides a real reason for consumers to read), direct mail stands alone. It must grab someone's attention without assistance; therefore, it is imperative that the message be designed in a format that combines verbal and illustrative elements attractively.

Image and Life Span

Direct mail is not a prestigious medium. Co-operative direct mailings are perceived by many consumers to be "junk mail" and are promptly discarded when they reach the household. Many consumers do not perceive the special offers to be all that special. Direct mailings to businesses may suffer the same fate (i.e., they may be discarded), particularly if several mailings from different suppliers are received at the same time. However, the physical form of direct mail enables consumers to retain it for future reference.

Potential Delivery Delays

Other print media have specific issue dates, so the time of message exposure is precisely controlled. Since direct mail relies on the postal service, and since it is delivered third class, there are no delivery guarantees. It is possible that a mailing will arrive at a destination after the offer has expired or the advertised event occurred.

*B*UYING *DIRECT MAIL*

There are three basic steps involved in buying direct mail: obtaining a proper prospect list, conceiving and producing the mailing piece, and distributing the final version.

OBTAINING DIRECT-MAIL LISTS

The direct-mail list is the backbone of the entire campaign. Both the accuracy and definition of the list can have a significant bearing on the success or failure of a direct-mail campaign. Lists can be secured from two basic sources: internal sources and external sources.

Internal Sources

Also referred to as *house lists*, internal sources can be a firm's own customer files—names of current customers and past customers can be made available. Also, the names of consumers who have returned warranty cards can be retained for future mailings.

External Sources

It is common for a list broker to make all the arrangements for one company to use the lists of another company. The buyer provides the broker with the profile of the target customer, and the broker supplies a list of possible prospects on a cost-per-name basis. Generally, a high-quality list is developed through a merge/purge process on a computer, whereby numerous lists are purchased, combined, and stripped of duplicate names. There are a few types of lists available: response lists, circulation lists, and compiled lists.

Response Lists   A response list is a list of proven mail-order buyers. Such lists include book-of-the-month-club buyers, subscribers to Maclean-Hunter business publications, or people who order from Carole Martin direct mailings or from other cooperative direct mailing firms.

Circulation Lists   Circulation lists are magazine-subscription lists that target potential customers by an interest or activity. A publishing company, for example, sells its list of subscribers to any other business that is interested in a similar target.

Compiled Lists   Compiled lists are prepared from government, census, telephone, warranty and other publication information. Often such lists are not personalized. For example, a business firm may be identified on the list but not the appropriate contact person within the firm. Names of business prospects are compiled from print sources such as the *Standard Industrial Classification (SIC), Fraser's Canadian Trade Index* or *Scott's Industrial Index.* Provincial and national associations such as the Canadian Medical Association commonly provide mailing lists of their physician members, or, in the case of other associations, lawyers, teachers and accountants.

PRODUCTION

When designing a direct-mail package, the advertiser usually engages the services of a specialist organization. In Canada, there are numerous advertising agencies specializing in direct-response advertising, and many of the larger agencies, recognizing the growth and opportunity in direct mail, have formed direct-response subsidiaries (e.g., J. Walter Thompson Direct Response, Vickers & Benson Direct Marketing, and Ogilvy & Mather Direct Response). An array of direct-mail consulting firms are also available to advertisers (see figure 12.3).

Once the mailing package is designed, it is ready for printing. Various factors such as size, shape, number of pieces, use of colour, and other variables all influence the cost. Costs are usually quoted on a per-thousand basis, with larger runs incurring lower unit costs.

Once printed, the mailing pieces are turned over to a letter shop that specializes in stuffing and sealing envelopes, affixing labels, sorting, binding, and stacking the mailers. Once this task is complete, the mailing units are sent to the post office for distribution.

DISTRIBUTION

The most common means of delivery is Canada Post. A number of options are available through the postal system: first-class mail, third-class mail, and business-reply mail.

First-Class Mail Although more costly, some direct mail is delivered first class. The advantages of first class are quicker delivery (if time is important), the return of undeliverable mail, and mail forwarding if the addressee has moved.

Third-Class Mail Most direct-mail pieces—be they single pieces, bulk, catalogues, or co-operative mailings—are delivered third class. The advantage over first class is the cost savings.

Business-Reply Mail For the benefit of the recipient, an individual can respond at the expense of the advertiser. A pre-printed reply card or envelope is included in the direct mail package. Postage-paid return envelopes are an incentive aimed at improving the rate of response (see figure 12.4).

Advertisers are now looking more closely at alternate forms of direct-response advertising, trying to find a way to break through the clutter of direct mail. Specifically, a lot of attention is being given to videocassette advertising. For information on this new form of advertising, read the Advertising in Action feature "Video Marketing: A New Era Beckons."

Figure 12.3 Trade advertisement for a direct-response advertising agency

J. WALTER RESPONSE

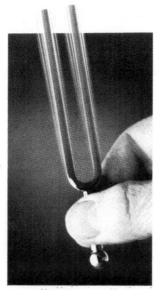

Indeed, we answer the needs of clients with sound direct response advertising. We're JWT Direct Response, the direct response instrument of J. Walter Thompson Canada.

RESPONDING TO CLIENTS' NEEDS

Our clients want high perform-ance direct response advertising *without* compromising their high quality image. So we analyze each problem very carefully before offering a solution and walk step by step with clients to achieve their goals.

DELIVERING RESPONSE

From mathematically planned strategy...through pin-point targeting...to canny creative – we deliver quality advertising that really gets response.

POSITIVE RESPONSE

Direct response advertising is unique. It is measurable. You always know how successful your latest campaign was. Judging by the response from our clients, *their* campaigns are measuring up to their highest expectations!

WE WANT YOUR RESPONSE

With offices around the world and a team of dedicated profes-sionals backed up by the full power of Canada's number one advertising agency, JWT Direct Response has the resources and expertise to ensure *your* adver-tising strikes a responsive chord.

Get the response *you* want – call JWT Direct Response today!

Call: Sherry Martin
Managing Director
(416) 926-7300

 Direct Response

Headline associates JWT Direct Response with the parent agency J. Walter Thompson Company Ltd.

Courtesy: JWT Direct Response. Reprinted with permission.

Figure 12.4 Business reply mail (postage prepaid by source)

HERE COME THE CANON COURIERS

Canon FAX

The courier service you can call your own.

Business Reply Mail
No postage required if mailed in Canada

Postage will be paid by

F-29

POSTES CANADA POSTAGE
810

Canon Canada Inc.
Attention: Steve Gasten
6390 Dixie Road
Mississauga, Ontario
L5T 9Z9

Printed in Canada

AD149

Advertising in Action
Video Marketing: A New Era Beckons

As direct marketers jostle to get attention-grabbing messages into the mailboxes of consumers, many are recognizing the truth in an old adage—that a picture is worth a thousand words.

The concept of video marketing has taken hold in the United States, so can Canada be far behind? In 1990, the Lincoln-Mercury division of the Ford Motor Company redesigned its Town Car and relaunched it by mailing videos to 200 000 pre-selected prospects. Toyota did the same thing when it mailed out 200 000 copies of a tape expounding the virtues of owning the company's new Previa mini-van. In recent years, marketers have experimented with a few new gadgets, including computer diskettes and musical microchips, but it is the video that has captured the attention of the marketplace. It stands out amid that deluge of mail that consumers like to refer to as "junk mail."

According to David Taylor, a noted direct-advertising expert and vice-chairman of Taylor-Tarpay Direct Advertising, a videocassette offers higher perceived value than a standard printed sales brochure. He says, "If somebody receives a videotape in the mail, they're going to be interested enough to watch at least a part of it."

Marketers are cautious about the use of videos, and many advise that the medium is not appropriate for all products. Videos will be far from commonplace in the media mix because of the high cost of producing and distributing them. In Canada, the cost of producing a 10-minute tape is estimated to be in the $10 000-to-$12 000 range. American companies have pegged average costs for a finished tape, produced and distributed, to be in the $12.00-$15.00 range. For Ford and Toyota, that meant an investment of around $3 million—no small amount, by any standard.

Despite the high cost, videos will find their way into the Canadian marketing fabric. They are very appropriate for high-ticket items such as cars, vacation resorts, and vacation destinations. They offer the unique advantage of making the product or service come alive through sound, imagery and action—things that are not possible in many other forms of direct-response advertising. Also, the market is a waiting target, as 62% of Canadian households are equipped with videocassette players.

And what about the Canadian experiences with videos thus far? The Audi division of Volkswagen Canada was one of the first to experiment with video marketing. Invitations to a "private screening" of a new video were mailed to a target audience of 15 000 Canadian professionals. The nine-minute video showed the Audi wending its way through a maze, encountering several obstacles along the way. According to marketing manager Deborah Woytenko, the video was "a visual metaphor for city driving." From a creative viewpoint, Woytenko stated that, "Cars are emotional things so you need to be able to give a feeling of what the car is all about." From a media perspective, "you're approaching people [upscale] with high entertainment standards, people who like to attend symphonies and live theatre, people who watch television selectively, so you have to send them a high quality package." On both counts, the video met the challenge.

Certainly there is potential for video marketing in Canada, but, given the small size of the market, its use will be much more conservative than in the United States. Progressive marketing organizations will find a use, and those firms that target carefully will be sending videos to prospects who are very likely to purchase. Get ready for your copy!

Adapted from David Todd, "Video: a new approach to direct mail," *Playback Strategy*, October 22, 1990, pp.21–24.

OUTDOOR ADVERTISING

Outdoor advertising has come a long way since it was first introduced to Canada in 1904. It is a highly visible and effective medium. Think about it. If you drive a car, travel by transit, or stroll through shopping malls, you are constantly exposed to outdoor advertising. Outdoor-advertising messages reach a massive cross-section of a city's population 24 hours a day, seven days a week.

In 1989, outdoor advertising in Canada generated a gross revenue of $718 million, which accounts for 8.5% of all advertising revenues in Canada.[4] This section of the chapter examines the various types of outdoor advertising, reviews the advantages and disadvantages of outdoor as an advertising medium, and discusses some basic points about buying outdoor space.

TYPES OF OUTDOOR-ADVERTISING UNITS

In Canada, there are several outdoor-advertising vehicles from which an advertiser can choose: *posters*, *bulletins* and *superboards*, *back-lit posters, transit shelters, mall posters, junior posters, pillar ads,* and *mural ads*.

Posters

The **poster** is the most commonly used form of outdoor advertising (see figure 12.5 for an illustration). The standard poster size is 10' × 20' (305 cm × 610 cm), and a poster of this size is commonly referred to as a "billboard." The poster is composed of 10 or 12 sheets of special paper designed to withstand the wear and tear of outdoor conditions. To maximize reach potential, posters are strategically located on major auto routes within, or leading to, the business and shopping districts of a community. To maximize the frequency of the message, to extend the daily viewing by consumers, posters are often illuminated. Advertisers can purchase poster space either in single panels or as a "showing" (i.e., in multiple panels). Which they choose would depend on what advertising weight level they are seeking.

Figure 12.5 An example of outdoor poster advertising

Courtesy: Labatt Breweries of Canada

Junior Posters

A junior poster is a small, low-cost version of a poster. The size of a junior poster is 6' × 12' (183 cm × 366 cm). They are currently confined to the core areas of six major urban centres in Canada. Junior posters are positioned close to eye level, and are visible to both pedestrian and vehicular traffic.

Superboards (Painted Bulletins)

A **superboard** (also referred to as a painted **bulletin**) is much larger than a poster, and more expensive to produce. The largest superboards are 14' × 48' (427 cm × 1464 cm), with smaller sizes available. The size of the boards available to advertisers is affected by location; the largest boards are only available in seven major markets; the smaller boards are available in an expanded list of markets.

The advertising design of a superboard is hand-painted on metal or plywood sections, and is transported to and installed in a designated outdoor structure. These painted panels are portable and can be moved to other locations in accordance with a predetermined rotation schedule. Being more expensive to produce and erect, superboards are located on high traffic routes, and offer up to twice the exposure opportunities of the standard poster.

A recent innovation is the introduction of a "superflex" board, a hand-printed or screen-printed flexible vinyl sheet that is stretched over the standard superboard frame.

Back-Lit Posters

A **back-lit poster** (often called a backlight or urban lite) is a luminous sign containing advertising graphics printed on translucent polyvinyl material. Colour reproduction and impact are among the advantages offered by a back-lit poster. At night, the lighted display takes on a three-dimensional effect. Back-lit posters are available in 30 major markets, and are strategically located on high-volume traffic routes. The primary advantage of back-lit posters is the image-enhancement they offer (i.e., they provide the illusion of product quality), and the fact that the panel faces are reusable. The cost of producing back-lit posters is quite high, but the opportunities for exposure are estimated to be twice that of a standard poster.

Transit Shelters

A **transit-shelter** advertising unit consists of two street-level 4' × 5' (122 cm × 168 cm) back-lit posters that are incorporated into the design of glass-and-steel transit shelters (see figure 12.6). Transit-shelter units are located on busy public-transit routes, and offer advertisers high levels of potential exposure to motorists, pedestrians, and transit riders. Similar to a back-lit poster, they offer the advertiser quality colour reproduction and good visual impact. These units are sold to advertisers on the basis of site-selection flexibility. That is to say, advertisers can select sites that reach certain age, income, or ethnic groups, or they can concentrate on a geographic trading zone, depending on the target they would like to reach.

Mall Posters

Mall posters make up an outdoor medium that does not rely upon vehicular traffic. A **mall poster** is a 3 1/2' × 5' (107 cm × 152 cm), back-lit, eye-level poster located in the main aisle of a shopping mall (see figure 12.7). Unlike other outdoor media, a mall poster and the message it bears are directed at a consumer who is actually on a shopping trip. The primary advantages of mall posters are their proximity to the

Figure 12.6 Examples of transit-shelter advertising

Courtesy: Mediacom

Figure 12.7 Examples of mall-poster advertising

Courtesy: Mediacom

shopping area (i.e., they can stimulate impulse purchasing), and their general location in an area where the advertised product can be purchased. Mall posters are good for supplementing other media, and for reinforcing the product's primary selling message.

Pillar Ads

Pillar ads are a relatively new outdoor-advertising concept, and at the moment they are confined to only five markets—Toronto, Vancouver, Calgary, Edmonton, and Windsor. A pillar ad is a four-sided, back-lit unit usually found in parking lots in the downtown area. The size of the advertising area is the same as that of a transit-shelter unit, so they are easily interchangeable.

Spectaculars

A **spectacular** is a nonstandardized outdoor unit erected according to the customized specifications of the advertiser. They are one-of-a-kind structures that are illuminated and frequently include protruding components such as objects that rotate. Spectaculars are located in extremely busy traffic areas, and require a long-term commitment from the advertiser, owing to the high expense of constructing them. Spectaculars are beyond the budgets of most advertisers.

Mural Advertising

Mural advertisements are handpainted outdoor extravaganzas on the sides of buildings. They are very large in size, often the entire height of the building. They can be three-dimensional in nature, which adds to their attention-getting capability (see figure 12.8).

ADVANTAGES OF OUTDOOR ADVERTISING

Target Reach and Frequency

Outdoor provides advertisers with the opportunity to reach a very large cross-section of a market's population in a short period of time. Depending on the weight level purchased (GRPs) and on the strategic location of outdoor boards on busy thoroughfares,

Figure 12.8   Example of mural advertising

Courtesy: Murad Communications

outdoor has the potential for multiple exposure. According to Mediacom data (Mediacom is one of Canada's largest sellers of outdoor space), up to 90% of a city's traffic is concentrated on 10% of the streets (streets where outdoor boards are located), and significant exposure levels are achieved during the first two weeks of a campaign.[5] From that point on, reach potential is marginal.

Geographic Flexibility

Advertisers only wanting to advertise in certain areas have the flexibility to do so with outdoor. Outdoor units can be purchased on a regional basis (say, for a total province or for an area within a province), or on a market-by-market basis. Therefore, advertisers wanting to increase weight levels in selected markets can use outdoor to supplement a national campaign in another medium.

In addition, there is the opportunity to have outdoor messages located in certain areas of a city. For example, an advertiser wanting to reach predominantly blue-collar workers can purchase units in an industrial area where factories are located. Other advertisers may choose mall posters so that the message is located close to the point of purchase.

Size and Quality of Message

Since the introduction of back-lit posters, mall posters, and transit-shelter advertising units, the reproduction quality of outdoor messages has improved considerably. Although the messages communicated by outdoor must be short, a strong visual impression can attract the attention of passersby.

Compatibility with Other Media

Outdoor can reinforce the message of other media in two ways. First, it can extend the total reach and frequency of a campaign beyond what a single medium can do. Therefore, it is a good complementary medium—a good means of reinforcing important sales messages. Second, outdoor can increase the total number of impressions made on a target market that may consume another medium lightly. For example, a light viewer of television, who is hard to reach regardless of the weight level purchased, may be easier to reach via outdoor.

Creating Product Awareness

Traditionally regarded as a complementary medium, outdoor can also be effective in generating product awareness when used as a primary medium, particularly if a shot-gun media strategy is employed (say, if an advertiser wanted to reach all adults of 18 to 49 years of age in specified markets). To illustrate the awareness potential of outdoor, let's consider the case of Jergen's Aloe & Lanolin bar soap. The product was introduced exclusively via mall posters over a 13-week period in major markets. The product exceeded sales expectations by 15%, and captured its market share objective in a very competitive bar soap category.[6]

Cost

When the absolute cost of outdoor advertising is evaluated with regard to the medium's reach potential—the opportunities for exposing consumers to outdoor messages—the medium begins to seem a fairly efficient media buy. Using the Vancouver market as an example, and assuming an advertiser purchased standard outdoor posters for a four-week period, we would calculate the CPM (cost of reaching a thousand people) as follows:[7]

$$CPM = \frac{Cost}{Population\ (000)}$$

$$= \frac{\$48\ 685}{1467.9}$$

$$= \quad 33.17$$

This is the cost of reaching an individual once. Therefore, when the daily-travel patterns of people are considered (and the potential for multiple exposure), the cost efficiencies of outdoor improve significantly.

DISADVANTAGES OF OUTDOOR ADVERTISING

Creative Limitations

The nature of the outdoor advertising medium (people pass by outdoor ads either in a vehicle or on foot) is such that it must rely upon instant visual impact to get attention. The message itself must be short, simple to read, and it must quickly draw attention to the brand name.

Lack of Target-Market Selectivity

The broad reach potential of outdoor (it reaches all adults and children) makes it impossible for an advertiser to focus on a target market. Therefore, owing to wasted circulation, the cost-per-thousand figures, which show efficiency, may be deceptively low (since the medium reaches many people who would never purchase the product).

Costs

Costs of outdoor are high in two areas. First, the costs of producing finished materials for vehicles such as back-lit posters, mall posters, and transit shelters are high (printing on a plastic vinyl material is expensive). Second, the absolute cost of buying media space is high. A four-week national showing of outdoor posters at a 25-GRP level would cost approximately $217 000.[8] For this reason, advertisers opt for geographic selectivity.

Lack of Prestige

Outdoor advertising does not always enhance the image of the product, whereas advertising in a quality magazine can rely on the surrounding editorial content to aid in image development. Also, the association of the product with a medium that clutters the landscape may have a negative impact.

Unobtrusive Medium

Despite the reach and frequency potential of outdoor, people who pass by may not notice outdoor ads. Unless the message catches the attention of passersby, the outdoor board will blend into the background, and not break through the perceptual barriers of the consumer.

BUYING OUTDOOR ADVERTISING SPACE

Regardless of the outdoor-advertising format under consideration (posters, super-boards, mall posters, etc.), there are similarities in the media-buying process. Outdoor space is sold in four-week periods, and is available on a market-by-market basis. Advertisers can purchase a single market, a group of markets (composing a regional buy), or a national buy if strategy demands it and budget permits it. The primary sellers of outdoor advertising space are Mediacom Inc. and Gallop and Gallop Advertising. A sample rate card for selected vehicles of outdoor advertising is shown in figure 12.9.

Media space is purchased on the basis of the advertising weight level desired by the advertiser. Advertising weight is expressed in terms of GRPs (gross rating points). As indicated in chapter 9 in the "Media Strategy" section, GRP is a weighting factor that combines reach and frequency variables. In the case of outdoor advertising, GRP is defined as the total circulation of a specific outdoor advertisement expressed as a percentage of the market's population. With reference to figure 12.9, a weight level of 100 GRPs delivers on a weekly basis exposure opportunities equal to the population of a market. A weight level of 50 GRPs offers one half the exposure opportunities, and so on for the various weight levels. GRPs for back-lit posters, mall posters, super-boards, and superflex are stated weekly, while GRPs for posters and transit shelters are stated daily.

Outdoor Advertising—Rates and Discounts

All outdoor advertising rates are quoted on a four-week basis. Both posters and transit shelters are sold on the basis of a four-week minimum purchase. The other options (back-lits, mall posters, superboards, and superflex) have a 12-week minimum purchase requirement. Rate examples are contained in figure 12.9.

A continuity discount is offered to advertisers who meet specified time commitments. The discount becomes a factor after the minimum purchase requirements have been met. In figure 12.9, the continuity discounts (i.e., percentage discounts based on dollar volume purchased) are offered at intervals of 24 weeks, 36 weeks, and 52 weeks. The period of time required to achieve continuity discounts can vary from one outdoor vehicle to another.

To illustrate outdoor cost calculations, let's consider a few media-buying examples. Rates and data from figure 12.9 are used to calculate costs.

Outdoor Buying Plan: Example 1

Medium:	Mall Posters
Markets:	Toronto, Montreal, Quebec City,and Winnipeg
Weight:	50 GRPs weekly
Contract Length:	24 weeks

Figure 12.9   Outdoor rate card

MO410
MALL POSTER RATES (4-wk. rates)

Market	Estimated 1990 population	25 GRPs weekly approx. panels	4-week rate	50 GRPs weekly approx. panels	4-week rate	75 GRPs weekly approx. panels	4-week rate	100 GRPs weekly approx. panels	4-week rate	% Continuity Discounts 24-wk	36-wk	52-wk
Toronto Metropolitan ESA	4,595,800	35	10,850	69	21,390	104	32,240	138	42,780	7	9	12
Montreal (CMA/RMR) & District	3,089,200	39	12,792	78	25,584	116	38,048	155	50,840	7	9	12
Vancouver (CMA/RMR)†	1,457,700	19	6,042	**39	11,817	*39	11,817	*39	11,817	3	6	9
Ottawa/Eastern Ontario ESA	992,900	11	3,113	23	6,509	34	9,622	46	13,018	7	9	12
Edmonton (CMA/RMR)†	812,300	9	3,150	18	6,300	27	9,450	35	12,250	—	—	—
Quebec City ESA	746,700	8	2,152	17	4,573	25	6,725	34	9,146	7	9	12
Winnipeg ESA	706,000	7	2,023	13	3,757	20	5,780	27	7,803	7	9	12
Calgary (CMA/RMR)†	702,000	10	3,350	19	6,365	29	9,715	38	12,730	—	—	—
London (CMA/RMR)/Sarnia (CMA/RMR)/Woodstock(C)†	458,500	7	2,100	14	4,200	*21	6,300	**21	6,300	*5	5	10
Kitchener (CMA/RMR)/Guelph (CA/AR)†	419,900	4	1,200	(8	2,400	**12	3,600	*12	3,600	*5	5	10
Central Quebec ESA	350,500	4	880	8	1,780	12	2,640	16	3,520	7	9	12
St. Catharines (CMA/RMR) & District+	349,700	4	1,200	9	2,700	**13	3,900	*13	3,900	*5	5	10
Halifax/Dartmouth (CMA/RMR) N.S./N.E.	306,200	#3	705	#3	705	#3	705	#3	705	7	9	12
Victoria (CMA/RMR)†	262,800	#3	840	#3	840	#3	840	#3	840	3	6	9
Sherbrooke District ESA	245,900	4	982	*7	2,455	12	3,437	16	4,419	7	9	12
Sudbury (CMA/RMR)/Elliot Lake (T-V)/Sault Ste. Marie (CA/AR)	242,300	*3	855	6	1,710	8	2,280	11	3,135	*3	6	9
Regina (CMA/RMR)/Moose Jaw (CA/AR)	231,500	2	580	*5	1,450	7	2030	9	2,610	7	9	12
Saskatoon (CMA/RMR)	220,400	*3	657	6	1,314	**9	1,971	*9	1,971	7	9	12
St. John's (CMA)/St. Jean (RMR) NFLD	165,800	*1	362	2	556	**3	834	*3	834	—	—	—
Thunder Bay (CMA/RMR)	120,700	*1	195	*2	390	3	585	4	780	7	9	12
Barrie (CA/AR)/Midland (CA/AR)/Huntsville (T-V)	120,100	1	285	*3	855	4	1,140	6	1,710	*3	6	9
Saint John (CMA)/St. Jean (RMR) N.B.	119,800	*2	554	**3	831	*3	831	*3	831	7	9	12
Moncton (CA/AR) N.B.	103,700	#2	832	#2	832	#2	832	#2	832	7	9	12
Renfrew (T-V) & County	88,100	1	250	1	250	2	450	3	645	*10	15	25
North Bay (CMA/RMR) & Dist.	84,800	1	250	2	450	3	645	4	748	*10	15	25
Timmins (C)	46,400	1	263	2	510	3	750	4	960	*3	6	9
Yorkton (CA) & District	41,300	*1	225	*1	225	1	225	1	225	5	5	10
The Pas (T) & District	10,000	*1	225	*1	225	1	225	I	225	5	5	10
TOTAL:	17,088,800	188	56,312	359	110,053	508	155,898	648	196,112			

*Rate is for closest available GRP. Consult your Poster Network representative for actual GRP delivery. **Maximum GRP level available. *Continuity discount applies to the total contract billing for continuous purchases of 20 GRPs or more. #Maximum GRP available is below 25 GRPs. Consult your Poster Network representative for actual GRP delivery. †A premium exists in this market for contracts less than 12 weeks; please see your Poster Network Representative for further information.

MO450
BACKLIGHTS SPACE FACTOR (4-week rates for 12-week contracts)

Market	Estimated 1990 Population	50 GRPs weekly approx. units	4-week rate	75 GRPs weekly approx. units	4-week rate	100 GRPs weekly approx. units	4-week rate	125 GRPs weekly approx. units	4-week rate	% Continuity 24-wk	36-wk	52-wk
Toronto (CMA/RMR)/Hamilton (CMA/RMR)/Oshawa (CMA/RMR)	4,434,700	15	18,765	23	28,773	30	37,530	38	47,538	7	9	12
Montreal (CMA/RMR)	2,924,500	6	7,542	9	11,313	13	16,341	16	20,112	7	9	12
Vancouver (CMA/RMR)	1,457,700	4	5,500	6	8,226	8	10,944	10	13,820	3	6	9
Ottawa/Hull (CMA/RMR)	857,400	4	5,004	6	7,506	8	10,008	10	12,510	7	9	12
Edmonton (CMA/RMR)	812,300	3	3,975	4	5,300	6	7,950	7	9,275	*5	5	10
Calgary (CMA/RMR)	702,000	*2	2,650	3	3,975	4	5,300	5	6,625	*5	5	10
Winnipeg (CMA/RMR)	645,600	2	2,440	*3	3,660	**3	3,680	*3	3,660	7	9	12
Quebec (CMA/RMR)	608,800	*3	3,660	4	4,880	6	7,320	7	8,540	7	9	12
London (CMA/RMR)	350,300	2	2,300	3	3,450	5	5,750	6	6,900	*5	5	10
St. Catharines-Niagara (CMA/RMR) & District	349,700	2	2,300	**4	4,600	*4	4,600	*4	4,600	*5	5	10
Kitchener (CMA/RMR)	328,600	2	2,300	3	3,450	5	5,750	6	6,900	*5	5	10
Halifax/Dartmouth (CMA/RMR) N.S./N.E.	306,200	1	1,220	2	2,440	3	3,680	4	4,880	7	9	12
Windsor (CMA/RMR)	253,800	*1	1,175	*2	2,350	**2	2,350	*2	2,350	—	—	—
Saskatoon (CMA/RMR)	220,400	*1	1,220	**2	2,440	*2	2,440	2	2,440	7	9	12
Regina (CMA/RMR)	194,200	1	1,220	*2	2,440	*2	2,440	2	2,440	7	9	12
Trois Rivieres (CMA/RMR) & District	193,400	**1	1,220	*1	1,220	*1	1,220	*1	1,220	7	9	12
St. John's (CMA)/St. Jean (RMR), Nfld	165,600	*1	1,190	*2	2,380	2	2,380	3	3,570	*5	5	10
Sudbury (CMA/RMR)	141,800	*1	1,000	*1	1,000	**1	1,000	*1	1,000	*5	5	10
Sherbrooke (CMA/RMR)	131,500	**1	1,220	*1	1,220	*1	1,220	*1	1,220	7	9	12
Kingston (CA/AR)	126,200	**1	1,220	*1	1,220	*1	1,220	*1	1,220	7	9	12
Thunder Bay (CMA/RMR)	120,700	*1	1,220	*1	1,220	*1	1,220	*1	1,220	7	9	12
Saint John (CMA)/St. Jean (RMR) N.B.	119,800	**1	1,220	*1	1,220	*1	1,220	*1	1,220	7	9	12
Moncton, (CA/AR) N.B.	103,700	**1	1,220	*1	1,220	*1	1,220	*1	1,220	7	9	12
Sarnia (CA/AR)	85,900	*1	1,150	*1	1,150	*1	1,150	1	1,100	*5	5	10
Barrie (CA/AR)	72,200	*1	1,360	*1	1,360	**1	1,360	*1	1,360	*3	6	9
Timmins (C)	46,400	*1	1,218	1	1,218	1	1,218	1	1,218	*3	6	9
Fredericton (C)	44,000	**1	1,220	*1	1,220	*1	1,220	*1	1,220	7	9	12
TOTAL:	15,797,400	61	75,729	90	111,776	113	140,541	138	169,353			

*Rate is for closest available GRP. Consult your Mediacom representative for actual GRP delivery. **Maximum GRP level available. *Continuity discount applies to total contract billing for continuous purchases of 40 GRPs or more.

Courtesy: Mediacom

According to figure 12.9, the costs for a four-week period for each market would be as follows:

Toronto	$21 390
Montreal	25 584
Quebec City	4 573
Winnipeg	3 757
	55 304

Since the length of the contract is 24 weeks, the cost of the markets above would be multiplied by six (24 weeks divided by four-week rates). The costs would be calculated as follows:

$$\$49\ 990 \times 6 = \$331\ 824.00$$

$$\textit{Less: } 6\% \text{ Continuity Discount } = \underline{\quad 23\ 227.68}$$

$$\text{Net Cost } = \$308\ 596.32$$

Outdoor Buying Plan: Example 2

Medium:	Backlights
Markets:	Toronto, Vancouver, Ottawa-Hull and Winnipeg
Weight:	75 GRPs weekly
Contract	Length: 24 weeks

Using the data from figure 12.9, we would calculate the appropriate costs for each market over a four-week period as follows (75-GRP column):

Toronto	$28 773
Vancouver	8 226
Ottawa-Hull	7 506
Winnipeg	3 660
	48 165

Since the length of the contract is 24 weeks, the total market costs above would be multiplied by six (24 weeks divided by four-week rate). Therefore, the total costs for this buying plan would be

$$\$48\ 165 \times 6 = \$288\ 990.00$$

$$\textit{Less: } 7\% \text{ Continuity Discount } = \underline{\quad 20\ 229.30}$$

$$\text{Net Cost } = \$268\ 760.70$$

TRANSIT ADVERTISING

The second major type of out-of-home media is transit advertising. Transit riders are a captive audience with a need for visual stimulation (they need relief from boredom, so they read advertising messages), and they are habitual transit users, so there is potential for the message to be seen repeatedly.

TYPES OF TRANSIT ADVERTISING

Interior Transit Cards

Interior **transit cards** or **car cards** are print advertisements contained in racks above the windows of public-transit vehicles (i.e., in buses and subway cars). The standard size of a car card is 23 1/4"× 11" (59 cm × 28 cm), with a double-sized option available (i.e., a card that is twice the length). Given that the audience is captive and that the average travelling time in a transit vehicle is estimated to be 28 minutes, the advertiser has the flexibility to include longer copy, which is not an option with other out-of-home media.[9] An interior transit illustration is included in figure 12.10.

Exterior Bus Posters

There are two options available in the **exterior-bus-poster** format. The first is a *large poster* (*king bus poster*) which is located on the sides of surface transit vehicles only. They are 139" × 30" (353 cm × 76 cm) in size, and are produced in two separate sections for creative flexibility. For example, one section could hold a permanent message, while the other section might carry special offers, sales advertisements, and so

Figure 12.10   Interior transit advertisement

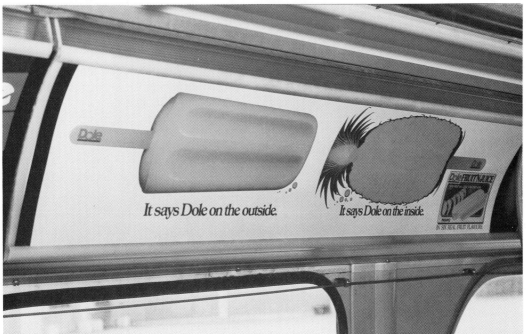

Courtesy: Trans Ad. A Jim Pattison Company. Reprinted with permission.

Figure 12.11 Exterior transit advertisement

Courtesy: Trans Ad. A Jim Pattison Company. Reprinted with permission.

on. The second option is a *smaller poster* that is normally located at the rear of surface-transit vehicles. These posters are somewhat smaller in size, conforming to the width of the bus. As with the larger side panels, *a channel strip* option is available, whereby three-quarters of the space is used for a permanent message, and the remainder for special offers and the like. The unique characteristic of exterior bus posters is their mobility. They move through every area of a city, and are seen by motorists, transit riders, and pedestrians. An illustration of an exterior bus poster is shown in figure 12.11.

Station Posters

Station posters are advertisements located on platforms and at the entrance and exit areas of the various subway and light-rail-transit systems in Canada. Trans Ad, one of the largest sellers of transit-advertising space in Canada, refers to this form of advertising as *SRO* (*Standing Room Only*), as the rider is exposed to the message while standing or walking in and out of a station. Station posters fall into two broad categories: *platform posters* and *subway back-lit*. Platform posters are located on the subway wall opposite the rider waiting on the platform. Two sizes are available: 62" × 48" (152 cm × 122 cm), composed of two sheets; or a much larger size of 144" × 65" (366 cm × 165 cm), composed of six sheets. In the Toronto subway system, posters are also attached to steel pillars in the area between rail lines. Passengers waiting on both platforms are exposed to these messages.

Figure 12.12   A digital-display-unit advertisement

Courtesy: Trans Ad.

The second option is subway back-lits, which are located above and below escalator stairwells throughout the Toronto and Montreal subway systems. Light-rail transit systems in Vancouver, Edmonton, and Calgary also have a variety of back-lit and poster options available.

Digital Advertising-Display Units

Digital-display units are located in high-profile positions on every Toronto-subway and Vancouver-Sky-Train platform. The display unit features the time, transit information, news items, weather, and advertising messages (see figure 12.12). Two of the unique characteristics of this medium are its immediacy and its flexibility. In terms of immediacy, copy can be changed up until the day before the message is communicated. In terms of flexibility, different messages can be run at different times of the day in accordance with the changing demographic profile of the riders (business people ride during the rush hours, shoppers in the daytime).

ADVANTAGES OF TRANSIT

Continuous Exposure

Commuters tend to be creatures of routine, so they are exposed to messages every day of the week. As indicated earlier, the average ride is 28 minutes in length, so messages are eagerly read by riders attempting to escape the boredom of the ride. In this regard, transit advertisements are a good vehicle for reinforcing the messages of in-home media.

Reach and Frequency

Very similar to outdoor advertising, transit advertising reaches a mass audience quickly. Transit riders cut across all demographics, with heaviest concentration in the adult category. Consumers generally encounter the message more than once because of daily ridership patterns, and the combination of high reach and frequency translates into an extremely high number of impressions on the target market. Factors such as the rising costs of running a car and the increasing numbers of commuters travelling to and from a city each day for work have had a positive effect on the reach potential of transit.

Flexibility

Certain transit media are flexible in that the message can be changed easily. For example, digital-display units can be changed up to the day prior to the communication of the message, and exterior bus posters offer merchandising flexibility. For example, a portion of a poster can display a permanent message and another portion can display a short-term message that can be changed periodically. In terms of geography, transit markets can be purchased on an individual basis, so it is a good complementary medium to add reach and frequency in a total advertising campaign.

Market Coverage

In any given market, transit advertising covers all sectors of an urban/suburban community—industrial, commercial, and residential areas—where other forms of out-of-home media may not be available.

Cost

On a market-by-market basis, the dollar outlay for transit-media space is relatively low, and, considering the number of consumers reached, the cost per thousand is low. Essentially, transit is a cost-efficient medium that reaches a mass audience. As a result, it is attractive to smaller-budget advertisers and retailers (assuming, of course, that a retailer's target market uses transit vehicles).

DISADVANTAGES OF TRANSIT

Lack of Target-Market Selectivity

In large urban markets, transit use reflects the general, non-specific demographic and socioeconomic characteristics of those markets.[10] Therefore, for an advertiser who is attempting to reach a precisely defined target, the use of transit results in waste circulation. Consequently, the cost-per-thousand efficiencies, which are based on high reach of a mass audience, may be artificially low.

Media Environment

Transit advertising is not granted the status of an important advertising medium. In the case of interior transit, the environment is often cluttered and crowded (particularly at peak-usage periods such as rush hour), a circumstance which makes the messages both less visible and less attractive. This environment may detract from the prestige of the product.

Creative Limitations

While transit advertising offers good colour reproduction, the actual amount of space it provides advertisers to work with is quite small. In the case of exterior bus posters and platform posters, there is a bit more creative flexibility.

BUYING TRANSIT ADVERTISING

Transit advertising rates are affected by variables such as the number of markets being covered, the length of the showing (which affects discounts), the weight level desired in any given market, and the size of the space required. Transit space is generally sold on the basis of four-week minimums and is available on a market-by-market basis. Advertisers can purchase space in a group of cities in a region to qualify for greater discounts: major Canadian market cities might compose a group, or cities within a geographic region. Trans Ad, a Jim Pattison company, is the largest seller of transit advertising space in Canada. This firm represents many urban transit properties across Canada.

The first thing to consider when purchasing transit space is the weight level desired in each market. As in outdoor advertising, transit weight is expressed in terms of GRPs (gross rating points), with GRP referring to the total circulation of a showing expressed as a percentage of a market's population. For an illustration of the GRP concept and its effect on costs, refer to figure 12.13.

Transit Rates and Discounts

As indicated earlier, all rates are based on the purchase of a four-week period of time, starting with a base rate for each market purchased. A continuity discount is available to advertisers who meet predetermined time commitments. As is shown in figure 12.13, discounts are available at 12-, 24-, 36-, and 52-week periods, with the percentage of the discount increasing with the time commitment. A market discount is available to advertisers that purchase a selected group of markets. As figure 12.13 shows, the purchase of all "A" markets results in an additional 5% discount. A national discount is also available if all markets are purchased for the same time period.

Let's consider a media-buying example, using the rates and data of figure 12.13 as a basis for calculating transit costs.

Transit Buying Plan: Example

Medium:	Exterior Bus Posters
Markets:	All "A" Markets
Weight:	300 GRPs
Contract Length:	24 weeks

According to figure 12.13, the costs for "A" markets over a four-week period would be as follows:

Figure 12.13 Exterior transit rate card

EXTERIOR KING BUS POSTERS: 139″ wide x 30″ high
RATES SHOWN ARE PER FOUR WEEK SHOWING

A MARKETS	WEEKLY GRP LEVEL									
	500		400		300		200		100	
	RATE	NO.	RATE	NO.	RATE	NO.	RATE	NO.	RATE	NO.
OTTAWA	$ 5,950	65	$ 5,010	52	$ 3,940	39	$ 2,745	26	$ 1,435	13
TORONTO	36,670	302	30,930	242	23,700	181	16,230	121	8,245	60
WINNIPEG	6,425	69	5,390	55	4,205	41	2,900	27	1,570	14
CALGARY	6,775	72	5,645	57	4,460	43	3,035	28	1,595	14
EDMONTON	7,145	78	5,975	62	4,740	47	3,270	31	1,770	16
VANCOUVER/FRASER VLY.	15,340	151	12,940	121	10,015	91	6,900	61	3,485	30
TOTAL	78,305	737	65,890	589	51,060	442	35,080	294	18,100	148
TOTAL INCL. 5% DISC.	74,390		62,595		50,805		33,325		17,195	

B MARKETS		WEEKLY GRP LEVEL									
		500		400		300		200		100	
		RATE	NO.	RATE	NO.	RATE	NO.	RATE	NO.	RATE	NO.
ATLANTIC REGION	HALIFAX/DARTMOUTH, N.S.	$ 3,775	32	$ 3,105	25	$ 2,510	19	$ 1,825	13	$ 890	6
QUEBEC REGION	HULL	1,835	20	1,545	16	1,215	12	845	8	440	4
ONTARIO REGION	LONDON	3,520	30	3,335	27	2,625	20	1,805	13	1,035	7
	HAMILTON	6,410	54	5,370	43	4,100	32	2,750	21	1,475	11
PRAIRIE REGION	REGINA. SASK.	2,560	22	2,080	17	1,700	13	1,110	8	595	4
	SASKATOON, SASK.	2,455	21	1,965	16	1,565	12	1,110	8	595	4
PACIFIC REGION	VICTORIA	3,535	30	2,975	24	2,340	18	1,665	12	875	6
	TOTAL	24,090	209	20,375	168	16,055	126	11,110	83	5,905	42
	TOTAL INCL. 15% DISC.	20,475		17,315		13,645		9,440		5,020	

NOTE: When B Markets are purchased in conjuction with Regional Markets the discount becomes 20%, with the exception of Hull.

RATES & DISCOUNTS

Rates are for four (4) weeks. Rates are for space only and subject to change without notice. Production is the responsibility of the advertiser.

Any contract less than four (4) weeks will be pro-rated to a weekly rate plus an installation fee equal to 10% of the four week rate.

12 WEEK DISCOUNT: deduct 6% per four (4) week showing for contracts of twelve (12) continuous weeks.

24 WEEK DISCOUNT: deduct 12% per four (4) week showing for contracts of twenty-four (24) continuous weeks.

36 WEEK DISCOUNT: deduct 16% per four (4) week showing for contracts of thirty-six (36) continuous weeks.

52 WEEK DISCOUNT: deduct 20% per four (4) week showing for contracts of fifty-two (52) continuous weeks.

REGIONAL DISCOUNT: if all markets within a region are purchased for the same time period, a discount of 20% per four (4) week showing is earned as shown.

NATIONAL DISCOUNT: deduct a further 2½% per four (4) week showing if all markets are purchased for the same time period.

CONTINUITY DISCOUNT: extensions to 12 week, 24 week, 36 week and 52 week contracts continue to earn the respective discounts.

MARKET DISCOUNT: If all A Markets/B Markets are purchased for the same time period, discounts are earned as shown.

REGIONAL MARKETS	WEEKLY GRP LEVEL							
	400		300		200		100	
	RATE	NO.	RATE	NO.	RATE	NO.	RATE	NO.
SYDNEY, N.S.	$ 1,250	10	$1,060	8	$ 705	5	$ 445	3
SAINT JOHN, N.B.	1,250	10	1,060	8	705	5	445	3
FREDERICTON, N.B.	625	5	530	4	430	3	300	2
TOTAL	3,125	25	2,650	20	1,840	13	1,190	8
TOTAL INCL. 20% DISC.	2,500		2,120		1,470		950	
GUELPH	870	7	790	6	560	4	305	2
KINGSTON	1,360	11	1,055	8	695	5	445	3
NIAGARA FALLS	870	7	790	6	560	4	305	2
SARNIA	995	8	790	6	560	4	305	2
ST. CATHARINES	1,485	12	1,180	9	840	6	445	3
THUNDER BAY	1,360	11	1,055	8	840	6	445	3
WINDSOR	2,840	23	2,230	17	1,530	11	740	5
WOODSTOCK	380	3	265	2	145	1	145	1
TOTAL	10,160	82	8,155	62	5,730	40	3,135	21
TOTAL INCL. 20% DISC.	8,125		6,525		4,585		2,505	
BRANDON, MAN.	495	4	395	3	280	2		
MOOSE JAW, SASK.	495	4	395	3	280	2		
GRANDE PRAIRIE, ALTA.	265	2	265	2	145	1		
LETHBRIDGE, ALTA.	625	5	535	4	420	3		
MEDICINE HAT, ALTA.	625	5	400	3	290	2		
RED DEER, ALTA.	625	5	535	4	420	3		
TOTAL	3,130	25	2,525	19	1,835	13		
TOTAL INCL. 20% DISC.	2,505		2,020		1,465			
KAMLOOPS	745	6	665	5	420	3		
KELOWNA	995	8	795	6	560	4		
KITIMAT	145	1	145	1	145	1		
NANAIMO	745	6	530	4	280	2		
NELSON	145	1	145	1	145	1		
PENTICTON	270	2	270	2	145	1		
PORT ALBERNI	270	2	270	2	145	1		
POWELL RIVER	270	2	145	1	145	1		
PRINCE GEORGE	745	6	665	5	420	3		
PRINCE RUPERT	270	2	145	1	145	1		
TERRACE	270	2	270	2	145	1		
TRAIL	270	2	145	1	145	1		
TOTAL	5,140	40	4,190	31	2,840	20		
TOTAL INCL. 20% DISC.	4,110		3,350		2,275			

ALL RATES AND SPECIFICATIONS SUBJECT TO CHANGE WITHOUT NOTICE

Courtesy: Trans Ad. A Jim Pattison Company. Reprinted with permission.

Ottawa	$ 3 940
Toronto	23 700
Winnipeg	4 205
Calgary	4 460
Edmonton	4 740
Vancouver/Fraser Valley	10 015
	51 060
Total (including 5% discount)	50 805

Since the length of the contract is 24 weeks, and the cost is $50 805 for four weeks, the cost would be multiplied by six.

$50 805 × 6	=	$304 830
Less: 12% Market Discount	=	36 580
Net Cost (24 weeks)	=	268 250

*P*OINT-OF-PURCHASE ADVERTISING

Point-of-purchase (POP) advertising can be defined as advertising or display materials set up at a retail location to build traffic, advertise a product, and encourage impulse buying. Unlike other forms of advertising, point-of-purchase is positioned where the product or service is immediately available to consumers. Thus it closes the gap between consumer advertising and actual sales. Gerald H. Long, the president and chief executive officer of R.J. Reynolds Tobacco Company, pointed out the effectiveness of point-of-purchase when he stated that "each form of advertising has its role, but, in very candid terms, POP is the only form that is at hand when consumers reach for their money."[11]

THE EFFECTIVENESS OF POINT-OF-PURCHASE ADVERTISING

The main reason for using point-of-purchase advertising is to remind consumers of a product just prior to their making a purchase decision. It is a medium that can provide a finishing touch to a well-integrated advertising and promotion program. Studies conducted by the Point-Of-Purchase Advertising Institute (POPAI) in the United States reveal that when the imagery of a television commercial is graphically repeated in an in-store display, sales increase significantly.[12] Figure 12.14 shows that a significantly higher purchase response is achieved if various combinations of in-store merchandising activities are implemented.

TYPES OF POINT-OF-PURCHASE ADVERTISING

On-premise signs, window displays, display racks, display shippers, wall displays, display cards, audiovisual displays, and vending machines are some of the more common types of point-of-purchase advertising.

Figure 12.14 Effectiveness of point-of-purchase advertising

Form of Advertising	Incremental Response (%)
Unadvertised price reduction	+35
Price reduction plus ad feature	+173
Unadvertised price reduction plus in-store display	+279
Price reduction plus ad feature plus in-store display	+545

The increased response is based on a comparison with an unsupported trade promotion

Source: Adapted from *1989 Topical Marketing Report*, Information Resources Inc., Chicago.

On-Premise Signs

The primary function of a store sign is to identify the business. The style and lettering of the sign (i.e., the store logo) become familiar to customers in the market area, and help draw them to the business. The logo style of the business sign is integrated with other forms of store advertising. McDonald's "golden arches" exemplify the familiar sign that can be seen from a great distance by passing motorists or pedestrian traffic.

Window Displays

Window displays can be an effective form of communication for retail outlets that rely on pedestrian traffic in shopping malls or in the main streets of a shopping district. For passersby who have never shopped in a particular store, the window display can help create a first impression. Since first impressions are often lasting impressions, the window display must create a positive impression, reflecting the store atmosphere and the quality of merchandise carried. The display should be appropriate for the nature of the business, and effective enough to grab consumers' attention as they pass by. In addition to showcasing merchandise, window displays can be used to promote in-store sales.

There are two types of window displays: promotional display windows and institutional display racks.

Promotional Display Windows As the name implies, the window displays a selection of the merchandise carried by the store.

Institutional Display Window A display which promotes the store itself, the institutional display window is used to instill a more positive image of the store in the consumer's mind. For example, many stores develop special window displays at Christmas time that highlight the spirit of the season rather than the store merchandise. Simpsons in Toronto is famous for its animated Christmas windows.

Modular Display Racks

A **modular display rack** is a permanent display unit, provided by a manufacturer to display a certain line of merchandise. These types of units are usually made of wire and metal (e.g., candy and gum counter-displays, potato-chip racks in variety stores) or plastic materials. The primary advantage of a display rack is that, for as long as the display rack remains, the merchandise is located outside its normal environment, by itself, away from the competition. Signage can be appended to the display unit to help draw attention to it. Depending on the size of the unit, a poster, shelf poster, or tear-off ad pad can be integrated into modular displays to communicate special sales or promotions.

Department Makers

A **department maker** is a more elaborate, often permanent, merchandise-display unit. The nature of a department maker is such that it creates a "store within a store," as it is used to merchandise a range of manufacturers' products. Permanent display units are popular for merchandising an assortment of colours and sizes of one product line. Department makers may be located with regular shelving (integrated into supermarket aisle-displays), or be located away from competing products. Spices and extracts are commonly sold from permanent merchandise-display units in grocery stores.

Display Shippers

A **display shipper** is a corrugated-cardboard shipping carton containing a predetermined amount of merchandise, which, when assembled, forms a temporary display at the point-of-purchase. These are designed to encourage impulse purchases, and they are often used to merchandise products that are seasonal in nature. Display shippers for Hallowe'en candies and for the summer barbecue season (exhibiting barbecue-related products such as spices and sauces) are quite common. Display shippers are very common in grocery and drugstore outlets, and are usually sold through the head office of the retail organization. The displays are used at the discretion of store management, and can be assembled by store personnel or the manufacturer's field sales representative.

Wall Displays

Wall displays are a more elaborate form of signage which draw attention to a certain brand of merchandise. In a restaurant or retail store, a clock displaying the name and logo of a soft drink or brand of cigarettes is not unusual. In a tavern or pub, a clock or mirror featuring the name of a certain beer is quite common. Such display units expose customers to last-second messages prior to their making a purchase.

Display Cards

Display cards include paper or paperboard posters, counter display posters (which are smaller in size than traditional posters), shelf talkers (small-size posters that hang from the store shelves where the product is located), and tear-off ad pads. Designed to encourage impulse purchases, these forms of advertising can be used in conjunction with display windows, display shippers, modular racks, or regular shelf merchandisers. Retailers utilize shelf talkers extensively in end-of-aisle displays and with regular shelf-merchandise to draw attention to weekly specials. Manufacturers commonly use tear-off ad pads to promote contests, refunds, and other sales promotion activity (see figure 12.15).

Figure 12.15 Point-of-purchase shelf pad/ad pad. Tear-off advertisements for special promotions that accompany product displays or shelf merchandise

Courtesy: Campbell Soup Company Ltd. Reprinted with permission.

Audiovisual Displays

Large department stores and national chain stores now utilize audiovisual displays frequently. Audiovisual displays can be short-term in nature, that is, they can be used to promote the sale of a special line of merchandise while it is on sale. For example, television monitors and videocassette units are sometimes integrated into aisle displays so that attention is drawn to special offers. On a long-term basis, television monitors are mounted into permanent display areas of department stores, and are used to draw attention to product lines carried in the department where the monitor is located (e.g., sporting goods, sportswear, men's and ladies' fashions). The displays are permanent, while the content of the message can be readily changed. For more information on the role and effectiveness of videos, refer to the Advertising in Action vignette "Closing the Loop."

Vending Machines

A long-standing tradition in the softdrink industry, vending machines are an effective form of point-of-purchase advertising. The design and advertising potential of softdrink vending machines have advanced considerably, to the point where the face panels (plastic front panels illuminated by interior lights) resemble a back-lit poster. Since significant softdrink sales are attributed to vending machines, softdrink manufacturers compete fiercely to improve the display power of their machines.

Other Point-of-Purchase Advertising

The supermarket industry in Canada has been particularly innovative regarding new forms of in-store advertising and merchandising concepts. In addition to using the traditional forms of POP advertising, such as window banners, colour posters, and shelf talkers, grocery chains are utilizing grocery-cart advertising, video television, and information centres that distribute direct-mail advertising.

Grocery-Cart Advertising **Grocery-cart advertising** is advertising done on 10" × 8" full-colour posters that are appended to the ends of shopping carts. Shoppers facing an

Advertising in Action
Closing the Loop

One of the hottest and fastest growing areas of advertising in retailing is the in-store video. For many retailers and advertisers whose goods are stocked by retailers, the in-store video closes the loop on major media campaigns, reinforcing the key selling message at the point of purchase. In Canada, the largest users of in-store videos are department stores such as the Bay, Eaton's, and Sears, and discount department stores such as K Mart and Zellers. They are used to promote sports videos, records and compact discs, sports equipment, major appliances, and fashion apparel. Sometimes the message is an elaborate demonstration of something technical, or a quick 20-second clip about a new product on display in the immediate selling area.

U.S. retailers are well ahead of their Canadian counterparts in the use of in-store video advertising. In the U.S., much research has been conducted into in-store advertising, and a series of basic guidelines have been established on the subject of how to improve the effectiveness of video-display messages. If used properly, video can provide both effectiveness (in terms of message) and efficiency (in terms of spending media dollars) to potential advertisers. For advertisers contemplating the use of in-store videos, there are several variables that must be considered in advance. For example, what should the tone and style of the message be? How long should the message be? How can the in-store message be integrated with broader-based messages in other media, and with marketing strategies?

Here are some of the known facts about in-store video advertising that should be considered:

1. The quantity of exposures a display generates is of concern to all advertisers. Maximizing exposure depends on one's knowledge of pedestrian-traffic patterns in the store. Sometimes a slight repositioning of a unit has a dramatic effect on the numbers of shoppers who see the display. Because of the nature of the medium, exposures come in strings—if one person stops to look, the likelihood of others stopping increases dramatically. For this reason, the display must always face the customer. Research studies have shown that the best location is not necessarily the busiest corridor where traffic congestion is likely to occur. Quieter locations within a department, where there is a captive audience, have proven to be better.

2. Consumers apparently perceive in-store video ads to be different from television ads they view at home. They are perceived to be more of an electronic poster than a television commercial. For this reason, advertisers are uncertain about how effective video messages are; they may only get a passing glance from shoppers. Another factor complicating the message issue is the competition from a stimuli-rich store environment where there are strange people, and a variety of sights, sounds, and smells. Further, research indicates that the average time of exposure to consumers is less than 15 seconds, so grabbing attention quickly is paramount. A good soundtrack is essential for grabbing attention, since people tend to respond to sound first. Shoppers tend to be attracted to quick and intimate exchanges between people, exchanges that have been preceded by a musical hook.

In-store videos are more effective with certain demographic target groups than with others. Not surprisingly, children and teenagers are the easiest groups to reach with a

continued

video message, for they are the video generation. Among adults, men in the 25-49-year age range are good targets, and generally speaking, men stop more frequently and for longer periods than women do.

Adapted from Paco Underhill, "In-store video ads can reinforce media campaigns," *Marketing News*, May 22, 1990, pp. 5,7.

approaching shopping cart are exposed to the message. The medium provides advertisers with last-minute exposure right at the point of purchase. Grocery-cart advertising is available in a variety of supermarket chains in major markets from coast to coast.

InfoCentre/InfoShelf Advertising These advertising media are located in major supermarket and drugstore chains across the country. InfoCentres are multi-dimensional display units equipped for poster advertising and the distribution of brochures and promotional material (coupons and contest-entry forms). InfoShelf is an on-shelf merchandising-and-promotion system that involves ad pads bearing coupons, contest entries, and recipes. Often the ad pads are contained in their own holder, and located on the shelf where the product is located.

ADVANTAGES OF POINT-OF-PURCHASE ADVERTISING

Message Reinforcement

While the display itself stimulates action, the incidence of consumer action increases when the display visuals are used to supplement the advertising done in other media (e.g., in-home media). Point-of-purchase reinforces prior messages, finalizing sales to consumers who have been preconditioned by other forms of advertising.

Message Receptiveness

POP addresses the message to consumers when they are shopping (i.e., it appeals in the right place, at the right time, and to the right audience). Since consumers generally shop in stores that they can afford, the selling message is visible to the desired target audience.

Commands Attention

The consumer's eye is drawn to the product or service by point-of-purchase. Effective use of colour and display will make a product stand out from among competitors in a retail outlet.

Impulse Purchasing

Especially in the case of frequently purchased product categories such as candies, snack foods, toiletries, and beverages, point-of-purchase advertising stimulates impulse purchasing. Since research indicates that many purchases in drug and grocery stores are unplanned, there is ample opportunity for point-of-purchase to influence last-minute decisions.

Last Chance (Deciding Factors) in Sale

For product categories where impulse buying is not a factor (such as expensive durable goods), point-of-purchase material can be used to inform and educate consumers. Automobile dealers rely heavily on the colour brochures in their showrooms to communicate some of the technological aspects of engine specifications, option lists, and so on, while other parts of the brochure illustrate the vehicle's more glamorous benefits. These types of advertisements go home with the customer, are perused in detail, and play a major role in bringing the customer back to the showroom.

Merchandise Tie-ins

Point-of-purchase advertising promotes the trial of new products, new packaging, and new sizes and flavours. It calls attention to warranties, rebate programs, contests, and other forms of promotion activity. It is also an effective vehicle for developing cross-promotions with related products sold in the same store (soup and crackers, potato chips and dips, bandages and antiseptics, etc.).

DISADVANTAGES OF POINT-OF-PURCHASE

Placement

The most eye-catching display will be ineffective if it is not located in the appropriate position in the store. The problem facing the retailer is the limited area in which to place the abundant display material available from manufacturers. If good placements are not found, the displays will not achieve sales objectives.

Clutter

Consider the number of displays you are exposed to while walking through a drug, grocery, or hardware store. Assuming a retailer grants a manufacturer permission to erect a display or poster material, the manufacturer's display will face considerable competition from other products in commanding consumers' attention. Due to clutter, some displays will be relegated to poor locations (and then they may as well not be there at all).

Design

The design of point-of-purchase display units is a specialty in itself. The display must get the attention of customers and make it easy for them to purchase the products. The display should not detract from the product; it should simply make the product noticeable and accessible.

Waste

Some displays and other point-of-purchase materials never get erected in the store. Manufacturers generally require permission from the retail store's head office to erect display units in corporate-owned retail stores such as Loblaws, Safeway, A&P, and Shoppers Drug Mart. Even if permission is granted, if and how the display units will be utilized is often left to the discretion of store managers. Securing co-operation from retail managers is the responsibility of the field sales force. This can be a difficult task at times.

OTHER FORMS OF OUT-OF-HOME ADVERTISING

It seems that there are always new ways to advertise products and services. Some of the new and unique vehicles for sending messages include: aerial advertising, bench advertising, coupon advertising, elevator advertising, sports advertising, stadium advertising, taxicab advertising, and theatre-screen advertising.

Aerial Advertising Aerial advertising includes advertising done by banner towing, remote-control inflatable balloons, hot-air balloons, and airships.

Bench Advertising This is advertising that appears on park benches and benches at or near transit stops.

Coupon Advertising Referred to as free-standing inserts, advertisements and product coupons are distributed in publications such as *Coupon Clipper*, and *Shop & Save*. These publications reach consumers through daily-newspaper distribution.

Elevator Advertising This sort of advertising entails glass display-cases on side panels adjacent to control panels in high-rise elevators.

Sports Advertising Sports advertising appears in the form of signs affixed to arena boards, plastic signboards on golf courses, and poster advertising on ski-lift towers.

Stadium Advertising This is an advertising medium used, for example, in the SkyDome. Options available in the SkyDome include back-lit signs on concourses, fixed signs in the bowl or seating area, product displays in concourses, commercial time on the world's largest videoscreen, and temporary signs during special events.

Taxicab Advertising Taxicab advertisements are roof-mounted back-lit panels or poster advertising on the backs of cab trunks.

Theatre-Screen Advertising These advertisements are one-minute commercials much like those appearing on commercial television; they are shown just prior to the start of the feature presentation.

Summary

Direct advertising is one of the largest advertising media in Canada. The major form of direct-response advertising is direct mail. Direct mail includes communications in the form of sales letters, flyers, statement stuffers, and catalogues.

The primary advantages of direct mail for advertisers are its audience selectivity (which makes it an excellent medium for the business advertiser), high reach potential, and its geographic flexibility. Disadvantages include the absence of editorial support, and poor image. The success of any direct-mail campaign largely depends on the quality of the list the advertiser uses. Lists are available from list suppliers and other secondary sources such as directories and trade indexes.

Out-of-home media are composed of outdoor, transit, and point-of-purchase media. The various forms of outdoor advertising are posters, superboards, back-lit posters, spectaculars, transit shelters, and mall posters. Outdoor advertising offers high target reach and frequency, and geographic flexibility. Among the weaknesses of outdoor advertising are its lack of target-market selectivity and the creative limitations related to the speed at which people pass by.

There are various forms of transit advertising, including interior and exterior cards, station posters, and digital-display units. Transit advertising offers continuous exposure (a result of transit users' consistent travel patterns), and high reach and frequency against a general target market. The major weaknesses of the medium are the lack of target-market selectivity it offers and the creative limitations owing to space restrictions.

Point-of-purchase advertising is designed to influence impulse purchasing and encourage shoppers to make last-minute purchase decisions. The benefits it offers are offset by the lack of use (or support) it receives from retailers who have an endless supply of manufacturers' display materials to choose from. The major types of point-of-purchase materials include signs, window displays, display racks and merchandise, and display cards. Some recent innovations include expanded utilization of video television, especially in department stores, and the use of information-display centres that distribute coupons and other promotional literatures. New forms of advertising media include aerial advertising, bench advertising, elevator advertising, sports advertising, stadium advertising, and theatre-screen advertising.

Review Questions

1. What is the difference between direct-response advertising and direct advertising?
2. What is the difference between a solo direct-mail campaign and a co-operative direct-mail campaign?
3. What characteristics make a product suitable for direct-mail advertising?
4. What are the advantages and disadvantages of direct-mail advertising for a business-product advertiser (e.g., a manufacturer of business equipment)?
5. What are the major types of transit advertising?
6. What types of products or services are suitable for transit advertising?
7. Evaluate the pros and cons of transit as an advertising medium.
8. Identify and briefly describe the major types of point-of-purchase advertising.
9. Explain the following terms in the context of the term in parentheses:
   a) superboard (outdoor)
   b) spectacular (outdoor)
   c) 75 GRPs (outdoor)
   d) continuity discount (outdoor)
   e) market discount (transit)
   f) continuity discount (transit)

Discussion Questions

1. "The dollars an advertiser invests in direct-mail advertising are wasted owing to the low image of the medium." Discuss this statement.
2. "Out-of-home media are primarily recognized as means of complementing other media forms." True or false? Discuss this statement, assuming the role of marketing manager—first for a television station, and then for an outdoor advertising company.
3. There is statistical evidence showing point-of purchase advertising to be effective in prompting purchase response, at least in the short term (see figure 12.14). Should advertisers be spending more or less on this form of advertising in the future? Should investment in this form of advertising come at the expense of traditional brand advertising in the mass media? Discuss these issues, using examples of your choice.

Illustrative Case for Part Four

Media-Cost Calculations

The purpose of this case is to provide the student with an opportunity to calculate the media costs for a variety of different media buys. Prior to starting the exercise, the student should refer to the sample illustrations in chapters 10, 11 and 12 to confirm their understanding of procedure. Also, a review of the content of certain rate cards in these chapters is necessary.

To complete this exercise, students will use the rate cards contained in the text-book to obtain cost information. The following rate cards are the ones needed to complete the exercises:

Figure 10.3	The *Globe and Mail* rate card
Figure 10.6	*Report on Business Magazine* rate card
Figure 11.2	CKCO-TV program schedule
Figure 11.4	CKCO-TV rate card
Figure 11.7	CKLC/CFLY rate card
Figure 12.9	Outdoor rate card
Figure 12.13	Exterior transit rate card

The objective of this exercise is to calculate the total net cost for each plan, taking into account any discounts that may apply.

Plan 1

Medium:	*The Globe and Mail/National Edition*
Ad Size:	3 columns wide by 5 units deep
Frequency:	2 insertions per week for 12 weeks
Specifications:	all ads are black and 1-colour

Plan 2

Medium:	*Report on Business Magazine*
Ad Size:	2/3 page and full page
Frequency:	8 insertions for 2/3-page ad
	2 insertions for full page (full-page ads on inside-back cover)
Specifications:	all ads are 4-colour

Plan 3

Medium:	CKLC/CFLY radio
Length:	all ads are 30–second spots
Daypart:	2 breakfast spots per day, Mon.–Fri. and 3 daytime spots per day, Mon.-Fri.
Period:	30 weeks

Plan 4

Medium:	CKCO-TV Kitchener
Length:	all ads are 30-second spots

Daypart:	3 AA spots per week
	4 A spots per week
	3 B spots per week
Period:	AA and B spots cover an 8-week schedule
	A spots cover a 16-week schedule

Plan 5

Medium:	mall posters
Markets:	Toronto, Montreal, Ottawa, and Winnipeg
Weight:	75 GRPs
Period:	24 weeks in all markets

Plan 6

Medium:	exterior transit space
Markets:	all "A" markets and the following "B" markets: Niagara Falls, St. Catharines, Thunder Bay, Brandon, Moose Jaw, Kamloops, Kelowna, Nanaimo
Weight:	300 GRPs in "A" markets for 16 weeks and 400 GRPs in "B" markets for 12 weeks

Plan 7

Media:	combination of CKCO-TV and mall posters
Market:	Kitchener

1. Television

Ad Length:	all television commercials are 30-second spots
Shows:	"Hunter" — 1 spot per week
	"Knots Landing" — 1 spot per week
	"Midnight Caller" — 1 spot per week
	"Scan News Hour" — 1 spot, 5 days per week, Mon.–Fri.
Period:	All spots cover a 12-week period, except the news spots, which are scheduled over 16 weeks

2. Mall Posters

Weight:	100 GRPS weekly
Period:	24-week schedule

Plan 8

Media:	combination of *The Globe and Mail* and back-lit posters

1. Newspaper

Markets:	*Globe and Mail* Metro Edition
Ad Size:	4 columns wide by 5 units deep
Frequency:	2 insertions per week for 10 weeks
Specifications:	all ads are black & white

2. Back-lits

Markets:	Toronto, Hamilton, Oshawa (CMA)
Weight:	100 GRPs weekly
Period:	24 weeks

Specialized Forms of Advertising

The basic objective of this section of the text is to describe the unique factors that influence three specific forms of advertising: sales promotion, business-to-business advertising, and retail advertising.

Previous sections of the book focused on the relationships between marketing planning and advertising planning, creative and media planning, and the process of developing objectives, strategies, and tactical plans in advertising. All of these variables influence the unique forms of advertising presented in this section. Chapter 13 presents the various sales-promotion techniques and activities that advertisers integrate into advertising plans. Chapter 14 introduces variables that have an influence on the planning of business-to-business advertising, and chapter 15 presents the considerations unique to retail advertising. Creative and media-strategy considerations for all of the specialized forms of advertising are discussed in this section.

PART V

CHAPTER 13 Sales
Promotion

In studying this chapter, you will learn about

- The promotion-expenditure trends and objectives for consumer-promotion and trade-promotion activities

- The various types of consumer- and trade-promotion activities

- The special creative and media-strategy considerations for advertising a promotion

This chapter focuses on sales-promotion activities. In the context of promotion and marketing planning, the manager must evaluate the contribution that sales-promotion activity will make to the achievement of overall objectives. A sales-promotion plan based on overall marketing direction is developed separately and then integrated into the promotion plan. The activities outlined in a sales-promotion plan complement the advertising effort.

Initial discussion reviews the nature and intent of promotion activity in general, and reviews some recent spending patterns of Canadian companies. The various types of consumer-promotion and trade-promotion activities are then presented, and the chapter ends with a brief look at some creative and media factors that should be considered in the development of sales-promotion activity.

SALES PROMOTION——WHAT IS IT?

Sales promotion can be defined as activity designed to generate a quick response from consumers, distributors (wholesalers and retailers), and the field sales force. Sales-promotion plans are developed with these three groups in mind. The consumer, or final user, must be motivated to take advantage of the promotion offer. The distributor must actively support the promotion to achieve its goals—greater volume of sales, higher profit margins, inventory movement, and so on. Finally, the sales force must be motivated to sell the promotion to the trade at the wholesale and retail levels, in order to make the promotion work successfully for their firm.

Sales-promotion activity can be subdivided into two broad categories: consumer promotion and trade promotion. **Consumer promotions** refer to those activities that are designed to stimulate consumer purchase, in effect to help pull the product through the distribution channel. Common types of consumer-promotion activities include coupons, free-sample offers, contests, and cash-back offers. **Trade promotions** refer to those activities designed to encourage distributors to purchase additional volume and provide additional support to stimulate consumer purchase. In effect, trade promotions help push the product through the distribution channel. Common types of trade-promotion activities include price discounts and allowances, co-operative advertising funds, and point-of-purchase display materials.

PROMOTION EXPENDITURE TRENDS

A problem facing marketing and advertising planners as they develop the various plans is determining how much money to allocate to the various areas. In the total marketing budget, the first decision to be made concerns the division between media expenditures and promotion expenditures. Whether the promotion budget should allocate more to consumer promotion or to trade promotion must be decided.

Most manufacturers would prefer to spend a greater proportion of their marketing budget on activities directed at the consumer or final user, but this is not generally feasible. The realities of business practice in the nineties do not allow for such a

Figure 13.1 Marketing budget allocations among Canadian packaged-goods companies

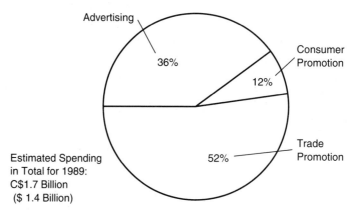

Source: A.C Nielsen Company of Canada Limited

practice. In fact, just slightly more than half of a marketing budget on average is allocated to trade-promotion activity, with the remainder being divided between media advertising and consumer promotions. Figure 13.1 summarizes the most recent statistics available for budget allocations in Canadian packaged-goods companies.

There has been a gradual shift away from national advertising and towards trade and consumer promotions as marketing organizations place more emphasis on regional-marketing strategies. Perhaps the most surprising figure is the amount being allocated to trade promotions. Certain factors have contributed to this shift toward trade promotions.

Recessionary Markets

When markets "flatten," that is, when there is no growth, manufacturers tend to scramble to protect the business they have (their market share). In so doing, they spend more to keep product flowing through the channel. Distributors are concerned with profit margins in this situation, and hence they are attracted to products with better trade-allowance packages.

Growth of Generic Products

Generics were originally made available to consumers solely on the basis of price advantage. In many product categories, such as paper goods, canned goods, and light snack foods, generics have become increasingly popular, owing to their price and reasonably good quality. In response, manufacturers have had to offer more in the way of trade allowances to keep their prices competitive (through more specials and feature pricing).

Buying-Power Concentration

Perhaps the most important factor contributing to increased spending on trade-promotion activity is the concentration of buying power in certain industries. Many

Canadian markets are "oligopolies," which means that buying power is controlled by a few large companies. Industries such as petroleum, communications, banking, and food-distribution have a significant portion of the buying power. The demands placed on manufacturers by distributors forces manufacturers to spend more on trade promotions than they would care to. In the case of allowances and co-operative advertising funds provided to the trade, the trade controls how the money will be spent, a situation not popular with manufacturers. In effect, there is a significant imbalance between funds allocated to pushing a product through the channel and those allocated to pulling a product through the channel. An example of buying-power concentration is the Canadian grocery business, which is dominated by a few buying groups (Canada Safeway, A&P, Steinbergs/Miracle Mart, Provigo, and Loblaws); these companies control approximately 80% of all purchases. To a lesser degree, hardware retailing is controlled by Canadian Tire and Home Hardware, and drug retailing by Shoppers Drug Mart and PharmaPlus.

Manufacturers must be concerned about the trend toward increased spending on trade, as trade promotions only offer short-term benefits (temporary volume increases), while media advertising tends to have a more long-term benefit. Continued high levels of spending in the area of trade promotion, then, may inhibit the achievement of long-term marketing objectives for any given product. For more information on the reasons for growth in consumer and trade promotions, read the Advertising in Action feature "The Move is On."

Advertising in Action

The Move is On

"Traditionally, sales promotion was looked on as advertising's little brother," said Scott Irwin, vice-president of advertising for Irwin Toys of Canada. "But now it's a full-fledged, highly disciplined partner." What has brought about this change? Why have more and more marketing-oriented organizations placed a greater emphasis on consumer- and trade-promotion activity?

Estimates of the size of sales promotion in Canada are in the $7–8 billion range; that's about the same amount that is spent on media advertising annually. Sales promotion, however, is growing at the rate of 12–14% per year whereas advertising is only growing at 6–7% per year. It is expected that, by 1990, 70% of all marketing and communication expenditures will be represented by sales promotion. Among the reasons for growth in sales promotion are the changing consumer (individuals today tend to be less brand-loyal and more brand-promiscuous); the media clutter that advertisers must deal with; increasing trade concentration (the shift in power within the channel, from manufacturers to distributors); and flat growth in many consumer markets. These developments have resulted in a greater degree of competition among brands as each brand tries to win market share from other brands.

According to John Cassaday, president of Campbell's Soup Company of Canada, marketers need to focus on "small wins" to ensure an eventual and gradual shift back to franchise

continued

building. In the short term, sales promotions are key ingredients in the small wins.

Cassaday points to three specific reasons why consumer-goods marketers have shifted to sales promotion and away from media advertising. The first, and most significant, reason is that it is extremely difficult to obtain a true measure of the short-term results of advertising. Advertising is the most visible form of marketing, and it is proof that you have actually done something—but what did it produce? Cassaday refers to a research study that shows that 10% of all advertising is exceptionally good, 10% is exceptionally awful, and 80% is just average. If those are the statistics, it is no wonder that there is a loss of confidence in advertising.

The second reason is that manufacturers are at the mercy of retailers, who, from one year to another, put additional pressure on them to support trade promotions. This is somewhat unfair to manufacturers, as the goal of the retailer is to increase its business, not build national brands. In the grocery business there is considerable pressure put on manufacturers to provide promotional fees and listing allowances. Listing allowances, or slotting fees, as they are sometimes called, are nothing more than fees manufacturers pay to secure shelf space—in effect, the manufacturer has to buy space. No longer is it up to the consumer to determine the success or failure of a product. That decision is now made by buyers for grocery stores. As one industry executive said, "If you don't pay the fee you are automatically disqualified. You don't get any space."

On the product side of things, the generic and private-label brands of grocery distributors have forced the hands of many prominent brand-name manufacturers. In Quebec, a major retailer reported that its private-label ketchup now has 50% of the volume in that category. If a private-label brand can do that to a dominant brand like Heinz, weaker brands are really in trouble if trade-promotion support is not forthcoming. Even the best of national brands are spending heavily with the trade to protect position and keep prices down.

What is the effect of such spending on sales volume? The average response to a 10% reduction in price in a supermarket item is a 20% increase in sales volume. If the price reduction is supported by retail advertising, volume goes up by about 70%. If an in-store display is added to the lower-priced feature item, volume goes up 105%. Such gains are short-term in nature—consumers buy more now and less later. This bothers manufacturers, since they don't have much choice. Given the clout of the retailers, manufacturers must plan for quarterly or even more frequent promotions of this kind, or lose out to the competition or to private-label brands.

The third reason why manufacturers have increased their concentration on sales promotion is the shift away from national planning. Companies are slowly learning that regional marketing plans are producing better results and that sales promotions offer greater flexibility in the creation and implementation of such plans. To illustrate, Cassaday points to Quebec, where Campbell's is number three in the market (hard to believe!). He blames the number-three position on Toronto marketing executives that have tried to tell French-Canadian consumers why they should buy Campbell's soup. There has been a lack of understanding. As a consequence, Campbell's has become more regional in its orientation. In fact, the flavour of the tomato soup sold in Quebec was changed to suit the taste preferences of the Quebec market—the only market in North America where it is different.

Adapted from Martin Mehr, "The beat goes on," *Marketing*, June 13, 1990, p.21 and John Cassaday, "Advertising: the great unknown," *Marketing*, February 20, 1988, pp.55-56.

Promotion planning

Promotion planning relies on input from the overall marketing plan—specifically, the marketing objectives and strategies. Very often, sales-promotion plans are developed at the same time as the advertising plan. The sales-promotion plan can be developed by the advertising agency, but more often a specialist agency does it. Regardless of who develops the plan, there is a direct relationship between advertising and sales promotion. The advertising agency creates a national advertising campaign to position the product or service in the marketplace. The promotion plan complements the advertising: it helps create demand for the product, encourages trial purchase, and/or builds loyalty through repeat purchase incentives. To be effective, to resolve clients' marketing problems, the agency's creative groups and those working on sales promotion must have a close working relationship.

PROMOTION OBJECTIVES

Before promotion activity is begun, clearly defined objectives must be established so that the relative success of the promotion can ultimately be measured. Since the time frame for promotion activity is relatively short, judgement as to the success or failure of a promotion can be passed quickly. Planning objectives are discussed below in the context of consumer-promotion and trade-promotion activity.

Consumer Promotion

Consumer promotions are designed to pull the product through the channel by encouraging consumers to take immediate purchase action. The most common objective of consumer-promotion activity is to have the consumer make a trial purchase. In the case of a new product, the marketer is concerned to have the initial trial and consumer acceptance of the product occur in a quick time frame. Even when a product is firmly established on the market, marketers will still attempt to secure trial purchase by non-users.

A second objective of consumer-promotion activity is to *protect loyalty* by offering incentives that encourage repeat purchase. For example, coupons distributed via the product itself are a good vehicle for maintaining customer loyalty—a reward for patronage. Current customers are very likely to use media-delivered coupons for products they normally purchase, in order to save money. Since the purchasers are already "sold" on the product's benefits alone, they view the coupon as an added bonus.

A third objective of consumer-promotion activity is to encourage *multiple purchase*. Promotions fulfilling this objective are designed to "load the customer up" or take them "out of the market" for a time. A well-conceived contest that encourages multiple entries, or a cash refund whose value increases with the number of purchases made, are examples of promotions that will achieve the multiple-purchase objective.

Trade Promotion

Trade-promotion activity is designed to push a product through the channel of distribution. Basically, manufacturers offer distributors incentives to improve the performance (volume movement) of the product in the channel and to gain the support of distributors in merchandising the product to the consumer. For any new product, the objective of trade-promotion activity is to secure a *listing* with distributors (wholesale and retail). A listing is defined as an agreement made by a wholesaler to distribute a manufacturer's product to the retailers it supplies. If, for example, the head office of A&P agrees to purchase a specific product, then it is available to all A&P retail stores. To secure a listing, manufacturers will offer distributors a combination of trade allowances and co-operative advertising allowances, which will cover the costs of the listing, of obtaining distribution, and possibly, of retailing the product at a special introductory price.

A second objective of trade promotions is to build volume, either on a seasonal basis or on a preplanned cyclical basis throughout the year. For example, it is quite common for a company to offer trade allowances and other merchandising programs quarterly for key products. The availability of trade allowances encourages retailers to purchase heavily during the promotion period, to support the manufacturer's promotion, and to "load up" at the end of the promotion to improve profit margins on products that will be regularly priced at retail after the promotion period. Very often, large retailers will carry inventories that will tide them over from one promotion period to another, a situation that manufacturers should be concerned about, because incremental volume sold on deal, particularly at the end of a promotion period, will reduce the sale of merchandise at regular prices. Short-term volume gains may not be to the manufacturer's advantage over a long period.

In the case of seasonal products, allowance programs are essential means of encouraging wholesalers and retailers to stock up before the season and to promote the product in the season. For example, suntan lotion will be promoted in the spring, canning and preserving supplies in the late summer, baking supplies in the late fall, before Christmas, and school supplies in the late summer.

A third objective is to secure sales support from distributors. For many products sold through drug, grocery, hardware, or department stores, manufacturers will offer complete promotion programs to encourage display activity, feature pricing, and retail-advertising support. Programs of this nature are often agreed to in a signed contract or promotion agreement, and the distributor is reimbursed only when the performance requirements of the agreement are met.

*T*YPES OF CONSUMER PROMOTION ACTIVITY

The major types of consumer-promotion activities implemented in Canada include coupons, free-sample distribution, contests, cash rebates, and premiums. A survey conducted by A.C. Nielsen Company of Canada Ltd. among packaged-goods companies (i.e., food, household-goods, personal-care-products, and pet-food manufacturers), revealed that 77% of the manufacturers viewed coupons as their most important form of consumer-promotion activity. Following, in order of importance, were sampling, contests, cash refunds, and premiums.

COUPONS

Coupons are price-off incentives offered to consumers to stimulate quicker purchase of a designated product. The array of products and services that use coupons are endless. Coupons are used to discount the price of movie and theatre tickets, to lower the price of restaurant meals and to encourage purchase of a popular brand of breakfast cereal. They are used more frequently by more marketers than any other consumer-promotion technique. In 1989 there were a total of 16.1 billion coupons distributed in Canada and over 209 million redeemed. The most recent trends in coupon distribution and redemption among packaged-goods manufacturers are outlined in figure 13.2.

Methods of Coupon Distribution

Coupons can be delivered to consumers in three different ways. The majority of coupons are delivered through two traditional channels: **media delivery** (through newspapers, magazines, co-operative direct mail, etc.), and **product delivery** (coupons inside or on a package). The third method of delivery is *in-store*, either through a product demonstrator or by special dispensers or ad pads. It is now common to receive coupons on the back of cash-register tapes, theatre tickets and parking stubs in city parking lots.

Coupon Redemption by Method of Distribution

The statistical information in figure 13.3 shows that instantly redeemable coupons and in-pack self coupons have the highest redemption rates among product-delivered coupons. **Redemption rate** is the number of coupons returned to the manufacturer expressed as a percentage of total distributed coupons. Among media-delivered vehicles, selective direct mail has by far the highest rate of redemption. Redemption rates for newspaper and magazine coupons are relatively low, compared with redemption rates for coupons distributed by other methods.

The method of delivery is only one factor that influences the rate of redemption for a coupon promotion. Other factors that play a major role are the face value of the coupon, and the consumer's perception of the value of the discount offered by the coupon in relation to the price of the product. For a complete list of factors that influence coupon-redemption rates, refer to figure 13.4.

Types of Coupons

Classified according to the methods of delivery available, the couponing alternatives for Canadian marketers to choose from are many. Whether one type of coupon is chosen over another is largely dependent upon the objectives of the coupon promotion: is the objective trial purchase, repeat purchase, or multiple purchase by consumers?

In-Pack Self Coupon These are coupons that are redeemable on the product in which they are distributed (the package is usually "flagged" to draw attention to the coupon inside).

Figure 13.2   Coupon distribution and redemption patterns in Canada

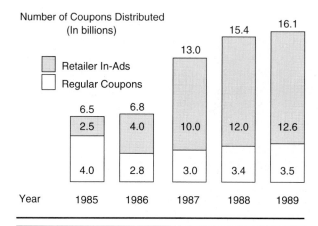

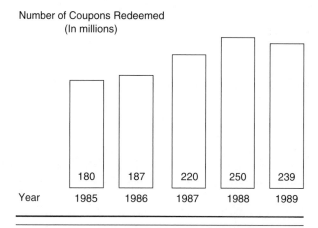

Source: A.C. Nielsen Company of Canada Limited

On-Pack Self Coupons There are two different types of on-pack self coupons:

1. *Regular On-Pack* These are valid for the future purchase of the product on which they are carried (they are usually located on the side or back panel of the package, or behind a label).

2. *Instantly Redeemable* These are valid for the immediate purchase of the product carrying the coupon (the coupon is removed from the package panel at the point of purchase).

Figure 13.3   Coupon redemption by method of distribution

Media	Range (%)	Median (%)
1. In & on package coupons		
In Pack-Self	1.5 – 44.3	13.6
On Pack-Self	2.8 – 33.8	12.4
Instantly Redeemable	19.2 – 89.2	43.9
In Pack-Cross	1.2 – 14.3	5.1
On Pack-Cross	0.6 – 30.4	3.0
2. Regular media coupons		
Coop Direct Mail	1.7 – 12.4	4.7
Free Standing Inserts	1.2 – 7.5	3.3
Newspapers (ROP)	0.1 – 3.9	1.0
Magazines	0.2 – 5.7	0.9
Selective Direct Mail	3.1 – 36.3	15.1
Cash For Kids		
(All Programs)	1.7 – 9.2	4.0
Rideau Kiwanis	3.8 – 9.9	5.1
3. In store coupons		
Selective In Store	0.3 – 18.2	N/P*
In Store Handout/Demo	3.7 – 75.2	25.1
In Store Shelf(Ad Pads)	4.3 – 39.8	17.3
Retailer Booklets	0.1 – 6.5	0.8

* Not published
Source: A.C. Nielsen Company of Canada Limited

In-Pack/On-Pack Cross Coupons   These are valid for the purchase of another product. Such coupons are commonly used to generate the trial purchase of complementary products (e.g., a soup product distributes coupons for crackers, and a cracker product distributes coupons for soup).

Co-operative Direct-Mail Coupons   These are distributed to households in selected postal walks by non-addressed mail. Figure 13.5 shows a co-operative direct-mail envelope for Carole Martin coupons and special offers.

Free-Standing Inserts   These are distributed in newspaper supplements (four-colour, magazine-quality, tabloid-size inserts are distributed in newspapers and contain coupons for numerous products).

Newspaper ROP (Run of Press) Coupons   These are included in manufacturer-sponsored newspaper advertisements.

Magazine Coupons   These are distributed via popular consumer magazines.

Pop-Up Coupons   These coupons are printed on heavier paper stock and stitched into a popular consumer magazine (they often appear directly before an advertisement for the couponed product).

Figure 13.4 Factors influencing redemption rates

REDEMPTION RATES

Redemption rates are influenced by many factors, including:
- The method of coupon distribution.
- The frequency of product purchase by a typical user – this is effectively categorized as the size of the product category in terms of total dollar sales at retail.
- The coupon's valid term as determined by the use or non–use of an expiry date.
- The couponed product's market share.
- The extent of a brand's consumer franchise.
- The coupon's face value.
- The percentage discount offered by the coupon, in terms of face value as a percent of the product's retail price.
- The geographic area in which the coupon is distributed.
- The product's distribution or availability at retail.
- Whether or not the coupon offers a discount on a single or multiple purchase.

Other factors such as coupon design and competitive activity tend to have less impact on redemption rates. Competitive couponing or refunding, however, may affect the redemption pattern of an offer by delaying its use, particularly if the competing offer has a much higher value.

Courtesy: A.C. Nielsen Company of Canada Ltd. Reprinted with permission.

In-Store Coupons These are delivered by in-store handout or by dispensers or ad pads at shelf level near or at the brand's product displays.

Selective Couponing This is a method of placing higher-value coupons with users of competitive brands or non-category users. There are two techniques used:

1. *Selective Direct Mail* Coupons are mailed to consumers who match a demographic profile compiled from consumer surveys.

Figure 13.5 Cooperative mailing envelope

Courtesy: McIntyre & Dodd Marketing—A division of O.E. McIntyre Ltd. Reprinted with permission.

2. *Selective In-Store "Printed-at-the-Check-Out"* These coupons are issued on the basis of the actual brand purchases that consumers make in a store. Through the use of scanning equipment and UPC codes, coupons are automatically generated when particular brands are bought.

The costs of these types of coupons are paid for out of the consumer promotion budgets discussed earlier in this chapter. Generally speaking, media-delivered vehicles encourage trial purchase, while product-delivered coupons encourage repeat purchase. Instantly redeemable coupons are ideal for both types of purchases.

Couponing Objectives

The traditional objectives associated with coupon promotions are to get non-brand users to make trial and first purchases of a brand, to maintain current users, to speed up acceptance of a new product, and to encourage current customers to repurchase the brand. Coupons are also useful in attracting users of competitive brands, and in encouraging multiple purchases and increasing seasonal sales.

How effective are coupons in achieving these objectives? In a report on coupon usage issued by Nielsen Promotion Services in 1989, it was found that 83% of grocery shoppers have used coupons within the past year and that 54% of coupon users used at least one coupon on a product or brand they had never tried before.[1] These statistics tend to uphold the view that couponing is an excellent promotional tool if the marketer's objective is trial or repeat purchase.

The stage the product has reached in its life cycle also has an impact on the objectives of a coupon promotion. In a product's introduction and growth stages, trial purchase is the marketer's main objective, so media-delivered coupons are popular. As the product moves into maturity and the marketers become concerned with repeat purchase by current customers, they attempt to defend their consumer franchise by means of product-delivered coupons. If an objective is still to attract competitive brand users (which is important, even at the mature stage), media-delivered coupons remain necessary.

Coupon Cost Calculations

The costs of a coupon promotion should be monitored closely by the marketing organization. A variety of factors have an impact on the total costs of a coupon promotion: the method of distribution, which affects delivery costs and redemption costs; the printing costs; the handling costs for the retailer and clearing house (the latter being the agent responsible for redeeming coupons, paying retailers, and reporting redemption and cost information to the marketing organization); and the coupon's face value.

The marketer should weigh the costs of a coupon promotion against the potential revenues to ensure that a positive financial payout will result from the activity. The following is a sample illustration of a coupon promotion plan that shows how a firm could estimate the payout.

Face Value	$00.40
Handling Charge (retailer)	$00.10
Handling Charge (clearing house)	$00.03
Distribution via Co-operative Direct Mail	$16.00/M
Printing Costs (digest size ad plus perforated coupon)	$8.00/M
Redemption Rate	10%
Retail Price (manufacturer receives 65% of retail price if wholesale and retail margins are excluded)	$1.89

Costs

Distribution	1 400 000 × $16.00/M	=	22 400
Printing	1 400 000 × $8.00/M	=	11 200
Redemption	(1 400 000 × 10%) × $0.53	=	74 200
Total Cost			107 800

[Redemption costs are calculated by multiplying the number of coupons distributed by the estimated rate of return, which in this case is 10%. This return figure(140 000) is then multiplied by the costs associated with each coupon return (face value plus all handling charges); in this case, the cost is $0.53.]

Revenues The revenue calculation is based on the number of actual purchases that the coupon generated, and takes into account misredemption of coupons. (A coupon is misredeemed if it was not used to purchase the product, but was sent to the clearing house anyway.) For the sake of the payout illustration, we assume a misredemption rate of 20% (80% are redeemed on an actual purchase). The revenue calculation considers the number of returned coupons multiplied by those legally redeemed, and multiplied by the revenue each purchase generates for the manufacturer.

Revenue Generated from Each Purchase: $1.89 \times 65\%$ = $1.23
Total Revenues: $(1\,400\,000 \times 10\%) \times 80\% \times \$1.23$ = $137 760

Therefore, the payout on the coupon promotion would be

Total Costs   = $107 800
Total Revenues   =   137 760
Payout   =   29 960

SAMPLES

A **sample** promotion program is a free distribution of a product to potential new users. Sampling is considered to be the most effective method of generating trial purchase, as it eliminates a consumer's initial financial risk. Unlike any other type of promotion, sampling is the only alternative that can convert a trial user to a regular user solely on the basis of product satisfaction. For a comparison of sampling and other promotion techniques that are best suited for achieving specific goals, refer to figure 13.6.

The most frequently used method of sample distribution is in-store. There are several variations on in-store sampling: product demonstrations and sampling, saleable sample sizes (small replica pack sizes of the actual product), and cross sampling. **Cross sampling** refers to an arrangement whereby one product carries a sample of another product (e.g., a regular-sized box of Cheerios cereal carries a small sample package of Pro-Stars cereal). The popularity of one brand is used to secure the trial usage of a less popular brand. Other alternatives for delivering free samples include co-operative direct mail (provided the sample is small and light enough to be accommodated by the mailing envelope), and finally, home delivery by private organizations. Distribution by these latter methods tends to be more costly.

Compared with coupon promotions, sampling programs tend to be an expensive proposition for the marketing organization because of the product, packaging, and distribution costs. In spite of these costs, sample promotions rank second in popularity among marketers, so clearly the potential long-run benefits outweigh the short-run costs.

CONTESTS

Contests and sweepstakes are designed and implemented to create temporary excitement about a product. The structure of a contest usually entails incentives for consumers to purchase; entrance often requires, for example, submission of a label or product symbol (or facsimile) and an entry form. Consumers are encouraged to enter as often as possible, resulting in multiple purchases by many consumers. Credit-card companies, for example, send entry cards to clients with their monthly statements. Each purchase made with the credit card over a given period must be entered on the

Figure 13.6 Consumer promotions best suited for achieving specific goals

Goals	Coupons	Sampling	Refunds	Contests	Premiums
–to generate trial on exisiting products	★	★			
–to gain trial on new products	★	★			
–to speed acceptance and first purchase of a new product by consumers	★★	★★	★		
to encourage multiple purchase of a new product and pantry loading	★		★★		★
–to encourage repurchase among current users	★		★	★	★
–to provide an extra tool to the sales force	★	★	★	★	★
–to increase seasonal sales	★				
–to help gain extra listings	★	★			
–to help gain off-self product displays	★	★		★★	
–to increase advertising effectiveness	★		★	★★	★
–to add excitement and focus to In Store displays				★	
–to focus bvrand advertising at specific target groups				★	★

Source: A.C. Nielsen Company of Canada Limited

entry form prior to the form's being submitted by the client—a multiple purchase incentive.

As a marketing vehicle, contests tend to attract current users, and since marketers only use contests occasionally (often during a peak selling season), they are not that effective at generating mass trial. Only a small portion of "prospects" (new users) enter a contest. Contests are appropriate in the mature stage of the product life cycle; they are a good vehicle for encouraging repeat and multiple purchase by current users. There are several types of contests: *sweepstakes* (cash prizes, cars, homes, and vacation give-aways); *instant wins* (prizes awarded in the package or at point-of-purchase); *match-and-win contests*; and *collect-and-win contests*. Instant wins are quite effective at reaching consumers who are not easily reached or influenced by other promotion techniques. Packaging and in-store promotion pieces are the major form of advertising support for instant-win promotions. Figure 13.7 is an in-store ad pad promoting a sweepstakes contest sponsored by many S.C. Johnson household products.

Figure 13.7 An example of a contest ad pad

SWEEPSTAKES RULES

1. No Purchase Necessary: To enter the 'FAMOUS HOMES' Sweepstakes, complete the entry form or print your name, complete address and telephone number on a plain piece of paper and mail to 'FAMOUS HOMES', P.O. Box 4095, Paris, Ontario N3L 3W9. Your entry must be received no later than March 31, 1989, the contest closing date.

2. One (1) grand prize will be awarded consisting of: Globus Gateway® 12-day motorcoach tour for two of Stately Homes and Castles in England, Scotland and Wales guided by a professional tour director. First-class hotels. Eleven full English breakfasts and eight 3-course dinners. Plus one night before and after your tour in a London hotel. Return air transportation via Air Canada to London from the international airport nearest to the winner's home; and $1,000 (Cdn.) spending money. The prize is non-transferable and must be accepted as awarded. No substitutions will be permitted. The trip must be booked 30 days in advance, space is subject to availability at time of booking and your travel must be completed by October 31, 1990. The approximate retail value of this prize is $6,000 (including $1,000 spending money).

3. Odds of winning depend upon the number of entries. A random draw will be made at 2 p.m. April 21, 1989, in Paris, Ontario from all eligible entries received on or before the contest closing date. Selected entrants will be contacted by mail and, in order to win, must correctly answer a mathematical skill-testing question enclosed therein, and will be asked to sign standard declaration forms confirming compliance with contest rules and acceptance of the prize as awarded. Decision of the judges will be final.

4. Contest is open to all residents of Canada of legal age in the province of residence, except employees of S.C. Johnson and Son, Limited, their advertising and promotional agencies, and the independent contest-judging organization and members of each of their respective immediate families living in the same household. All entries become the property of S.C. Johnson and Son, Limited who assumes no responsibility for lost, invalid, destroyed or misdirected entries. No entries will be returned and no correspondence will be entered into except with the selected contestants. However, by forwarding a stamped, self-addressed envelope to 'FAMOUS HOMES', P.O. Box 4095, Paris, Ontario N3L 3W6 on or after April 21, 1989, the name of the winner may be obtained. Decision of the judges is final.

5. The winner agrees to authorize S.C. Johnson and Son, Limited to announce and publish her/his name, address and photograph in any forthcoming publicity. Questions by a resident of the Province of Quebec concerning this promotion can be submitted to the Régie des loteries du Québec. This contest is subject to all federal, provincial and municipal laws.

® Can. Trade Mark Reg'd to S.C. Johnson & Son, Inc., Reg'd user S.C. JOHNSON AND SON, LIMITED, Brantford, Ontario, Canada N3T 5R1

To enter SWEEPSTAKES:
complete and mail to: 'FAMOUS HOMES', P.O. Box 4095, Paris, Ontario N3L 3W9 by no later than March 31, 1989.

NAME: _____

ADDRESS: _____

CITY: _____ PROVINCE: _____

POSTAL CODE: _____ TELEPHONE: _____

4283E   SP-991-1310-07/88E

Courtesy: S.C Johnson & Son Limited

A contest requires a significant investment in advertising. In effect, the focal point of a brand's advertising switches from the product to the contest in an attempt to build "excitement" for the brand. Because of consumer involvement, contests are usually well received and supported by the retail trade; indeed, they are often launched with trade-promotion programs to encourage feature pricing and maximize display activity at retail. To create awareness for the contest, a multi-media mix is frequently used (broadcast media to generate excitement and print media to communicate details). In a sweepstakes type of contest, it is point-of-purchase material such as ad pads and the package itself that are the key elements in the advertising strategy to promote the contest.

The success of a contest depends upon the consumer's perception of the value and number of prizes to be awarded, and of the odds of winning. Contest prizes should also be congruent with the image of the product. The contest prize shown in figure 13.8 is a trip for two around the world. This prize is a good match for the "quality" image of Black Magic and After Eight chocolates, and suitable for the product's target market. When designing a contest, the marketer must consider the above factors, and must either develop a high-value grand prize that will attract attention and create excitement, or have prizes of less value awarded frequently to compensate for the disappointment factor associated with most contests ("I'll enter, but who ever wins?").

A marketing organization considering the use of a contest must be familiar with the laws and regulations governing contests in Canada. Generally, contests are highly regulated by federal law (The Criminal Code—Section 189, and the Competition Act—Sections 52 and 59). Certain (fairly standardized) rules and regulations govern what must be communicated to participants. These rules state that the following information must be conveyed:

- The number of prizes and the value of each
- The odds of winning, if known
- Whether a skill-testing question will be administered
- Whether facsimiles are acceptable in the case of sweepstakes
- How to enter, and what proof of purchase is required
- The contest's closing date

CONSUMER REFUNDS AND REBATES

A **refund (rebate)** is a predetermined amount of money returned directly to the consumer by the manufacturer after the purchase has been made. For packaged-goods companies, cash refunds are a useful promotion technique in the mature stage of the product life cycle; they effectively reinforce loyalty by tempting consumers to make multiple purchases.

Cash refunds initially started with manufacturers offering the return of a stated amount of money for a single purchase. This concept has expanded, and now refund programs are quite common.

Refunds for Escalating Value

In the case of refunds for escalating value, the marketer offers a higher refund for added purchases—that is, the refund per unit is greater if the consumer buys the

Figure 13.8 Illustration of a coupon and contest combination offer. "Black Magic" and "After Eight" are registered trademarks of Rowntree Mackintosh Canada Ltd.

Courtesy: Rowntree Mackintosh Canada Ltd. Reprinted with permission.

product in maximum quantities. Refer to figure 13.9, the Schneider's "Lifestyle" products promotion. A refund of $1.50 is offered for three purchases, but for seven purchases, the refund is $5.00.

Multi-Product Refund Offers

In the case of multi-product refund offers, consumers are offered considerable savings if they buy combinations of products (usually products from the same company). A bingo-card format is quite popular, whereby a certain dollar amount is returned for the purchase of products on one line, two lines, etc. Purchasing enough products to gain a full card earns consumers the maximum refund.

The primary strategy for refund offers is to use them at the point of purchase, since a refund offer has the ability to increase sales when it is focused at store level. Ad pads are the medium most frequently used for advertising refund offers on consumer goods. Print media, particularly newspaper, is the medium most often used for promoting manufacturers' rebates on durable goods.

Rebate programs are now quite popular among manufacturers of durable goods such as kitchen appliances, other household durable goods (i.e., central-air-conditioning and heating equipment), and automobiles. They are usually advertised as "cash rebates," and are used to accomplish very specific promotion objectives—they are used to help liquidate inventories before the introduction of new models, to encourage purchase in traditionally weak selling periods, or to counter competitive activity. Refund offers are useful for gaining repeat and multiple purchases, encouraging size trade-up, and counteracting competitive activity.

PREMIUM OFFERS

A **premium** is an item that is offered free, or at a bargain price, to encourage consumers to buy a specific product. Premiums are available to consumers in four different forms: free mail-in premiums, self-liquidating premiums, in- or on-pack premiums, and near-pack premiums.

Free Mail-In Premiums These are offers that require the consumer to submit a specific number of proofs-of-purchase from the sponsoring brand in order to obtain the offered premium.

Self-Liquidating Premiums These offers require the consumer to send in a proof-of-purchase from the sponsoring brand plus money to cover all or part of the cost of the premium, postage, and handling. For example, a soup company may offer a "soup bowl" premium if a consumer sends in the required proofs-of-purchase and applicable charges. Often, the brand logo is a prominent feature of the premium—a factor that reinforces brand loyalty over the long term.

In/On Pack Premiums These offers only require that the consumer purchase the product carrying the premium to obtain it. Examples of such premiums are the small toys and games packed inside cereal boxes, or the towels packed in detergent boxes. Sometimes the premium can be a sample of another brand or product.

Near-Pack Premiums In the case of these offers, the premium is placed in stores near displays of the sponsoring brand, with some form of advertising advising consumers

Figure 13.9 Illustration of a cash refund offer. The value of the refund increases proportionately with the number of products purchased.

Courtesy: J.M. Schneider Inc. Reprinted with permission.

that they can obtain the premium either free or at low cost if the product is purchased. Near-pack premiums are frequently used to promote sales of perfumes and cosmetics in large department stores.

Premiums can be used to many ends: increasing the quantity of brand purchases made by consumers; helping to retain current users; and providing a merchandising tool to encourage in-store displays. Marketers generally rank premiums the lowest in importance among consumer promotion alternatives. They are used less frequently for two basic reasons. First, consumer response is generally low, so it is virtually impossible to predict what actual response levels will be. This complicates the budgeting process somewhat. Second, retail discounting and high postage and packaging costs make it difficult to create an attractive and profitable offer.[2]

COMBINATION OFFERS

In order to maximize the effectiveness of a promotion, marketers often combine the consumer-promotion techniques discussed in this chapter. The illustrations included in this chapter demonstrate how various combinations can be used to advantage by the marketer. Let's review these combinations:

1. *Rowntree Mackintosh* (figure 13.8) This offer combines a trial coupon on the initial purchase, with the coupon doubling as the entry blank for the trip-around-the-world contest.
2. *Schneider's Lifestyle Products* (figure 13.9) When consumers receive their cash refund, they will also receive a "Scratch-And-Win" card with a one-in-ten chance of winning a "Lifestyle" prize instantly.

For more insight into the influence of consumer promotion activity on consumer behaviour, refer to the Advertising in Action vignette "Trying Something New."

≡ *T*YPES OF TRADE PROMOTION ACTIVITY

The most commonly used types of trade-promotion activity are: quantity and performance allowances, co-operative advertising, dealer premiums, dealer-display material, collateral material, conventions, and dealer meetings.

Trade Allowances

A **trade allowance** is a temporary price reduction designed to encourage larger purchases by distributors (wholesalers and retailers). Such price reductions may be offered in the form of a percentage reduction from list price, a predetermined dollar amount off list price, or as a free-goods offer (e.g., buy 10 cases, get one free). These allowances can be deducted from the invoice immediately, and in such cases are called *off-invoice* allowances. Or, they can be offered on the basis of a bill back, in which case the manufacturer keeps a record of the amount of merchandise shipped to distributors, and, when the deal period is over, issues cheques to reimburse the retailers for the allowances they have earned.

Advertising in Action

Trying Something New

There's an old saying that "a little knowledge goes a long way." This saying has some direct implications for promotion planning. In today's cluttered marketing environment— there is a clutter of messages in the media, and a clutter of similar brands in the market-place—it is difficult to differentiate a brand, to make it stand out in a crowd. Consequently, marketing and advertising executives are always searching for new and unique ways to get consumers to buy their products.

On the promotion side of things, many options are available to help the cause. Marketing executives rank coupons first in terms of importance among the five basic types of promotions used frequently. Coupons remain best at gaining trial purchase among non-users and repeat purchase among current users of a product. A.C. Nielsen conducted a survey among grocery-products manufacturers in Canada to determine the importance of the various promotion alternatives. Not surprisingly, coupons were judged to be the most important form of consumer promotion. The rankings for all options were as follows:

Types of Promotion	Importance Ranking(%)
Coupons	77
Samples	52
Contests	31
Cash Refunds	25
Premiums	17

In a study conducted by the Promotion Marketing Association of America Inc., it was found that 76% of consumers in the study had participated in some type of sales promotion in the past six months. Further, 98% used coupons, 54% took part in a cash refund, 26% entered a contest, and 17% received some type of premium for a product they had purchased. With participation levels like these, it is no wonder that consumer promotion is increasing in importance in the promotion mix. The same study profiled the consumers most likely to take advantage of promotions offers. They are the affluent, educated, older individuals. Those who participate most are middle-aged college graduates earning $45 000 annually.

Which techniques have the most impact on this type of person? Not surprisingly, the results of the American study echo the sentiments of the Canadian marketing executives polled by A.C. Nielsen. The American study showed that:

1. Coupons have the most influence. Seventy percent of respondents purchased a brand for the first time, and another 70% purchased a different brand (switched brands at least temporarily) because of the coupon.
2. Refunds and premiums are equally effective in achieving repeat and multiple purchase. Of interest, however, is the fact that premiums are more effective than refunds in getting people to buy products they don't really need.
3. Sweepstakes were least effective in influencing purchase behaviour.
4. The likelihood of a consumer switching brands because of a promotion decreased as the age of the consumer increased. The age group most likely to switch brands is the one composed of 18-34 year olds.

With such knowledge, the promotion manager can start to plan better. The manager must determine which promotions are best suited for achieving specific brand objectives. In effect, it is the objective that determines the activity, though there is always a choice to be

continued

made by the manager. Sometimes, different promotion activities are combined in the hope that a combination will have a greater overall effect on consumers and their level of participation. Following is a list of some promotion objectives and the types of activities seen as most appropriate for each objective:

1. For trial purchase and the prevention of brand switching (maintaining present customers), coupons are effective.
2. To achieve trial purchase by new users and to retain (to reward, so to speak) current users, a free-sample distribution can be very effective—though expensive.
3. To encourage multiple purchase, a contest is always a good bet, since contests encourage consumers to enter often to increase the odds of winning—and they buy more product in the process.
4. For encouraging both repeat and multiple purchase, cash refunds or premiums offers are as effective as contests. Typically, the refund is higher if greater amounts of product are purchased.

Adapted from "Study: some promotions can change consumer behaviour," *Marketing News*, October 15, 1990, p.12.

Performance Allowance

A **performance allowance** is an additional discount (over and above a trade allowance) offered by manufacturers to encourage retailers to perform a specific merchandising function (often, to display the product at retail). Before paying the allowance, the manufacturer requires proof of performance from the retailer.

Co-operative Advertising Allowances

Co-operative advertising allowances are funds allocated to pay for a portion of a retailer's advertising. The weekly specials advertised by major supermarket chains, for example, are partially sponsored by the manufacturers whose products are part of the ads in any given week. In some cases, a manufacturer may agree to pay half of the retailer's cost of advertising (media and creative) if the retailer agrees to feature the manufacturer's product for a specified period of time. Frequently, the manufacturer provides advertising material that can be integrated into the retailer's own advertising.

To maximize the effectiveness of allowances offered to the trade, manufacturers combine the various allowances to develop a fully integrated promotion plan. The effective combination of all allowances can build short-term volume, possibly secure automatic distribution of a product to retail stores, encourage retail-display activity, and obtain an ad in a weekly flyer at a reduced retail price for a specified period of time. Complete package plans combining the various allowances are attractive to retailers— the financial rewards are much greater, and the package facilitates the efficient use of advertising dollars to support the retailers' own advertising and merchandising activities.

Retail In-Ad Coupons

A **retail in-ad coupon** is a coupon printed in a retailer's weekly advertising, either in run-of-press newspaper advertising or in supplements inserted into a newspaper.

These coupons, which are redeemable on national brands, are paid for by the manufacturers, not by the retailer. Such programs are usually developed by a manufacturer's sales representative and a buyer representing the retailing organization that is running the coupon promotion. Usually, the funds to cover the cost of these coupons come out of the trade-promotion budget, hence their inclusion as a trade-promotion activity even though they are designed to encourage consumer response. This type of coupon program is appropriate for achieving the following promotion objectives: reducing trade inventories, building distribution levels, gaining trade support at store level, and ensuring that some of a brand's trade spending is passed on to the consumer in the form of a lower retail price.

Dealer Premiums

A **dealer premium** is an additional incentive offered to a distributor by a manufacturer to encourage special purchase or to secure additional merchandising support from a retailer. Premiums are usually offered in the form of merchandise (e.g., a set of golf clubs, or other forms of sports- and leisure-oriented equipment and clothing); the value of the premium increases with the amount of product purchased by the retailer. The use of premiums is a delicate and often controversial issue for many manufacturers and retailers. Some retail organizations do not allow their buyers to accept premiums; they feel that the only party to benefit from the premium is the one who accepts it. The purchase of unnecessary volume by a buyer may be contrary to the objectives of the retail organization. The other side of the argument is that the purchase of manufacturer's products at a large savings (through allowances and premiums) offers direct, tangible benefit to the buying organization.

Collateral Material

To facilitate the selling process, the field sales force must provide considerable data in the form of collateral materials to customers (dealers, wholesalers, retailers, industrial companies, etc.). These materials include catalogues, sales brochures, pamphlets, specification sheets, product manuals, and audiovisual sales aids prepared by the manufacturer. Figure 13.10 includes an example of collateral material distributed in a Campbell's Soup promotion.

Dealer Display Material (Point-of-Purchase)

A variety of point-of-purchase material is available to support a manufacturer's promotion with the retail trade. Point-of-purchase display materials include posters, shelf-talkers, ad pads (tear-off pads that explain the details of the promotion), display shippers, and merchandising racks. Figure 13.11 is an example of an in-store poster promoting a combined cash refund/contest for Beatrice Yogurt. Display materials are used at the discretion of the retailers, and whether they are used often depends on the ability of sales representatives to convince retailers to provide merchandising support. Retailers usually have an abundance of manufacturer's display material to choose from, so they can be selective. Often, retailers refuse to use display material at all owing either to space considerations or to a need to protect their own image.

Figure 13.10   Collateral materials used by the sales force to communicate sales promotion plans to the trade

YOUR PARTNERS IN PROFIT

Increase sales by 213%* by merchandising **Campbell's** and **Christie's** together

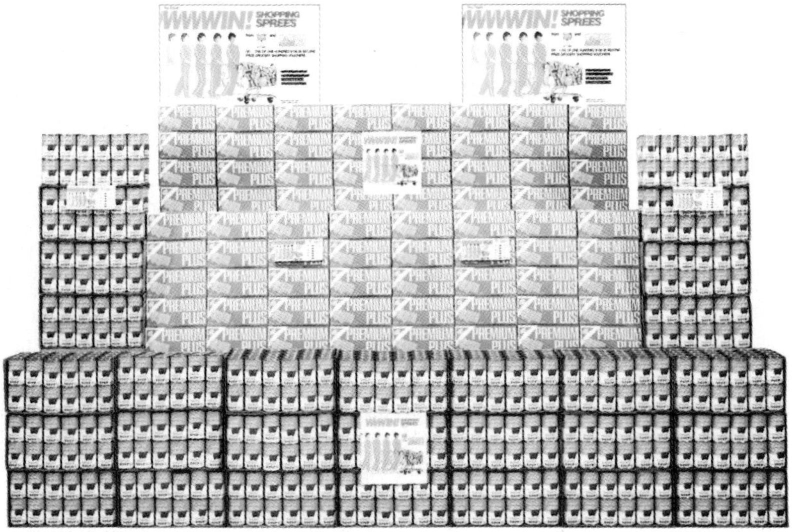

SUPPORT

- 14 Million specially flashed **Campbell's Soup** labels (Tomato)
- 2 Million specially flashed **Premium Plus** 450g packages
- Grocery Cart Advertising
- Impactful Point-of-Sale Material
- Ad Pad entry forms
- Promotional Ad Slicks
- Canadian Grocer advertisement in December announcing program

Stock up now for January Display and feature
Campbell's and **Christie's** – your **Partners in Profit**

Case Price	Deal Allowance	Net Price	Suggested Retail	Profit	% Mark-up	$ Return Per Case

* Based on Progressive Grocer Jan '81 article on Related-Items Display

® Registered Trade Mark of Nabisco Brands Ltd
™ Registered Trade Mark of Campbell Soup Company Ltd

Courtesy: Campell Soup Company Ltd. and Nabisco Brands Ltd. Reprinted with permission.

Figure 13.11   An example of an in-store poster

Courtesy: Beatrice Foods Inc.

Conventions and Dealer Meetings

Manufacturers often introduce new products or advertising campaigns to their dealer network at conventions and conferences. Such meetings are both informative and productive, because they can be used both as sales training sessions (the sales force always attends) and as opportunities to promote goodwill in the dealer network.

CONSIDERATIONS FOR ADVERTISING A PROMOTION

Promotion activity is not the focal point of the marketing strategy for a brand. In most cases, it is used to supplement regular brand advertising. It is a technique that can build volume at special times of the year. Regardless of the promotional direction the company takes, attention must be paid to certain creative-strategy and media-strategy considerations.

CREATIVE-STRATEGY CONSIDERATIONS

The marketer must consider that a promotion might be disruptive to the continuity of the regular sales message. It is possible that consumers not interested in the promotion will look elsewhere for product satisfaction. So that this potential problem is avoided, the creative should be designed as "supplemental" activity to regular advertising, and the following factors should be considered: the frequency of the promotion activity, and the promotion/product relationships.

Frequency of Promotion Activity

How frequently an activity should be used depends upon the type of the activity. Once a year is usually adequate to generate "excitement" over a brand (a contest might be used in peak season to counter competitive activity, or one during a traditionally low season to stimulate incremental volume). As a rule, coupon activity can be implemented much more frequently than cash refunds, premium offers, and contests, and it is less disruptive to the regular sales message.

Promotion/Product Relationships

In the case of contests, sweepstakes, and premiums, the promotion offer must fit the product image and be attractive to the target market. The Black Magic trip offer (figure 13.8) represents a logical promotion/product relationship. In a contest situation, the prize must be of interest to the target market. For example, an all-expenses-paid vacation in Disneyland may be appropriate for a soup or cereal manufacturer, but inappropriate for an expensive gourmet coffee. If the target market is not interested, the promotion will fail.

In terms of developing creative, separate but integrated strategies must be considered for promotion activity. Since a promotion is an added incentive, it temporarily becomes the unique selling point. It is logical, then, to integrate the offer into the regular sales message. The combination of a strong on-going sales message with the added bonus of a promotion offer should help achieve both short-term and long-term objectives for the advertised product.

When assessing the relative effectiveness of a promotional advertisement (particularly a print advertisement), marketers typically analyze the response generated by the specific advertisement or campaign. In a coupon promotion, how many coupons were redeemed? For a contest, how many entries were received? For a premium offer, how many premiums were shipped? Such evaluations provide direction for the design of subsequent promotion-oriented advertisements.

A recent study by Gallup and Robinson (Princeton, New Jersey) on promotion-oriented advertisements and their impact on consumer recall showed that certain types of promotion offers have a greater influence on advertising effectiveness than other types. Generally, ads with premiums, cents-off coupons and free samples have higher-than-average day-after-recall levels. Ads with sweepstakes or contest promotions and information-request coupons have lower-than-average recall levels. In terms of purchase interest, relative-to-average persuasion scores for all print advertising, coupon ads and ads with information-request coupons generate higher-than-average scores.[3]

The Gallup and Robinson research recommended that marketers determine what they want to accomplish before embarking on a specific promotional plan. The marketer should evaluate potential conflict between advertising the product and advertising the promotion. The research report stated that the ideal promotion offer draws attention to the ad and conveys a message about the product. Also, a strong association between the promotional offer and the advertised product tends to increase advertising recall and persuasiveness.[4]

Marketers should analyze their promotion-planning efforts, giving consideration to the following questions:

- Does the promotion support the product image?
- Does the promotion distract the reader's attention from copy points that describe product qualities?
- Should the promotion offer be the most prominent feature of the ad, or should it be secondary to the product sales message?

MEDIA-STRATEGY CONSIDERATIONS

Commitment to a sales-promotion plan requires commitment to media-advertising support. For any consumer promotion to have a chance, the target market must be made aware of the activity and the specific details of the promotion offer. Usually, a media mix is required to achieve the communications objectives of a promotion plan.

Broadcast Media

To create awareness and encourage consumers to respond quickly is largely the responsibility of television and radio. High-impact advertising in a short space of time (a blitz campaign) is quite common. In the case of a contest or sweepstakes promotion, television and radio can create excitement and convey a sense of urgency (to get consumers to take advantage of the offer—NOW!).

Print Media

Various combinations of print media are used to create awareness, and more importantly, to communicate essential details of the promotion offer.

It is the type of the promotion that determines the specific media mix that is used for it. For complex promotions, such as contests, a well-balanced mix is required. For a premium offer, free sample, or coupon, the marketer can be more selective.

In addition to advertising the promotion to the consumer, the marketer must take appropriate action to notify the trade. As discussed earlier in this chapter, consumer-promotion and trade-promotion activity (the combination of pull and push) is often integrated into a complete plan to maximize impact on, and response from, both customer groups—consumers and distributors. Therefore, the marketing organization must provide the sales force with appropriate sales aids (promotion literature and display material) so that more effective presentations can be made to distributors. In terms of media, marketers can use selective direct mailings to all distributors, or place advertising in appropriate trade journals to reach wholesale and retail buyers. Such advertising should provide promotion details, and encourage retailers to build inventories and participate in display activities in order to derive maximum benefit from the promotion.

Summary

The advertising manager must consider the impact that sales-promotion activity will have on the achievement of marketing objectives, so a sales-promotion plan is often developed concurrently with the advertising plan. Sales-promotion activities are designed to encourage immediate purchase response by consumers and distributors. There are two categories of sales-promotion activity: consumer promotions and trade promotions.

Consumer promotions are designed to pull the product through the channel of distribution. Specific objectives are to achieve trial purchase by new users, and to achieve repeat and multiple purchase by current users. The types of activities commonly used to achieve these objectives include coupons, cash refunds, samples, contests, and premium offers.

Trade promotions are designed to help push the product through the channel of distribution. Specific marketing objectives are to secure listings and distribution, build volume on a preplanned cyclical basis, and achieve merchandising support from distributors. Trade-promotion activities that help achieve these objectives include trade allowances, performance allowances, co-operative advertising, dealer premiums, point-of-purchase display materials, and collateral materials.

Sales promotion is generally regarded as supplemental activity that supports regular product advertising. Its goals are only short-term. Consequently, sales-promotion activity should not disrupt regular product advertising. In planning promotions, the manager must guard against running them too frequently so as not to harm the image of the product. Promotions that are implemented should complement the existing image of the product. From a media-strategy perspective, a combination of broadcast and print advertising is recommended as the means of creating awareness and communicating the details of the promotion offer.

Review Questions

1. What are the objectives of the consumer-promotion and trade-promotion activities?
2. What types of coupon distribution are appropriate for the early stages of the product life cycle? For the later stages?
3. What are the major reasons why marketing firms use coupons?
4. What benefits come from a manufacturer's implementation of a sample-promotion offer?
5. What elements contribute to the success of a contest offer?
6. Briefly describe the following consumer-promotion terms:
   i) Redemption rate
   ii) Instantly redeemable coupon
   iii) Instant-win promotions
   iv) Self-liquidating premium
   v) Rebate
7. What is the difference between a trade allowance and a promotion allowance?
8. What role does cooperative advertising play in the development of a manufacturer's product?
9. Briefly describe the following trade-promotion terms:
   i) Retail in-ad coupon
   ii) Dealer premium
   iii) Collateral material

Discussion Questions

1. "Contests and sweepstakes offers are only appropriate for products in the mature stage of the product life cycle." Discuss this statement in light of the competitive nature of the marketplace today.
2. "Spending less advertising money directly with consumers, and more advertising money with the trade, will ultimately harm a brand's consumer franchise." Discuss this statement from the manufacturer's viewpoint.
3. The trends of marketing budget allocations and the merits of various consumer- and trade-promotion techniques have been presented in this chapter. If you were responsible for developing a promotion plan for a brand in the mature stage of the product life cycle, what balance would you recommend between consumer promotion, media advertising, and trade promotion? Justify your position by using examples of your choice.

CHAPTER 14 Business–to–Business Advertising

In studying this chapter, you will learn about

- The types of customers who make up the business-to-business market

- The basic differences between consumer marketing and business-to-business marketing

- The way in which market-segmentation principles are used in the business-marketing process

- The buying characteristics affecting communications activity

- The role advertising plays in business communications

- The objectives and limitations of business advertising

- The special creative-strategy considerations in business advertising

- The factors affecting media strategy in business communications.

Business advertising can be defined as messages directed at industrial, institutional, commercial, and professional end users, as well as at purchasing agents or distributors whose occupation involves purchasing products and services. The business and industrial markets in Canada are composed of diverse organizations that require unique product and service mixes. These markets represent a wealth of purchasing opportunities, so marketing organizations must define target markets, identify the demand characteristics (the more precise needs of business and industry), and develop a responsive marketing program to present products and services so that they appear favourably to business customers.

Firms approaching the business market from a marketing and advertising viewpoint must fully understand the complex buying processes in business and industry. For example, there are users as well as influencers who must be communicated with, and there is a definite trend towards committee buying. Advertisers therefore must determine who to reach and how best to reach them. Traditionally, personal selling has been the most important means of communicating with business customers, but, in times of expensive selling costs, advertising's ability to reach business customers is being recognized, and hence advertising is playing a more important role. With the cost of an industrial sales representative now well over $200 per call, and as high as $500 and more in some industries, the demand for effective communications is immense.

This chapter endeavours to illustrate the factors that influence the decision-making process in business and industry. The various marketing variables affecting consumer and business marketing are contrasted, and various segmentation variables are discussed. (Refer back to chapter 4 for information on consumer behaviour and market segmentation.) Once the basic characteristics of the business market have been established, the role of advertising in the business-communications process is presented.

THE BUSINESS-TO-BUSINESS MARKET

TYPES OF CUSTOMERS

The business-to-business market can be divided into four distinct buying groups: business and industry, governments, institutions, and professional occupations.

Business and Industry

Business and industry buying organizations include users, original-equipment manufacturers, dealer and distributor networks, and a host of service businesses. Users purchase products to produce other products (i.e., to produce equipment, machinery, etc.). Original-equipment manufacturers (OEMs) purchase industrial products for inclusion directly in other products. General Motors would be classified as an OEM, based on their purchase of radios, spark plugs, and tires for their automobiles. Dealers (retailers) and distributors are middlemen who purchase products for resale to other middlemen or end users. Finally, service businesses comprise industries such as banks, real-estate companies, and insurance companies, which collectively require a variety of products and services.

Governments

Collectively, the federal, provincial, and local governments form Canada's largest buying group. Governments tend to have a more specialized buying procedure, involving detailed order specifications and tender submissions from potential suppliers.

Institutions

The third major buying group, institutions, includes hospitals, restaurants, and educational establishments. These customers require a varied mix of product and service items from potential suppliers.

Professional Market

The professional market comprises doctors, lawyers, architects, engineers, accountants, and so on. Professional market segments can be reached by publications that are tailored to the needs of the various segments.

Since we are primarily interested in advertising, let's focus specifically on some basic differences between consumer advertising and business-to-business advertising.

CONSUMER MARKETING VERSUS BUSINESS MARKETING

The characteristics of business markets are quite different from those of consumer markets. First, there are fewer potential buyers, and among the small number of buyers there is a concentration of buying power. Second, buying organizations can be very large, and as a consequence can dominate an industry (take, for example, the three largest auto makers: General Motors, Ford, and Chrysler). In contrast, smaller customers offer buying potential also, but there must be an efficient means of reaching them if their business is to be pursued. Finally, business markets tend to be concentrated geographically. For example, the Quebec-City-to-Windsor corridor encompasses 70% of all manufacturing establishments, and is the centre of banking and financial services in Canada.

In terms of planning, marketing, and advertising activity, consideration is given to positioning concepts, the four Ps (product, price, promotion, and place), buyer behaviour, and the decision-making process. Both consumer and business marketers employ these principles, but the manner in which they are used differs in accordance with the differences between the two markets. The following section summarizes some of the differences between consumer and business marketing.

Consumer Marketing	Business Marketing
Product:	
consumer products tend to be standardized, to rely on brand names, and to be purchased frequently.	business products tend to be complex or technical in nature. The focus is on price, quality, and service, and less on brand name. Generally, the products are purchased infrequently.

Price:

pricing in the channel is based on a list price and on a series of discounts that are in turn based on customer volume and marketing support.

basically the same as consumer marketing, but there is extensive price negotiation between buyers and sellers, or a contract-bidding process is used.

Promotion:

promotion activity focuses on advertising, with sales promotion acting as a support mechanism. Personal selling is important in securing distribution in the channel. Advertising is the most visible form of marketing support to end users.

the emphasis here is on personal selling, with sales promotion providing a support mechanism. Advertising is implemented through trade publications and direct mail, and generally plays less of a role in the promotion mix. Certain industries have moved towards more frequent use of mass media (e.g., business-equipment manufacturers).

Place:

basically traditional channels: manufacturer ➔ wholesaler ➔ retailer ➔ consumer.

shorter, direct channels based on personal selling and the higher dollar value of the transaction.

Decision Process:

generally, the purchase decision is made by an individual or household unit.

influence-centres within organizations have an impact on the purchase decision; various people (both users and non-users) influence the decision. Buying committees are also popular.

Buying Behaviour:

buyers tend to be influenced by emotion; hence the popularity of evocative advertising as a marketing tool.

buyers tend to be more rational, as the product and service mix requirements and the transaction costs require logical thought rather than emotional response.

Since we are primarily interested in advertising, let's focus specifically on some basic differences between consumer advertising and business advertising.

Advertising is Less Dominant in the Promotion Mix

In the eyes of business-marketing managers, personal selling remains the dominant and most influential form of customer communications. These managers recognize the role advertising can play in the selling process, namely, creating awareness and interest, but contend that personal selling creates preference, which leads to purchase.

Business Advertising Budgets are Smaller

In business-to-business advertising, the advertising funds are allocated to trade publications and direct-mail campaigns, which are directed at selective audiences (definite potential buyers). Consequently, with reach being low, particularly in trade publications, and with the rates such publications charge, the media used is efficient. This, combined with the dominance of personal selling in the promotion mix, adds up to smaller advertising budgets.

In recent years, this trend has been changing in certain industries. Several industries, including microcomputers, photocopiers and communications, have opted for more frequent use of the mass media to communicate with business customers. Advertising funds allocated to television and more general print media are quite significant. Firms in these industries are recognizing that business buyers are human, and that perhaps it is to their advantage to communicate with them when they are in a more relaxed frame of mind, away from the more stressful business environment.

For more insight into business-to-business advertising strategy, refer to the Advertising in Action vignette "Apple: The Strategy behind the Ads."

Advertising in Action
Apple: The Strategy behind the Ads

Since 1989, Apple has focused its communications on the general business market. In this market, Apple is attempting to build awareness that the MacIntosh is a superior computing solution for mainstream businesses. In 1990, Apple advertised via a broad range of media, including newspapers, television, and radio. The company's message emphasizes that its product is superior in terms of actual usability. The key phrase in many of Apple's ads was, "The most powerful computer is the one people actually use." As well, Apple addressed the market-place's negative perceptions regarding the price of Apple computers by introducing new affordable products such as the Mac Classic. Here's some additional information about these campaigns.

The Superiority Campaign

In the superiority campaign, Apple was attempting to enhance its credibility with the business market. In two of its advertisements (see pages 467 and 468), the aim of the message is to show what are the key requirements

of business customers—requirements concerning accounting and financial planning and networking capabilities—and to demonstrate that Apple Macintosh is superior in meeting every requirement. Further, each ad stresses the ease-of-use benefit offered by Apple computers. This campaign ran in national business magazines such as *Canadian Business* and many national daily newspapers.

Mac Classic Campaign

The advertisement shown on page 469 was part of the campaign to launch the new MacIntosh Classic in the marketplace. It too was based on the premise that "the most powerful computer is the one that people actually use." The ad focuses on the fact that the full benefit of a MacIntosh is now available at a more affordable price. The media mix for this campaign included prime-time television (to build awareness) and business print media and major-market daily newspapers (to provide potential buyers with more detailed information about the Classic).

"DEL C:\ LOTUS\ ACCOUNT\ $MM2\ *.WKS"

Gee, we would have just used [Trash]
(But then again, the language you see on our screen
is a lot less exotic. It's English.)

The wonder of using an Apple Macintosh computer for business is its uncanny ability to make even the most sophisticated functions look effortless.

Rather than forcing you to spew computer jargon, the Macintosh computer conforms to you. On our screen you'll see the most productive language known to business. English.

Other computers leave you staring at a daunting screen full of numerical syntax. We use simple visual icons.

Want to throw a file out? Drag the file icon to the trash can with your mouse. Done.

Want to open a file? Just click twice on the file folder icon. Presto.

It seems like magic. But we like to think of it as something else entirely.

Common sense.

See your authorized Apple dealer soon.

 The power to be your best.

Apple and the Apple logo are registered trade marks of Apple Computer, Inc. Macintosh and "The power to be your best." are trade marks of Apple Computer, Inc.

Courtesy: Apple Canada Inc.

We've spared no expense to cheapen our reputation.

In 1984, Apple® introduced the Macintosh™ computer on the simple premise computers should work the way people do.

Speak the same language they speak.

Think the way they think.

This revolutionary concept has given Apple a singular reputation as the one computer people actually enjoy using.

And we wouldn't dream of changing that for a second.

What we'd rather do is enhance that reputation by introducing more people to the Macintosh experience.

With a new series of Macintosh computers that everyone can afford.

The Macintosh Classic™ is one of these.

It's the most affordable Macintosh computer ever, yet it has everything that makes a Macintosh a Macintosh.

Built-in networking and a SuperDrive™ disk drive, which reads and writes both Macintosh and MS-DOS® compatible files.

Its amazing $1,349* price also includes a built-in monitor, key-

INTRODUCING THE MACINTOSH CLASSIC. $1,349*

board, mouse, system software and 1MB of RAM (a 40MB hard disk is optional).

And it outperforms the popular Macintosh SE.™

It can run thousands of programs from spreadsheets and word processing to graphics and design.

It's the perfect personal computer for business, education or home use.

Like every Macintosh computer, the Classic shares a compelling quality unavailable in any other PC, at any cost.

People really like using it.

And when you give people the power to be their best, an amazing thing happens.

They'll be it.

Call 1-800-668-1644 for the name of your nearest Authorized Apple Dealer.

 The power to be your best.™

Courtesy: Apple Canada Inc.

MARKET SEGMENTATION——BUSINESS AND INDUSTRY MARKETS

The principles of market segmentation presented in chapter 4 are applicable to business and industrial markets also. However, the variables considered in the development of a segmentation strategy for business and industrial markets are quite different. With consumer-market segmentation, markets are identified on the basis of groups of consumers with common needs and similar demographic characteristics and lifestyles. Target-market profiles are developed according to demographics (age, income, sex, education, etc.), psychographics (attitudes, opinions, and lifestyles), and geographics (regional location, and urban-versus-rural location differences).

In contrast, business and industry segmentation is based on macro and micro variables, and is primarily concerned with the organization profile (its size and its use of products) and the buyer profile (decision-making influences, styles, and buying procedures).

MACRO-SEGMENTATION

Macro-segmentation deals specifically with the characteristics of the buying firm and the buying situation. When marketing firms analyze potential buying organizations and their buying situation, three variables are important: basic organizational characteristics, product application, and purchase situation.

Buying Organization

When determining the most effective means of approaching business customers, marketing firms analyze the characteristics of the buying organization. Factors considered in this analysis include the organization's size and location, the potential usage rate of the product, and the organization's purchase procedure.

When the size of the buying organization is being considered, the goal is to determine where in the market the potential for sales is greatest. Will a firm pursue a smaller number of large firms, where competition may be fierce, or a larger number of smaller customers?

In terms of location, business and industrial markets can be divided into at least three distinct regions: East (Maritimes), Central (Quebec and Ontario), and West (Prairies and British Columbia). The location of potential customers definitely has an impact on the type of communications coverage used. As mentioned earlier, manufacturing concerns are dominant in Central Canada. Other resource-based industries, such as agriculture, forestry, and fishing, are dominant in other regions.

The rate at which a product is used by a customer is also taken into account when means of communication are being chosen. Marketing firms analyze potential usage rates to determine where potential is greatest. For example, will the fewer heavy users of the product be given priority, or do the many light users represent equally attractive opportunities?

The final aspect of the buying organization to be considered is its purchasing procedure. Generally, business customers are highly sophisticated when it comes to making decisions about purchases. Since the value of the transaction is high, there is a trend towards having buying committees (collective decision making) make decisions about purchases. This trend poses communications problems for marketing firms, as numerous individuals must be approached with the sales message.

All of the above factors—size, usage rate, location, and purchasing procedure—affect the marketing activity of supply firms. Recognizing that advertising and personal selling both contribute to the overall marketing approach, the supplier must develop the appropriate communications mix to create awareness, preference, and, ultimately, action by the purchaser.

Product Application

To identify and locate potential target markets, marketing firms can utilize the **Standard Industrial Classification (SIC) system**. The SIC system is a numbering system established by the federal governments of the United States and Canada. The system allows a supplier to track down customers who can utilize its products and services (i.e., customers with buying potential) within an industry. Each SIC category identifies a customer in terms of the number of firms in its classification, its sales volume, and the number of its employees.

The Canadian SIC system comprises 12 classifications ranging from agriculture to manufacturing, transportation, and communications, and to finance, insurance, and real estate. The system subdivides the major classifications into major industry segments (food and beverage manufacturers, for example, are a segment within the manufacturing classification). Within each subclass, companies are identified by product class and product line. The major benefit of the SIC system is that it refines target marketing to a point where specific lists are often appropriate for a targeted direct-mail campaign.

Purchase Situation

The final macro-segmentation variable is the purchase situation. The marketing firm is mainly concerned with the nature of the purchase. For example, is the purchase classified as a new task that will require a lengthy and careful scrutinizing process, and, therefore, significant marketing and advertising resources, or is it a re-order situation that only requires limited communication to get the customer to take action?

In addition, the marketing firm will consider what stage the customer has reached in the purchase-decision process. Have they started to conduct a new search for potential suppliers, or have they already conducted a search and streamlined potential suppliers to a short list? Having the answers to these types of questions allows a marketing firm to decide if a potential customer is worth pursuing.

MICRO-SEGMENTATION

Micro-segmentation variables are qualitative, and relate directly to the decision-making unit (DMU). These variables include buying motives, purchasing strategy, the relative importance of the purchase to the customer, and the personal characteristics of the buyer or of those who have influence on the buyer. These variables have a strong impact on the nature and content of the communications directed at potential business customers.

Buying Motives

As with consumer marketing, the identification of buying motives is imperative. Buying motives in business and industry are rational, that is, they focus on perceived relationships between quality and price, along with other factors. A knowledge of these motives would certainly help advertisers to develop successful business-oriented advertising messages. A list of buying motives is presented later in this chapter.

Purchase Strategy

It is common in buying-selling situations for a customer to be unwilling to accept new suppliers. There is a tendency for buyers to retreat to the familiar and conduct business with current suppliers or those dealt with in the past. Penetrating this type of buying organization is difficult for a sales representative. On the other hand, effective preparatory advertising communications may predispose buyers to new products and services. This predisposition may generate leads (through reply cards) and open up new doors for sales representatives.

Importance of Purchase

How important the purchase is to the customer is a factor in the type of communications chosen for use by a marketing firm. For example, the decision whether to purchase a photocopier may be quite significant for a small firm because of the investment required. If several sales calls must be made to complete the transaction, the seller must weigh the sales-call costs against the profit margin on the unit sale. For a much larger firm, the same decision may be relatively minor, and only a minimum of selling effort may be required; or, a less expensive form of communications (e.g., advertising) may be just as effective for a larger firm.

Personal Characteristics

Business buyers are human and behave like any other consumer; hence, the more knowledge there is regarding the buyer, the more impact the message can have. Depending on the buyer, emotional appeals might be added to the traditional rational appeals of the message presentation.

BUYING CHARACTERISTICS AFFECTING COMMUNICATIONS ACTIVITY

When a marketing firm is developing a communications mix with which to approach business customers, it is important that it understand the basic buying characteristics that influence the decision-making process. These characteristics include multiple buying influences, buying motives, time lags in the decision-making process, centralized purchasing practices, and the uniqueness of individual customers.

Multiple Buying Influences

In many business organizations, one individual may have the authority to sign the purchase order, but there can be many other individuals who influence the decision to buy. Two concepts come into play in this area of influencing decisions. First, a common tactic in business organizations today is to utilize buying committees, which bring together individuals to share the responsibility of making the purchase decision. Second, meetings of various informed groups of people may be held in order to arrive at a purchase decision. This informal meeting of several people in the organization is referred to as a **buying centre**.

Buying Committees To illustrate the concept of buying committees, we will assume that a firm is considering the purchase of a million-dollar piece of production equipment. Since the financial ramifications are significant, it is imperative that the firm make the best possible decision. Consequently, the firm may appoint a committee consisting of key personnel from Production, Engineering, Finance, Marketing, and Purchasing, so that the decision can be evaluated from a variety of angles. Theoretically, the decision-making process requires a great deal of thought, and there is certain comfort for the participants in knowing that a costly purchase decision is also a shared one.

Buying Centres In the more informal buying centre, certain roles are associated with the individuals who compose the buying centre. Researchers have identified five specific roles that a buying-centre unit can assume:

1. *Users*: those who will use the product (e.g., a word processor is used by a secretary).
2. *Influencers*: those who assist in defining specifications for what is needed (e.g., an engineer designs a production line).
3. *Buyers*: those with the authority and responsibility to select suppliers and negotiate with them (e.g., a purchasing agent).
4. *Deciders*: those with the formal or informal power to select the actual supplier (e.g., an expensive technical-equipment purchase may ultimately be the responsibility of a vice-president of Manufacturing).
5. *Gatekeepers*: those who control the flow of information to others who perform the other roles (e.g., a purchasing agent may prevent information from reaching influencers and deciders).[1]

From a marketing viewpoint, it must be determined who on the committee or within the buying centre has the most influence. Once that is known, the best means of communicating with the influence centre must be determined. Advertising can play a key role in this regard; targeted communications, sent through business publications and direct mail, can reach a variety of different individuals within the same organization. It is conceivable that the decision to purchase the textbook you are currently reading was made by a committee whose members were initially made aware of the text by a direct mailing piece similar to the one shown in figure 14.1.

Figure 14.1   A direct-mail piece designed to create awareness and interest

Buying Motives

In business and industry, the buying motives are generally rational. Emotional motives are present to a lesser degree. As indicated earlier, business organizations follow formal buying procedures to ensure that a good mix of quality and price is achieved. Quality, price, and a few other variables form the nucleus of rational buying motives in business and industry.

Price   Price is usually evaluated in conjunction with other factors. The lowest price is not always accepted, as the product may not satisfy other purchase criteria. In situations where the cash outlay is significant, cost information is analyzed over some time. Potential long-term savings potentially resulting from the purchase are weighed against the higher purchase cost in the short term.

Quality Business customers look for consistent quality, as the purchase could ultimately affect their own products (a supplier's product is integrated into the manufacturing process and so could negatively affect the quality of the end product, were the supplier's product of inconsistent quality). Generally, when business customers assess price-quality relationships, they do not sacrifice quality for price.

Service Customers frequently review a supplier's reputation for keeping its current customers satisfied. Also, there is frequently concern about the general availability of service (repair and replacement) when the need arises, particularly whether service is available on short notice.

The Pitney Bowes advertisement in figure 14.2 uses a humorous appeal technique to communicate its price, quality, and service benefits.

Continuity of Supply Customers are concerned about the consistent availability of a product or service. How reliable is the supplier in meeting customer demand? To maintain a steady flow of supply, it is common for customers to deal with numerous suppliers, knowing that factors such as strikes could halt the flow of product from any one supplier.

Emotional Buying Motives Among the emotional buying motives affecting business purchase decisions, two tend to stand out: desire for status and recognition, and reluctance to switch suppliers. A buyer who desires status and recognition may look for the purchase transactions that will enhance the organization's short-term productivity. In essence, the buyer looks for deals that highlight his or her own performance, and ultimately lead to promotion within the organization. The buyer may not be accountable for the purchase decision at a much later date.

A buyer with traditional-buyer syndrome has established a regular purchase routine, and is quite satisfied with current suppliers. Such situations suggest strong business relationships and, possibly, personal relationships with suppliers. Consequently, there is a reluctance to switch suppliers, even though a real need to do so may be there. This reluctance is quite contrary to the rational expectations of the buying organization; nonetheless it exists, and must be dealt with by new suppliers.

Time Lags in the Purchase-Decision Process

The decision-making process in the business market can be tedious. The length of time needed to make a decision for a product such as a computer system is determined by the financial outlay and the sheer complexity of the decision.

Centralized Purchasing

In today's current economic environment, buying organizations are looking for the best possible prices and value for dollars spent. Consequently, many firms have developed centralized purchasing systems, in order to secure better price discounts on volume purchases. For example, The Bay, Zellers, and Simpsons, all owned by The Bay, have formed one large buying division, which purchases for all three retail operations. In these situations, marketers must deal with fewer buyers, all of whom are likely to be upper-management, and this makes the marketing process much more complex.

Figure 14.2 Advertisement with an awareness objective. Pitney Bowes uses a humorous appeal technique supported by rational body copy emphasizing quality, service, and price

Courtesy: Pitney Bowes Canada Ltd. Reprinted with permission.

Uniqueness of Customers

Business customers are looking for products and services that will resolve specific problems and satisfy specific needs. For selling, tailor-made presentations and demonstrations can be developed. Business customers' need for uniqueness presents a challenge for advertising, however, as messages generally focus on the broader-based needs of a target market (group of customers). However, effective advertising that shows concern for productivity and profit improvement should open doors for more persuasive personal-selling messages.

THE ROLE OF ADVERTISING IN BUSINESS COMMUNICATIONS

The primary role of advertising in the business-communications process is to complement and supplement the efforts of the field sales force. Advertising is not intended to make the sale, but it should generate awareness of and interest in a product or service in such a way that it opens doors for more convincing presentations by the sales force. Advertising can make a contribution in two specific areas. First, it contributes to an integrated and efficient communications program, and second, it contributes to company recognition and product-line awareness.

Advertising Contributes to Efficient Communications

When used to advantage, advertising works in harmony with personal selling and sales-promotion activity to develop a unified presentation to prospective customers. In terms of efficiency, advertising can reach a large number of buyers at reasonable costs compared to personal selling, where costs per call are extremely high.

Advertising Creates Recognition and Awareness

Advertising can be a useful vehicle for establishing company recognition and product awareness in the minds of influence centres (i.e., those who influence the final decision). From a strategic-planning viewpoint, advertising that is placed in the right business publications or is directed at the right individual via direct-response advertising, will reach individual influencers that a sales representative may never be able to reach.

Some marketing studies have shown that sales to business customers have been higher among firms predisposed to advertising than among those who have not advertised. It is generally felt that prospects are more receptive to sales representatives from firms that advertise, probably due to the knowledge of the company and product they have received from advertising. Further, as an important information source, advertising in industrial and trade magazines ranks first among the five commonly-used communication channels for reaching business buyers. The other commonly used channels include direct mail, salespeople, trade shows, and catalogues.

SPECIFIC ADVERTISING OBJECTIVES FOR BUSINESS COMMUNICATIONS

Similar to the objective-setting process in consumer advertising, advertising objectives in business-to-business communications flow logically from marketing objectives and strategies. The planning process is the same as that discussed in chapter 5.

When advertising objectives are being established, no attempt should be made to draw direct relationships between advertising and sales targets. Sales targets are documented in the marketing plan, and all marketing activity, including advertising, contributes to their achievement. Business-to-business advertising objectives should be based on what advertising can accomplish, and therefore should be stated in terms of goals for awareness and recognition, for influencing buyer attitudes, and for communicating specific product information. Much like consumer-advertising objectives, business-to-business advertising objectives should be achievable within a reasonable period of time, and they should be quantifiable, so that success or failure can be eventually measured. Objectives that are achieved should have a positive impact on sales. Let us examine some of the more common objectives of business-to-business advertising.

To Develop or Improve Company Image

In the case of advertising aimed at developing or improving company image, the advertiser wants to inform customers about the company behind the products, to create, for the long term, a favourable impression of the company among potential customers. The development of a positive image, which often focuses on the strength of a company's resources (people, technology, progress, etc.), can enhance the reputation of the company and have an effect on customers' perceptions of individual product lines. The Dofasco advertisement in figure 14.3 achieves these types of goals.

To Create Awareness and Demand for Product Lines

If the objective is to create awareness and demand for product lines, a number of situations are possible. Advertising may be the form of communication initially used to introduce a new product line to the market. It can also be used effectively to inform new targets about established product lines, or to reach "influencers" that other communications, such as personal selling, cannot reach.

To Secure Leads

Perhaps the primary objective of a business-to-business advertising campaign is to generate leads for follow-up by the sales force. By analyzing advertising efforts of the past, advertisers may be able to predict the number of leads a particular campaign or advertisement will draw. Since this is an important objective, business advertisers include tear-out coupons or reply cards with their advertisments. Coupons and reply cards make it very easy for prospective customers to seek more information about a product or service. Accumulated coupons and reply cards can be used to develop prospect lists that can be passed on to the sales force for follow-up. Personal contact with an interested customer should result in lower sales costs and marketing costs

Figure 14.3 An image-oriented ad that stresses the resources of the company

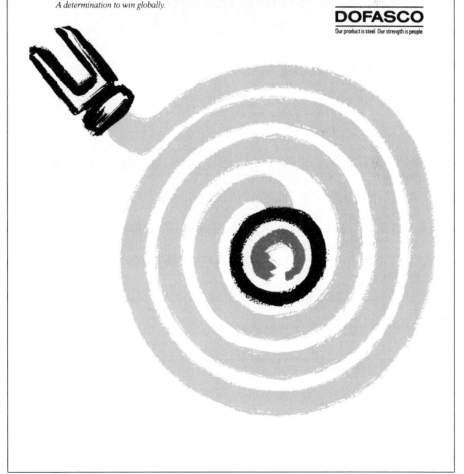

Courtesy: Dofasco Inc.

Figure 14.4 A print ad designed to create awareness and generate sales leads via a clipout return campaign (one execution in a series of advertisements)

Courtesy: Canon Canada Inc. Reprinted with permission.

overall, as the reply cards act as a means of qualifying customers. The Canon Fax ad in figure 14.4 shows a clipout coupon used as a means of generating sales leads.

LIMITATIONS OF BUSINESS ADVERTISING

As discussed earlier in this chapter, advertising is a supplementary activity that should be integrated into a total communications program. In terms of the hierarchy-of-effects model discussed in chapter 4—AIDA (attention, interest, desire, action)—business advertising is designed to draw *attention* to a product and generate customer *interest*. Advertising's role here is to provide basic facts about a product or service, and to enhance a company's image. Once these tasks have been accomplished, responsibility shifts to personal selling.

Business advertising does not create buyer preference; it is not a substitute for personal selling. Personal selling creates *desire* for a product. Getting a customer to this stage requires product demonstrations and a convincing, believable sales presentation that caters to individual buying needs. A carefully designed communications plan, which uses advertising to capture attention and initial interest, and personal selling to generate further interest and desire, should result in the intended response, specifically, buyer *action* or purchase.

*C*REATIVE STRATEGY IN BUSINESS COMMUNICATIONS

When messages for the business market and related markets (industry, trade, professional, etc.) are being developed, certain characteristics of the market must be considered. First, in comparison to consumer-directed advertising messages, which can be emotional in nature, messages for the business market rely more on rational appeals (functionality, cost-savings, dependability, etc.). Second, the needs of the individual business segments are quite diverse; their needs for and expectations of products and services vary considerably. One condition that all business market segments do have in common is a need for products and services that will resolve a problem. Consequently, messages for the business market tend to use more straightforward appeals and to provide potential buyers with sound reasons why they should consider buying the product. The message must be convincing enough to generate leads for the sales force.

Given the rational buying motives of business and industry markets, messages that answer the following questions affirmatively should appeal to buyers and influencers in business and industry:

* Will the product increase production capabilities?
* Will the product decrease operating costs?
* Will the product reduce production downtime?
* Will the product improve the saleability of another product?
* Will service facilities be adequate and readily available after purchase?

The subject matter of these questions can form the backbone of the advertising message. Although many more questions could be added, the intention of the list is to illustrate the importance of appealing to rational buying motives. If business and industry wants service, dependability, profit improvement, and production efficiency, suppliers must provide it, and let business consumers know about it through advertising.

In the past, business-oriented advertising messages tended to be quite dry in terms of presentation style. Illustration, such as it was, was supported with long copy explaining technical details. However, today's business advertising successfully combines the rational appeals needed for business situations with the emotional appeals used for consumer targets. Advertisers realize that there are different ways to reach business buyers, and given the fact that advertising's primary task is to create awareness, the increasing use of the mass media by business advertisers has changed the nature of business advertising dramatically. The Telemarketing advertising campaign (Telecom Canada) discussed in chapter 6 is a good illustration of the contemporary approach to dealing with business buyers. The campaign effectively combines humour with a few business facts to tempt buyers to investigate the savings opportunities the telephone can provide. The Canon-copier campaign discussed later in this chapter also illustrates the contemporary approach to business-oriented advertising.

CREATIVE-STRATEGY CONSIDERATIONS

The different customers in the various business-market segments all have unique problems that must be addressed by advertisers. Unlike personal selling, advertising cannot accommodate messages specifically designed for unique situations. Since messages are targeted at customer groups, copy must be fairly general in nature, catering to the basic motives of the various business segments. Print media are the vehicles most widely used for reaching the business-market segments. In the print media there are five necessary ingredients for obtaining higher readership.[2] These elements, if properly used, can together create an effective print advertisement for business-market segments.

Colour Some studies have indicated that the use of colour increases readership by as much as 50%; therefore, the costs of adding colour (of using the four-colour process) must be weighed against the higher potential readership. Does the increase in readership justify the cost?

Size of Advertisement There are many page options to choose from (full page, half page, third page, etc.). Generally, full-page ads attract more readers than do fractional-page ads, and indeed double-page spreads are becoming more popular with business advertisers. However, a very small ad such as the one for Federal Express shown in figure 14.5 can be just as effective in getting the message across.

Message Appeal Owing to the dominance of rational buying motives in the business market, it is preferable to communicate benefits in a straightforward manner. Emphasis should be placed on the headline and illustration so as to create attention and interest; body copy should be used to substantiate claims. The advertisement for the Banff Centre for Conferences shown in figure 14.6 follows these principles.

Figure 14.5 A small but effective ad reminding customers of a key benefit

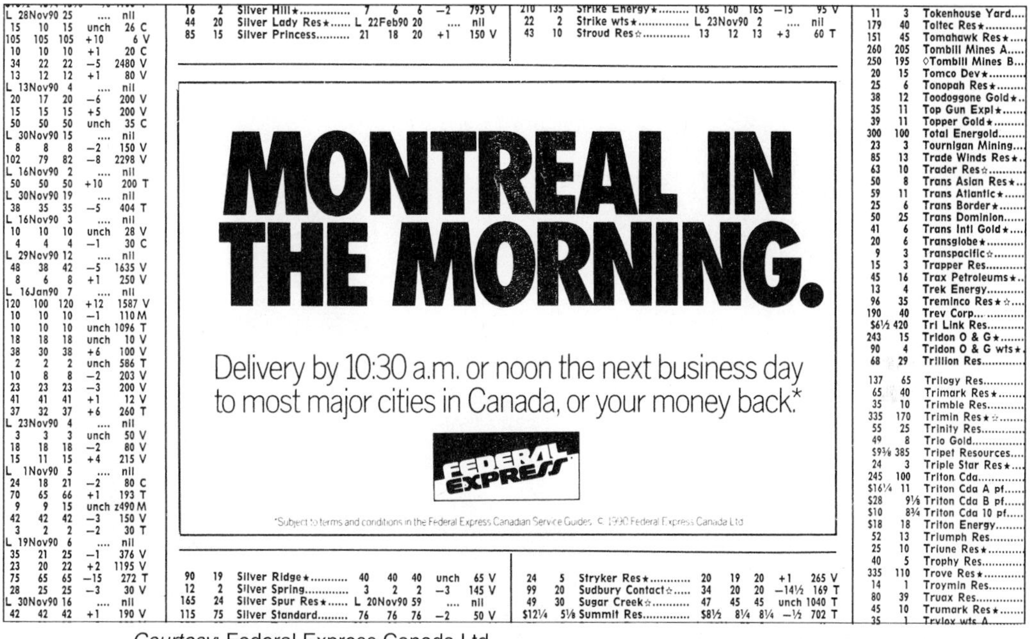

Courtesy: Federal Express Canada Ltd.

Reader Interest Homework and preparation are imperative for successful business advertising. Research should be conducted to find out reader interests. The layout, design, and copy should appeal to those interests.

A Hook Good business advertisements include a convenient means for prospective customers to take action (respond to the message). Consequently, advertisers frequently use tear-out coupons, business reply cards, or 1-800 telephone numbers (the "dial-free-for-further-information" type). Leads generated by such advertising initiatives can be a useful test of advertising effectiveness also. The Canon ad in figure 14.4 illustrates the use of a hook in a business advertisement.

APPEALING TO DIFFERENT BUSINESS-MARKET SEGMENTS

The nature of the message communicated to the various business-market segments varies according to their different needs and different problems. The communications appeal to the organization's rational buying motives and accommodate the uniqueness of each segment.

Business-to-Business Advertising

The term business-to-business advertising has become synonomous with the advertising of finished products and services that other business operations can use to advantage. Advertisers in this category include business-equipment manufacturers

Figure 14.6 An ad that uses an effective visual to grab attention

A Centre Beyond Compare.

Many conference centres promise customer service.

We provide it.

At The Banff Centre, our staff are given regular workshops on how they can serve you better. And it shows.

That is why almost 75% of our customers are repeat customers.

We offer your educational conference complete classroom facilities, comfortable accommodation for up to 600, and fine meals and banquet services.

And a setting beyond compare.

For more information, contact:
Catherine M. Hardie-Wigram
Director, Conference Services
(403) 762-6205
FAX: (403) 762-6388

The Banff Centre for Conferences

Courtesy: Banff Centre for Conferences

(photocopiers, data systems, office automation), communications- and networking-systems manufacturers, insurance and financial-services companies, transportation companies and hotels, to name just a few.

Advertisers in these product categories aim their messages at various management levels in an organization (at both influencers and purchasing agents), and, because of the competitive nature of their markets, they are adopting media strategies that include the use of mass media (television, newspaper, magazines), along with the more targeted business publications and direct mail. The mass media is used to create awareness, while the targeted business media communicates more precise product information.

Industrial Advertising

Industrial advertising is advertising for products that are used to produce and distribute other products. The majority of industrial advertising is directed at customers in the manufacturing sector. Product categories for which industrial advertising is frequently used include chemicals, steel, packaging, and transportation. Generally, advertisers are concerned with reaching buyers in specific industries who can utilize their products or services, and they frequently advertise in trade publications to reach those buyers.

As a general rule, advertising directed at industrial markets focuses on how one product (i.e., the seller's product) can improve either another product (i.e., the buyer's end-product), or the overall operations of the buyer's organization. Consequently, the messages that focus on quality, price, service availability, and dependability strongly appeal to buying organizations.

Trade Advertising

Trade advertising is directed at members of the distribution channel, providing distributors with sound financial reasons why they should carry a certain product line. A product such as canned soup is distributed via a traditional channel, from manufacturer to wholesaler to retailer, and, finally, to the consumer. A considerable amount of personal selling and advertising is implemented in the channel, particularly at the wholesale level, to ensure that the soup is properly distributed. Generally, wholesalers and retailers have two primary concerns: profit margin and saleability (turnover rate). Therefore, messages that communicate proven analytical data regarding these concerns will influence distributors. Messages are directed at the trade through specific trade publications: a food manufacturer may advertise in *Canadian Grocer* to reach retail buyers working for customers such as Safeway, Loblaws or Sobey's.

The Atlantic Packaging advertisement shown in figure 14.7 meets some of the message requirements for both industrial advertising and trade advertising.

Institutional Advertising

Institutional markets include governments, the military, restaurants, hospitals, and schools. These markets consume vast amounts of supplies and services, and since quantity is a factor, the buying concerns that must be addressed in advertising

Figure 14.7 An advertisement with a trade-oriented message

Courtesy: Atlantic Packaging Products Ltd.

messages are relationships between quality and price. The government market uses a bid-and-tender system when dealing with potential suppliers, meaning that the lowest bid that meets the specifications of the task is automatically accepted. In other segments the quality of the product may be of greater concern; this presents an opportunity for advertising to be effective.

Professional Advertising

This segment is diverse, and includes doctors, lawyers, engineers, accountants, architects, and so on. Most professional segments have their own publications that serve

Figure 14.8 An example of an awareness/image ad

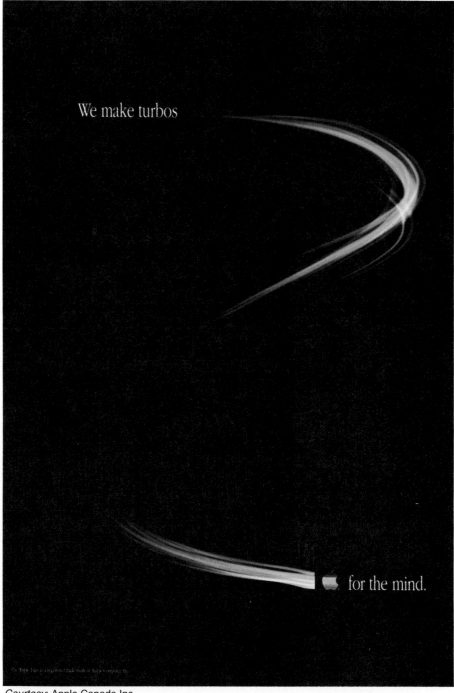

Courtesy: Apple Canada Inc.

their needs. The medical profession, for example, is served by periodicals such as *Geriatric Medicine*, *Modern Medicine of Canada*, and *Psychiatry in Canada*. Advertisements in these and other professional publications tend to focus on detailed product information or on how the professional can perform a job more efficiently and effectively by using the advertised product or service. As a result, messages that focus on convenience, time saving, or reducing cost will appeal to professionals. They may also be concerned about their professional image, so there is a good opportunity for ads that appeal to professionals' emotions by invoking prestige and status.

Corporate Advertising

Corporate advertising is designed to convey a favourable image of a company to its various publics. These publics include shareholders, potential investors, customers, employees, suppliers, and middlemen. Corporate campaigns involve long-term objectives, and messages that are designed to alter the public's attitudes toward and opinions of the organization. Corporate advertising can have an indirect effect on a customer's perception of the company's product lines or services. Some research studies have attempted to establish relationships between corporate advertising and its impact on the purchase of specific products. There is some support for the belief that buyers have a more favourable attitude towards corporate advertisers because of the awareness and image that advertising helped to create. The Apple Canada illustration in figure 14.8 is an example of an awareness/image ad. This ad ran in 1990 in event/theatre programs.

Corporate advertising can accomplish a variety of objectives. Some of the more common objectives of corporate campaigns are as follows:

1. To improve or establish a corporate identity (e.g., to bring all company products under a corporate name, logo, or slogan)
2. To attract potential investors (e.g., to communicate a positive image to an important target market, the firm's advertising may stress the strength of the firm's people or technology)
3. To create corporate goodwill (e.g., in a public relations vein, messages can be sent to customers, suppliers, employees, and other publics solely for the purpose of influencing public opinion favourably towards the firm)
4. To take a stand on an issue (e.g., to present the company's viewpoint on a government regulation that has an adverse effect on the firm and, potentially, its customers). Such advertising is referred to as **advocacy advertising**. This advertising takes a stand on an issue, for or against, and messages frequently appear in mass-circulation newspapers where high awareness and extensive communication of details can be achieved.

*M*EDIA STRATEGY IN BUSINESS COMMUNICATIONS

In selecting the media that will effectively and efficiently reach the various business-market segments, business advertisers must consider numerous strategic factors. As with the consumer-media strategies discussed in chapter 9, the key factors include the target market, the budget, the nature of the message, the combination of reach, frequency, and continuity, the coverage, and the best time to reach the target. There are, however, differences in approach between consumer and business media strategies.

FACTORS AFFECTING MEDIA STRATEGY

Target Markets

As discussed in the early sections of this chapter, business markets are segmented according to macro variables such as the size of the buying organization and its intended use for the product, and micro variables such as decision-making influences, styles, and buying procedures. Advertisers examine these variables in an effort to discover the best way to reach a target.

The availability of targeted publications in many business segments aids advertisers enormously in the communications process. There are two types of publication categories that service the needs of business segments: **horizontal publications** and **vertical publications**.

Horizontal Business Publications These publications reach people who hold similar jobs in different companies and business-market segments. Magazine titles such as *Marketing* and *Traffic Management* are titles of horizontal publications. Other, more general business publications, such as *Canadian Business* and *The Financial Post*, can also be classified as horizontal publications. The content of these magazines focuses on issues of concern to business generally, and appeals to a diverse group of management personnel.

Vertical Business Publications These publications reach people with different jobs in specific industries,and, consequently, are read by all employed within a buying organization or industry segment. Magazines such as *Food Service and Hospitality*, and *Canadian Plastics Directory and Buyer's Guide* are classified as vertical publications.

The choice between horizontal and vertical publications is largely dependent on the nature of the product or service to be advertised. In making the choice, business advertisers might consider the following two principles:

1. If the product or service is suitable for only a few industries, then vertical publications targeted to those industries is the best selection.
2. If many industries are potential customers, then horizontal publications will be more effective. In addition, there may be ample opportunity to utilize non-traditional media, such as television, to reach the same target.

Budget

As mentioned earlier, advertising budgets in business marketing are not necessarily large, since more money is traditionally allocated to personal selling. Nonetheless, even with smaller budgets, media choices can be cost-efficient. Once the decision has been made whether to use horizontal or vertical publications, or combinations of them, the advertiser must select from among the alternative means of reaching the target market. As in consumer media situations, advertisers look at the CPM figures for the alternatives. Advertisers also evaluate the quality of the publication (specifically, its editorial content) when choosing between alternatives.

Nature of Message

Creative considerations have already been discussed in detail. In relation to media-strategy factors, messages generally concentrate on product details, and are informative in tone and style. Commonly, ads use long copy to provide proof of product claims. Consequently, the print media (vertical and horizontal publications) and direct mail are very attractive media options.

Reach versus Frequency versus Continuity

Let's start by briefly reviewing these three media-strategy variables:

- *Reach*: refers to the number of customer buying organizations the message communicates with
- *Frequency*: refers to the number of times the message reaches the customer buying organization
- *Continuity*: refers to the length of time required to ensure impact on a target market through a particular medium

Since business publications offer targeted capabilities, they enable advertisers to effectively reach their audience. However, the numbers that are reached are very low compared to the numbers reached by consumer advertising. Considering the specific nature of the purchase decision in the business market (it is rational, more complex, and usually time-consuming), it is preferable to keep a message in front of the target in order to reinforce previous advertising and personal-selling messages. As a result, the frequency and continuity variables are more important strategy considerations than reach is. Because of possible budget restriction and low reach, it is preferable to concentrate messages in fewer publications.

Degree of Coverage

In business advertising, coverage refers to the number of business segments the message is directed at. The degree of coverage depends on the nature of the product and its potential application and usefulness to the variety of business segments. Both the targeting capabilities of business publications and the coverage capabilities of direct-response advertising ensure that messages can reach any segment, regardless of location.

Best Time to Reach Business Targets

Business publications and direct-response advertising are geared to reach prospective buyers in their working environment. But there are problems inherent in conveying advertising to the workplace. For example, the prospect may be pressed for time and read only portions of a publication, so many details of advertisements may be overlooked, and many ads will not be seen at all.

To counter this, numerous business advertisers are allocating more media dollars to approaching business customers and shifting their media strategy toward utilizing mass media. The advantages of using mass media (television, outdoor, and broader circulation magazines) include the following:

1. Customers are reached when they are in a relaxed environment (non-business hours); they are more receptive to messages, which means higher levels of product awareness.
2. More general media offer broader appeal to an expanded circulation base, which not only includes buyers and purchasing agents, but all of those within an organization who may influence the buying decision (e.g., those serving on a buying committee).

Consider the case of Canon Canada Inc. In recent years, Canon has been an extensive user of the mass media to advertise a variety of business products. Their investment in copier advertising has paid off, as Canon is the leader in the photocopier market with a 26.6% share of market (see figure 14.9). Xerox is second with 18.9%. Canon uses a balanced media mix that includes television, direct mail, and print ads in the business press and general print media like *Time* and *Maclean's*.[3]

Media Alternatives

The traditional and most commonly used media alternatives include business publications, direct mail, and trade shows, which combine advertising and promotional literature with personal selling.

Direct Mail Direct mail is frequently chosen as an alternative to trade publications. The primary advantage of direct mail is its ability to reach a predetermined and precisely defined target market (organizations the advertiser has defined as good prospects for its product or service). Direct mail, then, is cost-efficient, and provides a good conversion rate (i.e., conversion to actual sales) if proper follow-up procedures are in place in the marketing organization. Manufacturers can purchase lists from a variety of Canadian list sources, or they can develop their own lists, using the Standard Industrial Classification system.

Refer back to figure 14.4, and note the use of long copy in the Canon Fax ad. Since the mailing will be directed at interested prospects, it is effective to include in it a simple product picture accompanied by in-depth information and a tear-out reply card that can be sent away for further information. These creative considerations, communicated to qualified buying organizations, add up to a successful direct-response advertising campaign.

Trade Shows The purpose of participating in a trade show is to showcase any number of a company's product lines. For sellers, the primary advantage of a trade show is that it provides them with the opportunity to present product information on a personal basis, in a situation where the buyer comes to the seller. Essentially, the seller has a captive audience that is prepared to be very receptive to advertising messages. The success of any trade show depends on the integration of personal selling, demonstrations, displays, advertising, and promotion literature. Trade shows also present sellers with opportunities to secure business cards from prospects, which can be used at a later date as leads for a sales force or advertising follow-up.

However, trade shows will only be effective if the company commits enough financial resources to present an appropriate image of the product line and company.

Figure 14.9 The use of mass media (television) by a business advertiser to break through the clutter of business-publication advertising. The message reaches target in a different environment.

CLIENT: Canon Canada Inc.
DIVISION: Copiers
TITLE: "Performer"
LENGTH: 30 sec. English
AGENCY: Ian Roberts Inc.

MUSIC/FX: ELECTRONIC THROUGHOUT
V.O. ANNCR: Introducing a high-performance machine for your office. Canon's NP 7550 Copying System.

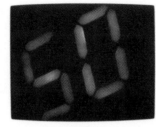

Zero to fifty in 60 seconds flat.

Automatically shifts to the right paper size.

Zooms up and down.

Does two-sided copying...

...from two sided originals.

And sorting. All automatically.

That's why Canon's NP 7550 is the automatic choice.

So step on it: you've got deadlines to meet.
MUSIC: (HOLD UNTIL END)

Courtesy: Canon Canada Inc. and Ian Roberts Inc. Reprinted with permission.

At trade shows, the competition is fierce, so the participants endeavour to leave a favourable impression with prospects. Companies concerned with marketing costs are probably wise to eliminate trade shows from their media mix and to focus on more traditional media alternatives.

Summary

In order to advertise effectively to the Canadian business market, advertisers must recognize that the variables and behaviour characteristics that influence business purchases are quite different from those that influence consumer purchases.

When developing communications programs for business markets, advertisers must consider macro-segmentation and micro-segmentation variables. Macro-segmentation is based on the characteristics of the buying firm and the environment surrounding the buying decision—specifically, the characteristics of the organization such as its size, location, and product-usage rate; product application; and the purchase situation.

Micro-segmentation is qualitative, a measure of rational buying motives, of the purchase strategy of the buyer (e.g., whom the buyer prefers to deal with), of the importance of the purchase (largely based on its dollar value), and of the personal characteristics of the buyer (e.g., is there potential for influencing the buyer's emotions?)

When a firm is developing communications programs for the business market, it must consider certain unique characteristics of that market. First, there can be multiple influences on a purchase decision. The use of buying committees and the various roles associated with influence centres means that the advertising message must be directed at numerous people in the buying organization. Second, messages must primarily appeal to rational buying motives and focus on price, quality, service, and continuity-of-supply benefits.

The primary role of advertising in the business-communications process is to complement and supplement the efforts of personal selling. Advertising creates awareness and interest for a business product or service, improves a company's image, and helps secure leads for the sales force to follow up.

In terms of creative strategy, effective business-oriented advertisements offer to resolve a problem for the prospect. The message is communicated in a straightforward manner and provides sound reasons why a company should buy the product or service advertised. Traditional media used in business advertising include the business press, direct response (direct mail), and trade shows. More recently there has been greater use made of the mass media. Advertisers now feel that reaching the same prospects when the prospects are in a more relaxed environment can work to the advertisers' advantage. The use of mass media has also changed the nature and content of business-to-business advertising messages: emotional appeals have been added to the base of rational-appeal techniques commonly used in business-to-business communications.

Review Questions

1. With respect to the four Ps and basic buying behaviour, how does business marketing differ from consumer marketing?
2. Identify and briefly explain the macro-segmentation variables that influence a business buy.
3. Identify and briefly explain the micro-segmentation variables that influence a business buy.
4. What do "multiple-buying influences" refer to, and how do they affect the communications process between advertisers and buyers?
5. Identify and briefly explain the rational buying motives that business-oriented advertising messages must appeal to.
6. Briefly describe the following:
   a) trade advertising
   b) professional advertising
   c) corporate advertising
   d) business-to-business advertising
   e) vertical publications
   f) horizontal publications
7. What are some objectives of business-to-business advertising?
8. What variables tend to positively influence the readership of business-oriented advertisements?

Discussion Questions

1. "The expanded use of mass media in business communications is a wise investment for business-to-business advertisers." Identify and discuss the pros and cons of this statement.
2. "Without effective follow-up by the sales force, a business firm's investment in direct-mail advertising is a waste of money." Discuss this statement.
3. "The future of business-to-business marketing lies in direct marketing and direct advertising strategies." True or false? Discuss this statement, using examples of your own choice.

CHAPTER 15 Retail Advertising

In studying this chapter, you will learn

- The role and importance of advertising in retail-communications activity
- The categories and types of retail advertising
- The roles of planning and objective setting in retail advertising
- The budgeting methods and allocation procedures common to retail advertising
- The process by which a retailer determines what to advertise
- The creative and media considerations exclusive to retail advertising

Retail advertising in Canada covers a broad spectrum of retail operations, from the local and independent sole proprietor to the largest national department-store chain. Consequently, the role and importance of advertising vary considerably from one advertiser to another.

The intent of this chapter is to highlight those aspects of advertising that are critical to the successful operation of a retail establishment. Many of the concepts have been discussed in other chapters, but this chapter brings them together in the context of retail applications.

THE ROLE OF RETAIL ADVERTISING

The role that advertising plays in the retailing environment can vary considerably depending on variables such as the size of the retail operation and the retailer's perception of advertising's importance in the promotion mix.

Small retailers, who often lack knowledge and expertise in marketing and advertising planning, tend to question the value of advertising. Small retailers often view advertising as an expense item that has an immediate—and negative—impact on profit margins. In contrast, large retailers such as department stores and national specialty-store chains always expect to advertise in order to remain competitive. The uppermost question in their minds is how much to spend on advertising. These retailers view advertising as a necessary investment that contributes to the long-term success of their operations.

Some retailers emphasize advertising at the expense of other elements such as sales promotion and personal selling. For example, many retailers have moved toward a self-serve concept to save money on salaries. Such a strategy, however, is usually a mistake. The principle of the promotion mix is the same for retailing operations as it is for nationally branded products: all promotion-mix elements must be considered as equals when a retailer is developing a marketing plan. All the advertising in the world may be ineffective if a retailer does not provide adequate levels of in-store service to keep customers satisfied. Therefore, each element of the promotion mix must be used according to the role it can play in achieving the objectives of the retail operation.

Regardless of the size of the retail operation or the importance of advertising in the promotion mix, all advertising activities must be carefully planned so that the short-term and long-term objectives of the organization are achieved as far as possible.

THE RETAIL PROMOTION MIX

Advertising is only one element of the promotion mix. Retail operations utilize the same promotion vehicles as do national brand manufacturers in order to inform consumers about their stores and the merchandise and services they offer, and to persuade them to take appropriate action. The four components of the retailing promotion mix are advertising, personal selling, sales promotion, and public relations.

Advertising In the case of a retail operation, advertising is any indirect or non-personal communication to a target market by a specific retailer.

Personal Selling Personal selling, in the context of retailers, involves face-to-face communications between a retail salesperson and a customer.

Sales Promotion Sales promotion is offering any direct or indirect incentive to retail customers (in the form of discount coupons, special sales events, contests, etc.). This form of activity also includes all in-store displays and merchandising exhibitions.

Public Relations The public-relations part of the promotion mix involves communications programs designed to sustain a positive image for the retailer and a favourable relationship between the retailer and its various publics. Generally, all retailers are interested in generating publicity about their operation. Publicity is free published information about the organization. In retailing, publicity often attends store expansions, openings of new locations, and personnel promotions.

In addition to these traditional elements of the promotion mix, there are two other significant factors determining where customers shop. These factors are customer service and availability of credit. The communication of information about customer service and the availability of credit is often part of a retailer's advertising.

Customer Service Customer service comprises additional benefits that can differentiate one retailer from another. For example, the availability of home delivery, layaway plans, free alterations, and merchandise-return privileges can make one store more appealing to consumers than another.

Credit Availability Credit availability refers to the retail operation's acceptance of major credit cards such as MasterCard, Visa, or American Express. Many of the large department stores, such as The Bay, Eaton's, Simpsons, Sears, and Canadian Tire, offer their own credit cards.

CATEGORIES OF RETAIL ADVERTISING

Prior to discussing the various types of retail advertising, we should first examine the categories of retail operations involved in advertising. Each category uses advertising in a different way, according to the nature of the products and services it offers consumers.

Retailers Selling Branded Merchandise

Retailers selling branded merchandise include department stores such as The Bay, Sears, and Zeller's; drug stores such as Shoppers Drug Mart and Guardian Drugs; and supermarkets such as A&P, Safeway, and Provigo. Much of the advertising in these operations focuses on the brand names of merchandise they carry or on their own private-label brands. Refer to figure 15.1, an example of Sears advertising for branded merchandise. Advertising content may also stress the extra services provided and the availability of credit in order to attract customers.

Figure 15.1 Print advertisement for "branded" merchandise (page from a newspaper advertising supplement)

Courtesy: Sears Canada Inc. Reprinted with permission.

Exclusive Dealerships and Franchises

Exclusive dealerships and franchises are retail operations such as car dealerships, car-rental agencies, and fast-food franchises, to name only a few. Advertising in these operations often originates from two sources. In the case of franchises such as McDonald's or Kentucky Fried Chicken, each franchisee (local owner) contributes funds towards advertising by the franchiser (national organization). The franchiser invests in advertising in the local markets, where its products are available, to create awareness and preference. The local franchisee may supplement this advertising with additional local advertising in order to attract customers to its store.

The situation is similar with car dealerships. The manufacturer advertises nationally to consumers to create awareness and preference for its automobiles, and suggests that customers visit their nearest dealer for a test drive. The local dealer advertises to advise customers where they can buy the automobiles, and to announce special sales events and other promotion activities.

Local Trades and Services

Local trades and services make up a group of advertisers who are entirely local and include the wide range of trades and services available in any given market. Included in this category are businesses such as independent retailers, restaurants, insurance agents, real-estate firms, electricians, plumbers, and other household-repair and renovation specialists. The amount of time, effort, and planning these businesses devote to advertising is usually limited, and they often rely on the services and expertise of local media representatives to help develop their advertising messages.

TYPES OF RETAIL ADVERTISING

Product Advertising

Product advertising, often referred to as promotional advertising, is designed to obtain immediate response from the target audience (that is, to increase store traffic). This type of advertising announces store sales on regular merchandise, inventory clearance sales, and so on, to urge the consumer to visit the store and buy. In many cases, a sense of urgency is associated with the advertising (declarations such as "only three days left," or "Best-Buys-Ever sale" are not uncommon). Refer to figure 15.2 for an illustration of promotion-oriented advertising. Product advertising does not have to be "sale"-oriented. Many retailers advertise the quality of their merchandise and differentiate their stores from competitors' on different bases. For example, a retailer may attract customers with its wide assortment of merchandise, its exclusivity, or its newness.

Institutional Advertising

Institutional advertising is designed to create a favourable image of a retail store. Generally, the objectives of such advertising are long-term. The advertising attempts to position the store in customers' minds so that they will consider a visit when they must make a specific purchase. A clothing store may, for example, attempt to position itself as a fashion leader, a leader in brand-name selection, or a leader in superior, personal service. A discount-drug-store chain may consistently position itself as having the lowest prices all of the time.

A generally accepted rule of thumb is that it is necessary to integrate the short-term components of product advertising with the long-term components of institutional advertising in all forms of retail-advertising communications. On the creative side, it is also important to be consistent in the use of type style, art work, and store logos and

Figure 15.2   Promotional advertisement designed to encourage immediate response

Courtesy: Clothe & Craft Shoppe. Reprinted with permission.

lettering in order to present a consistent image. Logos, in particular, are something that customers can easily remember.

Co-operative Advertising

Co-operative advertising is the sharing of advertising costs and materials between suppliers and retailers, or between several retailers working together on an advertising campaign. There are two different types of co-operative advertising: vertical, and horizontal.

Vertical Co-operative Advertising **Vertical co-operative advertising** is the sharing of costs by a supplier and a retailer. The supplier and retailer agree to a specified cost-sharing plan (e.g., a 50/50 split or some other agreed-upon ratio). The manufacturer may provide finished print and broadcast-advertising materials to which the retailer may ad the store's name, or which the retailer might integrate into the store's own advertising. A car dealer may utilize film footage from a national advertisement for a specific automobile; a grocery chain might use illustrations from a variety of suppliers and integrate them into its weekly newspaper ads and flyers. Point-of-purchase materials, which can be used to develop more effective in-store merchandising displays, are another form of vertical co-operative advertising.

Horizontal Co-operative Advertising **Horizontal co-operative advertising** is the sharing of costs by a group of retailers. Such advertising efforts are designed to encourage consumers to visit a specific shopping mall or shopping district in a certain area of a city. For example, local merchants might form a downtown business association, which could decide to advertise co-operatively to promote shopping downtown. The retailers in a shopping mall might contribute to a co-operative advertising fund to attract shoppers to special events such as annual sidewalk sales.

Co-operative advertising is common between manufacturers and retailers. For both, there are advantages and disadvantages in the co-op practice.

The advantages of co-operative advertising for retailers are as follows:

1. The frequency of advertising is increased since the co-operative advertising budget goes much further. For the retailer, there is a higher sales potential, with less direct investment in advertising.
2. The quality of the advertising (creative) improves, assuming that professionally prepared materials are available from the manufacturer.
3. The image of the retailer can improve because of its positive association with nationally advertised brands that have their own favourable image.

The disadvantages of co-operation advertising for retailers are as follows:

1. Co-operative advertising funds may be tied in with other trade allowances that encourage retailers to purchase more than the normal volume of product. In this case, the retailer may regret the extra purchase (remaining inventory) after the advertising has expired.
2. Very often, smaller retailers do not purchase enough volume to qualify for the

use of co-operative advertising funds. Therefore, such funds are of more bene-fit to larger retailers than to smaller retailers.

The advantages of co-operative advertising for manufacturers are as follows:

1. Co-operative advertising reduces local-market advertising costs, since rates in certain media are lower for local advertisers than for national advertisers. Therefore, investment in co-operative advertising is a good overlay for a national plan.
2. Co-operative advertising helps inform local consumers as to where a manufac-turer's product is available (e.g., an advertisement might say that a certain brand of socks is sold exclusively at ABC Department Store).
3. In combination with other trade-allowance programs, co-operative advertising assists in securing product distribution. Some retailers do not list (will not carry) products whose manufacturers do not provide co-operative advertising support.

The disadvantages of co-operative advertising for manufacturers are as follows:

1. Retailers control how and when the co-operative advertising funds will be spent, not the manufacturer.
2. Co-operative advertising funds are usually a trade-promotion expenditure. Monies allocated by the manufacturer to trade promotion are unavailable for consumer advertising, which means that there is less direct contact with the target market. While national brand marketers may value their own consumer advertising more, they recognize that they must spend money on co-operative advertising to maintain satisfactory relations with the trade.

RETAIL ADVERTISING PLANNING

So that there is guidance for retail advertising planning, proper advertising objectives must be established. Large retail advertisers such as department stores and national chain stores develop advertising plans very similar to plans for national-brand prod-ucts and services. They examine market conditions and competitive activity, evaluate past advertising efforts, assess problems and opportunities, and develop advertising objectives and strategies for the forthcoming year. In a retailing situation, the advertis-ing objectives can be classified as long-term objectives, which include institutional considerations; and short-term objectives, which include product- and event-oriented advertising considerations for the year. For more insight into how these variables affect retail advertising planning, refer to the Advertising in Action vignette "Image-Building at Eaton's."

Regardless of whether the objectives of the advertising are long-term or short-term, the advertising itself must elicit the proper behaviourial responses from the con-sumer. If you recollect the discussion of hierarchy-of-effects models in chapter 7, you will remember that these stages are awareness, comprehension, conviction, and

Advertising in Action
Image-Building at Eaton's

When you think of Eaton's, the image or perception that probably comes to mind is one of a department store with a strong, dependable reputation for quality. It is a traditional department store offering a wide range of products and services to customers. Its image is probably quite different from those of competitors such as The Bay or Zellers.

In today's competitive marketplace, there is a strong need for Eaton's to distinguish itself from the competition. Essentially, all department stores offer the same types of products, though the services each provides can differ. With shoppers being much more money-conscious, they must have a real reason to shop at one department store and not another. Nationally, the battle for market share is fierce. Among the big department stores, market shares are as follows:

Market share (%)

Sears	21.0
Zellers	15.2
Eaton's	14.6
The Bay	13.0
Woolco	12.7
All Other Stores	22.5
	100.0

In preparing its latest campaign (1990), Eaton's and its advertising agency assessed the market situation and considered a number of variables that would influence the direction of their advertising. Among these variables were the recessionary economy (e.g., if you spend in such an environment, how much do you spend?), the degree of competition (the market-share and media-spending patterns of

major rivals), the type of advertising Eaton's has traditionally done (i.e., a heavy emphasis on retail or promotion advertising and a smaller investment in national, image-building advertising), and the key benefits Eaton's offers customers (guaranteed quality, wide selection, and a reputation for being a customer-centred organization).

As a result of this situation analysis, Eaton's took a bold step, deciding to place a much heavier emphasis on image building. It described the new approach as "store-as-brand" advertising. In other words, the quality of its image advertising would be upgraded from a production viewpoint, and the style and themes would be more like those used in the advertising for a national brand—say, for Coke, Pepsi, or Maxwell House coffee.

Strategic highlights of the new approach include:

1. Higher production budgets that are close to those of national-brand advertisers (the typical cost of this type of ad is in the $80 000 to $130 000 range for a 30-second commercial). Eaton's developed a pool of five of these commercials.
2. Creative is much less focused on product, and price plays only a minor role.
3. A traditional benefit, one in which Eaton's had always had a tremendous equity, returned to centre stage. The "Goods-satisfactory-or-Money-Refunded" guarantee is a crucial aspect of the message.
4. The slogan "We are Canada's department store" was dropped. Instead, each advertisement stresses a different reason for shopping at Eaton's.

continued

5. The national media budget increased significantly, and less emphasis was placed on retail-or promotion-oriented advertising. The previous year, Eaton's spent $8.8 million on national advertising, the majority of it on radio (44% of the budget) and less on television (34% of the budget). Also, Eaton's spent $24.1 million on retail advertising in the previous year, the majority of it in daily newspapers. In the new campaign, the balance between national and retail advertising shifted, with greater emphasis placed on television.

To illustrate the new creative strategy, one commercial shows four young boys anxiously awaiting the arrival of a new dishwasher. Just when they think it won't be delivered, an Eaton's truck drives up the street. The viewer is puzzled by their excitement. The puzzle is resolved in the final scene when the boys are seen playing in their new cardboard fort. The voice-over says, "At Eaton's we know the purchase of a major appliance is usually a big event. That's why we stock a wide range of top-quality appliances priced right every day and back them up with the Eaton's guarantee."

Adapted from Jim McElgunn, "Store-as-brand policy returns in new TV campaign for Eaton's," *Marketing*, October 22, 1990, pp.1,3.

action. The advertising campaign should strive to obtain store preference—in other words, to establish the store within the consumer's frame of reference as a preferable place to shop for certain items.

LONG-TERM OBJECTIVES

Examples of a retailer's long-term institutional objectives might be as follows:

- To contribute to the overall profitability of store operations
- To develop a specific image in the mind of the target audience (e.g., an "upscale specialty boutique" or a "leader in price discounting")

Slogans usually play a key role in establishing the image of a retail operation. The use of slogans will be discussed in the section of this chapter entitled "Creative Strategy".

SHORT-TERM OBJECTIVES

Short-term objectives are more product-specific and operational in nature. Similar to advertising objectives for a nationally branded product or service, short-term retail-advertising objectives should be specific, quantifiable, and achievable within a realistic and specific time frame. Examples of such objectives could be as follows:

- To increase sales by 10% in traditionally slow sales months
- To create an awareness level of 75% in the store's trading area, among the store's target market

Once the measurable objectives have been established, the retailer can focus on the qualitative side of advertising planning. In this regard, the retailer must decide "what" to communicate—the actual content of the advertising message.

The retailer establishes a list of communications, or creative, objectives (recall the planning procedure outlined in chapter 5). There are a variety of creative objectives a retailer might consider when developing an advertising plan: increasing consumers' awareness of the store and of the merchandise it carries, developing the store's image, positioning the store, promoting special events, building store traffic, increasing the average number of purchases, and increasing sales.

Increasing Awareness of Store and of Merchandise Carried

The retailer must communicate important details about the store in order to attract customers. Hence, retail ads commonly focus on the store's name and location, the variety of merchandise it carries, and the services it offers. For the sake of current customers, anything that is "new" should be communicated (new lines, new services, or new policies). Once a reasonable level of awareness has been established, the retailer can consider adding some of the other creative objectives to the advertising scheme.

Developing a Store Image

Retailers must continuously strive to differentiate themselves from competitors; otherwise, they risk falling behind in the race for share of store traffic. The image a store strives for is based on the quality and variety of the merchandise it carries and on the additional services it provides for customers. There are a wide range of potential store images:

1. Image can be based on size, as is the case with some specialty boutiques, discount department stores, and department stores.
2. Image can be based on clientele: a store might stock designer labels to attract upscale adult targets, or price brands to attract lower-income groups.
3. Image can be based on price: a retailer might claim that it will not be undersold, or that it will match all competitive prices yet offer more personal service.

Positioning the Store

As discussed in chapter 4, positioning refers to the image the product (in this case, the store) has in the minds of consumers. Therefore, positioning and image objectives are similar, but positioning more clearly involves the competitive aspects of retailing practices today.

To illustrate the importance of positioning in retailing, consider the advertising of Black's and Home Hardware. Black's has spent a fortune in national television and print advertising, using Martin Short as a primary spokesperson for the chain. The company's message always stresses quality and uses the now familiar slogan "Black's is photography" to position the company in the consumer's mind. Home Hardware uses a multi-media campaign (television, direct mail, newspaper inserts, and in-store displays) to position itself as a store for the do-it-yourselfer. The company's slogan is "Home Hardware...home of the handyman."

In the food-distribution industry, Loblaws successfully positioned itself, through advertising, as the innovator of generic products. More recently, Loblaw's advertising has focused on the President's Choice line of merchandise (specifically on its good value) and on the company's line of green products to appeal to the environmentally-conscious consumer.

Promoting Special Events

A special event gives customers one more reason for visiting a store. Special events are often tied in with other forms of sales-promotion activity, and are usually planned well in advance. Event-oriented advertising usually revolves around a certain theme that the target market will find appealing. Refer to figure 15.3, a Father's-Day sale supplement issued by Sears. Eaton's has a "Trans-Canada" sale each year, a very big event for this company, which supports the event with a multi-media campaign. Examples of other event advertising might include the following:

- A fashion show in a local shopping mall, with all fashion-apparel retailers participating
- An annual "midnight-madness" sale organized by main street retailers in the downtown core. Such an event might involve expanded hours of operation and an emphasis on low prices.

Building Store Traffic

Traffic refers to the number of people who visit a store, and the frequency with which they visit. The surest way to improve retail sales is to attract more customers to the store. If they do not make a purchase on the first visit, at least they will have been exposed to the merchandise and services provided by the retailer. Stores such as The Bay and Sears frequently offer discounts on regularly priced merchandise to build traffic on Saturday (a key shopping day for department stores). These campaigns stress a sense of urgency—they tend to be one-day-only events. Retailers may easily measure the success of these types of promotions by comparing the average number of sales transactions on the discount Saturday with the average number of transactions on a regular Saturday. The value of the transactions is not important.

Increasing the Average Number of Purchases per Consumer

Many retailers adhere to the notion that it is easier to get current customers to make more purchases than it is to attract new customers to a store, so they direct their advertising messages toward current customers. For example, it is quite common for large department stores to send customers direct-mail offers (statement stuffers) with their monthly credit invoices. Smaller retailers can use customer receipts to develop their own direct-mail lists. In this area, some retailers send mailings to customers announcing a "preferred-customer sale" (special event). Tip Top Tailors has a preferred-customer list (members have cards), and direct mailings are made to the list announcing preferred-customer sales. Often incentives such as twenty-five-dollar and fifty-dollar vouchers accompany the mailing, offering customers additional incentive

Figure 15.3   A special event advertising supplement (Father's Day) (insert in major daily newspaper)

Courtesy: Sears Canada Inc. Reprinted with permission.

to visit a store. Shoppers taking advantage of such an offer means that the average number of purchases should increase for the retailer.

In another example of this sort of campaign, Zeller's has effectively increased average purchases through promotion of its "Club Z." Customers accumulate points every time they make a purchase at Zeller's, points which are later redeemable on merchandise. This type of promotion builds loyalty and increases the average number of purchases made by customers.

Increasing Sales

The most important business objective for any retailer is to increase sales (and profits) each year. As is the case with any product-advertising campaign, it is difficult, if not impossible, to link advertising effort directly to sales performance. Customer purchases are influenced by other factors such as price, store location, quality of merchandise, and service provided. For this reason, retailers should not establish advertising objectives that are related to sales.

DECIDING WHAT PRODUCTS TO ADVERTISE

If short-term advertising objectives focus on products and events, how does the retailer decide on what products to advertise? As a general rule, retailers should advertise items that traditionally move quickly. Mistakes made by a retailer in purchasing the wrong merchandise (merchandise that is unwanted by its customers) cannot be corrected by advertising.

In deciding what to advertise, the retailer should consider a number of factors:

1. If an item is offered on sale, the perceived value must be sufficient to attract customer attention and interest. The reduction must be significant in percentage and dollar terms.
2. Seasonal items and events are popular for advertising purposes. For example, Christmas, Valentine's Day, Mother's Day, and Father's Day (refer to figure 15.3) present advertising opportunities for a host of products. Other retailer-oriented occasions, such as year-end inventory clear-out sales or anniversary sales, are worthy of advertising support.
3. The retailer may re-advertise the manufacturer's product. As discussed earlier under co-operative advertising, the retailer may benefit from the prestige of the manufacturer's product.
4. Retailers tend to advertise related goods, as opposed to advertising single products. For example, a men's-wear store will advertise slacks, shirts, ties, and sports jackets all together.

RESPONSIBILITY FOR PLANNING

The size of the retail operation has a significant influence on how the advertising function is managed. Management practices vary between small retailers, medium-to-large-size retailers, and department stores. Who performs the advertising function, and how, varies considerably among these organizations.

Small Retailers

The owner or manager of a small business is usually responsible for advertising as well as a host of other duties. Small, local retailers do not use the services of an advertising agency, but they do work with media representatives, who help them prepare creative for their respective media. The local radio or newspaper sales representative, for example, will help the retailer develop a script or layout, and assist in commercial or print production.

Medium to Large Retailers (Multiple Store Operations)

Retailers in the medium-to-large classification can either form their own advertising departments—referred to as **in-house agencies** (involving creative specialists responsible for copy and art work for all product and institutional advertising, and, possibly, media specialists for media placement)—or they can work with an advertising agency. In either case, the advertising effort is the responsibility of an advertising manager. The advertising manager devises the budget, is responsible for creative and media planning and execution, and works internally with other managers to determine what to advertise. If an external advertising agency is employed, the advertising manager is the link between the organization and the agency.

Large Department Stores and National Chain Stores

The organization of the advertising department in large department stores and chain-store operations is similar to that of medium and large retailers. However, because of the size of the operation, the responsibility for advertising and promotion activities may be divided into functional areas. At the head of such an organization's advertising department is a marketing, or advertising, director (they may be one and the same, or advertising may report to marketing) who oversees the administration of advertising planning and provides direction to the advertising activities of the firm. Reporting to the director of advertising might be an advertising manager and a sales-promotion manager. The advertising manager's responsibility here is similar to that of the advertising manager in medium-to-large-sized retail operations. The sales-promotion manager assumes responsibility for all aspects of promotion planning (events, sale programs, etc.) and in-store merchandising and display activity.

It is very likely that large department stores and national chain-store operations will employ the services of an advertising agency. Since these organizations invest heavily in advertising, it is prudent to seek the knowledge and expertise of an agency. As discussed in chapter 3, there are agencies that specialize in retail accounts. This reflects the increased sophistication of retail advertising for all sizes of retail operations. Many retailers realize they can take advantage of the advertising and marketing strategies utilized for national-brand products.

CREATIVE STRATEGY IN RETAIL ADVERTISING

With its advertising and communications objectives defined, the retailer is ready to proceed with the development of creative strategy. As discussed in detail in chapter 6, creative strategy focuses on how the message will be communicated to the target audience. Generally, messages are developed to appeal to the rational or emotional buying motives of the customer.

The Use of Themes

As stated earlier in the chapter, all retail advertising should integrate product-specific (promotional) advertising with institutional advertising. Strategically, all advertising should revolve around a central theme or slogan, and provide continuity when it comes to style.

A theme may be explicitly or implicitly stated, but it should accomplish three major purposes:

- Impress the target audience with a unique and favourable image of the retail business
- Provide continuity for an advertising campaign that lasts for three months or more (the longer the better)
- Promote the achievement of the advertising objectives the retailer has established[1]

Themes usually involve a carefully worded slogan that helps position the store in the mind of the customer. The slogan is a summary statement of the key benefits the store is trying to communicate, so it should be short, easy to remember, and visible in all media advertising. To illustrate the use of slogans and their relationship to theme advertising and positioning, lets consider the following slogans:

> "Yes, that's all it costs when you shop at The Bay." (The Bay)
> "Your money's worth and more." (Sears)
> "Where the lowest price is the law." (Zeller's)
> "Black's is photography." (Black's)

When slogans are grouped together, certain observations can be made. The Bay, Sears, and Eaton's all stress value in the price-quality relationship, which is important in attracting retail shoppers. Refer to figure 15.4 for an advertisement stressing value. In contrast, Simpsons focuses on the consumer by implying that its merchandise will fit your life style (a more individualized approach), while K-Mart focuses on savings (rational appeals only), which is in line with that company's overall marketing strategy.

Themes and store image can also be communicated implicitly through the layout and design of advertisements. For example, an advertisement that appears cluttered suggests a discount- or bargain-oriented store. In contrast, advertisements that utilize space better and employ beautiful typography and art work may suggest a more upscale retail operation.

Creative-Design Considerations

Since newspaper is the medium most commonly used by retailers, the design considerations presented in this section focus mainly on print media. Nonetheless, broadcast advertising is employed by larger advertisers, so certain considerations regarding

Figure 15.4 Integration of product (promotional) advertising and institutional advertising via slogan. Note the use of research verification in lower portion of ad to substantiate promise.

Courtesy: Sears Canada Inc. Reprinted with permission.

broadcast media must be noted. For both television and radio commercials, two essential elements must be included:

- The identity of the store and its particular superiority over its competitors must be established during the flow of the commercial.
- A thematic event of high interest to the target audience should be included.

In addition, commercials should clearly establish the prices of the items in order to maximize the next day's sales response; finally, there should be continuity from promotion to promotion in terms of creative approach and production techniques in order to maximize long-term impact on consumers.

In the case of print advertising, the retailer must consider copy and design elements (discussed in chapter 7). Regarding copy and art work, there are four components which must be integrated if the ad is to form a complete message (one that will make an impression on consumers). These components are the headline, the body copy, the illustrations, and the signature. Since these concepts have been discussed previously, material presented here focuses on the retailing implications of each area.

Headlines The headline serves two basic purposes: to attract attention and to lure the potential customer into reading the body copy of the advertisement. Retail headlines tend to be "news-oriented;" they make announcements of special events and sales. Consider the following examples:

> "Huge Expansion Sale!"
> "Spring Fashions at Wholesale Prices"
> "Grand Opening!"
> "The Best-Buys-Ever Sale"
> "Dealer Invoice plus $100 Gets You a New Car."

As can be seen by these examples, the headline communicates the basic sales message; other components provide more specific details. The Canada Trust headline in figure 15.5 moves the reader into the body copy immediately.

Body Copy The body copy helps to develop interest and desire in the reader. To get the desired response, the copy should be simple and to the point. It should also be informative, and elaborate on the headline where applicable. A common practice in retail advertising is to use a series of subheadlines instead of body copy. Extraneous copy should be avoided at all costs. The Canada Trust RSP ad utilizes several subheadlines, and body copy elaborates on RSP details.

Illustrations In retail advertising, line drawings and photography are both popular. Regardless of the type of illustration used, the illustration must be meaningful and must grab the reader's attention. Since body copy is of less importance in retail advertising, the combination of headline and illustration must combine effectively to make a favourable impression on readers. To add visual impact to the advertisement, the retailer has the option of presenting the product alone or showing it in proper context. For example, the latest in fashion swimwear might be photographed by a pool or at the beach.

Figure 15.5 Headline dominates, and grabs attention; subheadlines and factual body copy substantiate headline claim.

Courtesy: Canada Trust. Reprinted with permission.

Signature A retailer should use the same signature in all forms of its retail-advertising and other communications (store sign, point-of-purchase displays, shopping bags and boxes, etc.). The store's distinctive logo and slogan should be in keeping with the image of itself the retailer is attempting to convey, and, wherever appropriate, should summarize the central theme of the institutional advertising message (refer to the examples of slogans for department stores presented earlier in this chapter). Logos are an important communications device, since they are easy to remember. For example, even very young children can identify McDonald's by the golden arches, which can be seen from a great distance.

The retailer must develop an appropriate layout for advertisements (see chapter 7). Developing the layout involves locating the various elements (i.e., blending together the headline, copy, illustration, and signature) so that they communicate the intended message effectively.

M*EDIA STRATEGY IN RETAIL ADVERTISING*

This section of the chapter focuses on the media considerations that surround retail advertising activity. The budgeting process is examined in the context of the retail environment, and then the various media alternatives are evaluated with regard to their role in retail advertising.

Budgets

A national product manufacturer must first develop a total budget, and then divide the budget among the various individual products that are to be advertised. In retailing, the situation is similar, but the manner in which the total budget is divided is quite different. In the case of a large department-store retailer, the first step is to develop the total budget and then divide it among departments, merchandise lines, media, and times (days, weeks, months). There are three budgeting methods that are specifically appropriate for retail operations: the all-you-can-afford method, the percentage-of-sales method, and the objective, or task, method.

All-You-Can-Afford Method While this method definitely restricts serious advertising planning, many retailers are forced to use it. For small retailers—particularly sole proprietors—who lack knowledge and expertise, there is no alternative but to examine last year's sales, advertising expenditures, and profits, and make a decision, based on those figures, as to what they can realistically afford the following year.

Percentage-of-Sales Method A budget can be based on a predetermined percentage of last year's sales, of this year's sales, or of the sales projected for the year in which advertising will occur. Alternatively, an industry-average percentage can be used (assuming it is known) as a basic starting point for developing a budget. The simplicity of these methods makes them popular with retailers, but neither method recognizes the value of advertising and the effect it can have on the business (i.e., they assume that the budget depends on sales, not vice versa).

Objective (Task) Method This is probably the best method, but it is the most complicated for any retailer to use. The task method uses a three-step procedure:

- Establish the quantifiable advertising objective—say, to increase awareness from 40% to 60% among the store's designated target market.
- Identify the advertising weight (type and amount) required to accomplish the objective.
- Determine the costs associated with the advertising weight.

This budgeting method requires a considerable knowledge of media planning, usually beyond the scope of the retail advertising manager. As a result, the use of an advertising agency is warranted if this budgeting approach is to be used. Occasionally when this method is used the budget is found to be beyond the actual means of the retailer. In this case, the objectives will have to be re-evaluated and the tasks reformulated in accordance with the revised objectives.

Budget Allocations

Once the budget has been developed and approved, the next task is to divide the budget between departments, merchandise, media, and seasons (times of year).

By Media The retailer can select from a variety of media, with local newspapers and radio being the most popular among smaller and medium-sized advertisers. Other media options include transit, outdoor, newspaper supplements, direct mail, and television, if it can be afforded. Media selection will be discussed in greater detail in a subsequent section of this chapter.

By Time of Year Retail advertising is usually distributed cyclically over one year. For example, an outboard-marine/motorcycle-dealer retail operation will advertise in the spring, as consumers prepare for approaching summer. For such an operation, advertising may also be heavy in the late summer and early fall period, when the retailer wants to clear out inventories.

Other retail businesses may not be influenced by seasonality factors. In this case, retailers normally schedule advertising in accordance with sales patterns throughout the year (advertising is generally scheduled before peak buying periods). Grocery-store and department-store advertising uses a straight-line weekly approach, with supplements being inserted in newspapers to communicate details of weekly specials and sales. For the average retailer, a month-by-month media plan is the logical approach, with the amount actually spent fluctuating in accordance with sales expectations.

Some retailers subscribe to the contracyclical theory of advertising timing. In this situation, the retailer will advertise more heavily in periods where sales are low, in order to improve sales and so remove cyclical sales patterns.[2] If advertising does not have the desired effect in the low sales period, it will at least get the retailer into the consumer's frame of reference so that it is there when consumers are ready to buy.

By Department and Merchandise For larger retail operations with a greater variety of merchandise and departments within the total operation, the selection of what merchandise to advertise may be linked to seasonality factors. The decision might also be made to allocate funds to fast-moving lines or slow-moving lines. Some retailers subscribe to the practice of promoting fast movers in order to sell more of them, while others prefer to promote slow movers to deplete inventories. Stores that do carry a wide assortment of merchandise may take a straight-line approach to advertising (media dollars allocated evenly), with the actual products to be advertised varying from season to season (or from month to month).

Media-Selection Considerations

A variety of media are suitable for retail advertising. As is the case with product advertising, the retailer's task is to select the media that will reach the greatest number of people within the target market, at the lowest possible cost (a mix of media effectiveness with media efficiency).

The advantages and disadvantages of the various media have been discussed in detail in chapters 11 through 13. A summary review is given here, with retail implications being noted where appropriate.

Newspapers Newspaper is the primary medium used by retailers, since it allows the visual illustration of the items offered for sale (the communication of sale items is a common advertising objective). Refer to figure 15.6 for an illustration of sale-oriented advertising. In most local markets, the daily newspaper is widely read; therefore, the advantages of cost and coverage come to the forefront. In addition, only short lead times are required, so last-minute copy changes can be accommodated with relative ease.

Supplements Supplements are prepared (preprinted) advertisements inserted into the fold of a newspaper, or delivered directly to households in a specified trading area. The costs of supplements are partially offset by co-operative advertising funds available to retailers from suppliers. Generally, the use of supplements is confined to larger retail advertisers who can afford it. Figure 15.3 shows part of a Sears supplement (the supplement is 40 pages long, all told) devoted to Father's Day items. Supplements for large department-store chains appear in major newspapers on a weekly basis. These ads often assist consumers in their shopping preparations, so if a retailer's advertisement does not appear in a given week, the store will be passed over by those shoppers who refer to supplements frequently.

Radio Radio is also popular with local-market retailers, since the medium offers selectivity and frequency. Station formats appeal to different target markets, so if the station target market matches the retailer's target market, radio can be an excellent media alternative. A jean manufacturer such as Levi's (Levi-Strauss) or GWG (Great Western Garment Company) will advertise heavily on local rock stations, while a car retailer might prefer to target a gold or easy-listening audience. The cost of radio is low compared to the costs of other media, so the medium offers the advantage of frequency-of-message to the retailer.

Catalogues Catalogues are an important form of communications for large national retail organizations. They are a constant reminder to customers of the products and

Figure 15.6 Illustration of sale-oriented retail advertising. Communication of sale items is a common advertising objective.

Courtesy: Clothe & Craft Shoppe. Reprinted with permission.

services available at the store, and they are a source of reference that customers refer to frequently when specific purchases are contemplated. Some of the biggest users of catalogues are Canadian Tire, Beaver Lumber, Ikea, Consumer's Distributing, and Grand & Toy.

Television From a retailing perspective, the store's image and personality can be portrayed effectively via television, but the costs of this medium are very high, making it an unrealistic alternative for smaller retailers.

Television can be used effectively by large retail advertisers. Canadian Tire and Home Hardware use the medium to achieve institutional advertising objectives (i.e., to establish an image and to assist in positioning the operation in the consumer's mind). Stores such as those mentioned above can advertise nationally and make local-market television buys also, in order to support those of their stores operating in local markets.

For local-market retailers who do use television, the quality of the commercials produced by the local television stations is generally poor. Very often, commercials for local retailers are indistinguishable from each other stylistically. The commercials show consumers the store from the outside and the inside, while an announcer comments on the products and services offered.

Outdoor and Transit These two media alternatives are grouped together, because the advantages they offer the retailer are quite similar. Both media are suited for reminder-oriented communications; they are good supplements to a primary medium such as newspapers. Also, they are useful for communicating a consistent message—they can focus on store image, while other media focus on sales merchandise, special events, and so on. On the negative side, messages must be brief, and both outdoor and transit lack prestige compared to other media.

Magazines Since most Canadian magazines are distributed regionally or nationally, they are unlikely candidates for retail advertising. However, the growth of city magazines such as *Toronto Life*, *Vancouver*, and *Montreal Magazine* has resulted in greater media usage by certain types of retail advertisers. These magazines generally appeal to an upscale target market, so they are appropriate for advertising high-fashion clothing stores, fine restaurants, and entertainment establishments.

Yellow Pages The yellow pages are a staple advertising medium for local-market advertisers, particularly for the trades and services group discussed at the beginning of this chapter. To illustrate the importance of the yellow pages for this group of advertisers, let's assume you want your leaking roof repaired. Probably no retailer is in your frame of reference, so the first source you are likely to check will be the yellow pages of the telephone directory. You could very well contact a few of the firms that are advertised "attractively" in the yellow pages. A consumer purchasing flowers for a special occasion may conduct the entire transaction by telephone. This again indicates the potential impact yellow-page advertising can have.

A final comment on the actual selection of media by a retail operation: the retailer's advertising objectives play a key role in the process of deciding what media to use. Retailers who seek to create a dominant impression of a store's—or a product's—uniqueness in the marketplace are wise to select a primary medium so that consumers become familiar with the advertising. If the advertising budget allows it, a secondary medium can be used either to complement the primary medium, or, perhaps, to perform a different task. One medium might be used for product-specific advertising, while another could carry institutional advertising.

Summary

The role of advertising in a retail operation is dependent upon the size of the retailer and the importance of advertising in the retail promotion mix. As with product advertising, the retail promotion mix includes four basic elements: advertising, personal selling, sales promotion, and public relations.

There are three basic types of retail advertising. Product advertising, or promotional advertising, is designed for immediate target response, and includes announcements of sale events and special offers. Institutional advertising is designed to develop an image for the retailer—that is, to provide an ongoing reason for consumers to shop at the store. Co-operative advertising refers to the sharing of advertising costs and materials between suppliers and retailers (vertical co-operative advertising) and between a group of retailers (horizontal co-operative advertising).

The objectives of retail advertising are both long-term and short-term. Long-term objectives are institutional, and focus on the image of the retailer. Short-term objectives are product-specific, and activities resulting from those objectives are designed to build store traffic, to create awareness of the store and its merchandise, to assist in positioning the store in the customer's mind, and to promote special events.

The management of the advertising function varies according to the size of the operation. In smaller firms, the owner, or manager, assumes the responsibility for advertising and works with local media representatives to develop creative. In larger firms, an advertising manager works with an advertising agency, and follows marketing-planning and advertising-planning procedures.

Creative considerations for retail advertising centre on the use of themes. Themes may have an institutional orientation. They involve slogans that give consumers a reason to consider shopping at a store, or they may be product- or event-oriented (announcements of annual sales, seasonal sales, etc.). In terms of creative execution, it is recommended that all advertising incorporate both institutional and product, or promotional, advertising elements.

With respect to media strategy, the newspaper and radio media are most popular with retailers because of the local-market coverage benefits they offer. Television is usually too expensive for small retailers, but is appropriate for large retailers who spend a considerable amount on image advertising. For small retailers who do not spend much on media advertising, local newspaper media and the yellow pages are important forms of advertising.

Review Questions

1. Distinguish between institutional advertising and promotional advertising.
2. What are the three basic categories of retail advertising? In terms of advertising activities, what are the differences between the categories?
3. What is co-operative advertising? What are the benefits and limitations of co-operative advertising from the retailer's point of view? From the manufacturer's point of view?
4. Identify the basic differences between retail advertising's long-term objectives and short-term objectives.
5. What factors influence the retailer's decision regarding what products to advertise?
6. What is the basic role of each of the following copy elements in retail advertising?
   i) headline
   ii) body copy
   iii) illustration
   iv) signature
7. What is meant by the "contracyclical theory of advertising timing?"
8. Briefly describe the following terms, as they apply to retail advertising:
   i) vertical co-operative advertising
   ii) horizontal co-operative advertising
   iii) in-house agency
   iv) event-oriented advertising
   v) traffic
   vi) supplements
   vii) all-you-can-afford budgeting

Discussion Questions

1. Themes play a major role in retail advertising. Discuss the role of themes, using examples of your choice to substantiate your opinions.
2. Assume you are an owner of an upscale dining establishment appealing to higher-income groups. You are located in the downtown core of a major Canadian city. Which media would you use to create awareness of and interest in your restaurant? In justifying your selection, provide appropriate rationale, and rank the media from most important to least important.

3. You are about to open an independent painting and decorating shop in a small town (population 10 000). Your store is located on the main street in the downtown area. How will you make the residents of this town aware of your store? Briefly discuss an appropriate media strategy, and provide supporting rationales for your decisions. Identify a specific town and specific media, if you like.

Illustrative Case for Part Five

Building a Strong Consumer Franchise

A key objective of most—if not all—marketing, promotion and advertising managers is to attract and retain a customer. Often referred to as "building a consumer franchise," the process of developing a relationship with a customer requires a manufacturer or retailer to constantly remind customers, through advertising, of the benefits offered by the manufacturer or retailer and then persuade customers to actually buy a particular brand rather than that of a competitor. Seldom will advertising alone accomplish all of this.

In meeting this challenge, the manager must decide what promotion mix is best. A crucial aspect of developing a balanced plan is deciding how much money to allocate to advertising, consumer promotion, and trade promotion.

Let's review a couple of examples:

1. Sears is Canada's largest department store retailer and a leading advertiser in its market. In 1991, Sears decided to invest heavily in advertising its popular Sears Club (a promotion concept). Sears launched a major campaign to encourage 3.2 million members of the Sears Club to use the frequent-buyer program more often. The campaign was the biggest ever for Sears. The club, open to Sears cardholders, awards points with each purchase; points can be used in buying in-store or catalogue merchandise. The objectives of the campaign were three-fold: to reward loyal customers, to attract casual shoppers more often, and to counteract the success of Zellers' "Club-Z" and "the-lowest-price-is-the-law" campaigns.
2. Red Lobster and Shell teamed up in a promotion that saw 1100 gas stations and 65 Red Lobster restaurants offer consumers coupons for each other's products. The promotion was supported by 30-second TV and radio spots. For the purchase of 25 litres of gasoline, Shell customers received coupons worth $9.99 at Red Lobster. Red Lobster customers received gasoline coupons worth $1.00 to $2.00. According to Linda Strachan, Red Lobster's director of marketing, "the promotion was designed to give customers added value in recessionary times." "Red Lobster was an excellent partner because its image targets families seeking good value," says Graham Jack, sales-promotion coordinator for Shell. Both companies saw the promotion as an exciting way to achieve trial purchase.

Both of these examples demonstrate the need for managers to consider alternatives other than advertising in order to build a strong customer base. Consumer promotions such as these provide consumers with an extra impetus to buy, and they are particularly good in persuading customers to buy a particular brand or shop in a certain location. Generally speaking, consumer promotions can accomplish numerous goals. For example, a well-conceived promotion can

- Position a brand in the marketplace
- Establish a brand's key benefits
- Provide a unique selling feature at the point of sale
- Remove some of the risk for consumers in trying a new product
- Create a theme around which a seasonal or special sales effort can be built
- Gain in-store displays and merchandising support

The objective of a campaign often dictates the type of consumer promotion the campaign employs. A coupon directly influences the price side of the price-value relationship by providing a direct price reduction to consumers. Coupons encourage trial purchase and are also effective in bringing back former customers. A cash refund is another direct price reduction that encourages repeat or multiple purchase among a current user group. Instant-win contests work best for frequently purchased items or items purchased on impulse. They increase the value of a brand and encourage multiple or repeat purchases. Sweepstakes also improve the value side of the price-value relationship by adding excitement to a brand's advertising and a theme for in-store displays. Sampling is effective when used to gain trial among new users or among users of competing products.

In Canada, trade promotion activity is also a priority. In industries such as food and beverages, it is the distributors of the products, not the manufacturers, who call the shots. Buying power is very concentrated in this segment; eight distributor organizations control 80% of the buying. Because of their organizational buying power and the sophisticated wholesaling and retailing network they control, these organizations actually determine the success or failure of a brand. A popular saying among these distributors (Loblaws, Safeway, and A&P, to mention a few) is that "you can do all of the advertising you want, but if I don't carry your product, my customers can't buy it." The implication of this statement is clear—retailers must be satisfied with the turnover and profit margin of the brands they carry. No longer can managers be satisfied with improving only their own profit goals. They must now focus more effort on satisfying the profit goals of their trade customers.

Trends now indicate that trade promotion is getting a fair share of the budget allocations in Canada. It is now estimated that 70% of total marketing budgets are allocated to trade promotion. In the U.S., the corresponding figure is around 50%. What, then, is to be gained from the high spending on promotion? Promotion money directed at the trade influences feature pricing and in-store merchandising support, both important influences on consumer purchases—that is to say, trade-promotion spending alters the price side of the price-value relationship.

Marketing research information from A.C. Nielson verifies the importance of trade spending. In the top 10 high-volume categories in food stores, the incidence of consumers purchasing a feature-priced product is quite high. The percentage varies from 32.5% for ready-to-eat cereals to 61.4% for packaged laundry detergent. More importantly, for the brand leaders in each of the 10 categories, there is a higher rate of purchase when the brand is feature priced. Refer to exhibit 1 for details.

Exhibit 1   Top Ten Product Categories—Share of Volume Sold at Feature Price

	Product Category— Percent of Sales at Feature Price	Leading Brand— Percent of Sales at Feature Price
Ready-to-Eat Cereal	32.5	50.3
Packaged Laundry Detergent	61.4	72.1
Fruit Juices	54.6	84.3
Packaged and Canned Soup	40.9	68.1
Bathroom Tissue	56.0	74.4
Frozen Dinners	40.9	n/a
Cookies	41.7	n/a
Regular Coffee	54.4	61.3
Instant Coffee	54.5	69.8
Drinks and Nectars	40.4	n/a

What can be concluded from this case? For building a consumer franchise, it is essential that strong, creative, and continual advertising be considered as a means of positioning a brand or company in the customer's mind and of clearly defining the benefits offered by the brand or company.

Consumer promotion helps pull a product through the channel of distribution, so it must be considered a crucial element in the mix. A well-conceived and well-executed promotion allows a manager to deal directly with the end users and to encourage them to buy and use more of a branded product. Much like advertising, a promotion is an activity that the manager can control.

Trade promotions ensure that products are available in the distribution channel. In today's price-sensitive environment, trade promotion helps ensure that a brand gets its share of feature pricing, cooperative advertising support, and in-store displays while it is helping trade customers to achieve their own profit objectives. Clearly, a balanced plan including all three elements—advertising, consumer promotion, and trade promotion—is crucial to the success of any brand or company.

Adapted from Ken Riddell, "Joint promotion targets recession," *Marketing*, February 18, 1991, p. 20., from Jim McElgunn, "Sears takes the outside track in major new push," Marketing, February 18, 1991, p. 3., and from Kevin Conners, "Trade marketing: Canada's promotion infant," Marketing, August 6, 1990, p. 19.

Experiential Learning

The objective of this simulation is to have you apply the advertising concepts and planning procedures you learned in the text. In developing an advertising plan, you will reinforce your understanding of advertising principles and procedures in Canada.

Through role playing, group interaction, strategic planning sessions, and sequential decision making, you will learn, first hand, how advertising campaigns are developed. The simulated planning process requires you to assess and evaluate a significant amount of background information in order to develop a properly researched advertising plan. You should refer back to appropriate sections of chapters 5, 6, 9, 10, 11, and 12 whenever you need reminders about planning procedures.

To participate in the simulated planning process, particularly in the media-planning section, you will need to have some exposure to *Canadian Advertising Rates and Data* (CARD), as this is the primary resource for developing the tactical portion of the media plan.

Advertising Planning— A Campaign Simulation

The material for the planning simulation is presented in the following order:

- Introduction and Organization
- The Simulation Process—a description of each step in the planning process
- Company and Brand Profiles
- Market Background
- Exhibits—statistical exhibits of relevant background information

INTRODUCTION AND ORGANIZATION

The market featured in this simulation is the condensed-soup market, which is a relatively large and thriving segment of the food industry in general. Within this market, there are three major brands, all competing for brand leadership. Over the course of this project, you and your classmates will simulate real-life competition between these brands. The nature of the game is competitive. You will be a member of a team representing one of the three major brands. The primary goal of each team is to produce an advertising campaign that will contribute to the profitability of the team's "firm" and improve its position in the marketplace relative to the competition (the other teams).

The abundance of information included in the simulation, combined with the planning sequence provided, should allow you to appreciate the relationship between various marketing disciplines. By the end of the simulation, you should understand fully the relationships between marketing research, marketing and market planning, sales, and advertising.

Advertising strategies cannot be developed until certain marketing strategies have been evaluated and agreed upon. It is with this fundamental planning principle in mind that you should analyze the abundance of information contained in the simulation. You need a thorough understanding of the existing market conditions, of the brand's past performance record in the market, and of the competitive activity of other major brands before you can commence with the planned series of strategy sessions, and make appropriate decisions for your brand.

Objectives of the Simulation Process

"Advertising Planning—A Campaign Simulation" is designed to give you greater insight into managerial problems in the areas of advertising and marketing planning.

The campaign simulation is designed so that the decision problems raised are fundamentally similar to those faced by real managers. The manager or decision-maker in the simulation, like his or her real-life counterpart, is concerned with making decisions in a dynamic, competitive, uncertain environment.

The market environment presented is only a simulation; hence, the strategic-planning-decision variables presented are generalized. The simulation environment is not intended to perfectly represent the condensed-soup market. Also, even though a large amount of information has been included, you will undoubtedly want access to even more. But in real life, as in the simulation, executives are forced to make marketing and advertising decisions on the basis of incomplete data. Your objectives in participating in the simulated planning process should be

- To develop an understanding of the sequence of steps that is involved in the planning and development of an advertising campaign
- To experience the working integration of various disciplines within marketing and advertising organizations
- To experience situation analysis, problem solving, and the process of strategic decision-making
- To participate with all members of your team in the decision-making process

Philosophy of Advertising Planning

The campaign simulation requires that you apply what you have learned in other marketing courses in your business program. Application of your knowledge of the following areas is important to your success in the simulation project:

- Analysis and application of market-research information
- Analysis and application of other supplementary data (i.e., Canadian census data)
- Application of management systems, based on a systematic procedure for establishing objectives and strategies
- Creative planning
- Media planning and placement
- Report writing
- Development of presentations (preparation and presentation of the advertising campaign)

Sample Team   Your team will be composed of four to five members, and will be responsible for the development of a new advertising plan for the following companies, agencies, and brands. The three competing organizations in the simulation are as follows:

Team A

Company Name:	Consolidated Foods Ltd.
Advertising Agency:	Lucas & Sommerhays Advertising Ltd.
Brand Name:	Souptyme

Team B

Company Name:	Power Foods Corporation
Advertising Agency:	Benson & Associates Advertising Ltd.
Brand Name:	Crown Soup

Team C

Company Name:	Select Foods Ltd.
Advertising Agency:	Klein-Mossman Advertising Ltd.
Brand Name:	Select Soup

For the purposes of the simulation, each company and each advertising agency has the same organizational structure. The organization charts are shown in figures A, B, and C.

PLANNING SESSIONS

Session 1: Student Familiarization

The purpose of the introductory session is to allow you to familiarize yourself with the concept of the simulation, and to give you an overview of what is expected.

Figure A   Consolidated Foods Ltd./Power Foods Corporation/Select Foods Ltd.

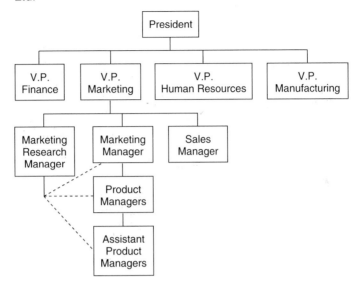

Figure B   Lucas & Sommerhays Advertising Ltd./Benson & Associates Advertising Ltd./Klein-Mossman Advertising Ltd.

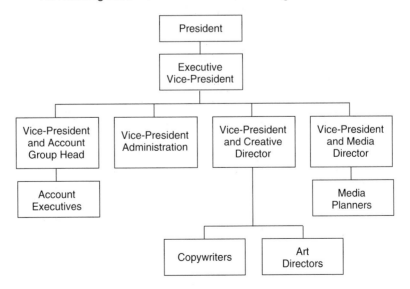

Figure C   The simulation process—schematic diagram of simulation

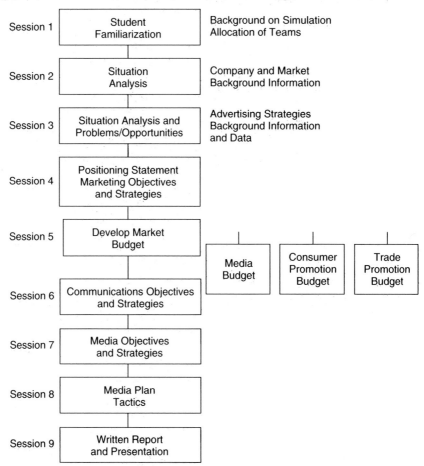

During the session, the competing teams will be organized, and each team will be assigned a brand. The three major brands will be distributed among teams of four to five members each, which could mean that several groups may be working independently on an advertising campaign for the same brand.

Session 2: Situation Analysis

Review of Company and Market Information In Session 2, your primary objective is to review all relevant company, market, and brand information. The purpose is to compile background information that will be included in the advertising plan. Each team will analyze the data presented in order to develop an understanding of market and brand performance. The task is to break the information down so that you can determine what conditions are having an impact on your brand's performance in the marketplace.

Typical information to review for this session includes

- Market-volume trends—national, regional, seasonal, and urban-versus-rural trends
- Market-share trends (major brands)—national and regional trends
- Consumer data—user profile(s)
- Category and brand loyalty
- Brand activity review—product, price, place

Note: Promotion considerations are included in Session 3.

At the conclusion of the session, all team members should be familiar with the competitive environment their company is operating in, and should be knowledgeable enough to discuss the position and activities of their particular brand.

Session 3: Situation Analysis and Identification of Problems and Opportunities

Review of Historical Advertising Strategies In Session 3 the focus shifts from the market and brand environment to advertising and promotion. Your objective is to analyze past advertising and sales-promotion activity to identify those activities which are contributing to the success or failure of the brand. Any observations that relate promotion activity to brand performance (share position, regional strengths or weaknesses, etc.) are worthy of note at this point.

To satisfy this objective, review

- Consumer media expenditures—national and regional dollar and percentage spending patterns
- Advertising share—national trends
- Seasonal media-expenditure trends—national and regional
- Spending trends by medium
- Consumer-promotion trends—major brands
- Trade-promotion trends—major brands
- Creative-strategy evaluation (major brands)—positioning review, image, tone, style, and appeal techniques

By the conclusion of the session, you should be familiar with the advertising strategies of all major brands.

Each team will undertake to develop a list of Problems and Opportunities for its brand. This list will act as a guideline for future marketing and advertising planning.

Session 4: Development of Positioning Statement, and Marketing Objectives and Strategies

At this stage of the simulation, you will have a thorough background knowledge of the condensed-soup market and the marketing and advertising activity utilized by the major brands.

Your primary objective in Session 4 is to establish the positioning statement and the marketing objectives and strategies for the forthcoming year. It is important to note that the scope of the marketing objectives will embrace the four Ps (product, price, promotion, and place) and any financial considerations important to the company. The underlying motivation is to generate ideas that will afford your brand competitive advantage in the marketplace. Each brand must consider the problems and opportunities identified in the previous planning session.

The only limit on each competing brand's objectives is that imposed by time. The objectives should be realistically achievable in a one-year period. All teams are encouraged to be aggressive, within reasonable financial limits. You and your team members should take note of the guidelines that follow:

1. *Positioning Statement* Positioning refers to the selling concept that motivates purchase—that is, the desired image a company tries to project for its product. Effective positioning statements are realistic, specific, and uncomplicated, and are working statements from which substrategies (four Ps) can be developed.

2. *Marketing Objectives* Objective statements identify "what" is to be accomplished in the planning year. The objectives that each brand establishes should be both quantitative and qualitative in nature. Quantitative objectives focus on variables such as sales volume, market share, and profit. Qualitative objectives focus more on product-related activities and changes. All teams should be aggressive with their objectives, within financial limits and time constraints.

3. *Marketing Strategies* Marketing-strategy statements indicate "how" objectives are to be achieved. Strategies usually include a profile of primary and secondary target markets (it's your product; you decide on the targets you want to reach). Do not feel restricted in this area to information included in the simulation.

Marketing strategies also outline the relevance of the four Ps, and where they will figure in the accomplishment of marketing objectives. Product changes and improvements, new products, price changes, promotion-mix changes, and methods for improving distribution levels are all important marketing strategies. (Refer to chapters 4 and 5 for more details.)

In the areas of positioning, marketing objectives, and marketing strategies, your instructor cannot provide firm direction. It is your brand; you make the decisions.

Hints on Procedure: Before establishing market-share and sales-volume objectives, your team must forecast total retail dollar volume for 1992 (refer to exhibit 1 on page 551), using the historical data provided. Manufacturers receive 75% of the total retail dollar volume. Once the team has agreed upon a market-share objective (based on historical trends and other objectives), you can calculate the corresponding sales-volume objective by expressing market share as a percentage of total manufacturer's dollar volume. (i.e., Retail dollar sales × market share × 75% = Manufacturer's Sales Revenue)

Session 5: Developing the Marketing Budget

The next step in the strategic planning process is to develop a marketing budget for your brand. In this planning session, your task is to analyze the factors that are considered when a budget is being developed, and then to employ an established budgeting method to generate a reasonable budget.

As a starting point you should review the information that was analyzed in Sessions 3 and 4. Pay particular attention to projected dollar-volume sales for the forthcoming year. By using the same expense-to-sales ratios as presented in the Financial Statements—Major Brands (see the chart on page 544), you can develop a reasonable marketing budget. It is unrealistic to spend for the sake of spending, but you can make significant increases in spending if you effectively justify doing so.

Consider the following factors when you are developing and rationalizing a budget:

- Total brand spending trends (degree of competition)
- Product category demand and product stage in life cycle
- Frequency of purchase
- Share of market versus share of advertising
- Profitability—profit (dollar/margin) after marketing expenses

For more details on budgeting, refer to chapter 9.

Your company must generate a total marketing budget for your brand. Existing budgets are summarized in the "Company and Brand Profiles" section of this simulation. In developing the budget for the upcoming year, utilize one or a combination of the following established budgeting methods:

- Percentage of sales
- Industry average
- Advertising share/market share
- Task (objective) method
- Combinations of the above

Experiment with several methods to arrive at a comfortable budget. *Hint*: limited knowledge may render the task method inappropriate in this situation.

When the total budget is ready, allocate funds to the various major sub-areas (media advertising, consumer promotions, and trade promotions). The weight you give each area is up to you, but base your decisions largely on your marketing objectives and strategies. Do not attempt to finalize budgets within the three major sub-areas, as they will change considerably when you get to the media-planning stage. Your objective, for now, is to get a sense of how (and why) funds will be allocated to the major areas.

By the conclusion of this session, your company will have formulated a total marketing budget, a budget allocation by type of activity, and a sound rationale to justify the budget requested.

Session 6: Communications Objectives and Strategies

Using input from marketing objectives and strategies, you will now develop communications objectives and strategies for your brand. To prepare for this, your team should review the information, compiled in previous sessions, on problems and opportunities, positioning, and marketing strategies, and analyze past and current creative strategies and competitive creative strategies.

Once the review is complete, your team will develop communications objectives and strategies based on discussion in the planning session. By the end of the session, all team members should agree on the creative direction the brand will take in the following year.

As guidelines for developing creative direction, your team should consider some or all of the following:

1. Creative Objectives

   • Outline the basic message content that is to be communicated to the target market, and what objectives are to be achieved by the content vis à vis awareness, acceptance, preference, or purchase response.
   • Describe the target group the message must reach.

2. Communications Strategy
   A review of "factors considered when developing creative strategy" (chapter 6) should result in clearly worded statements for some or all of the following:

   • Key fact or key benefits
   • Promise statement(s)
   • Reason why statement
   • Support claims (proof)
   • Tone of communications desired—appeal techniques, etc.
   • Themes to be considered
   • For more details on communications (creative) objectives and strategies, refer to the appropriate sections of chapters 5 and 6.

With objectives and strategies confirmed, the next stage is to develop the rough art work to be used in the presentation. Your own art work might turn out to be very rough indeed, but do not worry. This is a planning simulation, but some form (however unsophisticated) of creative art work is necessary for the presentation of the advertising plan. Refer to chapter 7 for script formats, storyboard formats, etc. Rough art work or scripts should be developed for each medium under consideration.

Session 7: Media Objectives and Strategies

Your task in this planning session is to develop a list of media objectives and strategies, based on input from the problems and opportunities sections, and marketing objectives and strategies. Prior to establishing media guidelines for the next year, your team should review relevant market and media background information, and any problems and opportunities considered earlier.

Make sure you look at the following:

• Market-share trends
• Brand media profile
    —Expenditure trends (dollars spent by activity, season, media, etc.)
    —Evaluation of past media strategy
• Competitor media profile
    —Expenditure trends
    —Evaluation of past media strategy

- Target-market profile
  - —Current target profile
  - —Potential new targets
- Problems and opportunities.

By the end of this planning session, your team members must be in agreement on media objectives and strategies. Working together as a team, you will develop the final media plan (final objectives, strategies, and execution details).

As a guideline for developing media objectives and strategies, and using input from the review of information suggested above, consider the following:

1. *Media Objectives* Media objectives clearly outline
   - WHO—target-market profiles
   - WHAT—summary of message to be communicated
   - WHEN—best time to advertise
   - WHERE—priority regions and markets
   - HOW—reach, frequency, continuity, etc.
2. *Media Strategies* The media-strategy section documents more specific details regarding the variables identified in the objectives section. Strategies rationalize why certain media activities and directions are being recommended, such as the use of specific media, the amount spent with each media, media timing, and media and market weight levels. For more complete details on media objectives and media strategies, refer to chapter 9.

To aid in the media-selection process, examine the following sample narrowing-down procedure:

- General Type of Media to Recommend (Choose one or more)
  - —Newspaper
  - —Radio
  - —Television
  - —Outdoor
  - —Transit
  - —Magazine
- Class of Media Within Type (Choose one or more)
  - —*Example: Magazine*—General Interest
    - —Special Interest
    - —Women's
- Particular Medium Within Class (Narrow your selection)
  - —*Example*: Newspaper—*Toronto Star*
    - Magazine—*Chatelaine.*

Session 8: Media Plan (Tactics)

In this session you will develop the actual media plan, which outlines how, when, and where the media dollars will be spent. As in other planning sessions, your team members will develop the final media plan on a co-operative basis.

By this stage you should be familiar with *Canadian Advertising Rates and Data* (CARD). Various media chapters in the text (chapters 10, 11, and 12) include some media cost-calculation examples, for which actual rate cards are used. These rate cards are the same as those contained in CARD. Refer to the examples again to develop a basic understanding of how to use CARD. *Canadian Advertising Rates and Data*, along with some supplementary media exhibits contained in this simulation, is the primary source for your media planning.

Charts and timetables that are appropriate for inclusion are

- Media Cost Sheets (Exhibits 39, 40, and 41)
    —Cost Breakdowns for Recommended Media
- Media Cost Summaries (Exhibits 42 and 43)
    —Spending by Media
    —Spending by Time of Year
- Media Schedule (Exhibit 44)
    —Media Placement (Timing) Summary.

This planning session gets each team started on the development of the tactical portion of the media plan, but you will no doubt find that you and your team need more time to develop an effective plan. Take it! Otherwise your plan might not be as good as it could be.

Session 9: Preparation of Written Report

At this stage of the simulation, your company will have completed all of the essential steps in the planning of an advertising campaign. The next step is to compile a formal report containing all of the key elements that have been discussed and agreed upon in preceding sessions.

Exhibit 38 contains a "Sample Advertising Plan" format that can be used as a guideline for developing the final report. The notes you have compiled throughout the planning simulation will be your primary resource.

Session 10: Presenting the Advertising Campaign

At the final stage of the simulation, your team will present your advertising campaign. A good approach is to play the role of an advertising agency presenting the complete advertising plan to the client for approval. For a presentation of this nature, it may not be practical to have each member participate at the same level. It is the responsibility of the group leader (vice-president, marketing) to determine who the presenters will be, and what content they will present.

To enhance the quality of the presentation, your team can use whatever resources are available to prepare suitable audio-visual aids (slides, overheads, tapes, etc.). The presentation must communicate all of the key elements of your advertising plan.

CONCLUDING COMMENTS

Throughout the simulation, your team will be assigned specific tasks, and you will be asked to analyze information, develop objectives and strategies, and make decisions, all in an effort to develop an advertising campaign. This is a challenging task.

The fact that you will not have at your disposal all of the information you would like reflects a real marketing and advertising environment. The challenge is to combine the factual data which is available with your own intuitive judgment. If you make proper decisions, and you take a logical direction in terms of advertising, the end result should be a campaign that will contribute to the growth of your brand in the marketplace.

You may supplement any lacking information by applying your knowledge of the economic environment that has prevailed in Canada for the past five years. This will add useful information and aid in the decision-making process.

COMPANY AND BRAND PROFILES

CONSOLIDATED FOODS LIMITED

Company Profile

Consolidated Foods Ltd. is a Canadian subsidiary of a large U.S. multi-national corporation. The Canadian headquarters is based in Toronto, and it is from this location that all marketing activity is generated. Branch sales offices are located in each of the five regions of Canada, and manufacturing plants are located in Bramalea, Ontario; Burnaby, B.C.; and Lachine, Quebec.

In 1991, company sales amounted to $225 000 000, generating a profit, after taxes, of $19 500 000. The overall company strategy in the past five years has been one of diversification. Working from a strong base in the manufacturing of food, the company has diversified into the fast-food restaurant business, launching a chain of pizza restaurants (Pizza Express) in most major markets across Canada. This venture has been very successful, and is now contributing 20% to overall company profits.

In its established food business, a cross-section of products is manufactured and distributed, including packaged goods, frozen food, dairy products, and canned goods. The company's soup line, under the brand name of Souptyme, is one of its original brands.

Advertising Agency

Since Consolidated Foods Ltd. is a large, diversified company, several advertising agencies are used by the firm. Souptyme is one of Consolidated's most heavily advertised brands. The account has been handled by Lucas & Sommerhays Advertising Ltd. for the past two years.

Lucas & Sommerhays is the Canadian arm of a world-wide advertising agency based in New York City. They are one of the largest agencies in Canada, billing approximately $140 000 000 annually. Known mainly as a packaged-goods agency, they handle numerous large Canadian packaged-goods manufacturers. Lucas & Sommerhays is a full-service agency, offering services in creative development, media planning and placement, public relations, sales-promotion planning, and advertising research. Its head office is located in downtown Toronto, and other offices are located in Montreal, Edmonton, and Vancouver.

Brand Profile—Souptyme Soup

Souptyme is an established brand on the Canadian market. It has been positioned as the "traditional" soup, and emphasis is put on the wholesome ingredients and delicious taste that each serving provides. Market research confirms that current users have a very positive attitude about Souptyme, and that the wholesome-ingredient benefit is firmly entrenched in the minds of consumers.

Souptyme is available in 20 different varieties, in two pack sizes (10-oz. and 19-oz. cans). Because of the brand's positive reputation, it is premium-priced in relation to other competitors. The marketing department does not feel that a higher regular price has had an adverse effect on market-share trends in recent years.

Up until the present time, advertising themes for Souptyme have concentrated on the "traditional" positioning of the brand. The typical ad uses the average female homemaker as a presenter, in a family context. Positive appeals based on family satisfaction with the taste and quality of Souptyme have been the backbone of recent creative execution. Souptyme relies on both television and consumer magazines to reach its target market.

The competitive nature of the market forces the brand to use trade promotions, which it does to its advantage. A considerable portion of the marketing budget is allocated to trade allowances, and special promotion funds are set aside for co-operative advertising with all food distributors across the country. The company offers the trade an attractive discount package on a quarterly basis. All trade promotions are planned by the marketing department, and are implemented by a nationwide sales force that calls on wholesalers and retailers.

Advertising and Marketing Budget

The advertising and marketing budget for Souptyme follows:

Souptyme Soup	*1990*	($'000) *1991*	*1992 Plan*
Media			
Television	432	425	
Print (Magazine/Newspaper)	144	141	
Radio	–	–	
Direct Mail	–	–	
Outdoor	–	44	
Transit	–	–	
Other	–	–	
Production Expenses	144	200	
TOTAL MEDIA	720	810	
Consumer Promotion			
Coupons	45	105	
Contests	–	70	

continued

Premiums	–	–
Samples	30	–
Other	–	–
TOTAL CONSUMER PROMOTION	75	175
Trade Promotion		
Deal Allowances	300	320
Co-Op Funds	230	335
TOTAL TRADE PROMOTION	530	665
TOTAL BUDGET	1325	1650
TOTAL $ SALES	20 966	22 596
M/S RATIO*	6.3	7.3

*Marketing to Sales Ratio (marketing budget expressed as a percentage of sales)

POWER FOODS CORPORATION

Company Profile

Power Foods Corporation is a publicly owned Canadian company. Originating, in 1923, as a small manufacturing plant in the core of downtown Toronto, the company has grown to become one of the largest food processors in Canada. The company has always been strong in the canned-goods segment of the food industry. Power manufactures a wide variety of canned goods, including vegetables, soups, juices, and sauces, under the brand names of Crown, Cabana, and Sunfresh. The company head office has recently moved to new facilities in Don Mills, Ontario, a suburb of Toronto. The Company recently opened a new manufacturing plant for soup in Mississauga, Ontario. Other plant locations are in Burlington, Ontario and Winnipeg, Manitoba. Regional sales offices are located in various major cities throughout Canada.

In 1991, total company sales were $250 000 000, with a profit after taxes of $31 500 000. The corporate strategy has remained constant over the years; the company's basic philosophy is to concentrate on and protect areas of strength. They remain the largest canned-goods processor in the country. Growth has been based on expansion of canned goods through the development of new lines and additional varieties of established brand names.

Advertising Agency

Since Power Food Corporation is a Canadian-owned company, it identifies with and actively promotes the use of Canadian suppliers. This philosophy has resulted in Power's recent appointment of Benson & Associates Advertising Ltd. as its agency of record.

Benson & Associates is a privately owned Canadian agency, with John Benson owning a controlling interest in the firm. Long on advertising experience, John Benson is an established name in Canadian advertising. Recognized as a creative innovator, he has won numerous advertising awards over the years. He has a background in marketing with a major Canadian beer marketer, and has worked with three large U.S.-based advertising agencies during his years in advertising. Five years ago, John and several associates decided to break way from the U.S. agencies and open up their own. Their agency has grown to the point where it is now billing $50 000 000 annually in Canadian advertising.

Power Food Corporation is one of their largest clients, and the advertising developed by the agency has played a key role in Crown Soup's market-share increases in the past three years.

Benson & Associates is a Toronto-based agency offering a full service to all clients. They have one other office, in Montreal, Quebec.

Brand Profile—Crown Soup

Crown Soup is also an established brand on the Canadian market. Throughout the years, Power Food Corporation has promoted the fact that Crown was the "original Canadian" soup. As the years passed, and other competitors entered the market, this positioning strategy had to change. Although numerous ideas were tried, none was truly successful. Once a dominant brand in the Canadian market, Crown Soup fell on hard times about five years ago. Market share dipped to an all-time low of 20% nationally. At that point, the company hired its new advertising agency (Benson & Associates), and, internally, placed direct emphasis on a share-recovery program for Crown Soup.

A new advertising campaign was developed by Benson & Associates, which was based on a unique creative concept that had never been used in the soup industry. Employing animation and a series of cartoon characters, Crown Soup was advertised as the "fun" soup. This had tremendous appeal to younger age groups, who have an indirect, yet significant, influence on the purchase patterns of homemakers. Since this new creative approach had tremendous appeal to the marketing executives of Power Food Corporation, the advertising budget was increased substantially. Research has confirmed a high level of awareness for the series of commercials promoting Crown Soup, and the brand has once again become a serious threat to competitors in the marketplace.

Coincident with the change in consumer advertising, Power Food Corporation also intensified its trade promotion activity. In an attempt to shake up the market, Crown Soup offered the trade more frequent discount allowances, which resulted in lower-than-normal retail prices. The frequency of trade deal activity allowed for more volume buying by distributors, and as a result prices remained low at the retail level. Hence, Crown Soup maintained a competitive advantage and provided an attractive alternative to the price-conscious segment of consumers.

As a result of renewed competitive activity, Crown Soup is gradually losing its competitive edge. Executives also feel that the animated advertising campaign may be facing wear-out. Because of these concerns, the company executives are considering a change in direction for future years.

Crown Soup is a national brand, available in 10-oz. and 19-oz. tins, and currently markets 15 different varieties. Because of recent trade promotion activity, retail prices are generally three cents to five cents a tin lower than prices of other major competitors.

Advertising and Marketing Budget

The advertising and marketing budget for Crown Soup follows:

	($'000)		*1992*
Crown Soup	*1990*	*1991*	*Plan*
Media			
Television	375	510	
Print (Magazine/Newspaper)	175	235	
Radio	–	–	
Direct Mail	–	–	
Outdoor	–	–	
Transit	–	–	
Other	–	–	
Production Expenses	100	150	
TOTAL MEDIA	650	895	
Consumer Promotion			
Coupons	–	–	
Contests	–	–	
Premiums	–	–	
Samples	–	–	
Other	–	–	
TOTAL CONSUMER PROMOTION	–	–	
Trade Promotion			
Deal Allowances	340	404	
Co-op Funds	393	456	
TOTAL TRADE PROMOTION	733	860	
TOTAL BUDGET	1383	1755	
TOTAL $ SALES	17875	20548	
M/S RATIO*	8.1	9.6	

*Marketing to Sales Ratio (marketing budget expressed as a percent of sales)

SELECT FOODS LTD.

Company Profile

In comparison to other competitors in the soup business, Select Foods Ltd. is a much smaller company. With headquarters in London, Ontario, the company is the Canadian subsidiary of U.S.-based Select Foods International. The Canadian operation is a dominant concern in the area of packaged dry goods. Product lines include a line of dehydrated soups and vegetables, pasta-based dinners, packaged dessert mixes, and a line of packaged dry sauce and seasoning mixes. Major brand names include London House, Catalina, and Select.

Select Foods Ltd. virtually owns the dehydrate segment of the soup market with its Select brand name. However, several years ago, the dehydrate segment of the market started to decline. Faced with a potential loss of business for an important brand name, the company made the decision to enter the canned-soup market and compete head on with Consolidated Foods and Power Foods Corporation. This venture proved to be successful with respect to share performance. It would appear that the strength of the Select brand name carried over to the company's canned-foods business, as the product has been widely accepted by consumers.

In 1991, company sales for Select Foods were in the $100 000 000 range, with net profit after taxes amounting to $7 840 000. The firm employs 500 people, and all manufacturing is located in the London, Ontario plant. Select Foods is a large employer in the London area.

Advertising Agency

Klein-Mossman Advertising Ltd. has been the agency for Select Foods Ltd. for the past eight years. Klein-Mossman handles all the advertising needs for all company brands, and has played a major role in establishing the London House, Catalina, and Select brand names in the minds of Canadian consumers.

Klein-Mossman is the Canadian arm of New-York-based Klein-Mossman International Advertising. Being one of the top 10 agencies in the U.S., they have also carved out a high ranking in the Canadian advertising business. Klein-Mossman has a diverse list of accounts, including several packaged-goods clients, a life insurance company, and numerous departments of the federal government.

Operating as a full-service agency, they are located in downtown Toronto, with other Canadian offices in Montreal, Winnipeg, Edmonton, and Vancouver.

Select Foods Ltd. is viewed as a medium-sized account by Klein-Mossman.

Brand Profile—Select Soup

Select Soup is a fairly new brand on the Canadian market. For years, the brand name was synonymous with dehydrated soup, due to its overall domination in that market segment. When Select's line of canned soups entered the market, the product was an instant success story, capturing 25% of market share in a short space of time. In the most recent years, share has levelled off, but the brand remains a solid threat to major competitors.

Although Select is a national brand, it is not a strong performer in all regional markets. It has become the number one brand in Ontario owing to tremendous marketing push in the region in the past four years. However, the brand is virtually non-existent in the Maritimes, and penetration in the Quebec market has been limited. Therefore, its market share is a distant third compared to Crown Soup and Souptyme.

Marketing support for Select Soup has been balanced between consumer advertising, consumer promotion activity, and trade promotions. The relative success of the brand is based on the premise that a balance of push and pull marketing activity will keep the trade and consumers satisfied.

The unique selling points of Select Soup are the generous portions of meat and vegetables packed in each tin. The positioning of the brand has been based on a "value-for-your-money" concept. Marketing executives feel that their soup offers the best value; this is promoted heavily in advertising.

Advertising for Select Soup has focused on a "quality" theme. Traditionally, Select Soup has been advertised in a straightforward, positive manner. Commercials simply present the facts, letting the consumer decide if this is the soup to purchase. Very recently, a new advertising approach has been tested in Vancouver. Convinced that Select Soup is the best-tasting soup, the company has launched a commercial involving a direct comparison with the other major brands. The commercial clearly communicates that Select Soup is the preferred choice of the average family. Company executives are considering expanded use of similar commercials in other markets, but they fear all-out war and retaliation by Souptyme and Crown, which could prove costly to the brand and company.

In the area of sales promotion, Select Soup places great emphasis on couponing (magazine, newspaper, and on-pack) to stimulate trial and repeat purchase. Also, the brand's package labels actively promote a recipe book, which is available free to consumers with every purchase of 50 tins.

Trade promotion activity is constant, as a trade-allowance program and special promotion funds are offered to all customers on a quarterly basis.

Select Soup is available in 20 flavours, in two pack sizes (10-oz. and 19-oz.). Retail prices of Select Soup are marginally lower than those of Souptyme, the market leader, and slightly above those of Crown Soup. During trade deal allowance periods, Select Soup does obtain a high degree of feature price activity at retail.

Advertising and Marketing Budget

The advertising and marketing budget for Select soup is as follows:

		($'000)	*1992*
Select Soup	*1990*	*1991*	*Plan*
Media			
Television	220	435	
Print (Magazine/Newspaper)	150	100	
Radio	–	–	
Direct Mail	–	–	
Outdoor	–	–	
Transit	–	–	
Other	–	–	
Production Expenses	80	140	
TOTAL MEDIA	450	675	
Consumer Promotion			
Coupons	100	150	
Contests	80	40	
Premiums	40	50	
Samples	–	–	
Other	–	–	
TOTAL CONSUMER PROMOTION	220	230	

continued

Trade Promotion		
Deal Allowances	288	300
Co-op Funds	236	276
TOTAL TRADE PROMOTION	524	576
TOTAL BUDGET	1194	148
TOTAL $ SALES	17069	1828
M/S RATIO*	7.0	8.1

*Marketing to Sales Ratio   (marketing budget expressed as a percent of sales)

FINANCIAL DATA—MAJOR COMPANIES AND BRANDS

Comparative Company Income Statements

Latest Year – 1991 ($'000)

	Consolidated Foods Ltd.	Power Foods Corp.	Select Foods Ltd.
Sales	225 000	250 000	100 000
Cost of Goods Sold	135 000	138 000	65 000
Gross Profit	90 000	112 000	35 000
Gross Margin	(40.0%)	(44.8%)	(35.0%)
Selling and Administrative Expense	62 000	67 000	23 800
Net Profit Before Tax	28 000	45 000	11 200
Income Tax	8 500	13 500	3 360
Net Profit After Tax	19 500	31 500	7 840
R.O.S.	(8.7%)	(12.6%)	(7.8%)

Comparative Financial Statements—Major Brands

1987–1988 Actual ($'000)

	1990	1991	1992 Plan
Souptyme			
Market Share	31.2	30.9	
$ Sales (75% of Retail Sales)*	20 966	22 596	
Gross Profit Contribution (20%)	4 193	4 519	
Marketing Budget	1 325	1 650	
Net Contribution Before Tax	2 868	2 869	

continued

Crown Soup

Market Share	26.6	28.1
$ Sales (75% of Retail Sales)*	17 875	20 548
Gross Profit Contribution(22%)	3 932	4 521
Marketing Budget	1 383	1 755
Net Contribution Before Tax	2 549	2 766

Select Soup

Market Share	25.4	25.0
$ Sales (75% of Retail Sales)*	17 069	18 281
Gross Profit Contribution(20%)	3 414	3 657
Marketing Budget	1 194	1 481
Net Contribution Before Tax	2 220	2 176

*NOTE: Margins for retailers vary from 20% to 30% on manufacturer's selling price. Since retail margins must be considered, dollar sales for each brand is estimated to be 75% of retail sales. (Refer to Exhibit 1 — Total Retail Dollar Sales)

MARKET BACKGROUND

CURRENT MARKET ENVIRONMENT

Market Size and Growth

Total retail dollar sales of all soups combined amounts to $130 000 000 in 1991. Within the soup market, there are two distinct categories: condensed soup, and dehydrated soup. The condensed-soup segment is by far the largest, comprising 75% of total retail dollar volume, or $97 500 000. Dehydrated soups account for the remaining 25%, or $32 500 000, in retail sales.

The nature of the product makes it a staple item in the average Canadian household. In spite of a rather sluggish economy in recent years, which has resulted in more cost-conscious shopping habits by consumers, the soup market has been able to maintain a rather enviable growth record. It seems that condensed soup remains a positive meal alternative in today's marketplace.

Regional Development*

The condensed-soup market is not a perfect reflection of current household population patterns in Canada. Current statistics reveal that the condensed-soup market is somewhat overdeveloped in relation to household population in the Ontario and British Columbia markets. The development of the Quebec market is about even with household population in that region, while the Maritimes and the Prairies remain underdeveloped markets.

*(Refer to National and Regional Market exhibits for statistical data.)

Within the five major regions of Canada, there is also a definite skew towards major urban centres. It seems that the success of any major brand is based upon a solid market base in large centres.

Consumer Data

Market-research information shows that the demographic profile of the condensed-soup market is as follows:

1. It is concentrated in large urban centres of 500 000 and over, with all centres exceeding 100 000 being relatively important.
2. Middle-aged to older female heads of households are the primary buyers of condensed soup. Priority is given to females 35 years of age and over.
3. Households with two children under the age of 10 years also dominate purchases.
4. Income is relatively unimportant in the purchase patterns of condensed soup.
5. By occupation, the blue-collar, professional, and managerial groups are all equally important.

Within this rather broad demographic profile of users, research information also indicates that two distinct user groups exist:

1. *Primary Target Group* These users are primarily concerned with the quality and taste of the product. They tend to be regular and heavy users. While they comprise only 30% of soup-purchasing households, they purchase 70% of soup volume. The impact of media, particularly television, influences their buying decisions. These heavy users are found primarily in large urban centres.
2. *Secondary Target Group* This user group comprises 70% of purchasing households and 30% of soup volume, hence they are classified as light and medium users. They are primarily concerned with price, even though they recognize the varying quality of soups which are available on the market. As a result, their purchase intent is stimulated through low-price featuring at retail stores.

Market Shares and Brand Loyalty

There are three major brands in the condensed-soup market: Souptyme (Consolidated Foods Ltd.), Crown Soup (Power Foods Corporation), and Select Soup (Select Foods Ltd.). Over the past five years, these brands have waged a bitter war in an attempt to build their respective market shares. Currently, Souptyme is the market leader, with a 30.9% market share, followed closely by Crown Soup, with a 28.1% market share, and Select Soup, with a 25% market share. A fourth entry, Friar's Soup, currently holds 6.2% of the market, but is considered to be only a fringe brand, with limited potential in the future. All other brands, including private-label and generic brands, make up the remaining market share.

The three major brands can take nothing for granted. Recent trends indicate that the gap between the three brands is getting smaller, almost to the point where any of the three has a chance of becoming the market leader. To be specific, Souptyme and Select Soup have suffered marginal share losses in recent years, at the expense of gains by Crown Soup.

The ongoing battle for market share is even more intense on a regional basis. For example, Crown Soup, the number-two brand nationally, is by far the most dominant brand in Quebec, and Select Soup, which is the number-three brand nationally, currently maintains a leadership position in the Ontario market. Similar situations exist in other regions of Canada.

As is not the case with other markets, private-label brands have only met with limited success in the condensed-soup market. Private-label shares reached a plateau of about 15% five years ago, but have declined to 10% in the past two years. Intense marketing activity by the three major brands has limited the success of private-label entries.

Because of market-share trends in recent years, and the insecure position of each brand, *it is concluded that there is a high degree of brand switching by purchasers within the market.* The exact extent of brand switching is not known, but it is felt that low-price featuring causes a positive (if only temporary) increase in volume and market share. Whether or not a satisfied purchaser remains loyal to the feature-priced brand is also not known. It should be noted that a loyal core of satisfied users is the base for the success of the three major brands.

Media Background

Media expenditures have increased dramatically in the condensed-soup market in recent years. Total media expenditures in the most recent year (1991) amounted to $2 100 000. This reflects a spending increase of 30% over 1990, and 82% over 1989. All of the three major brands have placed a greater emphasis on consumer advertising, in an attempt to attract potential users. In the years preceding this rapid media-spending increase, there was a greater emphasis placed on trade spending (co-operative advertising, discounts, etc.), and overall marketing budgets were significantly smaller than they are now.

In the past three years, all major brands have emphasized television in their media-spending patterns. Currently, about 70% of all media dollars are directed at television.

Distribution

All three major brands utilize the distribution channels common to the food industry.

Manufacturer	Wholesalers	Retailers	Consumers
PROCESSOR	CORPORATE OR INDEPENDENT	WHOLESALER OWNED/CONTROLLED OR INDEPENDENTS	END USER

	▼	▼	
	A&P	A&P/Dominion	
	Steinberg	Steinberg/Miracle/ Valdi	
	Loblaws	Loblaws/Zehrs/ Supercentre	
▼	Provigo	Provigo/Provibec	
Consolidated	Safeway	Safeway	
Foods Ltd.	Oshawa Group	IGA/Food City/	
Power Food		Dutch Boy	
Corp.	Kelly Douglas	Super Value	
Select Foods Ltd.	National Grocers	Red & White/ Lucky Dollar	
	Atlantic Wholesalers	Gordon's/Sobey's	
	M. Loeb	IGA/Much More	▼
	etc.	etc.	Mrs. Witherspoon-Smith

Mrs. Witherspoon-Smith
Mr. Melnychuk
Tamara Evans
Ana Gomez
Phillipe Boisvert
etc.

Distribution (%)

	National	*Chain Stores*	*"A" Cities*
Souptyme	88	100	94
Crown Soup	84	98	90
Select Soup	72	85	78
Friar's Soup	44	70	53

NOTE: Distribution is defined as the percentage of category sales accounted for by stores where the brand is available. Therefore, from the above chart, stores where Souptyme is sold account for 88% of all food-store soup-sales nationally.

Chains are defined as grocery organizations of four stores or more, under corporate or individual ownership. Chain stores typically account for 65% to 75% of all soup sales (chains versus independents).

"A" cities consititute those with 60 000 population and over.

Within the condensed-soup market, the three major brands have varying levels of distribution. National distribution and outlet distribution are as follows:

Pricing Strategy

The condensed-soup market is extremely competitive in terms of price. The three major brands are relatively close in price, but Crown Soup tends to offer more frequent trade discounts than do the other brands, which results in lower average retail prices for Crown Soup. A recent survey of chain-store retail prices reveals the following average retail prices for the three major brands:

	PACK SIZE	
	10 oz. fl.	*19 oz. fl.*
Consolidated Foods Ltd.		
Souptyme – Non-meat	$0.53–$0.59	$0.89–$0.99
– Meat	$0.65–$0.71	$1.09–$1.19
Power Food Corporation		
Crown Soup – Non-Meat	$0.49–$0.57	$0.79-–$0.95
– Meat	$0.59–$0.69	$0.99–$1.19
Select Foods Ltd.		
Select Soup – Non-Meat	$0.51–$0.57	$0.87–$0.97
– Meat	$0.63–$0.67	$1.03–$1.19

When the major brands offer discount packages to the trade, the resulting feature prices (temporarily lower prices) are usually five cents to ten cents below the average retail price on a per-tin basis. Multiple purchase is also encouraged by retailers through two-for-$0.89 and two-for-$0.99 specials, when the products are offered on deal by manufacturers.

Based on a random selection of varieties from the same pricing survey, the following chart outlines the current retail-price comparisons:

	Souptyme	*Crown*	*Select*
Non-Meat Varities(10 oz. fl.)			
Cream of Celery	$0.59	$0.55	$0.57
Vegetable	$0.54	$0.51	$0.54
Meat Varieties(10 oz. fl.)			
Vegetable Beef	$0.69	$0.65	$0.67
Cream of Chicken	$0.63	$0.59	$0.63
Beef	$0.69	$0.65	$0.67

EXHIBITS

1—Market Background
   (Condensed-Soup Market)
2—Canadian Population and Market Data
3—Supplementary Media Data
4—Sample Planning Formats

≡ *1. MARKET BACKGROUND*

A. National Market

Exhibit   1 Retail Dollar Sales
          2 Bi-Monthly Dollar Sales Trends—1991
          3 Market-Share Trends
          4 Bi-Monthly Market-Share Trends—1991
          5 All-Commodity Distribution—1991
          6 Dollar Volume by Store Type and City Size
          7 Media Expenditure Trends
          8 Advertising by Medium—1991
          9 Bi-Monthly Media Expenditure Trends—1991
        10 Regional Market Importance—1991
        11 Media Spending by Region—1991
        12 Percentage Media Spending by Region—1991

B. Maritimes Market

Exhibit 13 Market-Share Trends
        14 Advertising by Medium—1991

C. Quebec Market

Exhibit 15 Market-Share Trends
        16 Share of Advertising and Spending by Medium—1991
        17 Market-Share Trends—Metro Montreal
        18 Market-Share Trends—Remaining Quebec

D. Ontario Market

Exhibit 19 Market-Share Trends
        20 Share of Advertising and Spending by Medium—1991
        21 Market-Share Trends—Metro Toronto
        22 Market-Share Trends—Remaining Ontario

E. Prairies Market

F British Columbia Market

A. NATIONAL MARKET

Exhibit 1 National Market/Total Retail Dollar Sales

	1989	1990	1991	Forecast 1992
Dollar Sales($'000)	79 700	89 600	97 500	
Percentage Growth	+10.5	+12.4	+8.8	

Exhibit 2 National Market/Bi-Monthly Dollar Trends—1991 ($'000)

	J/F	M/A	M/J	J/A	S/O	N/D	TOTAL
Dollar Sales ($'000)	17 620	16 539	14 705	14 169	16 945	17 522	97 500
Percentage Growth Versus a Year Ago	+8	+9	+6	+10	+8	+8	+8.8

Exhibit 3 National Market/Market-Share Trends (Percentage)

	1989	1990	1991
Souptyme	34.2	31.2	30.9
Crown Soup	20.5	26.6	28.1
Select Soup	28.1	25.4	25.0
Friar's Soup	5.0	5.9	6.2
All Other and P.L.*	12.2	10.9	9.8
	100.0	100.0	100.0

*Private label.

Exhibit 4 National Market/Bi-Monthly Share Trends—1991 ($'000)

	J/F	M/A	M/J	J/A	S/O	N/D	AVG.
Souptyme	29.8	30.2	31.0	30.6	29.7	33.6	30.9
Crown	27.7	27.9	29.3	27.4	29.4	27.0	28.1
Select	24.5	26.9	24.1	26.0	24.3	24.2	25.0
Friar's	6.2	5.4	6.3	6.9	7.0	5.5	6.2
All Other and P.L.	11.7	9.6	9.4	9.1	9.6	9.6	9.8

Exhibit 5 National Market/All-Commodity Distribution—1991

	Percentage Distribution
Souptyme	88.0
Crown Soup	84.0
Select Soup	72.0
Friar's Soup	44.0

Exhibit 6 National Market/Dollar Volume by Store Type and City Size

Total Dollar Volume ($'000):   97 500

	Percentage
Chain Stores	68.9
Independent Stores	31.1
"A" Cities*	70.0
All Other Areas	30.0

*"A" Cities = 60 000 + population.

Exhibit 7 National Market/Media Expenditure Trends ($'000)

	1989	1990	1991	1991 Share of Advertising (%)
Souptyme	230	576	610	29.0
Crown Soup	464	550	745	35.5
Select Soup	289	370	535	25.5
Friar's Soup	102	65	100	4.8
All Other	65	80	110	5.2
TOTAL	1150	1641	2100	100.0
Percentage Increase Versus Previous Year	+43	+30	+29	

Exhibit 8 National Market/Advertising by Medium—1991

| | Percentage Weight | | |
	TV	PRINT/OTHER	TOTAL
Souptyme	70	30	100
Crown Soup	68	32	100
Select Soup	80	20	100
Friar's Soup	–	100	100
All Other	60	40	100

Exhibit 9 National Market/Bi-Monthly Media ExpenditureTrends 1991 ($'000)

	J/F	M/A	M/J	J/A	S/O	N/D	TOTAL
Souptyme	53.0	74.3	13.0	253.6	89.8	126.3	610.0
Crown	164.8	130.0	138.9	50.3	81.0	180.0	745.0
Select	64.6	20.8	137.6	202.3	49.7	62.0	535.0
Friar's	15.0	30.0	12.6	10.2	17.9	14.3	100.0
All Other	29.8	–	28.4	10.0	27.8	14.0	110.0
TOTAL	327.2	255.1	330.5	526.4	266.23	94.6 2	100.0

Exhibit 10 National Market/Regional Market Importance—1991

	Soup Market Volume (%)	Household Population (%)
Maritimes	6.0	8.0
Quebec	23.0	26.1
Ontario	46.0	36.4
Prairies	9.0	17.1
British Columbia	16.0	12.4
TOTAL MARKET	100.0	100.0

Exhibit 11 National Market/Media Spending by Region—1991 ($'000)

	Total	Maritimes	Quebec	Ontario	Prairies	B.C.
Souptyme	610	6.1	123.2	330.0	23.2	127.5
Crown	745	8.9	186.2	484.2	17.1	48.6
Select	535	–	119.8	285.7	54.6	74.9
Friar's	100	5.0	25.2	48.8	–	21.0
All Other	110	–	28.0	45.7	17.2	19.1
	2100	20.0	482.4	1 194.4	112.1	291.3

Exhibit 12   National Market/Percentage Media Spending by Region—1991

	Souptyme	Crown	Select	Soup Volume(%) Regional Market Importance	Household Population(%)
Maritimes	1.0	1.2	–	6.0	8.0
Quebec	20.2	25.0	22.4	23.0	26.1
Ontario	54.1	65.0	53.4	46.0	36.4
Prairies	3.8	2.3	10.2	9.0	17.1
B.C.	20.9	6.5	14.0	16.0	12.4
	100.0	100.0	100.0	100.0	100.0

B. MARITIMES MARKET

Regional Volume Importance 6.0%

Regional Dollar Volume ('000)—Retail $5 850

Exhibit 13   Maritimes Market/Market-Share Trends

	1989	1990	J/F	M/A	M/J	J/A	S/O	N/D	TOTAL 1991
Souptyme	42.2	36.0	33.2	33.3	35.1	32.4	34.6	31.2	33.3
Crown	23.8	32.2	31.3	34.7	30.7	33.0	29.4	33.7	32.1
Select	1.2	0.4	0.5	0.7	0.7	0.7	0.7	1.0	0.8
Friar's	–	–	–	–	–	–	–	–	–
All Other	32.8	31.4	34.9	31.2	33.4	33.8	35.3	34.0	33.8

Exhibit 14   Maritimes Market/Advertising by Medium—1991

	Percentage Weight		
	TV	PRINT	TOTAL
Souptyme	20.0	80.0	100.0
Crown	60.0	40.0	100.0
Select	–	–	–
Friar's	–	–	–
All Other	–	–	–

C. QUEBEC MARKET

Regional Volume Importance	23.0%
Regional Dollar Volume ($'000)—Retail	22 425
Metro Montreal ($'000)	14 576 (65%)
Remaining Quebec ($'000)	7 849 (35%)

Exhibit 15 Quebec Market/Market-Share Trends

	1989	1990	J/F	M/A	M/J	J/A	S/O	N/D	TOTAL 1991
Souptyme	34.7	30.0	26.6	28.6	33.1	29.5	25.6	35.2	30.0
Crown	30.4	40.3	42.9	42.6	40.2	42.4	42.3	37.6	41.2
Select	14.1	12.8	12.3	13.9	12.0	12.1	12.8	11.6	12.4
Friar's	6.7	6.8	7.2	5.2	5.7	6.6	8.4	5.5	6.4
All Other	14.1	10.1	10.9	9.7	9.0	9.4	10.9	10.1	10.0

Exhibit 16 Quebec /Share of Advertising and Percentage of Spending by Medium—1991

	% Share of Advertising	Percentage Weight			
		TV	PRINT	RADIO	TOTAL
Souptyme	25.5	74.0	26.0	–	100.0
Crown	38.6	65.0	35.0	–	100.0
Select	24.8	93.0	7.0	–	100.0
Friar's	5.2	–	–	100.0	100.0
All Other	5.9	–	100.0	–	100.0
	100.0				

Exhibit 17 Quebec Market/Market-Share Trends—Metro Montreal (65%)

	1989	1990	J/F	M/A	M/J	J/A	S/O	N/D	TOTAL 1991
Souptyme	37.8	33.0	28.8	32.8	36.2	33.0	28.5	39.6	33.5
Crown	25.9	34.3	37.4	35.9	34.0	36.0	35.6	31.5	34.8
Select	14.8	14.1	13.8	14.9	12.8	13.2	14.3	12.5	13.5
Friar's	6.8	7.8	8.5	6.1	7.0	7.8	9.6	5.9	7.5
All Other	14.6	10.8	11.5	10.4	10.0	10.1	12.1	10.5	10.7

Exhibit 18 Quebec Market/Market-Share Trends—Remaining Quebec (35%)

	1989	1990	J/F	M/A	M/J	J/A	S/O	N/D	TOTAL 1991
Souptyme	25.7	21.7	20.6	18.5	25.3	20.0	18.3	22.0	20.9
Crown	43.3	57.4	57.9	58.8	55.7	60.0	59.6	55.7	57.9
Select	12.0	8.9	8.4	11.4	10.0	9.2	9.0	8.9	9.5
Friar's	6.4	3.7	3.8	3.2	2.6	3.6	5.3	4.5	3.8
All Other	12.7	8.2	9.2	8.1	6.5	7.3	7.7	8.9	7.9

D. ONTARIO MARKET

Regional Volume Importance	46%
Regional Dollar Volume ($'000)—Retail	44 850
Metro Toronto ($'000)	21 528 (48%)
Remaining Ontario ($'000)	23 322 (52%)

Exhibit 19 Ontario Market/Market-Share Trends

	1989	1990	J/F	M/A	M/J	J/A	S/O	N/D	TOTAL 1991
Souptyme	30.1	28.3	27.1	28.4	27.6	27.9	28.1	30.4	28.3
Crown	16.5	20.2	20.3	20.6	22.7	19.6	24.3	20.3	21.3
Select	37.9	34.8	34.6	36.2	33.7	36.1	31.7	34.7	34.5
Friar's	5.6	6.7	7.3	6.6	8.6	9.4	8.9	7.0	8.0
All Other	9.8	10.0	10.7	8.3	7.4	7.0	6.9	7.5	7.9

Exhibit 20 Ontario /Share of Advertising and Percentage of Spending by Medium—1991

	% Share Of Advertising*	Percentage Weight			
		TV	PRINT	RADIO	TOTAL
Souptyme	27.6	76.0	24.0	–	100.0
Crown	40.5	60.0	40.0	–	100.0
Select	23.9	64.0	36.0	–	100.0
Friar's	4.1	–	20.0	80.0	100.0
All Other	3.9	–	100.0	–	100.0
	100.0				

*Calculations from data included in Exhibit 11

Exhibit 21 Ontario Market/Market-Share Trends—Metro Toronto (48%)

	1989	*1990*	*J/F*	*M/A*	*M/J*	*J/A*	*S/O*	*N/D*	*TOTAL 1991*
Souptyme	29.4	28.0	26.4	28.3	24.9	27.7	27.5	29.5	26.6
Crown	11.4	14.7	14.6	15.8	17.1	13.8	18.2	14.2	15.0
Select	44.5	41.8	41.3	42.2	42.0	41.5	38.2	42.2	40.5
Friar's } All Other }	n/a	n/a	n/a	n/a	n/a	n/a	n/a	n/a	n/a

Exhibit 22 Ontario Market/Market-Share Trends—Remaining Ontario(52%)

	1989	*1990*	*J/F*	*M/A*	*M/J*	*J/A*	*S/O*	*N/D*	*TOTAL 1991*
Souptyme	31.3	28.9	28.0	28.8	30.0	28.3	28.8	31.4	29.2
Crown	21.9	25.8	26.4	26.8	28.4	26.0	30.3	25.5	27.2
Select	30.6	27.4	27.4	29.1	25.4	29.8	25.0	28.1	27.5
Friar's } All Other }	n/a	n/a	n/a	n/a	n/a	n/a	n/a	n/a	n/a

E. PRAIRIES MARKET

Regional Volume Importance	9.0%
Regional Dollar Volume ($'000)—Retail	8 775

Exhibit 23 Prairies Market/Market-Share Trends

	1989	*1990*	*J/F*	*M/A*	*M/J*	*J/A*	*S/O*	*N/D*	*TOTAL 1991*
Souptyme	43.6	44.6	45.4	43.7	42.9	45.2	39.5	40.6	42.7
Crown	25.9	29.1	32.0	29.9	31.6	29.7	35.2	31.8	31.8
Select	22.0	21.3	18.5	21.8	21.7	21.1	20.3	22.7	21.1
Friar's	1.7	0.5	0.4	0.4	0.4	0.2	0.2	0.3	0.3
All Other	6.8	4.5	3.7	4.2	3.5	3.9	4.7	4.6	4.1

Exhibit 24 Prairies Market/Percentage Advertising Spending by Medium—1991

	Percentage Weight			
	TV	PRINT	RADIO	TOTAL
Souptyme	–	100.0	–	100.0
Crown	55.0	45.0	–	100.0
Select	90.0	10.0	–	100.0
Friar's } All Other }	–	100.0	–	100.0

F. BRITISH COLUMBIA MARKET

Regional Volume Importance	16.0%
Regional Dollar Volume ($'000)—Retail	15 600

Exhibit 25 British Columbia Market/Market-Share Trends

	1989	1990	J/F	M/A	M/J	J/A	S/O	N/D	TOTAL 1991
Souptyme	35.8	31.4	31.8	28.3	26.8	29.2	29.3	35.0	30.0
Crown	15.5	22.1	24.3	24.5	30.4	25.3	23.0	23.1	25.1
Select	32.0	29.2	26.2	31.9	27.3	31.0	32.6	27.0	29.4
Friar's	5.0	7.2	7.5	6.9	6.1	6.5	6.1	6.4	6.6
All Other	11.7	10.1	10.2	8.3	9.5	8.1	9.0	8.6	8.9

Exhibit 26 British Columbia Market/Percentage Advertising Spending by Medium —1991

	Percentage Weight			
	TV	PRINT	RADIO	TOTAL
Souptyme	75.0	25.0	–	100.0
Crown	50.0	50.0	–	100.0
Select	90.0	10.0	–	100.0
Friar's	–	–	100.0	100.0
All Other	n/a	n/a	n/a	n/a

2. *C*ANADIAN POPULATION AND MARKET DATA

Exhibit 27 Canadian Urban Markets (100 000 Population and over)
28 Canadian Regional Markets

Exhibit 27 Canadian Urban Markets (100 000 Population and Over)

	Total Population (000)	Percentage Canadian Total
CANADA	26 430	100.0
Toronto	3 646	13.8
Montreal	2 945	11.1
Vancouver	1 470	5.6
Ottawa-Hull	867	3.3
Edmonton	783	3.0
Calgary	683	2.6
Quebec City	635	2.4
Winnipeg	638	2.4
Hamilton	571	2.2
Halifax	302	1.1
Kitchener	334	1.2
St. Catharines-Niagara	357	1.3
London	360	1.3
Windsor	265	1.0
Victoria	269	1.0
Regina	187	.7
St. John's	168	.6
Saskatoon	201	.8
Oshawa	222	.8
Chicoutimi-Jonquière	159	.6
Sudbury	157	.6
Sherbrooke	138	.5
Saint John	122	.5
Kingston	136	.5
Trois Rivières	133	.5
Thunder Bay	122	.5
Sidney	121	.4

Source: Statistics Canada 1990

Exhibit 28 Canadian Regional Market

	Total Population (000)	Percentage Canadian Total	Households (000)
CANADA	26 430	100.0	9 568
Maritimes	2 316	8.8	765
Quebec	6 731	25.5	2 500
Ontario	9 714	36.7	3 483
Prairies	4 556	17.2	1 639
British Columbia	3 025	11.5	1 154
Yukon/N.W.T.	88	0.3	17

Source: Statistics Canada—1990 Estimates

3. SUPPLEMENTARY MEDIA DATA

A. Magazines

Exhibit 29 Leading Women's Magazines (Circulation, Page Rates, CPM)

B. Television Background Data

Exhibit 30 Television Viewing Patterns by Daypart
31 Summer Viewing Drop-off

C. Radio Background Data

Exhibit 32 Average Weekly Hours Tuned Per Capita
33 Audience Composition by Time Block
34 AM versus FM Reach and Share of Audience

D Newspaper

Exhibit 35 Audience Reach by Demographics
36 How a Newspaper is Read
37 Impact of Colour

A. MAGAZINES

Exhibit 29 Leading Women's Magazines (Circulation, Page Rate, and CPM)

English	Circulation	*Rate	CPM
Canadian Living	558 531	18 055	32.33
Chatelaine	1 010 152	29 200	28.91
City & Country Home	88 589	8 045	90.81
City Woman	200 000	11 795	58.98
Flare	214 291	10 770	50.26

Homemaker's	1 600 054	20 800	12.99
Reader's Digest	1 306 000	24 455	18.72
Western Living	250 673	13 575	54.15
TV Guide	826 973	15 870	19.19
Today's Parent	111 285	7 275	65.37

French

Chatelaine	258 166	9 540	36.95
Madame au Foyer	312 182	5 195	16.64
Sélection du Reader's Digest	361 371	8 880	24.57
Femme Plus	82 036	4 380	53.39
Coup de Pouce	140 197	6 485	46.26
TV Hebdo	349 885	5 920	16.92

Source: March 1990 CARD
*Rate: Based on one page, four colour rate

B. TELEVISION BACKGROUND DATA

Exhibit 30   Television Viewing Patterns by Daypart—Percentage

Daypart	*Women 18+*	*Men 18+*	*Teens 12-17*	*Children 2-11*
6:00 A.M. to 4:30 P.M., Monday to Friday	22	12	14	30
4:30 P.M. to 7:00 P.M., Monday to Friday	16	15	20	19
7:00 P.M. to 11:00 P.M., Monday to Sunday	45	50	44	27
11:00 P.M. to 2:00 A.M., Monday to Sunday	9	9	5	1
6:00 A.M. to 7:00 P.M., Saturday / Sunday	10	14	17	23

Source: BBM Fall 1989 and Television Bureau of Canada

Exhibit 31   Television Viewing—Summer Drop-off /Adults 18 and over, Monday to Sunday, 7:00 to 11:00 p.m.

	Percentage Difference
Halifax	-21
Montreal	-30
Toronto	-23
Winnipeg	-30
Calgary	-26
Vancouver	-21

C. RADIO BACKGROUND DATA

Exhibit 32 Average Weekly Hours Tuned Per Capita

	Women 18+	Men 18+	Teens 12-17	Children 7-11
Maritimes	21.1	18.3	12.5	7.0
Quebec	24.2	21.9	11.6	6.6
Ontario	22.5	20.7	13.5	4.8
Prairies	21.1	21.1	13.2	7.2
British Columbia	21.1	18.9	11.7	7.1
CANADA	22.4	20.6	12.7	7.0

Source: BBM, Fall 1989

Exhibit 33 Radio Audience Composition by Time Block (Percentage)

	Women 18+	Men 18+	Teens 12-17	Children 7-11
Breakfast (6:00 A.M. to 10:00 A.M.)	50	41	6	3
Mid-Day (10:00 A.M. to 10:00 P.M.)	56	41	2	1
Drive (4:00 P.M. to 7:00 P.M.	45	44	8	3
Evening (7:00 P.M. to 12:00 A.M.	41	43	12	3
Weekends (7:00 A.M. to 7:00 P.M.)	51	41	7	3

Source: BBM, Fall 1989

Exhibit 34 Radio AM/FM—Reach (Weekly) and Share of Total Hours by Demographics (Percentage)

	AM	FM	AM	FM
	Reach		Share	
Women 18+	74	64	55	45
Men 18+	72	66	51	49
Teens 12–17	65	62	49	51
Children 7–11	58	44	60	40
All Persons 7+	71	63	53	47

Source: BBM, Fall 1989

D. NEWSPAPER BACKGROUND DATA

Exhibit 35 Newspaper Audience Reach by Demographics

		Mon.–Fri. *Average* *Percentage*
	Total Adults 18+	66
SEX	Males	72
	Females	61
AGE	18–24	64
	18–34	64
	18–49	65
	50–64	72
	65+	65
INCOME	Under $15 000	56
	$15 000–$20 000	62
	$20 000–$25 000	61
	$25 000–$35 000	65
	$35 000+	69
REGION	Maritimes	77
	Quebec	62
	Ontario	66
	Prairies	68
	British Columbia	69

Source: NADBANK, 1988

Exhibit 36 How a Newspaper is Read

	Percentage *Adults*
(1) Go through newspaper page by page:	
Reading whatever is interesting	77
Scanning quickly	15
Looking at specific items only	4
(2) Look at newspaper ads:	
Whether interested in buying or not	68
When specifically interested in buying	30

Exhibit 37   Impact of Colour in Newspaper Ads

	Percentage *Noting Score* *(3)*
1000 B&W	25
1000 B + 1 Colour	41
1000 4 Colour	54

Sources: (1) NADBank, 1984
   (2) NNRS Study, 1976
   (3) CDNPA "New Dimensions Study"

4. SAMPLE PLANNING FORMATS

Exhibit   38 Advertising Plan (Sample Format)
   39 Media Cost Sheet—Magazine
   40 Media Cost Sheet—Newspaper
   41 Media Cost Sheet—Television/Radio
   42 Media Cost Summary (by Media)
   43 Media Expenditures by Quarter
   44 Media Schedule—Blocking Chart

The Advertising Plan (Sample Format) and Media Cost Summary charts included in this section are intended to provide you with a guideline. They are by no means a restriction; adapt them, or develop new charts to suit your own needs.

Exhibit 38   Advertising Plan (Sample Format)

1. Market Background*
   a. Market volume trends
   b. Market share trends
      i) National
      ii) Regional
   c. Competitive analysis (all major brands)
      i) Product U.S.P.'s
      ii) Pricing
      iii) Distribution trends
      iv) Sales promotion activity
      v) Media usage and expenditure trends

*Present your material in chart form, where appropriate, and support it with your observations regarding significant activity and trends.

2. Problems and Opportunities
a. Problems
b. Opportunities

3. Marketing Objectives and Strategies
a. Product positioning statement
b. Target market profile
   i) Current target market (demographic, psychographic, geographic)
   ii) New target markets (demographic, psychographic, geographic)
c. Marketing objectives (List: volume, share, product, price, distribution, etc.)
d. Marketing strategies

4. Budget
a. Marketing budget (as per illustrations in company and brand profile section of the simulation)
b. Budget rationale

5. Creative Plan
a. Competitive analysis (of past creative)
b. Communications objectives
c. Communications strategy
   i) Key benefits
   ii) Promise statements
   iii) Reason-why statement
   iv) Support claims
   v) Tone of communications desired (e.g., appeal techniques)
   vi) Themes to be considered

6. Media Plan
a. Media budget
b. Media objectives
   i) Who
   ii) What
   iii) When
   iv) Where
   v) How (type of media)
c. Media strategy (rationale for selection)
d. Media execution (refer to following exhibits)
   i) Media cost sheets
   ii) Media cost summaries (by media, time of year, etc.)
   iii) Media schedule

7. Sales Promotion Plan
a. Sales promotion budget
b. Promotion plan summary
   i) Activity
   ii) Costs

Exhibit 39   Media Cost Sheet/Magazines

PUBLICATION	CIRCULATION	COST/INSERT*	No. OF INSERTS	TOTAL COST

EXAMPLE ONLY

*Costs based on frequency discounts:
Canadian Advertising Rates and Data

Similar forms can be developed for other media.

Exhibit 40   Media Cost Sheet/Newspaper

NEWSPAPER	COST/LINE*	No. OF LINES	No. OF INSERTS	COLOUR COST	TOTAL COST

EXAMPLE ONLY

*Discounted Line Rate based on availability of discounts.

Exhibit 41 Media Cost Sheet /Television/Radio

MARKET & STATION	COST PER SPOT	SPOTS PER WEEK	No. OF WEEKS	TOTAL COST
		EXAMPLE ONLY		

Exhibit 42 Media Cost Summary

MEDIA	DOLLARS ALLOCATED
Television	
Radio	
Newspaper	
Magazine	
Outdoor	
Transit	
Other	_____
TOTAL MEDIA EXPENSES	_____
Production Expenses	_____
TOTAL MEDIA BUDGET	_____
Reserve	_____

EXAMPLE ONLY

Exhibit 43 Media Cost Summary/Dollar Expenditures by Quarter

ACTIVITY	1st QUARTER*	2nd QUARTER	3rd QUARTER	4th QUARTER	TOTAL COST
List details of media activity					

EXAMPLE ONLY

*Chart could be developed using a *bi-monthly* or *monthly* expenditure format.

Exhibit 44   MEDIA SCHEDULE—BLOCKING CHART

ACTIVITY	JAN	FEB	MAR	APR	MAY	JUN	JUL	AUG	SEP	OCT	NOV	DEC
TELEVISION —List Markets												
PRINT —List Publications												
…and so forth												

Endnotes

CHAPTER 1

[1] Martin Mehr, "Ad cutback not what it seems," *Marketing*, March 30, 1990, p.3.

[2] Philip Kotler and Gordon McDougall, *Marketing Essentials* (Toronto: Prentice Hall Canada Inc., 1985), p.13.

[3] *Advertising: An Advertiser's Overview*, booklet published by the Association of Canadian Advertisers Inc., n.d.

[4] *Why Advertisers Need ACA*, brochure published by the Association of Canadian Advertisers, n.d.

[5] Ibid.

[6] *Marketing*, December 11, 1989, p.23.

[7] *All About the Institute of Canadian Advertising*, booklet published by the Institute of Canadian Advertising, n.d.

[8] *About the Audit Bureau of Circulations*, booklet published by the Audit Bureau of Circulations, 1986.

[9] *Who Speaks for Advertising*, pamphlet published by the Canadian Advertising Foundation, n.d.

[10] Ibid.

[11] *Policy on Sex-role Stereotyping in the Broadcast Media* (Ottawa: Canadian Radio-television and Telecommunications Commission, December, 1986), p.23.

[12] *Guidelines for the Use of Research and Survey Data in Comparative Food Commercials*, pamphlet published by the Advertising Standards Council, 1986.

[13] Randy Scotland, "Remington TV Spot Has Kiam in Court," *Marketing*, October 29, 1990, p.1.

[14] *The Canadian Code of Advertising Standards*, booklet published by the Canadian Advertising Foundation, May 1986.

[15] "Lifestyle Approach for the New Cameo," *Marketing*, December 21, 1987, p.2.

[16] "Rothmans Challenges Legality of Advertising Ban," *Whig-Standard*, July 21, 1989, p.1.

CHAPTER 2

[1] John Blyth, "U.S. firms are becoming more realistic about global marketing," *Marketing News*, October 1, 1990, p.14.

[2] Randy Scotland, "Baker chief sees success, but not without some pain," *Marketing*, March 28, 1988, p.2.

[3] *How to Select an Advertising Agency*, brochure published by the Institute of Canadian Advertising, n.d., p.1.

[4] Ibid., p.6.

CHAPTER 3

[1] "Canada's Top 100," *Marketing*, Dec. 11, 1989, p.23.

[2] "What type of advertising agency would suit you best," *Stimulus*, June 1983, p.17.

[3] *So...You Want to Be in an Advertising Agency*, booklet published by the Institute of Canadian Advertising, n.d., p.2.

[4] Ibid.

[5] "What type of advertising agency would suit you best," p.18.

[6] "The Top 100 Agencies," *Marketing*, December 11, 1989, p.29.

[7] Randy Scotland, "The bottom line," *Marketing*, December 11, 1989, pp. 12, 16.

[8] Ibid.

[9] Ibid.

[10] Ibid.

[11] Mark Smyla, "Centralized media role a growing concern," *Playback Strategy*, August 27, 1990, p.1.

[12] Ibid.

[13] Ibid.

[14] *So...You Want to be in an Advertising Agency*, p.2.

[15] *Advertising Agency Compensation*, booklet published by the Institute of Canadian Advertising, n.d.

[16] Ibid.

[17] Ibid.

[18] Randy Scotland, "A clash over how the piper is paid," *Marketing*, May 12, 1986, p.1.

[19] "The hammer was down," *Marketing*, January 4, 1988, pp.1, 3.

[20] *The Agency Review: A Positive Step toward Client-Agency Relationships*, booklet published by the Institute of Canadian Advertising, n.d.

CHAPTER 4

[1] Christopher Gilson and Harold Berkman, *Advertising Concepts and Strategies* (New York: Random House Inc., 1980), p.100.

[2] James F. Engel, David T. Kollatt, and Roger D. Blackwell, *Consumer Behavior*, 2nd edition (New York: Holt, Rinehart and Winston, 1973), p.5.

[3] A.H. Maslow, *Motivation and Personality* (New York: Harper and Row Publishers, 1954), pp. 370-396.

[4] Clarkson Gordon/Woods Gordon, *Tomorrow's Customers in Canada*, 20th edition, 1985, p.2.

[5] Ibid.

[6] "BMW changes its approach to female market," *Marketing*, September 8, 1986, p.8.

[7] Ibid., p.16.

[8] Clarkson Gordon/Woods Gordon, *Tomorrow's Customers in Canada*, 21st edition, 1987, p.8.

[9] Gail Chiasson, "Seagrams launches a light rye," *Marketing*, November 12, 1990, p.4.

[10] Tomorrow's Customers in Canada, 20th edition, p.5.

[11] Statistics Canada, *Canada Yearbook 1988* (Ottawa: Supply and Services Canada, 1987, Cat. No. 11-402E/1987), p.2-7.

[12] Shlomo Schwartzberg, "Sun Life targets Toronto's Chinese community," *Playback Strategy*, November 20, 1989, p.36.

[13] Ian Pearson, "Social Studies," *Canadian Business*, December 1985, pp.69-70.

[14] Elliott Ettenberg, "Psychographics: The art of finding out why, not just who," *Sales and Marketing Management in Canada*, date unknown.

[15] John Douglas, George A. Field, and Lawrence S. Tarpey, *Human Behaviour in Marketing* (Columbus: Charles E. Merrill Publishing, 1967), p.5.

[16] Jim McElgunn, "Change of course for Carlsberg," *Marketing*, June 26, 1989, p.2.

CHAPTER 5

[1] M. Dale Beckman, Davie L. Kurtz, and Louis E. Boone, *Foundations of Marketing*, 2nd Canadian edition (Toronto: Holt, Rinehart and Winston of Canada Ltd., 1982), p.126.

[2] William Band, "Don't get trapped by the product life cycle," *Sales and Marketing Management in Canada*, September 1985, p.25.

CHAPTER 6

[1] Information provided by Ontario Foodland, Ontario Ministry of Agriculture and Food.

[2] Patrick Allossey, "Canada Pork hopes new ads create leaner image," *Playback Strategy*, October 22, 1990, p.12.

[3] Gail Chiasson, "The world of Alcan," *Marketing*, January 29, 1990, p.1.

[4] Information provided by London Life Insurance Company, London, Ontario.

[5] Harvey Skolnick, "When to use comparative ads," *Marketing*, August 5, 1985, p.11.

[6] Courtney and Wipple, *Sex Stereotyping in Advertising* (Toronto: Lexington Books, D.C. Heath Canada Ltd., 1983).

[7] Information provided by Pepsi-Cola Canada Ltd. and J. Walter Thompson Company Ltd.

[8] Colin Wright, "Only big stars shine before today's public," *Marketing*, July 8, 1985, p.8.

CHAPTER 7

[1] "Hard word is the key to success," *Advertising Age*, August 2, 1971, p.2.

[2] David Ogilvy, *Ogilvy on Advertising* (Toronto: John Wiley and Sons Ltd., 1983), p.139.

[3] McGraw Hill Research, Laboratory of Advertising Performance. Results reported by Jo Marney, "Sizing up ads: Bigger is better," *Marketing*, date unknown.

[4] Jo Marney, "Posters turn all heads," *Marketing*, September 8, 1986, pp.30ff.
[5] Comments from an Institute of Outdoor Advertising Seminar (U.S.), Jo Marney, *Marketing*, September 30, 1986, p.30.
[6] Ogilvy, *Ogilvy on Advertising*, p.146.

CHAPTER 8

[1] Cherie Hill, "In defense of DAR testing, *Stimulus*, June 1984, p.28.
[2] Timothy Hodapp, "You want to test a what?," *Stimulus*, October 1984, p.27.
[3] *TAM—BBM's Television Audience Meter*, booklet published by the Bureau of Measurement, n.d., p.6.
[4] *Canadian Media Directors' Council Media Digest, 1990-91*, p.12.
[5] Kathy Butler, "Radio research is entering the computer age," *Stimulus*, November-December 1984, p.31.
[6] *PMB Fact Sheets*, published by the Print Measurement Bureau, November 1986, p.4.
[7] *Market Data Report*, published by the Canadian Outdoor Measurement Bureau, September 30, 1986, p.3.
[8] Ibid.

CHAPTER 10

[1] *Facts about Daily Newspapers*, booklet published by the Daily Newspaper Publishers Association, n.d., p.3.
[2] *Canadian Media Directors' Council Media Digest, 1990-91*, p.41.
[3] "Canada's top dailies," *Financial Post Magazine*, Summer 1989, p.9.
[4] Ibid., p.44.
[5] *1985 Audited Circulation Report, The Globe and Mail.*
[6] "NAD bank '84", *Canadian Media Director's Council Media Digest, 1986*, p.41.
[7] "NNRS Study 1976," Ibid.
[8] "Southam Starch scores," Ibid.
[9] "*Toronto Star* 1974 test results," Ibid.
[10] *Canadian Media Directors' Council Media Digest, 1986-87*, p.39.
[11] *Canadian Media Directors' Council Media Digest, 1990-91*, p.10.

CHAPTER 11

[1] *Canadian Media Directors' Council Media Digest*, 1990-91, p.16.
[2] Ibid.
[3] *CBC Television Best on the Box*, Television Sales Brochure, 1986/87, Canadian Broadcasting Corporation, Toronto.
[4] *Canadian Advertising Rates and Data* (Toronto: Maclean Hunter Ltd.), January 1987, p.463.
[5] *Canadian Media Directors' Council Media Digest*, 1990-91, p.29.
[6] *BBM Television Data Book*, 1990, p.69.
[7] "Media Update: TV and radio facing new challenges in the 80's," *Stimulus*, June 1985, p.10.
[8] Ibid.

CHAPTER 12

[1] *Cooperative Direct Mail Coupons, Coupon Redemption Rates and Patterns*, 1985, A.C. Nielsen Promotion Services, p.20.

[2] From a speech delivered at the Canadian Direct Marketing Association Convention, Quebec City, *Marketing*, July 14, 1986, p.27.

[3] *Cooperative Direct Mail Coupons*, p.20.

[4] Net Revenues by Medium, *The Canadian Media Directors' Council Media Digest*, 1990-91, p.10.

[5] "Understanding outdoor media vehicles," *The Measure of Outdoor*, brochure published by Mediacom Inc., n.d., p.4.

[6] Gail Chaisson, "It's steady as she goes," *Marketing*, January 29, 1985, p.10.

[7] Rates and data obtained from *Canadian Advertising Rates and Data* (Toronto: Maclean Hunter Ltd.), November 1986, p.489.

[8] Ibid.

[9] *Just the Right Ticket*, brochure published by Trans Ad, n.d., p.1.

[10] Ibid, p.11.

[11] "The power of P.O.P.," insert to *Marketing*, n.d., p.1.

[12] "In-store merchandising," in "The power of P.O.P.," insert to *Marketing*, n.d., p.2.

CHAPTER 13

[1] *A Product Manager's Guide to Consumer Promotions*, Nielsen Promotion Services, 1989, p.B4.

[2] *The Marketer's Viewpoint, Special Presentation on Consumer Promotion Trends*, brochure published by Nielsen Promotion Services, a division of A.C. Nielsen Company of Canada Ltd., 1984, p.6.

[3] "Promotional offers can do more to bolster image," *Marketing*, February 24, 1986, p.10.

[4] Ibid.

CHAPTER 14

[1] Adapted from Frederick E. Webster and Yoram Wind, *Organizational Buying Behaviour* (Englewood Cliffs, New Jersey: Prentice-Hall, 1972), pp.78-80.

[2] Robert Black, "A weak advertisement with a strong message can still be a winner," *Business-to-Business Marketing*, March 1986, p.B14.

[3] Alvin Ng and Ann Sandy, "Who's on first?" *Financial Times of Canada*, December 4, 1989, p.A8.

CHAPTER 15

[1] John L. Beisel, *Contemporary Retailing* (New York: MacMillian, 1987), p.478.

[2] William Haight, *Retail Advertising: Management and Technique* (Morristown, New Jersey: General Press, 1976), pp.161-163.

APPENDIX I

Advertising Regulations and Legislation

The following is a summary of relevant broadcasting codes, industry guidelines, and government legislation which controls advertising activity in Canada. A cross-section of regulations is included. The intention of this section is to indicate the nature of advertising regulations and legislation which govern advertising practice. *It is by no means a complete reference on all regulations and legislation.*

The initial group of regulations are administered by the Standards Division of the Canadian Advertising Foundation and Le Conseil des Normes de la publicité.

The Canadian Code of Advertising Standards

November, 1990

Canadian Advertising Foundation

ADVERTISING'S SELF-REGULATORY PROCESS

The Canadian Code of Advertising Standards has been developed to promote the professional practice of advertising. The Code's clauses set the criteria for acceptable advertising and form the basis upon which advertising is evaluated in response to consumer or trade complaints. The Code is generally endorsed by advertisers, advertising agencies, media which exhibit advertising, and suppliers to the advertising process.

The code is the principal instrument of self-regulation for the advertising industry in Canada, supplemented by the standards set by individual media and by other advertising-related associations. The Code does not supersede municipal, provincial or federal regulation affecting advertising.

The Code is administered by the Advertising Standards Council, le Conseil des normes de la Publicite, and by regional councils located in Vancouver, Edmonton, Calgary, Regina, Winnipeg and Halifax,. The Council/Conseil and the regional bodies are supported and coordinated by the Standards Division of the Canadian Advertising Foundation.

DEFINITION OF ADVERTISING

For the purpose of this Code, "advertising" is defined as any paid message communicated by Canadian media with the intent to influence the choice, opinion or behaviour of those addressed by the commercial messages.

APPLICATION

The Code applies to advertisers promoting the use of goods and services, to corporations or institutions seeking to improve their public image, and to governments, government departments and crown corporations, provided such advertising meets the criteria set forth in the definition.

EXCLUSIONS

The Code does not govern or restrict the free expression of public opinion or ideas through advocacy advertising, or election advertising.

SCOPE OF THE CODE

The Code deals with how products or services may be advertised, not with which products or services may be advertised. Thus, the authority of the Code applies only to the content of commercial messages and does not prohibit the promotion of legal products or services or their portrayal in circumstances of normal use. The content of the advertisement and audience reached or intended to be reached by the message are relevant factors in assessing its acceptability.

The Code

The Canadian Code of Advertising Standards has been approved and is supported by all participating organizations, and is designed to help set and maintain standards of honesty, truth, accuracy, fairness and taste in advertising. The principles underlying the Code and more detailed descriptions of its application are presented in the Manual of General Guidelines for Advertising.

No advertising shall be prepared or knowingly exhibited by the participating organizations which contravenes this Code of Standards.

The clauses should be adhered to both in letter and in spirit. Advertisers and advertising agencies must be prepared to substantiate their claims promptly to the Council, if and as required, upon request.

1. **Accuracy, Clarity**
   (a) Advertisements must not contain inaccurate or deceptive claims, statements, illustrations, or representations, either direct or implied, with regard to price, availability or performance of a

product or service. In assessing the truthfulness and accuracy of a message, the concern is not with the intent of the sender or precise legality of the presentation. Rather, the focus is on the message as received or perceived, that is, the general impression conveyed by the advertisement.

(b) Advertisements must not omit relevant information in a manner which is deceptive.

(c) All pertinent details of an advertised offer must be clearly stated.

(d) Disclaimers or asterisked information must not contradict more prominent aspects of the message and should be located and presented in such a manner as to be clearly visible.

2. **Disguised Advertising Techniques**
No advertisement shall be presented in a format or style which conceals its commercial intent.

3. **Price Claims**
(a) No advertisement shall include deceptive price claims or discounts, unrealistic price comparisons or exaggerated claims as to worth or value. "Regular Price", "Suggested Retail Price", "Manufacturers's List Price", and "Fair Market Value" are deceptive terms when used by an advertiser to indicate a savings, unless they represent prices at which a reasonable number of the item was actually sold within the preceding six months in the market place where the advertisement appears.

(b) Where price discounts are offered, qualifying statements such as "up to", "XX off", etc., must be in easily readable type, in close proximity to the prices quoted, and, where practical, legitimate regular prices must be included.

(c) Prices quoted in advertisements in Canadian media, other than in Canadian funds, must be so identified.

4. **Bait And Switch**
Advertisements must not misrepresent the consumer's opportunity to purchase the goods and services at the terms presented. If supply of the sale item is limited, or the seller can fulfil only limited demand, this must be clearly stated in the advertisement.

5. **Guarantees**
No advertisement shall offer a guarantee or warranty, unless the guarantee or warranty is fully explained as to conditions and limits and the name of the guarantor or warrantor is provided, or it is indicated where such information may be obtained.

6. **Comparative Advertising**
Advertisements must not discredit, disparage or attack unfairly other products, services, advertisements, or companies or exaggerate the nature or importance of competitive differences.

7. **Testimonials**
Testimonials, endorsations, or representations of opinion or preference must reflect the genuine, reasonably current opinion of the individual(s), group or organization making such representations, and must be based upon adequate information about or experience with the product or service being advertised, and must not otherwise be deceptive.

8. **Professional or Scientific Claims**
Advertisements must not distort the true meaning of statements made by professionals or scientific authorities. Advertising claims must not imply they have a scientific basis which they do not truly possess. Any scientific, professional

or authoritative claims or statements must be applicable to the Canadian context, unless otherwise clearly stated.

9. **Imitation**
No advertiser shall imitate the copy, slogans, or illustrations of another advertiser in such a manner as to mislead the consumer.

10. **Safety**
Advertisements must not display a disregard for public safety or depict situations which might encourage unsafe or dangerous practices, particularly when portraying products in normal use.

11. **Exploitation of Persons with Disabilities**
Advertisements must not hold out false hope in the form of a cure or relief, either on a temporary or permanent basis, for persons who have disabilities.

12. **Superstition and Fears**
Advertisements must not exploit superstitions or play upon fears to mislead the consumer.

13. **Advertising to Children**
Advertising which is directed to children must not exploit their credulity, lack of experience, or their sense of loyalty, and must not present information or illustrations which might result in their physical, emotional or moral harm.

Child-directed advertising in the broadcast media is separately regulated by the Broadcast Code for Advertising to Children, also administered by the Canadian Advertising Foundation. Advertising to children in Quebec is prohibited by the Quebec Consumer Protection Act.

14. **Advertising to Minors**
Products prohibited from sale to minors must not be advertised in such a way as to appeal particularly to persons under

legal age and people featured in advertisements for such products must be, and clearly seen to be, adults under the law.

15. **Taste, Public Decency**
It is recognized that standards of taste are subjective and vary widely from person to person and community to community, and are, indeed, subject to constant change. Advertising must not present demeaning or derogatory portrayals of individuals or groups; must not exploit violence, sexuality, children, the customs, convictions or characteristics of religious or ethnocultural groups, persons with disabilities or any other person, group or institution in a manner which is offensive to generally prevailing standards.

SELF-REGULATION OF ADVERTISING IN CANADA

The Canadian Code of Advertising Standards was originally sponsored by the Canadian Advertising Advisory Board, the predecessor organization of the Canadian Advertising Foundation (CAF). First published in 1963, it has since been reviewed and revised periodically to keep it contemporary, and has been supplemented by other industry Codes. Change in the provisions of the Code is an ongoing process.

The CAF - Standards Division in Toronto handles all national advertising complaints and complaints from the Ontario region, when these concern English-language advertising; complaints from Quebec and all national French-language complaints, are handled by le Conseil des normes de la Publicite in Montreal. The majority of these complaints are processed at the staff level and only unresolved complaints are referred to the Advertising Standards Council or le Conseil.

Across the country, regional councils — in the Atlantic provinces (Halifax), Manitoba

(Winnipeg), Saskatchewan (Regina), Alberta (Calgary and Edmonton), and British Columbia (Vancouver) — handle local advertising complaints in their respective areas. Each council operates autonomously and, generally speaking, it is the full regional advertising council which reviews and rules on each complaint received.

Each council includes public representatives, nominated by consumer, academic or special interest groups, as well as representatives from advertisers, agencies and media.

PRE-CLEARANCE PROCEDURES

All English language broadcast commercials directed to children as well as English-language television commercials for feminine sanitary protection products, must be pre-cleared by special committees of the CAF prior to acceptance. Scripts and storyboards are checked by CAF staff but a final approval number is not given until the finished commercial has been viewed by the appropriate clearance committee.

Cosmetic advertising for broadcast must be pre-cleared by the appropriate government regulatory body or the CAF. Scripts for cosmetic products may be cleared through the Toronto and Montreal offices of the Canadian Advertising Foundation. This service is offered in cooperation with the Health Protection Branch of the Department of Health and Welfare Canada.

A Pharmaceutical Advertising Advisory Board (PAAB) Code of Advertising Acceptance applies to advertisements for pharmaceutical products appearing in health-services magazines — directed to doctors, dentists, hygienists, nurses and pharmacists. Such messages must also be pre-cleared. Because these messages are often highly technical, they are cleared by the Commissioner of the Pharmaceutical Advertising Advisory Board, of which the CAF is a member.

ROLE AND RESPONSIBILITIES OF COUNCIL

The Advertising Standards Council, le Conseil and the regional councils are pledged to:

1. Review and, where appropriate, resolve public complaints regarding advertisements.
2.. Work within the advertising industry and with consumer bodies in developing, updating, administering, and publicizing self-regulatory standards and codes.
3. Counsel individual advertisers and agencies on laws, regulations, standards and codes affecting advertising.

CAF staff in Toronto and Montreal maintain a tracking process to monitor trends in advertising, trends in advertising complaints, and to bring to the attention of the various advertising standards councils new developments so that the councils can review the information gathered and consider the appropriate action to be taken.

HOW TO COMPLAIN

If you are exposed to advertising carried by Canadian media which you believe contravenes the Canadian Code of Advertising Standards, write to the Advertising Standards Council nearest you.

If it is a print advertisement, it helps if you can enclose a copy of the advertisement; with a broadcast message, identify the station, approximate time, the name of the product, etc. Give a brief written explanation as to why you think the message contravenes the Code.

The addresses of the various Councils are listed on page 11.

HOW COMPLAINTS ARE RECEIVED AND HANDLED

All written complaints directed to the Toronto or Montreal office of the Canadian Advertising Foundation will be initially handled by Standards Division/le Conseil staff. Complaints to the Regional Councils are processed by the full council in that region. All written complaints will be acknowledged and reviewed and if there appears to be a Code violation, the advertiser will be notified of the nature of the complaint. The advertiser is required to respond to the enquiry and to provide the requested information so that a determination can be made as to whether the Canadian Code of Advertising Standards has been violated. If a violation has occurred, the advertiser is requested to amend the advertising in question or withdraw it. Once the advertiser has take either of these two steps, the complaint will be closed and the complainant informed in writing of the corrective action taken by the advertiser.

If the complaint is not sustained, the complainant will be informed of the reasons why it has been determined that the advertising does not violate the Code.

If the advertiser or complainant disagrees with a staff or Council ruling, an appeal may be requested. The matter will be referred to, or back to, the Advertising Standards Council/le Conseil des normes de la Publicite for a further review. If Council/Conseil sustains the complaint, the advertiser is notified, and asked to amend or withdraw the advertising. Generally, this closes the matter. Regardless of whether the complaint has been sustained or not, both the complainant and the advertiser will be notified of the outcome of an appeal. Occasionally an advertiser will be reluctant to take corrective action. When this occurs, the media involved will be notified, indicating that this message has been judged to have contravened the Code. In general, this means that supporting media will not exhibit the advertising in that form.

Communications regarding the interpretation and application of the Code should be addressed to:

Canadian Advertising Foundation - Standards Division

350 Bloor Street East
Suite 402

Toronto, Ontario
M4W 1H5

or to:

le Conseil des normes de la Publicite
4823 ouest, rue Sherbrooke
suite 130
Montréal, Québec
H3Z 1G7

PARTICIPANTS

The Canadian Code of Advertising Standards has been reviewed and approved by the following participating organizations:

Advertising and Sales Executive Club of Montreal
Association of Canadian Advertisers
Association of Medical Advertising Agencies
Association of Quebec Advertising Agencies
Better Business Bureau of Canada
Canadian Association of Broadcasters
Canadian Broadcasting Corporation
Canadian Business Press
Canadian Cable Television Association
Canadian Community Newspapers Association
Canadian Cosmetic, Toiletry and Fragrance Association
Canadian Daily Newspaper Publishers Association
Canadian Direct Marketing Association
Canadian Farm Press Association
Canadian Magazine Publishers Association
Canadian National Yellow Pages Association
Direct Sellers Association
Grocery Products Manufacturers of Canada
Institute of Canadian Advertising
Le Publicite Club de Montreal
Magazines Canada
Non-Prescription Drug Manufacturers of Canada
Outdoor Advertising Association of Canada
Pharmaceutical Advertising Advisory Board
Retail Council of Canada
Society of Ontario Advertising Agencies
Telecaster Committee of Canada

Trans Ad Limited
Trans-Canada Advertising Agency Network
Welcome Wagon Ltd.

The Canadian Advertising Foundation and the regional advertising standards councils also endorse in principle the International Code of Advertising Practice, developed by the International Chamber of Commerce and now adopted in some 30 countries.

LEGISLATION AFFECTING ADVERTISING

FEDERAL ACTS

Broadcasting Act (Sections 5(1),(2), 8(1),(2),(3),(4), 16)
Regulations: Advertising Generally
             Liquor, Beer, Wine and
             Cider Advertising Criteria
             Food and Drugs

Circular

Pre-clearance of ads for food and drug commercials
Food advertising
Registration procedures for television commercials
Canadian Human Rights Act
Competition Act
Consumer Packaging and Labelling Act
Copyright Act
Criminal Code
*Department of National Revenue - Customs and Excise Tariff
Items 99221-1, Schedule C, June 30, 1972
Food and Drugs Act
Canada Hazardous Products Act
*Income Tax Act (Section 19)
National Trade Mark and True Labelling Act
Official Languages Act
Textile Labelling Act
Trade Marks Act

PROVINCIAL ACTS

British Columbia
Trade Practices Act

Consumer Protection Act and Regulations
*Closing Out Sales Act
Motor Dealer Advertising Guidelines
Liquor, Beer and Wine Advertising Regulations

Alberta
The Unfair Trade Practices Act
Credit and Loan Agreements Act
Liquor, Beer and Wine Advertising Regulations

Saskatchewan
Consumer Products Warranties Act
Cost of Credit Disclosure Act
*Liquor, Beer and Wine Advertising Regulations

Manitoba
Consumer Protection Act
Trade Practices Inquiry Act
*Liquor, Beer and Wine Advertising Regulations

Ontario
Business Practices Act
Consumers Protection Act
Human Rights Code
*Regulation 12B (credit advertising)
Liquor Control Act

Quebec
Charter of the French Language
(under above heading) Regulations - Language of Business and Commerce
Consumer Protection Act
(under above heading) Regulation - Children's Advertising
Lotteries Act - Publicity Contests and Lotteries
*Broadcast Advertising Tax Act
Agricultural Products, Marine Products and Food Act
Liquor, Beer and Wine Advertising Regulations
Pharmacy, Professional Advertising Regulations
Roadside Advertising Act
Quebec Class Actions Act

New Brunswick
Consumer Product Warranty and Liability Act
Cost of Credit Disclosure Act

Nova Scotia
Consumer Protection Act
Liquor, Beer and Wine Advertising Regulations

Prince Edward Island
Business Practices Act
Consumer Protection Act
Highway Advertisements Act
Liquor, Beer and Wine Advertising Regulations

Newfoundland
Trade Practices Act
Consumer Protection Act
Exhibition of Advertisements (Billboards) Act
Liquor, Beer and Wine Advertising Regulations
*in question

OTHER INDUSTRY CODES

Broadcast Code for Advertising to Children
Cosmetic Code for Advertising Acceptance
CBC Advertising Standards
Code of Consumer Advertising Practices for
    Non-Prescription Medicines
Guidelines for the Use of Comparative
    Advertising in Food Commercials
Guidelines for the Use of Research and Survey
    Data in Comparative Food Commercials
Pharmaceutical Advertising Advisory Board
    Code of Advertising Acceptance
Telecaster Committee of Canada Guidelines
Television Code of Standards for the Advertising
    of Feminine Sanitary Protection Products

WHERE TO WRITE

You may obtain free copies (up to 5) of the
Canadian Code of Advertising Standards, in
French or English, by writing to:

    CAF - Standards Council
    350 Bloor Street East
    Suite 402
    Toronto, Ontario
    Canada M4W 1H5

or

le Conseil des normes de la Publicite
4823 ouest, rue Sherbrooke
suite 130
Montréal, Québec
Canada H3Z 1G7

REGIONAL COUNCILS:

Advertising Standards Council - B.C.
P.O. Box 3005
Vancouver, B.C.
Canada V6B 3X5

Alberta Advertising Standards Council -
Calgary
Box CH 3000
Calgary, Alberta
Canada T2P 0W8

Alberta Advertising Standards Council -
Edmonton
Box 5030, Postal Station E
Edmonton, Alberta
Canada T5P 4C2

Advertising Standards Council -
Saskatchewan
P.O. Box 1322
Regina, Saskatchewan
Canada S4P 3B8

Advertising Standards Council - Manitoba
P.O. Box 848
1700 Church Avenue
Winnipeg, Manitoba
Canada R2X 3A2

Advertising Standards Council - Atlantic
P.O. Box 3112
Halifax, Nova Scotia
Canada B3J 3G6

AAB Advisory
Committee on

Sex-Role
Stereotyping

The following regulations are administered by the Advocacy Division of the Canadian Advertising Foundation.

GUIDELINES

The intent of these guidelines is to encourage advertising in all media to portray women and men in a manner which reflects their emotional and intellectual equality and which respects their equal dignity.

1. Authority

Advertising should take steps to attain significant positive change in the balance of women and men in roles of authority such as announcers, voiceovers, experts, and on-camera authorities.

Comment

Research conducted on broadcast advertising in 1984 revealed a heavy imbalance in the number of male versus female voiceovers, as well as in roles of experts and product/service authorities. Further, no data could be found to prove greater effectiveness of males in these roles.

This area of advertising remains a male-dominated bastion because the pool of extensively trained male voices exceeds the availability of female voices with comparable backgrounds in radio announcing or other equivalent training. The advertising industry should work toward correcting this imbalance and encourage promotion of demonstration tapes and lists of female talent to the industry to facilitate positive change in the use of women in these roles.

2. Sexuality

Advertising should avoid exploiting sexuality.

Comment

Exploiting is interpreted as a presentation in which sexuality is on display merely for the gratification of others. Some examples of exploitative used are double entendres, camera as voyeur, unnatural physical positions, etc.

There is, however, nothing wrong with tasteful, positive, relevant sexuality in advertising which portrays a person in control of and celebrating her/his own sexuality.

3. Decision-making

Both women and men should be portrayed as decision-makers, particularly as buyers and users of big-ticket items and major services, as well as smaller purchases.

Comment

Both women and men are active decision-makers for major personal and household purchases and in the workforce. Decisions on life insurance, cars, major appliances, office equipment and systems, travel, etc. are often team decisions - whether in the workplace or at home. Many women make major purchasing decisions on their own and many men are frequently the purchasers of household items, grocery and drug products.

4. Household

Males and females should be portrayed as equally sharing and benefiting from household management and tasks.

Comment

Canadians live in a variety of household arrangements and this should be reflected in advertising. Advertising should portray home management — organizing, care-giving, decision-making — as a shared responsibility of members of a unit and give equal dignity to domestic and wage-earning roles.

Non-traditional households, e.g., childless couples, single parent families, "empty nesters", etc., are all important purchasing units and should be used in advertising as well as the more traditional family unit.

5. Diversity

Women and men in a variety of ages, backgrounds and appearances should both be portrayed in a wide range of contemporary occupations, hobbies, activities and interests.

Comment

Advertising should portray an expanded range of roles for both women and men reflecting more accurately contemporary Canadian society.

Women as doctors, politicians, parachutists, men as care-givers, computer operators, are lifestyles and occupational choices commonly seen in real life situations. Further, Canadians of all ages, appearances and backgrounds should be considered when creating advertising. The goal is to show a significant broadening in the diversity of characters and their assigned roles in advertising.

6. Language

Advertising should use generic terms which include both sexes.

Comment

Language should be used which recognizes the equal treatment of women and men and does not exclude one sex, provided these terms have common understanding in vocabulary across the country. Contemporary Canadian language is changing and now includes terms in common usage such as Business Executive and Firefighter in place of Businessman and Fireman. Advertising should reflect this.

BACKGROUND

Sex-role Stereotyping guidelines were originally developed by a Canadian Radio-television and Telecommunications Commission Task Force on Sex-role Stereotyping in the Broadcast Media in 1981. They have been administered by the Canadian Advertising Foundation since then and applied to all media.

The revised guidelines (dated 24 July 1987) were developed in 1987 through a consultation process with the advertising industry and public representatives. They are administered by the Canadian Advertising Foundation through French and English Advisory Panels on Sex-role Stereotyping.

These guidelines represent one important element of the Canadian advertising industry's commitment to self-regulation in the area of portrayal of women. Past experience has shown that self-regulation, involving industry and public representatives, has been effective in creating positive change and is more flexible and less costly to administer than government regulation.

The advertising industry collectively supports these guidelines and encourages all individual advertisers and agencies to reflect them in responsible, realistic and ultimately more effective advertising executions.

The following Associations and organizations have endorsed the guidelines and support the activities of the Panels:

Association of Canadian Advertisers Inc.
Canadian Association of Broadcasters

Canadian Broadcasting Corporation
Canadian Cosmetic, Toiletry and Fragrance
    Association
Canadian Daily Newspaper Publishers
    Association
Canadian Manufacturers' Association
Canadian Toy Manufacturers' Association
Grocery Products Manufacturers of Canada
Institute of Canadian Advertising
Magazines Canada
Nonprescription Drug Manufacturers Assoc.
    of Canada
Outdoor Advertising Association of Canada
Publicité Club de Montréal
Retail Council of Canada

Soap and Detergent Association of Canada
Trans Ad

THE ADVISORY PANELS ON SEX-ROLE STEREOTYPING

Composition and Mandate

Each Panel includes members from the following sectors:
• Advertiser • Advertising Agency • Broadcast Media - CBC and Private • Print Media • Public

The Panel is responsible for on-going information and sensitizing programs with the advertising industry, complaint-handling and public awareness programs.

The Panel meets at least once a quarter, more frequently if circumstances warrant.

Should a message be found in violation of the guidelines, the Panel will seek the co-operation of the advertiser, advertising agency and the media in having the message amended or removed.

ADMINISTRATION

1) An advertiser's need to target identified purchasing groups is recognized within the context of the guidelines. For example, if an identified market consists solely of female homemakers, an advertiser has a clear priority to identify this market in advertising providing the portrayals within this advertising adhere to the guidelines.

2) In interpreting the guidelines it should be noted that, particularly in TV advertising, a combination of sound, visual effects and performance nuances can result in a violation of the spirit of the guidelines, while not directly violating any individual guideline.

3. These guidelines apply to both Canadian produced and imported advertisements which appear in or on Canadian media.

4. Advertisers and their agencies are encouraged to seek counsel and advice from the CAF Advisory Division when they have any doubt as to whether certain creative concepts might conflict with the guidelines.

5) Members of the public are encouraged to send the Panel complaints about advertising which they feel is not in accord with the guidelines, keeping in mind:

a) The Panel makes no judgement on products or services which may be advertised, only the manner in which they are advertised in the context of these guidelines.

b) While the CAF has no influence with out-of-country media or advertisers, it is recognized that advertising from outside Canada can cause offence. When complaints are received about such advertising, they will, when possible, be forwarded to the advertiser in question.

English complaints should be sent to:
Canadian Advertising Foundation
Advisory Division
350 Bloor Street East,
Suite 402
Toronto, Ontario
M4W 1H5
(416) 961-6311

Les plaintes d'expressions française doivent être acheminées ":
La Fondation canadienne de la publicité
4823 Ouest rue Sherbrooke
Suite 130
Montréal, Québec
H3Z 1G7
(514) 931-8060

APPENDIX II

Advertising Lexicon

Account director   The senior member of the account-management group in an advertising agency, responsible for the agency's performance in handling client accounts.

Account executive   The liaison between the agency and client, responsible for co-ordinating the agency's services for the benefit of the client, and for representing the agency's point of view to the client.

Account shifting   Moving an advertising account from one agency to another.

Account supervisor   A mid-manager in an agency who manages the activities of a group of account executives; generally takes a longer-term perspective on product-advertising assignments.

Advertising   A persuasive form of marketing communications designed to stimulate positive response from a defined target market.

Advertising manager   Generally, the individual in the client organization who is responsible for advertising planning and implementation.

Advertising plan   An annual planning document that outlines the advertising activities (creative and media) for the forthcoming year. The plan includes discussion of objectives, strategies, and tactics for both creative and media plans.

Advertising research   Any form of research providing information useful in the preparation or evaluation of creative, of media alternatives, and of media usage.

Advertising share   A brand's media expenditure, expressed as a percentage of total product-category media expenditures.

Advocacy advertising   Advertising that is designed to communicate a company's stand on a particular issue (usually an issue, such as pollution control, that will affect a company's operations).

Affiliates   Independent stations that carry network programming.

Agency commission   Compensation that a medium pays an agency for placing advertising with the medium. Agencies use the commission system, a fee system, or a combination of both.

Agency of Record (AOR)   A central agency, often used by multiple-product advertisers that use more than one advertising agency, responsible for media negotiation and placement.

Aided recall A research situation where respondents are provided with certain information to stimulate thought.

AM (Amplitude Modulation) Refers to the height at which radio waves are transmitted.

Animated commercials A commercial technique involving the use of hand-drawn cartoons or stylized figures and settings.

Answerprint The final post-production stage of a television commercial, where film, sound, special effects, and optics are combined and printed (final copy of an advertisement for distribution to television stations).

Appeal The creative angle taken to motivate a consumer to purchase a particular product or service.

Art director The individual responsible for the visuals in an advertisement (illustrations in a print ad and storyboards in a broadcast ad).

Attitudes An individual's feelings, favourable or unfavourable, toward an advertised product.

Audience flow In radio, the change in audience demographics based on the time of day.

Back-lit poster A luminous sign containing advertising graphics printed on translucent polyvinyl material.

Balance The relationship between the left side and the right side of a print advertisement. Equal weight (left versus right) refers to *formal balance,* and unequal weight is *informal balance.*

Bleed (bleed page) A situation where the coloured background of an advertisement extends to the edge of the page so that there is no margin.

Blitz media schedule A schedule characterized by heavy media spending in a short space of time (saturation), with spending gradually tapering off over an extended period of time.

Body copy Informative or persuasive prose that elaborates on the central theme of an advertisement.

Build-up media schedule A schedule characterized by low media weight initially, gradually building to an intensive campaign.

Business-to-business advertising Advertising of finished products and services that is directed at other businesses that can use the advertised items to advantage.

Buying centre Informal buying groups within an organization; composed of several individuals who either make or influence purchase decisions.

Buying committees The formal buying groups in a business organization (a cross-section of individuals who will be affected by the product purchase) who share equally in the purchase-decision process.

Cash refund (rebate) A predetermined amount of money returned directly to a consumer by a manufacturer after specified purchases have been made.

Circulation The average number of copies of a publication sold by subscription, or through retail outlets, or distributed free to predetermined recipients.

Cluster The grouping of commercials in a block of time during a program break or between programs.

Clutter The clustering of commercials together in a short space of time.

CNU (Canadian Newspaper Unit) A standardized newspaper format that divides a 13"-wide broadsheet into six columns and a 10 1/4"-wide tabloid into five columns. Each unit has a depth of 30 modular agate lines. A broadsheet contains 60 CNUs; a tabloid has 30 CNUs.

Comparative advertising A form of advertising whereby a brand is compared with a competitive brand on the basis of similar attributes that are judged to be important to the target market.

Comprehensive A mechanical art layout that has all copy and illustrations pasted precisely into place (often referred to as camera-ready art work).

Consumer behaviour The acts of individuals in obtaining and using goods and services; the decision processes that precede and determine these acts.

Consumer promotion Promotion activity directed at consumers, and designed to encourage quicker purchase response.

Contest A consumer promotion technique that involves the awarding of cash or merchandise prizes to consumers when they purchase a specified product.

Continuity The length of time required to insure impact on a target market through a particular medium.

Continuity discount A discount based on the purchase of a minimum number of designated spots, over an extended period of time (usually 52 weeks).

Controlled circulation Publications that are distributed free to individuals who fall within a specific demographic segment or geographic area.

Co-operative advertising The sharing of advertising costs and materials by suppliers and retailers; or, by several retailers.

Co-operative direct mail Mailings containing specific offers from non-competing products (e.g., coupons, samples, subscription offers).

Copywriter The individual responsible for developing the headline, body copy, and signature in a print advertisement, or the script in a broadcast ad.

Corporate advertising Advertising designed to convey a favourable image of a company to its various publics.

Coupons Price-off incentives offered to consumers to stimulate quicker purchase of a designated product (coupons are usually product-delivered or media-delivered).

Coverage The percentage of individuals reached by a publication in a specific geographic area.

CPM (Cost Per Thousand) The cost of delivering a message to 1000 individuals.

Creative boutique An advertising agency that specializes in the development of creative concepts and executions.

Creative concept The central theme, or basic sales message, that an advertisement communicates through verbal and visual devices.

Creative department The department in an advertising agency that provides creative services such as copy and art.

Creative execution A more precise definition of creative strategy (i.e., tactical considerations regarding the best way to present products for maximum impact—celebrity spokespersons, dramatizations, use of colour, etc.).

Creative objectives   Clearly worded statements that outline the basic content of an advertising message (i.e., brand name, and benefits that are of high interest to potential buyers).

Creative research   Evaluating and measuring the impact of an advertising message on a target market.

Creative strategy   Clearly worded statements that provide direction regarding how the message will be presented. Such statements usually consider appeal techniques, tone, style, and theme.

Cross couponing   One product carrying a coupon offer for another product (often done by complementary products, such as coffee and biscuits).

Cross sampling   One product carrying a free sample of another product.

Custom-designed research   Primary research that focuses on resolving a specific problem or obtaining specific information.

DAR (Day-after recall)   Research conducted the day following the respondents' exposure to a commercial message to determine the degree of their recognition and recall of the advertisement, the brand, and the selling message.

Daypart   The blocks of time during the day, in television and radio, used to distinguish viewing and listening patterns.

Dealer premium   An incentive (usually merchandise) offered to distributors to encourage special purchase or additional merchandising support for a manufacturer's product.

Demographic segmentation   The process of dividing a large market into smaller segments on the basis of various combinations of age, sex, income, occupation, education, race, and religion.

Department maker (POP)   An elaborate, often permanent merchandise-display unit (store-within-a-store concept).

Dialogue copy   Messages delivered from someone's point of view.

Direct advertising   Advertising directly to prospects via mail, sales people, and dealers (does not use traditional mass media).

Direct mail   A form of direct advertising that uses the postal service as the vehicle for delivering the message.

Direct marketing   A market system, controlled by the marketer, whereby products are developed, then promoted to a variety of end users through a variety of media options, and then distributed to the customer.

Direct-response advertising   A message that prompts immediate action (e.g., advertisement with a coupon), usually communicated via direct mail or other forms of mass media.

Display advertising   Advertising that appears anywhere in a newspaper, excluding the classified section.

Display cards (POP)   Small advertisements located at the point of purchase (shelf talkers, tear-off ad pads, counter posters) and designed to encourage impulse purchases.

Display shipper (POP)   A shipping carton containing a predetermined amount of merchandise that, when assembled, will form a temporary display at the point of purchase.

Efficiency   The relative cost-effectiveness of a particular medium, based on CPM.

Endorsement advertising   Advertising that uses a celebrity (e.g., rock star, television personality, sports star) to present the product message.

End-product advertising   Advertising by a firm that makes part of a finished product (e.g., Kodak advertises the benefits of processing film on Kodak paper).

Even media schedule   The purchase of media time and space in a uniform manner over an extended period of time.

Event-oriented advertising   Retail advertising that revolves around a central theme that a target market will find appealing, such as an annual midnight-madness sale.

Execution (tactics)   Action plans that outline specific details of implementation.

Exterior bus poster   A poster-type advertisement appended to the side or rear section of a bus.

Eye camera test   A test whereby a hidden camera records eye movement to gauge the point of immediate contact in an advertisement, how a reader scans the ad, and the amount of time spent reading.

Fade   An optical effect in a television commercial, whereby one scene gradually disappears and another gradually appears.

Family life cycle   The stages an individual progresses through during a lifetime (bachelor stage to solitary survivor).

Feature sheet   A sheet, commonly used in radio personality announcements, that provides the station with the key benefit and with the slogan for the product advertised.

The DJ develops the specific message-wording from the sheet.

Flexibility   The ability to modify media-spending plans throughout the media-spending (planning) period.

Flights   Periodic waves of advertising, separated by periods of total inactivity.

Flow   The reader's eye movement (e.g., from left to right and from top to bottom) when reading an advertisement.

FM (frequency modulation)   The speed at which waves travel in thousands of cycles per second (kilohertz).

Format   A term that, in the context of radio, describes the nature of the programming done by an individual station.

Fragmentation   A situation where a television- or radio-station audience has numerous stations to choose from.

Freelancer   A self-employed, independent creative specialist (e.g., a graphic artist, a copywriter, or an art director).

Frequency   The average number of times an audience is exposed to an advertising message over a period of time, usually a week.

Frequency discount (broadcast)   A discount based on a minimum number of spots being purchased over a specified period of time.

Full-service agency   An advertising agency that provides a complete range of services to the client (i.e., creative- and media-planning, marketing research, sales promotion, and, possibly, public relations).

Functional management   A system whereby advertising responsibility is distributed according to the type of advertising activity (corporate advertising versus product advertising versus sales promotion).

Gatefold   A printed magazine advertisement that consists of a series of folded pages, with the folded pages conforming to the publication's page size.

Geographic management   A system whereby advertising responsibility is managed on a regional basis (different strategies for different regions).

Geographic segmentation   The process of dividing a large geographic market into geographic units (e.g., Canada is divided into Maritimes, Quebec, Ontario, Prairies, British Columbia).

Grid card   A price schedule, in broadcasting, that quotes different price levels, depending on certain criteria such as demand for time, frequency of advertising, volume of advertising, and time of year.

Grocery-cart advertising   Advertising (small posters) appended to the ends of shopping carts and visible to approaching shoppers who are moving about the supermarket.

GRP (Gross Rating Points)   An aggregate of total ratings in a schedule, as determined by reach times frequency, usually in a weekly period, against a target audience.

Group head (or associate media director) The member of the Media Department who carries an administrative workload and is responsible for the management of the Media Department.

Guaranteed position   A specific position for an advertisement, with a premium rate charged for such positioning.

Gutter   The blank space on the inside page margins in a bound publication, or the blank space between two facing pages in a newspaper.

Hiatus   The period of time between advertising flights.

Hierarchy of effects   Various theories concerning how advertising influences the behavioural stages an individual passes through prior to making a purchase decision.

Hooker (tag)   The local dealer's name added to national advertisements in newspapers.

Horizontal co-operative advertising   The sharing of advertising costs by a group of retailers.

Horizontal publications   Publications appealing to people who occupy the same level of responsibility in a business.

Horizontal rotation   The placement of radio commercials based on the day of the week.

Horizontal split   A situation in the layout of a print advertisement where the page is divided across the middle, with illustration in one half, copy in the other.

Impressions   The total audience delivered by a media plan. Often referred to as "total exposures," impressions are calculated by multiplying the number of people who receive a message (reach) by the number of times they receive it (frequency).

Industrial advertising   Advertising of products that are used to produce and distribute other products.

In-house agency   An organization structure used in a manufacturer's or retailer's operation that handles its own advertising function: creative is developed by staff copywriters and artists; media time and space are purchased by in-house specialists; external agencies are used only on an as-needed basis.

Insert   A preprinted advertisement (e.g., a leaflet, a reply card) that is specially placed in a newspaper or magazine.

Insertion order   A statement of specifications for an advertisement sent by an advertising agency to print media, including insertion dates, size, position, and rates.

Insert layout   The inclusion of a secondary visual (an insert) in a print layout.

Institutional advertising   Advertising designed to create a favourable image of a store or of a product in the minds of potential and current customers.

Interlock   The synchronizing of sound and picture for a television commercial through the use of a special editor's projector.

Key-market media plan   Purchasing media time on the basis of market priorities (i.e., on a market-by-market basis).

Layout   The design and orderly formation of the various elements of an advertisement, within specified dimensions. A layout integrates all copy elements with the illustration to create a complete message.

Lifestyle advertising   A form of advertising that attempts to associate a product with the lifestyle of a certain market segment.

Line rate   The newspaper advertising rate charged for one modular agate line.

Live-action commercials   Advertisements that use real-life situations with live actors.

Local advertising (television)   Purchase of television time by local-market advertisers.

Long copy   A copy-dominant advertisement, one that makes little or no use of illustration.

Long list   In the agency-selection process, a listing of the advertising agencies that could potentially meet the advertising needs of a client.

Make good   A rerun of an advertisement at the publisher's expense, to compensate for an error in or substandard printing of the original insertion.

MAL (Modular Agate Line)   A standardized unit of space equal to one column wide and 1/14" deep. Broadsheet column-widths are 2 1/16"; tabloids 1 15/16".

Market discount (transit)   A discount based on the purchase of a predetermined list of markets.

Marketing objectives   Statements identifying what a product will accomplish over a one-year period of time.

Marketing plan   An annual planning document for a product, service, or company that includes background analysis (of the market, the product, and the competition) and objectives, strategies, and tactics for the forthcoming year.

Marketing research   The systematic gathering, recording, and analyzing of data to resolve a marketing problem.

Marketing strategies   The process of identifying target markets and satisfying those targets with a blend of marketing-mix elements.

Marketing tactics   Detailed activity plans that contribute to the achievement of marketing objectives.

Market segmentation   The process of dividing a large market into smaller homogeneous markets (segments) according to common needs and/or similar lifestyles.

Media billings The total dollar-volume of advertising handled by an agency in a one-year period of time.

Media buyer A media specialist conversant with the competitive claims of the various media alternatives. The media buyer's primary function is to purchase media time and space for clients as efficiently as possible.

Media-buying service An advertising agency that specializes in media planning and placement.

Media-delivered coupons Coupons distributed by various print-media alternatives, including newspapers, magazines, direct mail, or via in-store merchandising methods such as demonstrations or information centres.

Media director The most senior media-position in an advertising agency; responsible for the management of the Media Department and accountable for media planning and placement for all clients.

Media mix The combination of media used in a media schedule.

Media placement The actual purchase of media time and space, once a media plan has been approved.

Media planner A media specialist who assesses the strengths, weaknesses, costs, and communications potential of various media in order to develop a media plan.

Media planning Preparation of a plan that documents how the client's money will be spent to achieve advertising objectives.

Media supervisor A senior-level media specialist who supervises the activities of media planners and buyers.

Mission statement A statement of purpose for an organization that usually reflects the organization's operating philosophy.

Mixed interlock The addition of sound effects and music to the interlock.

Mixed tape The finished radio-commercial tape containing the spoken words, music, and special effects.

Modular display rack (POP) A permanent display unit, provided by a manufacturer, to display a certain line of merchandise.

Multiple illustrations In a print-advertisement layout, the use of many individual illustrations in sequence.

Narrative copy Messages presented in the third person.

Narrowcasting Specialized programming designed to attract a narrowly defined target market (a special age or interest group).

National advertising Advertising of a trademarked product or service wherever that product or service is available.

Network advertising Advertising that comes from one central source and is broadcast across the entire network of stations.

Noise Competitive advertising messages aimed at a specific target market.

Objectives Statements outlining what is to be accomplished in a plan (corporate, marketing, or advertising plan).

Omnibus study (syndicated service) Research data collected by, or available to, participants in a common study (Print

Measurement Bureau data bank, for example, provides such studies).

Opinion-measure testing A form of research yielding information about the effect of a commercial message on consumers' brand-name recall, their interest in a brand, and their purchase intentions.

Outdoor advertising Advertising that is directed at vehicular or pedestrian traffic (e.g., posters or billboards, back-lit posters, transit shelter advertising, and mall posters).

Pace (television) Designing message content so that it falls within the time parameters of the commercial—usually 15, 30, or 60 seconds.

Package plans (television) Discounted rate plans that combine prime-time spots with fringe-time and day-time spots.

Passalong reader (secondary reader) A person who reads a magazine after having received it secondhand.

Perception How individuals receive and interpret messages (three levels have been defined: selective exposure, selective perception, and selective retention).

Performance allowance Additional trade discounts (beyond trade allowances) used to encourage retailers to perform a specific merchandising function.

Personality announcement In radio, a situation where the disc jockey presents a commercial message in his or her own style.

Planning The process of anticipating the future business environment, and determining the courses of action to take in that environment.

Point-of-purchase (POP) Advertising or display materials located in a retail environment so as to build traffic, advertise a product, and encourage impulse purchasing.

Pop-up coupon A coupon printed on heavier paper stock and stitched into a popular consumer magazine (it is usually positioned directly before an advertisement for the couponed product).

Positioning The place a brand occupies in the minds of consumers; or, in other words, the selling concept that motivates purchase.

Poster A picture-dominant advertisement (i.e., one with a minimum of copy).

Post-testing The evaluation and measurement of a message's effectiveness during or after the message has run.

Pre-emption A situation where regular programming is interrupted by special programming. Advertisers of the regularly scheduled programs are rescheduled for comparable time slots at a later date.

Premium An item offered free, or at a bargain price, to encourage consumers to buy a specific product (usually offered to consumers through the mail or through in- or on-pack communications).

Premium rates In radio, an extra charge the advertiser pays for sponsoring a special program.

Pre-testing Evaluating commercial messages or advertisements, prior to final production, in order to determine the strengths and weaknesses of the communications.

Primary reader A person qualifying as a reader who lives in a household (or works in an office) that receives the publication initially.

Primary research data Data observed, recorded, and collected on a first-time basis with a view to resolving a specific problem.

Prime/fringe/day time (television) In television, the basic dayparts sold—prime time is normally 6:30 P.M. to 11:00 P.M.; fringe time is usually 4:30 P.M. to 6:30 P.M. and 11:00 P.M. to sign-off; day time is sign-on until 4:30 P.M.

Product advertising (promotional advertising) In retailing, advertising that is designed to encourage immediate response by consumers (e.g., the announcement of a major sale event).

Product-delivered coupons Coupons distributed in the product or on the product package (side panel, back panel, etc.).

Product life cycle The path a product follows from its introduction to its eventual withdrawal from the market (it is a four-stage process).

Product manager (brand manager) A manager in the client organization who is assigned responsibility for carrying out the marketing planning (four Ps) for a product or a group of products.

Professional advertising Advertising directed at professionals such as doctors, lawyers, accountants, and engineers.

Profile-matching strategy Matching the demographic profile of a product's target market with a specific medium that has a compatible profile.

Psychographic segmentation Market segmentation based on the activities, interests, and opinions (in short, the lifestyles) of consumers.

Publicity The communication of newsworthy information about a product, a service, or an idea.

Public relations The firm's communications with its various publics (shareholders, employees, suppliers, governments).

Publisher's statement A statement of circulation data issued by a publisher to the Audit Bureau of Circulations. The statement, used in ABC's compilation of circulation data, is unaudited at the time of issue, but is subject to audit by the ABC.

Pulse media schedule The grouping of media in flights over a predetermined period of time.

Pupillometer A device that measures the pupil dilation (enlargement) of a person's eye when the person is reading.

Qualitative research Data collected from a small sample size; usually the initial step in assessing target-market feedback for an idea or concept.

Quantitative research Data, collected from a much larger sample size, that quantifies respondents' feelings, attitudes, and opinions.

Reach The total unduplicated audience (number of people reached) potentially exposed, one or more times, to an advertiser's message over a period of time (week).

Reach plan (total audience plan) A plan that involves rotating a radio commercial through the various dayparts so that the same message can reach different groups of people.

Readers per copy The average number of persons who read a single issue of a publication.

Recall testing Measuring an advertisement's

impact by asking respondents to recall specific elements (e.g., the selling message) of the advertisement.

Recognition testing   Testing of a target audience's awareness of a brand, of its copy points, or of the advertisement itself after the audience has been exposed to the message.

Redemption rate   Refers to coupons actually redeemed. The rate of redemption for a specific coupon offer equals the number of coupons redeemed divided by the number of coupons distributed.

Reference groups (peer groups)   A group of people with a common interest who have an influence on the individual member's attitudes and behaviour.

Related recall   The percentage of a test-commercial audience who claim to remember a test commercial, and can provide, as verification, some description of the commercial.

Reply card (business reply card)   A type of mail that enables the recipient of direct-mail advertising to respond without paying postage (encourages response).

Repositioning   Changing the place a product occupies, relative to competitive products, in the consumer's mind.

Residual   The additional payments granted to an actor, actress, or model for appearing in a commercial over an extended period of time. Individuals are paid for each time the advertisement appears on screen (paid in 13-week cycles).

Retail advertising   Advertising by a retail store (the advertising of a store name, image, and location, and the re-advertising of branded merchandise carried by the retailer).

Retail in-ad coupon   A coupon printed in a retailer's weekly advertising, either via

run of press or supplements inserted in a newspaper.

Rifle strategy   A strategy that involves using a specific medium that reaches effectively a target market defined by a common characteristic.

ROP (Run of paper)   Advertisements placed anywhere within the regular printed pages of a newspaper.

ROP colour   A colour process printed in a newspaper during the regular press run.

ROS (Run of schedule)   A discount offered to advertisers who allow the television or radio station to schedule the commercial at its own discretion.

Rotation plan   A selection of radio time slots, specified by the advertiser and based on time of day (vertical rotation) and day of week (horizontal rotation).

Rough art   The drawing of an advertisement, done to actual size and with the various elements (i.e., headline, copy, illustration, and signature) included to show relative size and position.

Rough cut   The best film takes (as shot on location or in a studio) spliced together to form the video portion of a television commercial.

Sales promotion   Activity designed to generate prompt response from consumers, distributors, and the field sales force.

Sample   Free distribution of a product to potential new users.

Satellite paper   A publication whose typesetting signal is sent to distant printing facilities via satellite for regional or expanded national distribution.

Script   A document used in the production of television and radio commercials. In the case of television, the script describes the video presentation on one side, the audio on the other. In the case of radio, the audio presentation and sound effects, music, etc., are described in the script.

Seasonal discounts (television) Discounts offered to advertisers in traditionally slow seasons (television viewership drops in the summer, so additional summer discounts are offered).

Seasonal media schedule A schedule whereby media spending is heavier in the pre-season (to create awareness), with media spending tapering off during the season of usage.

Secondary research The compiling and publishing of data by disinterested sources; the data is used by companies for purposes other than resolving a specific problem.

Selective media plan (rifle strategy) A plan for reaching a specific target market via a specific interest medium.

Selective spot (spot television) In a network show, some commercial time is not allocated and is left to regional or local stations to sell. Advertisers can purchase this time on a station-by-station basis.

Self-concept An individual's understanding of him- or herself. (In advertising, four categories of consumer self-perception are significant: real self, self-image, looking-glass self, and ideal self.)

Short list A brief list of the advertising agencies that a prospective client is interested in hiring; the agencies are invited to make a business presentation to the client (to win an account).

Short rate A charge incurred by an advertiser who does not meet a contractual estimate of advertising time or space.

Shotgun strategy A strategy involving the use of mass media to reach a more loosely defined (i.e., more general) target market.

SIC system A numbering system, established by the Canadian and U.S. federal governments, that provides business firms with a means of tracking down potential customers. It can be used to compile direct-response-advertising mailing lists.

Simulcasting A situation in which an episode of a U.S. network program is scheduled to appear on a Canadian station at the same time. Cable companies must carry the Canadian signal, and, therefore, viewers are exposed to Canadian advertising.

Skip media schedule A schedule whereby media time and space are purchased on an alternating basis (every other week, month, etc.); alternate use of media types, over time.

Social classes Hierarchically ordered groups whose members share similar values, interests, and beliefs.

Solo direct mail Individually prepaid and distributed direct-mail offers.

Spectacular A non-standardized outdoor-advertising unit constructed according to the customized specifications of the advertiser (these often have protruding components, to attract attention).

Split run A situation in which an advertiser splits the full circulation of a newspaper to test two different advertisements—half the circulation contains one ad; the other half, another ad. It is commonly used to test the effectiveness of different advertising layouts.

Spot television The purchase of local broadcast time on a station-by-station basis (sometimes called selective spot).

Starch test A recognition-testing procedure that measures readers' recall of an advertisement (noted), their ability to identify the sponsor (associated), and whether or not they read more than half of the written material (read most).

Station posters Transit advertisements located on platforms and exit areas of subway and light-rail transit systems.

Storyboard A set of graphic renderings in a television-frame format, accompanied by appropriate copy, depicting what a finished commercial will look like.

Strategic planning The process of determining objectives and identifying strategies and tactics that will contribute to the achievement of objectives.

Strategies Statements that outline how objectives will be achieved.

Subculture Subgroups of a larger culture that have distinctive lifestyles, yet maintain important features of the dominant culture.

Super A print message superimposed on a television frame.

Supplements Prepaid and preprinted advertisements inserted into the folds of newspapers (commonly used by large department-store chains).

Tachistoscope A device measuring what respondents see when they are submitted to a flashed exposure (lasting a fraction of a second) of a message.

Tagline An alternate expression for the signature portion of an advertisement. Usually includes the brand name, a distinctive logo, and a slogan.

Target audience A specific group of individuals at whom an advertising message is directed.

Target-market management A system in which advertising responsibility is managed according to the nature of the customer (industrial versus institutional versus consumer customer groups).

Tear sheet A page supplied to an advertiser by a newspaper that is carrying the advertiser's insertion; the tear sheet verifies that the advertisement ran as scheduled.

Telecommeter A device that pinpoints a person's focus of attention (demonstrating which elements of an advertisement are noted, in what order, and which ones are re-examined).

Testimonial advertising A form of advertising in which a credible source, usually a typical consumer, presents the product message.

Thumbnail sketches Small, experimental sketches of a variety of design concepts.

Total paid circulation In print, the total of all classes of a publication's distribution for which the ultimate purchasers have paid (single-copy sales plus subscription sales).

Trade advertising Advertising by manufacturers to channel members to secure distribution of a product and resale of the advertised product.

Trade allowance A temporary price reduction intended to encourage larger purchases by distributors.

Trade promotion Promotion activity directed at distributors, and designed to encourage volume purchases andmerchandising support for a manufacturer's product.

Traffic   The number of people who visit a retail store.

Transient rate   The base rate, or open rate, charged to casual advertisers in a newspaper; it is the maximum rate charged.

Transit cards (car cards)   Print advertisements contained in racks above windows of public transit vehicles.

Unaided recall   A research situation where respondents are provided no information to encourage thought.

Unity (print)   The blending of all elements in a print advertisement to create a complete impression.

Unity (television)   The visual and aural flow of a broadcast commercial, from the customer's perspective.

Vertical co-operative advertising   The sharing of advertising costs between a supplier and a retailer.

Vertical publication   A publication that reaches people with different jobs in the same industry.

Vertical rotation   The placement of radio commercials, based on the time of day.

Vertical split   A type of print-advertisement layout in which copy dominates one side, illustration the other—left and right sides are divided by an imaginary line down the middle of the page.

Voice-over   Spoken copy or dialogue delivered by an announcer who is heard but not seen.

Volume discount (broadcast)   A discount that is based on the dollar volume purchased over a period of time (13, 26, 52 weeks).

Wipe   An optical effect, in a television commercial, that involves one scene pushing the other away.

White space   The part of an advertisement that is not occupied by any elements.

Zapping   The practice of channel switching, usually by means of a remote control device, to avoid commercial messages.

Zipping   A method of reducing commercial viewing that involves using the fast forward device on a VCR while watching a pre-recorded program.

Index